THE INSIDE, OUTSIDE, AND UPSIDE DOWNS OF CHILDREN'S LITERATURE
From Poets and Pop-ups to Princesses and Porridge

Jenifer Jasinski Schneider, Ph.D.

The Inside, Outside, and Upside Downs of Children's Literature: From Poets and Pop-ups to Princesses and Porridge

Jenifer Jasinski Schneider, Ph.D.

Copyright

Published by The University of South Florida Library, 4202 E. Fowler Avenue, Tampa, FL 33620. Copyright ©2016 by Jenifer Jasinski Schneider. All rights reserved.

This work is licensed under a Creative Commons Attribution-NonCommercial-NoDerivatives 4.0 International License.

Author and Editor in Chief: Jenifer Jasinski Schneider
Editorial Director: Monica Metz-Wiseman
Media Project Manager and Producer: Christine Brown
Video Producers and Editors: Jared Brown, Jason Su, Ian Crenshaw, Jessica Brennen, Diana Trueman, Jeremy Willis
Art Director: Stephanie Rivera
Illustrators and Multimedia Designers: William Tillis and Elise Michal
Copyright Coordinator: LeEtta M. Schmidt
Open-Access Editor: Jason Boczar
Editorial Manager: Carol Ann Borchert
Editorial Project Manager: Chelsea Johnston

Library of Congress Cataloging-in-Publication Data
Schneider, Jenifer Jasinski, 1968-
The Inside, Outside, and Upside Downs of Children's Literature: From Poets and Pop-ups to Princesses and Porridge / Jenifer Jasinski Schneider.
ISBN- 978-0-9776744-1-1 eBook
ISBN- 978-0-9776744-2-8 print

The Internet addresses listed in the text were accurate at the time of publication.

Dedication

To my daughters, Bethany and Mary.

To Bethany, my reader of animal facts, biology books, and all things fantasy or science fiction. Through you, I learned that it's really true—a love of books starts at bedtime (Figure i). I love you madly!

To Mary, my reader of fairy tales and fiction (Figure ii). Through you, I learned that a love of books delays bedtime, or invites *more* reading, depends on how you look at it.

Me: Go to bed, Mary.
Mary: Can I read?
Me: Yes.
(20 minutes later)
Me: OK, Mary, that's enough.
Mary: Just five more minutes?
Me: OK. Five minutes, but that's it.
(20 minutes later)
Me: Go to sleep now.
Mary: Can I finish this page?
Me: Yes.
(10 minutes later)
Me: That's the longest page in the history of books. Goodnight, Mary.
Mary: Good night, Mommy. I love you. Sweet dreams. Sleep tight.
Me: Goodnight, Mary. I love you. Sweet dreams. Sleep tight.

To Troy, my "fox" in socks (Figure iii). Through you I've learned that Johnny Cash rules the world. I've also witnessed the inevitable truth; kids love to *Hop on Pop* (Figure iv). **We won the game!**

Figure i
Bethany's reading before naptime. Photo copyright 2002 by Jenifer Schneider.

Figure ii
Mary's reading before bedtime. Photo copyright 2011 by Jenifer Schneider.

Figure iii
Troy is my "fox" in socks. Photo copyright 2003 by Jenifer Schneider.

Figure iv
The girls love to "hop on their pop!" They also love to read with their pop. Photo copyright 2003 by Jenifer Schneider.

With Appreciation
To the People, Objects, and Events that Created a Reader

To my parents, Ziggy and Mary Jasinski (Figure v), who filled my life with love, laughter, and books. Have you ever known what it's like to have a fan club? My parents are mine. Buzi!

To Dr. Seuss, P.D. Eastman, and the Berenstains (in the universe) (Figure vi). You were sheer perfection to my toddler self. I have vivid memories of reading pages from your books (Figure vii).

To Charles M. Schultz (in the universe). Somewhere, in a drawer, box, or attic, I have a letter from you. I told you that I wanted to grow up and draw cartoons—just like you. You wrote back and told me that you believed in me. You also sent me a drawing of the whole Peanuts gang. You were an inspiration.

To Mrs. Jerry Hines, my elementary school librarian. You were gregarious, outrageous, and mad about books. You showed me (and my whole class) all of the Newbery and Caldecott winners. You read aloud each week. You let us check out more than one book. You helped us find the books we wanted. You helped us want the books we needed. You read books about Black people, White people, Wild Things, and Lonely Dolls. What a role model!

To Judy Blume, what can I say that you haven't heard from every other fan in the world? I read all of your books as a kid. I loved them. They changed me as a reader and a person. I follow you on Twitter. I'm a huge fan. By the way, my dad's nickname is Ziggy (for Zygmunt) and when I was little, he had an alter ego named Iggy. When my sister and I played alone for too long, Iggy (my dad on his knees) knocked on the bedroom door to "come play" and check on us. When Iggy arrived, our playtime became a wrestling match or we decorated Iggy with make-up and bows (Figure viii). I expected Iggy's House to be about my dad. Boy, I was wrong. Thanks for opening my eyes to the rest of the world.

Figure v
My mom and dad with me. Photo copyright 1968 by Al Scanio.

Figure vi
Inside, Outside, Upside Down by Stan and Jan Berenstain, 1968, New York, NY: Random House. Copyright 1968 Stan and Jan Berenstain.

Figure vii
Hanging out in my bookpen. Photo copyright 1969 by Zygmunt Jasinski.

Figure viii
My dad in role as "Iggy." Photo copyright 1976 by Jenifer Jasinski.

To Dr. Fran Goforth (in the universe), when I decided to become a teacher, you taught my first children's literature course. You taught me how to teach reading with children's literature and to provide spaces for children's authentic, aesthetic responses. As a Masters student, you taught my second children's literature course. When I mentioned that I was interested in a doctorate, you told me that Ohio State had a wonderful program in literacy and children's literature. That suggestion, dear lady, changed my life.

Figure ix
Ohio State doctoral students meet with Jeanne Chall in 1994. Photo copyright unknown.

To all of my Ohio State professors who changed my mind: Theresa Rogers, Anna Soter, Janet Hickman, Cecily O'Neill, Karin Dahl, Rob Tierney, Diane DeFord, Gay Su Pinnell, Rudine Sims Bishop, Vladimir Sloutsky, and Patti Lather. Of course, I can't forget my fellow Ohio State doctoral students who experienced the mind-blowing with me (Figure ix): Sue Constable, Carrie Blosser Scheckelhoff, Christi Hovest, Larry Sipe (in the universe), Beth Murray, Janis Harmon, Tom Crumpler, Ernie Bond, Nancy Anderson, Adrian Rogers, Emily Rogers, Ron Kiefer and so many others.

Figure x
Got butterbeer? Escaping into The Wizarding World of Harry Potter™. Photo copyright 2010 by Troy Schneider.

Finally, to J.K. Rowling. I don't think I had a better literary experience than when I read Harry Potter alongside my daughters. Then, when we visited Harry's World, the stories came to life before our eyes (Figure x). Rarely, as an adult, can a person experience magic. I did.

Acknowledgements

I would like to thank Provost Ralph Wilcox for your foresight in creating an open-access textbook program at the University of South Florida. With a focus on student success and textbook affordability, your vision set this work in motion.

Thank you to Dr. Cynthia Deluca, Assistant Vice Provost for Innovative Education, for your encouragement and administrative navigation throughout the book creation process. I appreciate your support and guidance.

Thank you to Christine Brown (Media Project Manager and Producer) and your entire Media Innovation Team: Jared Brown, Stephanie Rivera, Diana Trueman, Jason Su, Ian Crenshaw, Jessica Brennen, William Tillis, Jeremy Willis, and Elise Michal (Figure xi). You took my thought bubbles, visions, and harebrained schemes and made them come to life. Thank you for your countless hours of filming, editing, designing, and building. You are incredibly talented people and amazing collaborators. Did you know there's just one more video I want to make?

Figure xi
The members of the Media Innovation Team, USF Innovative Education at the University of South Florida. Copyright 2016 by the University of South Florida.

Thank you to my colleagues in the USF Library:
Monica Metz-Wiseman (Coordinator of Electronic Collections), Todd Chavez (Interim Dean of the USF Library), LeEtta M. Schmidt (Resource Sharing and Copyright Librarian), Jason Boczar (Digital Scholarship and Publishing Librarian), Carol Ann Borchert (Coordinator for Serials), Melanie Griffin (Children's Literature & Young Adult Literature Special Collections Librarian), and Susan Ariew (Education Librarian). As I said somewhere in this book, librarians have mad skills. None madder than you!

Thank you to the current and former doctoral students in the Literacy Studies program who share my interest in and passion for children's literature. In particular, I would like to thank those who have taught the children's literature course with me: Csaba Osvath, Aimee Frier, Anne W. Anderson, Margaret Branscombe, Lindsay Persohn, Sarah Pennington, Rebecca Powell, Stephanie Branson, Allison Papke, and Erin Margarella. You read the chapters, piloted projects with students, taught me, and gave me outstanding feedback and advice. Of course I didn't listen to all of it, but I love you anyway (Figure xii)

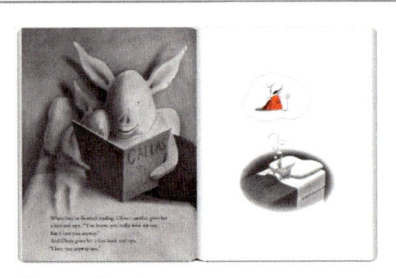

Figure xii
Just like Olivia, the Literacy Studies doctoral students wear me out. But I love them anyway! Illustration from Olivia, by Ian Falconer, 2000, New York, NY: Simon & Schuster. Copyright 2000 by Ian Falconer. Reprinted with permission.

Table of Contents
The Inside, Outside, and Upside Downs of Children's Literature: From Poets and Pop-ups to Princesses and Porridge

Book Cover

Title Page

Copyright

Dedication

With Appreciation

Acknowledgements

Contents

Section 1: Introduction and Overview of Children's Literature

    Chapter 1: Why are you reading kids' books?
          (An Introduction)
        Purpose
        Different Uses for Different Audiences
            Audiences with Professional Interests in Connection to Children
            Audiences with Professional Interests in Library Science, English, or Education
            Audiences with Personal Interests in Children's Literature
            Audiences in the U.S. and Around the Globe
        Key Features
        About the Author

    Chapter 2: What is Children's Literature?
          (Definitions and Delimitations)
        Children's Books on Trial
        A Working Definition
        A Brief History of Children's and Young Adult Literature

    Chapter 3: Got Books?
          (Access, Collections, and Digital Resources)
        Access to Books
            The Library
                Ancient libraries
                University, religious, and government libraries
                Public libraries
                The Librarians and the American Library Association (ALA)
                Children's story hour and reading rooms

- Children's Libraries
  - Advice from a Librarian by Melanie Griffin
- Collections
  - Locations and Access
  - Special Collections Online
- The Booksellers Gruff
  - The Itty-Bitty Book Shop
  - The Bigger Box Bookstore
  - The Mega eCommerce Retailer
- Museums
- Get Books

Section 2: Hot Topics and Curious Quandaries

pp. 59-97

Chapter 4: Important Books
(The Problems and Politics of Importance; Notable Lists, Awards, & Associations)

- The Experts Who Study Children's Literature
  - The Librarians
    - Association for Library Service to Children (ALSC)
    - Young Adult Library Services Association (YALSA)
    - Ethnic Materials Information Exchange Round Table Task Force (EMIERT)
  - The Literary Scholars
    - Children's Literature Association (ChLA)
  - The Teachers
    - National Council of Teachers of English (NCTE)
    - International Literacy Association (ILA)
  - The Content Experts
    - National Science Teachers Association (NSTA)
    - American Phytopathological Society
    - Mathematical Sciences Research Institute
    - National Council for the Social Studies (NCSS)
  - The Creators: Children's Book Writers and Illustrators
    - Society of Children's Book Writers and Illustrators (SCBWI)
    - Society of Illustrators
    - American Academy of Poets
    - American Folklore Society (AFS)
    - Science Fiction and Fantasy Writers of America (SFWA)
  - The Publishers and Booksellers
    - Horn Book Magazine
    - Boston Globe-Horn Book Award
    - Kirkus
    - American Booksellers Association (ABA)
    - Children's Book Council (CBC)
  - The Fans
    - Cybils
    - Children's Choices- Revisited
- Other Indicators of Importance
  - Popularity and Sales
  - Social Networks
  - Circulation Reports
  - The Lists
- The Problem with Awards and Lists
  - The Dangers of a Single Story
  - More Awards and Different Labels
- Whose Story? Additional Considerations

Chapter 5: The Right Book for the Right Reader at the Right Time
    (Literary Analysis, Quality, and Developmental Perspectives)

pp. 98-158

- Determining Quality
- Question #1: What is the author's and/or illustrator's purpose?
  - Literary Purpose and Text Structures: A Vehicle for Communication
    - Narration (fiction)
    - Information (nonfiction)
    - Description
    - Argumentation
  - Visual Purpose and Illustrative Style: Another Vehicle for Communication
    - Narrative Illustration
    - Informative Illustration
    - Descriptive Illustration
    - Argumentative Illustration
  - Genres: The Makes and Models of Children's Literature
    - Picture Books
    - Wordless Books
    - Poetry
    - Traditional Literature
    - Fantasy
    - Contemporary Realistic Fiction
    - Historical Fiction
    - Graphic Novels/Texts
    - Biography
    - Information
    - Diverse Books
    - Many Languages Literature
    - Classics
- Question #2: How do we select and apply the appropriate criteria to evaluate books?
  - Elements and Expectations: Overview of the Working Parts
    - Narration
    - Information
    - Description
    - Argumentation
- Question #3: How do we match books to readers?
  - Reading Development and the Role of Children's Literature
  - Babies
    - Short List of Recommendations for Babies
  - Toddlers
    - Short List of Recommendations for Toddlers
  - Young Children
    - Short List of Recommendations for Young Children
  - Older Children
    - Short List of Recommendations for Older Children
  - Young Adults
    - Short List of Recommendations for Young Adults
  - Book Recommendation Services
- Question #4: How do we judge the overall product to know what works?
  - Know Your Financing Options: Library or Bookstore? Print or eBook?
  - Preview the Book: Take a Test Drive and Don't Fall for Gimmicks
  - Library of Bookstore/Print or eBook: Know Your Financing Options
  - Ask Around

    An Opinionated Journey through Children's Literature: Through the Eyes and Mind of an Almost Teenager by Mary Schneider
    Exploring Literary Analysis: Techniques for Understanding Complex Literature by Lindsay Persohn
 Chapter 6: The Reading Wars
    (Children's Literature and the Intervening Effects of School and Politics)
  The Reading Wars
    Reading Readiness and Phonics (First Grade Studies)
      Conventional Basal Readers
      Phonics-Emphasis Instructional Systems
      Language Experience Approaches
      Linguistic Materials
      i.t.a. Initial Teaching Alphabet
    Reading to Learn
    Students with Learning Disabilities
    From Emergence to Adolescence
    Whole Language
    Second Language Learners
    Balanced Literacy Solutions
  The US Government Attempts to Settle the Reading Wars
    Five Pillars of Reading
      Phonemic Awareness
      Phonics
      Fluency
      Teaching Vocabulary Words
      Reading Comprehension Strategies
    Accountability and Scripted Instruction
  The US Governors Attempt to Settle the New Reading Wars
    Common Core State Standards, Close Reading, and the Text Complexity Canon
    Motivation, Purpose, and the Return to Children's Literature
  The Role of the School Library and Programs to Promote Reading with Kathleen Edwards
    Library Spaces
    Collection Development
    Budget
    Book Promotion through Story Time and Book Talks
    Classroom Support
    Pleasure Reading Programs
      Sustained Silent Reading
      Book Fairs, Book Orders, & Book Clubs
    Author/Illustrator Visits
    Battle of the Books
    Reading Incentive Programs
    Middle and High School Libraries
  Other Public and Private Programs to Promote Reading
    Dolly Parton's Imagination Library
    Book Mobiles
    RIF
    Reading Rainbow
  Interventions and Intended Consequences
 Chapter 7: American Typo
    (Ghost, Fan, Serial, and Celebrity Writers—and Illustrators)
  Natural Born Serial Killers
    A Series Sampler
    Number of Sales
    Number of Uses

           Number of Critiques
           Number of Promotions
           Number of Readers
      The Making of a Serial Writer (or Illustrator)
           The Prolific and Profound
                Personalities and Products
                Pedigree and Product
           The Ghosts
           The Celebrities
           The Fans
      Revisiting a Number of Things

Chapter 8: Beyond the Page and Behind the Scenes
           (Writing, Publishing, & Marketing Children's Literature: Books, Cinema, Cartoons, Toys & Apps)
      The Work of Authors and Illustrators: Learning to Write or Draw
           The Writers
                Forms and Feedback
                Processes and Procedures
                Writing Instruction and Training
           The Illustrators
                Forms and Feedback
                Processes and Procedures
                Art Instruction and Training
      Getting Published
           Learn from Mentors
           Engage in Professional Networks
           Listen to Good Advice
      Where do Authors and Illustrators Get Their Ideas?
           Read, Read, Read
           Look, Look, Look
           Write, Write, Write or Draw, Draw, Draw
      Whose idea is it anyway? Big ideas in *Jurassic Park*, *Jumanji*, and *The Cat in the Hat*
           by Anne W. Anderson
      Take Offs, Spin Offs, and Paraphernalia
      Please, Sir. I Want Some More

Section 3: Textual Tendencies and Open and Close Readings

      Chapter 9: Gore & Grimm, Princesses & Porridge
           (The Roots of Story and Narration)
           Passing Down Stories
           Writing Down Stories
           Exploring Story
           From Tradition to Modern Fiction

      Chapter 10: Waxing Poetic with Deliberate Description and Aesthetic Argument
           (Reading Aloud, Choral Reading, and Performance)
           Who's Who
                The Popular Ones: Shel Silverstein, Jack Prelutsky
                The Award Winners
                The Weirdos, Novelties, and Outliers
           Finding Poetry
                For Extensive Biographies and Information about Poets
                To Search for Complete Poems
                To Search "Best Of" Lists
                Sharing Poetry
                      Reading Aloud and Recitations

                Choral Reading
                Poetry Slams and Spoken Word
                Performing and Embodying Poetry
                    Dramatic Interpretation
                    Musical Interpretation
                    Visual Interpretation
            Creating Poetry by Csaba Osvath
        Exploring Poetry

        Chapter 11: Past Presidents and Evading Inventors: Not Your Grandmother's Information Books
            (Portraying People, Arguing Positions, and Presenting Disciplinary Content)
            The Quest for Information
                Relevant Topics and Professional Interests
                Your Personal Interests and Passions
                Limited Topics and Perspectives
            Expertise and Interesting Writing
                Author Expertise
                Language Features and Readability
                The Importance of Illustration
            Looking Past Dead Presidents and the Same Ol' Inventors

        Chapter 12: Banned and Burned: Why worry? It's just Kiddie Lit
            (Children, Banned Books, and the Right to Read)
            Most Wanted
            The Right to Read
            Supreme Court Rulings

Appendices

List of Figures

List of Videos

Contributors

References

Children's, Young Adult, and Adult Literature Cited

Key Words Index

INTRODUCTION AND OVERVIEW OF CHILDREN'S LITERATURE

SECTION 1

CHAPTER 01 | WHY ARE YOU READING KIDS' BOOKS?

AN INTRODUCTION

Children's literature is the foundation for youth's literacy development. Children and young adults need to engage in literary and aesthetic acts because they are essential for human growth. In other words, kids must read books in order to learn and grow. You are an adult. What are you doing here?

Why are **you** reading kids' books? I'll take a few guesses.

- You are interested in children's literature because you have fond memories of books from your youth (Figure 1.1). You enjoyed these books as a child and you would like to revisit them as an adult.

Welcome! I will review some old favorites and introduce you to new ones as well.

- You are a writer or artist (or both) and you want to create books for children; therefore, you want to know more about the field. Or, you might have a strong literary background in other areas of literature and you want to build complementary knowledge in children's literature (Figure 1.2).

Great. You are in the right place.

Figure 1.1

A classic image from *The Polar Express*, by Chris Van Allsburg, 1983, New York, NY: Scholastic. Copyright 1983 by Chris Van Allsburg.

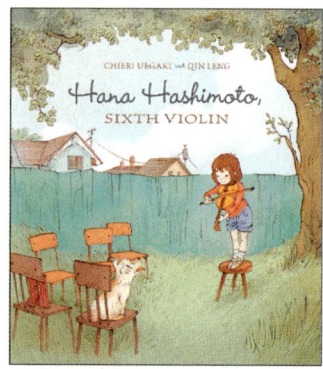

Figure 1.2

Explore newer books. *Hana Hashimoto, Sixth Violin* by Chieri Uegaki and illustrated by Qin Leng, 2014, Toronto, CA: Kids Can Press. Copyright 2014 by Qin Leng.

- You have (or will have) children in your life and you want to know how to select books for them. Alternatively, you might also want to know which books are best for reading aloud (Figure 1.3). You probably want to know when you should stop reading aloud to kids or when kids are too old for books with pictures. (Short answer: Never!)

 I will provide a thorough response to these questions and address many more.

- You have children in the *center* of your career path (nurse, doctor, dentist, social worker, psychologist, lawyer, minister), and you need to know what children read, why children read, and how children's books work in connection with children's social, emotional, and physical developmental progression (Figure 1.4).

We definitely will explore these topics.

- You have children in the *margins* of your career path (children in waiting rooms, employees with children, working with children's charities, designing, building, or decorating schools, libraries, hospitals or offices, for example), and you want to know how or where children read (Figure 1.5).

Yes, I will discuss the faces, places, and spaces of children's literature.

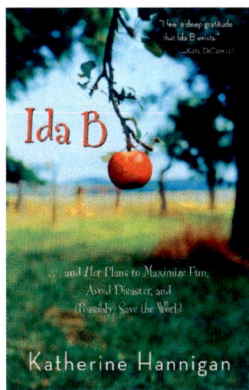

Figure 1.3
A wonderful book, perfect for reading aloud. *Ida B... and Her Plans to Maximize Fun, Avoid Disaster, and Save the World* by Katherine Hannigan and cover illustration by Dana Tezarr, 2004, New York, NY: Greenwillow/HarperCollins. Cover art copyright 2004 by Greenwillow/HarperCollins.

Figure 1.4
Peter H. Reynolds' *The Dot* demonstrates how small moments can make significant changes to a child's life. *The Dot* by Peter H. Reynolds, 2003, Somerville, MA: Candlewick Press. Copyright 2003 by Peter H. Reynolds.

Figure 1.5
The waiting room at the office of Gerald Copeland, D.D.S., Tampa, FL. Photo copyright 2015 by Jenifer Jasinski Schneider.

- Or perhaps children are the *beneficiaries* of your career path. You are a musician, graphic designer, computer programmer, lawyer or advertiser, for example, and you are interested in the entertainment industry or business aspects of children's literature, games, apps, and movies (Figure 1.6).

This book has something for you too.

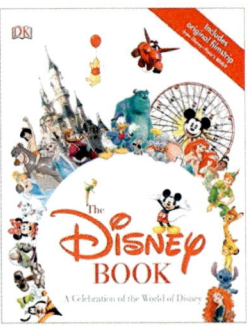

Figure 1.6
The Walt Disney Company is one example of an enterprise that has impacted the production of children's books. For an overview of the Disney industry, Jim Fanning's *The Disney Book* provides visual highlights and an historical synopsis. *The Disney Book*, by Jim Fanning, 2015, New York, NY: DK. Cover art copyright 2015 by Disney.

- You don't have children in your personal life or crossing your professional career path, but you want to know the ways in which children's literature socializes youth, politicizes identity, represents history, and becomes art (Figure 1.7).

Yes, we will go there.

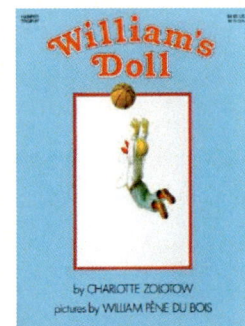

Figure 1.7
Explore what can happen when boys love dolls. *William's Doll* by Charlotte Zolotow and illustrated by William Pene du Bois, 1972, New York, NY: Harper & Row. Copyright 1972 by William Pene du Bois.

- You are taking a class in children's literature because you think it will be an easy A. After all, children's literature is written for children and youth; therefore, children's books must be easy to comprehend with simplistic plots and lots of pictures (Figure 1.8).

Wrong! You need to stop, go back to the beginning of this chapter, re-evaluate your life, and make better choices.

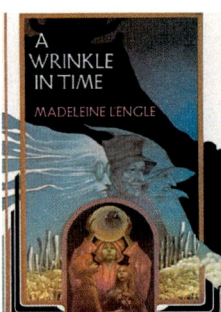

Figure 1.8
If you think children's books are "easy," think again. One example of young adult fiction with complex plots and characters is *A Wrinkle In Time* by Madeleine L'Engle, 1962, New York, NY: Farrar, Straus, and Giroux. Cover illustration copyright 1979 by Leo and Diane Dillon.

Children's literature is written for children and youth, but the analysis of children's literature requires careful attention to text as well insightful interpretation of the ways in which authors and illustrators present the human condition, the physical world, imaginative experiences, and global forces. Children's literature is also a $4-billion-a-year industry that impacts social practices, politics, financial markets, schools, literacy rates, history, and art. Whatever the reason for your interest, children's literature is a big deal.

According to IBISWorld (2015), the children's literature industry "designs, edits and markets books for children aged 17 and under, including coloring and picture books. It does include e-books, but excludes online-only publishers and authors, as well as textbook publishing." The Children's Book Publishing market research report indicates $4 billion in annual revenue. (http://www.ibisworld.com/industry/childrens-book-publishing.html)

In addition, the children's market is driving growth across the publishing industry with a trend for increasing sales (Jarrod, 2015).

Video 1.1 Why are you reading kids' books? (An Introduction) http://www.kaltura.com/tiny/yn1jr

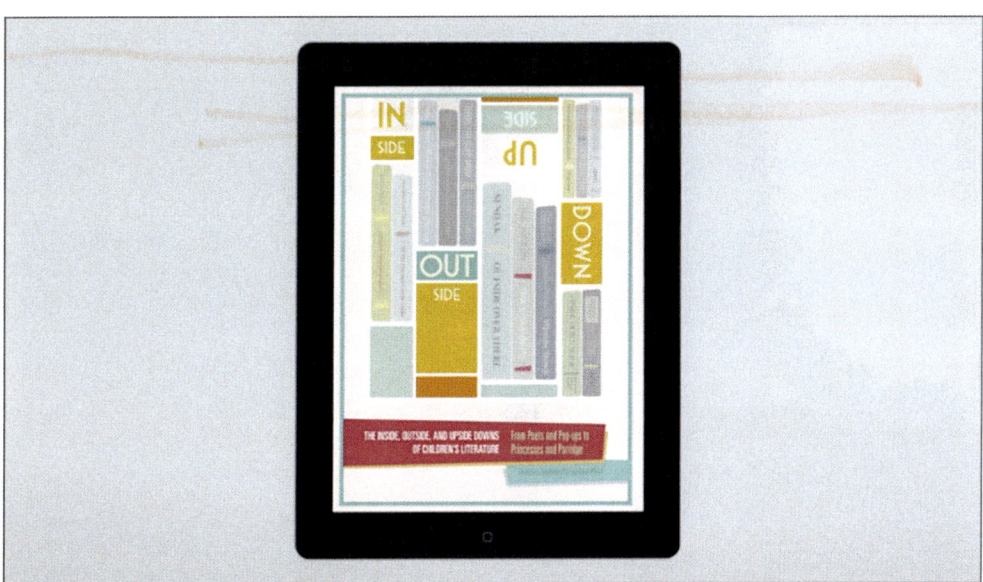

Overview of *The Inside, Outside, and Upside Downs of Children's Literature: From Poets and Pop-ups to Princesses and Porridge*. Copyright 2015 Jenifer Jasinski Schneider.

Purpose

The purpose of this book is to introduce you to the field of children's literature. My goals for you are as follows: develop an appreciation of children's literature as a literary art form, learn how children's books and text structures work to create meaning, and to acquire strategies for critically evaluating books written for children and youth. In addition, you will examine societal trends and cultural issues in connection to particular texts and across the field of children's literature.

Different Uses for Different Audiences

By creating an e-textbook, I have integrated relevant digital resources and provided an interactive space for exploring the content that meets the needs of many audiences.

Audiences with Professional Interests in Connection to Children

This book is relevant for professionals who work with children in the fields of medicine, health, sports, entertainment, arts, journalism, politics, or business, etc. Knowing what children read, how children's books work, and the value of children's literature in society is relevant information for your career (Figure 1.9). For example, you need to know what children read so you can fill your waiting rooms with appropriate books of interest. You need to know how children's books work so you can select the right books for the right children. And you need to understand the importance of children's literacy development so you will be motivated to support literacy in all of your workspaces.

Figure 1.9
With thousands of children's and young adult books published each year, it's important to know how to select books. Copyright 2015 by Jenifer Jasinski Schneider.

Audiences with Professional Interests in Library Science, English, or Education

This book is relevant for literacy specialists, librarians, and literary critics at the undergraduate and graduate levels. Given my broad focus on enjoyment, critical judgment, and appreciation, those of you in the fields of library, education, and English can use this book to advance your knowledge of the history of children's literature, stay updated with current trends, and pursue thematic study in your areas of interest. The book could be used in study groups, professional learning communities, university courses, and professional development seminars at the local, national, and international levels.

Audiences with Personal Interests in Children's Literature

Many children's literature texts are written for K-12 educators or librarians, but you won't find lesson plans in this book. Instead, for those of you with a personal interest in children's literature, I have written a topical textbook in which you can explore broad issues such as the banning of books, the writing and marketing of series books, and diversity and cultural portrayals.

Audiences in the US and Around the Globe

This book is relevant to US audiences as most of the examples are drawn from children's literature published in English. However, the book also includes specific references to international children's literature and guides readers to explore databases and collections of diverse examples (e.g., International Children's Digital Library http://en.childrenslibrary.org or the USF Children's and Young Adult Literature Special Collection http://www.lib.usf.edu/special-collections/childrens-young-adult-literature/). Therefore, this book also crosses political, cultural, and social borders.

Key Features

The Inside, Outside, and Upside Downs of Children's Literature: From Poets and Pop-ups to Princesses and Porridge integrates relevant digital resources and provides an interactive space for learning that is affordable and accessible and meets the needs of multimodal readers and learners.

GRAPHICS
Each chapter includes graphics to help you navigate the book and to provide quick visual summaries or questions to guide your thinking.

COMMENT BUBBLES
Throughout the book, comment bubbles provide a space for me to post additional information or add behind-the-scenes commentary. In other words, comment bubbles are the spaces where I let you know what I really think.

PHOTOGRAPHS/VIDEO
Visual images of children's books are important features of the book. I included photographs of cover art and illustrations. I also embedded video content from Youtube, TED talks, and I also created my own—with a little help from my friends.

WEB LINKS

There is much to learn about children's literature and a great deal of content has been created by museums, libraries, and organizations such as the *American Library Association*. When appropriate, I have linked to reliable, relevant information that is already posted in digital spaces. By providing links to other sources, I hope you explore content beyond the information provided in this book.

About the Author

I spent my life as an avid reader and fan of children's literature. I also spent my career reading and studying children's literature as an elementary teacher and then as a professor of literacy studies at the University of South Florida.

I am obsessed with arts-based approaches to literacy education including the ways in which children's literature, process drama, and technological tools support symbolic development and meaning-making strategies. I appreciate the literariness of children's literature and derive aesthetic pleasure from the images (if present). I also greatly respect the roles of librarians as mediators of collections and keepers of the texts.

I believe (actually, I know) children's literature is relevant to adults because children's literature includes some of the highest quality writing, art, story, and informational content available. Children's literature is worthy of reading, discussion, study, and critique.

I have high expectations for the quality of children's literature, but with that said, I do not care what children and young adults read as long as they read. I believe it is the role of adults (parents, teachers, and other mentors) to expose reluctant readers to outstanding exemplars and to encourage broader reading and lifelong habits because, let's face it, passionate readers will find quality. It is the struggling readers who need help finding motivating and interesting texts that are relevant to their lives. Struggling readers do not need competitions, leveled books, or colored dots to encourage their reading. They need to be guided by role models who can help them find the right books (Figure 1.10).

I do not care what adults read. I am a passionate defender of the right to read. I believe banning books is un-American, and "scholars," critics, or other individuals who defend free speech and the freedom to read should not shame adults who read children's literature or tell youth what they should or should not read.

Children's literature is important, the stories are relevant, and the information will change the way you see the world.

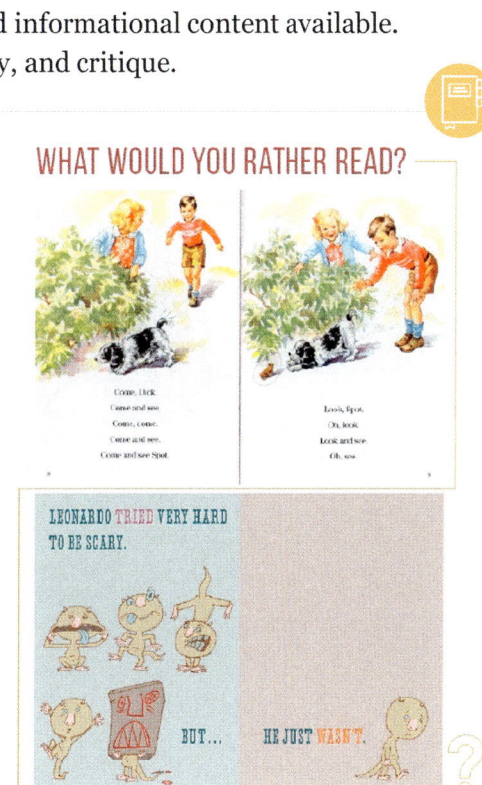

Figure 1.10

Which book would *you* rather read?
Dick and Jane by William S. Gray and illustrated by Zerna Sharp, 2004, New York, NY: Grosset & Dunlap. Illustration copyright 2004 by Zerna Sharp. *Leonardo the Terrible Monster* by Mo Willems, 2005, New York, NY: Hyperion. Illustration copyright 2005 by Mo Willems.

CHAPTER 02 | WHAT IS CHILDREN'S LITERATURE?
DEFINITIONS AND DELIMITATIONS

Children's Books on Trial

Children's Literature, the term conjures images of baby books, predictable plots, and basic illustrations (Figure 2.1). Or, perhaps, you might equate children's literature with the artless, pointless stories in classroom basal readers, the ones with contrived vocabulary built around particular reading levels (Figure 2.2), or the purified stories, stripped of real life in order to pass the scrutiny of state textbook selection committees and school boards (Figure 2.3). Yes, it's true. Some examples of children's literature can be inane. But the same can be said about books for adults; the quality varies.

Basal readers are anthologies of stories and other texts grouped together for students at certain reading or grade levels. Basal readers contain contrived stories and stilted vocabulary. Many people do not consider basal stories to be "literature" because the texts are often altered for readability purposes.

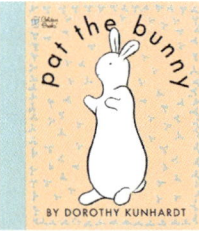

Figure 2.1
Dorothy Kunhardt's *Pat the Bunny* is a classic example of a predictable baby book in which the content, layout, illustration, and language are designed to match young children's developmental levels. *Pat the Bunny* by Dorothy Kunhardt, 1940/2001, New York, NY: Golden Books. Copyright 1940 by Dorothy Kunhardt.

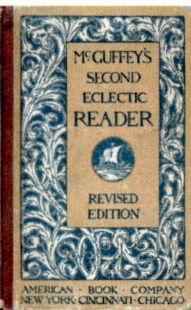

Figure 2.2
The McGuffey Readers were a popular series beginning in the early 1800's and used until the 1950's. *McGuffey's Second Eclectic Reader (revised edition)* by William H. McGuffey, 1879, Van Antwerp, Bragg & Co. (https://archive.org/stream/mcguff2ndeclreader02mcguf#page/n3/mode/2up).

Figure 2.3
Current basal readers include "real" children's literature in their collections. The publishers rewrite the stories, controlling for content and embedding vocabulary words. *Treasures* by Macmillan/McGraw-Hill, 2011, New York, NY: Macmillan/McGraw-Hill. Copyright 2011 by Macmillan/McGraw-Hill.

At its best, children's literature includes books of the highest caliber, representing complex plots or concepts in both word and art. Children's literature is often defined as a **collection of books written for children, read by children, and/or written about children**. But this definition may be too simplistic for a not-so-simple genre. Below, I offer a series of exhibits to test your knowledge and this definition.

Is children's literature a collection of books?

Is children's literature read by children?

Is children's literature written about children?

Exhibit A:
A Game of Thrones by George R. R. Martin
(Figure 2.4)

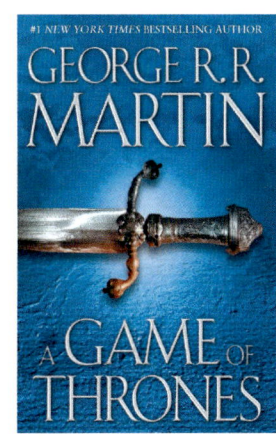

A Game of Thrones, which is the first book in the series, *A Song of Ice and Fire*, is an epic fantasy set in medieval times. The book, written by George R.R. Martin, is wildly popular and was developed into a television series for HBO. Based on three interwoven storylines, *A Game of Thrones* is told from individual character's perspectives and recounts a complex, dark, and epic story of family dynasties.

Figure 2.4

A Game of Thrones by George R. R. Martin, 1996, New York, NY: Random House. Cover art copyright 2011 by Bantam Books.

Is *A Game of Thrones* children's literature?

 A Game of Thrones is a book. But its plot was used as the basis for a television show and other adaptations.

 A Game of Thrones was not written for children. George R.R. Martin is a writer of adult fiction, known for his fantasy, horror, and science fiction. *A Game of Thrones* was not intended for youthful readers; however, it is a popular book among teenagers.

School Library Journal lists *The World of Ice and Fire: The Untold History of Westoros and the Game of Thrones* (Martin, Garcia & Antonsson, 2014) as one of its choices for best fantasy (nonfiction companion). In fact, so many books crossover from adult to "child" readers that *School Library Journal* hosts a blog by Angela Cartensen and Mark Flowers entitled, *Adult Books 4 Teens* (http://blogs.slj.com/adult4teen/).

Children read adult books. Of course you may not refer to teenagers as children, but the United Nations (1989) recognizes anyone under the age of 18 as a minor child (http://www.ohchr.org/en/professionalinterest/pages/crc.aspx). The United States Citizenship and Immigration Services (2015) defines children as unmarried persons under 21 years of age (http://www.uscis.gov/policymanual/HTML/PolicyManual-Volume12-PartH-Chapter2.html). And the United Stated criminal code code (18 U.S. Code § 2256) defines a "minor" as any person under the age of 18 years (2015, https://www.law.cornell.edu/uscode/text/18/2256).

In the book industry, teenagers form their own demographic and they are a separate, targeted group. Young Adult is the common term for literature written for youth aged 12 to 18. The young adult label took hold in 1957 when the American Library Association (ALA) (www.ala.org) divided the Association of Young People's Librarians (established in 1941) into the Children's Library Association and the Young Adult Services Division for the purposes of providing differentiated services to groups of youth who have different social, emotional, and literacy needs (Starr, 2015).

When does "childhood" begin and end? The differences are fluid and debatable, yet often randomly demarcated by certain organizations such as movie theaters, restaurants, libraries, credit card companies, and the US criminal justice system. If jail sentences vary state-by-state and judge-to-judge, why are book audiences held to rigid age limitations? Some people make a career obsessing over age limits and reading habits, judging what is or is not children's literature. For example, Ruth Graham (2014a) levied harsh criticism against adults who read YA novels (http://www.slate.com/articles/arts/books/2014/06/against_ya_adults_should_be_embarrassed_to_read_children_s_books.html). But as Mark Medley (2014) explained, her position is nonsensical (http://news.nationalpost.com/2014/06/11/stick-with-your-kind-getting-adults-off-ya-books-doesnt-go-nearly-far-enough/).

To me, it's all academic (code for irrelevant—unless you are concerned about library classification systems or marketing, profits, and awards—but more on that later) and easily decided through an operational definition: Kids under the age of 18 read *A Game of Thrones*, some as young as 10 or 11; therefore, some adult books crossover into the YA category because they are read by teenagers. *A Game of Thrones* is read by adults, teenagers, and children. Therefore, what is it?

A Game of Thrones is not written about children, although children exist in this fantasyland. There are many examples of children's books that feature adults, but they are written for children. Think about biography books featuring US Presidents or famous scientists (more on that later as well).

 ## Exhibit B:
The Kite Runner by Khaled Hosseini
(Figure 2.5)

The Kite Runner is a story of two youths, Amir and Hassan, and their friendship built around kite flying. The story is set in Kabul and includes scenes of violence, rape, and racial discrimination along with themes of loyalty, betrayal, family, and war. Told over a period of many years, the story comes full circle through a series of acts of redemption.

Is *The Kite Runner* children's literature?

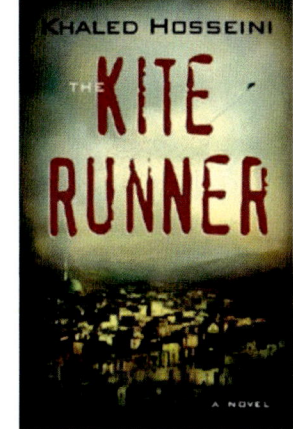

Figure 2.5

The Kite Runner by Khaled Hosseini, 2003, New York, NY: The Berkeley Publishing Group. Cover art copyright 2003 by Honi Werner.

 The Kite Runner is a book.

 The Kite Runner was not written for children. The book is marketed to adults. It was on the *New York Times* Bestseller List and reviewed by adult fiction critics. The author writes for adults.

As with *A Game of Thrones*, young adults read *The Kite Runner*. It is assigned as summer reading and used in high school English classrooms. Due to the subject matter, *The Kite Runner* is often "banned" and placed on the American Library Association's list of frequently challenged books (http://www.ala.org/bbooks/frequentlychallengedbooks/top10).

 People commonly refer to "banned" books. Legally, we don't ban books in the United States. Books are "challenged" and they can be removed from shelves or restricted for purchase. More on that later...

Unlike *A Game of Thrones*, the book begins with two children as the main protagonists, yet young adults read the book. The content of *The Kite Runner* is clearly intended for mature audiences. It seems as if the age of the protagonists may not be the best criterion for classification.

Exhibit C:

Fanfiction (e.g., Wrenfield Hall by Wannabe Charlotte, 2015, Retrieved from https://www.fanfiction.net/s/6369019/1/Wrenfield-Hall)

Fanfiction is fiction written by fans of the characters, plots, and settings borrowed from other works of fiction including movies, books, comics, anime, cartoons, and games. Fanfiction.net boasts the largest collection of fanfiction (https://www.fanfiction.net/) holding millions of stories. But sites such as Archive of Our Own (AO3) (http://archiveofourown.org/) boasts refereed content and better search capabilities, winning a place on a *Time* magazine list of best websites (2015, Retrieved from http://techland.time.com/2013/05/06/50-best-websites-2013/).

Two popular fandomes are based on the *Harry Potter* Series by J.K. Rowling and the *Twilight* Series by Stephanie Meyer. For demonstration purposes, let's examine *Wrenfield Hall*, which is fanfiction based on the characters, Bella and Edward, from *Twilight*.

Is *Wrenfield Hall* children's literature?

 Wrenfield Hall is not a book. In other words, it is not printed on paper and sold in bookstores. It is, however, a fully-developed story, freely available to anyone with an Internet connection. Stories are the basis of many books, but not all stories are published as books.

Some fanfiction is published in book form. For example, *Fifty Shades of Grey* by E.L. James began as fanfiction, but then James distributed her stories in other forms. Following her success, some fanfiction writers resented her cross publication using different outlets (Miller, 2015; http://nypost.com/2015/02/07/fan-fiction-writers-speak-out-against-50-shades-of-grey/).

Does publication format determine what is or is not children's literature? Books are one physical method of sharing text and images, but other methods exist. Some books, like the one you are reading, are shared digitally. "Open-source" or "ebooks" are the more specific labels; yet, they are still defined as books. Before the digital age, authors and illustrators relied on publishing companies to select, produce, and distribute children's literature because the process was too expensive for an individual to pursue mass distribution. Now, self-publishing platforms make it possible for almost anyone to publish in any form.

Do the materials (paper, skin, wood, ivory, computer screen) or the methods of production (binding, gluing, sewing, coding) determine the definition of a book? Of course not. Artistic explorations with format, binding, layout, and design have always been a part of book production.

Perhaps "books" are privileged in definitions of children's literature because there is an assumption of quality and selectivity? Books are reviewed and published by editors and critics. However, book status does not necessarily indicate quality (See Chapters 4 and 5). Also, famous authors, including S.E. Hinton, Neil Gaiman, and Meg Cabot, write fanfiction (Romano, 2014; http://www.dailydot.com/culture/10-famous-authors-fanfiction/). Therefore, literary texts of high quality can be found outside the printed pages of books.

Video 2.1 What makes a book? www.youtube.com/watch?v=x4BK_2VULCU

What makes a book a book? That's a great question. For one answer, read *It's a Book* by Lane Smith, 2010, New York, NY: Roaring Book Press. Copyright 2010 by Lane Smith.

Wrenfield Hall is not written for children. However, the story is rated as "T" which is the Fanfiction.net rating that indicates "Suitable for teens, 13 years and older, with some violence, minor coarse language, and minor suggestive adult themes" (https://www.fanfiction.net/guidelines/). Again, when does childhood end? Given the age restrictions, pre-teens should not read teen fanfic. But they do. What is suitable for children and who decides?

The author of *Wrenfield Hall* did not intend to write the story for children, but children read the posts. Once an author writes and places the story into the public sphere his or her control over readership is lost. Is authorial intent the best way to define a book?

 Wrenfield Hall features young protagonists. Children are part of the plot. Again, the age of the protagonists may be a strong indicator of the best audience for a particular piece of literature; however, there are many examples (such as *Wrenfield Hall*) in which character age is not the best criterion for classification.

 ### Exhibit D:

Unspoken: A Story from the Underground Railroad by Henry Cole (Figure 2.6)

Figure 2.6

Unspoken: A Story from the Underground Railroad by Henry Cole, 2012, New York, NY: Scholastic. Copyright 2012 by Henry Cole.

Set during the time of slavery in the U.S., in *Unspoken*, Henry Cole presents the story of a young girl who discovers a runaway slave hiding in her family's barn. Frightened at first, she eventually decides to help the person by providing food, water, and safety, receiving a special gift in return.

Is *Unspoken* children's literature?

 Unspoken is a book, printed, bound, and distributed by Scholastic Press.

Unspoken is not written for children; it is *illustrated* for children. Tricky! Beyond the title, *Unspoken* does not include any words to advance the plot. Beautiful, brown, charcoal images capture the story with scenes spanning two full pages (Figure 2.7) or broken into panels (Figure 2.8).

Figure 2.7

A full-page spread from *Unspoken: A Story from the Underground Railroad* by Henry Cole, 2012, New York, NY: Scholastic. Copyright 2012 by Henry Cole.

Figure 2.8

Panel illustrations from *Unspoken: A Story from the Underground Railroad* by Henry Cole, 2012, New York, NY: Scholastic. Copyright 2012 by Henry Cole.

How many words are required in order for a story to become "literature?" Must books include text or print? How many pictures are too many? If pictures are juvenile, why do adult texts include images and cover art? For example, graphic novels include images and text. If a viewer can interpret the story from the images, are words necessary?

The author, or in the case of *Unspoken*, the illustrator, intended to *create* a story for children. *Unspoken* is marketed to children and listed as a children's book. However, the history of slavery in the US is filled with stories of horrific cruelty. Wouldn't these issues come up when children wonder why the person had to hide in the straw and was so afraid of being discovered? The power of a wordless book lies in the interpretation by the reader, and readers can take the story in many directions beyond what is "appropriate" for children. Therefore, author or illustrator intention is not a foolproof test for defining children's literature. In addition, the interpretation rests with the reader.

 Henry Cole tells the story from the perspective of a child. In this case, the protagonist is a strong indicator of the intended audience. *Unspoken* features children and it was created for children.

 **Exhibit E:**

The Littlest Bitch by David Quinn and Michael Davis, illustrated by Devon Devereaux (Figure 2.9)

The Littlest Bitch is a story about Isabel, a bossy little girl who aspires to have a corporate career as a venture capitalist and business tycoon. Unfortunately, her thoughtless behavior fuels her physical demise as she literally shrinks into obscurity.

Is *The Littlest Bitch* children's literature?

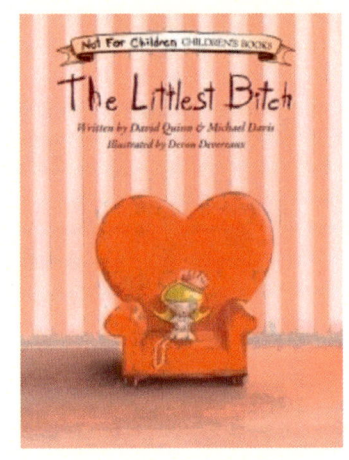

Figure 2.9

The Littlest Bitch by David Quinn and Michael Davis, illustrated by Devon Devereaux, 2010, Portland, ME: Sellers Publishing. Cover art copyright 2010 by Devon Devereaux.

 The Littlest Bitch is a book.

 The Littlest Bitch is not written for children. The book cover clearly states "a not-for-children children's book." The Littlest Bitch, along with many other books with similar intent, uses the format of a picturebook along with a child protagonist to create an illusion of children's literature, but the content is not appropriate for children. Or is it?

What is appropriate for children? How do we decide? In the Grimm Brothers' version of Cinderella, the step-sisters chop off portions of their feet to fit into the shoe. Is this behavior appropriate for children? What levels of violence are acceptable in children's books? What portrayals do we want to reinforce or call into question? The content of children's literature is broad and reaches into adult topics whether we like it or not.

The Littlest Bitch refers to a child, and she is pictured on the cover and throughout the fully-illustrated book. In this case, *The Littlest Bitch* looks like a children's book, reads like a children's book, and features a child. Yet, it is not for children. What gives?

I would like to submit these exhibits into evidence. They represent the outliers and renegades that stand as counterclaims against a simple definition that children's literature consists of books written for children, read by children, and/or written about children. As a result, I revise the previously provided definition of children's literature:

Children's literature is an assortment of books (and not books) written for children (and adults), read by children (and adults), and written about children (but not necessarily).

That was a better definition. But it is not completely inclusive. As further evidence, I submit the following:

Children's literature is a collection of books as old as the printing press (Figure 2.10)

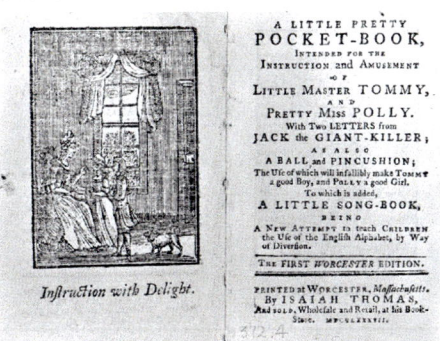

Figure 2.10

Gutenberg invented movable type printing around 1439 and children's books evolved alongside changes in the printing process. Although not the very first children's book, *A Little Pretty Pocket Book* was an influential publication. *A Little Pretty Pocket Book* by John Newbery, 1744, Worcester, MA: Isaiah Thomas. Copyright expired.

WHAT IS CHILDREN'S LITERATURE?
DEFINITIONS AND DELIMITATIONS

and as new as the latest app (Figure 2.11).

Figure 2.11
Popular book characters can lead to popular apps. *Don't Let the Pigeon Run This App* by Mo Willems and you, 2011, Glendale, CA: Disney Enterprises Inc. Cover art copyright 2011 by Disney Enterprises Inc.

Children's literature portrays all aspects of humanity (Figure 2.12),

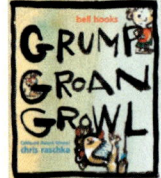

Figure 2.12
Some children's literature deals with everyday emotions as demonstrated in *Grump, Groan, Growl* by bell hooks and illustrated by Chris Raschka, 2008, New York, NY: Disney-Hyperion. Cover art copyright 2008 by Chris Raschka.

inhumanity (Figure 2.13)

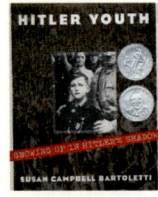

Figure 2.13
Many forms of children's literature explore the dark side. For example, learn how Hitler exploited children in *Hitler Youth: Growing Up in Hitler's Shadow* by Susan Campbell Bartoletti, 2005, New York, NY: Scholastic. Copyright 2005 by Susan Campbell Bartoletti.

and non-humanity (Figure 2.14),

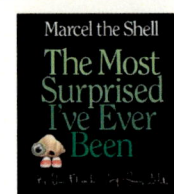

Figure 2.14
Children's literature is full of memorable characters. He's not human, but he acts like one. *Marcel the Shell: The Most Surprised I've Ever Been* by Dean Fleischer-Camp and Jenny Slate, 2014, New York, NY: Razorbill. Copyright 2014 by Dean Fleischer-Camp.

all periods of human history (Figure 2.15)

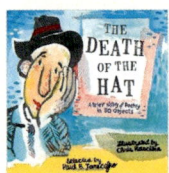

Figure 2.15
Children's literature includes unique views of history. *The Death of the Hat: A Brief History of Poetry in 50 Objects* by Paul B. Janeczko and illustrated by Chris Raschka, 2015, Somerville, MA: Candlewick. Cover art copyright 2015 by Chris Raschka.

and all places of this world (Figure 2.16)

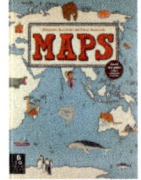

Figure 2.16
Children's literature covers the whole world. *Maps* by Aleksandra Mizielinski and Daniel Mizielinski, 2013, New York, NY: Big Picture Press. Copyright 2013 by Aleksandra Mizielinski and Daniel Mizielinski.

as well as worlds beyond (Figure 2.17).

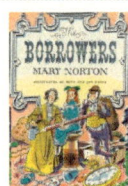

Figure 2.17
Explore the secret worlds of your imagination in children's literature. *The Borrowers* by Mary Norton and illustrated by Beth Krush and Joe Krush, 1953, New York, NY: Harcourt Brace. Cover art copyright 1953 by Beth Krush and Joe Krush.

Children's literature is poetry (Figure 2.18),

Figure 2.18

Children's literature claims world famous poets. *Where the Sidewalk Ends* by Shel Silverstein, 1974, New York, NY: Harper & Row Publishers. Copyright 1974 by Shel Silverstein.

fiction (Figure 2.19),

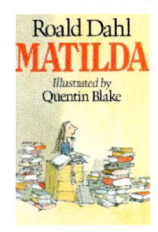

Figure 2.19

Children's literature includes world famous storytellers. *Matilda* by Roald Dahl and illustrated by Quentin Blake, 1988, New York, NY: Penguin. Cover art copyright 1988 by Quentin Blake.

nonfiction (Figure 2.20),

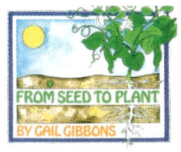

Figure 2.20

Children's literature explains everything we need to know. *From Seed to Plant* by Gail Gibbons, 1993, New York, NY: Holiday House. Copyright 1993 by Gail Gibbons.

argument (Figure 2.21),

Figure 2.21

Children's literature portrays human qualities, desires, and perspectives. *No, David!* by David Shannon, 1998, New York, NY: Blue Sky Press. Copyright 1998 by David Shannon.

and biography (Figure 2.22).

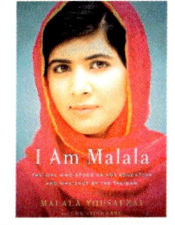

Figure 2.22

Children's literature demonstrates human resilience and power. *I am Malala: The Girl Who Stood Up for Education and Was Shot by the Taliban* by Malala Yousafzai and Christina Lamb, 2013, New York, NY: Little, Brown and Company. Copyright 2013 by Malala Yousafzai and Christina Lamb.

Children's literature includes picturebooks (Figure 2.23)

Figure 2.23

Jumanji by Chris Van Allsburg, 1981, New York, NY: Houghton Mifflin Harcourt. Copyright 1981 by Chris Van Allsburg.

and pop-up books (Figure 2.24; Video 2.2),

Figure 2.24

Encyclopedia Prehistorica Dinosaurs: The Definitive Pop-Up by Robert Sabuda and Matthew Reinhart, 2005, New York, NY: Candlewick. Copyright 2005 by Robert Sabuda and Matthew Reinhart.

paper books (Figure 2.25)

Figure 2.25

It's a Book by Lane Smith, 2010, New York, NY: Roaring Brook Press. Copyright 2010 by Lane Smith.

plays (Figure 2.26)

Figure 2.26

Peter Pan: The Boy Who Wouldn't Grow Up by J.M. Barrie, 1904, London, England: Hodder & Stoughton. Copyright 1988 by Great Ormond Street Hospital.

and digital texts (Figure 2.27).

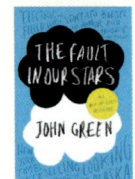

Figure 2.27

The Fault in Our Stars by John Green, 2012, New York, NY: Penguin. Copyright 2012 by John Green.

Children's literature includes many stories (Figure 2.28)

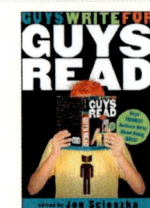

Figure 2.28

Guys Write for Guys Read edited by Jon Scieszka, 2005, New York, NY: Viking Press. Copyright 2005 by Jon Scieszka.

and single stories (Figure 2.29),

Figure 2.29

Delores Huerta: A Hero to Migrant Workers by Sarah Warren and illustrated by Robert Casilla, 2012, Seattle, WA: Two Lions. Cover art copyright 2012 by Robert Casilla.

happy stories (Figure 2.30),

Figure 2.30

Mr. Happy by Roger Hargreaves, 1971, London, England: Price Stern Sloan. Copyright 1971 by Roger Hargreaves.

sad stories (Figure 2.31),

Figure 2.31

Sad Underwear and Other Complications by Judith Viorst and illustrated by Richard Hull, 2000, New York, NY: Antheneum. Cover art copyright 2000 by Richard Hull.

scary stories (Figure 2.32),

Figure 2.32

Scary Stories to Tell in the Dark by Alvin Schwartz and illustrated by Stephen Gammell, 1981, New York, NY: Scholastic. Cover art copyright 1981 by Stephen Gammell.

mad stories (Figure 2.33),

Figure 2.33

Babymouse #14: Mad Scientist by Jennifer Holm and illustrated by Matthew Holm, 2011, New York, NY: Random House Books for Young Readers. Cover art copyright 2011 by Matthew Holm.

and not stories (Figure 2.34).

Figure 2.34

Locomotive by Brian Floca, 2013, New York, NY: Atheneum Books for Young Readers. Copyright 2013 by Brian Floca.

Children's literature is created for and read by children, adolescents, and adults. Children's literature is high art, extraordinary writing, and everything in-between.

 Video 2.2 Look, Touch, Shake, and Swipe: Pop Up Books and Interactive eBooks http://www.kaltura.com/tiny/wlrn1

LOOK, TOUCH, SHAKE, AND SWIPE: POP UP BOOKS AND INTERACTIVE eBOOKS

WITH JENIFER SCHNEIDER

THE INSIDE, OUTSIDE, AND UPSIDE DOWNS OF CHILDREN'S LITERATURE | From Poets and Pop-ups to Princesses and Porridge

It's difficult to appreciate the 3D art of pop-up artists like Robert Sabuda and Matthew Reinhart in a 2D, non-moving, space. To see some of the intricacies in pop up books, watch this pop up video.

A Working Definition

Children's literature is a label for collections of texts that are specifically written and/or illustrated for and/or about youth as well as texts that are not specifically written and/or illustrated for and/or about youth but which youth choose to read, view, and/or write. Adults are welcome to read children's literature too—many do.

Children's literature provides encounters with the world that shape the meaning children make of the world (Kiefer, Hepler, Hickman, Huck, 2007). Having a vicarious or "lived through" experience with literature, builds readers' aesthetic responses and perceptions (Rosenblatt, 1978). Reading literature increases one's sensitivity to the power of the written word (Sipe, 2008) and contributes to visual expression (Brenner, 2011; Sipe, 2011). For these reasons, adults study children's literature as scholars, critics, educators, librarians, entrepreneurs, and social commentators.

A Brief History of Children's and Young Adult Literature

With my almost anything goes orientation toward children's literature broadly detailed, let's take a look at how this body of literature came to be through selected examples and important artifacts.

The origins of children's literature are hard to nail down. Do cave illustrations count? In my opinion, why not? There is evidence cave paintings included children (2015, November 10, Retrieved from http://www.telegraph.co.uk/news/earth/earthnews/8798392/Childrens-prehistoric-cave-paintings-discovered.html).

I accept different formats of text as representatives of children's literature (and by text I am referring to symbolic systems of meaning). I realize cave paintings are not "books," but they were a form of communication most relevant and accessible to the people of that time.

I am not obsessed with the content of the cave drawings either. If hunting deer was the trending topic of ancient people, then children and young adults needed to know about it. Cave youth needed to access others' thoughts and ideas. They needed information.

Somewhere between prehistoric cave people and the Renaissance, the Sumerians and others invented cuneiform to represent sounds that captured human speech, the Egyptians developed hieroglyphs for record-keeping, and the Chinese used oracle bones and inscriptions to communicate with their ancestors (2015, November 10, Retrieved from http://www.britishmuseum.org/explore/themes/writing/historic_writing.aspx). Gutenberg created a printing press and the speed of information exchange increased dramatically (2015, November 10, http://www.history.com/topics/middle-ages/videos/mankind-the-story-of-all-of-us-the-printing-press). Here are a few examples.

1400's : A 1485 Italian edition of *Aesopus Moralisatus* by Bernardino di Benalli (Figure 2.35).

Figure 2.35

An Italian translation of Aesop's Fables was published as *Aesopus Moralisatus* by Bernardino di Benalli, 1485, Venezia, Italy. Copyright 1485 by Bernardino di Benalli. The book is available for viewing at https://en.wikipedia.org/wiki/Aesop%27s_Fables#/media/File:Aesopus_-_Aesopus_moralisatus,_circa_1485_-_2950804_Scan00010.tif.

1500's: Michael Agricola's ABC book published in 1559 (Figure 2.36)

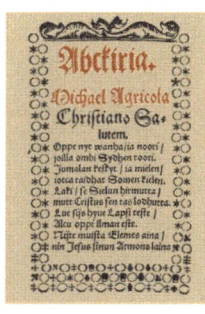

Figure 2.36

Abckiria is the first children's book in Finnish, written by Bishop Michael Agricola (c. 1510-1557), 1559, Helsinki, Finnland: Finnish Literature Society. Copyright 1559 by Michael Agricola. The complete book is available for viewing at http://www.childrenslibrary.org/icdl/BookPreview?bookid=agrabck_00070001&route=advanced_327_326_0_English_0_all&lang=English&msg=&ilang=English.

1600's: Johannes Amos Comenius' *Orbis Pictus*, 1657, is widely considered to be the first picturebook school book (Comenius, 1896) (Figure 2.37).

Figure 2.37

Johannes Amos Comenius' *Orbis Pictus*, 1657, is widely considered to be the first picturebook school book (Comenius, 1896). *Orbis Pictus* by Johannes Amos Comenius, 1685, London, England: Charles Mearne. Copyright expired. The 1728 edition is available for viewing at http://www.gutenberg.org/files/28299/28299-h/28299-h.htm.

1700's: *The Catechism of Nature for the Use of Children* by Dr. Martinet published in 1793 (Figure 2.38).

Figure 2.38

The Catechism of Nature for the Use of Children by Dr. Martinet was published in 1793. Figure 2.38 is an English version translated from Dutch. The Catechism of Nature for the Use of Children by Dr. Martinet, 1793, Boston, MA: Young and Etheridge. Copyright expired.

As these representative texts indicate, writing evolved across cultures and through various modes and media. Tablets, stones, pamphlets, and books were vehicles for conserving history or sharing information among scholars, the wealthy, and royalty.

Eventually, the creation of chapbooks, and other forms of cheaply-produced texts, increased people's access to books. Chapbooks often featured rhymes, fairy tales, or alphabet books along with crime stories, songs, and prophecies; however, children were not the only target audience of these texts (2015, November 10, Retrieved from http://www.vam.ac.uk/content/articles/n/national-art-library-chapbooks-collection/).

Fairy tales, collected by the Brothers Grimm as part of their study of linguistics, were oral stories that were shared among adults. Their work was not necessarily intended for children either (Ashliman, 2013, Retrieved from http://www.pitt.edu/~dash/grimm.html).

Of course, children read the texts of their times, or listened to the stories around them, but they only had access to the books that were placed within their lives.

Parallel to the publication of chapbooks, publishers developed instructional materials specifically for children (Video 2.3). Spelling books, primers, and alphabet books were intended to support religious and/or academic instruction for children. Yet, the notion of reading for pleasure or the production of texts specifically for children's amusement was not a priority.

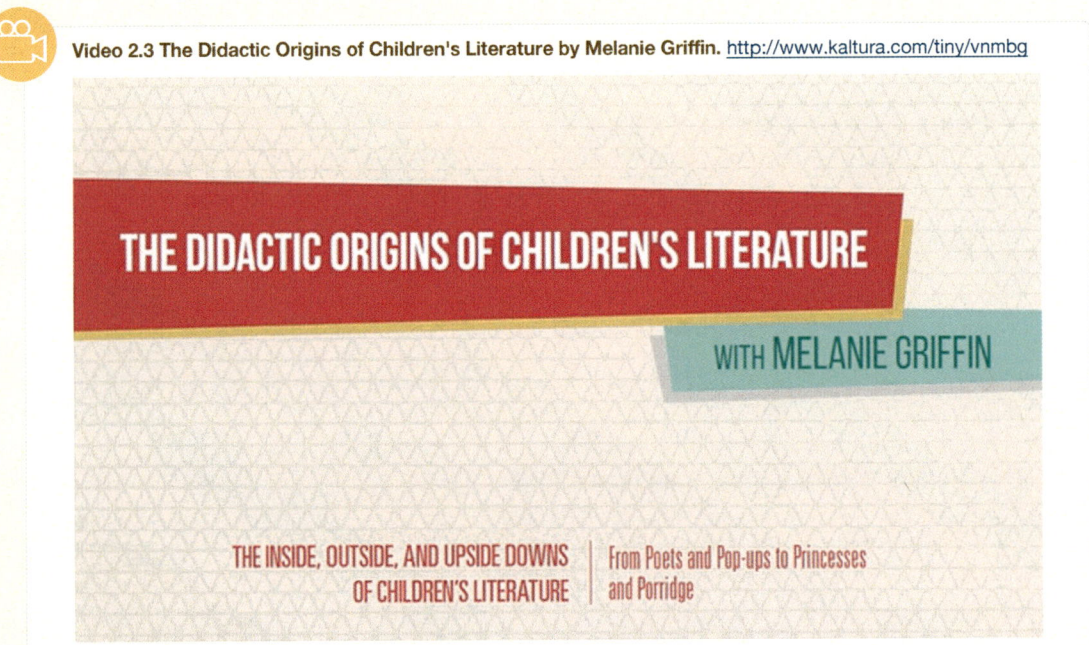

Video 2.3 The Didactic Origins of Children's Literature by Melanie Griffin. http://www.kaltura.com/tiny/vnmbg

For the most part, the 18th century was the time period in which "children's literature" became a thing. According to Professor M.O. Grenby (2015), Professor of Eighteenth-Century Studies in the School of English at Newcastle University,

A cluster of London publishers began to produce new books designed to instruct and delight young readers. Thomas Boreman was one, who followed his *Description of Three Hundred Animals* (Figure 2.39) with a series of illustrated histories of London landmarks jokily (because they were actually very tiny) called the Gigantick Histories (1740-43). Another was Mary Cooper, whose two-volume *Tommy Thumb's Pretty Song Book* (1744) is the first known nursery rhyme collection, featuring early versions of well-known classics like 'Bah, bah, a black sheep', 'Hickory dickory dock', 'London Bridge is falling down' and 'Sing a song of sixpence' (Figure 2.40). But the most celebrated of these pioneers is John Newbery, whose first book for the entertainment of children was *A Little Pretty Pocket-Book Intended for the Instruction and Amusement of Little Master Tommy and Pretty Miss Polly* (c.1744) (Figure 2.41). - See and read more at: (Grenby, 2015, Retrieved from http://www.bl.uk/romantics-and-victorians/articles/the-origins-of-childrens-literature#sthash.6MIH4V0M.dpuf).

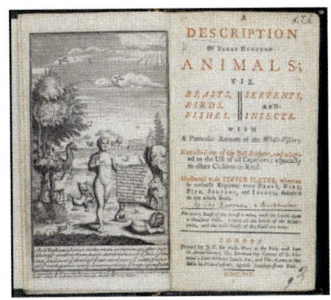

Figure 2.39

A Description of Three Hundred Animals by Thomas Boreman, 1730, London, England: Thomas Boreman. Copyright expired.

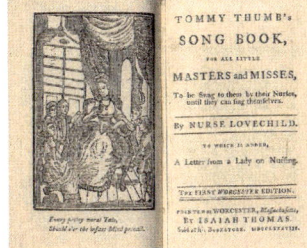

Figure 2.40

Image from *Tommy Thumb's Pretty Song Book* by Mary Cooper, 1788, Worcester, MA: Isaiah Thomas. Copyright expired.

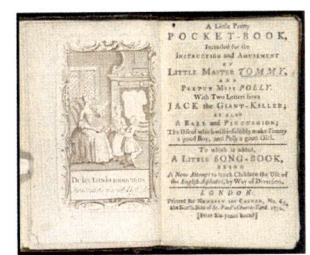

Figure 2.41

John Newbery published *A Little Pretty Pocket-Book Intended for the Instruction and Amusement of Little Master Tommy and Pretty Miss Polly* in 1744. Image from *A Little Pretty Pocket-Book Intended for the Instruction and Amusement of Little Master Tommy and Pretty Miss Polly* by John Newbery, 1770, London, England: Newbery and Carnan. Copyright expired.

With the development of improved printing processes and the recognized value of books and literacy, the field of children's literature shifted and expanded.

1800's: *The Adventures of Robinson Crusoe* written by Daniel Defoe and illustrated by Paul Adolphe Kauffman (1884) is still widely read and this version boasts "coloured illustrations" on the book cover (Figure 2.42).

1900's: By the 1900's, children's literature was more pervasive in homes, libraries, and schools. The global importance of children's literature is represented in books published in many languages all over the world (Figures 2.43, 2.44, 2.45, 2.46)

2000's: More recently, children's literature has taken a digital turn. In addition to ebooks, attempts to reflect diverse perspectives have increased with open access publishing and grass-roots promotion through social networking. For example, the Anna Lindh Foundation promotes Arab children's literature (http://www.arabchildrensliterature.com/about).

Children's books are an important part of civilization. The creation of children's literature led to changes in how children read, how children learn in school, and how children understand the world. Yet none of the changes would have been possible without access to books.

Figure 2.42

The Adventures of Robinson Crusoe written by Daniel Defoe and illustrated by Paul Adolphe Kauffman, 1884, London, England: T. Fisher Unwin. Copyright expired. The book is available for viewing at http://www.childrenslibrary.org/icdl/BookPage?bookid=defthea_00360697&pnum1=1&twoPage=false&route=advanced_329_326_0_English_0_all&size=0&fullscreen=false&lang=English&ilang=English.

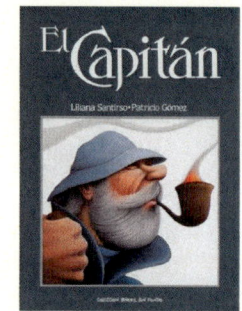

Figure 2.43

El Capitán by Liliana Santirso and illustrated by Patricio Gómez, 1998, Mexico: Celta Amaquemecan. Cover art copyright 1998 by Patrico Gómez. The book is available for viewing at http://www.childrenslibrary.org/icdl/BookPreview?bookid=sntcptn_00160004&route=advanced_335_326_0_English_0_all&lang=English&msg=&ilang=English.

Figure 2.44

All We Need Are Dragons by Ljubivoje Ršumović and illustrated by Dušan Petričić, 1990, Serbia: Rad. Cover art copyright 1990 by Rad. The book is available for viewing at http://www.childrenslibrary.org/icdl/BookPreview?bookid=rsujosn_00380094&route=advanced_335_326_0_English_0_all&lang=English&msg=&ilang=English.

Figure 2.45

Intik'a: How the Taquileo island was not an island but a very tall mountain that was called Intik'a by Cronwell Jara Jiménez, 1995, Lima, Peru: Ironyodla. Copyright 1995 by Cronwell Jara Jiménez. The book is available for viewing at http://www.childrenslibrary.org/icdl/BookPreview?bookid=jarinti_00510025&route=advanced_335,389_326,359_0_English_0_all&lang=English&msg=&ilang=English.

Figure 2.46

Mbegu Ya Ajabu (The Amazing Seed) by Deus. M. Richard, 1997, Kenya: Sasa Sema. Copyright 1997 by Readit Books. The book is available for viewing at http://www.childrenslibrary.org/icdl/BookPreview?bookid=ricmbeg_00590008&route=advanced_335,380_326,359_0_English_0_all&lang=English&msg=&ilang=English

CHAPTER 03

GOT BOOKS?
(ACCESS, COLLECTIONS, AND DIGITAL RESOURCES)

Access to Books

Identifying and categorizing examples of children's literature is an important skill but *finding* children's literature is a whole different story. In this chapter, I focus on the central conduits for the collection, curation, and distribution of children's literature: libraries, booksellers, and museums.

The Library

For some individuals, the library is an archaic place, filled with memories of dusty books and shushing librarians. Some stuffy libraries still exist, but they are fading away as modern libraries are now equipped with hi-tech hubs, collaborative meeting areas, green designs, and cafes. In fact, the ALA offers resources for library-building design to help architects and planners achieve a shared vision for library space usage (http://www.ala.org/acrl/academic-library-building-design-resources-planning).

If you dig **libraries** as I do, THEN FOLLOW THESE LINKS TO A SERIES OF LISTS of the "best" libraries in the world:

62	World's Most Beautiful Libraries
25	Most Famous Libraries
35	Best Libraries in the World
20	Libraries So Beautiful They'll Bring Out the Bookworm in Everyone
45	Most Majestic Libraries in the World
18	Libraries Every Book Lover Should Visit

I have worked with students who haven't visited a library in 10 or more years. As a book lover, it's hard for me to believe. As a professor, it's the reason I make people go—the library is an amazing resource. Yes, yes, yes, you can find information online. But I guarantee you'll find more in a library because you will search differently. In addition, you will find better stuff if you work with a librarian. There is an art to searching for books and librarians have mad skills in online databases and in the stacks.

Go on a library scavenger hunt! Find the following:

- One book of poetry for children written by Eloise Greenfield or Arnold Adoff.
- One Newbery winner.
- One Caldecott winner.
- One book about a science concept (any topic will do, but it has to be for kids—college textbooks do not count).
- One biography written for children.

Video 3.1 Jenny's Tour Through the Wackety Stacks http://www.kaltura.com/tiny/rr3ev

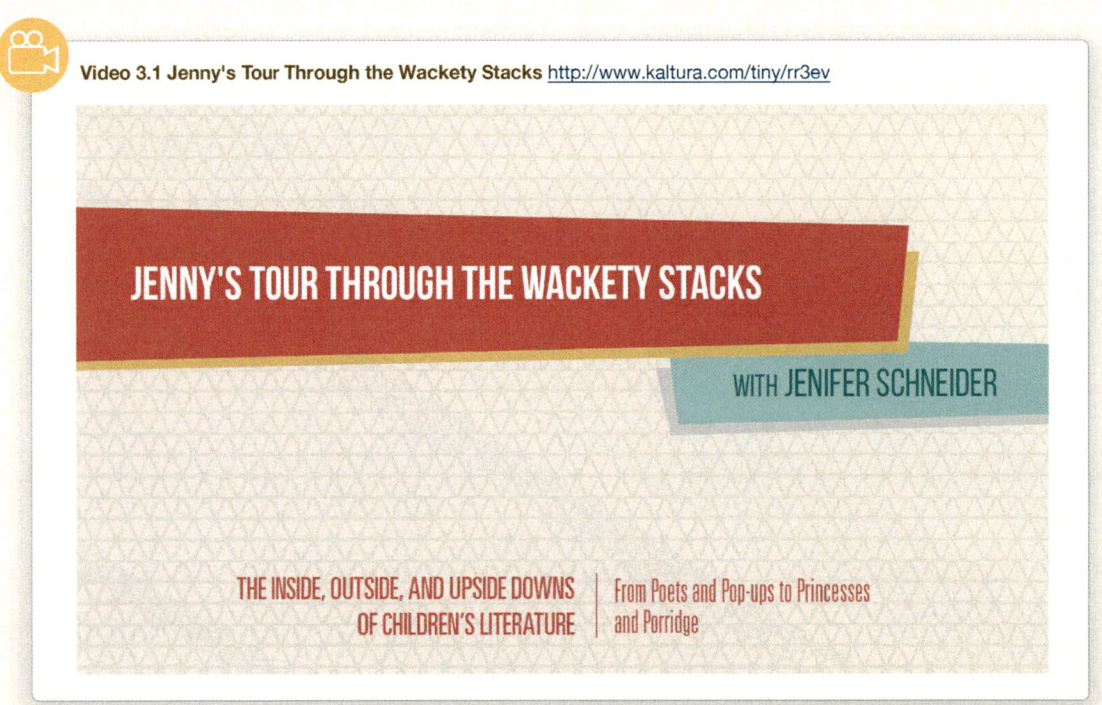

I have also worked with students who come from countries in which public libraries are not available or accessible. A free, public library is an unprecedented resource for them. Similarly, I have worked with students who are traveling, living, or studying abroad and they are shocked by the limited availability of books in other countries. It's true. The library is the cornerstone of democracy and the key to an educated public.

Why do you think Hitler burned books?
(http://www.ushmm.org/outreach/en/article.php?ModuleId=10007677)

Why do you think North Korea censors what people read?
(http://www.nytimes.com/2015/04/22/world/eritrea-and-north-korea-are-worlds-most-censored-countries-advocacy-group-says.html?_r=0)

Why do you think US slaves were forbidden to read or write?
(http://www.pbs.org/wnet/slavery/experience/education/history2.html; http://www.yale.edu/glc/archive/927.htm)

OK, so this isn't a book about the history of the United States or a political treatise on democracy, but understanding the history of the library is important when we think about children's literature and access to books.

- Did you know libraries did not have special sections for children until the late 1800's (Hanaway 1897)?

- Did you know some library hours were often limited for girls, giving priority to working boys; and some libraries were only open to boys of a certain class or employment level (Powell, 1917; Sayers, 1963)?

- Did you know many libraries were segregated and Black people were not allowed to use all public libraries until the Civil Rights Act of 1964 (Lee, 1991, 1998; Malone, 1995)? (That's just a few years before I was born.) Even then, many libraries refused service.

As with all history lessons, it is important to understand the origins of the library because this knowledge enhances our awareness of the cultural, social, and political structures that shape our experiences. In this case, the library shapes our experiences with books. Think about it. The policies to segregate libraries or deny access to particular individuals certainly affected the children at that time (Figure 3.1). We know, for example, parent-preschooler reading is related to outcome measures such as language growth, emergent literacy, and reading achievement (Bus, Van Ijzendoorn, & Pellegrini, 1995). Book reading also affects children's acquisition of the written language register (i.e. their ability to speak or write in standard ways) (Bus, Van Ijzendoorn, & Pellegrini, 1995). Therefore, if you limit access to books, you limit opportunities.

Figure 3.1

Reading lesson in African American elementary school in Washington, D.C., by Marjory Collins, 1942. Library of Congress Prints and Photographs Division Washington, D.C. 20540 USA. No known restrictions.

If you limit access to books, you limit opportunities.

But the impact of book reading extends to the next generations as well. Children with limited literacy experiences can grow into adults with lower literacy levels. Adults with lower literacy levels often doubt their ability to support their children as readers, providing them with fewer books and fewer literacy experiences in the home (Neuman & Celano, 2001). In other words, adults with limited literacy do not have the personal experiences from which to draw upon as they make parental choices for their children. It takes time and intervening actions to undo cycles of illiteracy that are brought about by public policies and social practices.

The library plays a central role in the education of the populace. For this reason, let's examine the evolution of the modern library in relation to its focus on children.

 Want to know more about the evolution of libraries? Check out the "History of Libraries" http://eduscapes.com/history/index.htm.

Ancient libraries. The oldest known library in the world is in Ebla, Syria (Figure 3.2), where archeologists discovered "a vast archive of thousands of clay tablets dating from about 2600 to 2300 B.C." (Wellisch, 1981). Other ancient libraries, such as the Library of Alexandria in Egypt (283 B.C.E.) and libraries in Athens and Rome held significant texts for scholars to study (Casson, 2001). No children allowed.

Figure 3.2
The oldest known library in the world is in Ebla, Syria, 2008. Photograph by Effi Schweizer. Reprinted with permission.

 No children allowed!

University, religious, and government libraries. Monks, rabbis, clergy, clerics, and other religious persons maintained institutional libraries to store historical scrolls and other documents to conserve history and religious doctrines. Churches also funded parochial libraries that included religious texts as well as books of law, math, natural history, and medicine (Steiner, 1896).

 No children allowed!

Of note, in 1695, Thomas Bray, a clergyman in the Anglican Church, devised and developed a system of parochial libraries that were funded by English citizens and eventually supported by public funds in the colonies. Thomas Bray initiated the idea and directed donations as the "best Inducement to Pious and Sober Ministers to come and live amongst us; And will be the Cause of such Education be given, both to our own People, and Native Indians, as will best promote the Interest of Religion and Morality in this province" (Steiner, 1896, p. 67). As a predecessor of the branch library, these small outreach initiatives of the church/state, were managed by ministers and meant to socialize people (Figure 3.3).

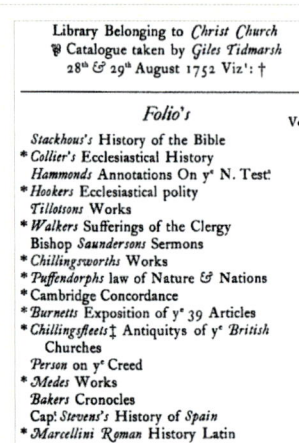

Figure 3.3

Excerpt of catalog from the Old North Church, 1752. Photograph by Percival Merritt. The parochial library of the eighteenth century in Christ Church, Boston. Boston: Merrymount Press, 1917. Public domain.

Universities also maintained libraries for students. Given most universities did not admit women or people of different races or ethnicities until the 1900s, access was limited to the student body and mediated by scholars. Of course, children were not given access to any of these libraries.

  No children allowed!

Public libraries. The United States, as a former Spanish, French, and British colony, borrowed heavily from European practices and idealistic visions for information exchange. With little attention to American Indian philosophies and traditions of poetics, performances, and texts (Figure 3.4) (See Swann & Krupat, 1987), the US's evolving creation of a democratic government along with free libraries and compulsory schooling, necessitated a focus on the book to both conserve and promulgate Western ideas and practices.

Figure 3.4

American Indian cultures included literate and artistic practices, and they were ignored in favor of European trends. "The Red Child of the Forest" by Eleanor Stackhouse Atkinson in The *How and Why Library,* 1909. Public domain.

During the Colonial years, Benjamin Franklin's recognition of the importance of access to books led to his involvement in the creation of the Library Company of Philadelphia (http://www.librarycompany.org/) (Hayes, 2008). Benjamin Franklin and his friends owned impressive personal libraries. Books were extremely expensive and required shipping from Europe to the Colonies. Benjamin wanted his friends to share books with each other, but the men did not want to give away their prized possessions. Instead, they combined resources and made donations to develop a subscription-service library. *The Library Company* (est. 1731) (Figure 3.5) offered subscribers the opportunity to read more books than they could purchase on their own, and from this concept, the public library emerged (Fletcher, 1894).

A short Account of the LIBRARY.

THE Library-Company was form'd in 1731, by Constitutions or Articles entred into by 50 Persons, each obliging himself to pay 40 s. for purchasing the first Parcel of Books, and 10 s. *per annum* to defray Charges and encrease the Library.

Ten Directors or Managers of the Library, and a Treasurer, are chosen yearly by Vote, at a General Meeting of the Company.

The Number of Members are now encreased to upwards of 70. Persons enclining to be admitted, apply to any one of the Directors, who nominates them at the next monthly Meeting of Directors; and being allowed, and paying to the Treasurer the Value of a Share at the Time, and signing the Articles, they become Members.

Any Member may borrow a Book for 2, 3, or 4 Weeks, leaving his Note for double Value, and paying a small Penalty if 'tis not return'd at the Time agreed; which Penalties are applied to defraying Charges, or purchasing more Books.

Every Member has an absolute Property in his Share; may devise it in his Will, or dispose of it when he pleases to any Person the Directors approve. And Shares so sold have always hitherto yielded as much as they had cost. As Shares encrease yearly in Value 10 s. so much being yearly added by each Subscriber to the Stock of Books, a Share which at first was worth but 40 s. is now valued at 6 *l.* 10 s. But for this small Sum, which, laid out in Books, would go but a little Way, every Member has the Use of a Library now worth upwards of 500 *l.* whereby *Knowledge* is in this City render'd more cheap and easy to be come at, to the great Pleasure and Advantage of the studious Part of the Inhabitants.

Those who are not Subscribers may notwithstanding borrow Books, leaving in the Hands of the Librarian, as a Pledge, a Sum of Money proportion'd to the Value of the Book borrow'd, and paying a small Acknowledgment for the Reading, which is apply'd to the Use of the Library.

The Library is open and Attendance given every Saturday Afternoon from 4 a Clock 'til 8.

Besides the Books in this Catalogue given to the Library, the Company have been favour'd with several generous Donations; as, a curious Air-Pump, with its Apparatus, a large double Microscope, and other valuable Instruments, from the Hon. JOHN PENN, Esq; A handsome Lot of Ground whereon to build a House for the Library, from the Hon. THOMAS PENN, Esq; Proprietaries of the Province; and the Sum of 34 *l. Sterl.* (to be laid out in Books) from Dr. *Sydserfe*, late of *Antigua*.

At present the Books are deposited in the West Wing of the State-House, by Favour of the General Assembly.

It is now TEN Years since the Company was first establish'd; and we have the Pleasure of observing, That tho' 'tis compos'd of so many Persons of different Sects, Parties and Ways of Thinking, yet no Differences relating to the Affairs of the Library, have arisen among us; but every Thing has been conducted with great Harmony, and to general Satisfaction. Which happy Circumstance will, we hope, always continue.

NOTE, *A Copy of the Articles or Constitutions is left in the Library, for the Perusal of all that desire to be more fully inform'd.*

THE END.

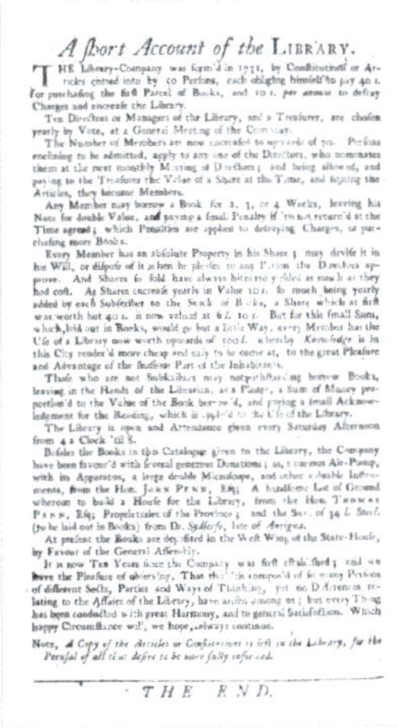

Figure 3.5

The Library Company of Philadelphia was founded in 1731 by Benjamin Franklin. Image scan of "A Short Account of the Library," in *A Catalogue of Books Belonging to the Library Company of Philadelphia* (Philadelphia: B. Franklin, 1741). No known restrictions.

Selected youth were allowed.

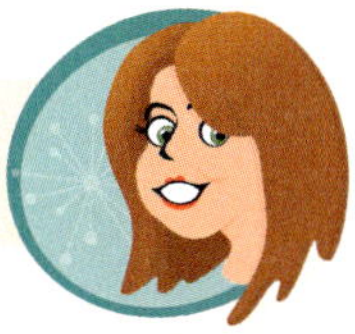

Another influential figure, Thomas Jefferson, also accumulated a vast personal collection of books from all over the world. When the Library of Congress collection was burned as a result of the War of 1812, Jefferson agreed to sell his books to Congress (Jefferson & Wilson, 2010). According to the Library of Congress website, "Jefferson anticipated controversy over the nature of his collection, which included books in foreign languages and volumes of philosophy, science, literature, and other topics not normally viewed as part of a legislative library" (https://www.loc.gov/about/history-of-the-library/).

Jefferson's extensive collection and eclectic interests established a diverse national library (Figure 3.6). The "Jeffersonian concept of universality, the belief that all subjects are important to the library of the American legislature, is the philosophy and rationale behind the comprehensive collecting policies of today's Library of Congress" (https://www.loc.gov/about/history-of-the-library/).

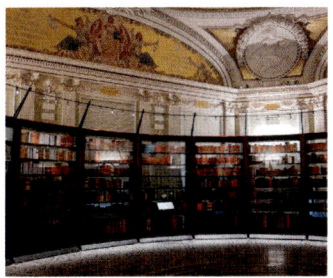

Figure 3.6

An exhibit featuring Thomas Jefferson's library in the Thomas Jefferson Building at the Library of Congress in Washington, DC, 2015. Photograph by Smash the Iron Cage. Reprinted with permission.

In addition to Franklin's and Jefferson's contributions, Andrew Carnegie's enormous wealth provided the funding for large philanthropic initiatives, one of which was the Carnegie library system (Figure 3.7). Andrew Carnegie made his fortune in steel but he gave away over 90% of his money to build libraries and fund other educational endeavors. As a youth, Carnegie experienced the benefits of a library when a Civil War Colonel opened his personal library to the working boys of the neighborhood (Van Slyck, 1995). Carnegie felt he owed his business success to the knowledge he gained through exposure to the Colonel's books. As a result, Carnegie established a corporation to distribute his money to build over 2,500 libraries across the United States, and throughout Europe, 1880 to 1920. The Carnegie Corporation approved each free, public library based on local need for library facilities. Carnegie paid for the building only upon agreement that the local city or town maintained the libraries through taxes (Van Slyck, 1995). Carnegie also built libraries for colleges and universities often supporting colleges for African American students.

Figure 3.7

The West Tampa Free Public Library is a Carnegie Library built in 1913. The library continues to serve the West Tampa community. Photograph by Ebyabe, 2007. Reprinted with permission.

 Youth were allowed but segregated.

Franklin's and Jefferson's libraries were foundational in concept and collection to what currently exists in libraries today. Additionally, Andrew Carnegie's libraries provided unprecedented access for some, along with public funding and changes in design that improved the user experience (Figure 3.8).

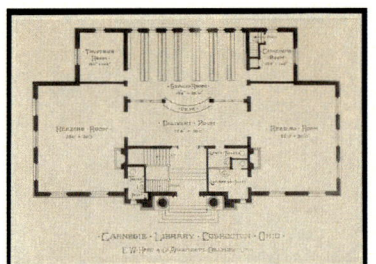

Figure 3.8

Carnegie libraries featured large reading rooms to encourage extended visits. Carnegie Library, Coshocton, Ohio / E.W. Hart, architects, 1903. Library of Congress Prints and Photographs Division Washington, D.C. 20540 USA. No known restrictions.

However, none of these early libraries focused space or programming for children. As Deborah Stevenson (2011) points out, "Literate children have often been a minority; even among them, many have had neither money with which to buy books, other opportunities to access them, especially in the pre-library days, nor the school or the leisure time in which to read them…. The 'children' in 'children's literature' have been a privileged subset of a much larger group" (p. 180).

Service to children came at the insistence of the librarians. In addition to recognizing the emergence of books and buildings, it is necessary to acknowledge the corresponding significance of the librarians who worked within them.

The Librarians and the American Library Association (ALA). Beginning in 1853 a group of librarians made their first attempt to form the American Library Association to promote library service and librarianship. Officially founded in 1876, the current mission of ALA is to "provide leadership for the development, promotion, and improvement of library and information services and the profession of librarianship in order to enhance learning and ensure access to information for all" (http://www.ala.org/aboutala/). For a complete history of the organization, visit the ALA website (http://www.ala.org/aboutala/history/details-ala-history).

Since its founding years, members of the ALA have fought for the direction of public libraries (Jevons, 1881; Quincy, 1876). Librarians also debated the design of library spaces and access to the stacks (Figure 3.9). As Van Slyck (1995) describes these early years of the ALA, "the traditional understanding of the library as a treasure house, protecting its books from untrustworthy readers, was falling out of currency. Increasingly, the library profession sought to use the public library to bring readers and books together, rather than to keep them apart" (p. 25).

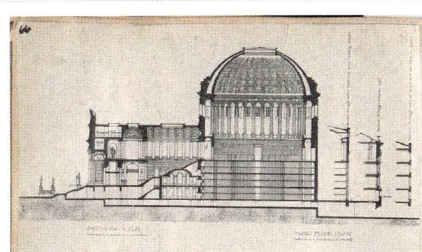

Figure 3.9
Librarians frequently debated library design. Competitive design for the New York Public Library / Brite & Bacon, architects, 1897. Library of Congress Prints and Photographs Division Washington, D.C. 20540 USA. No known restrictions.

By the early 1900s, Bostwick (1910) reported that open-shelf libraries in which the user selected his or her own books were replacing closed-shelf libraries in which books were stored in large alcoves where library staff scaled ladders to retrieve them (Figure 3.10).

Figure 3.10
View of library with stacks and skylight by George Gardner Rockwood, 1832-1911. Image scan of Robert N. Dennis collection of stereoscopic views. Stephen A. Schwarzman Building / Photography Collection, Miriam and Ira D. Wallach Division of Art, Prints and Photographs. Public domain.

Librarians also debated issues of access in other ways. Some libraries required users to provide certificates of character (Figure 3.11) to ensure the users would return books or pay fines (Williamson, 1919). The librarians also debated the type of shelving (Godfrey, 1892) and classification system needed to manage collections (Dewey, 1891) as well as the loan charging process and the best template for borrowers' cards and cataloging (Bullock, 1901). They reviewed national data regarding lost or stolen books (Lord & Wilcox, 1908). And they discussed the amount of fines (Bostwick, 1910).

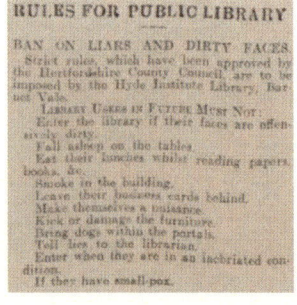

Figure 3.11

Library patrons agreed to follow the rules and often signed certificates of character, which were intended to guarantee the return of books. Rules for Public Library, Hertfordshire, 1930. No known restrictions.

In addition to administrative issues, librarians also discussed the social and cultural practices that impacted the library. For example, some librarians explicitly discussed the "colored" population and how to support, or in some instances dissuade, library usage along racial lines (Bell, 1917). Bostwick (1910) described the situation as one in which open access was the theory in Northern libraries where very few "Negroes" actually used the library. He sensed they felt unwanted. In contrast, "in the South separate accommodation for the colored people, if they are to be accommodated at all, is, of course, a postulate [sic]" (p. 52).

Bostwick stated that the problem was addressed in one of three ways: "by the tacit understanding that the Negroes are not to use the libraries [sic]" (p. 52), by the creation of separate branch libraries near residential districts where Black people lived, or by separate accommodations in the same building (Figure 3.12). Other librarians wrote of varying success using branch libraries for segregated populations (Yust, 1913) including accommodations for immigrants (Figure 3.13) and those who spoke and read in languages other than English (Bostwick, 1910).

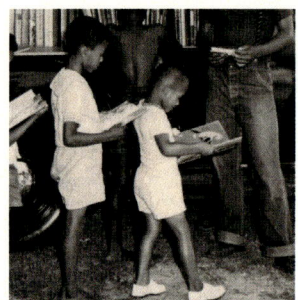

Figure 3.12

African-American children line up outside of Albemarle Region bookmobile. Colored Children's Library [sic], North Carolina Digital Collections, 1950s. No known restrictions.

Figure 3.13

Branch libraries segregated immigrant populations. Art and Picture Collection, The New York Public Library. [Interior of the Aguilar Library, Lower East side, ca. 1898.] Public domain.

In most of the publications and papers presented in the early years of the ALA, including those written by African Americans (e.g., Bell, 1917), many librarians conserved segregation practices while trying to elevate services in separate facilities (Harris, 1915; Jones, 1917; Rose, 1922). Still, a fringe group of librarians led the way to equal access (Lee, 1991; 1998; Malone, 1995).

The same exclusionary practices directed toward African Americans and immigrants were also directed toward children. Whereas some librarians balked at the idea of library services for children (Figure 3.14), others gave the concept serious consideration and engaged in contentious debate.

Figure 3.14
When we think about libraries, we think about open stacks. In the late 1800s and early 1900s, librarians pulled reading materials for patrons. Children were not the priority. Inside the Buffalo Public Library, New York, 1900s. Public domain.

Children's Story Hour and Reading Rooms. In the Colonies, "social libraries" were founded in small towns. Similar to Benjamin Franklin's Library Company and Thomas Bray's provincial libraries, groups of people gathered books for children to read (Powell, 1917). But these libraries were underfunded, underdeveloped, and hard to find. They operated more along the lines of book clubs than public libraries. One of the earliest social libraries for children, The West Cambridge Social Library (est. 1835), was created by Dr. Ebenezer Learned. In his last will and testament, he left $100 to create the library for the small town where he first taught school (Jordan, 1913).

 Social libraries functioned like book clubs rather than libraries.

In the early days of public libraries, children were banned. Library services were restricted to those who were 12 and older and usually limited to boys who served as apprentices (Sayers, 1963). According to Sophy Powell (1917), "as early as 1797 there was an Artisans' library in Birmingham, England, which could be used upon payment of a penny a week" (p. 4) (Figure 3.15). Other libraries followed with "mechanics' institutes in England and the United States, each with its library, reading room, museum, and lecture courses" (Powell, 1917, p. 34).

Figure 3.15
Mechanics institute and free libraries were intended to educate the working class, nd. Public domain.

Emily Hanaway (1887), the principal of a grammar school, described her idea for a children's reading room. Soliciting donations and collaborating with librarians, civic leaders, and representatives from different faiths, the reading room was located in different rented spaces and children were issued tickets for admission. Upon entering the room, children could read books within the confines of the space.

> The idea for a children's reading room came from a grammar school principal in 1887.

Caroline Hewins, the librarian at the Hartford Young Men's Institute (private subscription library) is credited with creating the first children's story hour in Hartford, Connecticut (Figure 3.16). She also shared methods for developing expertise in the reading preferences of children (Hewins, 1882; 1896). As Caroline Hewins described it, she paid special attention to the books that one particular family read and reread over a period of years. Based on her observations of children's reading habits, she built her expertise and contributed to her library's publication of a quarterly bulletin called "Library Notes" in which they made recommendations for reading. In addition,

Figure 3.16
Caroline Hewins is credited with creating the first children's story hour. Image of Caroline Hewins – Hartford History Center, Hartford Public Library - See more at: http://connecticuthistory.org/the-public-library-movement-caroline-hewins-makes-room-for-young-readers/

Hewins developed the library's collection based on her knowledge of children and their interests. Of course Caroline Hewins avoided books that included "unwholesome mental food" (1882). Once the library became public, the library opened a branch for children in 1895, and Caroline Hewins continued publishing recommendations in Publishers Weekly and developing the children's library. She also published a history of children's literature (Hewins, 1888), which can be accessed freely (http://tinyurl.com/zecgqfg). Due to Caroline Hewins' focused efforts over several years, the Hartford Free Library was influential in the area, and Hewins' presentations and published papers impacted the field.

> Caroline Hewins created the first children's story hour. In selecting books she avoided the ones that included "unwholesome mental food."
> Do librarians make different choices today?

In 1897, Mary Wright Plummer, reported on the "Work for Children in Free Libraries." She reviewed data from 15 libraries across the US and reported on a range of indicators. She discussed circulation rates, number of volumes, and staffing of libraries that provided services for children. Of these 15 locations, 11 libraries actually circulated books to children, allowing them to take the books home while the remaining four libraries required children to read on the premises in a children's reading room. In addition to providing information on usage, Mary Plummer also provided commentary on the quality of reading materials available to children.

> We have passed the time when reading in itself was considered a vast good. The ability to read may easily be a curse to the child, for unless he be provided with something fit to read, it is an ability as powerful for evil as for good. When we consider the dime-novels, the class of literature known as Sunday-school books, the sensational newspapers, the vicious literature insinuated into schools, and the tons of printed matter issued by reputable publishers, written by reputable people, good enough in its intention but utterly lacking in nourishment, and, therefore, doing a positive harm in occupying the place of better things—when we consider that all these are brought within a child's reach by the ability to read, we cannot help seeing that the librarian, in his capacity as selector of books for the library [sic], has the initial responsibility. Certain classes of the printed stuff just spoken of do not, of course, find their way into children's libraries, since they are barred out from all respectable shelves; but we are still too lenient with print because it is print, and every single book should be carefully examined before it goes into a library where children should have access to the shelves. (Plummer, 1897, p. 78).

You are what you read.

Is this entirely true? Children's literary diets build up within them, allowing them to make connections between themselves and others. Can this be harmful? What happens when children read about dangerous topics or contrasting opinions? Can reading change their minds, bodies, and souls?

After lamenting the quality of books for children, Mary Wright Plummer then questioned whether children should spend so much time reading in the first place.

> Are there not here and there children who are reading to the lasting detriment of their memories and powers of observation and reflection, stuffing themselves with type, as it were? Nearly every observant librarian knows of such cases. Are there not days when the shining of the sun, the briskness of the air, the greenness of the turf and of the trees, should have their invitation seconded by the librarian, and the child be persuaded away from the library instead of to it? We are supposed to contribute with our books toward the sound mind, but we should be none the less advocates of the sound body—and the child who reads all day indoors when he ought to be out in the fresh air among his kind, should have our especial watching. (Plummer, 1897, p. 79)

 Sounds like arguments about kids playing video games, watching TV, and engaging in all other forms of screen time.

Other librarians, such as Alice Hazeltine, published papers to support librarians who wished to engage children. She discussed the type of programming children needed, disciplinary measures for unruly children, and programming to support development. By 1917, the ALA published enough papers and presentations to warrant a book on the topic—*Library Work with Children*—a collection edited by Alice Hazeltine (1917).

For the most part, "noise" kept children out of libraries because they disturbed adult patrons (Figure 3.17). However, many people held beliefs about children that prohibited them from using the libraries. In a speech presented to the Massachusetts Library Club, Caroline Matthews (1908) summarized her own beliefs; it is a speech that captures disparaging views about children that were prevalent at the time. Her speech was also published by the ALA in the Library Journal and reprinted in an edited collection by Hazeltine (1917). I have selected a few quotes to share:

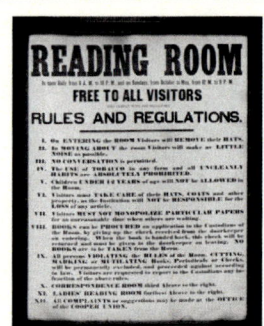

Figure 3.17

Library rules for the Cooper Union Reading Room, nd. Cooper Union for the Advancement of Science and Art. No known restrictions.

- [On children's rooms] I grew to have a horror of children's rooms—as distinct from children's departments. Intellectually, physically, morally, I believe them harmful. Neither can I see their necessity (Matthews, 1917, p. 96).

 Here is that old mantra: Children should be seen and not heard.

- [On attention to the Child] Everywhere, in city, town and suburban library, the effort to reach the Child is apparent. Special attendants are in readiness to meet him the instant he comes into reading room and station after school hours. Thoughtful women are assigned to overlook and guide his reference work. Entertainment is offered him in the form of blocks to play with, scrap-books to look at, story hours to attend. Books specially selected with regard to his supposedly individual needs are placed on the shelves. Picture bulletins are made for his use in the schools. Where he is not segregated he is allowed to monopolize tables and chairs. I find no corresponding effort made to reach the adult, to reach the young mechanic, to draw to the library the parent. (Matthews, 1917, p. 97)

What a hater? Clearly Miss Caroline Matthews had no understanding of child development, the impact of literacy on adult employment options, or the correlation between education and the economy.

- [On the role of women librarians] I next noticed and with some alarm the feminization of the library corps. And I confess to see no remedy. The schools are facing the same difficulty, but eventually it will be solved for them in the raising of certain salaries to a man's standard. This is not likely to happen in library work. Consequently we have this feminization to reckon with… for women far more than men are prone to indulge individual fads. (Matthews, 1917, p. 95) [In this case, the fad was a children's reading room.]

Ok, so this just angers me. I'm baffled by women putting down women.

What? Are you saying men don't care about children?

Librarians and patrons also worried about the destruction of property and the transmission of germs as many librarians wrote extensively about the ways to clean books in between users (all users, not just children) (Bostwick, 1910). In addition, children's literature was in its infancy. Challenges, such as "Why waste good books on children?" were eventually replaced with "What books would the children read?" and "What services could the library provide?"

During the early years of the library, schools such as the Pratt Institute graduated influential women, such as Anne Carroll Moore, who challenged traditions, gained recognition within ALA, and secured services for children (Figure 3.18). In particular, storytelling, reading aloud, and gaining personal knowledge of children were characteristics of library services at Pratt (Eddy, 2006). Storytelling was useful in rural districts with short supplies of books. Reading aloud enticed readers by example.

Figure 3.18

Anne Carroll Moore, nd, was hired by the Pratt Institute and she altered the library program to secure services for children. No known restrictions.

And building personal relationships helped librarians find the right book for each child. The librarians who trained within this system had a lasting impact on children's rooms and libraries across the country.

  The Pratt Institute had a lasting impact on children's rooms and libraries with a focus on storytelling and reading aloud.

By 1919, children's reading rooms and libraries were firmly in place and the demand for more and better books for children was increasing. In particular, Frederic Melcher, editor of *Publishers Weekly*, and Franklin Mathiews, chief librarian of the Boy Scouts of America decided to create "Children's Book Week" to encourage the quality of juvenile reading (Eddy, 2006). To support their efforts, they reached out to Anne Carroll Moore and Alice Jordan, the supervisors of children's services in the New York and Boston public libraries (Figure 3.19). Both women were considered experts in children's books, savvy in navigating social, political, and professional networks, and they knew how to reach into neighborhoods to find children.

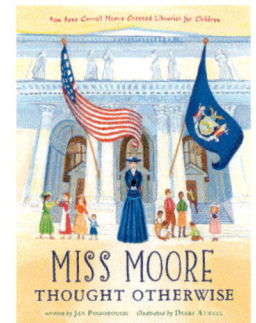

Figure 3.19

Anne Carroll Moore was a pioneering librarian. Her story is told in a children's book: *Miss Moore Thought Otherwise: How Anne Carroll Moore Created Libraries for Children* by Jan Pinborough and illustrated by Debby Atwell, 2013, New York, NY: HMH Books for Young Readers. Copyright 2013 by Debby Atwell.

  Children's Book Week encouraged the quality of juvenile reading.

Enterprising librarians recognized the value of books for children and with the expansion of public libraries, dedicated attention to children grew in spite of continued criticism.

Children's Libraries

In modern children's libraries, children's books are usually located in special locations. Why? Because children are still loud! Young children do not read silently and they enjoy discussing books when they take them from the shelves. Children are also playful. Based on decades of transdisciplinary research, we now have greater understanding of how children learn to read. Educators, librarians, and parents know to encourage children to have embodied responses to books by acting out stories, laughing out loud, asking questions, and sharing personal connections to the text. The days of quiet children's libraries are over.

 Children are loud!

Video 3.2 Toddler Story Time - Webster Library http://www.nypl.org/audiovideo/toddler-story-time-webster-library

Toddler Story Time. Webster Library. New York Public Library. Retrieved from http://www.nypl.org/audiovideo/toddler-story-time-webster-library.

GOT BOOKS?
(ACCESS, COLLECTIONS, AND DIGITAL RESOURCES)

However, libraries are also responsive to children with special needs. For example, many libraries hold separate storytimes for children with sensory processing issues. The librarians adjust the amount of stimulation to create the best environment for the children (e.g., http://wgntv.com/2015/05/27/chicago-libraries-start-a-new-kind-of-storytime/).

Children need their own special areas where they can be themselves and engage in reading and its associated responses. Rather than separating children from adults and limiting the books they are allowed to read, children's libraries are designed to encourage reading and interaction.

In children's libraries, you will notice tiny chairs and tables, beanbags, stages, carpeted areas, oversized chairs, and character cut-outs. The newer books will be prominently displayed, advertising popular authors and illustrators and the librarians' recommendations.

Check out my Pinterest page for a collection of my favorite library designs for children. https://www.pinterest.com/jschneidusf/childrens-library-and-bookshelf-design/

Young adult books are typically located near the children's section, but they seem to have less interesting furniture and fewer book-themed decorations. Why? I'm not sure. Most teenagers appreciate interesting spaces, unique lounging furniture, and literary displays. In spite of the fact that young adults appreciate good design, their books tend to be placed in the same stacks and arrangements used for adult books.

KEEP CALM AND ASK A LIBRARIAN

Advice from a Librarian. One of the unsung benefits of studying children's literature is how easy it is to find relevant texts in libraries. Unlike textbooks, which most libraries do not collect, children's literature is very accessible—for free!—in libraries, if you know where to look. Here are some tips and tricks to get you started:

Public libraries. Public libraries typically have extensive collections of children's literature, although their collections tend to skew toward the recently published or perennial favorites and classics. Looking for an obscure title from 1976? You probably won't find it at the public library, particularly at a smaller branch.

In order to obtain a library card, most public libraries require you to show proof of residency in the city or county in which the library is located. Even if you do not have a library card, though, you can visit a public library and use their resources in the building for free. If you are uncertain if you qualify for a borrower's card or if you need help, just ask— librarians will be happy to provide additional information.

Ebooks and libraries. Many children's books are available in ebook format, and many public libraries provide free access to ebook downloads (note that while many college and university libraries have ebooks in their collections, almost none have children's literature in ebook format). In order to access ebooks from a public library, you will need to have a library card. On a public library's homepage, look for the world "ebook." This link will take you to a database with ebooks, including children's literature, for you to check out and download to your iPad or other tablet device.

Your college or university library. College and university libraries, particularly those at schools that offer degrees in education, typically have representative samples of children's literature in their collections. Children's literature holdings at university and college libraries tend to be smaller than those found at public libraries and often focus on award winners or titles that support curriculum development studies. Nevertheless, in a pinch, you should be able to find some children's literature titles at your college or university.

- Melanie Griffin

Associate Librarian for the Children's and Young Adult Literature Collection at the University of South Florida

Collections

In contrast to public librarians, children's-literature archivists and special-collections librarians assemble and curate original manuscripts, artwork, and published books in libraries across the world (e.g., the de Grummond Children's Literature Collection, the Kerlan Collection, the International Youth Library, National Collection of Children's Books in Ireland).

The University of Southern Mississippi houses the De Grummond Collection, a collection of manuscripts and illustrations from more than 1300 authors and illustrators and including more than 160,000 books. http://www.lib.usm.edu/degrummond

The University of Minnesota houses the Children's Literature Research Collections (https://www.lib.umn.edu/clrc). The extensive collections include:

- The Kerlan Collection includes over 100,000 books, manuscripts, illustrations, and materials related to children's literature. Click here for access to Kerlan Newsletters dating back to 1998 https://www.lib.umn.edu/clrc/kerlan-newsletter-archive

- The Borger Collection centers on the 40,000 volume comic book collection of John Borger. https://www.lib.umn.edu/clrc/borger-collection

- The Hess Collection also features dime, pulp, and series books. https://www.lib.umn.edu/clrc/hess-collection

- The Oz Collection includes books, memorabilia, and paraphanalia related to L. Frank Baum and the Oz books. https://www.lib.umn.edu/clrc/oz-collection

- The Paul Bunyan Collection features books, papers, and documents related to Paul Bunyan. https://www.lib.umn.edu/clrc/paul-bunyan-collection

- The Treasure Island Collection includes over 450 books that represent various published versions of Treasure Island. https://www.lib.umn.edu/clrc/lionel-johnson-collections

The International Youth Library preserves, documents, and shares international children's and youth literature through collections, catalogues, and outreach efforts. Located in Munich, Germany, the library's complete libraries holdings are listed in an online database. http://www.ijb.de/en/about-us.html?noMobile=0%27A%3D0

The National Collection of Children's Books in Ireland is an online database that facilitates the exploration of over 250,000 children's books written in over 90 languages from five libraries in Dublin, Ireland. https://nccb.tcd.ie/about

Many of these collections are housed in universities with the primary intention of acquiring and preserving a living history of literary text and art that can be accessed through online databases and in person (Hoyle, 2011). For example, The Baldwin Library of Historical Children's Literature is a model of ease and access with searches available by genre, creator, publication date, publisher, or text excerpt (See http://ufdc.ufl.edu/juv).

For those of you who live near me (Tampa, Florida), the following collections are open to visitors.

The Baldwin Collection. The Baldwin Library of Children's Literature in the Department of Special Collections (http://web.uflib.ufl.edu/spec/) at the University of Florida's George A. Smathers Libraries (http://cms.uflib.ufl.edu) contains more than 130,000 books and periodicals published in the United States and Great Britain from the mid-1600s to present day.
http://ufdc.ufl.edu/juv

USF Children's and Young Adult Literature Special Collections. The USF Children's and Young Adult Literature Collections currently feature over 25,000 titles of American fiction for adolescent and young readers, dating from 1870 to the present. The collections comprise three distinct parts: the Hipple Collection of young adult literature, the children's literature collection, and the dime novel collection.
http://www.lib.usf.edu/special-collections/childrens-young-adult-literature/

Additionally, many archives and special collections may be viewed by appointment during supervised site visits (Video 3.3).

Video 3.3 Using Special Collections http://www.kaltura.com/tiny/pcd3b

When I visited the Peter Pan Collection at the Great Ormond Street Hospital in London (http://www.gosh.org/about-us/peter-pan), I met with Christine De Poortere, the Peter Pan Director, who led me into an empty reading room where she assembled portions of the collection that were typically stored away (Figure 3.20). Together, we examined variations in illustrations across versions of the story/play (Figure 3.21), memorabilia from the first performance of Peter Pan (Figure 3.22), and programs from various pantomimes (Figure 3.23). I examined the collection through her passion and insight—a very different experience in person.

These same interpersonal connections I experienced with the Peter Pan Collection can be recreated for people who live across diverse social, geographic, and economic regions. As Marcus (2011) observed, "now that special collections have web sites on which are sometime posted detailed finding aids and even virtual exhibitions, it has become easier to scope out the archival portion of the research landscape…" (p. 393).

Figure 3.20
The reading room for the Peter Pan Collection at the Great Ormond Street Hospital. Photo copyright 2015 by Jenifer Schneider.

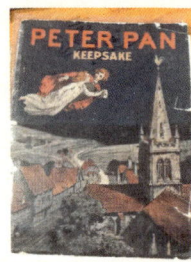

Figure 3.21
Original program artwork for the performance of Peter Pan by J.M. Barrie, 1904, London, England: Hodder & Stoughton. Copyright 1988 by Great Ormond Street Hospital. Photo copyright 2015 by Jenifer Schneider.

Figure 3.22
Peter Pan memorabilia in the Peter Pan Collection at the Great Ormond Street Hospital. Photo copyright 2015 by Jenifer Schneider.

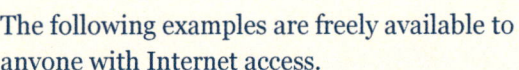

The following examples are freely available to anyone with Internet access.

The International Children's Digital Libarary. The ICDL is a collection of historical and contemporary children's books from throughout the world. The books represent different cultures and they are written in different languages. In addition, search tools use different languages. http://en.childrenslibrary.org/

The Children's Literature Comprehensive Database. The CLCD provides search access to all important and relevant information about Pre K-12 media of all types, including reviews from respected publications for those professionals who work with Pre K-12 media. http://www.library.arizona.edu/applications/quickHelp/tutorial/childrens-literature-comprehensive-database.

Figure 3.23
Programs from various Peter Pan pantomimes are available in the Peter Pan Collection at the Great Ormond Street Hospital. Photo copyright 2015 by Jenifer Schneider.

Although children's literature collections may lack the geographic convenience of a local public library, and they are not typically targeted for audiences of children, the collections house a depth and breadth of materials that provide unprecedented access to the texts and processes of children's book creation. In addition, these collections and archives are mediated through the scholarly lenses of archivists, librarians, and passionate collectors.

Locations and access. For expert insight into special collections, I turn to my colleague, Melanie Griffin, Associate Librarian for the Children's and Young Adult Literature Collection at the University of South Florida (http://www.lib.usf.edu/special-collections/childrens-young-adult-literature/).

> Most public libraries and college or university libraries collect current or very popular children's literature due to the nature of the populations that they serve. If you are looking for obscure, old, or less popular works of children's literature in libraries, you may need to consult a special collections department. These departments collect children's literature more broadly and holistically, typically with goals of ensuring long-term preservation and providing access to texts that are not widely available. Some special collections of children's literature are broad, covering the entire history of children's literature across the globe, while others are more specific, focusing on particular genres, such as contemporary young adult literature, or geographic areas, such as Japan. Many special collections of children's literature also include manuscript and archival material related to the production of specific texts or the careers of specific authors.
>
> Special collections libraries are typically part of a university library or a very large public library, such as the New York Public Library or the San Francisco Public Library; there are also some independent research libraries, such as the Newbery Library in Chicago, that include special collections departments with collections of children's literature. Unlike the materials found in public and university libraries, the books and manuscript materials housed in special collections departments cannot be checked out and taken home; instead, researchers consult these materials in the department's reading room. It pays to plan ahead if you need to conduct research in a special collections library: they are typically open fewer hours than other libraries, materials may be stored off site and require advance notice for retrieval, and you may need to travel to visit the library.

Despite these challenges, conducting research in children's literature at a special collections library will let you investigate questions that are difficult to answer elsewhere. Using special collections materials, you can:

- See how the text of a book, such as the first Nancy Drew novel, for example, has changed over time to reflect changing social and cultural values (Video 3.4).

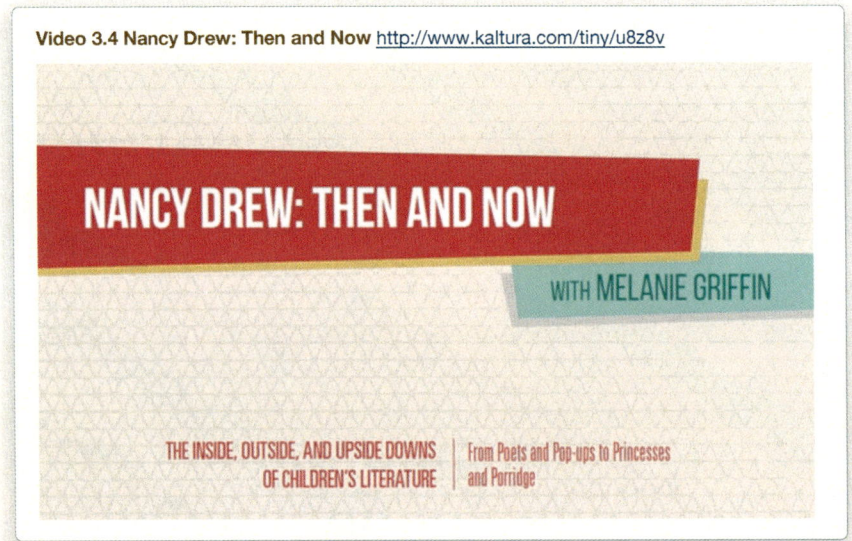

- Compare manuscript and early drafts of novels to explore the textual and editorial evolution of a well-known text (Video 3.5).

- Consult editorial notes, correspondence, and press releases to trace the publication history of a text.
  - Columbia University's collection of literary agents' personal papers proved pivotal in classifying Harper Lee's *Go Set a Watchman* as a precursor to *To Kill a Mockingbird* rather than a sequel; for more information, see https://blogs.cul.columbia.edu/rbml/2015/07/14/go-set-a-watchman-in-the-papers-of-harper-lees-literary-agents/)
- Trace the reception history of a text through its subsequent publications, its reviews, and its spin-offs (Video 3.6).

Video 3.6 The Alice in Wonderland Collection at the University of South Florida
http://www.kaltura.com/tiny/vbkud

- Read texts outside of the current canon of children's literature that are not included in other circulating collections.

> There are many excellent online listings of children's literature research collections in special collections libraries. Two particularly notable bibliographies are:
>
> - The Special Collections in Children's Literature Wikiography, maintained by the Association for Library Services to Children (http://wikis.ala.org/alsc/index.php/SPECIAL_COLLECTIONS_IN_CHILDREN%27S_LITERATURE_WIKIOGRAPHY). This wiki provides collection name, location, and very brief collection overviews.
>
> - The Collections of Children's Literature is a listing maintained by the Social Sciences, Health, and Education Library at the University of Illinois at Urbana-Champaign: (http://www.library.illinois.edu/sshel/s-coll/usebks/collections.htm). This listing is more selective in nature than the wikiography, but it contains more detailed collection descriptions for the collections that it highlights.
>
> **Special collections online.** Can't travel but still interested in studying historical or international children's literature? There are some online collections that will be of particular interest. These digital collections present a select portion of larger special collections freely online; they typically include only material not currently under protection by copyright (in the United States, this covers the vast majority of books published from 1923 to the present).
>
> - The Baldwin Library of Historical Children's Literature at the University of Florida provides free, online access to over 6,000 of the titles in the collection (http://ufdc.ufl.edu/juv).
>
> - The Rosetta Project's Children's Books Online offers online access to illustrated children's books published in the 19th century (http://rosettaproject.org).
>
> - The International Children's Digital Library includes both historical and contemporary children's books from around the world in a wide variety of languages (http://en.childrenslibrary.org/index.shtml). The homepage may look a bit outdated, but the content is extraordinary in terms of its scope, breadth, and diversity.
>
> Newbery and Carnegie Award winner Neil Gaiman famously (on the internet, at any rate) quipped that "libraries are our friends." For students of children's literature in particular, Gaiman is right, especially if you know where to look.

- Melanie Griffin
Associate Librarian for the Children's and Young Adult Literature Collection
at the University of South Florida

The Booksellers Gruff

Outside of public and private libraries, bookstores and book sellers provide access to children's literature. Many retailers allow reading without buying, but their underlying mission is to function as a business.

The Itty-Bitty Book Shop. We've heard the predictions that little retailers are dead. We've seen the plot in romantic movies—an independent bookseller loses her business to the big, bad book store around the corner. The potential for extinction is there, but independent bookstores are actually on the rise (Video 3.7).

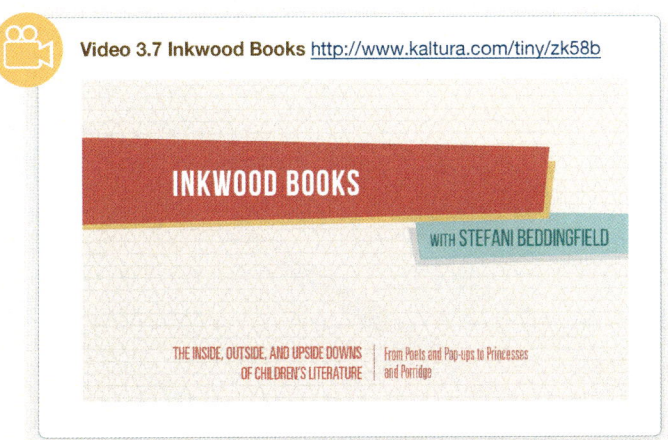

Customers rely on expert booksellers to develop the book inventory and recommend good books for individual clients. Customers value a bookseller who understands their reading interests and shares their love of particular authors and illustrators. For example, in my itty-bitty book shop, Inkwood Books (Figure 3.24), the employees use bookmarks to indicate their recommended books. The owner, Stefani Beddingfield, also sponsors author talks, social gatherings, and book clubs.

Figure 3.24
Inkwood Books in Tampa, Florida. Photo copyright 2015 Stefani Beddingfield. Reprinted with permission.

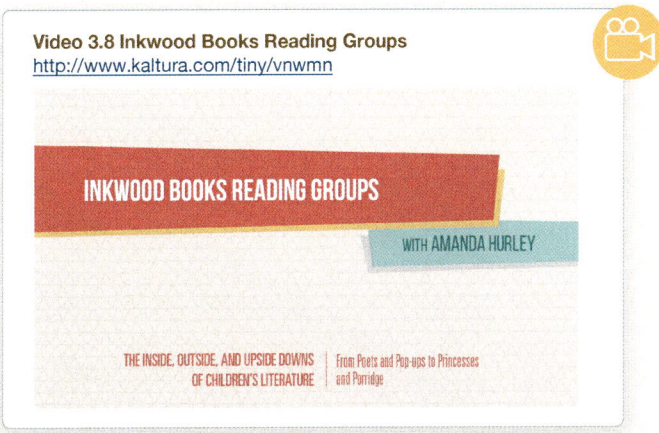

Independent bookstores also keep an inventory of old and new books because people reread classics and they also search for new titles. In a recent article, Zachary Karabell (2014) explains the reasons for the success of small, independent bookstores and the failures of larger stores such as Borders and Barnes and Noble:

> To demonstrate higher profitability, retail stores have an incentive to turn over their inventories quickly. For clothing and electronics and automobiles, that workflow is in sync with consumer behavior. Consumers want new fashion, the newest flat-screen, the latest model car. Book consumers aren't the same. Yes, new titles can drive sales, but book buyers also look for forgotten classics and hidden gems. That means poring over shelves, and that requires old inventory.
> (http://www.slate.com/articles/business/the_edgy_optimist/2014/09/independent_bookstores_rising_they_can_t_compete_with_amazon_and_don_t_have.html)

In addition to the expertise of the bookseller and the care given to the selection of books in a small bookshop, initiatives such as Small Business Saturday (the Saturday after Thanksgiving) and IndieBound (http://www.indiebound.org/) encourage people to shop locally. For more information, the American Booksellers Association (ABA) offers a list of local stores and provides helpful information about the independent bookseller industry (http://www.bookweb.org/).

The Bigger Box Bookstore. Many people enjoy shopping for books in large bookstore chains. Yes, children's literature is also found in grocery stores, drug stores, and retail stores such as Target or Walmart, but bookstores have larger collections that are developed in response to market trends. The major bookstore chains will often have what you want or they can order it within days. Major bookstores often create an atmosphere for reading with classical music playing and a coffee shop area for refreshments.

At first sight, big box retailers appear very similar to libraries: children's sections are separated from young adult and adult books, the children's area includes small furniture and spaces for interactive reading, and they tend to have knowledgeable staff. Big stores also have large collections that include new and old best sellers across a variety of genres. But this is where the similarities end.

Unlike libraries and small bookstores that have a catalogue created with local readers in mind, bookstores are stocked for sales. If there is an upcoming holiday (even Hallmark holidays), the big stores will have a display of books to match the theme. The big box stores also sell stuffed animals, games, and toys that correspond to the best selling books of the day. Try to find great poetry for children, or a selection of Coretta Scott King Award winners, and you will find very little. But if you need a wand for your Harry Potter purchase, or a Dr. Who alarm clock for your nightstand, the big box store will meet your needs.

The Mega eCommerce Retailer. If the big box store has a large selection, it is nothing in comparison to the mega ecommerce retailer known as Amazon. On Amazon.com you can find any book that is still in press and many that are not. You can find the most obscure and the wildly popular, and if you aren't sure what you want, you can search by topic, author, genre, or bestsellers. You can find new and used books and they arrive within days.

Open catalog searching is a key feature of online retailers. Open searching is also available for the library. However, library databases and Amazon are not equivalent searches. As with big box stores, Amazon is guided by sales as well as the analytic assessment of your searching patterns and online shopping history. Therefore, Amazon search results are skewed to match your buying tendencies. The library is guided by key words, not best sellers or your recent purchases.

Amazon is great if you know what you want and if you want to keep the books in your personal collection. Amazon is also helpful because it includes book reviews from other patrons as well as professional book reviews from sources such as *School Library Journal*. But don't confuse Amazon's recommendations with expertise. Just because a book is popular or trending, doesn't mean it's good.

 Don't confuse online recommendations with expertise.

Museums

Children's literature museums function to construct community spaces in which children and families view, interpret, and manipulate various media and artifacts. The museums may also simulate the experiences and artistic processes of specific authors and illustrators. In doing so, effective children's museums address spatial affordances, aesthetic education goals, and informal learning strategies to promote children's engagement in space through exploratory movement, visual contact, and active engagement with exhibit elements (Ishikawa, 2012; Valance, 2007; Wineman & Peponis, 2010).

When I entered the Roald Dahl Museum and Story Centre in Great Missenden, England (Figure 3.25), I was transported into the life of the author, his characters, and his local places of inspiration. I read the story about Roald's British Airforce experience and then looked at a life-sized cut out of a giraffe and a palm tree that functioned as a height chart (Figure 3.26). The names of Roald and his characters, Matilda, Willie Wonka, the BFG, and many others, were carved on pieces of wood and tacked onto the tree, giving museum visitors a very real sense of Roald's height in comparison to his characters and in relation to a giraffe. (The fact that adults between the heights of 5'6 and 5'10 corresponded to the heights of "The Twits" was not lost on me.)

Moving on from this display, I could have chosen to sit in the cockpit of a mock WWII airplane, play dress-up with items held in a 1940's suitcase, or turn around and walk to the center of the room to enter Roald's actual writing hut, preserved and opened up like a doll house in the middle of this intimate and engaging exhibit space (Figure 3.27). When I entered the hut and saw his old, beat-up chair, his collection of candy wrappers, and his pencil sharpener, I felt a connection to Roald Dahl through physical contact with and close proximity to his artifacts.

Many popular museums have sprung from the birthplaces or writing spaces of beloved authors such as Beatrix Potter's Hill Top Farm near Sawrey, Hawkshead, Ambleside, UK (http://www.peterrabbit.com/en) or Louisa May Alcott's Orchard House in Concord, Massachusetts (http://www.louisamayalcott.org/) (Figure 3.28). These museums take visitors back in time to understand the ways in which authors lived and how they drew inspiration from their environments.

Figure 3.25
The Roald Dahl Museum and Story Centre in Great Missendon. Photo copyright 2015 by Jenifer Schneider.

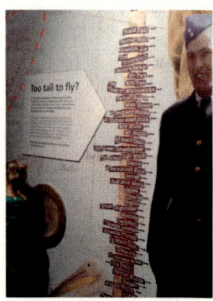

Figure 3.26
I'm as tall as a Twit. Photo copyright 2015 by Jenifer Schneider.

Figure 3.27
Walk through Roald's writing hut! Photo copyright 2015 by Jenifer Schneider.

Figure 3.28
Louisa May Alcott's Orchard House. Photo copyright 2015 by Jenifer Schneider.

Other museums are focused on curating children's literature as fine art or literature. For example, Eric Carle Museum of Picture Book Art in Amherst, Massachusetts (http://www.carlemuseum.org/) is focused on inspiring a love of art and reading through picture books (Figure 3.29). The Carle includes a gallery, movie theater, library, and studio where children and adults can explore picturebook art creation. In fact, even the bathroom tiles contain art (Figure 3.30). In another example, the Mazza Museum in Findley, Ohio (http://www.mazzamuseum.org/) is one of the largest and most diverse collections of original picturebook art in the world. Unlike other museums with exhibits that focus on one artist or one theme, the Mazza includes an amazing gallery with examples from hundreds of children's book illustrators and authors (Figure 3.31), representing different illustration styles and techniques (Figure 3.32).

Figure 3.29
My visit to the Eric Carle Museum of Picture Book Art. Photo copyright 2015 by Jenifer Schneider.

Figure 3.30
The bathrooms tiles are a space for art at the Eric Carle Museum of Picture Book Art. Photo copyright 2015 by Jenifer Schneider.

Figure 3.31
The Mazza Museum gallery, an amazing collection of children's book illustration. Photo copyright 2015 by Jenifer Schneider.

Figure 3.32
Different illustrative styles and techniques are on display at the Mazza Museum. Photo copyright 2015 by Jenifer Schneider.

Still other museums maintain the collection and preservation of a nation's literature, for example Australia's Dromkeen (http://www.dromkeen.com.au/) or Britain's Seven Stories Centre (http://www.sevenstories.org.uk/) (Hammill, 2011).

Children's literature museums provide a focus on certain collections of literature and they create multimodal experiences with texts.

Get Books

Ultimately, you have many choices when it comes to finding children's literature. It all comes down to personal preference. Do you know what you want or do you need help searching? Do you want to shop from home, shop in a store, or not shop at all? Are you comfortable exploring shelves for the right book or do you like to plan, organize, and search with a list? Unless you really know the field of children's literature, I recommend that you try the Goldilocks approach. Try different locations (library, museum, or bookstore) and find the place that is "just right" for you.

HOT TOPICS AND CURIOUS QUANDARIES

SECTION 2

CHAPTER 04 | IMPORTANT BOOKS

(THE PROBLEMS AND POLITICS OF IMPORTANCE; NOTABLE LISTS, AWARDS, & ASSOCIATIONS)

Given the origins of children's literature as a mode of communication, an instructional resource, and a literary object, the study of children's literature is most often pursued by scholars in the fields of English, Library Science, and Education.

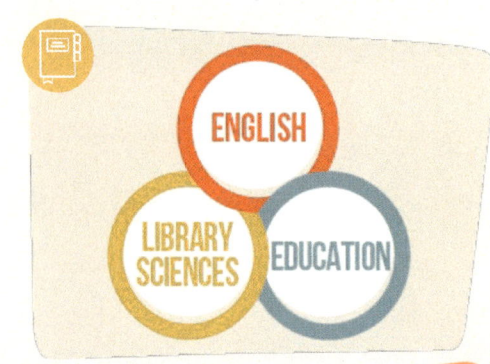

However, with the moneymaking potential of children's literature, its ability to communicate political and social messages, as well as its documentation of shifting instantiations of culture and language, children's literature is also studied by anthropologists, sociologists, psychologists, historians, business analysts, and content experts.

In this chapter, you can find book awards from the following groups.:

Librarians p. 60	Writers & Illustrators p. 75
Literary Scholars p. 66	Publishers & Booksellers p. 78
Teachers p. 68	The Fans p. 84
Content Experts p. 73	

Children's literature has wide appeal and broad impact. With so much attention from various fields, the value experts place on children's literature can appear contradictory. Understandably, different experts attend to the aspects of children's literature that are most relevant and important to them. In a nutshell, it's all relative.

The Experts Who Study Children's Literature

As in any field, quality is rewarded with recognition and awards. But what exactly do the experts look for and who gets the recognition?

Let's take a look at my view of the field of children's literature. Who are the experts? What do they value? Does it really matter?

The views expressed in this book are those of the author and do not necessarily reflect the views of those who view themselves as experts in the field of children's literature.

The Librarians

In the field of children's literature, the primary group that serves to collect, catalogue, monitor, distribute, and recognize books for children and youth are the librarians.

In the US, the American Library Association (www.ala.org) is the leading organization for librarians. The ALA advocates for libraries and librarians, provides education and lifelong learning for all people, actively defends the right to read and other forms of intellectual freedom, advocates for equitable access to information, spaces, and library services, and supports literacy initiatives. Just as books have transformed from bounded, printed texts, the library manages and maintains all forms of text including books, electronic resources, graphic material, and multimedia.

OK, if this is the first time you've heard of the ALA, you did not read the previous chapters. Go back, read about the history of the ALA, and then come back here.

ALA is divided into 11 divisions to meet the needs of librarians who work in different types of libraries or library specializations. Two divisions focus on children's and young adult literature: the Association for Library Service to Children (ALSC) and the Young Adult Library Services Association (YALSA).

Two divisions of the ALA focus on children's and young adult literature:
Association for Library Service to Children http://www.ala.org/alsc/;
Young Adult Library Services Association. http://www.ala.org/yalsa/ .

The ALA recognizes children's and young adult books, print, and media with over 30 awards and prizes for authors, illustrators, librarians, and educators. The awards are searchable and listed on the ALA website (http://www.ala.org/awardsgrants/awards/browse/bpma/all/cyad).

IMPORTANT BOOKS
(THE PROBLEMS AND POLITICS OF IMPORTANCE: NOTABLE LISTS, AWARDS, & ASSOCIATIONS)

Association for Library Service to Children (ALSC). The ALSC is the world's largest organization dedicated to the support and enhancement of library service to children. The ALSC administers nine book awards for children's literature. Of these awards, the Newbery and Caldecott Medals are widely considered to be the most prestigious.

The Newbery Medal. The Newbery Medal is named after John Newbery, a London publisher, who is credited with creating the first book written and published for the *entertainment* of children (e.g., *A Little Pretty Pocket-Book Intended for the Instruction and Amusement of Little Master Tommy and Pretty Miss Polly*, c.1744, Figure 4.1). As such, John Newbery is often called the "father" of children's literature. The Newbery Medal is awarded to the author of the most distinguished contribution to American literature for children.

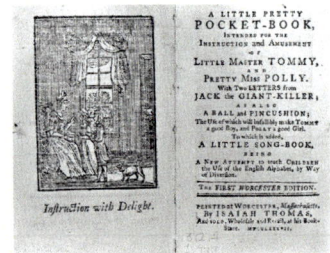

Figure 4.1
A Little Pretty Pocket Book by John Newbery, 1744, Worcester, MA: Isaiah Thomas. Copyright expired.

  Prior to Newbery, other books were written for children, but they were focused on moral development or literacy instruction. John Newbery recognized the entertainment potential of text.

The author wins the award, but the book is recognized with acclaim as well. In particular, the book must demonstrate excellence across the following criteria (http://www.ala.org/alsc/awardsgrants/bookmedia/newberymedal/newberyterms/newberyterms):

- Interpretation of the theme or concept;
- Presentation of information including accuracy, clarity, and organization;
- Development of a plot;
- Delineation of characters;
- Delineation of a setting;
- Appropriateness of style.

The first Newbery was awarded in 1922 for *The Story of Mankind* by Hendrik Willem van Loon (Figure 4.2). A more recent winner was The Crossover by Kwame Alexander (Figure 4.3). The Newbery is clearly a writing prize that focuses on the literariness of the text.

Figure 4.2
The first Newbery Medal was awarded to *The Story of Mankind* by Hendrik Willem van Loon, 1922, New York, NY: Boni and Liveright. Copyright 1922 by Hendrik Willem van Loon.

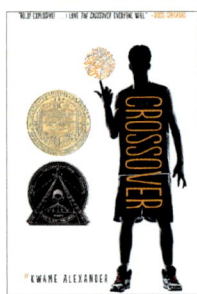

Figure 4.3
Kwame Alexander won the Newbery for *The Crossover* by Kwame Alexander, 2014, New York, NY: Houghton Mifflin. Copyright 2014 by Kwame Alexander.

Below, you'll read about other awards that have different agendas.

The Caldecott Medal. The Caldecott Medal is named after Randolph Caldecott, a 19th century illustrator from England. In 1878, he illustrated *The Diverting History of John Gilpin*, a poem by William Cowper (Figure 4.4). Caldecott wasn't the first illustrator of children's books, but his work was notable, original, and acclaimed at the time (Figure 4.5).

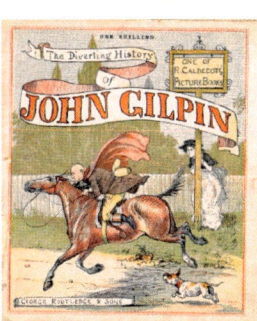

Figure 4.4
Randolph Caldecott was a prominent illustrator of his time. For example, one of his early books was The *Diverting History of John Gilpin* by William Cowper and illustrated by Randolph Caldecott, 1878, London, England: George Routledge & Sons. Reprinted with permission from http://www.randolphcaldecott.org.uk/gilpin.htm.

The Randolph Caldecott Society developed an extensive website of Caldecott's biographic and publication information (http://www.randolphcaldecott.org.uk/index.htm).

The website is out of date, but it's a fantastic resource if you appreciate specific details and historical accuracy (http://www.randolphcaldecott.org.uk/rhymes.htm).

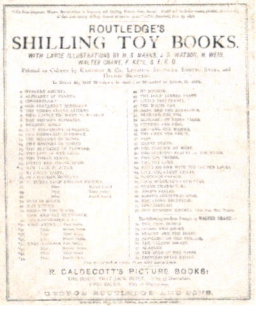

Figure 4.5
Did you know that back covers were used by the publisher to advertise other books? Visit the Randolph Caldecott Society website for other details about various editions (http://www.randolphcaldecott.org.uk/editions.htm).

The Caldecott Medal is awarded annually to the artist of the most distinguished American picture book for children published by an American publisher in the United States in English during the preceding year.

In the case of the Caldecott, the illustrator wins the award for creating a high-quality visual experience. In particular, the book must be individually distinct and demonstrate eminence across the following criteria (http://www.ala.org/alsc/awardsgrants/bookmedia/caldecottmedal/caldecottterms/caldecottterms):

- Excellence of execution in the artistic technique employed;
- Excellence of pictorial interpretation of story, theme, or concept;
- Appropriateness of style of illustration to the story, theme or concept;
- Delineation of plot, theme, characters, setting, mood or information through the pictures;
- Excellence of presentation in recognition of a child audience.

The first Caldecott was awarded in 1938 for *Animals of the Bible, A Picture Book*, illustrated by Dorothy P. Lathrop with text selected by Helen Dean Fish (Figure 4.6).

A more contemporary winner was *The Adventures of Beekle: The Unimaginary Friend* by Dan Santat (Figure 4.7).

The Newbery and Caldecott medals are awarded every year for work published in the previous year. The medal winners and Honor Books (runners up) are adorned with gold or silver medallions on their covers. Libraries, bookstores, and school libraries often create special displays for these books to introduce students to the winners.

Figure 4.6
The Caldecott Medal was created several years after the Newbery. The first Caldecott was awarded to *Animals of the Bible, A Picture Book*, illustrated by Dorothy P. Lathrop with text selected by Helen Dean Fish, 1938, New York, NY: Lippincott. Cover art copyright by Dorothy P. Lathrop.

Figure 4.7
Artwork and illustrative styles have changed over the years. A more recent Caldecott winner is *The Adventures of Beekle: The Unimaginary Friend* by Dan Santat, 2014, New York, NY: Little, Brown Books for Young Readers. Copyright 2014 by Dan Santat.

You may have noticed the preachy nature of the early award winners. To combat religious or instructional motives, ALA's current criteria specifically state that Newbery and Caldecott awards are not for books with didactic intent. In addition, the award specifically guards against popularity as the award committee does not consider sales or the creator's body of work.

Other Notable ALSC Awards. In addition to the Newbery and Caldecott Medals, the ALSC division of ALA offers seven other prestigious book and media awards to recognize specific populations or in recognition of particular content. I highlighted some of them here:

 If a book wins an award, and no one reads it, does it make a noise?

Why do you think it became necessary for ALA to focus on authors and illustrators who portray or represent specific populations?

The *Belpre Medal* (Figure 4.8) is awarded to a Latino/Latina writer and illustrator whose work best portrays, affirms, and celebrates the Latino cultural experience in an outstanding work of literature for children and youth (http://www.ala.org/alsc/awardsgrants/bookmedia/belpremedal).

Figure 4.8
The 2015 Pura Belpre Award was given to *I Lived on Butterfly Hill* by Marjorie Agosín and illustrated by Lee White, 2014, New York, NY: Atheneum Books for Young Readers. Cover art copyright 2014 by Lee White.

IMPORTANT BOOKS
(THE PROBLEMS AND POLITICS OF IMPORTANCE: NOTABLE LISTS, AWARDS, & ASSOCIATIONS)

The Geisel Award, named in honor of Dr. Seuss, is awarded to the author(s) and illustrator(s) of the most distinguished American book for beginning readers published in English in the United States during the preceding year (http://www.ala.org/alsc/awardsgrants/bookmedia/geiselaward).

The Sibert Medal (Figure 4.9) is awarded to the author(s) and illustrator(s) of the most distinguished informational book published in the United States in English during the preceding year (http://www.ala.org/alsc/awardsgrants/bookmedia/sibertmedal).

Figure 4.9
The 2015 Sibert Medal was awarded to *The Right Word: Roget and His Thesaurus* by Jen Bryant and illustrated by Melissa Sweet, 2014, New York, NY: Eerdmans Books for Young Readers. Cover art copyright 2014 by Melissa Sweet.

The Wilder Medal is awarded to the author or illustrator whose books, published in the United States, have made, over a period of years, a substantial and lasting contribution to literature for children (http://www.ala.org/alsc/awardsgrants/bookmedia/wildermedal).

Young Adult Library Services Association (YALSA). The Young Adult Library Services Association is another division of the American Library Association. YALSA is a national association of librarians, library workers and advocates whose mission is to expand and strengthen library services for teens, aged 12-18 (http://www.ala.org/yalsa/aboutyalsa).

YALSA administers six book awards for young adult literature. Of these, the Michael L. Printz Award and the Nonfiction Award are considered the most prestigious.

Michael L. Printz Award. Similar to the Newbery, the Printz Award is given to a book that exemplifies literary excellence in young adult literature. A recent Printz Award was given to *I'll Give You the Sun* by Jandy Nelson (Figure 4.10).

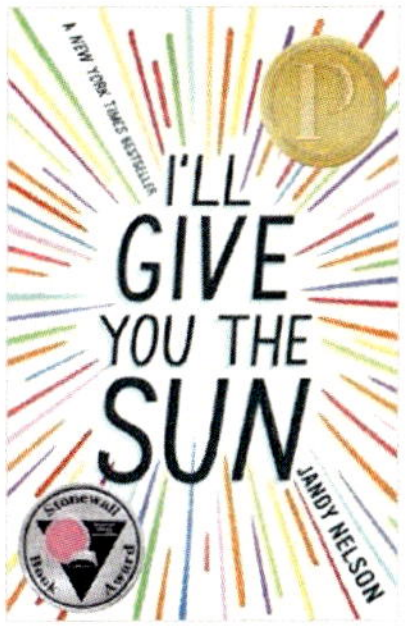

Nonfiction Award. The YALSA Award for Excellence in Nonfiction is given to the best nonfiction book published for young adults (ages 12-18). One of the latest Nonfiction Awards was given to *Popular: Vintage Wisdom for Modern Geek* by Maya Van Wagenen.

Figure 4.10
The Printz Award is given to young adult literature. A recent winner was *I'll Give You the Sun* by Jandy Nelson, 2014, New York, NY: Dial Books. Copyright 2014 by Jandy Nelson.

Ethnic Materials Information Exchange Round Table Task Force (EMIERT). ALA offers 20 Round Table groups which function as a Special Interest Group within the organization. In particular, EMIERT serves as a source of information on recommended ethnic collections, services, and programs.

> Why do you think it became necessary for ALA to create a group specifically charged with serving as a source of information on ethnic collections, services, and programs?

Coretta Scott King Awards. In 1970, EMIERT established the Coretta Scott King Award to recognize outstanding African American authors and illustrators of books for children and young adults that demonstrate an appreciation of African American culture and universal human values (http://www.ala.org/emiert/cskbookawards).

The first winner of the Coretta Scott King Author Award was Lillie Patterson for *Martin Luther King, Jr.: Man of Peace* in 1970 (Figure 4.11). The first illustrator award was presented in 1974 to George Ford who illustrated *Ray Charles* (written by Sharon Bell Mathis) (Figure 4.12).

Figure 4.11
The first Coretta Scott King Author Award was given to *Martin Luther King, Jr.: Man of Peace* by Lillie Patterson, 1969, New York, NY: Dell. Copyright 1969 by Lillie Patterson.

A contemporary winner of the author award was *brown girl dreaming* by Jacqueline Woodson. Christopher Myers recently won the illustrator award for *Firebird* (written by Misty Copeland).

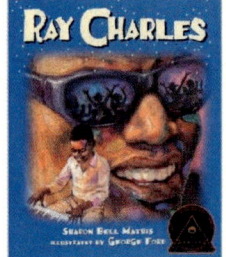

Figure 4.12
The first Coretta Scott King Illustrator Award was given to George Ford for illustrating *Ray Charles* by Sharon Draper. Ray Charles by Sharon Draper and illustrated by George Ford, 1973, New York, NY: Crowell. Cover art copyright 1973 by George Ford.

John Steptoe New Talent Award. John Steptoe, well known for his contributions to children's literature (*Mufaro's Beautiful Daughters, The Story of Jumping Mouse, Stevie*) is the namesake for this award which honors new talent in authorship or illustration.

The first John Steptoe Award was given to Sharon Draper in 1996 for *Tears of a Tiger*. The first illustrator award was given to Eric Valasquez in 1999 for The Piano Man (written by Debbi Chocolate).

Recent winners include Theodore Taylor III for illustrating *When the Beat was Born: DJ Kool Herc and the Creation of Hip Hop* and Jason Reynolds for writing *When I was the Greatest*.

Virginia Hamilton Award for Lifetime Achievement. The lifetime achievement award, named in honor of Virginia Hamilton, is presented in even years to an African American author and/or illustrator of children's literature. The inaugural winner was Walter Dean Myers in 2010, Ashley Bryan won in 2012, and Patricia and Frederick McKissack won in 2014.

Get to know the authors and illustrators who have received the Virginia Hamilton Award for Lifetime Achievement:

Walter Dean Myers (https://www.youtube.com/watch?v=nUJ37nrfNV4);

Ashley Bryan (https://www.youtube.com/watch?v=7REBumHUzPM);

Patricia and Frederick McKissack (https://www.youtube.com/watch?v=nCjNWnmvWg8).

The Literary Scholars

By definition, literature scholars focus their attention and analysis on books. Literary scholars have academic homes in many different disciplines, but the fields most closely associated with literary analysis and interpretation are English and the Humanities. However, English and the Humanities were (and in many cases, still are) slow to welcome children's literature as a serious area of focus. Aren't Sendak, Blume, and Rowling as crucial to human experience and literary development as Shakespeare, Austin, or Hemingway? Of course! As Francelia Butler (1973) wrote:

> To many humanists...in languages, philosophy, psychology, sociology, anthropology, or history, the most embarrassing literature to study is not about autoeroticism or cunnilingus. On such work scholars pride themselves on their broadmindedness. What truly embarrasses them is literature for their own children—'kiddy lit,' they call it." (Butler, 1973, p. 8)

Whoa! The times have changed since 1973. I don't know about you, but I would be more embarrassed to write about autoeroticism and cunnilingus than children's literature. Yikes!

IMPORTANT BOOKS
(THE PROBLEMS AND POLITICS OF IMPORTANCE; NOTABLE LISTS, AWARDS, & ASSOCIATIONS)

It is true. For some academics, children's literature does not meet the qualifications to join the world of comparative literatures. Fortunately, there are many gifted scholars who find those views to be outdated and unwarranted. Plus, it is hard to deny the relevance of books that form the basis of a multi-billion dollar industry. In fact, since the 1980's several universities have developed children's literature programs to support interest and provide a space for faculty to engage in scholarly pursuit. Programs such as those at the University of Pittsburgh, Ohio State, Kansas State, San Diego State, University of Florida, and the University of North Carolina-Charlotte demonstrate the robust nature of the field.

In spite of varying opinions on the subject, many English and Humanities publications and annual conferences often include articles and papers focused on children's literature (Neumeyer, 1987; Taylor, 1978). Prestigious organizations, such as the Modern Language Association, have included children's literature sessions in its annual conference for years.

Children's literature is too big, too important, and too profitable for writers, scholars, and critics to ignore. Fortunately, over 40 years ago, a group of scholars recognized the value of this body of literature and organized themselves into a collective to systematically explore children's literature.

[Handwritten note: Formerly Laura Ingalls Wilder Award]

Children's Literature Association (ChLA). This is an association of scholars, critics, professors, students, librarians, teachers and institutions dedicated to the academic study of literature for children. ChLA members define children's literature as "books, films, and other media created for, or adopted by, children and young adults around the world, past, present, and future" (http://www.childlitassn.org/about).

> Of all of the organizations listed in this chapter, ChLA is the only one that exists as a stand-alone association with a sole focus on children's literature. It also pulls members from different fields and backgrounds.

Phoenix Award and Phoenix Picture Book Award. ChLA recognizes high-quality literature through the Phoenix Award and the Phoenix Picture Book Award. Unlike most awards, which are given to books published in the last year, the ChLA offers their recognition to authors and illustrators whose books did not win a major award during the year of publication. Instead, the awards are given to books published 20 years previously and which have stood the test of time (Phoenix Award http://www.childlitassn.org/phoenix-award; Phoenix Picture Book Award http://www.childlitassn.org/phoenix-picture-book-award).

For example, the 2016 Phoenix Award Winner was *Frindle* by Andrew Clement. The 2016 Phoenix Picture Book Award Winner was *Goose* by Molly Bang (Figure 4.13).

In contrast to ALA's Newbery and Caldecott, the ChLA awards consider quality as well as popularity among a generation of readers in recognizing books that have had an impact on the field.

Figure 4.13

Goose by Molly Bang won the Phoenix Award from ChLA. Goose by Molly Bang, 1996, New York, NY: Blue Sky Press. Copyright 1996 by Molly Bang.

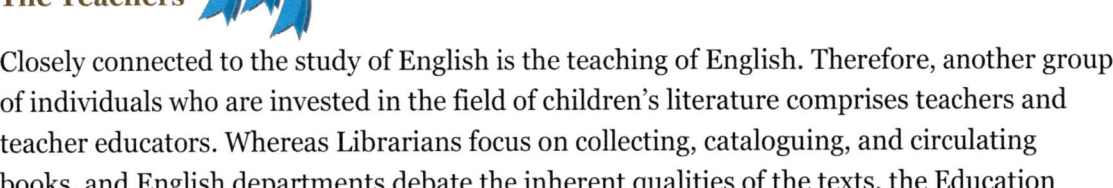

The Teachers

Closely connected to the study of English is the teaching of English. Therefore, another group of individuals who are invested in the field of children's literature comprises teachers and teacher educators. Whereas Librarians focus on collecting, cataloguing, and circulating books, and English departments debate the inherent qualities of the texts, the Education scholars focus on the reader's experience in relation to the text.

Reading literature increases a student's sensitivity to the power of the written word (Sipe, 2008) while reading picturebooks increases a student's exposure to visual modes (Brenner, 2011; Sipe, 2011). As such, children's and young adult literature is the foundation for youth's literacy development (Short, 2011). Youth need to be familiar with all genres of literature in order to create texts within recognizable written and artistic genres. They also need to know, as captured in picturebooks or graphic novels, how written and artistic modes can reflect their unique experiences and ideas.

In the US, two major literacy organizations provide extensive support, resources, and professional development for teachers—Kindergarten to College. Both of these organizations also give annual recognition to children's literature texts and they acknowledge authors' and illustrators' valuable contributions to children's literature.

National Council of Teachers of English (NCTE). This organization is "devoted to improving the teaching and learning of English and the language arts at all levels of education" (http://www.ncte.org/mission). NCTE was formed in 1911 "primarily out of protest against overly-specific college entrance requirements and the effects they were having on high school English education" (http://www.ncte.org/history). With such a focus on English education, NCTE has maintained consistent attention to the issues of teaching composition, rhetoric, and literature. Over the years, NCTE's range expanded to include a focus on teaching "language arts" in the elementary and middle school as well.

IMPORTANT BOOKS
(THE PROBLEMS AND POLITICS OF IMPORTANCE; NOTABLE LISTS, AWARDS, & ASSOCIATIONS)

To encourage the teaching of English, with particular attention to quality children's and young adult literature, NCTE offers the following awards for books for children.

NCTE Charlotte Huck Award for Outstanding Fiction for Children. Charlotte Huck was a Professor of Children's Literature at The Ohio State University. This NCTE award honors her incredible legacy with recognition of an outstanding book of fiction that also has the potential to transform children's lives by inviting compassion, imagination, and wonder.

 O-H-I-O, as a graduate of The Ohio State University, I can attest to the incredible impact of Charlotte Huck's work, her contributions to the education of teachers of reading and language arts, and the advancement of the field of children's literature. Her textbook, which is now revised and authored by Barbara Kiefer, is foundational reading for all teachers and anyone with an interest in children's literature.

In 2015, the inaugural Charlotte Huck Award was given to *Rain Reign* written by Ann M. Martin (Figure 4.14).

Figure 4.14

Rain Reign won the inaugural Charlotte Huck Award. *Rain Reign* by Ann M. Martin, 2014, New York, NY: Feiwel & Friends. Copyright 2014 by Ann M. Martin.

NCTE Orbis Pictus Award for Outstanding Nonfiction for Children. Johannes Amos Comenius was a 17th Century educational philosopher and reformer who wanted to change the ways in which boys learned in school (girls didn't go to school or really matter at this time). Rather than rote memorization of facts in Latin, Comenius wanted the boys to learn more about the world through active engagement and scholarly pursuit (Comenius, 1896). He published textbooks, such as *Janua*, which changed instructional methods. His popular textbook, *Orbis Pictus* (1657), was recognized as the first picturebook schoolbook for children. Therefore, the Orbis Pictus Award is given for excellence in the writing of nonfiction for children.

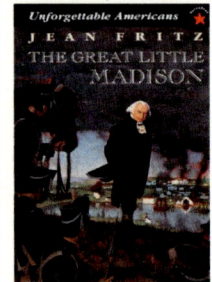

Figure 4.15

The winner of the first Orbis Pictus Award was *The Great Little Madison* by Jean Fritz, 1988, New York, NY: Puffin. Copyright 1988 by Jean Fritz.

The inaugural winner of the Orbis Pictus Award was Jean Fritz for *The Great Little Madison* (Figure 4.15). A more recent winner was *The Family Romanov: Murder, Rebellion & the Fall of Imperial Russia* by Candace Fleming (Figure 4.16).

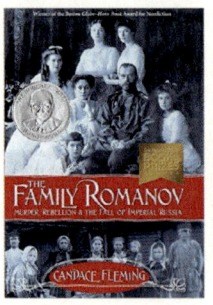

Figure 4.16

A recent Orbis Pictus winner is *The Family Romanov: Murder, Rebellion & the Fall of Imperial Russia* by Candace Fleming, 2014, New York, NY: Schwartz & Wade. Copyright 2014 by Candace Fleming.

Similar to the Sibert Medal from ALA (est. 2001), the Orbis Pictus (est. 1989) marked a shift in children's literature to recognize the aesthetic values of nonfiction and the need for quality writing in information books.

NCTE Award for Excellence in Poetry for Children. NCTE designates an Award for Excellence in Poetry for Children to honor a living American poet for his or her aggregate work for children ages 3–13. NCTE specifically targeted children's poetry in an effort to "recognize and foster excellence in children's poetry by encouraging its publication and by exploring ways to acquaint teachers and children with poetry through such means as publications, programs, and displays" (http://www.ncte.org/awards/poetry). The winners include a "who's who" of children's poetry: David McCord (1977 inaugural), Myra Cohn Livingston (1980), Eve Merriam (1981), Valerie Worth (1991), Arnold Adoff (1988), Eloise Greenfield (1997) (Figure 4.17), X.J. Kennedy (2000) and Marilyn Singer (2015).

Figure 4.17
Eloise Greenfield is one of my favorite poets of all time. And my favorite Eloise Greenfield book is *Honey I Love and Other Love Poems* by Eloise Greenfield and illustrated by Diane and Leo Dillon, 1978, New York, NY: HarperCollins. Cover art copyright 1978 by Diane and Leo Dillon.

Children's Literature Assembly of the National Council of Teachers of English (CLA). The Children's Literature Assembly is a Special Interest Group of NCTE. This group advocates for the centrality of literature in the classroom, believing that every teacher needs extensive knowledge of children's and young adult literature. The CLA believes it is a "teacher's responsibility to help students discover the joy of reading while they also teach students the skills and strategies of fluent reading" (http://www.childrensliteratureassembly.org/index.html).

Each year, the Children's Literature Assembly committee selects 30 titles for the Notables Award. Books considered for this annual list are works of fiction, non-fiction, and poetry written for children, grades K-8. The books must meet one or more of the following criteria:

- Deal explicitly with language, such as plays on words, word origins, or the history of language;
- Demonstrate uniqueness in the use of language or style;
- Invite child response or participation (http://www.childrensliteratureassembly.org/notables.html).

This is an interesting award that focuses on a specific type of writing that elicits children's responses and participation rather than focusing on the identity of the author or the range of the content.

International Literacy Association (ILA). ILA is a "worldwide advocate for excellence in literacy instruction, actively participating in advancing thought leadership for the literacy profession and shaping sound public policy on education" (http://literacyworldwide.org/about-us/where-we-stand).

Founded as the International Reading Association (IRA) in 1956, the organization changed its name in 2015 to reflect a shift from "reading" research toward a broader focus on all aspects of literacy. Yes, "reading" is still a focus of ILA, but the organization also concentrates on writing, speaking, listening, viewing and visual expression. According to the ILA, "Literacy is the ability to identify, understand, interpret, create, compute, and communicate using visual, audible, and digital materials across disciplines and in any context" (http://literacyworldwide.org/why-literacy).

ILA Children's and Young Adults' Book Award. These ILA awards are presented to newly published authors who show unusual promise in the children's and young adults' book field. Awards are given for fiction and nonfiction published in the previous year and intended for each of three audiences: primary, intermediate, and young adult (http://www.literacyworldwide.org/about-us/awards-grants/ila-children's-and-young-adults'-book-awards).

The ILA book award focuses on writing targeted at different audiences. Rather than considering literary merit alone, the committee recognizes the developmental differences of readers and offers awards to those who write exceptionally well for different age levels.

Recent ILA Book Award winners include:

Primary Fiction: *Maddi's Fridge*. Lois Brandt. 2014. Illustrated by Vin Vogel. Flashlight Press.

Primary Nonfiction: *Polar Bears and Penguins: A Compare and Contrast Book*. Katharine Hall. 2014. Arbordale Publishing.

Intermediate Fiction: *The Night Gardener*. Jonathan Auxier. 2014. Amulet Books.

Intermediate Nonfiction: *The Industrial Revolution for Kids: The People and Technology That Changed the World*. Cheryl Mullenbach. 2014. Chicago Review Press.

Young Adult Fiction: *Beauty of the Broken*. Tawni Waters. 2014. Simon Pulse.

Young Adult Nonfiction: No award was recommended in 2014.

Children's Literature and Reading Special Interest Group of the International Literacy Association (CL/R). The mission of the CL/R is to "promote the educational use of children's books by focusing on recently published children's literature, supportive professional books, issues relative to children's literature, and current research findings" (http://www.clrsig.org/nbgs.php). Founded in 1979, CL/R includes members who are teachers, librarians, teacher candidates, administrators, university professors, authors and publishers.

Notable Books for a Global Society (NBGS). In 1995, the CL/R formed the Notable Books for a Global Society Committee to help students, teachers, and families identify books that promote understanding of and appreciation for the world's full range of diverse cultures and ethnic and racial groups. Each year, the NBGS selects 25 outstanding books for grades K-12 that reflect a pluralistic view of the world (http://clrsig.org/pdfs/2015%20NBGS%20flyer.pdf). The 25 titles represent the committee's selection of the best in fiction (Figure 4.18), nonfiction (Figure 4.19) and poetry (Figure 4.20). Of primary importance are accuracy and authenticity. The books must accurately and authentically depict people in terms of physical characteristics, social and economic status, intellectual and problem-solving abilities, and displays of leadership and cooperation. The books must also include thought-provoking content that invites reflection, critical analysis, and response. Rather than including a minority group for purposes of tokenism, NBGS books are selected because they provide a richness of detail concerning the group or groups depicted (http://www.clrsig.org/nbgs.php).

Figure 4.18

NBGS books are selected because they accurately portray diverse cultures and groups of people. *No Crystal Stair: A Documentary Novel of the Life and Work of Lewis Michaux, a Harlem Bookseller* by Vaunda Michaux Nelson and illustrated by R. Gregory Christie, 2012, Minneapolis, MN: Carolrhoda Lab/Lerner. Cover art copyright 2012 by R. Gregory Christie.

Figure 4.19

A nonfiction NBGS book is *Denied, Detained, Deported: Stories from the Dark Side of Immigration* by Ann Bausum, 2009, Washington, D.C.: National Geographic. Copyright 2009 by Ann Bausum.

In addition to NCTE and ILA, there are many other organizations whose missions focus on literacy research and who attend to quality in children's literature texts. However, most of those organizations are for researchers and scholars and they do not offer awards or have sustained initiatives to recognize high-quality books, authors, or illustrators.

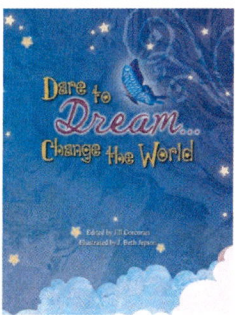

Figure 4.20

Poetry books are also included in the NBGS selection process. An example is *Dare to Dream.. Change the World* edited by Jill Corcoran and illustrated by J. Beth Jepson, 2012, Tulsa, OK: Kane/Miller. Cover art copyright 2012 by J. Beth Jepson.

IMPORTANT BOOKS
(THE PROBLEMS AND POLITICS OF IMPORTANCE; NOTABLE LISTS, AWARDS, & ASSOCIATIONS)

The Content Experts

Children's literature isn't just about reading and literacy. Children's literature is also a vehicle for sharing information about the world. Neal deGrasse Tyson (2004) said:

> My parents didn't know much science; in fact, they didn't know science at all. But they could recognize a science book when they saw it, and they spent a lot of time at bookstores, combing the remainder tables for science books to buy for me. I had one of the biggest libraries of any kid in school, built on books that cost 50 cents or a dollar. (http://www.pbs.org/wgbh/nova/space/conversation-with-neil-tyson.html)

Scholars in the fields of science, social studies, and mathematics have found untapped potential in the form of information books for children. In addition to the nonfiction awards offered by the American Library Association (Sibert Medal) and the National Council of Teachers of English (Orbis Pictus), other professional organizations have created awards to recognize the role of children's literature in the development of disciplinary knowledge.

> The Sibert and Orbis Pictus Medals are awarded to books covering a broad range of topics. Therefore, other organizations created awards to recognize books that represent their specific areas of expertise.

National Science Teachers Association (NSTA). This organization works with the Children's Book Council (CBC) to create an annual list of Outstanding Science Trade Books for Children. Originally, the list targeted grades K-8 (Figure 4.21), but as the genre of science information texts has developed to include advanced topics (Figure 4.22), the list was expanded to include high school students as well (http://www.nsta.org/publications/ostb/).

Figure 4.21
Science books are recognized by the National Science Teachers Association. *Egg: Nature's Perfect Package* by Robin Page and Steve Jenkins, 2015, New York, NY: Houghton Mifflin Harcourt. Copyright 2015 by Robin Page and Steve Jenkins.

American Phytopathological Society. The American Phytopathological Society created the DeBary Children's Science Book Award. Selected by scientists in the fields of botany and biological sciences, the awards are presented to the best science books for children. There is a slight bias towards botany and biological science, but books on all topics, from Astronomy to Zoology, are eligible http://www.apsnet.org/edcenter/K-12/Pages/DeBary.aspx.

Figure 4.22
Advanced science trade books are published for high school students as well. *Food Engineering: From Concept to Consumer* by Michael Burgan, 2015, Framingham, MA: C. Press/F. Watts Trade. Copyright 2015 by Michael Burgan.

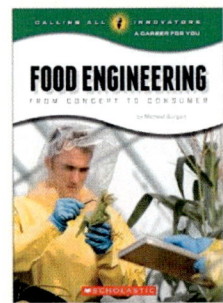

Mathematical Sciences Research Institute. The Mathematical Sciences Research Institute also works with the Children's Book Council (CBC) to create a list of outstanding mathematics books for children. Identifying winners in five categories, the "Mathical Prize" is awarded to popular, math-related fiction and nonfiction for very young children through teenagers (http://mathicalbooks.org/). The books are selected if they inspire youth of all ages to cultivate a love of mathematics in the world around them (Figure 4.23). Similar to book awards from NCTE or IRA, the Mathica books are sorted by the intended reader's age level.

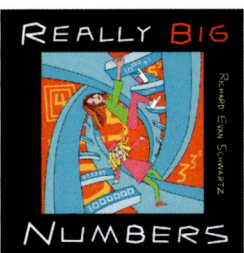

Figure 4.23

Math books have come a long way. Check out a Mathica winner, *Really Big Numbers* by Richard Schwartz, 2014, Providence, RI: American Mathematical Society. Copyright 2014 by Richard Schwartz.

The Mathica Prize comes from math people, not teachers or librarians. The MSRI is primarily funded by the National Science Foundation (NSF) and its mission is the advancement and communication of fundamental knowledge in mathematics and the mathematical sciences.

National Council for the Social Studies (NCSS). NCSS awards two prizes for outstanding children's literature. Working with the Children's Book Council (CBC), NCSS recommends Notable Social Studies Trade Books for Young People. The annual reading list is selected by social studies educators and includes exceptional books for use in social studies classrooms (http://www.socialstudies.org/notable).

NCSS also established the Carter G. Woodson Book Awards for the most distinguished children's books that depict ethnicity in the United States. First presented in 1974, this award is given to a book written for elementary (K-6) and middle grades (5-8) and it is intended to "encourage the writing, publishing, and dissemination of outstanding social studies books for young readers that treat topics related to ethnic minorities and race relations sensitively and accurately" (http://www.socialstudies.org/awards/woodson/winners).

Content expertise resides in many different places. Many of the aforementioned awards come from professional associations that are focused on teaching disciplinary content (e.g., National Council for the Social Studies, National Science Teachers Association). But others represent the broader discipline. In these cases, the disciplinary concepts or subject matter might take precedence over other important aspects of children's books, such as the quality of the illustrations or the author's writing style, but not necessarily so.

The Creators: Children's Book Writers and Illustrators

You would think, in a book about children's literature, that I would feature the authors and illustrators as the foremost experts in the field. Truthfully, they are. They create the stuff of which we all obsess ("we" being children's literature people). They are the ones "doing" while everyone else is "consuming." But there is no single method for writing children's books and no single way to illustrate children's literature. The writers and illustrators are a collection of artists, nomadic thinkers, literary wonderers, and stylistic voyagers who create literature and art differently. Therefore, the creators' expectations for quality vary. In addition, they come from different backgrounds and schools of practice, leading to the fact that they do not approach the field of children's literature with one particular point of view.

In the previous sections, I discussed awards for children's literature that are as much about a targeted agenda as they are about the creators' products. Similarly, when writers and illustrators get together, they promote their own agendas as well.

Society of Children's Book Writers and Illustrators (SCBWI). The SCBWI offers five awards for *authors* in support of their manuscript development and five awards for *illustrators* to recognize work in progress or illustrators of promise. SCBWI also offers nine awards for those who are already published and whose work is deserving of recognition (http://www.scbwi.org/awards/grants/for-illustrators/).

Several of the SCBWI awards are focused on the business of children's book creation. For example, the Book Launch Award provides authors and illustrators with recognition and funding to support the promotion of their newly published work and to allow them to "take the marketing strategy into their own creative hands" (http://www.scbwi.org/awards/book-launch-grant/). The Jane Yolen Mid-List Author Grant honors the contribution of mid-list authors and aims to help raise awareness about their current works-in-progress (http://www.scbwi.org/awards/grants/jane-yolen-mid-list-author-grant/). The Spark Award is given to an author or illustrator who self-published a Board Book, Picture Book, Chapter Book, Middle Grade, or Young Adult book through an established self-publishing enterprise or an individually self-published outlet. The Tomie dePaola Award, selected by Tomie himself, is given to an illustrator of promise. The selected illustrator receives $1000 plus tuition and attendance paid to attend the SCBWI winter conference.

In addition to the awards that focus on the professional development of the authors and illustrators of children's literature, SCBWI also recognizes books for their excellence.

IMPORTANT BOOKS
(THE PROBLEMS AND POLITICS OF IMPORTANCE; NOTABLE LISTS, AWARDS, & ASSOCIATIONS)

Golden Kite Awards. In contrast to awards given by experts in children's literature, the Golden Kite Awards are the only children's literary award judged by a jury of author-and-illustrator peers. The Golden Kite Awards recognize excellence in children's literature in the following categories: Fiction, Nonfiction, Picture Book Text, and Picture Book Illustration. (http://www.scbwi.org/awards/golden-kite-award/)

Current Golden Kite winners include:

Fiction: *Revolution* by Deborah Wiles (Figure 4.24);

Nonfiction: *The Family Romanov* by Candace Fleming;

Picture Book Illustration: *The Right Word: Roget and His Thesaurus* illustrated by Melissa Sweet and written by Jen Bryant;

Picture Book Text: *A Dance Like Starlight: One Ballerina's Dream* written by Kristy Dempsey and illustrated by Floyd Cooper (Figure 4.25).

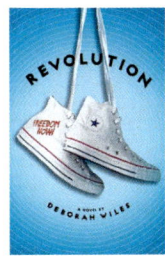

Figure 4.24
A Golden Kite Award for Fiction was awarded to *Revolution* by Deborah Wiles, 2014, New York, NY: Scholastic Press. Copyright 2014 by Deborah Wiles.

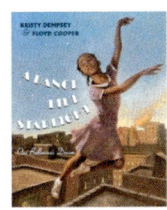

Figure 4.25
A Golden Kite Award for Picture Book Text was awarded to *A Dance Like Starlight: One Ballerina's Dream* written by Kristy Dempsey and illustrated by Floyd Cooper, 2014, New York, NY: Philomel. Cover art copyright 2014 by Floyd Cooper.

Sid Fleischman Humor Award. Children's literature is serious business, and much like the Academy Awards for Motion Pictures, the highest acclaim often goes to the dramatic. Humor is difficult to do well; however, humor is often dismissed in favor of profound and deeply emotional work. Therefore, the SCBWI created the Sid Fleischman Humor Award in 2003 to recognize authors whose work exemplifies excellence in writing in the genre of humor. The award is named after its inaugural awardee, Sid Fleischman, author of over 35 books for children (Figure 4.26). Recently, the award went to Michelle Knudsen for *Evil Librarian* (Figure 4.27).

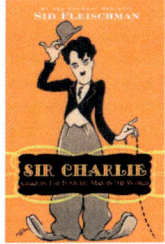

Figure 4.26
Humor wasn't often recognized as a literary quality until the Sid Fleischman Humor Award came along. One of Sid Fleischman's books was *Sir Charlie: Chaplin, the Funniest Man in the World* by Sid Fleischman, 2010, New York, NY: Greenwillow. Copyright 2010 by Sid Fleischman.

Figure 4.27
The *Evil Librarian* is one example of a humorous book recognized by the Sid Fleischman Humor Award. *Evil Librarian* by Michelle Knudsen, 2014, Somerville, MA: Candlewick. Copyright 2014 by Michelle Knudsen.

Humor and laughter are emotional responses and always associated with children. It makes sense that high-quality children's literature should feature humor too. Right?

Society of Illustrators. Founded in 1901, the mission of the Society of Illustrators is "to promote generally the art of illustration and to hold exhibitions from time to time." The Society of Illustrators includes members who are illustrators across various forms including children's book illustrators, comic book illustrators, and designers. The Society offers juried exhibitions of children's book art and an annual award for comic and cartoon art (http://www.societyillustrators.org).

Academy of American Poets. The Academy of American Poets was founded in 1934 to foster an appreciation for contemporary poetry and to support American poets through all stages in their careers. The Academy offers prizes, programs, and publishing opportunities for poets. Although the organization is not exclusive to children's or young adult poetry, they offer programs and support targeted for youth (http://www.poets.org).

American Folklore Society (AFS). This organization is an association of people who study and communicate knowledge about folklore throughout the world. The AFS was founded in 1888 by university-based humanities scholars, museum anthropologists, and private citizens--including author Mark Twain.

Aesop Prize. The Aesop Prize and Aesop Accolades (runners up) are conferred annually by the Children's Folklore Section of the AFS (Figure 4.28). The award is given to English language books for children and young adults, both fiction and nonfiction. The books must have folklore as central to the book's content and illustrations (http://www.afsnet.org/?page=aesop).

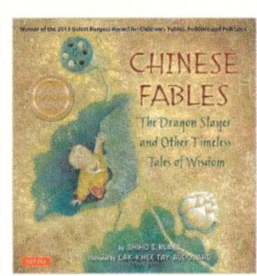

Figure 4.28

The Aesop Prize was awarded to *Chinese Fables: The Dragon Slayer and Other Timeless Tales of Wisdom*, by Shiho S. Nunes and illustrated by Lak-Khee Tay-Audouard, 2013, Tokyo/Rutland, Vermont: Tuttle Publishing. Cover art copyright 2013 by Lak-Khee Tay-Audouard.

Science Fiction and Fantasy Writers of America (SFWA). The Society is a professional organization for published authors. It informs, supports, promotes, defends and advocates for its members. Interestingly, SFWA makes loans available to authors who are engaged in writing-related disputes in court.

Norton Award. The SFWA presents the Norton Award to outstanding young adult and middle-grade fiction that includes speculative content, such as science fiction and fantasy (http://www.sfwa.org/nebula-awards/the-andre-norton-award/).

As mentioned throughout this section, authors and illustrators are a collective group of self-employed business owners who have particular needs and agendas. Their organizations tend to focus on the logistics of navigating the publishing industry rather than literary or artistic issues because, quite honestly, they know how to do the literary and artistic stuff. Children and young adults are their targeted audiences, but not the central focus of their organizations.

The Publishers and Booksellers

Speaking of agendas, the motives of the children's book publishers and booksellers are very clear—sell books. I like to characterize the publishers, and their entourages (sales staff, production staff, editors, etc.), in three ways.

First, there are the sales extremists for whom profit is the bottom line. They sell anything, anywhere. Most of their books are junky, trendy, and sentimental. They are the copy-cats of innovative ideas and the outsourcers of talent. The fact that they sell literature is irrelevant. It's about profit margins.

 Grocery Store Books: "Grocery Store Books" is the term I use for the junky, trendy, sentimental, and cheaply-made books you can find in the check-out line, in a rounder by the deli, or in a display in the magazine aisle.

Next, you have the selective stewards and picky promoters of the children's literature world—the ones who are passionate about the product, adamant about quality, and savvy in business. They are consumers of children's literature and admirers of creativity but they know what works and what sells, and they usually go with that.

Finally, you have the creative types—the open-access/not-for-profit/start-up believers who are passionate and idiosyncratic. They work hard and have groundbreaking ideas, and their business is not solely about sales.

As with all of the other awards for children's literature, you have to understand the motivations of the entity that confers the honor. In the case of publishers and booksellers, it's ultimately about pushing product.

IMPORTANT BOOKS
(THE PROBLEMS AND POLITICS OF IMPORTANCE; NOTABLE LISTS, AWARDS, & ASSOCIATIONS)

Horn Book Magazine. Bertha Mahony opened a children's bookshop, The Bookshop for Boys and Girls, in Boston in 1916. As the proprietor, she implemented innovative ideas such as a traveling bookstore (called The Caravan) (Eddy, 2006). Bertha also authored "Books for Boys and Girls" which was a list of over 1000 titles of recommended books organized by age and subject. This suggestive purchase list eventually turned into a children's book review service called Horn Book Magazine (http://www.hbook.com/).

Boston Globe-Horn Book Award. The Boston Globe-Horn Book Award is given to outstanding books published in the United States. The books may be written or illustrated by citizens of any country.

In 1967, the inaugural winners were:

Fiction: *The Little Fishes by Erik Christian Haugaard* (Figure 4.29);

Picture Book: *London Bridge is Falling Down* by Peter Spier (Figure 4.30).

Figure 4.29

The inaugural Boston Globe-Horn Book Award for Fiction was given to *The Little Fishes* by Erik Christian Haugaard in 1967. *The Little Fishes* by Erik Christian Haugaard and illustrated by Milton Johnson, 1967, Boston, MA; Houghton Mifflin. Cover art copyright 1967 by Milton Johnson.

I love to compare the early award winners to the more recent ones, especially for an award that spans decades. What do you notice?

Figure 4.30

The inaugural Boston Globe-Horn Book Award for Picture Books was given to *London Bridge is Falling Down* by Peter Spier in 1967. London Bridge is Falling Down by Peter Spier, 1967, London, England: Doubleday and Company. Copyright 1967 by Peter Spier.

In 1976, **nonfiction** books were added as a separate category and Alfred Tamarin and Shirley Glubok won the award for *Voyaging to Cathay: Americans in the China Trade* (Figure 4.31).

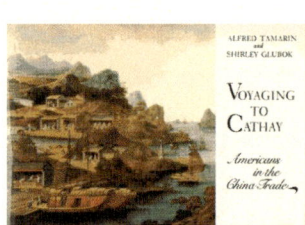

Figure 4.31

The inaugural Boston Globe-Horn Book Award for Nonfiction was given to *Voyaging to Cathay: Americans in the China Trade* by Alfred Tamarin and Shirley Glubok, 1976, New York, NY: Viking Press. Copyright 1976 by Alfred Tamarin and Shirley Glubok.

Contemporary winners include:

Fiction: *Cartwheeling in Thunderstorms* by Katherine Rundell (Figure 4.32);

Picture Book: *The Farmer and the Clown* by Marla Frazee (Figure 4.33);

Nonfiction: *The Family Romanov: Murder, Rebellion, and the Fall of Imperial Russia* by Candace Fleming (Figure 4.34).

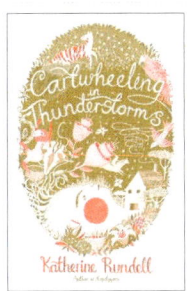

Figure 4.32

A contemporary winner of the Boston Globe-Horn Book Award for Fiction is *Cartwheeling in Thunderstorms* by Katherine Rundell, 2014, New York, NY: Simon & Schuster. Copyright 2014 by Katherine Rundell.

Figure 4.33

A contemporary winner of the Boston Globe-Horn Book Award for Picture Books is a wordless book, *The Farmer and the Clown* by Marla Frazee, 2014, New York, NY: Beach Lane Books. Copyright 2014 by Marla Frazee.

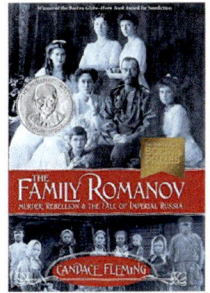

Figure 4.34

A contemporary winner of the Boston Globe-Horn Book Award for Nonfiction is *The Family Romanov: Murder, Rebellion & the Fall of Imperial Russia* by Candace Fleming, 2014, New York, NY: Schwartz & Wade. Copyright 2014 by Candace Fleming.

Kirkus. *Kirkus* is a literary review magazine founded in 1933 by Virginia Kirkus. Her idea to sell review services to booksellers originated under the threat that she was losing her job during the Great Depression. Virginia was the head of the Department for Boys and Girls at Harper & Brothers Publishers. In her role, she visited booksellers across America to secure sales. It occurred to her that booksellers ordered books from publishing lists without any insight about the book's quality or style. Virginia decided booksellers needed assistance and she offered her discerning eye. Virginia sold her services (book critiques) to help the booksellers make informed decisions about purchasing.

Whereas Virginia Kirkus delivered her reviews by mail or in person, today, *Kirkus Reviews* magazine provides industry professionals a preview of the most notable books being published through a weekly email newsletter and on their website (https://www.kirkusreviews.com/). *Kirkus* also provides other services for authors such as editing and reviews.

The Kirkus Prize. A Kirkus Star is awarded by editors, in consultation with reviewers, to demarcate noteworthy books of excellence. Any of the books that earn a Kirkus Star are eligible to win the yearly prize. The Kirkus Prize is awarded to the best in Fiction, Nonfiction and Young Readers' Literature.

A writer, a bookseller or librarian, and a Kirkus critic judge each of the three categories. In the Young Readers' Literature category, the finalists include two picture books, two middle-grade books, and two teen books and one winner is selected among them.

The Kirkus Prize for Young Readers' Literature was inaugurated in 2014 and given to *Aviary Wonders Inc.: Spring Catalog and Instruction Manual* written and illustrated by Kate Samworth (Figure 4.35).

Figure 4.35

The inaugural Kirkus Prize for Young Readers was awarded to *Aviary Wonders Inc. Spring Catalog and Instructional Manual* by Kate Samworth, 2014, New York, NY: Clarion. Copyright 2014 by Kate Samworth.

American Booksellers Association (ABA). Founded in 1900, the ABA is a national not-for-profit trade organization that works to help independently owned bookstores grow and succeed (http://www.bookweb.org/about-aba). The ABA creates programs; provides education, information, business products, and services; and engages in public policy and industry advocacy.

Indies Choice. The annual Indies Choice Book Awards honor best-loved titles of indie booksellers. ABA member bookstores may vote literature for in eight (8) categories. The Indies Choice Awards recognize the handselling expertise of independent booksellers, and the Book of the Year winners and Honor Award recipients are all titles nominated by ABA member booksellers to the Indie Next Lists.

E.B. White Read-Aloud Awards. These awards were established in 2004 and previously administered by the Association of Booksellers for Children. The award honors books that reflect the read aloud standards that were created by the work of E.B. White in his classic books for children: *Charlotte's Web* (Figure 4.36), *Stuart Little*, and *The Trumpet of the Swan*. In other words, the books should include playful, well-paced language and have universal appeal.

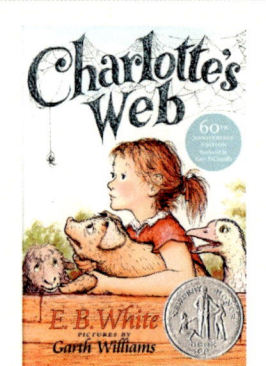

Figure 4.36

E.B. White wrote our most beloved contributions to children's literature, and the ABA named their read aloud award in honor of his collection of books. Here's one example, *Charlotte's Web* by E.B. White and illustrated by Garth Williams, 1952, New York, NY: HarperCollins. Copyright 1952 by Garth Williams.

 Parent/child read alouds play an important role in children's literacy development. Children learn how books work (front to back, left to right, top to bottom), what tells the story/information on each page (text), and how written language sounds (writing and talking are two different things).

IMPORTANT BOOKS
(THE PROBLEMS AND POLITICS OF IMPORTANCE; NOTABLE LISTS, AWARDS, & ASSOCIATIONS)

In the first two years of the award, a single book was selected. In 2006, in recognition of the fact that reading aloud is a pleasure at any age, the award was expanded into two categories: Picture Books, and Older Readers (http://www.bookweb.org/general-marketing-resources). In addition to honoring current titles, the E.B. White Award also inducts books into its Hall of Fame, and this list is a great resource for finding old favorites.

The E.B.White Award was recently awarded to:

Middle Reader: *brown girl dreaming*, by Jacqueline Woodson (Figure 4.37);

Picture Book: *Sam and Dave Dig a Hole*, by Mac Barnett, Jon Klassen;

The Hall of Fame inductees include:

Blueberries for Sal, by Robert McCloskey;

Frog and Toad, by Arnold Lobel (Video 4.1);

If You Give a Mouse a Cookie written by Laura Numeroff and illustrated by Felicia Bond.

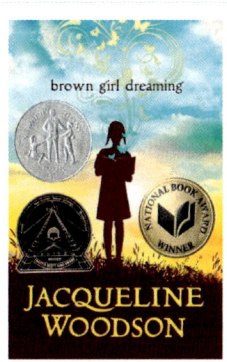

Figure 4.37

brown girl dreaming has won many awards, including the E.B. White Read-Aloud Award. *brown girl dreaming* by Jacqueline Woodson, 2014, New York, NY: Penguin. Copyright 2014 by Jacqueline Woodson.

Video 4.1 Frog and Toad Are Friends by Arnold Lobel http://www.kaltura.com/tiny/x7ypm

Children's Book Council (CBC). This is the nonprofit trade association of children's book publishers in North America. The Children's Book Council came into being as an organizing structure to manage activities associated with Children's Book Week, activities that were originally managed by Anne Carroll Moore and Alice Jordan, the supervisors of children's services in the New York and Boston public libraries in 1919 (Eddy, 2006). Over time, the Children's Book Council developed into an organization that advocates for the children's publishing industry through educational programming, professional development, marketing and promotion.

This is where the history of the library has relevance to today.

In joint sponsorship with the International Literacy Association, the Children's Book Council administers the Choice Book Awards. According to the CBC website,

> Teams of ILA-affiliated educators in five geographic regions receive copies of each submitted title to provide to students to read and rate in classrooms across their region. The votes from the five regions (from approximately 12,500 children) are compiled and the five titles with the highest number of votes in each category (K-2, 3-4, 5-6) become the finalists for the Children's Choice Book Awards.
>
> Teen Book of the Year finalists are chosen by 4,000+ teens via voting conducted by Teenreads.com.
>
> The five finalists in each of the Children's Choice Debut Author, Teen Choice Debut Author and Children's Choice Illustrator categories are determined by two selection committees comprised of librarians, educators, booksellers, and children's literature experts appointed by Every Child a Reader (http://ccbookawards.com/about.php).

Children's Choice Book Award. The *Children's Choice Book Award* is given to a "book of the year" for K-2, 3-4, and 5-6 grades following the procedures outlined above.

Teen Choice Book Award. The *Teen Choice Award* is given to a young adult "book of the year" following the procedures outlined above.

Although The Children's & Teen Choice Book Awards promote themselves as "the only national book awards program where the winning titles are selected by children and teens," this proclamation is skewed by the intervention of the International Literacy Association and Children's Book Council members who select the books to be voted upon and who make the final choices for some of the awards. For unfiltered reviews from children and teens, one must look elsewhere. In addition, to eliminate the influence of big publishing, one must take a look at small publishing houses and self-published authors and illustrators.

The Fans

Seriously, the fans are experts? Yes, the fans are experts. The people (children, teens, and adults) who stand in line for book signings (Figure 4.38), attend lectures, follow authors and illustrators on Twitter, and wear book-themed clothing—they are experts? Yes, the fans are experts. The people who use children's literature quotes in their email signatures, dress up like book characters for Halloween, take children's-literature-themed vacations (Figure 4.39), and populate numerous Pinterest pages with the "best of" guide to some (fill-in-the-blank) sub-genre of children's literature—they know how to judge quality. Yep. Experts.

Figure 4.38
Book fans meet Henry Cole at the USF CLICK Conference (Children's Literature Collection of Know How). Photo copyright 2015 by Jenifer Schneider.

Figure 4.39
Yes, I flew through platform 9 ¾ in London's Kings Cross Station. Photo copyright 2015 by Troy Schneider.

The people who obsess about children's literature—the avid readers, booksellers, beach goers, grad students, individual teachers and librarians, and all others who have a passion for children's and young adult literature—know more about books, authors, trends, and literary events than most scholars or critics I've ever met or read. Why? Fans are passionate, not posturing. They study deeply and broadly. And they share their responses freely; they are open-access.

Unlike other awards that are predominantly managed and/or filtered by the publishers via preview copies and marketing campaigns, the fans vote with their purchases, lending records, fanfiction tributes, and other networked methods. However, unlike other groups of experts, the fans are harder to organize. There are book clubs, fan clubs, and individual bloggers, but it is difficult to pull these distinct entities together; albeit, some have tried.

IMPORTANT BOOKS
(THE PROBLEMS AND POLITICS OF IMPORTANCE; NOTABLE LISTS, AWARDS, & ASSOCIATIONS)

Cybils. The Cybils are the Children's and Young Adult Bloggers' Literary Award. In other words, the Cybils are an organizing entity for independent book bloggers. Cybils judges are a group of selected bloggers who "read, discuss, think about, blog about, narrow down, and select the year's best (and most kid-friendly) books (http://www.cybils.com/information-for-bloggers/judging-overview)."

According to their website, "The Cybils Awards aims to recognize the children's and young adult authors and illustrators whose books combine the highest literary merit and popular appeal. If some la-di-dah awards can be compared to brussels sprouts, and other, more populist ones to gummy bears, we're thinking more like organic chicken nuggets. We are yummy and nutritious" (http://www.cybils.com/about-the-cybils-awards).

The Cybils began in 2006 and the awards continue today, covering a range of children's literature: best book app (Figure 4.40), fiction picture book, non-fiction, easy reader (Figure 4.41), early chapter book, graphic novel, poetry, middle grade fiction, and speculative fiction.

The Cybils are also awarded to a range of young adult literature: fiction, graphic novel (Figure 4.42), non-fiction, speculative fiction.

Graphic Novels are popular with readers and gaining lots of attention from publishers and award committees as well.

For example, First Second books (http://www.firstsecondbooks.com/) publishes and blogs about graphic novels. Their website includes an award list as well.

Figure 4.40

The Cybils selected *Kalley's Machine Plus Cats* as the best book app of 2014 (https://itunes.apple.com/us/app/kalleys-machine-plus-cats/id905722643?mt=8&ign-mpt=uo%3D4). *Kalley's Maching Plus Cats* by Jon, Carrie, Corbett, & Kalley Alexander, 2014, RocketWagon: Retrieved from http://rocketwagon.com/app/kalleys-machine/.

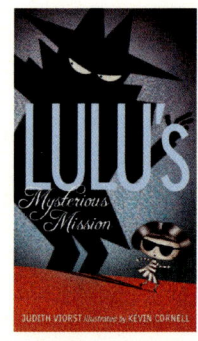

Figure 4.41

You don't see many awards for easy readers or early chapter books. The Cybils categorizes their awards based on ages and stages in reading development. A Cybils Early Chapter Book winner was *Lulu's Mysterious Mission* by Judith Viorst and illustrated by Kevin Cornell, 2014, New York, NY: Atheneum. Cover art copyright 2014 by Kevin Cornell.

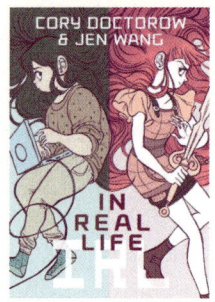

Figure 4.42

The Cybils also gives awards to graphic novels for children and young adults. A recent winner was *In Real Life* by Cory Doctorow and Jen Wang, 2014, New York, NY: First Second. Copyright by Cory Doctorow and Jen Wang.

Children's Choices—Revisited. Children's Choices is a program initiated by the International Literacy Association and Children's Book Council in 1974. Each year, children choose favorite books among the approximately 500 titles donated by children's book publishers. Team Leaders from five different areas around the US distribute the books and collect responses. Each year, thousands of children participate in the voting and review experience. The Children's Choices are organized by reading level and published as an expansive list (http://www.cbcbooks.org/wp-content/uploads/2013/04/childrenschoiceslist_2015.pdf).

Children's Choices is marketed as a list created by children. However, the children choose from a predetermined list and the results are clearly marketed to teachers. Although there are enough titles (about 500) to allow for variation and to get a sense of children's preferences, Children's Choices is a list of books aggregated within boundaries. According to Beach (2015), there is a significant divergence between the providers and consumers of children's literature. Beach compared the lists from ALA's Notable Children's Books (chosen by a committee of librarians) and the ILA's Children's Choices (chosen by children) from 1974 until 2004. He found that there was only a 4.36% overlap between the lists across the 30-year period. In fact, he also noted that the award winning books that were prominent on the adult list seldom appeared on the children's list. So much for awards, right?

 If children choose within a predetermined list, are we really getting a sense of their choices?

Other Indicators of Importance

I have presented my opinion of the experts in the field of children's literature and described the awards they offer to recognize and reward quality. Why? Experts are important. They challenge, guide, and direct the field. They spark excellence. Beyond personal preferences (which, of course, they possess), they have a sense of the history and trends of the field and they can compare books as well as creators' contributions. But sometimes experts are wrong (see the Phoenix award). And sometimes experts are right. And sometimes experts are right, but no one listens.

Popularity and Sales

Oftentimes it's not the inherent qualities of a book that determine its excellence; it is the book's commercial success. Metrics, such as the New York Times Best Sellers List or Amazon Best Sellers often dictate which books are created, marketed, and sold.

IMPORTANT BOOKS
(THE PROBLEMS AND POLITICS OF IMPORTANCE; NOTABLE LISTS, AWARDS, & ASSOCIATIONS)

New York Times. The *New York Times* list reflects sales reported by vendors. According to the *New York Times* website the following statement reflects their methodology (http://www.nytimes.com/best-sellers-books/picture-books/list.html):

Many people think that the *New York Times* list has a mechanism to measure sales. The reality is they aggregate sales numbers based on self-report from the vendors.

The sales venues for print books include independent book retailers; national, regional and local chains; online and multimedia entertainment retailers; supermarkets, university, gift and discount department stores; and newsstands. E-book rankings reflect sales from leading online vendors of e-books in a variety of popular e-reader formats.... The universe of print book dealers is well established, and sales of print titles are statistically weighted to represent all outlets nationwide. The universe of e-book publishers and vendors is rapidly emerging, and until the industry is settled sales of e-books will not be weighted.

Among the categories not actively tracked at this time are: perennial sellers, required classroom reading, textbooks, reference and test preparation guides, journals, workbooks, calorie counters, shopping guides, comics, crossword puzzles and self-published books.

Interesting! E-books are included, but they aren't weighted because that industry isn't predictable or controlled—yet.

In addition, the *New York Times* documents when bookstores report that a book has been ordered in bulk. Bulk orders can happen for a variety of reasons. For example, in the State of Florida, the Sunshine State Young Readers program is a reading motivation program for students in grades 3-8. If the Sunshine readers are required summer reading, libraries and bookstores might order the books in bulk.

Amazon Best Sellers. Amazon ranks 100 books based on sales from their website. Unlike the *New York Times* list, which provides a singular ranking based on sales for the week, Amazon updates the best sellers hourly. In addition, Amazon provides an overall best sellers list of children's books, but they also provide the opportunity to look for best sellers by category (e.g., art, biographies, political, science, sports, women, etc. (http://www.amazon.com/Best-Sellers-Books-Childrens/zgbs/books/4)

Bestseller lists offer consumers an opportunity to monitor trends and make purchases with the idea that books are popular and well-received by children.

Sometimes popularity indices are correct (e.g. the Harry Potter series), and sometimes they are wrong, because children don't buy books; parents do. For example, when Dr. Seuss' lost book, *What Pet Should I Get*, was set for publication (7-28-2015), Amazon started taking orders and the book was listed as the #1 best seller for weeks prior to its release. Not a single child had read the book at that point.

Remember, children don't typically buy books on the Internet; adults do. You should view "bestsellers" as adult purchases, not necessarily children's choices.

When it comes to popularity and sales, celebrities such as Jamie Lee Curtis (actress), Julie Andrews (actress), or Madonna (singer) write books, their books tend to skyrocket to the top of the New York Times and Amazon bestsellers lists. Why? Parents and grandparents buy the books.

Social Networks

For a more accurate indicator of children and young adults preferences, I use natural resources—I talk to kids.

Since I can't talk to kids all over the world, I also use digital resources such as Twitter. In the world of children's literature, Keith Richards (guitarist for the Rolling Stones), Bob Dylan (singer/songwriter), and Bruce Springsteen (singer/songwriter) have written books for children, but they are not rock stars. The rock stars of children's and young adult literature are J.K. Rowling (4.29 million), John Green (4.28 million), and Neil Gaiman (2.18 million) who have millions of followers on Twitter.

Here are some suggestions for following illustrators of children's books.

18 Illustrators to Follow on Instagram

Picturebook Authors & Illustrators on Twitter

Don't Follow the Pigeon
Follow Mo Willems on Twitter https://twitter.com/The_Pigeon, but watch this video first: http://www.cbsnews.com/news/for-kids-book-author-mo-willems-childhood-is-an-awful-time/

Check Out the Children's Illustrators Showcase

Find Information Through Author & Illustrator Websites
Search the professional Society of Children's Books Writers and Illustrators: http://www.scbwi.org/

In addition, recommendation sites, such as Goodreads (www.goodreads.com), offer reader ratings and feedback on books. The sites query a reader's book preferences and then use algorithms to determine which books are likely favorites. Sites such as Goodreads also allow members to create their own lists of favorites that can appear in diverse categories such as best books about animals, best books about sports, or popular books about trains. The categories are almost endless.

Whereas Twitter or Goodreads may serve as a more accurate indicator of author or illustrator popularity, if you want to know about particular books, youth tend to leverage their "buying" power at the library.

Circulation Reports

Libraries, without a financial stake in any particular book's success, offer circulation reports for an accurate assessment of children's and young adult preferences. Resources, such as the *Library and Book Trade Almanac* (2015) provide statistical data and other information to determine trends. Although the almanac is expensive, librarians use the data to make purchases for their collections. Similar resources are available for school libraries as well.

The Lists

For an encompassing list of lists, the Junior Library Guild has compiled extensive resources to help you navigate the following:

- Outstanding Book Lists (https://www.juniorlibraryguild.com/awards/list.dT/outstanding-book-lists);

- State awards (https://www.juniorlibraryguild.com/awards/list.dT/state-awards);

- National Book Awards (https://www.juniorlibraryguild.com/awards/list.dT/national-awards);

- Themed Lists (https://www.juniorlibraryguild.com/awards/list.dT/themed-lists);

- Yearly Awards (https://www.juniorlibraryguild.com/awards/list.dT/award-winning-titles).

The Problem with Awards and Lists

Children's literature awards, especially the Newbery and Caldecott Medals, have a long and important history. These awards have clearly elevated children's literature as Art and Literature. But along the way, librarians, scholars, readers, authors and illustrators began to notice a few trends…

- The Caldecott is awarded to far more men than women.

- The Newbery is awarded to Caucasian authors more than any other racial group.

- The Newbery and Caldecott books predominantly feature Caucasian characters who are mostly male.

- The Orbis Pictus winners feature limited portrayals of people from diverse backgrounds, with different religions, who represent different developmental abilities, and who represent a range of sexual identities (Crisp, 2015).

Remember the history of the library? Many libraries and schools were segregated until the 1960's. How can children dream of growing up to write or illustrate children's books, if quality books were not part of their lives? It takes generations to recover from institutional racism, and just because a law is passed doesn't mean the changes happen immediately. Look at Obamacare. Look at marriage equality.

According to the ALA, when the Newbery Medal was approved in 1922, its purpose was as follows: "To encourage original creative work in the field of books for children. To emphasize to the public that contributions to the literature for children deserve similar recognition to poetry, plays, or novels. To give those librarians, who make it their life work to serve children's reading interests, an opportunity to encourage good writing in this field" (http://www.ala.org/alsc/awardsgrants/bookmedia/newberymedal/aboutnewbery/aboutnewbery).

Yet, in 1922, good writing focused on the White, middle- or upper-class experience. Children from different races, ethnicities, and religious backgrounds did not see themselves in books. Similarly, nonfiction texts have not evolved to reflect diverse perspectives on history, science, technology and our encounters with the world. As Crisp (2015) wrote: "It is discouraging that… the world of nonfiction texts continues a long-standing tradition of excluding minority populations from children's media and other artifacts of popular culture" (p. 253).

The Dangers of a Single Story

Watch Chimamanda Adichie's story about books and her childhood.

Chimamanda Adichie's TED talk: The Danger of a Single Story. Retrieved from http://www.ted.com/talks/chimamanda_adichie_the_danger_of_a_single_story?language=en.

Rudine Sims-Bishop, a literacy professor and children's literature expert, wrote: "Literature transforms human experience and reflects it back to us, and in that reflection we can see our own lives and experiences as part of the larger human experience. Reading, then, becomes a means of self-affirmation, and readers often seek their mirrors in books." (Bishop, 1990 p. ix)

For this reason, calls for diverse portrayals and different perspectives have consistently remained since the early days of the library. Throughout the 20th century, many individuals and groups called for better literature featuring diverse populations. Some of the calls were heard, especially in the 1990's, but the problem remains.

Two noted children's authors, Christopher Myers (2014) and Walter Dean Myers (2014), clearly identified the continuance of this problem and its consistent effects on generations of readers. Of the "apartheid" of children's literature, and the lack of characters of color in books, Christopher Myers noted that today's children don't view literature as a mirror, but more as a map. In limiting their view of what's possible for others, "children of color remain outside the boundaries of imagination," following a "flawed cartography" of limited possibilities for their lives. Similarly, Walter Dean Myers wrote of his own experiences and limitations in a world in which people's views of himself and others were limited by their lack of experiences with people of color. Books, he believes, can change perceptions. He wrote,

> Books transmit values. They explore our common humanity. What is the message when some children are not represented in those books? Where are the future white personnel managers going to get their ideas of people of color? Where are the future white loan officers and future white politicians going to get their knowledge of people of color? Where are black children going to get a sense of who they are and what they can be?

If we can't physically interact with different people in our own lives, books have the potential to give us the vicarious experiences that change minds. Books shape and shift our identities.

More Awards and Different Labels

To combat the dangers of privileging certain voices and books, other awards and honors have been created to highlight diverse perspectives. Yet these awards are also criticized for being overly myopic.

Lambda Literary Award (http://www.lambdaliterary.org/awards/guidelines.html). The Lammy's identify and celebrate the best lesbian, gay, bisexual and transgender books of the year and affirm that LGBTQ stories are part of the literature of the world. Most of the Lammy's identify quality books in adult literature categories, but there is one Lammy award given for children's and young adult literature (Figure 4.43). Individual works and collections of fiction, nonfiction, picture books, and poetry whose intended audience is young readers are all eligible; anthologies are not eligible (see more at http://www.lambdaliterary.org/overview-of-llf-awards/#sthash.SR0SH1N6.dpuf).

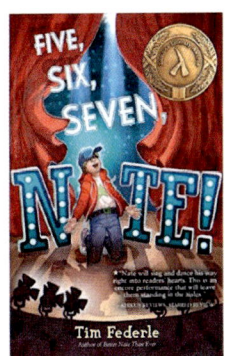

Figure 4.43

The 2015 Lammy was awarded to *Five, Six, Seven, Nate!* by Tim Federle, 2015, New York, NY: Simon & Schuster Books for Young Readers. Copyright 2015 by Tim Federle.

IMPORTANT BOOKS
(THE PROBLEMS AND POLITICS OF IMPORTANCE; NOTABLE LISTS, AWARDS, & ASSOCIATIONS)

 The Lammy is typically awarded to one book, representing all categories of fiction, nonfiction, picture books, and poetry. Occasionally, the committee selects more than one book. For example, in 2014, two novels won a Lammy (Figure 4.44 and Figure 4.45).

Notable Books for a Global Society (http://clrsig.org/nbgs.php). The Children's Literature & Reading Special Interest Group of the International Literacy Association selects 25 outstanding trade books for enhancing student understanding of people and cultures throughout the world.

Schneider Family Book Award (American Library Association) http://www.ala.org/Template.cfm?Section=bookmediaawards&template=/ContentManagement/ContentDisplay.cfm&ContentID=172663#). The award honors an author or illustrator for a book that embodies an artistic expression of the disability experience for child and adolescent audiences (Figure 4.46). The book must portray some aspect of living with a disability or that of a friend or family member, whether the disability is physical, mental or emotional. The award is given to a teen book, a middle school book, and a children's book.

Jane Addams Children's Book Award (http://www.janeaddamspeace.org/jacba/). The award is given to children's books that effectively promote the cause of peace, social justice, world community, and the equality of the sexes and all races as well as meeting conventional standards for excellence (Figure 4.47).

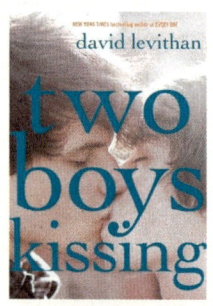

Figure 4.44
The novel, *Two Boys Kissing*, won a Lammy for fiction in 2014. *Two Boys Kissing* by David Levithan, 2013, New York, NY: Alfred A. Knopf Books for Young Readers. Copyright 2013 by David Levithan.

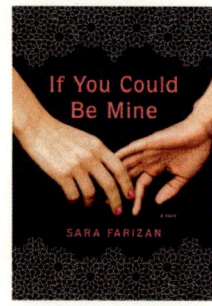

Figure 4.45
The novel, *If You Could Be Mine*, also won a Lammy in 2014. *If You Could Be Mine* by Sara Farizan, 2013, New York, NY: Algonquin Books. Copyright 2013 by Sara Farizan.

Figure 4.46
An award that focuses on the portrayal of disability is the Schneider Family Book Award. *Girls Like Us* by Gail Giles, 2014, Somerville, MA: Candlewick Press. Copyright 2014 by Gail Giles.

Figure 4.47
A recent Jane Addams Children's Book Award was given to *The Girl From the Tar Paper School: Barbara Rose Johns and the advent of the Civil Rights Movement* by Teri Kanefield, 2014, New York, NY: Abrams Books for Young Readers. Copyright 2014 by Teri Kanefield.

Mildred L. Batchelder Award (American Library Association) (http://www.ala.org/awardsgrants/mildred-l-batchelder-award). This citation is given to an American publisher for the most outstanding children's book originally published in a foreign language in a foreign country, and subsequently translated into English and published in the United States (Figure 4.48).

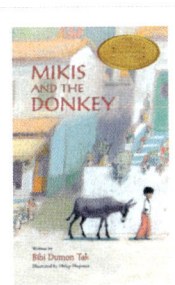

Figure 4.48

The Batchelder Award goes to a publisher. Eerdmans Books won the 2015 award for *Mikis and the Donkey*, written by Bibi Dumon Tak, illustrated by Philip Hopman, translated by Laura Watkinson, 2014, Grand Rapids, MI: Eerdmans Books. Copyright 2014 by Philip Hopman.

 Valerie Knight, a reference librarian at Wayne State College maintains an excellent LibGuide of Children's Award Winning Books. She updates the lists with the newest winners and provides short summaries of the books (http://libguides.wsc.edu/content.php?pid=404952&sid=3899399).

Whose Story? Additional Considerations

Sometimes awards and recognition are important because they give voice to the voiceless and recognition to the unrecognized. Some awards have provided inspiration to authors and illustrators, drawing their attention, and with it, more diverse portrayals in books.

In addition, "more" portrayals are not necessarily desirable portrayals. In his article, "It's Not the Book, It's Not the Author, It's the Award," Thomas Crisp (2011) recounts his experience reading his first young adult novel featuring a gay main character (Figure 4.49). Overwhelmed with emotion, it was important to Thomas that the author was also gay. For reasons he described in his article, his reading became more authentic when the author shared the same gay, male identity as the main character, and the same identity as Thomas. Therefore, when the Lammy's were criticized for limiting their selection criteria to LGBT authors, Thomas supported their decision although he recognized the move as

Figure 4.49

Thomas Crisp wrote about the impact of reading *Rainbow Boys*. *Rainbow Boys* by Alex Sanchez, 2003, New York, NY: Simon & Schuster Books for Young Readers. Copyright 2003 by Alex Sanchez.

contrary to the nature of vicarious reading and writing experiences in which imagination and creativity are the focus. In this instance, Thomas' feelings were not about the importance of books or the authors who write them. Instead, Thomas wanted recognition for LGBT people who have been systematically persecuted. He wanted LGBT people to have the award.

Even though awards and labels were developed with the intention of creating opportunity structures and recognition for many people's stories, debates continue.

> Here is a selection of articles and blogs on the subject:
>
> **Are Whites Entitled to Write Black History?**
> http://www.pbs.org/wnet/tavissmiley/blogs/staff-guest-blog/are-whites-entitled-to-write-black-history/
>
> **N.Y. Teacher Runs Into a Racial Divide**
> http://www.washingtonpost.com/wp-srv/national/frompost/dec98/hair3.htm
>
> **Heads of Joy**
> https://www.nytimes.com/books/99/11/21/bib/991121.rv143629.html

An Example

Nightjohn (Figure 4.50) is a story about two Black slaves written by a White man (Gary Paulsen). The main character is *Nightjohn*, a Black, male adult. The other main character is Sarny, a Black, female girl. Gary Paulsen wrote *Nightjohn* from Sarny's perspective using African American English (AAE).

According to a book review, Paulsen succeeded in presenting the story.

Figure 4.50

Gary Paulsen, a White man, wrote *Nightjohn*, a story about a Black slave. *Nightjohn* by Gary Paulsen and illustrated by Jerry Pinkney, 1993, New York, NY: Delacorte Press. Cover art copyright 1993 by Jerry Pinkney.

> Among the most powerful of Paulsen's works (*Hatchet*; *The Winter Room*; *Dogsong*), this impeccably researched novel sheds light on cruel truths in American history as it traces the experiences of a 12-year-old slave girl in the 1850s. Narrator Sarny exposes the abuse (routine beatings, bondage, dog attacks, forced "breeding") suffered by her people on the Waller plantation. The punishment for learning to read and write, she knows, is a bloody one, but when new slave Nightjohn offers to teach her the alphabet, Sarny readily agrees. Her decision causes pain for others as well as for herself, yet, inspired by the bravery of Nightjohn, who has given up a chance for freedom in order to educate slaves, Sarny continues her studies. Convincingly written in dialect, this graphic depiction of slavery evokes shame for this country's forefathers and sorrow for the victims of their inhumanity. (http://www.publishersweekly.com/978-0-385-30838-0)

Happy to be Nappy (Figure 4.51) is a concept book about Black girls' kinky hair and all of the ways nappy hair can be worn and styled. *Happy to be Nappy* is written by a Black woman. Not only is *Happy to be Nappy* written by a Black woman, but it's written by bell hooks, one of the most acclaimed Black, Feminist, cultural theorists of our time.

Figure 4.51

bell hooks, a Black woman, wrote *Happy to be Nappy*, a book about girls' hair. *Happy to be Nappy* by bell hooks and illustrated by Chris Raschka, 1999, New York, NY: Jump at the Sun. Cover art copyright by Chris Raschka.

> This joyous ode to hair may well restart conversations that began last year with the controversy over Carolivia Herron's *Nappy Hair*. Bubbling over with affection, and injecting a strong self-esteem boost for girls, hooks's ebullient, poetic text celebrates the innate beauty and freedom of hair that's "soft like cotton,/ flower petal billowy soft, full of frizz and fuzz." Waxing poetic about "short tight naps" or "plaited strands all," hooks conjures all the lovely varieties of hairstyles that "let girls go running free." She sings the praises of "girlpie hair," subtly reinforcing her theme with a chorus of descriptive words like "halo" and "crown." She also evokes the intimate warmth of mother-daughter time--"sitting still for hands to brush or braid and make the day start hopefully." A powerful, uplifting and, above all, buoyantly fun read-aloud, the text receives a superb visual interpretation by Raschka (*Like Likes Like*)... (http://www.publishersweekly.com/978-0-7868-0427-6)

Jerry Pinkney illustrated *Nightjohn's* cover art. Jerry Pinkney is a Black man. Jerry Pinkney is a renowned, Caldecott-winning illustrator. Chris Raschka illustrated *Happy to be Nappy*. Chris Raschka is a White man. Chris Raschka is also a renowned, Caldecott-winning illustrator.

Who can tell whose stories? Is it acceptable for a White man or woman to write about nappy hair or write about being a slave? Would he or she be able to do so with authenticity?

On the other hand, aren't these works of fiction? Who is to say that a White man can't understand the emotions of slavery or the dialect of the times given the proper research? Isn't it possible that experiences in Paulsen's own life, the language of his own family, might be very similar to those of *Nightjohn*? Wouldn't his ability to create believable characters demonstrate his ability to write? bell hooks has short hair. I can't tell if it's nappy or kinky, but who is to say she experienced the rituals she wrote about in her book?

What about the illustrations? Do the same arguments hold true? Should Black people only draw Blacks and White people only draw Whites? Who gets to draw animals and aliens?

The issues surrounding awards, recognition, publication preferences, and "importance" are complex.

- Who gets to tell whose story?

- Is the award really about literary quality or illustration excellence if the criteria are about race, ethnicity, religion, or sexual identity, etc.?

- Do specific awards, based on other criteria, actually create more opportunities for diverse characters and content, or do these awards limit books and their creators?

- Is the award for the book, the artistry, or a label?

What do you think?

There isn't a right answer. On a basic level, I believe that anyone may, can, and should write whatever story he or she chooses. I believe people are inherently similar in their desires, feelings, and dreams. Therefore, good writers and illustrators can authentically capture someone else's experience through writing and art. I also know that people have different life experiences, and even though people may share similar traits, qualities, or identities, no two people are the same. Therefore, I don't need my authors or illustrators to be of the same background as the people and content they create in books. In other words, Black people can write about White people, Jewish people can write about Christians, adults can write about children. To be more specific, J.K. Rowling created my Harry Potter, John Green created my Hazel Grace, and Gary Paulsen created my Nightjohn. However, I know institutional racism, sexism, classism, and other forms of discrimination exist. Just because laws are created, schools are integrated, and equal rights are guaranteed does not mean that people have the same rights, the same benefits, the same pay, or the same opportunities. Social, political, and cultural obstacles exist well beyond the legal removal of barriers. Barriers exist for generations. Therefore, I understand the need for awards, recognition, and opportunities for people.

 See, I told you. Children's literature isn't just about kids, happy times, and love. Children's literature, like other forms of literature and art, offers a space for all of us to engage in insightful interpretation of the ways in which authors and illustrators present the human condition, the physical world, imaginative experiences, and global forces.

It's all relative.

CHAPTER 05

THE RIGHT BOOK FOR THE RIGHT READER AT THE RIGHT TIME
(LITERARY ANALYSIS, QUALITY, AND DEVELOPMENTAL PERSPECTIVES)

Although there is deep literary value in children's literature resulting in critical acclaim as well as commercial success, each year, authors, illustrators, and publishers also produce a lot of duds. When selecting books, you can rely on the awards to determine literary value, but as previously discussed, the "best" books may not interest children, young adults, or you. In order to select books and determine the right book for the right reader at the right time (including yourself), let's review criteria for evaluating books and then connect those criteria to how and what readers read.

Determining Quality

Considering that, "rhetorical tradition has too often distorted issues of intention and purpose by setting up unnatural distinctions" (DiPardo, 1990, p. 66), I hesitate to dwell on brief and narrow descriptions of categories for literary analysis. However, I want you to understand how good books work, and just like a car mechanic, we have to go under the hood, identify the parts, determine if they function successfully, and put everything back together. Therefore, we can determine quality through the following process:

(1) identifying the author's purpose,

(2) selecting and applying the appropriate criteria to evaluate books,

(3) matching books to readers, and then

(4) judging the overall product in connection with the intended audience.

 I know absolutely nothing about cars. It's just a simple and common analogy. I promise there won't be any talk of overhead cams and drive shafts—or windshield wipers.

Question #1: What is the author's and/or illustrator's purpose?

Literary Purpose and Text Structures: A Vehicle for Communication

In books, linguistic features are embedded in text structures and they combine to form various modes of discourse. The modes of discourse in children's literature are the same modes in adult literature. According to Bain (1866, as cited in DiPardo, 1990), literary modes include narration, exposition, description, and argument.

 Think about literary purpose in connection to the phrase, "form follows function." The text will take a different shape depending on its purpose—just like different types of vehicles are used for different purposes: Sedan, Pickup, Van, Convertible.

Narration (fiction). Narratives are a linguistic structuring of events in a manner similar to the actual or imagined sequence of lived events (Bowditch, 1976; Labov, 1972). Narratives include action and events multiplied into a series or, as Sternberg (2010) described it, "sequentiality-plus" (p. 546). Narratives tell a story, set in a particular place with characters and a plot. Another common term is "fiction" which refers to the notion that the story did not actually happen and the characters and events were "made up." Fictional stories *could* happen, but they haven't actually happened, such as the events in *Pointe* (Figure 5.1).

> I wish I could say the day Donovan came home was extraordinary from the start, that I woke up knowing something special would happen that Thursday evening in October. But the truth is, it's like any other day of the week (Colbert, 2014, p. 1).

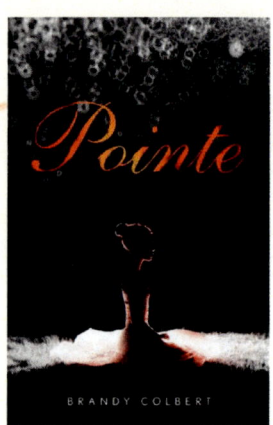

Figure 5.1

Fictional stories *could* happen, but they haven't actually happened. An example of a fictional story with an authentically flawed protagonist and realistic plot twists is *Pointe* by Brandy Colbert, 2014, New York, NY: G.P. Putnam's Sons Books for Young Readers. Copyright 2014 by Brandy Colbert.

Or, in the case of fantasy, (Figure 5.2), the events could never happen (finding a fountain of youth), but the author forms a story around them.

> There was something strange about the wood. If the look of the first house suggested that you'd better pass it by, so did the look of the wood, but for quite a different reason. The house was so proud of itself that you wanted to make a lot of noise as you passed, and maybe even throw a rock or two. But the wood had a sleeping, otherworld appearance that made you want to speak in whispers (From *Tuck Everlasting* by Natalie Babbitt, 1975, p. 6).

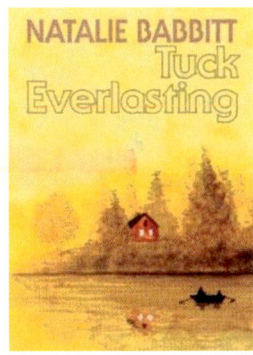

Figure 5.2

Tuck Everlasting is a story about living forever. *Tuck Everlasting* by Natalie Babbitt, 1975, New York, NY: Farrar, Straus and Giroux. Copyright 1975 by Natalie Babbitt.

Or, in the case of fictionalized biography, the characters were real people and the life events were real, but the details of the events may be imagined or made up to illustrate the real and tell a better story (e.g., creating dialogue) (Figure 5.3).

> On a continent of many songs, in a country shaped like the arm of a tall *guitarrista*, the rain drummed down on the town of Temuco.
>
> Neftalí Reyes sat in his bed, propped up by pillows, and stared at the schoolwork in front of him. His teacher called it simple addition, but it was never simple for him. How he wished the numbers would disappear! He squeezed his eyes closed and then opened them.
>
> The twos and threes lifted from the page and waved for the others to join them. The fives and sevens sprang upward, and finally, after much prodding, the fours, ones, and sixes came along. But the nines and zeros would not budge so the others left them. They held hands in a long procession of tiny figures, flew across the room and escaped through the window crack. Neftali closed the book and smiled (From *The Dreamer* by Pam Muñoz Ryan, 2010, p. 1-2).

Figure 5.3

Fictionalized biographies are stories based on the true lives of real people. The story of Neftalí Reyes (also known as Pablo Neruda, the Nobel Prize-winning poet) is recreated by Pam Muñoz Ryan and illustrated by Peter Sís. *The Dreamer* by Pam Muñoz Ryan and illustrated by Peter Sís, 2010, New York, NY: Scholastic Press. Cover art copyright 2010 by Peter Sís.

The key determinant for fiction is the telling of a story (plot, setting, characters) of an *actual* or *imagined* sequence of lived events.

Information (nonfiction). In expository texts, the purpose is to explain. As such, expository text structures are used to present information or to describe phenomena (See Berman & Katzenberger, 2004; Caswell & Duke, 1998). More commonly called "information books" or "nonfiction," the authors and illustrators of these books explicate a topic (Figure 5.4). Informational books are defined as those written to present, organize, clarify, and interpret documentable, factual material (ALA, nd, Sibert Medal). The "presentation" of factual material can take many forms and this is where the writer's skill comes into play. For example, in the *Family Romanov: Murder, Rebellion, and the Fall of Imperial Russia*, Candace Fleming writes the story of one family, weaving together different chains of events while also using maps, charts, definitions, and primary source documents to substantiate her points and to contextualize the circumstances and resulting actions.

Figure 5.4

Nonfiction authors use expository text structures to present information. For example, Melissa Stewart used labels and short explanations to explore different types of feathers in *Feathers Not Just for Flying* by Melissa Stewart and illustrated by Sarah S. Brannen, 2014, Watertown, MA: Charlesbridge Publishing. Cover art copyright 2014 by Sarah S. Brannen.

 Listen to *Text Messages Episode 79*, A Conversation with Candace Fleming, 2014, as Candace discusses historical story telling and her research process.

Audio 5.1 *Text Messages Episode 79*

Interactive 5.1 *I Face The Wind* by Vicki Cobb

Good nonfiction writers use engaging writing techniques to capture the audience's attention. For example, Vicki Cobb uses real life examples and directly asks readers to think through problems in her nonfiction text, *I Face The Wind* by Vicki Cobb and illustrated by Julia Gorton, 2003, New York, NY: HarperCollins Publishers.

Description. Descriptive writing includes a main topic with related sub-topics that are explained clearly and in detail (Sanders & Moudy, 2008). Similar to expository texts, descriptive texts may present information; however, descriptive writing offers more elaborative detail. For example, in *Witches: The Absolutely True Tale of Disaster in Salem*, Rosalyn Schanzer (2011) uses bold imagery and straightforward language to describe the Salem Witch trials (Figure 5.5).

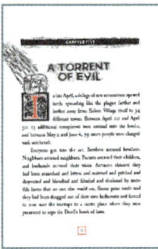

Figure 5.5

Rosalyn Schanzer uses honest prose and straightforward examples to describe numerous people, places, and events surrounding the Salem Witch Trials. Excerpt from *Witches!: The Absolutely True Tale of Disaster in Salem*, by Rosalyn Schanzer, 2011, Washington, DC: National Geographic Books. Copyright 2011 by Rosalyn Schanzer.

THE RIGHT BOOK FOR THE RIGHT READER AT THE RIGHT TIME
(LITERARY ANALYSIS, QUALITY, AND DEVELOPMENT PERSPECTIVES)

Descriptive writing can be found in many fictional stories (Figure 5.6) such as Jane Yolen's *Owl Moon*. In contrast to Schanzer, Yolen creates quiet imagery by selecting delicate words that describe owling in the late night.

The writers of horror, myths, and legends rely on descriptive writing to build suspense, describe surroundings, and relate emotions. J.R.R. Tolkien's *The Hobbit* (1937, p.1), is filled with rich, descriptive language:

> In a hole in the ground there lived a hobbit. Not a nasty, dirty, wet hole, filled with the ends of worms and an oozy smell, nor yet a dry, bare, sandy hole with nothing in it to sit down on or to eat: it was a hobbit hole, and that means comfort.

Descriptive writing is often used to present complex ideas or events. For example, Peter Sís (1998) wrote and illustrated *Tibet* based on his father's personal diary, which his father kept while he separated from the family to work in Tibet for two years (Figure 5.7).

Some poetry is also a form of descriptive writing. For example, Langston Hughes (1994) uses specific objects, repetition, and dialect to visually and spiritually portray the content and theme of his poem, *Mother to Son* (Figure 5.8). Descriptive writing provides elaboration and sensory detail.

Figure 5.6

Jane Yolen's text for *Owl Moon* captures the main character's feelings as well as the quiet of the snow and the still of the late night. Excerpt from *Owl Moon* by Jane Yolen and illustrated by John Schoenherr, 1987, New York, NY: Philomel Books. Text copyright 1987 by Jane Yolen and illustration copyright 1987 by John Schoenherr.

Figure 5.7

Peter Sís uses his father's diary as inspiration for *Tibet Through the Red Box* by Peter Sís, 1998, New York, NY: Farrar, Straus and Giroux. Copyright 1998 by Peter Sís.

Figure 5.8

Poetic language is often descriptive. For example, Langston Hughes uses sensory detail in his poem, Mother to Son, in *The Dream Keeper and Other Poems* by Langston Hughes and illustrated by Brian Pinkney, 1994, New York, NY: Alfred A. Knopf. Text copyright 1932/1960 by Langston Hughes and 1994 by the Estate of Langston Hughes, illustrations copyright 1994 by Brian Pinkney.

Argumentation. Argument is not about "winning" a debate. Rather, a literary argument reflects the writer's ability to engage in mature reasoning and to think through issues in order to evaluate them (Crusius & Channell, 2009; Knoblauch, 2011). In an argument, just like a position paper, the author uses different writing techniques, but with an evaluative perspective. Authors who present an argument may use descriptive or narrative techniques but they also use techniques specific to argument such as how they organize the text or address the reader's ethics, reason, and emotions (Lauer, et.al., 2000) (Figure 5.9). For example, in *Separate is Never Equal: Sylvia Mendez and her Family's Fight for Desegregation*, Duncan Tonatiuh writes about Sylvia's courtroom experience, sharing her emotional reactions to unethical behavior:

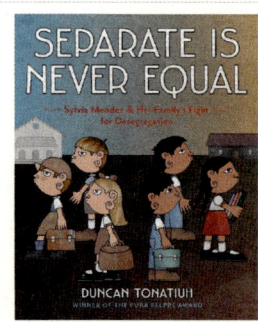

Figure 5.9

Duncan Tonatiuh tells the story of Sylvia Mendez using narrative techniques and argumentation. *Separate is Never Equal: Sylvia Mendez and her Family's Fight for Desegregation* by Duncan Tonatiuh, 2014, New York, NY: Abrams. Copyright 2014 by Duncan Tonatiuh.

> On the first day, Mr. Kent, the superintendent of the Garden Grove district was questioned. He said that he sent children to the Mexican school to help them improve their English.
>
> That is a *lie* thought Sylvia. Her English was as good as the English of any of the children at the Westminster School.
>
> "Do you give the children any tests?" asked Mr. Marcus.
>
> Mr. Kent claimed he did. "We do so by talking to them."
>
> That is another *lie*! Sylvia wanted to yell. No one had questioned her. They rejected her from the Westminster school without asking her a thing (Tonatiuh, 2014, p. 25).

Speeches, essays, nonfiction, science fiction, and dramas are examples of genres in which authors frequently use argumentation.

With these authorial purposes in mind (narration, information, description, argumentation), we can use applicable criteria to determine quality across children's literature texts (Video. 5.1).

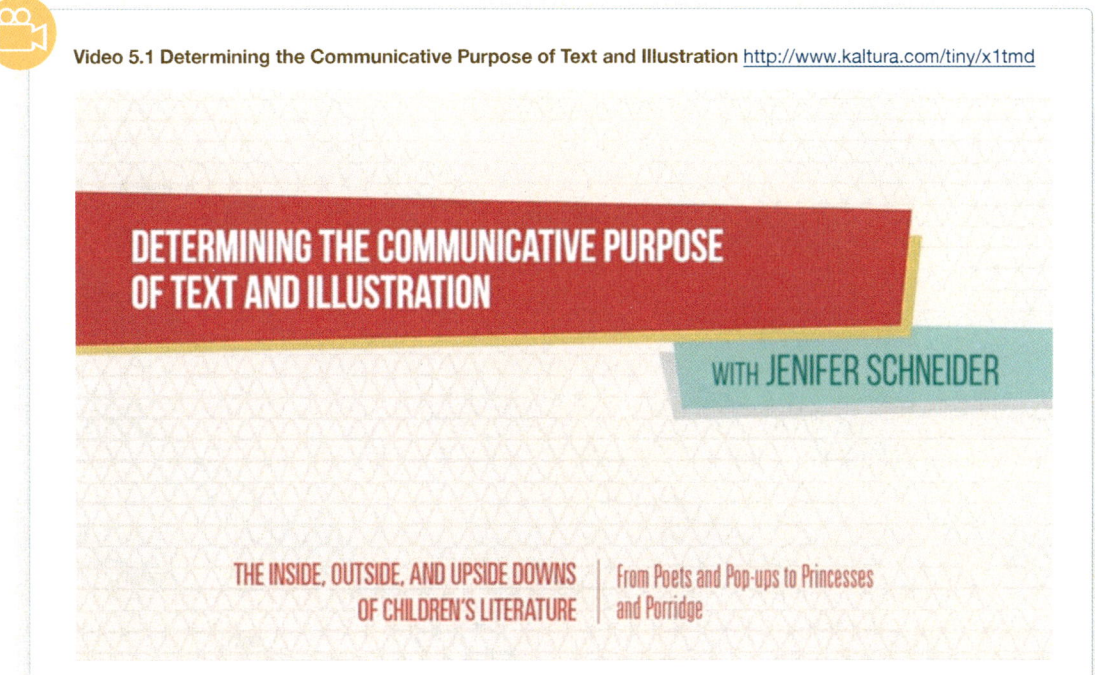

Video 5.1 Determining the Communicative Purpose of Text and Illustration http://www.kaltura.com/tiny/x1tmd

Wait! Not so fast. What about the pictures? In the previous examples, I used the author's rhetorical devices and compositional techniques to determine the communicative purpose of the text. Some of the examples were illustrated, but I focused on the text as the predominant carrier of the message. Picture books are different. Picture books represent the *illustrator*'s intent through visual imagery. What do we do about the pictures? We do the same thing.

Visual Purpose and Illustrative Style: Another Vehicle for Communication

Illustrations are created for all of the same purposes described above (narration, information, description, argumentation). The difference between picture books and illustrated texts is the role of the illustrations. Many books include illustrations as cover art, as chapter introductions, or to illustrate selected ideas throughout the text. In picture books, text and images are the conduits of meaning; they work together.

 Other forms, other functions: Convertible, Muscle, Hybrid, Coupe

To analyze illustrations, readers typically examine the *elements* of artistic representation such as line, value, shape, form, space, color, and texture. The reader might also consider the *principles of design* that integrate the elements such as balance, contrast, movement, emphasis, pattern, proportion, and unity. Several experts have explored these concepts and they offer excellent criteria for "seeing" illustrations and engaging in formal analysis (See Bang, 2000; Moebius, 1986; Nodelman, 1988; Serafini, 2010; Serafini, 2011; Sipe, 1998). Other children's literature texts go into great detail and provide numerous examples to illustrate the elements and principles of artistic representation (e.g., Charlotte Huck's Children's Literature; Kiefer, 2010).

Several online resources are available to help you understand the
Artistic Elements:
Line; Value; Shape; Form; Space; Color; Texture;

Principles of Design:
Balance; Contrast; Movement; Emphasis; Pattern; Proportion; Unity.

J. Paul Getty Museum: http://www.getty.edu/education/teachers/building_lessons/formal_analysis.html

http://www.getty.edu/education/teachers/building_lessons/formal_analysis2.html

The Kennedy Center ArtsEdge:
https://artsedge.kennedy-center.org/educators/how-to/from-theory-to-practice/formal-visual-analysis

I thought I would go in a different direction. Formal analysis works really well if I want to examine one piece of art, one photograph, one collage. But picture books and illustrated texts are constructed differently. Picture books move. Not in the sense of a motion picture, which captures segments of constructed, yet fluid, movement; but more along the lines of stop-motion animation, which freezes selected moments along a continuum of time. Even so, stop-motion carries a sense of fluidity and a more detailed documentation of movement. Picture books are more episodic. So are illustrated texts. Come to think of it, so is the writing.

 "Picture books are more episodic. So are illustrated texts. Come to think of it, so is the writing."

Authors compose text on a blank page and we use their words to comprehend the larger message. Illustrators also create images on a blank canvas and we tend to look more myopically at their techniques. Why not give illustrators the same consideration and look at the broader communicative purposes to determine what they did artistically? Why should I only examine the illustrator's use of color, shape, texture, or pattern?

 A caveat—if teachers are using children's literature as a mentor text for teaching writing and/or illustration, then students will examine the author's or illustrator's craft in order to learn from good models. In other words, teachers analyze words, sentence construction, and paragraphing in children's literature in order to help students emulate good writing. This chapter is not about using children's literature mentor texts to teach writing or illustration (that's a different book)—this chapter is about understanding criteria to analyze children's literature for the purposes of knowing what's good and what's a dud. For those of you who are teachers, determining quality is the first step in text selection.

Therefore, let's explore visual analysis as a mode of discourse that indicates the illustrator's intent as well as the way in which the artist communicates the message.

Narrative Illustration. Narratives include action and events multiplied into a series. In narrative illustrations, events are depicted in a sequence of actions that advance the plot. For example, in *Make Way for Ducklings*, Robert McCloskey created elaborate illustrations of important incidents as they occurred in chronological order (Figures 5.10 and 5.11).

Figure 5.10
A scene from *Make Way for Ducklings* shows elaborate detail of the setting and tells the story from the perspective of the ducks. *Make Way for Ducklings* by Robert McCloskey, 1941, New York, NY: Viking Press. Copyright 1969 by Robert McCloskey.

Figure 5.11
Another scene from *Make Way for Ducklings* by Robert McCloskey shows the progression of the plot. *Make Way for Ducklings* by Robert McCloskey, 1941, New York, NY: Viking Press. Copyright 1969 by Robert McCloskey.

In other books, the illustrations may be more episodic through the selection of big ideas presented in small moments. In a book about the Civil War, Patricia Polacco's portrayals of simple interactions speak volumes about the characters and their evolution as people in *Pink and Say* (Figure 5.12). The illustrations tell a visual story in a particular place (setting) with character development occurring within the plot.

Figure 5.12
Pink and Say tells a big story using illustrations of small details and events. *Pink and Say* by Patricia Polacco, 1994, New York, NY: Philomel. Copyright 1994 by Patricia Polacco.

In addition to illustrating plot sequences and character actions, illustrators also narrate by providing the right visual at the right time. In Video 5.2, I share my reading of *Olivia*, looking specifically at the ways in which Ian Falconer isolated key examples to illustrate the story of a little pig who is good at lots of things. Watch this video to learn how to "read" a picture book by exploring book design, by interpreting the visual illustrations, and by understanding the rhetorical moves of the printed words.

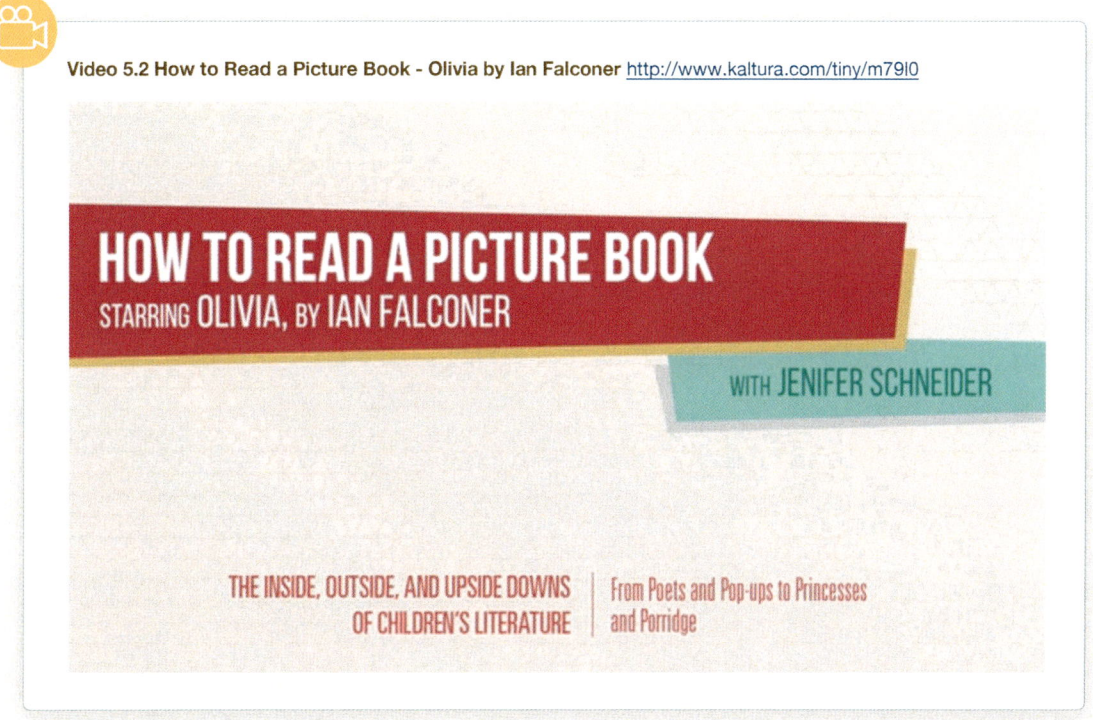

Video 5.2 How to Read a Picture Book - Olivia by Ian Falconer http://www.kaltura.com/tiny/m79l0

Overall, narrative illustration tells a story. Yet, just as a writer makes authorial choices with regard to sequencing, point of view, pacing, voice, and tone, the illustrator makes the same choices. The illustrator is not retelling the author's story; the illustrator is creating his or her own visual story.

Informative Illustration.

Informational books are defined as those illustrated to present, organize, and interpret documentable, factual material (ALA, nd, Sibert Medal). Informative illustrations replicate these purposes. Often the illustrations provide thick, rich details that are not always readily apparent or interpretable from the text (Figure 5.13). For example, Katharine Roy illustrates the idiosyncrasies of a shark's circulatory system demonstrating how blood impacts body temperature (Figure 5.14). Unless a reader has an extraordinary ability to visualize the internal workings of a shark, the illustrations are essential for the reader's comprehension of the concepts.

Often informative images are realistic, such as the actual photographs and documents used in *The Family Romanov: Murder, Rebellion, & The Fall of Imperial Russia* (Figure 5.15). Yet, other books are illustrated to capture a different feeling. For example, In *The Right Word: Roget and his Thesaurus*, Melissa Sweet chose to emphasize Roget's work, his keeping of lists, and his aggregation of words over time (Figure 5.16), highlighting different scenes and events from his life (Figure 5.17). The spirit of Roget's obsessive collecting and word documentation was interpreted by Sweet's collage illustrations that have the feeling of a junk-drawer or a treasure chest (Figure 5.18).

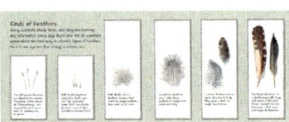

Figure 5.13

Sarah S. Brannen used panels and labels to highlight the features of different types of feathers in *Feathers Not Just for Flying* by Melissa Stewart and illustrated by Sarah S. Brannen, 2014, Watertown, MA: Charlesbridge Publishing. Copyright 2014 by Sarah S. Branne

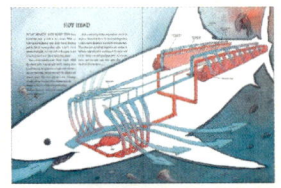

Figure 5.14

Katherine Roy's illustrations provide essential visual details in *Neighborhood Sharks: Hunting with the Great Whites of California's Farallon Islands* by Katherine Roy, 2014, New York, NY: David Macaulay Studio. Copyright 2014 by Katherine Roy.

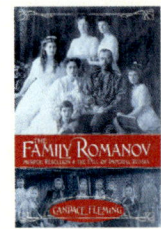

Figure 5.15

The cover image features the use of photographs and primary sources in *The Family Romanov: Murder, Rebellion & the Fall of Imperial Russia* by Candace Fleming, 2014, New York, NY: Schwartz & Wade. Copyright 2014 by Candace Fleming.

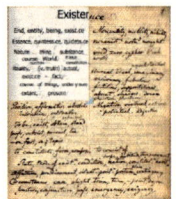

Figure 5.16

Roget's lists are viewable at the Karpeles Manuscript Library. The online site includes an interactive tool that allows users to view the document's transcription (http://www.rain.org/~karpeles/index.html). Roget's entry for Existence, 1805, Retrieved from http://www.rain.org/~karpeles/rogfrm.html.

Figure 5.17

Melissa Sweet uses collage to represent Roget's process of collecting words in *The Right Word: Roget and his Thesaurus* by Jen Bryant and illustrated by Melissa Sweet 2014, New York, NY: Eerdmans Books for Young Readers. Excerpt art copyright 2014 by Melissa Sweet.

Figure 5.18

Sweet's illustrations are highly detailed and accessible to readers. *The Right Word: Roget and his Thesaurus* by Jen Bryant and illustrated by Melissa Sweet 2014, New York, NY: Eerdmans Books for Young Readers. Excerpt art copyright 2014 by Melissa Sweet.

 Describing Melissa Sweet's illustrations as a junk-drawer might seem derogatory. I don't have this intention. I use this analogy because her illustrations have a lot of visual interest; everything has its place; and it captures and collects the necessities of life. Melissa Sweet's illustrations do just that!

Illustrators, just like authors, use different structures to inform readers. Some informational illustrations are organized by concept (Figure 5.19). Others dramatically recreate sequences of events (Figure 5.20). Still others use captions, comparisons, labels, titles, charts, graphs, fonts, and other text features to convey meaning (Figure 5.21).

Descriptive Illustration.

Descriptive illustration is focused on the presentation of elaborative detail. The illustrations provide a visual that corresponds to or extends the details from the text. For example, in *Owl Moon*, Jane Yolen's language reflects the quiet of the snow and the stillness needed to find an owl in the late night. John Schoenherr's illustrations move beyond the main character's thoughts to reflect her relationship with her father as well as their interactions with the expansiveness of nature (Figure 5.22).

In contrast to *Owl Moon*, Rosalyn Schanzer uses harsh black and white scratchboard illustrations with striking accents of red to portray the hysteria and horror of the Salem witch trials in *Witches!* (Figure 5.23). In *Owl Moon* and *Witches!*, the illustrations add descriptive details, elucidating themes that are not specifically mentioned in the texts.

Figure 5.19

Seymour Simon has written approximately 300 books for children. Most of his books focus on a particular concept such as snakes, planets, and coral reefs. *Coral Reefs* by Seymour Simon, 2013, New York, NY: HarperCollins. Copyright 2013 by Seymour Simon.

Figure 5.20

In *Drowned City,* Don Brown illustrates the tragedy of Hurricane Katrina with a perspective that is more disturbing than the media coverage of the storm and its aftermath. *Drowned City: Hurricane Kartrina & New Orleans* by Don Brown, 2015, New York, NY: HMH Books for Young Readers. Copyright 2015 by Don Brown.

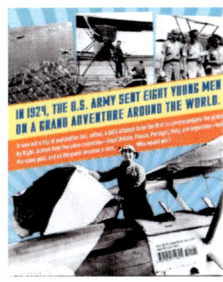

Figure 5.21

Captions, labels, titles, and charts are a few of the text features used in informative illustrations. Excerpt from *First Flight Around the World: The Adventures of the American Fliers Who Won the Race* by Tim Grove and the National Air and Space Museum, 2015, New York, NY: Henry N. Abrams. Copyright 2015 by Tim Grove and the National Air and Space Museum.

Figure 5.22

John Schoenherr's illustrations for *Owl Moon* capture more than a story. They explore human interaction in nature. Excerpt from *Owl Moon* by Jane Yolen and illustrated by John Schoenherr, 1987, New York, NY: Philomel Books. Illustration copyright 1987 by John Schoenherr.

Figure 5.23

Rosalyn Schanzer uses color, line, and a scratching technique to illustrate the events surrounding the Salem Witch Trials. Excerpt from *Witches!: The Absolutely True Tale of Disaster in Salem*, by Rosalyn Schanzer, 2011, Washington, DC: National Geographic Books. Copyright 2011 by Rosalyn Schanzer.

In another example, *The Boy Who Loved Math*, the title informs the reader that the book is about a boy who loves math, but the illustrations show the depth of his love (Figure 5.24). Illustrator, LeUyen Pham, creates the vivid details of someone who not only loves math, but he lives, breathes, and thinks with math (Figure 5.25). This is what math obsession looks like (Figure 5.26).

Argumentative Illustration. Argumentation through illustration is the illustrator's ability to present issues with an evaluative perspective. For example, one of the rhetorical structures for argument is to compare and contrast. Illustrators can make this move as well. In *Hey, Little Ant* (Figure 5.27), Debbie Tilley uses size differences, along with character gestures and facial expressions, to help the reader understand the ant's argument for why he should not be squashed.

Argumentative illustration also presents a point of view. In *Separate is Never Equal: Sylvia Mendez and her Family's Fight for Desegregation*, Duncan Tonatiuh could have illustrated Sylvia's courtroom experience from any number of perspectives (from above, close up to the main character, from the judge's bench, from the witness stand), but he chose to place the reader behind Sylvia (Figure 5.28). As readers, when we view the page, we watch the whole scene unfold as an objective audience even though the words are written from Sylvia's point of view.

Figure 5.24
Illustrator, LeUyen Pham, creates the details of math obsession in *The Boy Who Loved Math* by Deborah Heiligman, 2013, New York, NY: Roaring Book Press. Illustration copyright 2013 by LeUyen Pham.

Figure 5.25
If you know someone who loves math, you will recognize the math-centric behaviors of the main character, Paul Erdős in *The Boy Who Loved Math* by Deborah Heiligman, 2013, New York, NY: Roaring Book Press. Illustration copyright 2013 by LeUyen Pham.

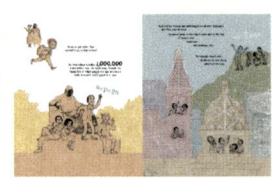

Figure 5.26
Seriously. My husband loves math and he sees the world in numbers and formulas. This is real. *The Boy Who Loved Math* by Deborah Heiligman, 2013, New York, NY: Roaring Book Press. Illustration copyright 2013 by LeUyen Pham.

Figure 5.27
Debbie Tilley uses comparison in her illustrations of the characters in *Hey, Little Ant* by Phillip M. Hoose and Hannah Hoose and illustrated by Debbie Tilley, 1998, New York, NY: Tricycle Press. Illustration copyright 1998 by Debbie Tilley.

Figure 5.28
Duncan Tonatiuh manipulates the reader's point of view to alter our relationship to the character and our interpretation of the courtroom scene in *Separate is Never Equal: Sylvia Mendez and her Family's Fight for Desegregation* by Duncan Tonatiuh, 2014, New York, NY: Abrams. Copyright 2014 by Duncan Tonatiuh.

Illustrators use argumentative techniques to appeal to the reader's ethics, reason, and emotions (Figure 5.29). In the classic picture book, *The True Story of the Three Little Pigs*, Jon Scieszka tells the story of a misunderstood wolf who "accidentally" causes a series of calamities in which pigs must be eaten, otherwise, their carcasses would go to waste. Beginning with the cover, Lane Smith presents the wolf's story as journalistic truth. The wolf is a bespectacled, respectable citizen whose newspaper article is crumpled by a pig's wicked-looking hoof. Whose side are you on?

Figure 5.29

Was it an accidental sneeze or an intentional blow? Illustrators, such as Lane Smith, appeal to the reader's ethics, reason, and emotions. Excerpt from *The True Story of the Three Little Pigs* by Jon Scieszka and illustrated by Lane Smith, 1989, New York, NY: Penguin. Illustration copyright 1989 by Lane Smith.

All genres, including speeches, essays, nonfiction, science fiction, and dramas use argumentation in illustration (Watch Video 5.3). Even poetic texts use argumentative illustration. For example, when you read the title of Douglas Florian's book, *Poem Runs*, you may not understand the meaning or intention of the text. But take a look at the illustrations (Figure 5.30) and the author's playfulness is apparent as he appeals to the reader's sense of humor.

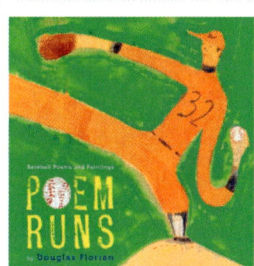

Figure 5.30

Douglas Florian has a series of poetry books (*Poem Depot, Poem Runs, Poetrees*) in which the illustrations alter the ways in which the titles are read. Cover from *Poem Runs* by Douglas Florian, 2012, New York, NY: HMH Books for Young Readers. Copyright 2012 by Douglas Florian.

Video 5.3 Visual Purpose and Illustrative Style http://www.kaltura.com/tiny/lfhu3

So far we have identified the text's communicative purpose across rhetorical and visual modes. In other words, we determined the literary form of the textual "vehicle" and assessed its intended function.

Next, let's take a look at assorted makes and models to get a sense of the range and variation across different vehicles.

  I said I didn't know anything about cars, but I never promised to abandon my analogy. I'm going to stick with it.

Genres: The Makes and Models of Children's Literature

Literary genres are categories of text based on any number of different criteria:

> literary purpose (narration, information, description, argumentation);
> author's tone (humor, serious, unbiased);
> content (science topics, social substance, subject matter);
> style (prose, poetry, technical);
> format (board book, wordless book, novel, games);
> length (short story, booklet) etc.

There are many different genres and no single agreement on the number of genres, names of genres, or sub-categories of genres. In other words, "genres" are the categories that make up a taxonomy of children's literature.

  The Makes and Models are equivalent to the different vehicle brands (Chevy, Ford, Toyota) and the variations in the forms of each vehicle (Corolla, Camry, Prius).

Although many other children's literature textbooks are organized by genre, I chose to organize this book by purpose. Here's why—I want you to know how to evaluate children's literature quality. Rather than providing extensive details about choosing books across the field of children's literature, which can include 15-20+ genre categories (depending on who's counting), I wanted a more simplified approach and I chose to organize around four major communication purposes. However, genre knowledge is important. Therefore, you need to familiarize yourself with some of the most common genre categories as well as some of the authors and illustrators who write or draw in particular genres.

"Genres" are the categories that make up a taxonomy of children's literature. This is why I chose to use "rhetorical purpose" to help you determine quality children's literature. It's easier to familiarize yourself with four categories of evaluative criteria rather than use different criteria across 15 to 20+ genres.

Picture books. Picture books are stories or content presented through text and illustrations. All topics are covered. The author's words and the illustrator's images are interwoven and equally important. Picture books are written for any purpose and on all topics.

Notable Authors and Illustrators.
Dr. Seuss, Tomie dePaola, Eric Carle (Figure 5.31), Maurice Sendak, Jane Yolen, Jerry Pinkney, Chris Van Allsburg, Mo Willems, Judith Viorst, Kadim Nelson, Beatrix Potter, Floyd Cooper (Figure 5.32), Henry Cole, Doreen Cronin, Chris Raschka, David Diaz, Jon Scieszka, Robert McCloskey, Leo Lionni, Ezra Jack Keats, Paul Goble, Eve Bunting, Marc Browne, Anthony Browne, Eric Velasquez, Betsy Lewin, Ted Lewin, Donald Crews, Anno, Pat Hutchins, Molly Bang, Helen Oxenbury.

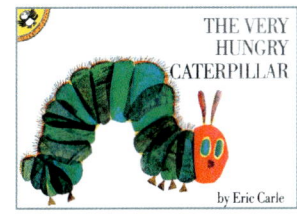

Figure 5.31
Magical, beautiful, interesting, and just overall lovely! I'm sure you have read *The Very Hungry Caterpillar* by Eric Carle, 1969, New York, NY: World Publishing Company. Image from a later publication, 1982, New York, NY: Penguin. Copyright 1969/1982 by Eric Carle.

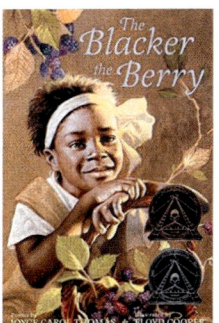

Figure 5.32
I don't know of any artist who paints faces like Floyd Cooper. I am drawn to his artwork. He is able to capture an internal spirit that is indescribable. This example is a book of poetry *The Blacker the Berry* by Joyce Carol Thomas and illustrated by Floyd Cooper, 2008, New York, NY: Amistad. Cover art copyright 2008 by Floyd Cooper.

Best-of lists.

- School Library Journal's Top 100 Picture Books: Great overview of famous books
  - http://www.slj.com/wp-content/uploads/2012/08/SLJ_Fuse8_Top100_Picture.pdf
- Goodreads: Lists categories of "best" picture books (Indie, modern, 'green', bedtime)
  - https://www.goodreads.com/list/tag/picture-books

Comment: OK this is very difficult. I could go on and on and on with lists of authors and illustrators. I've tried to select people with different styles and who have created several books-- some old and some new. So view my recommendations as a starter list. Then create your own.

Wordless books. Wordless books look like picture books, but they do not have words. The story or information is shared through illustrations or other images. The images can be simple or elaborate and created in all mediums, but the meaning is in the illustrations. All topics are covered.

Notable Authors and Illustrators. David Wiesner (Figure 5.33), Henry Cole, Marla Frazee, Raul Colon, Chris Raschka, Jerry Pinkney, Molly Idle, Barbara Leyman Mercer Mayer, Brinton Turkle, Alexandra Day, Peter Spier, Raymond Briggs, Emily McCully.

Figure 5.33

In wordless books, the illustrations do all of the work. Most illustrators don't have a whole career in wordless books, but David Wiesner's has had several and his are famous. Here is a page from *Flotsam* by David Wiesner, 2006, New York, NY: Clarion. Copyright 2006 by David Wiesner.

Best-of lists.

- Goodreads Wordless Picture Books: Nice overview of popular wordless books
  - https://www.goodreads.com/list/show/722.Wordless_Picture_Books
- Children's Books Guide, Wordless: Top 10 list of wordless books
  - http://childrensbooksguide.com/wordless

Poetry. Poetry is published in anthologies or single-authored poem books. Single poems are often turned into picture books. Poetry expresses feelings, thoughts, and events in brief and meaningful ways. Poetry is rhythmic, emotional language and it is written to cover the range of human experience.

Notable Authors and Illustrators.

Arnold Adoff, Eloise Greenfield (Figure 5.34), Myra Cohn Livingston, Jack Prelutsky, Shel Silverstein, Douglas Florian, Nikki Giovanni, Nikki Grimes, Langston Hughes, A.A.Milne, Byrd Baylor, Lee Bennett Hopkins, Paul Fleischman, Judith Viorst, Pat Mora, Eve Merriam, Marilyn Singer, X.J. Kennedy, Kenn Nesbitt, J. Patrick Lewis (Figure 5.35).

Best-of lists.

- School Library Journal, Introducing Students to NCTE's Notable Poetry Titles
    - http://www.slj.com/2014/04/collection-development/introducing-students-to-nctes-notable-poetry-titles/
- Goodreads Best Children's Poetry Books
    - http://www.goodreads.com/list/show/1340.Best_children_s_poetry_books

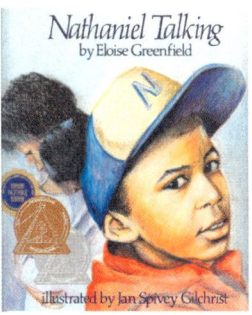

Figure 5.34

Eloise Greenfield's poetic texts are written from different perspectives and focus on unique characters, but they all relate powerful emotions and stories. *Nathaniel Talking* is one example of Eloise Greenfield's many contributions. *Nathaniel Talking* by Eloise Greenfield and illustrated by Jan Spivey Gilchrist, 1998, London, England: Writers & Readers. Cover art copyright 1998 by Jan Spivey Gilchrist.

Figure 5.35

J. Patrick Lewis and Kenn Nesbitt are award-winning, prolific poets. In *Bigfoot is Missing*, they take on the creatures of childhood nightmares. MinaLima's illustrations play with all of the hype. *Bigfoot is Missing* by J. Patrick Lewis and Ken Nesbitt and illustrated by MinaLima, 2015, New York, NY: Chronicle Books. Illustration copyright 2015 by MinaLima.

Traditional literature. Traditional literature is the label for stories that have been passed from generation to generation through oral storytelling. These folk tales, fables, myths, legends, and tall tales may be published as single story picture books (Figure 5.36) or in collections and anthologies (Figure 5.37). Most people associate the Brothers Grimm, Joseph Jacobs, and Charles Perrault as the "writers" of these stories, but they were more like collectors and interpretive transcribers. They collected the stories and published them, with their own twists and spins, of course, but they didn't "create" them.

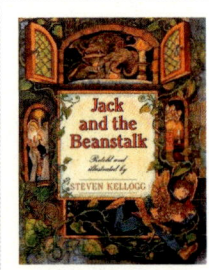

Figure 5.36

Steven Kellogg wrote and illustrated several tall tales and legends as separate books. One example is *Jack and the Beanstalk* by Steven Kellogg, 1997, New York, NY: HarperCollins. Copyright 1997 by Steven Kellogg.

Sometimes writers and illustrators use traditional stories to create spin-offs, parodies, or fractured fairy tales (Jon Scieszka and Lane Smith are a famous duo). There are many variations. Most often readers have concepts of the Disney versions of these tales. Read the older versions and you will see a huge difference.

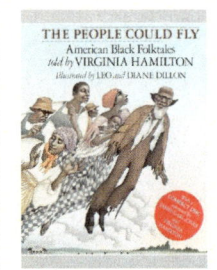

Figure 5.37

Virginia Hamilton wrote a collection of Black folktales in *The People Could Fly: American Black Folktales* by Virginia Hamilton and illustrated by Leo and Diane Dillon, 1993, New York, NY: Knopf Books for Young Readers. Cover art copyright 1993 by Leo and Diane Dillon.

Notable Authors and Illustrators. Modern variations or retellings by Arnold Lobel, Paul Galdone, Steven Kellogg, Jon Scieszka, Virginia Hamilton, James Marshall (Figure 5.38).

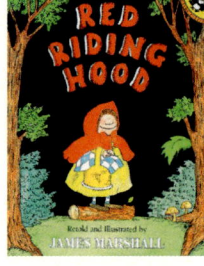

Figure 5.38

James Marshall put his own spin on well-known fairy tales such as The Three Pigs, Goldilocks, and Hansel & Gretel. Check out *Little Red Riding Hood* by James Marshall, 1993, New York, NY: Puffin. Copyright 1993 by James Marshall.

Best-of lists.

- LibGuide, Traditional Literature: Comprehensive review of traditional literature with a description of the genre and sub-categories
    - http://libraryschool.libguidescms.com/content.php?pid=342934&sid=2804433
- Goodreads: Popular Traditional Literature Books
    - http://www.goodreads.com/shelf/show/traditional-literature
- School Library Education Consortium: Traditional Literature
    - http://uwsslec.libguides.com/c.php?g=186921&p=1236147
- Collection of Grimm Brothers' Tales compiled, translated, and classified by D.L. Ashliman.
    - http://www.pitt.edu/~dash/grimmtales.html

Fantasy. Fantasy stories are most often presented as novels, although they often include chapter illustrations or sporadic illustrations throughout. Fantasy is a category of fiction (the story is created by the writer) except the events are fantastical and cannot happen in real life. Fantasy is imaginative and borrows elements of style, characters, and themes from traditional literature as well. For an excellent overview of different types of fantasy, click here: http://www.yalsa.ala.org/thehub/2013/04/03/discovering-your-brand-of-fantasy/.

Notable Authors and Illustrators.
Madeleine L'Engle, C.S. Lewis, Susan Cooper, R.L. Stine, Lois Lowry, Natalie Babbitt, Roald Dahl (Figure 5.39), Jon Scieszka, P.L. Travers, Mary Norton, Lloyd Alexander, Hans Christian Andersen, J.K. Rowling, Neil Gaiman.

Figure 5.39

Roald Dahl was simply fantastic and his book are still loved and read all over the world. One of my favorites is *James and the Giant Peach* by Roald Dahl and illustrated by Nancy Ekholm Burkert, 1961, New York, NY: Penguin. Cover image copyright 1961 by Nancy Ekholm Burkert.

Best-of lists.

- Goodreads Best Children's Fantasy (under 10)
    - http://www.goodreads.com/list/show/461.Best_Children_s_Fantasy

- School Library Journal Middle Grades Fantasy (ages 10-13, easier to read)
    - http://www.slj.com/2012/11/collection-development/focus-on-collection-development/middle-grade-fantasy-believe-it-focus-on-believe-it-november-1-2012/

- NPR's Top 100 Science Fiction & Fantasy books (young adult)
    - http://www.listchallenges.com/npr-top-100-science-fiction-and-fantasy-books

Contemporary Realistic Fiction. Contemporary realistic fiction stories deal with all aspects of life within current or recent times, usually set within the parameters of a generation. However, some books begin as contemporary fiction, and due to their longevity, they transfer toward the historic. For example, many of Judy Blume's novels are set in the early 1970's before cassette tapes, CD's, and iPads. At some point, books that reference rotary dial phones will lose their contemporary feel. Contemporary realistic fiction is often referred to as a collection of "problem novels" because they deal with a range of subject matter from drug abuse and suicide to family problems and learning disabilities.

Notable Authors and Illustrators. Lois Lowry, Judy Blume, Walter Dean Myers (Figure 5.40), Gary Paulsen, Avi, Gary Soto, Katherine Paterson, Johanna Hurwitz, Cynthia Rylant, Phyllis Reynolds Naylor, John Green, Sharon Draper.

Best-of lists.

- Goodreads Best Young Adult Realistic Novels

    - http://www.goodreads.com/list/show/8460.Best_Young_Adult_Realistic_Novels

- Goodreads Popular Children's Realistic Fiction Books

    - http://www.goodreads.com/shelf/show/childrens-realistic-fiction

- YALSA (Young Adult Library Services Association) Best Fiction for Young Adults Archive: Search by year

    - http://www.ala.org/yalsa/2015-best-fiction-young-adults

Figure 5.40

One of the most important and impactful writers of contemporary fiction is Walter Dean Myers. Although his books span 40 years, his stories are relevant today. One award winning example is *Monster* by Walter Dean Myers and illustrated by Christopher Myers, 1999, New York, NY: HarperCollins. Cover art copyright 1999 by Christopher Myers.

Historical fiction. Historical fiction is the label for stories that are set in the past. Exactly how far in the past is debatable. Does the book reference cell phones, rotary phones, or no phones? Some people set the cut-off date at 25 years, or a generation. Some people set an historical marker such as the Civil Rights Act. Others use the year of the reader's birth. There isn't a correct answer to what makes fiction historical, but I tend to use the reader's birth as the general line for what "feels" historical; it's relative. Another issue in categorizing historical fiction is the author's intention. Some books get old and they become historical; whereas new historical fiction is written with contemporary insight and reflection on the past. The whole point is that historical fiction is set in the past and it provides insight into a different time period. Historical facts may or may not be used but the text must accurately reflect the historical time period in which it is set. Most of all, historical fiction must tell a good story.

Notable Authors and Illustrators.
Katherine Paterson (Figure 5.41), Mildred Taylor (Figure 5.42), Laura Ingalls Wilder, Lois Lowry, Lawrence Yep, Jean Fritz, Patricia MacLachlan, Paul Fleischman, Avi, Scott O'Dell, Jane Yolen, James Collier.

Best-of lists.

- Pinterest Collection of Best Historical Fiction for Kids
    - https://www.pinterest.com/pragmaticmom/best-historical-fiction-for-kids/
- Keene Public Library: Search a list of historical fiction sorted by setting/location
    - http://keenepubliclibrary.org/library/kids/historicalfiction
- Notable Social Studies Trade Books: Provides 15 years of notable lists, although some of the books are not "historical fiction."
    - http://www.socialstudies.org/notable

Graphic novels/texts. Graphic novels are compilations and original works published in a sequential art format. They are reminiscent of cartoons or comic books and they can have varying amounts of text. They can feature fictional, nonfiction, descriptive, or argumentative content.

Notable Authors and Illustrators.
Dav Pilkey, G. Neri (Figure 5.43), Jeff Kinney, Jullian Tamaki (Figure 5.44), Hope Larson, Lucy Knisley, Faith Erin Hicks, Kevin O'Malley.

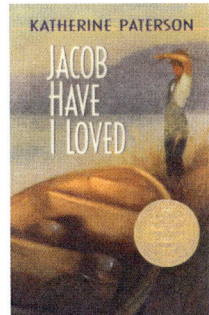

Figure 5.41

Katherine Patterson is probably best known for writing *Bridge to Terebithia* or *The Great Gilly Hopkins*, but my favorite book of all time is *Jacob Have I Loved*. I have read it over and over again. This is an older cover, but it's the one I love. *Jacob Have I Loved* by Katherine Paterson, 1980, New York, NY: HarperCollins. Cover art copyright 2007 by Chris Sheban.

Figure 5.42

Roll of Thunder, Hear My Cry is one of a series of novels set during the time of segregation in the US. *Roll of Thunder, Hear My Cry* by Mildred Taylor, 1976, New York, NY: Dial Books. Frontispiece copyright 1976 by Dial Books.

Figure 5.43

Neri writes all types of fiction, but *Yummy* was one of the first graphic novels I read. *Yummy* by G. Neri and illustrated by Randy DuBurke, 2010, New York, NY: Lee & Low Books. Cover art copyright 2010 by Randy DuBurke.

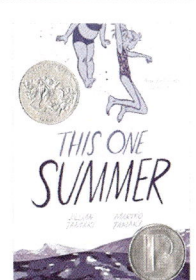

Figure 5.44

Graphic novels are insanely popular for young adults. The illustrations are elaborate and intense with developed characters and quick dialogue. Jullian Tamaki created *This One Summer* with her cousin, Mario Tamaki. *This One Summer* by Jullian Tamaki and Mario Tamaki, 2014, New York, NY: First Second Books. Copyright 2014 by Jullian Tamaki and Mario Tamaki.

Best-of lists.

- ALA Graphic Novels Reading Lists
  - http://www.ala.org/alsc/graphicnovels2013
- Goodreads Best Graphic Novels for Children

  https://www.goodreads.com/list/show/5038.Best_Graphic_Novels_for_Children
- School Library Journal Comic Relief: Thirty-nine graphic novels that kids can't resist
  - http://www.slj.com/2011/07/collection-development/comic-relief-thirty-nine-graphic-novels-that-kids-cant-resist/#_
- Pinterest Best Graphic Novels
  - https://www.pinterest.com/pragmaticmom/best-graphic-novels/
- First Second Books is a publisher of graphic novels and their website highlights creators and collections of graphic novels for all ages.
  - http://www.firstsecondbooks.com/

Biography. Biographies are fictionalized or authentic stories about a real person. Biographies can appear in picture book, novel, or information book formats.

Notable Authors & Illustrators. David A. Adler (Figure 5.45), Jean Fritz, Diane Stanley, Robert Lawson, Russell Freedman, Aliki, Kadir Nelson (Figure 5.46), Jennifer Fisher Bryant, Jacqueline Briggs Martin, Jeanette Winter, Kathleen Krull, Matt de la Pena.

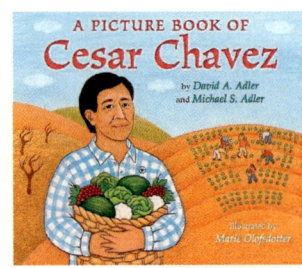

Figure 5.45

David Adler is a prolific writer of biographies. Check out *A Picture Book of Cesar Chavez* by David A. Adler and Michael S. Adler and illustrated by Marie Olofsdotter, 2011, New York, NY: Holiday House. Cover art copyright 2011 by Marie Olofsdotter.

Best-of lists.

- Goodreads Popular Children's Biography Books
  - http://www.goodreads.com/shelf/show/childrens-biography
- YALSA Booklists for Biography: An expansive lists of biographies that covers all people and time periods.
  - http://www.ala.org/yalsa/booklistsawards/booklists/outstandingbooks/biographyoutstanding

Figure 5.46

Kadir Nelson creates amazing illustrations and he also writes incredible tributes for important individuals. One example is *We Are The Ship: The Story of Negro League Baseball* by Kadir Nelson, 2008, New York, NY: Jump at the Sun. Copyright 2008 by Kadir Nelson.

Information. In information or nonfiction books, text is the primary source of information but pictures may play an equal role and they are usually desired. Text and pictures must be accurate, authentic and current. Information books cover a range of topics from history to science to culture.

Notable Authors and Illustrators. Seymour Simon, Russell Freedman, Kadir Nelson, Peter Sis, Joanna Cole, Gail Gibbons (Figure 5.47), Aliki, David Macaulay, Vicki Cobb, Susan Campbell Bartoletti, Jim Murphy, Marc Aronson.

Figure 5.47

Gail Gibbons writes information books for youth of all ages, but she is particularly strong at creating concept books for young children. She writes about a range of topics as well. *Tornadoes* by Gail Gibbons, 2010, New York, NY: Holiday House. Copyright 2010 by Gail Gibbons.

Best-of lists.

- Goodreads Best Children's Nonfiction: Great list of favorites from different years
    - http://www.goodreads.com/list/show/1557.Best_Children_s_Nonfiction
- Pinterest Best Nonfiction for Kids
    - https://www.pinterest.com/pragmaticmom/best-non-fiction-for-kids/
- YALSA Nonfiction Award for notable information books for young adults. Listed by year of publication/award.
    - http://www.ala.org/yalsa/booklistsawards/bookawards/nonfiction/previous
- Time Magazine's All Time 100 Best Nonfiction: Not necessarily for children, but definitely for young adults
    - http://www.goodreads.com/list/show/12719.Time_Magazine_s_All_TIME_100_Best_Non_Fiction_Books

Diverse books. Children's literature is a window, a mirror, and a map (Sims-Bishop, 1990; Myers, 2014). It is important for children and young adults to read realistic portrayals of people who share similar identities. For these reasons, books are labeled as multicultural books or they are labeled with specific markers to promote the inclusion of diverse characters from different races, classes, nations, and genders. Maybe we won't need labels, but for now, the world of children's literature is still "all white" (Horning, 2014; Larrick, 1965), and the labels bring attention to the issue that #WeNeedDiverseBooks (http://weneeddiversebooks.org/).

Notable Authors and Illustrators. Floyd Cooper, Kadir Nelson, G. Neri, Jacqueline Woodson, Eloise Greenfield, Pat Mora, Nikki Grimes, Angela Johnson, Allen Say (Figure 5.48), Ed Young, Shaun Tan, Matt de la Pena.

Best-of lists.

- School Library Journal: #WeNeedDiverseBooks Realistic Fiction with Diverse Protagonists
    - http://www.slj.com/2014/10/reviews/spotlight/weneeddiversebooks-realistic-fiction-with-diverse-protagonists-slj-spotlight-2/
- We Need Diverse Books
    - http://weneeddiversebooks.org/
- Book Dragon: Books for the Multi-Culti Reader, sponsored by the Smithsonian Asian Pacific American Center
    - http://smithsonianapa.org/bookdragon/about/
- Kids Like Us is an organization that promotes literacy learning of children in city schools and city neighborhoods. You can browse for books by age, genre, gender, and race.
    - http://www.kidslikeus.org/books/
- Pat Mora (author) has collected a list of Latino Authors and Illustrators
    - http://www.patmora.com/sampler-latino-authors-illustrators-for-children-ya/
- Valerie Knight, a librarian at Wayne State College created an excellent guide to books that reflect religious diversity as well as a guide to books about family diversity and social issues
    - http://libguides.wsc.edu/content.php?pid=488998&sid=5512404
    - http://libguides.wsc.edu/content.php?pid=488998&sid=4010447

Figure 5.48

Allen Say often creates paintings and tells stories that reflect his Japanese heritage. He won the Caldecott for *Grandfather's Journey*, which is a must-read about his grandfather's emigration to the US, but he has many other books as well. *Kamishibai Man* is about a man who performs the dying art of paper theater. *Kamishibai Man* by Allen Say, 2005, New York, NY: HMH Books for Young Readers. Copyright 2005 by Allen Say.

Many languages literature. Not everyone speaks English, and children need books written in a language that is comfortable and easy for them. In addition, many children who speak English are also learning different languages. They could benefit from reading children's books written in other languages. Many languages literature includes books specifically written in other languages as well as books translated into different languages.

Notable Authors and Illustrators. Maria Teresa Andruetto, Victor Carvajal, Edna Iturralde, Jordi Sierra i Fabra, Alma Flor Ada (Figures 5.49 & 5.50), Bibi Dumon Tak.

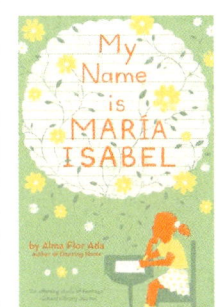

Figure 5.49

Alma Flor Ada writes books in English that focus on Latina/o culture. *My Name is Maria Isabel* is about a girl whose teacher calls her Mary, not Maria, and the struggle the child feels about her name and her identity. *My Name is Maria Isabel* by Alma Flor Ada and illustrated by K. Dyble Thompson, 1995, New York, NY: Atheneum Books for Young Readers. Cover art copyright by K. Dyble Thompson.

Best-of lists.

- International Children's Digital Library: A searchable database for books written in many languages

  - http://en.childrenslibrary.org

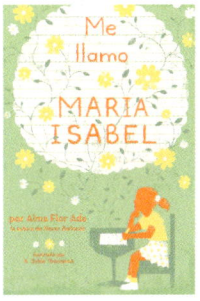

Figure 5.50

Alma Flor Ada translates children's books from English to Spanish. She translated *My Name is Maria Isabel* into *Me Llamo María Isabel* by Alma Flor Ada and illustrated by K. Dyble Thompson, 1996, New York, NY: Atheneum Books for Young Readers. Cover art copyright by K. Dyble Thompson.

- ALA Batchelder Award: Lists of the most outstanding children's book originally published in a language other than English in a country other than the United States, and subsequently translated into English for publication in the United States.

  - http://www.ala.org/alsc/awardsgrants/bookmedia/batchelderaward

- S-Collection: Foreign Language & Bilingual Children's Books, find books in French, Spanish, Navajo, etc. You can also find translations.

  - http://www.library.illinois.edu/sshel/s-coll/findbks/s-collbibs/forlang.htm

  - http://www.childrensbooksonline.org/library-translations.htm

Classics. Classics are books from any genre that have stood the test of time. They should tell good stories and have well-constructed plots, worthwhile themes, and convincing characterization.

Notable Authors and Illustrators. J.M. Barrie, C.S. Lewis, J.R.R. Tolkien, Beatrix Potter (Figure 5.51), Maurice Sendak (Figure 5.52), Beverly Cleary, Shel Silverstein, Ludwig Bemelmans, Judy Blume, A.A. Milne.

Best-of lists.

- New York Public Library 100 Books/100 Years: A review of best loved books in alphabetical order
    - http://www.nypl.org/childrens100
- Real Simple 40 Classic Children's Books Even Adults Love: Definitely includes sentimental favorites
    - http://www.realsimple.com/work-life/entertainment/classic-childrens-books

Figure 5.51

You can download Beatrix Potter's books for free from Project Gutenberg (http://www.gutenberg.org/ebooks/author/292), and you can browse the Beatrix Potter Collections at the Victoria & Albert Museum in London (http://www.vam.ac.uk/page/b/beatrix-potter/) or in the private collections of rare book dealers (http://www.peterharrington.co.uk/blog/first-editions-of-peter-rabbit/), but there is something about holding them in your hands. Cover of the first, privately printed edition of *The Tale of Peter Rabbit* by Beatrix Potter Retrieved from http://www.abebooks.com/

Figure 5.52

Images of Max's "wild rumpus" are immediately recognizable by people across generations. Image from *Where the Wild Things Are* by Maurice Sendak, 1963, New York, NY: Harper & Row. Copyright 1963 by Maurice Sendak.

Question #2: How do we select and apply the appropriate criteria to evaluate books?

In the previous section, I focused on the author's and illustrator's purpose for creating children's and young adult literature. I also provided a list of genres (categories) that are often found in children's literature. Now that you have a sense of the field, how do you know what's good?

Elements and Expectations: Overview of the Working Parts

To determine the effectiveness of the working parts in children's literature, I like to borrow from the experts and use their *suggested criteria* for choosing award winning children's literature. Yes, awards have issues (see chapter 4), but the award criteria are in our hands now. Again, rather than focus on genres, I prefer to focus on the mode of visual and rhetorical discourse.

> When selecting a vehicle (literature) and a particular make and model (genre), the buyer (reader) expects certain standard parts: tires, steering wheel, engine, seats (plot, characters, setting). But then, certain manufacturers/engineers (publishers/authors/illustrators) tweak the formula to enhance the driving experience: mirrors, cup holders, hands-free systems, music players (innovative design, new media, contemporary topics).
>
> In many cases, what starts off as "optional" can become "standard." Therefore, to evaluate books, consider what comes standard and then look for the manufacturers and engineers (artists and illustrators) who do a better job of making a vehicle with higher levels of design and craft (art and aesthetics of writing and illustrating).

Narration. To evaluate narrative books (i.e., books that tell a story) based primarily on the text, such as contemporary realistic fiction, historical fiction, fantasy, or novels in verse, I use a combination of criteria from the Newbery Medal (http://www.ala.org/alsc/awardsgrants/bookmedia/newberymedal/newberyterms/newberyterms) and the Printz Award (http://www.ala.org/yalsa/booklistsawards/bookawards/printzaward/aboutprintz/criteria). Depending on the book, one or more of these criteria apply:

- Development of a plot (beginning, middle, end)
- Delineation of characters
- Delineation of a setting
- Distinctive interpretation of the theme or concept
- Excellent presentation of information including accuracy, clarity, and organizational flow
- Appropriateness of style for the audience
- Design and layout of the book

If the narrative is presented in the form of a picture book or graphic novel, or if it includes sufficient illustration, I use the following criteria from the Caldecott Medal as well (http://www.ala.org/alsc/awardsgrants/bookmedia/caldecottmedal/caldecottterms/caldecottterms).

- Excellence of execution in the artistic technique employed;
- Excellence of pictorial interpretation of story or theme;
- Appropriateness of style of illustration to the story or theme;
- Delineation of plot, theme, characters, setting, mood through the pictures;
- Excellence of presentation in recognition of the intended audience.

Don't expect to find excellence in each of the named elements. The book should, however, have distinguished qualities in all of the elements pertinent to it.

Information. To evaluate nonfiction books based primarily on the text, such as life cycle books, concept books, specialized books, and some biographies, I use a combination of criteria from the Sibert Medal (http://www.ala.org/alsc/awardsgrants/bookmedia/sibertmedal/sibertterms/sibertmedaltrms) and the Orbis Pictus Award (http://www.ncte.org/awards/orbispictus). Depending on the book, one or more of these criteria will apply:

- Interesting and timely subject matter;
- Excellent, engaging, and distinctive use of language;
- Excellent, engaging, and distinctive use of visuals in illustrated texts (for picture books see below);
- Appropriate organization with clear sequencing and logical development;
- Thorough documentation and author's qualifications;
- Clear, accurate, and stimulating presentation of facts, concepts, and ideas;
- Appropriate style of presentation for subject and for intended audience;
- Supportive features (index, table of contents, maps, timelines, etc.);
- Respectful and of interest to intended audience.

INFORMATION

If the information is presented in the form of a picture book, or if it includes sufficient illustration, I use the following criteria from the Caldecott Medal as well (http://www.ala.org/alsc/awardsgrants/bookmedia/caldecottmedal/caldecottterms/caldecottterms).

- Excellence of execution in the artistic technique employed;

- Excellence of pictorial interpretation of theme or concept;

- Appropriateness of style of illustration to the theme or concept;

- Delineation of information through the pictures;

- Excellence of presentation in recognition of the intended audience.

Description. To evaluate descriptive books based primarily on the text, such as biography, poetry, journals, and essays, I use a combination of criteria from the NCTE Award for Excellence in Poetry for Children (http://www.ncte.org/awards/poetry), the John Burroughs Riverby Award (American Museum of Natural History, http://research.amnh.org/burroughs/awards.html), the Newbery Medal (http://www.ala.org/alsc/awardsgrants/bookmedia/newberymedal/newberyterms/newberyterms) and the Printz Award (http://www.ala.org/yalsa/booklistsawards/bookawards/printzaward/aboutprintz/criteria). Depending on the book, one or more of these criteria will apply:

- Perceptive and aesthetic accounts of direct experiences in the world;

- Demonstrate authenticity of voice;

- Use of language and form in fresh ways;

- Excellent, engaging, and distinctive use of clear and concise language;

- Excellent, engaging, and distinctive use of vivid language;

- Excellent, engaging and distinctive use of sensory language;

- Appropriate structure to highlight the topic;

- Appropriate organization with clear sequencing and logical development.

DESCRIPTION

If the description is presented in the form of a picture book, or if it includes sufficient illustration, I use the following criteria from the Caldecott Medal as well (http://www.ala.org/alsc/awardsgrants/bookmedia/caldecottmedal/caldecottterms/caldecottterms).

- Excellence of execution in the artistic technique employed;

- Excellence of pictorial interpretation of theme or topic;

- Appropriateness of style of illustration to the theme or topic;

- Delineation of description through the pictures;

- Excellence of presentation in recognition of the intended audience.

Argumentation. To evaluate argumentation based primarily on the text, such as historical nonfiction, current nonfiction, and essays, I use a combination of criteria from awards designed to address a point of view or perspective [e.g., Jane Addams Peace Award (http://www.janeaddamspeace.org/jacba/subguide.shtml), Scott O'Dell Award for Historical Fiction (http://www.scottodell.com/pages/scotto'dellawardforhistoricalfiction.aspx), Sibert Medal (http://www.ala.org/alsc/awardsgrants/bookmedia/sibertmedal/sibertterms/sibertmedaltrms) and the Orbis Pictus Award (http://www.ncte.org/awards/orbispictus)].

Depending on the book, one or more of these criteria apply:

- Establishes a central claim;

- Provides clear and accurate evidence to support the claim;

- Appropriate organization with clear sequencing and logical development;

- Appropriate style of presentation for subject and for intended audience;

- Consistency and coherence within the chain of reasoning;

- Honest and intimate accounts of experience that are relevant.

ARGUMENTATION

If the argumentation is presented in the form of a picture book, or if it includes sufficient illustration, I use the following criteria from the Caldecott Medal as well (http://www.ala.org/alsc/awardsgrants/bookmedia/caldecottmedal/caldecottterms/caldecottterms).

- Excellence of execution in the artistic technique employed;
- Excellence of pictorial interpretation of theme or argument;
- Appropriateness of style of illustration to the theme or argument;
- Delineation of argument through the pictures;
- Excellence of presentation in recognition of the intended audience.

Although I selected these criteria to evaluate quality in children's literature, your use of criteria will be subjective. Rather than attempting to seek inter-rater reliability, the purpose of sharing the criteria is to help you see the books differently.

For example, many people love the books, *Guess How Much I Love You* (McBrantney, 1995) or *Love You Forever* (Munsch, 1986). These books are popular and people buy them when they have babies or young children at home. If you view the books from the warm and wonderful experience of being read to as a child, then you will value them. However, if you consider text structures, authorial intent, rhetorical moves, and cultural implications, you will understand why children may not be interested in reading this book on their own without parent initiation. You might also understand how others might critique the book.

Children's literature, while seemingly innocent and simple to those unfamiliar with its depth and scope, can provide the opportunity for deep structural analysis and cultural criticism.

 Interested in learning how to engage in close reading and how to write literary critiques, read Lindsay Persohn's guide.

Question #3: How do we match books to readers?

Reading Development and the Role of Children's Literature

Reading interests vary person to person. In the US, there is a cultural tendency to divide children and youth by gender. But gender is an arbitrary category and reading interests are more complicated than gender assignment. There aren't "girl" books or "boy" books. There are books. Girls read books about boys (*Harry Potter*) and boys read books about girls (*Hunger Games*). Girls read genres typically associated with boys such as fantasy, science information books, and graphic novels. Boys read genres typically associated with girls such as poetry, fiction, and biographies. That is—if people (parents, teachers, librarians, friends, siblings, booksellers, media and television personalities, filmmakers, and social networks) let them read what they want. In fact, the individuality of book choice becomes even more pronounced if youth are encouraged to pursue their interests.

Hey, this is important. When you go to McDonalds and order a happy meal, there aren't girl toys and boy toys. There are toys. Just let the kids pick the toy.

There aren't girl colors and boy colors. Colors are colors. We are constructing gendered notions of color.

If you don't believe me, then believe the Smithsonian: http://www.smithsonianmag.com/arts-culture/when-did-girls-start-wearing-pink-1370097/?no-ist

Or NPR: http://www.npr.org/2014/04/01/297159948/girls-are-taught-to-think-pink-but-that-wasnt-always-so

Or the BBC: http://www.bbc.com/future/story/20141117-the-pink-vs-blue-gender-myth

Why do we do such a thing?

Shaming and shunning have been used as a form of public humiliation for centuries. Today, many criminal courts use shaming instead of incarceration or financial penalties. Shaming is a form of social control, which is precisely why gay-shaming and fat-shaming are forms of bullying.

Read more about shaming as a form of public humiliation:

http://www.latimes.com/opinion/op-ed/la-oe-0525-morrison-sentencing-shame-judges-20140525-column.html

http://www.npr.org/2013/08/24/215097279/some-judges-prefer-public-shaming-to-prison

http://www.slate.com/articles/news_and_politics/view_from_chicago/2015/04/internet_shaming_the_legal_history_of_shame_and_its_costs_and_benefits.html

Along the same lines, shaming has no place in children's literature selection. Public ridicule for a child's book preference (or toy or color preference, for that matter) is not appropriate. Book choices are personal preferences, not punishable offenses. My book preferences are not indicative of my sexual, social, gender, or professional identities, nor do my reading preferences alter my behavior. Just because I read about someone's heroin addiction doesn't mean I will become addicted to heroin (or want to try heroin, or even know where to buy it or what to do with it.) But reading about a character with a heroin addiction will help me understand someone else's perspective and experiences as I think about my own. Alternatively, if someone with different life experiences and different tendencies toward drug use reads about heroin addiction, he or she may have a different personal reaction than me. However, there are many people and intervening events between books and the real, live people who read them. Books are mirrors, and windows, and maps!

"Book choices are personal preferences, not punishable offenses."

With an understanding that idiosyncratic factors are at play in the determination of book preferences, we can examine reading trends and develop strategies for selecting books based on developmental considerations for youth. Please remember, these are generic recommendations based on broad patterns of physical, cognitive, and social development (Video 5.4). The only way to know what a particular child will read is to ask the child, offer different types of books, and encourage reading. Plus, you have to pay attention and look and listen very carefully.

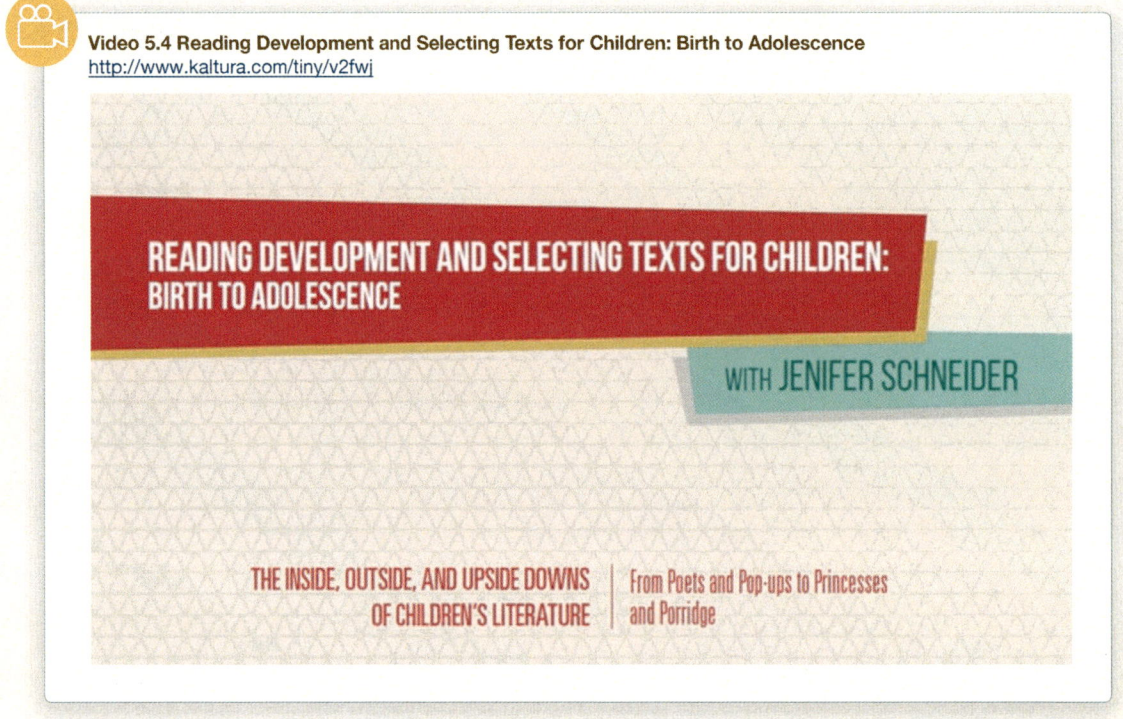

Video 5.4 Reading Development and Selecting Texts for Children: Birth to Adolescence
http://www.kaltura.com/tiny/v2fwj

Babies

"Babies can't read." This statement is true only if you have a very formal, school-based conception of reading. Babies don't go to school or sit at desks; therefore, don't expect them to read the same way a 6-year-old reads (Figure 5.53). Instead, newborn babies *experience* reading (Video 5.5).

Figure 5.53
Babies read differently than older children. Photo copyright 2015 by Aimee Frier.

 Books are expensive. Here is an idea. I had a book shower when my daughter was born. I registered for books on Amazon and received books as gifts. Diapers get dirty. Books last a lifetime.

 Video 5.5 Reading to a Newborn http://www.kaltura.com/tiny/m3fdp

READING TO A NEWBORN
2 MONTHS OLD

WITH JENIFER SCHNEIDER

THE INSIDE, OUTSIDE, AND UPSIDE DOWNS OF CHILDREN'S LITERATURE | From Poets and Pop-ups to Princesses and Porridge

THE RIGHT BOOK FOR THE RIGHT READER AT THE RIGHT TIME
(LITERARY ANALYSIS, QUALITY, AND DEVELOPMENT PERSPECTIVES)

Babies exhibit emergent reading behaviors when they have access to books. In other words, little babies read with their eyes, their hands, and their body language (Figure 5.54). Older babies learn how to hold books, turn the pages, and follow along (Figure 5.55). Parents, family members, teachers, and caregivers who recognize and encourage these behaviors (Figure 5.56) can significantly effect a child's attitude toward reading, can help a child develop the persistence necessary to be receptive to later reading instruction, can help a child develop higher-level thinking skills, can increase a child's language proficiency, and can help a child acquire basic academic knowledge (Gregory and Morrison, 1998; High et.al., 2014).

The key figure in baby reading is the adult who recognizes early reading behaviors and encourages them, not discourages them (Video 5.6).

Figure 5.54
Babies read with their eyes. Photo copyright 2000 by Jenifer Schneider.

Figure 5.55
Babies exhibit emergent reading behaviors when they have access to books. They learn how to hold books, turn the pages, and follow along. Photo copyright 2015 by Aimee Frier.

Figure 5.56
Family members, including older siblings and cousins, who recognize and encourage reading behaviors can significantly affect a child's attitude toward reading. Photo copyright 2015 by Aimee Frier.

I'm reminded of a quote: "Children are made readers on the laps of their parents." — Emilie Buchwald

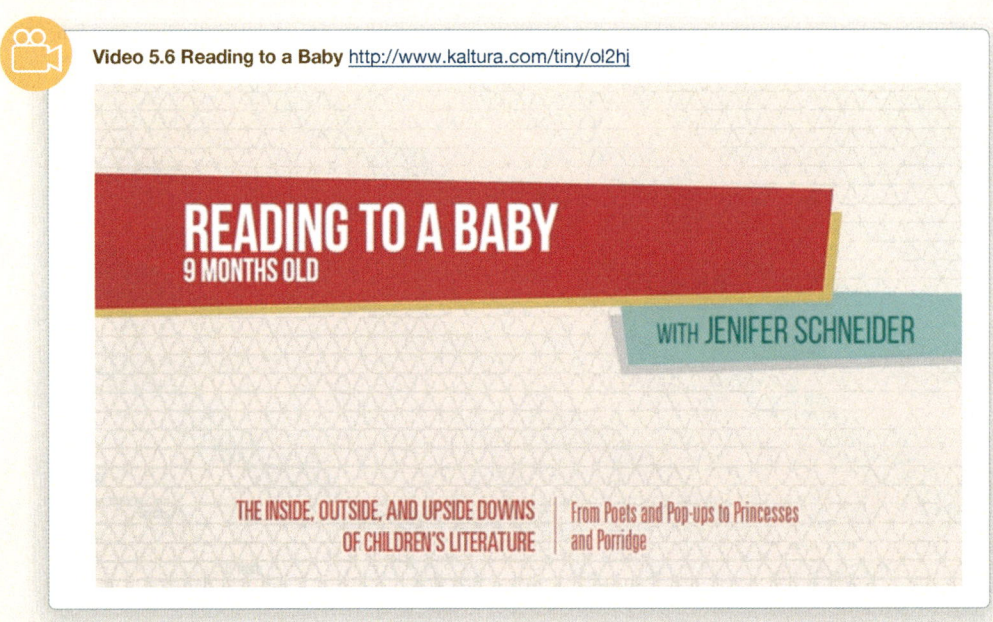

Video 5.6 Reading to a Baby http://www.kaltura.com/tiny/ol2hj

READING TO A BABY
9 MONTHS OLD

WITH JENIFER SCHNEIDER

THE INSIDE, OUTSIDE, AND UPSIDE DOWNS OF CHILDREN'S LITERATURE | From Poets and Pop-ups to Princesses and Porridge

Babies will gnaw on books. That's ok; babies explore the world with their mouths. That's why publishers make baby books. As a parent, I used all forms of baby books, depending on where I was going.

Short List of Recommendations for Babies:

- Soft books for teething time. Soft books are great for quiet places like church or doctor's waiting rooms. Soft books work well for the car seat or in restaurants (Figure 5.57). On a personal note, I loved soft books because my older daughter spit up a lot. Soft books are washable!

- Waterproof books for bath time (also good for the babies who spit up a lot). But they will get moldy inside, so squeeze and sniff for smelly funk.

- Touch and feel books for bedtime.

- Board books for the stroller.

- Baby books are great because they are small, the pictures and text match, the images are clear, and babies can hold them.

- Sandra Boynton has wonderful board books (Figure 5.58).

- I love anything with Sesame Street characters. Sesame Street publishes lots of board books.

- But babies also need bigger books with more elaborate language and pictures. It's ok if the babies can't "read" them. They will "read" them in their own way by looking, touching, and licking.

- When babies are read to, and someone turns the pages and guides their attention, babies will learn to look at the pictures, follow the pages, and hear the language (which is different than talking).

Figure 5.57
Soft books work well for many reasons. Babies can read, chew, or throw them. *Find the Ball* by Manhattan Toy, nd, Minneapolis, MN. Copyright 2015 by Manhattan Toy Company.

Figure 5.58
Sandra Boynton has collections of board books that feature simple illustrations and funny, rhythmic, and repetitive text. *Moo, Baa, La La La* by Sandra Boynton, 1982, New York, NY: Little Simon. Copyright 1982 by Sandra Boynton.

Warning for parents! Babies are captive. They can't wiggle off a lap and walk away. So parents and caregivers should create the habit of reading while a baby can't bolt. Also, there isn't much "reward" in reading to a newborn baby. Hang in there. Read whatever you like—just keep reading. Make reading a routine (Bath, Bottle, Book, Bed). When you feed a baby, read to a baby.

Bath, Bottle, Book, Bed— When you feed a baby, read to a baby.

Suggestions for others: If you feed a baby, read to a baby. In other words, if you work in industries that deal with food, food products, or baby products (e.g., infant formula development, engineering baby products, grocery stores, food banks, homeless shelters, social work, healthcare), keep this motto in mind. How could your business or industry educate families about the importance of baby books?

Toddlers

As babies grow into toddlers, they will develop a general sense of how books work if they see how books work. That is, they learn that books are read from front to back, top to bottom, and left to right. Adults have to show them how (Video 5.7).

 Kids don't learn to read by osmosis. Remember, reading is a human creation. Book reading is shaped, just like talking and walking.

Video 5.7 Reading with a Toddler http://www.kaltura.com/tiny/mg2he

When toddlers read books with their parents, they learn that squiggly black lines (text) carry the messages on each page, telling the reader what to say. It's an amazing phenomenon to toddlers, and they will ask for the same book over and over and over again. When children ask for the same book, just read it. I know it's annoying, but get over it. Here's why.

 You exhibit the same annoying behavior when you incessantly listen to your favorite songs or watch reruns of your favorite shows.

- If adults read the same book over and over again, toddlers learn that the message stays exactly the same every single time. In other words, print has lasting power.

    Think about how comforting that may seem to a toddler. In a world full of information and different experiences every day, sameness and routine are comforting.

- When a toddler hears the same book over and over again, he or she is matching the spoken words to the text. The child will start to remember the story and the words.

    This is when many parents will say, "She's not really reading." Trust me, she is reading. When she says dada, she's talking, right?

- Reading the same book helps the child gain a sense of story and begin to understand the structure of the rhetorical presentation (depending on the book's purpose).

- The child is making predictions and watching them come true, over and over again. The child is feeling smart. This is rewarding, motivating, and enjoyable—all things needed for a child to become a reader.

Short List of Recommendations for Toddlers:

- Dr. Seuss' Beginner Books Series is fantastic. The stories are clever. The language is predictable in some books. In fact, many of Dr. Seuss' beginner books were written with the same 100 words to facilitate children's learning (Figure 5.59).

Figure 5.59
Dr. Seuss' Beginner Books have repetitive, rhyming language that is easy for toddlers to memorize. Excerpt from *Hop on Pop* by Dr. Seuss, 1963, New York, NY: Random House. Copyright renewed 1991 by Dr. Seuss Enterprises L.P.

  Some people don't like the Berenstain Bears. I do. They are the book version of TV sitcoms—goofy characters and repetitive plots.

- The Berenstain Bears books are also excellent for toddlers with simple phrases, rhymes, and repetition.

Rhyming books are perfect for toddlers. The rhythm and rhyme will help children remember the words; and remembering is a sign of reading.

  Remembering is a sign of reading.

- Interactive books are important as well. I'm not talking about elaborate pop-ups, but peek-a-boo type books create suspense and playfulness around reading.

- I love anything with Sesame Street characters for this age as well. I think Sesame Street does a great job with their books (Figure 5.60).

Figure 5.60
Elmo is a favorite, recognizable character. This lift the flap book features letters, characters, and labels. *Sesame Street: Elmo's ABC Lift-the-Flap* by Sesame Street, 2014, New York, NY: Reader's Digest. Copyright 2014 by Sesame Street.

THE RIGHT BOOK FOR THE RIGHT READER AT THE RIGHT TIME
(LITERARY ANALYSIS, QUALITY, AND DEVELOPMENT PERSPECTIVES)

Warning for parents! Toddlers are not captive. They will wiggle off a lap and run away. It's ok. Don't take it personally. And don't give up. Don't ever give up! One minute of reading is better than no minutes. Make book reading enjoyable. Choose books that the child will love. But also choose books that you love. Make reading a routine (Bath, Brush (teeth), Book, Bed). If the child won't sit on your lap, then read the book aloud in the same room where he or she can hear you while playing. Read the book to another family member. Do anything to draw attention to the importance and enjoyment of the event.

Make a reading routine (Bath, Brush (teeth), Book, Bed).

 I'm not above bribery. "Hey, do you want to have some cookies when we read our book tonight?" Make it Bath, Biscuit, Brush, Book, Bed!

Suggestions for others: Toddlers do not sit still. They need to move. How could your business or industry incorporate movement into literacy events? For example, many malls have play spaces for young children, but I haven't seen any with books. If you work in industries that deal with toys, children's programming, or educational products, is there a place for books, play, and movement?

Young Children

Young children can exhibit many of the same preferences and behaviors as toddlers (Video 5.8). They may wiggle away and prefer to play rather than read. They may enjoy reading books over and over again or they may like reading a different book each day.

> If a child is 5 or 6 and raised in a home of daily reading, the parents have read aloud approximately 2000 times. It gets old. If you are responsible for reading to young children, read books that you like. Enthusiasm for reading is as important as the quality of the text. Don't give up!
>
> And if you are a parent and you gave up, start again. It's never too late.

Video 5.8 Reading with Young Children http://www.kaltura.com/tiny/k4ktd

The best thing to do for young children is to vary the selection of books to get their attention. Alternatively, you may have to read the same book over and over to get their attention.

Short List of Recommendations for Young Children:

- Predictable books with a strong picture and text match are ideal for young children. Books from Eric Carle, Donald Crews, Molly Bang, and Lois Ehlert are excellent choices.

- Many Dr. Seuss books are elaborate with detailed stories (e.g., *Horton Hears a Who; The Lorax*). Toddlers can't sit still through a long Dr. Seuss book, but young children can. The language is interesting and some of the vocabulary is made up. When you come across funny words, play with the pronunciation and tone.

- I like funny books. So do young children. Check out the books on the Sid Fleishman Humor Award list. http://www.scbwi.org/awards/sid-fleischman-award/.

- The Ted Geisel Award is given to books that are perfectly suited for young, emergent readers. http://www.ala.org/alsc/awardsgrants/bookmedia/geiselaward

- Anything by Maurice Sendak. Wild Things. Enough said.

- Some classics include:
    - Arnold Lobel—Frog and Toad;
    - Richard Scarry—Busy books (Figure 5.61);
    - Rosemary Wells—Max and Ruby, Sophie, Yoko, Nora.

Figure 5.61
I loved Richard Scarry as a child. His illustrations were intricate with hidden sub-plots. Excerpt from *What Do People Do All Day?* by Richard Scarry, 1968, New York, NY: Random House. Copyright 1968 by Richard Scarry.

- I also love anything by Mo Willems for this age group. He is funny for kids and funny for adults. He used to work for Sesame Street and he really knows how to write for young children and their grown-ups.

- Henry Cole and Doreen Cronin are also excellent picture book creators for this age group.

- Picture books come in all shapes and sizes. Check out pop-up books. Young children can visit the library and check out several at a time. It's great to have variety.

THE RIGHT BOOK FOR THE RIGHT READER AT THE RIGHT TIME
(LITERARY ANALYSIS, QUALITY, AND DEVELOPMENT PERSPECTIVES)

Warning for parents! Early reading is not a sign of giftedness. Late reading is not a sign of developmental delays. I used to teach first grade. I have two children of my own. I've been a literacy professor for almost 20 years. I promise—early readers are not necessarily gifted. Early readers are children with book experience. Now, that's not to say that lots of exposure to books and having conversations about the content isn't an intervening factor in a student's success. It most certainly is. But do not fret if your child is a late reader. Also, don't call Harvard if your child is reading at the age of 2 or 3. Early reading gives a child an advantage with the start of school, but many other factors come into play along the way.

Suggestions for others: Programs like Accelerated Reader, which level books and administer computerized tests, claim to be effective; but research indicates that external motivators can have a negative impact (Cox, 2012; Huang, 2012 Schaffner, Schiefele, & Ulferts, 2013). Asking students to take a test after every book is not fun. In fact, it's counter to the purposes of reading. Assigning a reading level and telling kids to read books that are coded to that level, is also demotivating. Books should be selected based on children's interests. Competing with others to read more books? That works for a very small minority of highly competitive people. Plus, those of you with knowledge of psychology know that competition is no way to motivate a reader. If you work in computer programming or product development, keep developmental issues in mind when your company develops software. Reading isn't a race.

On Lexiles and reading competitions: I know, you competitive types disagree. But remember, not everyone is like you. Why in the world would anyone read to earn dots, jelly beans, or pizzas. It makes no sense. There is no immediate reward. Also, how do jelly beans, dots, and awards connect to the author's or illustrator's purpose for creating the book? They don't.

Teachers, the world is full of people who say that the only thing that got them (or their child) reading was Captain Underpants or Harry Potter. They recall books with memorable characters, funny or moving plotlines, and shared experiences with friends. I have yet to hear any adult recall fond memories of books with dots and Lexiles (https://lexile.com/). That's a teacher thing; not a reader thing. Please, know the difference. Yes, you need to find a kid's reading level to provide instruction that isn't too hard or too easy, but don't let Lexiles and levels undermine the benefits of reading choice. If a kid knows his or her Lexile, but hates reading, YOU get an F-.

Older Children

Once children can read on their own, parents and teachers often abandon the read aloud routine. Parenting is exhausting and relentless. Adults have so many other things to do. But reading aloud is essential throughout a child's developmental years.

> My daughters laugh about the times when I fell asleep mid-sentence. Or when they were annoyed because I read the same sentence over and over again (because I was sleepy). And they don't even know about the times when I chose to read the shortest book on the shelf. I get it. You don't have to be perfect. Just don't give up.

Here's why. Reading time can be bonding time. Books allow parents to discuss topics that may not come up during the regular normal routine (Video 5.9). The same is true for teachers during the school day.

Reading aloud offers children exposure to many different books and linguistic styles. If parents or teachers read aloud books on topics of their choice, then the child will be exposed to those books.

Children can comprehend a larger vocabulary than what they can produce. When children are read to, adults expose them to new words and concepts they won't get on their own.

Video 5.9 Reading with Young Children http://www.kaltura.com/tiny/ng9aq

Parents also use book reading to introduce children to cultural connections and they reinforce language learning.

In addition, older children like to read about people and places that are different from their own lives. They especially enjoy topics that are interesting, scary, and often inappropriate in the eyes of parents and teachers. I say, let them read. Let them read what they want. Let them read above and below their reading "level." Let them read how they want, where they want, and when they want.

Short List of Recommendations for Older Children:

- Older children will venture out to find their own preferences. Most kids love book series like *Diary of a Wimpy Kid* by Jeff Kinney or *Captain Underpants* by Dav Pilkey.

- Picture books are not only acceptable, they are encouraged! Older readers should certainly continue to read picture books. Good choices are anything by Jon Scieszka and Lane Smith, Chris Van Allsburg (Figure 5.62), and Patricia Pollacco.

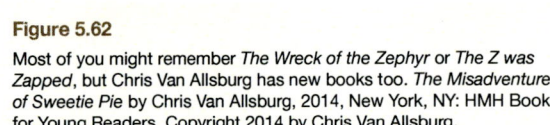

Figure 5.62
Most of you might remember *The Wreck of the Zephyr* or *The Z was Zapped*, but Chris Van Allsburg has new books too. *The Misadventures of Sweetie Pie* by Chris Van Allsburg, 2014, New York, NY: HMH Books for Young Readers. Copyright 2014 by Chris Van Allsburg.

- You might see a spike in information book reading in older children. Kids like to learn about the world. This is the age where obsessions begin to develop—horses, video games, sports, dogs, cats, music, etc. Go with it. You might even try reading some aloud. Imagine what your kids would think if you read about farts.

- Graphic novels are excellent forms of literature for all children.

- Many children like to read stories about urban youth. Authors like G. Neri, and Jacqueline Woodson (Figure 5.63) create modern, relevant books for a variety of readers.

Figure 5.63
Jacqueline Woodson writes about Lonnie, a boy in foster care who finds hope through poetry. *Locomotion* by Jacqueline Woodson, 2003, New York, NY: G.P. Putnam & Sons. Copyright 2003 by Jacqueline Woodson.

- Older children also enjoy series books. This is the age to start reading *Harry Potter*.

- This is also the age to start learning about the world through a more critical lens. Books by Lois Lowry and Katherine Paterson will provide exposure to a broad range of topics through excellent stories and beautiful writing.

Warning for Parents! This is the age when children encounter intervening effects of school—good and bad teachers, good and bad friends, good and bad books, good and bad reading habits. I see nothing wrong with "bad" books, but you have to make the call for your own child (see banned books chapter.) You will have to make the call on the good and bad friends as well. Here are a few strategies to support young adolescents' reading habits.

- *Barter tech time for reading time. In other words, if they read x minutes, then they get x minutes to game, chat, text or whatever.*

- *Alternate reading aloud. Older kids start to play sports, join clubs, and have social lives. You might find it difficult to read aloud every night so alternate reading aloud with reading on their own.*

- *Get audiobooks for the car. If you commute to school or sports, play audiobooks. OK, so they aren't "reading" the text, but they are hearing the stories or information. When you know books, you make more connections.*

Suggestions for others: Unlike books for babies or toddlers, older children know how books work and they take care of them for the most part. Therefore, books can be "littered" in many spaces beyond a library and bookstore. I think it's an incredible waste of opportunity when I visit doctors' and dentists' offices and there aren't any books for kids. There are many spaces in which books could replace televisions. Can you think of any? If not, use some ideas from Little Free Library (http://littlefreelibrary.org).

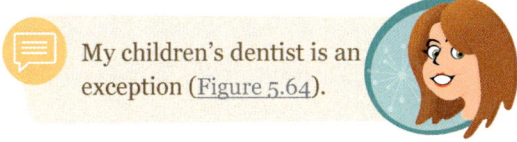

My children's dentist is an exception (Figure 5.64).

Figure 5.64

My daughters' dentist, Dr. Gerald Copeland, is an exception—his office has a large selection of books for children of all ages. He also has an extensive array of interesting magazines of all types. He invests in his patients' literacy and he is thoughtful about parent, child, and teen wait time. Photo copyright 2015 by Jenifer Schneider.

Young Adults

Young adults have varied interests. They read across many genres including biography, history, military history, science, mythology, video games, celebrities, current events, fan fiction, realistic fiction, outdoor, TV shows, and teens (Moeller & Becnel, 2015).

In good schools, with enterprising teachers, students are encouraged to join book clubs and other forums for reading and sharing literature. I know one AP English teacher, in a public high school, who created an LGBT Book Club during lunch. All students in the school were invited and about 30 students showed up to talk about books. Why can't parents have book clubs at home?

  I try to read the same books as my children so we can talk about them.

A popular genre for teens is urban literature or street lit. Different than multicultural literature which often depicts characters of color in a variety of settings, urban or street literature is set in lower-income, city neighborhoods (Morris, 2012). Organizations such as *Kids Like Us* (http://www.kidslikeus.org) and *Street Literature* (http://www.streetliterature.com/) promote urban literature for children in city schools. Young adults from all backgrounds enjoy reading street lit.

  I never read *Treasure Island* as a kid. But when my daughter read it in 7th grade, she asked me to read it so we could talk about it!

In the young adult years, books can serve as a social conduit, bringing teens and adults together. Young adults also engage with authors and illustrators through social networking and fan clubs. Another hallmark of young adults is an interest in fanfiction.

Short List of Recommendations for Young Adults:

- Young adults love edgy, authentic writing. Some of their favorite authors are:

  - John Green
  - Neil Gaiman
  - J.K. Rowling
  - Philip Pullman (Figure 5.65)
  - Cassandra Clare
  - Susan Cooper
  - Lauren Oliver

- Also, young adults are still reading the same books you read in high school. If there are books you loved, there are kids who will read them today.

  - *The Outsiders* by S.E. Hinton
  - *Treasure Island* by Robert Louis Stevenson
  - *The Chocolate War* by Robert Cormier
  - *The Hobbit/The Lord of the Rings* trilogy by J.R.R. Tolkien
  - *The Princess Diaries* by Meg Cabot

- Many picture books are targeted at young adults. Intricate picture books, along with graphic novels, combine art and text. Don't think about picture books as baby books. Think of them as fine art coupled with short stories or graphic representations of current information.

Figure 5.65
Edgy and authentic are two words that describe Philip Pullman's books. For example, *His Dark Materials* are best selling books that continue to be read by new generations. The 20th anniversary edition of *Northern Lights* was published in 2015. *Northern Lights (His Dark Materials)* by Philip Pullman, 1995, London, England: Scholastic UK. Copyright 1995 by Philip Pullman.

> *Warning for parents! Stay open to changes in expertise. When children are young, parents guide their choices in books. When children reach middle and high school, they get recommendations from friends, teachers, librarians, social networks, and websites. Maintain literary connections with children—even when they are grown.*

Also, as children develop into young adults, many people assume they don't read paper copies of books because young adults read on the computer or on e-reader devices. Young adults read on the computer or on e-reader devices. This is true for many, but not for all. Many young adults continue to prefer paper-bound books.

> Suggestions for others: As mentioned above, doctors' and dentists' offices tend to provide limited numbers and poor quality books for children to read. But when it comes to young adults, they are completely ignored! When was the last time you saw young adult reading material in a waiting room, airport, or train station? Newspapers and magazines are prevalent, but how about thinking outside the box? Young adults have more sophisticated reading tastes, but they don't have time to complete a novel during a doctor's visit. Alternative reading sources include graphic novels, manga and anime, and elaborate information books. If you work in a business or industry where people wait, linger, or shop, consider young adults' interests.

Book Recommendation Services

There is a lot to consider when choosing a book for a reader. If it feels overwhelming, you can always go the computer-programming route and have an algorithm choose a book for you. Just like vehicle recommender programs and dog matching quizzes, there are book recommender services that take into account several factors such as the reader's age, interests, favorite books, etc. Unlike data analytics software, such as the programs used by Amazon, other reader programs use the information you provide rather than previous purchase data. On the surface, the idea seems better suited to book selection practices since the user (reader) provides the information. For example, Amazon often gives me false results because I don't necessarily like every book I buy and I don't always look for books I want. However, many of the recommendation services target adults and the book information is only as accurate as the person who read and coded the keywords to describe the book.

In any case, here are a few book selection sites:

- Whichbook (http://www.openingthebook.com/whichbook/)

- What Should I Read Next? (http://www.whatshouldireadnext.com/)

- Your Next Read (http://www.yournextread.com/us/)

 Recommendation Services are Internet dating sites for book selection.

Question #4: How do we judge the overall product to know what works?

At the beginning of this chapter, I discussed the modes of discourse in children's literature and I reviewed criteria to analyze particular texts. Then I discussed the impact of family literacy events and emphasized the type, quality, and quantity of experiences a child can have with books. Now, let's get back to the books.

Know Your Criteria: Comparison Shop

Choosing books is like buying a car: some of it's rigged (by publishers), some of it's luck, and everyone is happy if there's a match. First, in choosing books, your priority must be the reader. Your priorities and interpretation of the criteria will change depending on whether you are you selecting books for yourself, or a toddler, or a 9th grader. Second, you have to know the books. Do some research and become familiar with books. Read—a lot! Third, make a guess. Of course it's not a shot in the dark. Your guess is based on knowledge.

Preview the Book: Take a Test Drive and Don't Fall for Gimmicks

The "match" extends beyond the child and the books. You have to consider the family as well. Will the parents support the book purchase? Will parents be the primary readers or will they object to the content? Drew Magary (2012) wrote a funny article with advice for parents about reading books to kids. He offered 10 tips for avoiding terrible books. You should read the whole article for his commentary (if you don't mind a lot of cursing). Here's a nutshell version of his advice:

1. Check for length and textual density. Long books are "medieval torture devices."
2. Make sure the text rhymes. Rhyming is more fun.
3. Avoid one-trick ponies. Too formulaic.
4. Avoid repetitive books. Too annoying.
5. Do not buy fancy pop-up books. Too tedious.
6. Buy any book that features textures (e.g. Pat the Bunny). Fun and quick.
7. Do not buy any Amelia Bedelia books. She's too stupid.
8. NEVER buy a DK reader book. Written by a "corporate spambot."
9. Never buy any book that's a movie or TV tie-in. It's like buying an advertisement.
10. Never buy a children's book written by a celebrity. Epic fails.

Of course I don't agree with everything listed, but Magary's advice is written from a parent's perspective and that could be very helpful to you.

 I disagree with 5. Pop ups are great.

And I also disagree with any of the other suggestions if the child is the one who is choosing. Now, parents don't have to read the books they don't like, but if the kid wants it, then I buy it or check it out. There are too many non-reader, alliterate people to play around with a child's motivation to read.

 Yes, I'm a parent, but I'm a parent with a literacy obsession.

Bottom line: Preview the book and look for the elements you expect. You can preview books online and in the library or bookstore. It's called browsing. Visit sites such as Goodreads.com or Pinterest.com and search for books that match your criteria.

Know Your Financing Options: Library or Bookstore? Print or eBook?

When you select a book, you have to know *a lot* about *a lot* of things. In addition to thinking about the mode of discourse (e.g., narration, information, description, or argumentation), you need to think about the genres because they blend and share rhetorical and visual purposes. You have to know the authors and illustrators—there are thousands from which to choose. And you have to phrase your response in the form of a question—what would the reader want? Given there is as much art as there is science in the process of book selection, you need to think about the long-term use of the book. Do you think the book will be read again and again? Will it become a favorite? Or, is the book for a short-term purpose such as a school report, a life event (starting school/college/a new job), or does the book feature a topic with a short life span (e.g., a biography of the latest boy band)?

Ask Around

Ultimately, if you want to select the right book for the right reader at the right time—ask the reader! They have opinions and they know good books. If they don't know "good," they know what they like; and therein lies the answer.

*An Opinionated Journey through Children's Literature
Through the Eyes and Mind of an Almost Teenager*

By: Mary Schneider

Children have many different ideas of entertainment—from sports stories to science fiction to fantasy. The authors of books need to adjust the language of their writing to fit the interests of the audience.

Part 1: Fiction Books

Sports books. An obvious example would be a sporty book. The author might use slang or simpler words. Sports are not really labeled as a place to learn or fantasize. Children reading this type of book will most likely be reading it for the sport. They would choose a book that represents a sport of their liking. One where the focus is on the sport, not the players. The topic of almost every conversation would be about the sport. The point is, the audience of sports books are in it to read about the sport, and maybe a basic heartwarming story about a disabled player or the underdog team in a town. They are not in it as much for the highly intelligent and complicated plot line. Sports books should be an easy read. Not a book for toddlers, but simple and straight forward.

Science fiction. Another example would be sci-fi books. Sci-fi books should have a plot line that makes sense, but have multiple branches. Almost like mini-plots. Sci-fi books should also contain a few facts that blend into the story and make logical sense. Not like a nonfiction book, but also not like a fantasy novel. Take the science fiction show *Doctor Who* for example. (If you are unfamiliar with this television series, then take *Star Wars* or *Star Trek* as another example.) Although it is not a novel, it is the perfect example of a would-be amazing sci-fi book. The main character is a Time-Lord, which is a species from a different planet and different Galaxy. It provokes the audience to think deeply. It provokes wonder, and that infamous question: What if? What if there really is a world out there filled with creatures like this? What if there was actually a war going on in a different galaxy? A war between some of the most powerful beings in the cosmos? What if a few of them walk among us, tricking us into believing that they are one of us? What if there is a place on Earth that acts as a substitute for the notorious area 51? No one knows, but there are many theories in the form of Science Fiction novels, because that is what they are about. Science fiction novels induce a sense of wonder and questioning. They pull the reader in and make them think deeply through a series of events connected to create a complicated yet enthralling plot.

When writing a sci-fi book the author should be caught up on their facts. Science Fiction authors are more committed to logic than fiction authors, but they can still create brilliant imaginary plots that have some facts in them. Like in *Doctor Who*, they harness the stability and power of the space-time continuum and manipulate it by using highly advanced technology to do their bidding. This may seem like a form of magic to some, but this is really just highly advanced technology that was made possible by an advanced species. The authors must always be creative.

Fantasy. Then there is Fantasy. Fantasy does not have to be logical. Fantasy includes books and series such as *Harry Potter*, *Twilight*, and *Percy Jackson*, etc. These books pull the reader into a world filled with magic, mystery, excitement, and adventure. The characters are whimsical, mysterious, and interesting. These worlds can abandon reason almost completely. Fantasy books can range from something like the *Hunger Games* which could possibly happen in the future, and contains only technical and manual activities, supplies, and happenings, to a series such as *Harry Potter*, which could not happen, and is filled almost completely with magical doings. Fantasy books are kind of like Sci-fi books, because of the fact that they should be enthralling and slightly complicated. They are unlike sci-fi books because they do not really provoke many deep questions. They may provoke some, but not ones like the "What if" question. These books are more meant to entertain the reader, and to unleash their imagination. These books enable the reader to wander a world unknown. And connect with the characters and their adventures.

When writing fantasy books the author might use a large vocabulary, create an intricate plot, and intelligent characters. Multiple events create a chain reaction that makes the book. Fantasy books are not really meant for a level 1 reader, so the author would be able to fill the pages with intelligent language and intelligently interesting events. The author should fill the book with action and adventure, along with some mysterious and mystical events, because that is what keeps the reader interested. The more time spent building up for the event the more the world that the audience is in fades. By this I mean that the transitions between the heartwarming, action-packed, hysterical, suspenseful, and tragic scenes should be quick: just a page or two that lets the reader catch their breath and get filled in on the happenings. Not every event has to be the extreme of one or two emotions, though. There can still be calm points, but they still have to be interesting. One basic calm point would be the aftermath of an extremely suspenseful event, or an ordinary day or activity in the life of the main character. These happenings are not necessarily exciting, but it gives the reader some insight into what the main characters are really like. These moments are extremely necessary because if the entire book was one big climax, then the reader would become confused and lost. A book that is all one note, whether that note is suspenseful or boring, is never a good read.

Audience. So, basically, when the author begins to write a book, they should determine their audience. This is an instruction coming all the way from elementary school, but this is a very important one indeed. The type of audience is not just a matter of age or gender, but of interests. If the author chooses to create a sporty novel, then the reader will most likely be a sporty person, or at least a person that enjoys watching sports. While they may enjoy reads from other genres, they chose the sports novel to read about sports, not to get engaged in some intricate plot. Science fiction novels would be for a person who enjoys science to some degree, and someone who is able to think critically. Fantasy is for the reader just looking to be entertained and get away for a while. There will always be the extremely intelligent and scientific lover of sports. Just because they are intelligent does not mean that they are always looking for an advanced piece of literature. The author is always writing for a specific person in a specific mood, whether they know this or not. Authors are taught from a young age to first determine their audience. To many, this means a specific kind of person, and they should always write like they are reading the book in the mind of that one specific reader. This, however, could be a fatal flaw to many novels. People reading sports novels are not always dumb jocks. Throwing some science, math, or another more advanced topic into the book is not a bad idea, just like adding a little bit of sports into a Fantasy book is a good idea. Take Quidditch as an example. J.K. Rowling added sports into her novels, and made it a big thing. This way someone who loves sports would get a little taste of sports within the Fantasy novel. It widens the range of audience members for the book.

Relatable action. Another thing that makes novels interesting to kids would be the author injecting something that they can relate to into the book. Maybe there is a bully that uses verbal insults or practical jokes to bring down the protagonist ("ahem" Draco), or the stress of finding a date or having to look pretty all of the time, exams, grades, competitions, friends, and etc. If the main character is an adult, then the author might make him or her out to be a person that either is trying to find a date, or has trouble with their girlfriend or wife, because there is not really much that a child has to relate to an adult. The more the main characters are similar to the reader, the deeper the felt connection is, and the deeper the connection is, the more the reader enjoys the book.

Part 2: Nonfiction

Nonfiction books are often dreaded by children. For me, they are the last resorts as I mainly use them for reports and research projects. Nonfiction books are very necessary and very helpful when it comes to research projects, and I am sure that there are many people who read them for recreation, but basically every single average teenager or child I know would not read a nonfiction book for fun (except my sister). I hate to be the one to say this, but the sad truth is that nonfiction books are just not that fun to read.

> I love her, but I totally disagree with Mary on this one. What you have here is a matter of opinion and preference—which is the whole point of this chapter. You have to match the right book to the right reader at the right time.
>
> Mary's point is a good one and her experience is indicative of the instructional choices of her teachers. If nonfiction books are read as encyclopedias and children must hunt and peck for information in order to regurgitate it accurately, then they will not enjoy reading nonfiction. If, however, nonfiction books are used to explore a topic and if well-written nonfiction books are used to entice reading, then they can be engaging.

Animal books. However, some books are better than others. Most class reports now are about animals, technology, or history. The basic information needed for practically every project on animals nowadays would be: Where are they found? Are they endangered? How many are there on Earth (approximately)? What is the species' scientific name? What are the animal's basic predators and prey? What effect do humans have on this species? And finally, what are at least three interesting facts about this species? When writing a nonfiction book about a specific species, the author should put most of this information into the manuscript. If not, the book will most likely only frustrate the reader.

Biography questions. Some questions asked constantly about current technologies are: How does it work? When was it invented? Who invented it? How old were they? Do they have any other inventions? What was their childhood like? How did this invention affect humans? What are the pros and cons of this invention? How much does the human race depend on this invention? What effect does it have on the environment? Much of the information used to create reports on technologies is either about the inventor or the effect that the invention itself had on the environment and on the human race. Strangely enough, teachers do not ask for much information on the actual technology.

Historical biographies and important questions. The questions constantly asked about people in history are: Who are they? What place did he or she have in society? What did the person do, have, or invent to become well known and remembered? In what era did he or she live? What year was the person born? What was the name of his or her spouse and children, if he or she had any? What year did this person die? Where did the person live? How did he or she get to be where they were when the person died? What are two or three important things that he or she did in his or her life? When did he or she do these things? And finally, once again, what are a few interesting facts about this person?

Many times, historic figures create a lot of headaches for students, because of all of the dates, accomplishments, and names of acquaintances and relatives that need to be included as well. The more packed with important information a biography is, the more helpful the book would be to a student.

History questions. Some questions commonly asked about events in history are: When did this event occur? What led to it? Why did this happen? Who participated in this event? What effect did it have on the future? What effect did it have on the people of that era? What are the pros and cons of this event occurring? Has this event had a lasting impression on the way things function? Why or Why not? Was this an international affair? There are normally fewer questions asked about events on reports because all that can really be asked is: How? When? Where? What? Why? And Who? The basics. There really isn't a way to embellish these questions, to add information. What you see is what you get. However, because there is not much more than the basics, the author must be sure to include everything. One piece of forgotten information will decrease the likeliness of a student reading the book and using the information.

If these questions are asked and answered, along with a few more extra facts, the nonfiction book will be very helpful to students, and it will be more likely to be bought by schools and libraries for their students.

Important features. When looking for nonfiction books for projects, students will most likely look for three main features. These features are pictures, level of detail, and citations.

Pictures. On most research projects, the child will most likely need pictures. Therefore, the author should include multiple pictures. These pictures should be placed in the corners of the pages to leave the maximum amount of space for the actual information. The child will most likely also need a few random facts, so when writing a nonfiction book, the author would need to be sure to add some seemingly unnecessary information, because to the child reading the book, those few sentences could make or break their paper or presentation. However, one would need to balance this out. If the author fills the book with more random facts than basic and important information, then the reader will have to sort through the information to get what they need, which is not helpful.

Balancing length, detail, and reading level. Research projects are normally done in a short amount of time in a span of 1 ½ to 2 weeks. Because of this, the students would need a shorter book, but one that has all the necessary information and is written for their grade level. For students in the fifth, sixth, and even seventh grades, there is a shortage of books that can be used for most research projects. Many books are either too short, lacking in information, and written for a younger student; too long with too much information and written for an older student; just the right length but too much random information; and then there is the glorious book that has just the right number of facts, written for the middle school level, and only takes about fifteen minutes to read. The other types of books are necessary, but there is an excess of them, and a shortage of middle school level books. There is a very distinct balance of information to length to reading level that makes a nonfiction book interesting and worth reading. When writing this type of book, the author must always pay attention to this balance.

Citations. One problem that comes up constantly is the citations. Many times citations take up much of the time spent on creating the project, because the information is so hard to find sometimes. Some books have the information needed to create a citation separated between the cover, the back, and the front. If the author takes the extra few steps to either make sure that all of the basic information needed for citations, such as dates, publication companies, names, and addresses are all in the same place, or creates a citations page in the book, students will be that much more likely to pick up the book.

CHAPTER 06 | THE READING WARS

(CHILDREN'S LITERATURE AND THE INTERVENING EFFECTS OF SCHOOL AND POLITICS)

A child's literacy development and literary interests are interconnected. One doesn't precede the other; they work in tandem. In other words, children don't learn to read and then choose interesting books as a result; they learn to read because they have the right books and someone to guide and encourage them. Good reading begets reading. Sure, a child can learn some of the components of reading by completing worksheets and playing with phonics apps, but how do you define reading?

I can learn aspects of playing Cricket by watching YouTube videos and taking a vocabulary test on Cricket terms. But am I playing Cricket? If I swing the bat and toss the ball to myself in my living room, I might learn Cricket skills, but am I playing Cricket? I can only learn to play Cricket by playing the game—the real game. Yes, I need to learn skills and strategies for fielding and batting, but none of those are worthwhile if I don't feel like I'm getting better at Cricket. It's all about the game. Therefore, my development as a player is interconnected with my opportunities to play and my increasing acquisition of skills and strategies that motivate me to practice and succeed.

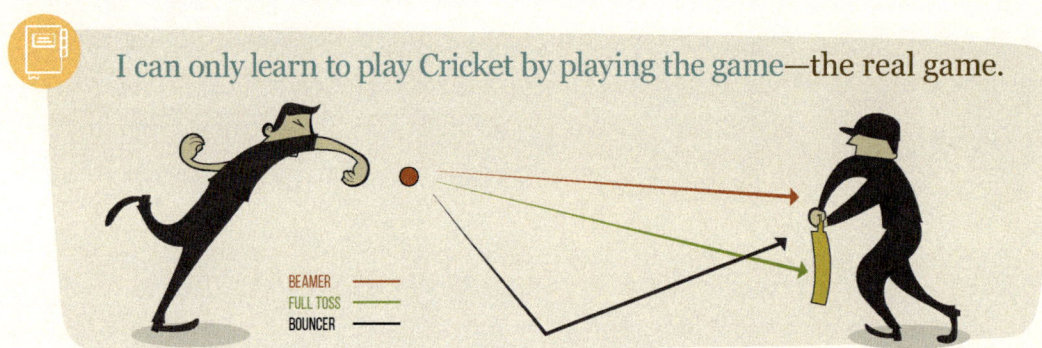

I can only learn to play Cricket by playing the game—the real game.

Just like with anything in life, the more one practices, the better one gets, especially with better coaching and training. More importantly, one must be motivated to perform and motivation comes from feelings of success, enjoyment, and accomplishment. The same is true for reading.

Motivation is a key factor in reading. Watch this video about a child who loved to read so much he used junk mail to practice reading (http://www.huffingtonpost.com/entry/boy-asks-mailman-junk-mail-books-read_55b6b002e4b0224d88338ba4)

As revealed in the previous chapter, a child's literacy experiences at home can have a tremendous impact on the child's developmental and academic trajectory. Children can come to school with thousands of hours of literacy experiences or with very few. Children from high-poverty homes, where there is little food, inconsistent healthcare, and inadequate shelter, rarely have parents with the time and resources to provide thousands of hours of literacy experiences. This is one way poverty negatively impacts literacy rates. Similarly, children from affluent homes can come to school with extensive screen time, but they may have had very few hours of quality interactions around books. Fostering reading is a matter of time, attention, books, and knowing what to do.

> I want to be perfectly clear—poor parents love their children. Poverty affects the amount of time, attention, and resources parents can devote to visits to the library, reading for pleasure, and monitoring literacy development. The effects of poverty have nothing to do with love, care, and concern. Affluent parents also love their children, but many people incorrectly assume that a reading app on a smartphone can replace lap time. It can't.

According to the International Reading Association (2005):

> Based on the best research evidence, access to appropriate, high-quality early language and literacy experiences will enhance young children's development. The preschool curriculum, therefore, should emphasize a wide range of language and literacy experiences including, but not limited to, story reading, dramatic play, storytelling, and retelling.

School is important, and after 100+ years of systematic research, the field of literacy studies knows a lot about reading instruction and the role of children's literature. However, along the way, politics, funding, and the court of public opinion have had a tremendous impact on reading as well.

> Good reading experiences beget good reading, but there are some kids who won't like to read no matter what you do. For those kids, read to them. It's better for a child to hear reading than to experience no reading at all.

In the following sections, I provide a quick review of some of the trends in reading instruction over the last 50 years. Why? Because the way in which your adult relatives were taught to read impacted the ways in which they shared books with you. The ways in which you were taught to read at home and school impacted your perceptions of reading and your exposure to books throughout your lifetime. And your experiences with books will impact your interactions with the next generation.

Beliefs and practices are inherited within families and further shaped by cultural expectations and social practices. School, as the ultimate shape-shifter, becomes an intervening factor.

 What year were you born? As you read this section, place yourself and your parents/guardians in the context of the reading instruction they received and think about how you were taught to read at home and at school.

The Reading Wars

Although the field of reading has amassed a strong body of research about the reading process and the effects of instructional strategies, there is no single path to reading achievement and no single instructional approach to get there. As a result, researchers study approach reading from different theoretical orientations, resulting in different views about the impact of the cognitive, social, physical, emotional, cultural, and text-based components of reading. The result—the reading wars—a time when researchers duked it out over books, words, letters and sounds.

The Reading Wars

Reading Readiness and Phonics

Prior to the 1970s, most "reading" instruction occurred in the primary grades. Getting "ready" to read was the reading method of choice as young children were first taught the alphabet (Figure 6.1), then phonics, followed by sight words, phrases, and controlled sentences (Singer, 1970).

Figure 6.1
If you were in school in the 60s or 70s, you may have met Mister M with the munching mouth. The Letter People represent a systematic approach to teaching the alphabet letter names and corresponding sounds. A brief history of The Letter People is available at http://www.retrojunk.com/article/show/1448/the-letter-people.

There is nothing wrong with teaching the alphabet and phonics. In fact, they are necessary for solving unknown words. However, teaching the isolated parts before kids get the big picture of the whole book inhibits many kids from understanding how reading makes sense. Plus, learning to read doesn't work in isolated, sequential steps.

Beginning reading instruction in the United States varies along an historically related methodological continuum from emphasis upon decoding print to speech at one end of the continuum to stress upon meaning at the other end of the continuum. The methods involved in this continuum can be categorized into one or the other of the two major classes of learning theories, stimulus-response and cognitive or field theory models (Singer, 1970, p. 25).

A massive investigation of reading programs (Bond & Dykstra, 1967), often referred to as the First-Grade Reading Studies, led to a number of reports and projected paths for classroom practice based on stimulus-response or field theory reading models. Specifically, Bond and Dykstra identified five categories of instructional methods used across the 27 first-grade studies.

- **Conventional basal readers:** Popularized by William S. Gray, basal reading programs used individual student reading books, workbooks, and assessments. The readers were leveled based on increasing complexity of controlled vocabulary (Figure 6.2). Teachers often used flash cards and the look/say method to help students remember whole words (Figure 6.3);

Figure 6.2
Teachers used basal readers, workbook pages, and assessments to teach reading. My elementary school used the Holt Reading Series, and I specifically remember feeling happy when I moved through different levels. *People Need People* by Eldonna L. Evertts, 1973, Holt Basic Reading System Level 9, New York, NY: Holt, Rinehart and Winston. Copyright 1973 by Holt, Rinehart and Winston.

Figure 6.3
Flash cards were a prevalent instructional material for teachers who used basal readers. Image retrieved from https://cdn.shopify.com/s/files/1/0817/7493/files/blog_vintage-flashcards.jpg?2371429416518442553.

- **Phonics-emphasis instructional systems:** Phonics methods focused on matching the letters of the alphabet with specific sounds. According to Bond and Dykstra (1967),

    > Phonics can be further classified as either synthetic or analytic. The synthetic method is based upon the belief that the child should be taught certain letter-sound relationships of word elements before beginning to read and then be taught to synthesize word elements learned into whole words...The analytic method is based upon the belief that children should be taught whole words and then, through various analytic techniques, be taught to apply letter combinations learned in familiar words to sounding out new words (p. 14).

    Phonics-emphasis methods could include "a formidable program of drill on the sounds of letters and letter combinations organized into some kind of 'system' of phonics which was introduced at the beginning of instruction in reading, and usually continued through several elementary school grades" (Gates, 1961, p. 248). Phonics drill-type methods included the Carden method (1949) or the Hay-Wingo method (1954) (Figure 6.4). Less formal word analysis methods were also used.

    Figure 6.4
    Reading with Phonics by Julie Hay and Charles Wingo was a reading series using phonics lessons. The teacher's edition included directions for teaching single sounds, blending, recognizing digraphs, dipthongs, and silent letters, and word lists for practice. Excerpt from *Reading with Phonics* by Julie Hay and Charles Wingo, 1954, Philadelphia, PA: Lippincott. Copyright 1954 by Julie Hay and Charles Wingo.

- **Language Experience Approaches:** In the Language Experience Approach, teachers replaced published texts and controlled-vocabulary passages with their own reading materials that were created through collaborative writing and group dictation. These texts, which were composed in the classroom, were believed to be more motivating because they reflected the students' interests and experiences. The texts were written using the children's oral language levels; therefore, the children should be able to read the texts they wrote and they should be able to develop individualized sight vocabulary. It was expected that the children would learn about letters, syllables, and words through spelling and writing activities (Figure 6.5).

    Figure 6.5
    The Language Experience Approach was based on the development of student-created texts with the intention of helping students learn to read the words they knew and used. The method is described in *The Language Experience Approach to Reading* by Denise D. Nessel and Margaret B. Jones, 1981, New York, NY: Teachers College Press. Photo copyright 2009 by Jenifer Schneider. Click here to see other examples of the method (http://edp1f2012.blogspot.com/2012_03_01_archive.html).

- **Linguistic materials:** The role of grammar came into play as many educators promoted the relationship between reading, oral language, and the structure of sentences. In linguistic methods, lessons could include word recognition activities based on phoneme-grapheme analysis, writing tasks, and structural pattern analysis of reading passages (Figure 6.6).

- **i.t.a.:** Initial teaching alphabet materials were based on a special alphabet consisting of 44 characters representing the basic sound units of spoken English. Lower case letters were used to reduce the number of characters students needed to remember. The i.t.a. was used with the whole-word method, phonics methods, or language experience methods (Figure 6.7).

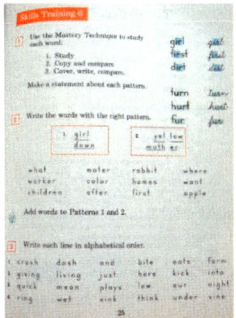

Figure 6.6

Linguistic methods included a focus on grammar and the structure of language. Excerpt from *Patterns and Spelling in Writing* by Morton Botel, Cora Holsclaw, and Aileen Brothers, 1964, Chicago, IL: Follett Publishing Company. Copyright 1964 by Morton Botel, Cora Holsclaw, and Aileen Brothers.

Based on the analysis of the First-Grade Studies, Dykstra (1968) concluded that early phonics instruction is highly related to early success in word recognition and spelling achievement. He stated, " there is some indication that the method by which phonics is taught may not be as important as the fact that direct attention is given to helping the pupil learn sound-symbol relationships" (p. 8). In addition, Dykstra stated that children needed to be taught the letters of the alphabet, and he claimed that reading materials needed some control of vocabulary in relation to sound-symbol correspondence. Interestingly, all of the focus on phonics did not translate into comprehension success; therefore, Dykstra stated that direct instruction in comprehension was essential as well.

Figure 6.7

A basic chart of the Pitman Initial Teaching Alphabet (i.t.a.). The i.t.a. included Roman and Latin characters and it was a semi-phonetic orthography of English mainly intended to make learning to read easier.

The First-Grade Studies were so important in the history of literacy research that John Readance and Diane Barone, editors of *Reading Research Quarterly*, reprinted The First-Grade Studies in 1997. As editors, they also invited retrospectives from Lyn Searfoss and P. David Pearson who are two influential researchers who were involved with the studies as doctoral students. Arlette Willis and Violet Harris were asked to provide their reflections on the First-Grade Studies and to specifically comment on the missing attention to marginalized students.

THE READING WARS
(CHILDREN'S LITERATURE AND THE INTERVENING EFFECTS OF SCHOOL AND POLITICS)

During this time, basal readers and phonics programs were widely used (Figure 6.8). In many schools, children were discouraged from reading whole books until component skills were mastered (Bissett, 1969). Teachers used basal readers that included stories with predictable vocabulary and formulaic plots. They also used leveled reading kits (SRA kits) with controlled reading passages and corresponding quizzes (Figure 6.9). Reading was broken into its component parts and children had to put the pieces together through workbook pages, oral language recitation, and leveled readers.

Figure 6.8
Mrs. Miles (in green) taught me to read in the first grade using reading groups, workbook pages, and SRA kits. She also sang to us, recited poetry every morning and afternoon, taught us how to make Rice Krispy treats, and she took us out to play.

Reading to Learn

Once children entered the intermediate and middle grades, they were expected to already know "how to read" and instruction focused on processing content or "reading to learn." In the intermediate grades, reading instruction focused on disciplinary

Figure 6.9
The SRA Reading Laboratory kits were used extensively in schools. The materials included tests and color-coded levels. I remember working through the books and levels on my own. Image from https://s-media-cache-ak0.pinimg.com/736x/87/a7/aa/87a7aadf278dba630ddc441a1e226442.jpg.

information or content-area reading strategies such as pre-reading, using graphic organizers, and other techniques to help students read textbooks (Moore, Readence, & Rickelman, 1983; Smith & Feathers, 1983; Tierney, 1985).

When students entered high-school they moved into content-area courses and they were no longer "taught" to read. In fact, subject-area teachers resisted the idea that they should teach reading (Dupuis, Askov, & Lee, 1979; Ratekin, Simpson, Alvermann, Dishner, 1985). Literature was for the library. Nonfiction picturebooks were practically non-existent in middle and high schools. Literature instruction was the work of English teachers but the materials were narrowly focused and often racist (Figure 6.10).

Figure 6.10
Literature collections and reading materials were limited in their representation of writers from different races, ethnicities, and genders. *Norton Anthology of English Literature* (3rd Ed.), 1975, New York, NY: Norton & Co. Copyright 1975 Norton & Co.

 Don't you read differently depending on whether you are reading a novel vs. a science textbook vs. a global studies textbook? Of course you do. That's why disciplinary literacies are taught.

In fact, the NCTE was compelled to create a Task Force on Racism and Bias in the Teaching of English that developed criteria for teaching materials in reading and literature (NCTE, 1970)

> Specifically, educational materials now suffer from the following crucial deficiencies: (1) inadequate representation of literary works by members of non-white minorities in general anthologies, (2) representation of minority groups which is demeaning, insensitive, or unflattering to the culture, (3) inclusion of only popular and proven works by a limited number of "acceptable" writers, (4) biased commentaries which gloss over or flatly ignore the oppression suffered by non-white minority persons, and (5) other commentaries in anthologies which depict inaccurately the influence of non-white minority persons on literary, cultural, and historical developments in America. It is recommended that: (1) Literature anthologies commit themselves to fair and balanced inclusion of the work of non-white minority group members; (2) Illustrations and photographs present as accurate and balanced a picture of non-white minorities and their environments as is possible in the total context of the educational materials; (3) Dialect be appropriate to the setting and characters; and (4) Literary criticism draw as heavily as possible from the critical writers of non-white minorities.

NCTE's stand on the content of reading materials marked a shift in the recognition that reading instruction had to account for the reader's interests and life experiences.

Do you think these issues are from long ago? Think again. Look at these reading books, which were purchased by a school district in 2015 (Figure 6.11). Read the full story (https://www.washingtonpost.com/news/morning-mix/wp/2015/09/11/lazy-lucy-and-other-painfully-offensive-racial-stereotypes-lead-a-school-district-to-recall-books/).

Figure 6.11

Racist literature still exists. *An African Fable* by Reading Horizons Staff, 2012, North Salt Lake, Utah: Reading Horizons. Copyright 2012 by Reading Horizons.

Students with Learning Disabilities

For students with learning disabilities, reading instruction was frustrating and often inappropriate. In 1970, a special issue of *The Reading Teacher* focused on students with learning challenges but the contributors viewed the students as deficient with clinical pathologies. One contributor discussed children with "neurotic" factors, such as aggression and hostility, as the cause of reading failure (Abrams, 1970). She also described brain-damaged children as "hyperdistractable" with "severe deficiencies in both perceptual and conceptual skills" (Abrams, 1970, p. 300). Another contributor described children with dyslexia as 'retarded readers' as she suggested therapy groups in combination with reading groups (Edelstein, 1970). During this time period, students with learning disabilities were often considered to have "modality deficiencies, cognitive deficits, aptitude weaknesses, and varied verbal performance abilities," requiring teachers and psychologists to use multiple forms of diagnostic assessment to determine the "ultimate truths about retarded readers" (Reed, 1970, p. 393).

If a child was treated as deficient, imagine the subsequent impact on school performance and self-perception. Since this time, researchers and educators have learned to look for assets and strengths, rather than deficits.

From Emergence to Adolescence

The practices of "reading readiness" were expanded in the 1980s when emergent literacy researchers recognized the contextual nature of reading as they observed children interact with books in classrooms rather than in controlled studies in a lab (Clay, 1972; Goodman, 1978). Researchers identified how children developed concepts about print (Clay, 1989) and literacy knowledge (e.g. Sulzby & Teale, 1991; Teale & Sulzby, 1986). Researchers recognized children's reading mistakes as strategic indicators rather than random errors; and they gained insight into the child's reading process by analyzing the miscues (Goodman, 1969; Goodman & Goodman, 1978) (Figure 6.12), conducting running records (Figure 6.13), and providing "diagnosis and early intervention" (Clay, 1985).

Figure 6.12
Miscue analysis was an important tool in helping teachers identify a reader's use of cueing systems (syntactic/semantic/graphophonemic or meaning/structure/visual). Teachers used the symbols to take notes on reading passages as the student reads them aloud. Running Record Symbols and Marking Conventions, 2015, Reading A-Z, Retrieved from https://www.readinga-z.com/guided/runrecord.html#markingsample.

Figure 6.13
A completed running record gives a teacher qualitative data about reading errors (meaning/structure/visual) and quantitative information about a student's errors, self-corrections, and strategies. Running Record Symbols and Marking Conventions, 2015, Reading A-Z, Retrieved from https://www.readinga-z.com/guided/runrecord.html#scoring.

Note the shift in language from getting "ready" to read (learning the parts before the whole) toward the emergence or evolution of reading over time.

Marie Clay studied how children developed concepts about print and her materials helped teachers understand what children know and do while they read (https://www.youtube.com/watch?v=nK02cLJjZMU).

Researchers also developed theories of comprehension (Guthrie, 1980) that focused on the reader's mental imagery and meaning-making strategies (Anderson & Pearson, 1984) as well as the relationship between reading and writing (Tierney & Pearson, 1983). The focus on comprehension moved teachers' instruction beyond a narrow application of phonics lessons and precise word reading (Pearson & Gallagher, 1983) and toward a focus on reader response (Beach, 1983). Researchers also documented the importance of parent interactions and family literacy events at home (Taylor, 1983).

> There are many important scholarly contributions during this time period. For an excellent historical review of reading research over time, I suggest reading the many iterations of the *Handbook of Reading Research*:
>
> Pearson, P. D., Barr, R., & Kamil, M. L. (1984). *Handbook of Reading Research* (Vol. 1). London, England: Psychology Press.
>
> Barr, R., Pearson, P. D., Kamil, M. L., & Mosenthal, P. B. (1996). *Handbook of Reading Research* (Vol. 2). London, England: Psychology Press.
>
> Kamil, M.L., Mosenthal, P.B., Pearson, P.D. & Barr, R. (2000). *Handbook of reading research* (Vol. 3). London, England: Psychology Press.
>
> Kamil, M. L., Pearson, P. D., Moje, E. B., & Afflerbach, P. (Eds.). (2011). *Handbook of Reading Research* (Vol. 4). London, England: Routledge.

Simultaneous to a focus on the needs of the young child, reading researchers also directed attention to the different needs of intermediate and middle-grades readers (Atwell, 1987; Taylor & Frye, 1992), adolescent readers (Alvermann, 1987; Hynds, 1985), and adults (Gambrell & Heathington, 1981; Rasinski, 1989). Calling for teachers to learn from the students and to acknowledge the wealth of personal experiences readers bring into the classroom, researchers explored reading preferences (Fisher & Natarella, 1982; Terry, 1974) and students' personal responses to literature (e.g., Weaver, 1990). Researchers also investigated effective reading strategies for comprehending text (e.g., thematic organizers, prereading strategies) and for thinking about thinking (metacognition) (Alvarez & Risko, 1988; Olshavsky, 1976; Paris, Cross, & Lipson, 1984).

Whole Language

Throughout the 1970s and 1980s, the Whole Language Movement (http://www.ncte.org/wlu/beliefs) gained momentum alongside a surge from children's literature advocates, redirecting the focus of reading instruction toward the *construction of meaning* rather than the breakdown and analysis of the alphabetic code and corresponding phonics instruction.

Children and youth began to read real literature (complete texts, not excerpts) in school. They read literature under the guidance of their teachers during small group reading instruction (Cullinan, 1987) (Figure 6.14) as well as during whole class explorations of genres, themes, and selected books [Huck, 1992 (Figure 6.15); Norton, 1992]. Whole language teachers repeatedly read big books and word charts to help students learn words and language structures (Martinez & Roser, 1985) (Figure 6.16). Researchers called for students to engage in leisure reading and to read widely (Krashen, 1993).

Borrowing from traditions in the library, K-12 teachers used book clubs to motivate reading and foster discussion (Eeds & Wells, 1989; Raphael & McMahon, 1994). Teachers focused on authors and illustrators by helping their students critically analyze texts and identify the author's values and underlying messages, as well as the voices that are not present in a text (Harris, 1992; Martinez & Teale, 1993; Short, 1995). In other words, the use of literature and the promotion of aesthetic reading, writing, and art-making were goals of many teachers from Kindergarten through high school (Applebee, 1993; Dutro & McIver, 2011).

Figure 6.14

Literacy experts, such as Bernice Cullinan, helped teachers understand how to use real books to teach reading. Her book, which has successive editions, includes chapter contributions from leading literacy researchers. *Children's Literature in the Reading Program*, by Bernice Cullinan, 1987, Newark, DE: International Reading Association.

Figure 6.15

Charlotte Huck and Doris Young Kuhn, first published their comprehensive overview of children's literature in 1961. They helped teachers find a place for children's literature across the curriculum, providing book suggestions and genre overviews. Although Charlotte Huck passed away, iterations of her book continue by her co-author, Barbara Kiefer. *Children's Literature in the Elementary School* by Charlotte S. Huck and Doris Young Kuhn, 1968, New York, NY: Holt, Rinehart and Winston.

Figure 6.16

Whole language instruction prioritizes book reading and writing activities that have relevance to children's lives. Teachers use big books and charts for whole class instruction. Teachers reread texts frequently, helping children remember the words they read. Image retrieved from http://www.tunstallsteachingtidbits.com/wp-content/uploads/2014/08/IMG_4295.jpg.

During the 1980s and 1990s, thematic units were commonly used to integrate the curriculum and support the use of nonfiction texts in the content-areas (Lipson, Valencia, Wixson & Peters, 1993; Pappas, 1990). Teachers found information books to teach science, math, and social studies and they taught reading and writing in the service of disciplinary goals.

Teachers also selected children's literature and elicited personal responses in connection to integrated explorations of disciplinary content.

Oftentimes, teachers focused on whole reading practices such as reading aloud, sustained silent reading, and building a love of reading at school and at home (e.g. Goodman, 1986) without attending to word study instruction or understanding the importance of students reading text accurately and within their instructional levels (reading between 90-94% accuracy). In doing so, many teachers moved away from systematic phonics instruction, word study, and comprehension strategies, allowing students to memorize texts without learning reading strategies. In other words, many teachers were too global in their approach, and the students who needed more explicit instruction in how written language works could not decipher the relevant strategies to develop as readers.

These issues (skill and drill vs. holistic approaches) were the basis of the reading wars (Chall, 1967; Goodman, 1969).

 In contrast to my "anything goes" approach to the books people choose to read, when it comes to teaching reading, the text really matters. So does the instruction.

Second Language Learners

Within the years of the reading wars, a series of lawsuits regarding the education of language minority students was shaping public policy and classroom practice (Figure 6.17). Court rulings across the US mandated that schools must provide instruction in English for students who spoke other languages because they were not yet proficient in English, and because they needed fluency in English to succeed in classrooms. In addition, courts ruled that schools must teach English Language Learners (ELL) the same academic content as their English proficient peers (Wright, 2010). Teaching reading to second language learners required extensive professional development and changes in teacher education across the US. What strategies did ELL students need to learn? What books would they read?

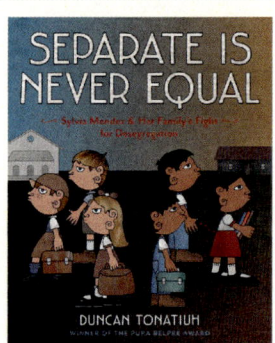

Figure 6.17

Remember Sylvia Mendez? *Separate is Never Equal: Sylvia Mendez and her Family's Fight for Desegregation* by Duncan Tonatiuh, 2014, New York, NY: Abrams. Copyright 2014 by Duncan Tonatiuh.

Balanced Literacy Solutions

An outcome of the reading wars was the purposeful selection of effective methods from phonics research coupled with best practices from whole language research to form a balanced approach. In other words, teachers needed to approach reading instruction with the global understanding of when, why, and how to teach different types of reading skills while understanding social and cultural factors involved in motivating and engaging readers (e.g., Stanovich, 1990). Proponents of balanced approaches recommended authentic reading and writing activities across the curriculum, and they recognized reading as a balance of skills and strategies across cueing systems (meaning, structure, visual).

Balanced literacy is a combination of activities that include language and word study as well as reading and writing for communicative purposes. For an overview of balanced literacy, read this brochure from the Ohio State University Literacy Collaborative (http://www.lcosu.org/training/LCbrochure.pdf).

Teachers were taught to assess students' reading abilities using miscue analysis and running records and then to select texts that were at the students' instructional levels (90-94% accuracy). By doing so, the text would not frustrate the reader, but the text was challenging enough to allow the teacher to teach the necessary skills or strategies (Pinnell, Lyons, Deford, Bryk, & Seltzer, 1994). This means that teachers needed access to texts that were specifically created to increase in difficulty across levels of vocabulary, grammar, and content.

Leveled books, such as those that use Lexiles or grade level equivalents, are important materials for reading instruction. Leveled books are not, however, the best materials for reading aloud, parent/child reading, or reading for pleasure. Children need to read real children's literature on their own and with adults. They need to read books that interest them whether those are too easy, too hard, or just right. The controlled, leveled texts are for teaching.

By focusing on individual needs and students' strengths, teachers could provide differentiated instruction based on assessment data. This approach allowed teachers to address the needs of all students including second language learners as well as those students with reading disabilities.

Teachers provided explicit instruction in fluency, comprehension, and vocabulary development while phonemic awareness and phonics instruction were taught as students engaged in reading and writing. Teachers also engaged in word study and the systematic exploration of word families. Literacy instruction followed a "gradual release of responsibility" model in which teachers moved from demonstration and explicit teaching to guided practice and independent problem solving (Campione, 1981; Pearson & Gallagher, 1983). Teachers also used a combination of leveled, specially-designed texts along with authentic children's and young adult literature.

> This is a completely different topic for another type of textbook, but students learn a lot about phonics and how language works when they write. During the 'reading readiness' years, students were not encouraged to write until they knew how to read. Just like baby reading is the beginning of "real" reading, scribbling is the beginning of writing.

The US Government Attempts to Settle the Reading Wars

In the late 1990s, the field of literacy studies and the use of children's literature was drastically altered when Congress asked the National Institute of Child Health and Human Development to work with the Department of Education to create a coalition of researchers to study reading instruction. The National Reading Panel reviewed published research dated from 1966 through 1999 to make determinations about reading instruction.

The Five Pillars of Reading

The National Reading Panel (NRP) (National Institute of Child Health and Human Development, 2000) concluded that a combination of techniques is effective for teaching students to read. The following bulleted points highlight their major findings and are directly quoted from the NRP report (https://www.nichd.nih.gov/research/supported/Pages/nrp.aspx).

- **Phonemic awareness**—the knowledge that spoken words can be broken apart into smaller segments of sound known as phonemes. Children who are read to at home—especially material that rhymes—often develop the basis of phonemic awareness. Children who are not read to will probably need to be taught that words can be broken apart into smaller sounds.

> Here's where the importance of the library becomes clear. Families need access to books in the home. Support at home is also connected to a parent's literacy level and ability to discuss language concepts with children.

THE READING WARS
(CHILDREN'S LITERATURE AND THE INTERVENING EFFECTS OF SCHOOL AND POLITICS)

- **Phonics**—the knowledge that letters of the alphabet represent phonemes, and that these sounds are blended together to form written words. Readers who are skilled in phonics can sound out words they haven't seen before, without first having to memorize them.

> I think many people approach reading as a process of "sounding it out." If sounding it out always works so well, what do you do with words like "the"? There is more to reading than sounding out. That's what babies and toddlers learn when someone reads to them—they learn the big picture.

- **Fluency**—the ability to recognize words easily, read with greater speed, accuracy, and expression, and to better understand what is read. Children gain fluency by practicing reading until the process becomes automatic; guided oral repeated reading is one approach to helping children become fluent readers.

> On the surface level, fluency practice makes sense—practice makes perfect. But what happens when students are forced to read the same passages over and over and over? That's right—they become bored and they lose motivation because repetition for the sake of fluency is contrary to the communicative purposes of reading.
>
> Here's the problem. If researchers review studies in isolation, they lose sight of the big picture. Reading is more than sounding out words and reading quickly, it's also about reading books that are interesting and important. Books that children and adolescents want to read over and over again.

- **Teaching vocabulary words**—teaching new words, either as they appear in text, or by introducing new words separately. This type of instruction also aids reading ability.

> Absolutely—a strong vocabulary is necessary to understanding texts. But again, how many times in your life did you apply new vocabulary words that you wrote in English class. It doesn't work that way. Students need experience with language and experiences within which to learn language.

- **Reading comprehension strategies**—techniques for helping individuals to understand what they read. Such techniques involve having students summarize what they've read, to gain a better understanding of the material.

> Teaching comprehension strategies is a no-brainer. However, the texts students read have to be worth comprehending.

The NRP findings were (and are) problematic because the NRP only reviewed one type of research (quasi-experimental or experimental designs with controlled interventions). By ignoring qualitative research, the NRP overlooked more holistic approaches to reading methods including the effects of teachers reading aloud, the effect of students' independent reading of children's literature, and impact of students' responses to literature (e.g., Krashen, 1993; 2011).

For years, the tobacco industry denied that smoking causes cancer because research couldn't "prove" it (Brownell & Warner, 2009; Warner, 2005). Unfortunately, in the realm of scientific "rigor" the tobacco industry was technically correct, the only way to scientifically "prove" effects is to randomly place a representative sample of people into groups and conduct controlled experiments. Well, researchers couldn't randomly select participants (from all ethnicities, genders, and ages) and force people to smoke. So the tobacco industry manipulated science and public opinion. That is, until the results of other forms of research became overwhelming.

When the NRP chose to limit their review of reading studies to "scientifically-based research," they essentially ignored all forms of qualitative research and "kid watching" including teacher reports, interviews, observational studies, case studies, and surveys. They followed the model of big tobacco and created a very narrow version of reading-- one that could be systematized and teacher proofed and then published, marketed, and sold.

Children's literature went bye-bye and scripted reading lessons with controlled vocabulary came back. Oh, and NCLB also brought in high-stakes tests to hold everyone accountable for teaching with prescribed methods and controlled texts.

The NRP's findings were also problematic because its conception of reading did not correspond to the ways in which children's literature texts are written. Children's books are not written with phonics lessons in mind. Children's books are not written with controlled vocabulary (except for Dr. Seuss or the Berenstains, but those aren't meant for older students). Good writing is interesting writing. Therefore, the NRP report harkened back to phonics and basal reading programs.

Members of the NRP issued minority reports and published dissenting reviews of the data (Yatvin, 2000). Other literacy scholars condemned the findings as well (Allington, 2002). But to no avail.

Accountability and Scripted Instruction

Despite the criticism of the NRP, President George W. Bush acted upon the findings by signing the No Child Left Behind Act (NCLB) in 2001. Unfortunately, this law ushered in an era of rigid accountability and scripted instruction. Teachers were required to teach the 5 pillars of reading (whether students needed those forms of instruction or not). Reading materials and textbooks were revised to conform to the NRP findings and teachers were given scripts to follow.

> Don't even get me started on the billions of dollars made by companies that produce the scripted textbooks, create the tests, and score them each year. Are you defined by your SAT score? Why are we defining kids by one test given on one day and then judging teachers based on the results of these tests as if families, reading materials, instructional resources, facilities, time, food, health, and wellness don't have any role in reading performance?

Children's literature became a peripheral instructional material. And most damagingly, school funding was tied to test performance. Accountability and standards are fine within a controlled context of sameness. But when students come from different homes, with different families, and different experiences and support, their teachers can't be held accountable for all of the differences between them. In addition, teachers have varying levels of skill and expertise. It is unethical to "use" students' scores to weed out bad teachers, and you can't hold students to the same standards when they have different teachers with varying levels of effectiveness.

But most importantly, real reading can't be measured by a multiple choice, standardized test. Reading assessment requires time and expert analysis as the teacher listens to and watches a child read. Reading behaviors are far too complex for standardization; and more authentic forms of assessment are far too expensive for massive testing. The result, President Bush asked teachers to teach to the test.

> When it comes to our schools, dollars alone do not always make the difference. Funding is important, and so is reform. So we must tie funding to higher standards and accountability for results.

> I believe in local control of schools. We should not, and we will not, run public schools from Washington, DC. Yet when the Federal Government spends tax dollars, we must insist on results. Children should be tested on basic reading and math skills every year between grades three and eight. Measuring is the only way to know whether all our children are learning. And I want to know, because I refuse to leave any child behind in America.

> *Critics of testing contend it distracts from learning. They talk about teaching to the test. But let's put that logic to the test. If you test a child on basic math and reading skills and you're teaching to the test, you're teaching math and reading. And that's the whole idea. (President George W. Bush's Address Before a Joint Session of Congress, February 27, 2001)*

In his edited book, *Literacy as a Civil Right* (2008), Stuart Greene used former Education Secretary Rod Paige's pervasive mantra "the achievement gap is the civil rights issue of our time" as an opportunity to reframe the discourse surrounding underachievement and low graduation rates for populations of African American, Latino/a, Native American, and Asian American students. Specifically, Greene wrote that the No Child Left Behind Act purported to eliminate the achievement gap through increased accountability and testing practices. Accountability, standards and grades were touted as vehicles for civil rights and educational equity, yet, the "move toward educational reform actually masks racist and deficit ideologies that have contributed to the failure of the very students it seeks to help" (Greene, 2008, p. 3). Greene and his contributing authors predicted, "as long as low-income, minority students are defined by the low-level skills required to succeed on standardized tests, the gap will increase between these schools and those serving middle-class White students" (p. 7).

Time and, ironically, additional testing, have brought to light this reality. After more than a decade of accountability and teaching to the test, the US literacy rates for minority students have not "closed" and the "gap" across racial or gender divides still exists. In fact, gaps are growing in areas such as technology usage and in mathematics. We haven't seen the huge reading gains as promised. For example, in the 2015 National Assessment of Educational Progress (NAEP) Fourth and Eighth Grade Assessment, reading scores were not different at grade 4 and lower at grade 8 than in 2013. Female students had higher percentages at or above the Proficient level than male students at both grades. The stark discrepancies among racial groups continues to exist (http://www.nationsreportcard.gov/reading_math_2015/#reading?grade=4).

The National Assessment of Educational Progress (NAEP) measures student performance on reading, writing, math and other subject area tests. NAEP provides results about subject-matter achievement, instructional experiences, and school environment, and reports these results for populations of students (e.g., fourth-graders) and subgroups of those populations (e.g., male students or Hispanic students). (https://nces.ed.gov/nationsreportcard/faq.aspx).

Large gaps still exist across student groups:

46% of White students were at or above Proficient / 79% at or above the Basic;

18% of Black students were at or above Proficient / 52% at or above Basic;

21% of Hispanic students were at or above Proficient / 55% at or above Basic;

57% of Asian students were at or above Proficient / 84% at or above Basic;

21% of American Indian/Alaska Native were at or above Proficient / 52% at or above Basic.

See for yourself. Explore the reading and math scores for different groups and regions. Click on this link and scroll to the bottom of the page where you can build custom data tables for reading and math scores across testing iterations and racial groups:
http://www.nationsreportcard.gov/reading_math_2013/#/executive-summary

If scientifically-based research was the gold standard, then the Department of Education and participating states who enacted high-stakes accountability requirements failed to meet their own standards by using faulty research designs. In other words, all teachers were asked to use the same instruction and all students were held to the same standards without controlling for all of the variables in students' lives or in their teachers' training.

Following NCLB legislation, President Obama's Race to the Top provided a successor regime of reading-instruction guidelines by funding grants for states to implement reforms. Aesthetic reading and visual creation continued to give way to formalized skills instruction as high-stakes testing persisted as the gold standard. As Allington and Pearson (2011) explained, high-stakes testing and accountability measures have resulted in a reduction in the amount of time children spend reading for meaning, a reduction in meaningful discussions about literature, and an overemphasis on scripted instruction.

Literacy scholars were outraged. Regardless of their position during the reading wars, no one wanted to see the de-professionalization of teachers and the mandates of scripted instruction.

From the moment the NRP report was published, individual teachers, school boards, and several education organizations swung into action to combat the stifling requirements of subsequent NCLB policies and the detrimental effects of high-stakes testing. For example, individual teachers published articles to discuss the impact of NCLB policies and practices and major research associations issued policy briefs, data, and position statements:

- The American Education Research Association issued a position statement against high-stakes testing based on recommendations from the American Psychological Association and the National Council on Measurement in Education. They questioned harmful measurement practices and flawed results based on one-test/one-time practices (http://www.aera.net/AboutAERA/AERARulesPolicies/AERAPolicyStatements/PositionStatementonHighStakesTesting/tabid/11083/Default.aspx).

- The International Literacy Association (formerly the International Reading Association) issued a position statement about evidence-based reading instruction and how reading could or should be "measured" (http://www.reading.org/Libraries/position-statements-and-resolutions/ps1055_evidence_based.pdf).

- The International Literacy Association also issued position statements about early reading instruction, adolescent reading and other facets of literacy education (http://literacyworldwide.org/docs/default-source/where-we-stand/high-stakes-assessments-position-statement.pdf?sfvrsn=4).

- The National Council for Teachers of English issued a call to action and position statement: *What We Know About Adolescent Literacy and Ways to Support Teachers in Meeting Students' Needs*. They specifically decried the labeling of adolescent readers as "struggling" and the systematic use of phonics in secondary classrooms. They made specific recommendations for students and teachers based on a more comprehensive review of the research (http://www.ncte.org/positions/statements/adolescentliteracy).

By attempting to "end" the reading wars, the government created a new war of aggression against teachers, students, administrators, researchers, and scholars who know there isn't one way to teach reading to all students. They also made the testing industry a lot of money.

 If there was "one" way to teach reading, it would have been invented. Heck, I would have invented it. Then I would be rich! There is no magic recipe. Remember Hooked on Phonics?

The US Governors Attempt to Settle the New Reading Wars

The NCLB raised "standards" but not necessarily literacy rates. In addition, individual states were allowed to use their own tests and measures to document "annual yearly progress". Working as an association of governors and school administrators, the Common Core State Standards (CCSS) initiative was meant to refocus the vision for public schools and prepare students for the workforce and college. The CCSS were intended to create more cohesive goals across the country including elements of standardization for comparison.

If success is measured by different assessments, then the Department of Education can't make causal claims. Again, the rules of good measurement were not applied.

Common Core State Standards, Close Reading, and the Text Complexity Canon

With the implementation of the CCSS in 2014 (National Governors Association, 2010), the role of literature and the arts was again uncertain.

The CCSS focused on close reading, which is a method of paying very close attention to the text. As stated in the CCSS, students should "read closely to determine what the text says explicitly and to make logical inferences from it" (p. 10).

In particular, the CCSS recommend the use of "mentor texts" (i.e., the systematic study of literary models) as a way to increase students' awareness of text structures, organizational patterns, and authorial strategies (Clark, Jones, & Reutzel, 2013). Mentor texts provide teachers with literary "exemplars" that help them teach students how to comprehend text as well as how to compose text (National Governors Association and Council of Chief State School Officers, 2010).

The good news is that the use of "mentor texts" puts an emphasis back on children's literature and high-quality writing. The bad news is that many current recommendations for the use of mentor texts suggest a static interpretation of literature as mere words on a page. In fact, the CCSS have identified a specific set of books to serve as mentor texts based primarily on their linguistic complexity rather than literary value or students' interest levels (See Appendix B, National Governors Association and Council of Chief State School Officers, 2010).

Come on, you know better than this. What motivates reading? Apply what you've learned so far. Linguistic complexity will not entice youth to read. Neither will literary value. Reading happens when the right book is put in the right reader's hands at the right time and with the right support. There is no magic list of books that works for all kids.

Similarly, teachers' use of mentor texts to guide literacy instruction is often isolated from the process of artistic creation. For example, Clark, Jones, and Reutzel (2013) state, "teachers need to scaffold young students' text structure knowledge development by using well-structured exemplar texts... [that] make use of signal or clue words and other text features" (p. 266). Researchers, such as Donovan and Smolkin (2011) have also created developmental sequences for tracking writing progression based on text analysis. None of these models mention drawing nor do they integrate art.

Do not get me started on the role of drawing and art! Writing comes from drawing. They are semiotically linked. Some youth think in images and they create through visual modes. Any developmental sequence that excludes drawing or art is narrow and incomplete.

Granted, the mechanics of text creation are essential skills for students (Graham, McKeown, Kiuhara, & Harris, 2012), yet, in order for youth to understand how texts work, they must also appreciate the aesthetics.

Motivation, Purpose, and the Return to Children's Literature

The "research-based strategies" recommended by the NRP didn't work as anticipated. Guess what? Ninth graders don't need phonics instruction and all readers need texts that match their interests and abilities (Dennis, 2013).

The CCSS are an improvement to previous policies because, rather than dictating instructional strategies with blanket mandates, the CCSS offer standards as a guidepost without prescribing the instructional methods to get there. Teachers and school districts are implementing the Common Core (some states are doing their own versions), and as a field, we are starting to show some early signs of instructional relief and potential recovery. Some school boards, principals, and parents are starting to reject excessive testing (Emma, 2015; Wallace, 2015). Children's literature markets are picking up (Bluestone, 2015) and students are starting to read books in school. Teachers are returning to children's literature as models for teaching reading and writing (Louie & Sierschynski, 2015).

Think about the best teachers you have ever had. What made them unique and interesting? I'm confident it wasn't their ability to administer tests. I'm confident their teaching expertise wasn't scripted in a teacher's manual.

 I'm not exaggerating when I tell you that the literacy world was upended by the National Reading Panel. Their recommendations were shortsighted and based on a skewed selection of research. Literacy is more than a gathering of sub-skills. And it definitely involves the appropriate selection of text. The combination of the NRP and NCLB pushed children's literature to the periphery of reading instruction.

With all of the poking and prodding we have done to students to make sure they know how to read, it's understandable that many of them stop reading. A focus on decontextualized skills negates the purpose of reading; and the removal of interesting literature demotivates readers. We lost all of the benefits of whole language and phonics instruction. As Gallagher (2009) describes it, schools are committing "readicide."

To combat destructive testing and instructional practices, Richard Allington and Rachael Gabriel (2012) remind teachers, librarians, and parents of six elements of effective reading instruction:

- Every child reads something he or she chooses.
- Every child reads accurately.
- Every child reads something he or she understands.
- Every child writes about something personally meaningful.
- Every child talks with peers about reading and writing.
- Every child listens to a fluent adult read aloud.

Click here for the complete article that includes brief summaries of research to support each point: (http://www.ascd.org/publications/educational-leadership/mar12/vol69/num06/Every-Child,-Every-Day.aspx)

In addition, effective reading education in the adolescent years is marked by different challenges than teaching beginning reading. According to Biancarosa and Snow (2004), there are two reasons for the difficulty in teaching adolescent reading, "first, secondary school literacy skills are more complex, more embedded in subject matters, and more multiply determined; second, adolescents are not as universally motivated to read better or as interested in school-based reading as kindergarteners" (p. 1).

To combat the challenges of working with adolescents, the National Council of Teachers of English (2004) asserts that all students, regardless of reading ability, need opportunities to read and respond to literature beyond basal readers and other programmed materials. In addition, students should use adolescent literature throughout the reading and writing curriculum, and as part of their content-area studies.

Given that leisure reading has been on the decline, the International Reading Association (2014), in collaboration with the National Council of Teachers of English and the Canadian Children's Book Centre issued a joint position statement calling for teachers to facilitate leisure reading in students' lives, support students' reading choices, and provide daily opportunities for leisure reading in school. In particular, teachers should "model fiction and nonfiction book selection, conference with students during Sustained Silent Reading (SSR), and hold students accountable for their reading (Reutzel, Fawson, & Smith, 2008)" (IRA, 2014). In particular, the International Literacy Association recommends the following principles to support leisure reading.

> Principle I: Readers should choose their own reading materials (Krashen, 2011). Students are better able to choose engaging and appropriate reading materials when teachers and family members scaffold their selection of leisure reading materials (Reutzel, Jones, & Newman, 2010; Sanden, 2014).

> Principle II: The benefits to students' fluency, comprehension, and motivation from engaging in leisure reading are increased when teachers scaffold school-based leisure reading by incorporating reflection, response, and sharing in a wide range of ways that are not evaluated (Parr & Maguiness, 2005; Pilgreen, 2000; Reutzel, Jones, Fawson, & Smith, 2008; Walker, 2013) and when students' home environments support their self-selected reading (Sonnenschein, Baker, Serpell, & Schmidt, 2000).

If youth actually make it to, and through, high school as engaged, well-read readers, they have extraordinary choices when it comes to books. That's why many adults are drawn to Young Adult (YA) literature; YA literature includes complex plots and exceptional writing. As Madeleine L'Engle once said:

> You have to write the book that wants to be written. And if the book will be too difficult for grown-ups, then you write it for children.
> — Madeleine L'Engle

The Role of the School Library and Programs to Promote Reading

With our attention back on books, in this section I provide an overview of the school library and supportive reading programs that work in connection to school reading instruction. I also invited Kathleen Edwards, an amazing school librarian at Berkeley Preparatory School in Tampa, FL, to share her perspectives about the inner workings of the library as well. I have observed Kathleen's work in two other school settings and she exemplifies the best in school librarianship. Fortunately, she currently works in a school that appreciates her knowledge and funds her ideas and best practices.

I am painfully aware that most school libraries, if they exist, are underfunded and under-resourced. However, I am choosing to focus on best practices because you should understand what youth need from a school library. Although many of the following ideas can be implemented for free, you should understand that schools need funding.

Library Spaces

Just like public libraries and bookstores, school libraries have specific uses and corresponding spaces (Video Series 6.1). The librarian makes choices about space planning, materials, organization, and programming—all within the constraints of physical boundaries and finances.

View this interactive map of a school library to learn about space planning and design.

Video 6.1.1 Interactive school library video series:
The Rudolph Library introduction
http://www.kaltura.com/iny/j1b7w

Video 6.1.2 Interactive school library video series:
The Rudolph Library Teaching area
http://www.kaltura.com/tiny/ogxtt

Video 6.1.3 Interactive school library video series:
The Rudolph Library Computer Stations
http://www.kaltura.com/tiny/qbm2m

Video 6.1.4 Interactive school library video series:
The Rudolph Library read around the world
http://www.kaltura.com/tiny/ s7hyu

Video 6.1.5 Interactive school library video series:
The Rudolph Library Storytime area
http://www.kaltura.com/tiny/jque8

Video 6.1.6 Interactive school library video series:
The Rudolph Library collections development
http://www.kaltura.com/tiny/o63fo

THE READING WARS
(CHILDREN'S LITERATURE AND THE INTERVENING EFFECTS OF SCHOOL AND POLITICS)

> Library programming is similar to preparing a banquet table. One would want to have many enticing selections to delight the guests. As a Librarian, I want to prepare a banquet of reading pleasure for students. Our passion is promoting the joy of reading. The physical space of the library is one of enchantment. The library staff work within the physical space to promote gathering, reading, creativity, and community. It is a space where all members of the learning community should feel welcomed and enriched. It is a cozy and inviting space.
>
> It is possible to maintain this inviting atmosphere while at the same time providing the latest in digital tools. In my library, we have a research area with 11 computers for student use. Our 4th and 5th grade students bring their iPads to library to read and do research. We have a teaching area with a screen and projector and we also have a large TV in the story time area. I use technology to integrate multimedia content. For example, I may share a story about moles then I will show a short video on the star nosed mole to enrich the story. I also use rocking chairs for students in library. The children benefit from having the motion so that they are not sitting still for long periods.
>
> Ideally, the library should have enough space to house reading nooks and projects that the children may want to explore. My students enjoy setting up a tent in October with a fake campfire. We dim the lights and create night sounds in the library. We put on glow stick bracelets. Then we share campfire stories to celebrate fall. After doing this activity one fall, the students were quite reluctant to see the tent come down. So I said, "What can we create to be our next cozy story time setting?" The students decided that we would create an igloo for winter. They brought in shoeboxes that we covered with heavy-duty white paper. We explored igloo construction in the online encyclopedias and in books then we created our igloo. The children came to library during recess or DEAR time (Drop Everything and Read) to sit in the igloo and read. Children love cozy reading spaces and they especially enjoy designing and creating them. Library programming is about creating magic in the lives of children.
>
> Our library is staffed with one full time librarian, one full time assistant, and one part time assistant. This level of staffing allows us to work closely with our students to ensure that every student is connected with just-right reads. We will often work individually with a student to browse the shelves, explore the card catalog, and databases such as Novelist K through 8 in search of their next great read. Our students can email a request for a reference session or just come to the library during the day with teacher permission.

- Kathleen Edwards

Collection Development

In contemporary schools, librarians create programs that promote reading, acquiring appropriate materials for diverse learners.

The library staff in the Rudolph Library all participate in collection development. One library assistant enjoys reading journal reviews and developing suggested lists based on the reviews from *Kirkus*, *Booklist*, and *School Library Journal*. I add books based on curriculum needs for units of study in the classrooms. Teachers ask me to purchase books relating to social studies, science and language arts content. A second library assistant also works in the science lab. She helps develop the library collection by making suggestions for science units. I use two online databases to help make selections. They are Novelist K through 8 and the Children's Literature Database. We pay an annual fee for access to each of these. I order from Follett, Amazon, Inkwood Books in Tampa, and Barnes & Noble. Follett is a well-known vendor for books for school libraries. I also encourage my students to use Novelist K through 8 and to let me know if they would like for me to purchase books that they have discovered in Novelist that are not in our collection. Novelist is a readers' advisory platform. Parents, teachers and students can use it to explore book recommendations by genre and age level.

Our students enjoy over 5,000 eBook titles through a platform called MyOn. We do not pay for this platform. The Children's Board of Hillsborough County (http://www.childrensboard.org/) along with The Tampa Hillsborough Public Library Cooperative (http://www.hcplc.org/) partnered to bring this eBook platform to the Tampa Bay area. We are able to access and use this platform, which provides eBook access to students in PreK through 8 any time/anywhere.

-Kathleen Edwards

Budget

In spite of documented evidence of success, school libraries have historically experienced reductions in funding alongside changes in school reading curricula that correspond to government mandates and assessment practices (Ellis, 1963). For the most part, school administrators must understand the role of the library or they tend to cut services (Lance & Kachel, 2013). The librarian must work with the principal to educate the administrator about library services. The school librarian must demonstrate her or his value through visible programming and instructional support. Library budgets vary widely depending on the school's resources and number of students.

> Our current annual budget is approximately $26,000 for a library that serves 400 students. Budget categories include materials and supplies, subscriptions, library books, audio visual supplies and expense and miscellaneous. This budget ensures that we can maintain a collection in both print and online that is considered exemplary. Additionally, we have two rolling accounts that help fund library programming. They are our book fairs account and the Birthday Book Club account.

Book Promotion through Story Time and Book Talks

Story time is an important opportunity for young children to learn about the library collection through interesting examples. Librarians choose books that are best read aloud and they often incorporate dramatic play, movement, and visual components to the stories.

> Story times for the emerging reader are fun and engaging. We have a special place in our library that is designated as the story time area. This year we added a large screen television so that short videos or pictures that enrich the story may be viewed. We could also use this display and teach the children a song or poem. Another favorite of our young students are the felt storyboard stories such as the *Three Little Pigs*, *Rapunzel*, and *There was An Old Lady Who Swallowed a Fly*. Sometimes the children take turns adding the felt pieces to the story as I tell it. The children are delighted with the Folkmanis puppets in the library. Petey the Pack Rat is a big hit with PreK as Petey will wear a banner with the letter of the week that they are learning and he will bring interesting items in his backpack for the children to view. Sometimes, Petey may also have a treat in his pack for the children. He had huckleberry gummy bears to go with a story set in Montana where the characters eat huckleberries.

For older students, school librarians often create booktalks to advertise particular books. Booktalks can create a lot of interest in a new book; and they give the librarian an opportunity to provide individual guidance to help students select the "right" book to read (Everhart, 2013).

Check out these links to booktalks:

SchoolTube Booktalks http://www.schooltube.com/channel/scholastic_booktalks/;

Book Winks http://www.podfeed.net/podcast/Bookwink,+video+booktalks+for+kids/10030;

Digital Book Talks http://www.digitalbooktalk.net/;

JLG's Book Talks To Go http://www.slj.com/category/collection-development/jlg-booktalks/#_.

Classroom Support

School librarians also work with classroom teachers to support the reading curriculum. According to Lance and Kachel (2013) "when administrators believe students receive excellent library instruction in inquiry-based learning, students are consistently more likely to score advanced and less likely to score below basic on both reading and writing tests" (p. 12). In other studies, the school library is a consistent factor in standards-based assessment and library media specialists have a quantifiable, positive impact on student achievement (Francis & Lance, 2011).

> I work closely with classroom teachers to support the curriculum taught in the social studies, language arts, and science curriculum. Each month, I meet with a liaison from each grade level team to plan ahead. One of my main focuses is to ensure that our students learn to use online databases and to cite their sources properly when doing research. Research skills that are taught outside of the curriculum are not retained and have little meaning to children. It is essential that these skills are taught within the units of study in the classroom. For example, students learn that multiple sources often need to be consulted when answering essential questions. Our students are taught that pictures taken from the Internet must also be cited. They are taught to search for photos through Creative Commons as well as through databases such as Britannica Image Quest.

> For example, our units of study with library collaboration are as follows:
>
> 2nd grade: country and biography units;
>
> 3rd grade: planet unit and Florida Studies;
>
> 4th grade: Colonial America;
>
> 5th grade: Immigration unit.
>
> For the 3rd grade Florida Studies unit, the library collaborates by preparing the children for their visit to the Ringling Estate in Sarasota, FL (https://www.ringling.org/history-ringling). We have a circus poster contest and award prizes that are purchased at the Museum store. Also for the Florida Studies unit, the Library coordinates a visit by the Florida Public Archaeology Network (FPAN) whereby two members of FPAN come to our school campus and teach the children to toss arrows using a tool called the atlatl that was used by the Timucua Indians. This is a big hit each year. I also prepare 3rd grade for their visit to the Henry B. Plant Museum (http://www.ut.edu/plantmuseum/) by hosting a visit with local author Robin Gonzalez who wrote *Maggie and Max at the Museum*. We also read Robin's book, *If Our Hotel Could Talk*, to learn about the history and architecture of the Plant Museum.

Pleasure Reading Programs

Hopefully, leisure reading and SSR (sustained silent reading) are making a comeback in schools. Many of these programs are administered and promoted by library media specialists. Therefore, the school librarian/media specialist plays a key role in helping students find motivating books for sustained leisure reading. To do so, the librarian needs a budget to maintain a current and motivating collection of books and she or he needs the time to create programs that encourage and support reading.

Sustained Silent Reading

"Sustained Silent Reading" (SSR) is an umbrella term that teachers and librarians use to give students time to read for pleasure in school. The parameters of reading vary, but the intention is the same—get kids reading books.

DEAR Day: Drop Everything And Read!

"D.E.A.R. programs have been held nationwide on April 12th in honor of Beverly Cleary's birthday, since she first wrote about D.E.A.R. in Ramona Quimby, Age 8 (pages 40-41) (Figure 6.18). Inspired by letters from readers sharing their enthusiasm for the D.E.A.R. activities implemented in their schools, Mrs. Cleary decided to give the same experience to Ramona and her classmates. As D.E.A.R. has grown in popularity and scope, the program has expanded to span the entire month of April . . . offering classrooms and communities additional time to celebrate!" (http://www.dropeverythingandread.com/NationalDEARday.html)

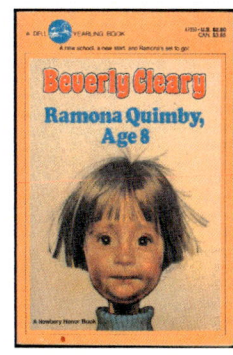

Figure 6.18

April 12th is Beverly Cleary's birthday and national DEAR day. She is the author of *Ramona Quimby, Henry Huggins, Dear Mr. Henshaw, Ralph S. Mouse* and so many more (http://www.beverlycleary.com/characters.aspx#Ramona). *Ramona Quimby, Age 8* by Beverly Cleary, 1981/1982, New York, NY: Dell. Cover art copyright by Joanne Scribner.

Below I have listed the various names of "sustained silent reading" programs. These alternative titles demonstrate the teachers' and librarians' awareness of the importance of the right book for the right reader as well as the benefits of encouragement, enjoyment, and time. Essentially, teachers give students uninterrupted time in class (10-30 minutes) and students can read books of their choice.

BARF: Be A Reader Freak

DEAR: Drop Everything and Read

DIRT: Daily Independent Reading Time

ELVIS: Everybody Loves Very Interesting Stories

FUR: Free Uninterrupted Reading

GRAB: Go Read A Book

KBAR: Kick Back and Read

OTTER: Our Time to Enjoy Reading

SQUIRT: Super Quiet Uninterrupted Reading Time

SSR: Sustained Silent Reading

SURF: Silent Uninterrupted Reading Fun

USSR: Uninterrupted Sustained Silent Reading

WEB: Wonderfully Entertaining Books

ZYLAR: Zip Your Lip And Read

For more information about independent reading programs in classrooms, visit the ILA website (http://www.literacyworldwide.org/blog/literacy-daily/2016/02/18/making-independent-reading-work).

Book Fairs, Book Orders, & Book Clubs

You may remember book fairs. The library shuts down for a week and big carts roll in with the latest books for sale. Students shop for books before and after school. You may also remember book orders. Teachers send home a little newspaper that advertises the latest books. Students check off the books they want and the teacher/librarian collects money and places the order. Within days, the books arrive for distribution.

Book fairs and book order programs serve as fundraisers for the school or school library. However, the success of these initiatives requires school populations of families who can afford to spend money on books. For many families, books are a luxury. To get books in the hands of children, other programs take alternative routes to reach children.

Each year we have two book fairs. One is in the fall after Thanksgiving and the other is in early May. Our combined book fair profits total approximately $7,000.

We currently use Scholastic for our book fair. The profits from the fairs are used to fund author visits throughout the year.

Our Birthday Book Club is a voluntary program in which students come to the library on or near their birthday to pick a new book out of the Birthday Book Closet. The closet includes the books that we have already purchased, but have not yet circulated. A plate is put in the front of the book indicating that the book was purchased for the library in honor of that student. The student is the first one to check it out and read it. Then they return it to the collection. A customary donation is $20 to $25 dollars for birthday book club. In schools with fewer resources, any donation amount would be acceptable.

Author/Illustrator Visits

Students enjoy meeting authors and illustrators in person. During school visits, the authors or illustrators typically present hour-long sessions to groups of children. The authors and illustrators show images of their work, discuss their creation process, and provide the students with insights about their books. The sessions end with autographs and/or question and answers. Many school library budgets have diminished with regard to school appearances, but there are librarians who make these events a priority. Author/illustrators can charge $250-$3000, depending on the person's popularity. The school must also pay for transportation and accommodation.

> The USF CLICK Conference borrowed the idea of author/illustrator school visits and expanded the concept to create a centralized author visit opportunity for local schools. Rather than paying for one author, schools send students to the CLICK conference to hear several authors/illustrators. In addition, the children break into small groups to participate in writing, reading, drawing, and performance activities in connection to books (https://www.facebook.com/ClickChildrensLiteratureCollectionOfKnowHow/).

> Author visits are an excellent avenue for fully engaging students with high quality literature. We invite authors, illustrators, and master storytellers to visit our school. We fund these visits through book fair earnings as well as through our Birthday Book Club program. Additionally, we have collaborated with a local independent bookstore to bring authors for school visits. The bookstore arranges for authors to come visit the school and we pre-sell the books to our students. Presentations are done in large groups as well as small break-out sessions whereby students may learn a specific skill such as how to begin to develop a character for a book. The energy generated by these visits propels students to read more as well as to create stories of their own.

Battle of the Books

Each year the Florida Association for Media in Education and the Office of Library Media selects 15 titles for grades 3rd through 5th and 15 titles for grades 6th through 8th. These titles are the Sunshine State Young Reader Award nominees. Students read the books and can vote on their favorite. In the Battle of the Books Program, students compete in teams answering questions about the book titles.

> At Berkeley, we select 5 titles for each grade 3 through 5. Students in those grades become an expert on one of the titles. They read their selected book and fill out a journal on the characters, setting, and key events. At winter break, we have class battles and the team that wins for each class then battles the other teams in that grade for a grade winning team. Additionally, students who wish to read all 15 titles can try out for the team that will battle other independent schools in the Tampa Bay Area. Berkeley hosts this event each year in May.
>
> ## Mock Caldecott
>
> The Caldecott Medal is awarded each year in January for the best American picture book published the year before. The award is given by the American Library Association. Mock Caldecott is a library program whereby students read and review approximately 20 potentially nominated books and vote on whether the book would be a winner, an honor book, or left out of the running. I begin in advance of the students by reading book reviews as well as several Caldecott blogs which attempt to predict the winners. I develop the list of 20 books that will be previewed. I have done this activity with students in grades 2 through 5 and it is well received. Students learn about the medal including the history of how the medal came to be. They learn that the American Library Association has a committee each year to review the nominated books and decide on which book receives the medal and which books will be given the status of honor books. Students review the visual elements of art and types of art mediums prior to reading the books. We use a graphic organizer form that students fill out as they read a book. These forms are tallied to make our predictions. This activity is done for about a month to six weeks prior to the actual award announcements. Students engage with the books deeply learning how written word and picture come together artfully to create the story. They learn about art mediums and reflect on why the illustrator may have chosen that particular medium to bring out the story.

Reading Incentive Programs

Reading incentive programs, such as Reading Counts or Accelerated Reader, are commonly used to promote independent reading or family reading time. Students are required to create reading logs, obtain parent signatures, or take tests. I am not a fan. For children who do not love to read, these programs are not conducive to fostering a love of reading. In fact, these programs often cause struggles in families when children are forced to read for so many minutes or from color-coded books. In addition, children who love to read are often forced to read books on a certain level or in their color code. Sometimes children want to read books that are off the grid—and they should. Reading incentive programs are counter-intuitive to the purpose of reading. More importantly, research indicates they do not improve reading scores or motivation to read (Huang, 2012). Kathleen has a different opinion, and her school uses an incentive program as an option.

> Reading Counts is an optional reading incentive program whereby students read books then take a 10 question quiz on the book. They earn points for successfully passing quizzes. Reading related prizes are awarded for certain attained point levels for students who score 85% or above. At 175 points, we award a book as a prize. Students are able to select a paperback for their prize. We have some on hand or will special order for them provided that the book falls within our price point range. At 250 points (200 for 2nd grade and 225 for 3rd grade), students are awarded the Reading Counts hat, which is designed by the rising 5th grade at the end of the school year.

Middle and High School Libraries

Middle and high school libraries share many of the same characteristics and qualities as the elementary school library. The main difference is the developmental level of the youth and a change in their reading interests and literacy skills. For example, libraries for adolescents will feature young adult and classic literature as well as collections of literary criticism.

Upper-level librarians must also address collections development and pleasure reading programs in relation to their adolescent population. The librarian must be able to select and recommend books that the students will want to read. This means the library staff must interact with the students and get to know them as individuals.

A major focus of the middle or high school library is research. The library must have updated computers and relevant databases to provide students with access to the materials they need. The librarian also works with classroom teachers to provide research skills training and instructional support relevant to the content. Often, student volunteers work in middle or high school libraries by operating the circulation desk and recommending books to other students. They also shelve books, maintain order in the library and perform special projects for the library staff.

The middle and high school library has a different look and feel than an elementary library. It is accessible and comfortable. But it is more suited to adolescents' tastes and desires to work in small groups, hide out in isolated coves, and lounge in comfortable chairs. The library space will often feature student work and special projects as middle and high school libraries are a central hub and study space for students (Video 6.2).

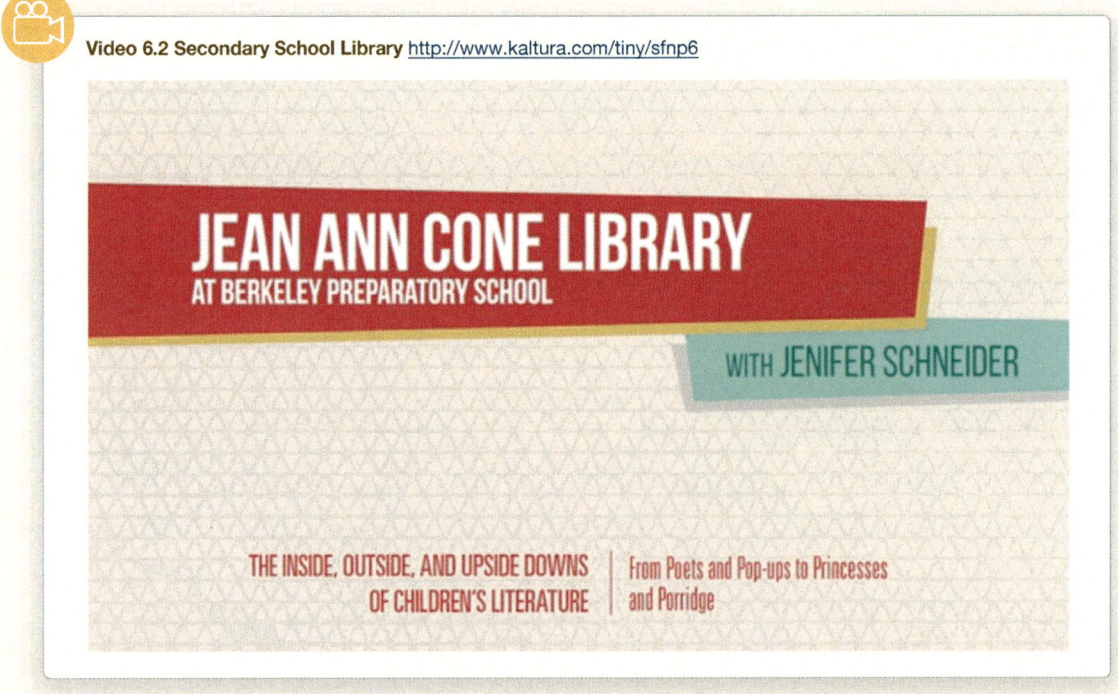

Video 6.2 Secondary School Library http://www.kaltura.com/tiny/sfnp6

Other Public and Private Programs to Promote Reading

Outside of the school library, there are many other initiatives that promote reading and intend to provide students with the right books.

Dolly Parton's Imagination Library

Have you heard about Dolly Parton's Imagination Library? Inspired by her father who couldn't read, Dolly Parton created a program to send a book a month to every child in her home county in Tennessee (https://imaginationlibrary.com/). The library has grown to include duplicate programs around the world, and Dolly's charity has given away more than 70 million books. Dolly Parton had a great idea that emerged from her personal experiences. How have your experiences with books impacted your life? How can your business or industry impact the lives of young readers?

Book Mobiles

Book mobiles have existed since the creation of free libraries and the invention of vehicles to transport books. In the US, Mary Titcombe is credited with the first book mobile. For a history on book mobiles, watch this video (https://www.youtube.com/watch?v=dm7qDYyrETA).

Luis Soriano, an elementary teacher in Columbia's Magdalena Province, uses two donkeys to travel to children's homes delivering books. You may have heard about the Donkey Library or BiblioBurro. His story was featured in a documentary (http://www.pbs.org/pov/biblioburro/). Luis brings books to children in the hopes that reading and education can combat drugs and poverty. Luis created his own unique version of a book mobile.

Book mobiles are still used across the US. Bess the Book Bus (http://bessthebookbus.org/) is a mobile literacy outreach program dedicated to distributing books to underprivileged children and fostering a love of reading (Figure 6.19). Jennifer Frances named the program after her grandmother, Nana Bess, who taught her the joy of reading. Jennifer fills her mini-bus with enough donations to travel throughout the US to freely share books with children (Figure 6.20). Sponsors generously support her vision for widespread free reading (Video 6.3).

Figure 6.19
Jennifer Frances, founder of Bess the Book Bus, stocks her bus shelves with hundreds of books, which she gives away to underprivileged children. Photo copyright 2015 by Jenifer Schneider.

Figure 6.20
Bess the Book Bus travels all over the US, distributing books to children who don't own many, if any, of their own. Photo copyright 2015 by Jenifer Schneider.

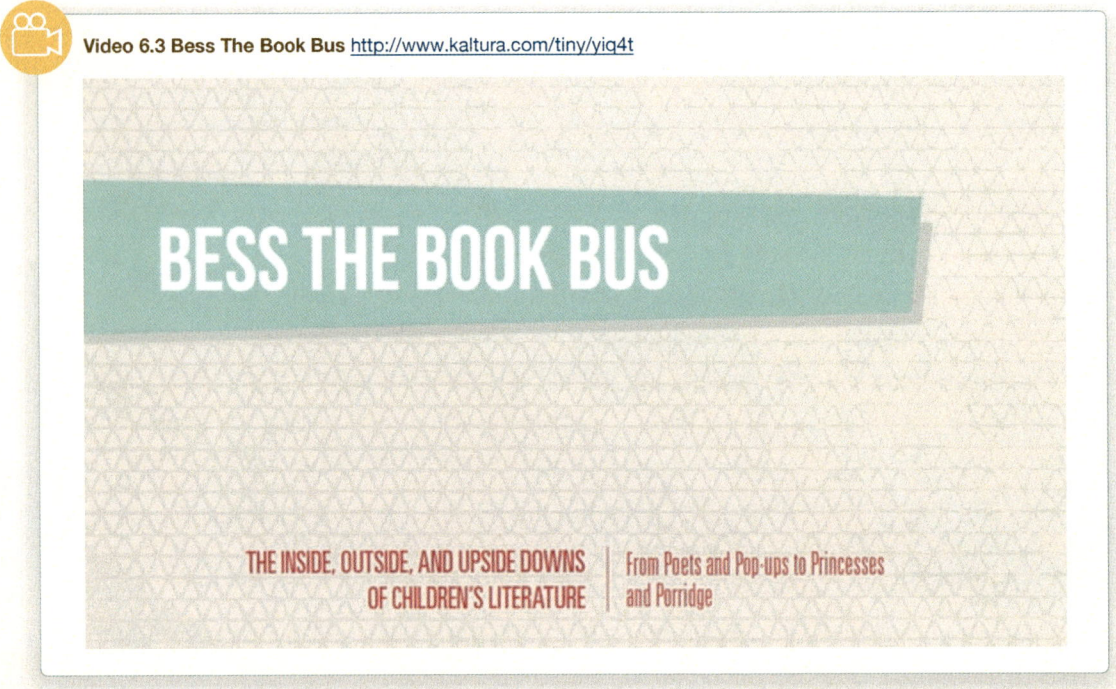

Video 6.3 Bess The Book Bus http://www.kaltura.com/tiny/yiq4t

RIF

RIF is a book distribution and reading motivation program. Founded by Margaret McNamara in 1966, Reading Is Fundamental (RIF) is a non-profit organization dedicated to serving low-income and disadvantaged youth through literacy initiatives. According to the RIF website, RIF prepares and motivates children to read by "delivering free books and literacy resources to those children and families who need them most. We inspire children to be lifelong readers through the power of choice. RIF provides new, free books for children to choose from and make their own" (http://www.rif.org/us/about-rif.htm). Focused on children from birth to age eight, RIF provides 15 million new, free books to 4 million children in all 50 states each year. RIF works through schools, community centers, Boys & Girls Clubs, migrant communities, churches, hospitals, and clinics.

Reading Rainbow

Reading Rainbow (https://www.readingrainbow.com/) is a television show focused on reading books. The show, which aired on PBS from 1983 until 2009, featured short stories about literacy events (literary field trips), people (and kids) making a difference, and the show always included a celebrity read aloud. Once the show ended, LeVar Burton, the host, created RRKIDZ. The website features old Reading Rainbow videos, teacher resources, community initiatives, and the Skybrary, which is an interactive library of books and videos available through a subscription service.

Interventions and Intended Consequences

In this chapter, I summarized a series of political, educational, and cultural events that derived from a desire to increase US literacy rates. Undergirding these broad, sweeping efforts is the concept of the right book for the right reader at the right time with the "right" instruction. But there is no "right" way. The debate over the best methods to teach reading continues; however, reading specialists understand the individualized nature of teaching and they have a repertoire of strategies that support literacy development. The people who have spent their lives studying reading know what to do and they will continue to work to help every student because teaching and learning are evolutionary processes.

There are clear benefits to a populace when children and adolescents know how to read and when they can read for pleasure and for information. But what happens when the kids choose books that adults don't like? In the remaining chapters of this book, I will explore some of the issues related to books, choice, and audience.

CHAPTER 07 | AMERICAN TYPO
(GHOST, FAN, SERIAL, AND CELEBRITY WRITERS —AND ILLUSTRATORS)

Natural Born Serial Killers

Series books are a "menace" (Kinlock, 1935); they capture "swaggering and infantile art," (Powell, 1917), and their content will "blow out boys' brains" (Mathiews, 1914). In the early years of the American Library Association, some librarians believed series books killed the creative spirit and allowed readers to whither in redundancy. Church leaders, civic associations, and parents agreed.

Certainly, modern sensibilities have changed the perceptions of literary experts. Certainly not!

Modern cultural critics are often quoted about the embedded racism or outright sexism associated with series books. Literary scholars detest the repetitive plots and stagnant characters. Teachers, on the other hand, have found that consistent characters and simplified plot structures are supportive vehicles for children who struggle with or who are disinterested in reading, especially boys (Senn, 2012). However, boys are often bullied away from particular book series due to the content (e.g., see Shannon Hale's essay on the exclusion of boys: http://oinks.squeetus.com/2015/02/no-boys-allowed-school-visits-as-a-woman-writer.html)

 What a double standard for boys! Girls have no problem reading "boy" books (you know I don't believe in such a thing, but for the sake of argument, stay with me), but boys can't read girl books? Let kids read. Why so judgy?

Love them or hate them. Series books are different things to different people. And many series have solid stories and high literary values in addition to all kinds of fan-love.

A Series Sampler

In a previous chapter, I read *Olivia* (Video 7.1).

Video 7.1 Olivia, by Ian Falconer http://www.kaltura.com/tiny/rtws0

Now find out what happens when she goes to the circus (Video 7.2).

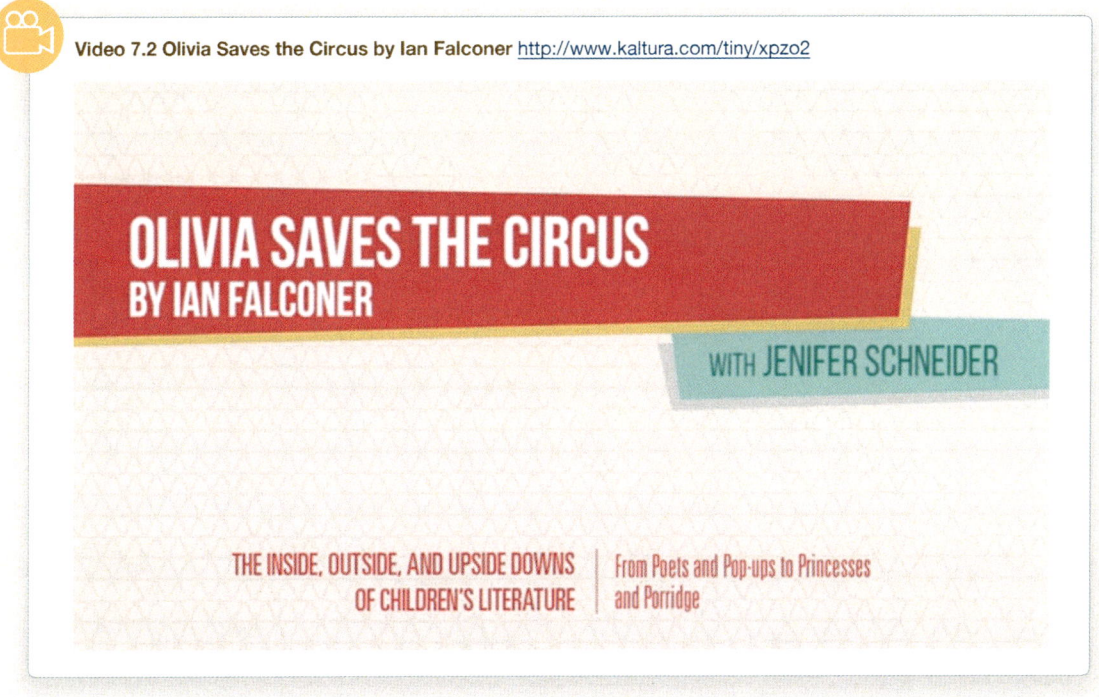

Video 7.2 Olivia Saves the Circus by Ian Falconer http://www.kaltura.com/tiny/xpzo2

Or, perhaps you've developed a Math Curse (Video 7.3)?

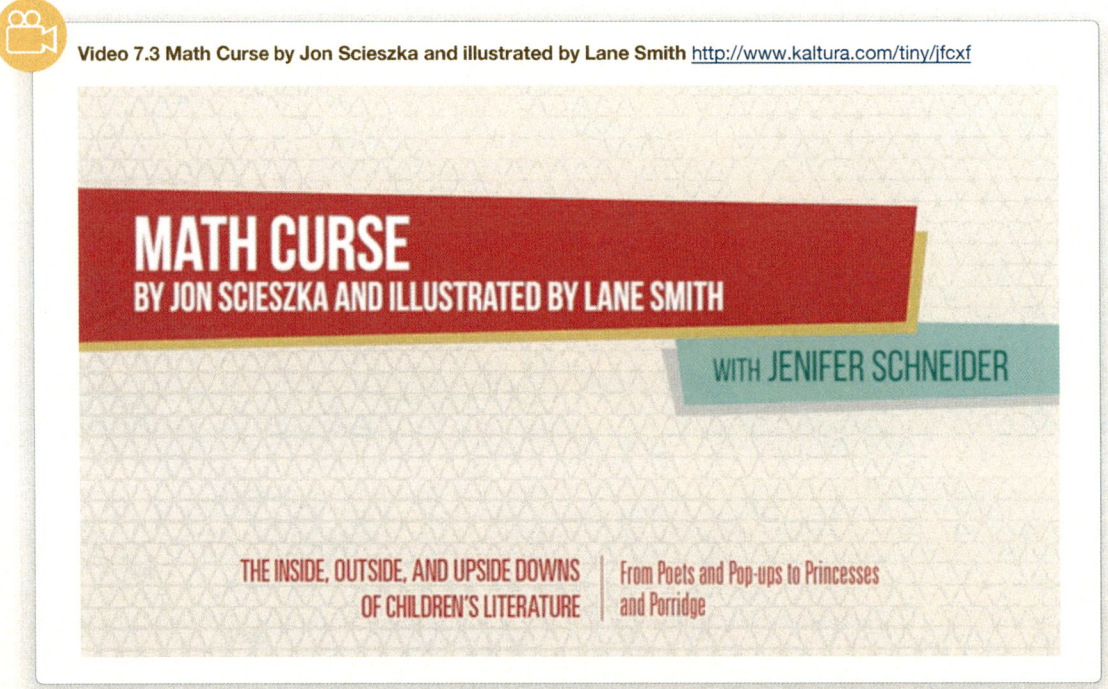

Video 7.3 Math Curse by Jon Scieszka and illustrated by Lane Smith http://www.kaltura.com/tiny/jfcxf

Science Verse, by Jon Scieszka and illustrated by Lane Smith (Video 7.4)?

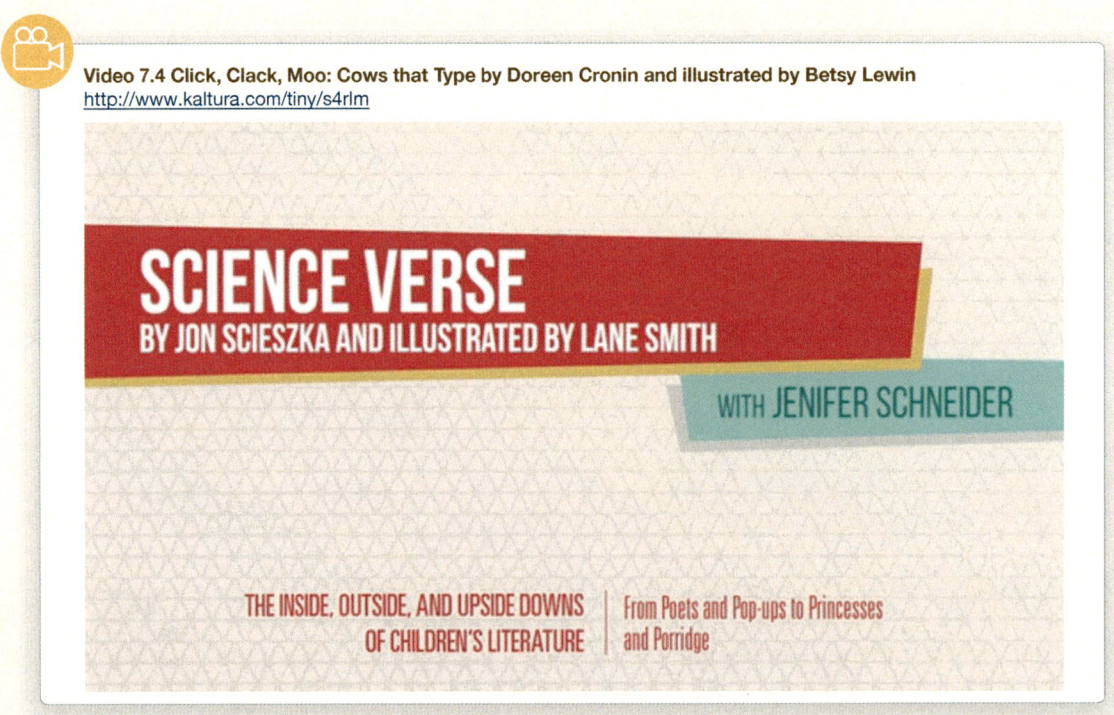

Video 7.4 Click, Clack, Moo: Cows that Type by Doreen Cronin and illustrated by Betsy Lewin http://www.kaltura.com/tiny/s4rlm

How about a duck and some cows? Are you interested in what Clicks, Clacks, or Moos (Video 7.5)?

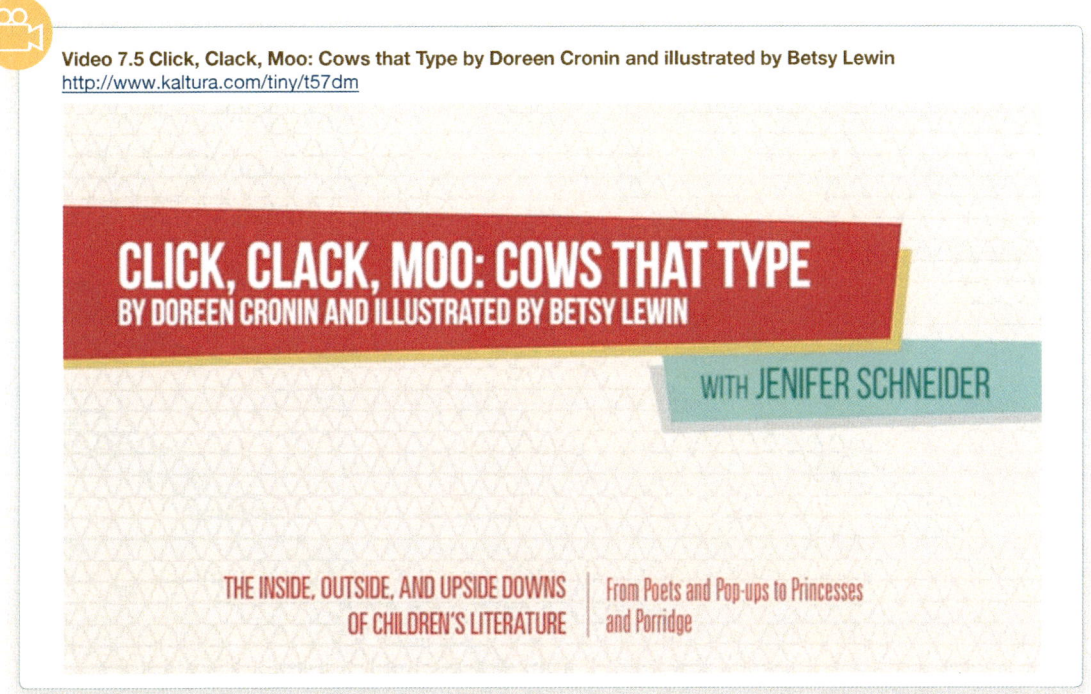

Video 7.5 Click, Clack, Moo: Cows that Type by Doreen Cronin and illustrated by Betsy Lewin
http://www.kaltura.com/tiny/t57dm

Haven't had enough? How about cows that quack, snooze, and Dooby-Dooby-Moo (Video 7.6)?

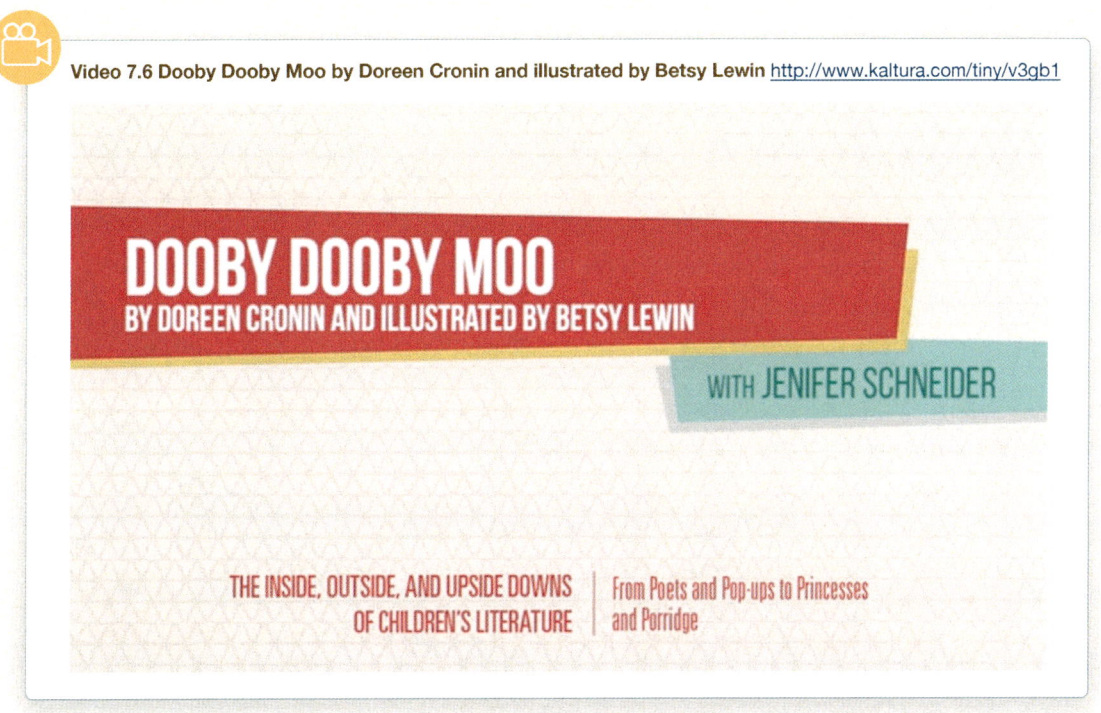

Video 7.6 Dooby Dooby Moo by Doreen Cronin and illustrated by Betsy Lewin http://www.kaltura.com/tiny/v3gb1

These books are certainly not the stuff to cause menace or the blowing of brains. What's the problem?

In this chapter, I focus on how series books are made and how their creators become serial writers or illustrators. It has a lot to do with success, time, opportunity, and demand. Of course, series books are tied to audience reception and sales, but is there something inherently valuable that attracts readers in the first place? What do you notice about the books I just shared with you?

Number of Sales

Many scholars, librarians, and teachers dislike series books for their stilted plots, flat characters, and predictable dialogue (e.g., Zipes, 2002, p. 171). As Caroline Hewins wrote: "The series habit should not be encouraged" (1915, p. 10). But it's hard to disagree with the numbers.

- In 2013, Veronica Roth's series of three books about a dystopian future, *Divergent*, *Insurgent*, and *Allegiant* sold 6.7 million copies: 3 million hardcover, 1.7 million paperback and 2 million ebook.
- In 2012, Suzanne Collins's *The Hunger Games* trilogy sold 27.7 million copies: 15 million print books and 12.7 million e-books (Roback, 2013).
- In 2011, *The Hunger Games* books found their audience and sold 9.2 million copies.
- In 2010, Jeff Kinney's *Diary of a Wimpy Kid* sold 11.5 million, followed by Rick Riordan's *Percy Jackson* series, which sold over 10 million copies.
- In 2009, *Twilight* was the winner with 26.5 million copies sold.

What comes first: the series or the success?

Number of Uses

What is it about series books that makes them so appealing? As we know, sales are not indicative of quality. So perhaps the success of a series rests with different numbers.

Success could stem from the number of classroom uses. For example, some children's books are trolled for vocabulary keywords (Liang, 2015). Others are reread to build vocabulary, comprehension, and fluency (Korat, 2010). Some books are read, and deplored, for their focus on banal topics that are ironically entertaining for children (McKenzie, 2005) (Figure 7.1). And some teachers use series books to support vocabulary acquisition for second language learners (Cho & Krashen, 1994).

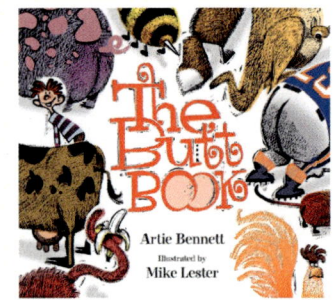

Figure 7.1

Come on! Who isn't laughing at this cover and concept? Artie Bennett also wrote *Poopendous* and *Belches, Burps, and Farts, Oh My!* Cover from *The Butt Book* by Artie Bennett and illustrated by Mike Lester, 2009, London, UK: Bloomsbury. Cover art copyright 2009 by Mike Lester.

Classroom usage can be convincing. In fact, when I searched for teacher resources on www.ReadWriteThink.org, I found over 350 classroom lesson plans and afterschool resources focused on series books. However, teachers rarely target one particular series as the focus for their instruction unless that series is already popular. In other words, instructional uses do not make a book popular.

Number of Critiques

Another factor in the success of series books is the number of condemnations it draws. Jessica Roy, of www.Fusion.net gathered several of the initial reviews of *Harry Potter* and found consistent commentary from the irrelevant, old, white, British guys (I added the irrelevant part). *Publisher's Weekly* gave a favorable review of J.K. Rowling's *Harry Potter* debut (Figure 7.2), comparing Rowling to P.L. Travers and Roald Dahl. The *New York Times* was fond of Harry as well. But the reviewers from *The Guardian, Christianity Today*, and the *Wall Street Journal* found fault.

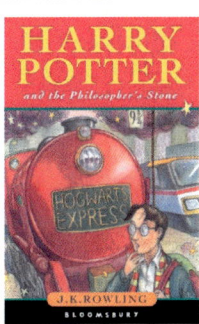

Figure 7.2

You may not know that Harry's British title is *Harry Potter and the Philosopher's Stone*. Either way, critics on both sides of the pond wrote mixed reviews. *Harry Potter and the Philosopher's Stone* by J.K. Rowling and illustrated by Thomas Taylor, 1997, London, UK: Bloomsbury. Cover art copyright 1997 by Thomas Taylor.

The same is true in music and movies. Taylor Swift is often too popular to be good. I'm sorry, but Taylor Swift captures the human experience of adolescence, societal expectations, and bullying. She lays bare the unrealistic expectations placed upon girls and the slander levied against them when they don't want to be the cheerleader in short skirts. She's also criticized as a faux feminist. Oh, so there's one brand of feminism? I wasn't aware.

For a different crowd, Jimmy Buffett's lyrics, made pleasant with rhythmic melodies and steel drums, capture reflections on life, love, and loss.

I hear depth in Metallica and Eminem. Listen to what they are saying then pay attention to how they say it musically.

Look at the acting of Bradley Cooper, Zach Galifinakis, and Ken Jong in the Hangover. I'm really serious about this. I see layers and depth.

Scholars and critics seem to hate popularity. From the early ALA rants against vulgarity in dime novels (West, 1985) to the recent rage against adults who like to read YA books (Burnes, 2014; Graham, 2014a; Wolitzer, 2014), if it's popular; it's never quite good enough. Yet, those who levy sweeping dismissals should be more conditional in their admonitions. As Moses (1907) warned, "Democracy in literature is falsely associated with mediocrity" (p. 8).

Those who abhor the popular (similar to those who must have Henri Jayer Cros Parantoux wines and nothing less will do), are not revealing the depth of their literary palates nor are they thinking of the literary diets of the proletariat. They are holding forth, and in doing so, exposing their personal issues. Rather than seeking audience with the scholar class, they should take a reprieve to the psychiatrist's couch and whilst there, curl up with some Karl Marx, Walter Benjamin, Theodor Adorno, and the newest Harper Lee. Then put on their Beats by Dre and reflect on the linguistic stylings and musical renderings of Taylor Swift as she explores the layers of teenage angst because she, better than they, knows the *intended* audience.

> Marx, Benjamin, and Adorno are associated with forms of literary criticism and views of the "popular." My reference to Harper Lee is associated with the sales of and buzz about *Go Set a Watchman*, which were completely based on the popularity of *To Kill a Mockingbird* a book that some believe was ghostwritten by Truman Capote. And I think it's funny that highbrow critics are so dismissive of popular literature when I know they are obsessed with other forms of pop culture such as which devices they use (headphones, phones, watches) or how many Twitter followers they have.

I find thoughtless, erudite-light criticism amusing. This positioning of grandeur is rampant among the children's literature crowd who find they aren't quite as respected as those who write about Russian literature, Holocaust studies, or Arthurian traditions. Thoughtless positioning is also pervasive among the High Literature crowd because they seem to resent it when good books are written for other audiences. Of course some series are formulaic and some authors are stilted, but others are complex and well-written. Of course "the job of criticism is to make distinctions between good things and bad things and between complicated things and simplistic things" (Graham, 2014b). But the critics do more than "evaluate the text" when they condemn the reader.

> My point is this: one's theoretical approach to literature serves as justification for different kinds of critical activity. In other words, there are different ways to read and critique literature. And these different ways of reading are why some people dislike English literature or poetry courses—the professor/instructor tries to retrain the students' approaches to reading. At times, this is a good thing. It's helpful to learn how to think and see differently. The problem comes from the snobbish attitudes surrounding certain schools of thought or rigidity in thinking. There is more than one way to read a book.

Children's literature is *intended* for children and young adults. Unlike dead literature studies, children's literature is an active, evolving collection whose consumers, not only vote with their feet, they vote with their Likes, Tweets, and Cosplay. Working in the field of a living literature requires some intellectual risk taking, the willingness to be connected to kids (even if it is in circumstantial ways), and the ability to study literature as integral to social existence, not isolated from it. Popularity is social existence.

Number of Promotions

Some series books are hyped up. As Zipes (2002) pointed out, much of the hype about Harry Potter was due to the rags-to-riches story surrounding J.K. Rowling. For example, *New York Times* writer, Michael Winerip (1999), wrote:

> On the whole, "Harry Potter and the Sorcerer's Stone" is as funny, moving and impressive as the story behind its writing. J. K. Rowling, a teacher by training, was a 30-year-old single mother living on welfare in a cold one-bedroom flat in Edinburgh when she began writing it in longhand during her baby daughter's nap times. But like Harry Potter, she had wizardry inside, and has soared beyond her modest Muggle surroundings to achieve something quite special. (https://www.nytimes.com/books/99/02/14/reviews/990214.14childrt.html)

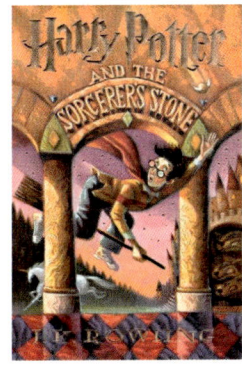

Figure 7.3

Harry Potter was re-titled, repackaged, and re-illustrated for the US market. *Harry Potter and the Sorcerer's Stone* by J.K. Rowling and illustrated by Mary GrandPré, 1998, New York, NY: Scholastic. Cover art copyright 1998 by Mary GrandPré.

Certainly there is legitimacy in examining the publishing machine, which explains some of the success of *Harry Potter* (Figure 7.3) and other series such as *Nancy Drew*, the *Bobbsey Twins*, and many books in the Stratemeyer Syndicate. Even in the early 1900s, the literary market was influenced by publishers and profits (Video 7.7). The same is true today. Perhaps current series success is also a function of social networking and the speed with which trends are promoted digitally: all reasonable explanations for a book's success.

The Girls' and Boys' Series Books Collection at USF is one of the most extensive collections of twentieth century American juvenile series books in existence. Many can be viewed online: http://www.lib.usf.edu/special-collections/childrens-young-adult-literature/girls-boys-series-books/#

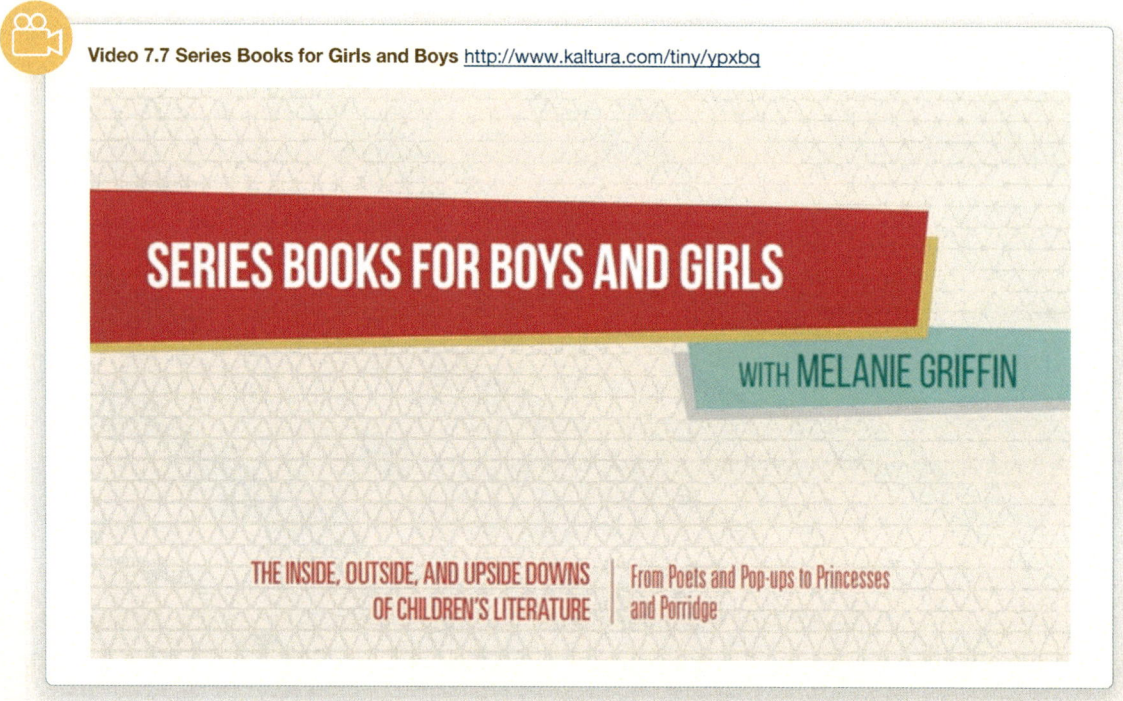

Video 7.7 Series Books for Girls and Boys http://www.kaltura.com/tiny/ypxbq

Yet, Zipes dismissal is off-base. Children and young adults don't read publisher previews or literary critiques. Kids don't care that Rowling was single, a mother, on welfare, and wrote on paper rather than a computer. Kids liked *Harry Potter* when they read the book and that's why it spread like wildfire.

In positioning series books as a viable option for struggling readers and a bridge between picturebooks and novels, Dubrovin (1979) found 12 common characteristics recommended by publishers of formulaic books:

- Fast-paced opening;
- Simple and direct story line;
- Limited number of characters;
- Viewpoint of the main character;
- Short time span;
- Tight writing;
- Brief, carefully woven descriptions;
- Short chapters;
- Lots of dialogue;

- Plenty of action scenes;
- Short sentences, simple constructions, everyday vocabulary;
- Snappy conclusion.

But these characteristics do not explain the success of the rest of the books in any series. Perhaps, as suggested by Zipes, the publicists and publishers "push" these books and the librarians (lemmings that they are), blindly recommend books without reading them? This might be true in some cases, but millions of copies? Someone is reading. Someone is liking. Somehow the children are finding the books and making a choice whether to come back for round two or move on. There is something in the book that resonates with readers.

Librarians as lemmings? I'm joking here. As Neil Gaiman famously wrote, you don't "mess" with librarians:
http://journal.neilgaiman.com/2004/12/world-aids-day-post.asp

Number of Readers

The reality of any series success is the connection between the author, the text, and the reader. Kids read what they like: what's funny, interesting, scary, dangerous, and different. Sequels are written due to the success of the previous book. Without success, the second book wouldn't go under contract because publishers have to make money. Series books are working books; they are books that people read. As Catherine Ross (1995) wrote: "series books do not enfeeble readers or render them unfit for reading anything else. It is not helpful to establish a hierarchy in reading in which a reader's passionate engagement with a pleasurable book somehow does not count as 'real reading'" (p. 233).

I couldn't agree more. Series books can be formulaic, repeating the same story lines in different spaces and times (e.g, *Nancy Drew, Goosebumps*). Series books can also be more intricate, garnering lots of attention and mixed critical acclaim. As with all children's literature, the quality varies and attracts readers for different purposes.

The Making of a Serial Writer
(Or Illustrator)

Like any other gift, writing for children cannot be taught; it has to be born. If possible, with the exception of drama, it is the most difficult art to master, since its narrative will not stand imitation, since its simplicity must represent naturalness and not effort, since its meaning must be within reach, and without the tone of condescension (Moses, 1907, p. 6)

Whereas some devalue the writing of series books, others recognize the creator's ability to write or illustrate for a massive, exacting audience as a laudable task. In this section, I explore the serial authors and illustrators who create successful series as well as non-series books. First, I highlight famous series creators, the people you know and love. I also feature authors and illustrators who are prolific creators, the people you should get to know. Second, I share information on ghostwriting, a common practice in children's, young adult, and adult literature. Third, I delve briefly into celebrity authorship and, fourth, conclude with a look at fanfiction: the literary equivalent to MMOGs (Massive, Multiplayer, Online Games).

You can find lists of great authors and illustrators here:
http://www.balkinbuddies.com
http://www.scbwi.org

The Prolific and Profound

Think of an author or illustrator from a children's book series-- someone you read during your childhood or someone with whom you are familiar. What do you remember about her or him? Back in the day, before the Internet, it was hard to get to know authors and illustrators (Video 7.8). Sure, some of them made school visits, but those experiences were rare. Now, take a look at these authors' and illustrators' websites. What do you notice?

J.K. Rowling. You know her name. You know her characters (*Harry Potter*). Now get to know her through her website. This is not a basic website (http://www.jkrowling.com).

AMERICAN TYPO
(GHOST, FAN, SERIAL, AND CELEBRITY WRITERS—AND ILLUSTRATORS)

Video 7.8 Meeting Authors and Illustrators: Autographs, Materials, and Tweets
http://www.kaltura.com/tiny/z8k2b

 Marketing and publicity have always played a role in the children's literature industry. Check out the old ways of author and illustrator promotion.

Nikki Grimes. Author of books such as the *Dyamonde Daniel* series (Figure 7.4), Nikki Grimes is also an author of award-winning poetry and picture books. What's featured on her website? (http://www.nikkigrimes.com/)

Neil Gaiman. Neil Gaiman is hugely popular and critically acclaimed for his books. What does his website reveal about his work? (http://www.neilgaiman.com/)

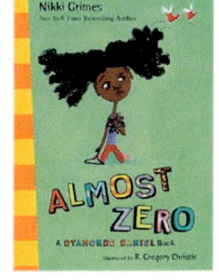

Figure 7.4
Dyamonde Daniel is a memorable character, and Nikki Grimes' series focuses on her normal, everyday life experiences. *Almost Zero: A Dyamonde Daniel Book* by Nikki Grimes and illustrated by R. Gregory Christie, 2010, New York, NY: G.P. Putnam's Sons Books for Young Readers. Cover art copyright 2010 by R. Gregory Christie.

Suzanne Collins. Author of the *Hunger Games*. View Suzanne Collins' website. What do you think about the content and coverage? (http://www.suzannecollinsbooks.com)

Jeff Kinney. Author of *Diary of a Wimpy Kid*. Jeff's books are really popular. How does his website target his audience? (http://www.wimpykid.com)

Mo Willems. Mo has several series (Pigeon, Elephant & Piggie (Figure 7.5), Knuffle Bunny) and they are wildly popular. How does his website reflect his authorial and illustrator personas? (http://www.mowillems.com/)

Figure 7.5
Elephant & Piggie books are one of several series written and illustrated by Mo Williams. *I Broke My Trunk (An Elephant & Piggie Book)* by Mo Willems, 2011, New York, NY: Disney-Hyperion. Copyright 2011 by Mo Willems.

Personalities and products. Commercially successful series authors or illustrators often develop a brand. In addition to writing books, they license products, make appearances, and sign movie deals. What starts with a book can turn into an entire enterprise including theme parks and West End plays. As you may notice, most of their websites are professionally designed and feature opportunities for games, author connections, and book, video, or toy purchases. Of these series writers, only Suzanne Collins' website is reminiscent of an older website that feels as if she wrote it and manages it herself. Her website also focuses on critical acclaim and sharing information rather than the user's experience.

Mo Willems is particularly good at interacting with his audience. He creates videos of read alouds, posts coloring pages, and he posts on Twitter.

Other successful series authors and illustrators manage their own websites, book their own visits, and run more of the business of publishing and selling books. Here are a few examples of some other award-winning authors and illustrators who are successful, but they don't have theme park rides (yet):

Vicki Cobb http://www.vickicobb.com;

Henry Cole http://www.henrycole.net;

Ethan Long http://www.ethanlong.com;

Elizabeth Levy http://elizabethlevy.com;

More on the commercialization of children's literature in a later chapter.

Organizations such as the Society of Children's Book Writers and Illustrators (SCBWI) offer resources to help the creators succeed in the business end of book publication (http://www.scbwi.org/online-resources/frequently-asked-questions/). Authors and illustrators are good at writing and art, not necessarily talent management, sales, accounting, and all of the other components connected to creating books. Most authors and illustrators can be contacted directly via email or they may use a personal assistant (often a partner, sibling, adult child, or friend). Either way, marketing and publicity have a major impact on sales and the "enterprise" of creating children's books. The publishers do not strongly advocate for the small or mid-level authors and illustrators and they rarely market their books appropriately.

Pedigree and product. While some critics, teachers, and librarians are quick to summarily disregard popular series (Schurman & Johnson, 2002), many authors and illustrators create extraordinary books that engage readers. These writers and artists don't happen upon success by chance; they study, prepare, write and illustrate incessantly. They work at their craft and along the way their work pays off.

Children's book authors attend well-respected and prestigious schools, colleges, and universities to study English, literature, writing, illustration, design, and languages

- J.K. Rowling studied at the University of Exeter;
- Nikki Grimes attended Rutgers University;
- Suzanne Collins attended the Alabama School of Fine Arts and Indiana University;
- Neil Gaiman went to Whitgift School and Ardingly College;
- Jeff Kinney attended the University of Maryland;
- Mo Willems graduated from the Tisch School of the Arts at New York University.

Children's book illustrators attend the top art and design schools

- Molly Bang attended the University of Arizona;
- Anthony Browne attended Leeds College of Art and Design (Figure 7.6);
- Eric Carle attended the Academy of Fine Arts in Vienna;
- Floyd Cooper graduated from the University of Oklahoma;
- David Diaz went to the Fort Lauderdale Art Institute;
- Jerry Pinkney attended the Philadelphia Museum College of Art aka The University of the Arts;
- Chris Van Allsburg went to the Rhode Island School of Design and the University of Michigan;
- Nina Crews attended Yale University and earned a BA in art (Figure 7.7);
- Dr. Seuss attended Dartmouth College and Oxford University.

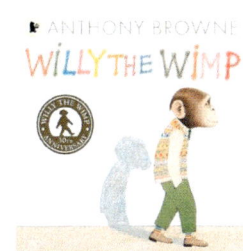

Figure 7.6
Anthony Browne, a prolific and award-winning artist, created an illustrated series based on Willy a wimpy chimp. *Willy the Wimp* by Anthony Browne, 2008, London, UK: Walker Books. Cover from 2014 edition, copyright 2014 by Anthony Browne.

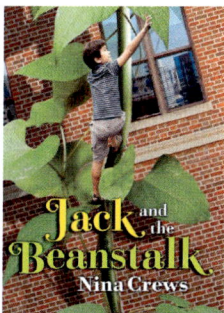

Figure 7.7
Nina Crews takes familiar folk tales and sets them in modern, urban settings. One example is *Jack and the Beanstalk* by Nina Crews, 2011, New York, NY: Henry Holt and Co. Copyright 2011 by Nina Crews.

Of course, a lot of persistence and a little luck are associated with the types of series that create international buzz and garner movie deals. But for the most part, series are successful because readers fall in love with the characters, plots, and styles of the creators.

The Ghosts

When people think about book series, *Nancy Drew* and the *Hardy Boys* often come to mind. Or they may like the *Babysitter's Club* or the *Magic Tree House*. "Series books" are familiar and memorable because they are often written on a concept of sameness through recurring characters, themes, and plot structures. In these instances, series books are often written by ghostwriters.

Amy Boesky is a ghostwriter. In her essay, *The Ghost Writes Back*, she reveals some insider perspectives on the process. https://www.kenyonreview.org/kr-online-issue/2013-winter/selections/amy-boesky-656342/

> Writing for *Sweet Valley High*, I wasn't supposed to be original. Or different. My job was to pick up somebody else's thread and follow it: *just write the story*. Spice it up with dialogue, add a toss of a blond curl here, a sparkle of a blue-green eye there. Create a subplot and weave it through the narrative.
>
> I liked the discipline of writing SVH, the structure. Francine created the story plots, which arrived in my mailbox in manila envelopes and, when I took them out and studied them, read like long, free-verse poems. Eight or nine pages of single spaced directives that laid out exhilarating and implausible fables of duplicity, innovation, risk, and triumph. My task was to turn these into "chapter outlines," adding my own subplots, mailing them back to my editor, and waiting for his approval. Once I got the green light, I worked with the precision of a Swiss clock.

Other ghostwriters tell of similar tales. R.L. Stine conceptualized each *Goosebump* book (Figure 7.8), outlining the plot and providing general information to his ghost; the ghost added the dialogue and details (Dudak, 2013). Most ghostwriters have very little contact with the named author (less so when the author is dead). The writers typically deal with an editor who hands over the details of the book. According to Gross (2015), the ghostwriter benefits

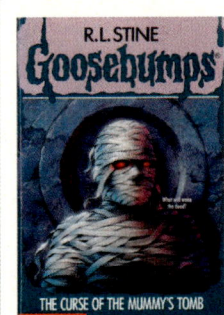

Figure 7.8
R.L. Stine created one of the most famous series of children's books—the Goosebump Series. *The Curse of the Mummy's Tomb*, by R.L. Stine, 1993, New York, NY: Scholastic. Cover art copyright 2003 by Scholastic.

from a consistent paycheck, the continual practice, and the freedom to write without scrutiny. However, ghostwriters never receive credit, acclaim, or great financial reward.

Series, such as *Sweet Valley High* or *Goosebumps* are representative of the series books bemoaned by critics. Their predictable plots are intended for repeat readers, not representative of high literary art. Similar to the writing of a television series, in which all of the successive iterations are replications of the pilot, to write such a repetitive story, requires a system.

Yes, Goosebumps are ghostwritten. R.L. Stine started the series and had to use ghostwriters to keep up with the demand. He developed the concept for each book and outlined the plot, but ghosts wrote the rest.

The secret behind the longevity of Nancy Drew and the Hardy Boys is simple. They're still here because their creators found a way to minimize cost, maximize output, and standardize creativity. The solution was an assembly line that made millions by turning writers into anonymous freelancers—a business model that is central to the Internet age (Gross, 2015).

But not all ghostwriting occurs with such writing rigidity. Shel Silverstein was a ghostwriter for Johnny Cash and other singers such as Dr. Hook. He also published cartoons and stories in *Playboy* (Silverstein, 2015).

Watch Shel Silverstein sing with Johnny Cash (https://www.youtube.com/watch?v=Dmt7woOTnr8).

The Celebrities

Many celebrities use ghostwriters or "co-authors." But you probably figured that out. The celebrities, who may have success as actors, comedians, or musicians, write children's books figuring anyone can write for children. But it's just not true.

Many celebrities use ghostwriters For example, Dustin Warburton co-wrote with several celebrities: http://www.csmonitor.com/The-Culture/Family/Modern-Parenthood/2014/1020/Children-s-books-written-by-celebrities-The-good-the-bad-the-charming

First, notice the fact that celebrities write short children's picturebooks that are often pulled along by the artwork. For example, LeUyen Pham illustrates Julianne Moore's text in *Freckleface Strawberry* (Figure 7.9). LeUyen Pham also illustrates the *Alvin Ho* series by Lenore Look, *The Princess in Black* series by Shannon and Dean Hale (Figure 7.10), and a series of board books by Jabari Asim (Figure 7.11).

Second, notice that celebrities who do not have "writing" backgrounds never write novels. There are a few individuals who have some level of fame in other "writing" careers (e.g., Mike Lupica is a sports writer and he's created a series of sports-themed novels for kids), but a successful non-writer is rare.

Sometimes the celebrities are inspired by their own children and occasionally these individuals have backgrounds writing for television or stand-up (Jimmy Fallon is one example, Figure 7.12). Other times the celebrities are merely searching for other revenue streams (e.g., Dennis Rodman's book was co-written with Dustin Warburton; Mary Kate and Ashley Olson's books were ghostwritten). Sure, celebrity authors get an initial bump in sales due to marketing and name recognition, but if the quality isn't there, the sales drop off quickly.

A recent example of a celebrity flop is a book by Kim Kardashian http://radaronline.com/celebrity-news/kim-kardashian-naked-selfies-selfish-book-flop/

Figure 7.9

Freckleface Strawberry started as a successful book by a celebrity author and now there is a book series and musical. *FreckleFace Strawberry* by Julianne Moore and illustrated by LeUyen Pham, 2007, London, UK: Bloomsbury. Cover art copyright 2007 by LeUyen Pham.

Figure 7.10

Shannon Hale writes an excellent essay on boys and series books. *The Princess in Black* Series by Shannon and Dean Hale and illustrated by LeUyen Pham, 2015, New York, NY: Random House. Cover art copyright 2015 by LeUyen Pham.

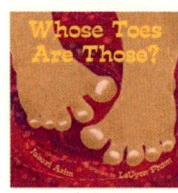

Figure 7.11

LeUyen Pham illustrates several series. One series is by Jabari Asim. *Whose Toes Are Those?* By Jabari Asim and illustrated by LeUyen Pham, 2006, New York, NY: LB Kids. Cover art copyright 2006 by LeUyen Pham.

Figure 7.12

Jimmy Fallon is an example of a celebrity author who has a writing background as a comedian. He also writes children's books from his personal experience as a father. But notice that this picture book does not list the illustrator, Miguel Ordóñez, on the front cover. *Your Baby's First Word Will Be Dada* by Jimmy Fallon and illustrated by Miguel Ordóñez, 2015, New York, NY: Feiwel & Friends. Cover art copyright 2015 by Miguel Ordóñez.

Behind closed doors, children's book authors and illustrators dislike the phenomenon of celebrity authors. Here's why—children's book creation seems romantic and lucrative, but it's not. Authors and illustrators work years, and suffer countless rejections, to get published. Then, if they get published, they have to work their way up the publicity ladder to get promoted and marketed by their publishers. They travel to schools and talk to a lot of kids. Remember all of those book awards and literary reviews? Someone has to send copies of the books. Publishers push and promote the books that they believe will sell. Sales are tied to trends and fluctuations in the market. Celebrities bypass the traditional routes of literary scrutiny with their name recognition. Then they re-direct the publishers' time, attention, and marketing away from those who have made children's books a career.

Again, if a kid likes a celebrity book, read it. But don't be surprised if they don't like it. Celebrity books are targeted for parents or adults—the people who actually recognize the celebrity's name. If a parent likes the book and will read it aloud, I encourage it. As I said before, good readers find quality. You have to make the reader first, and the parents who read to their kids make readers.

Do babies like caviar?
Does one's first sip of beer or wine taste good?
Taste develops with experience. Experience comes from motivation and success.

The Fans

The book publishing field is complex and filled with roadblocks. It is the fans who must endure long waits for the next book in the series. Taking matters into their own hands, the fans created their own literature series that are easily disseminated across digital networks—fanfiction.

Did you know that *Fifty Shades of Gray* is fanfiction for the *Twilight* Series? A book, popular with teens, can become another book popular with millions of adults.

I discuss issues of "appropriateness" and fanfiction ratings in another chapter.

Did you know that the *Harry Potter* series and the *Twilight* series have spawned more fanfics and fandoms than any other book series?

Fanfiction is a series book gone wild. Fanfiction is a genre of literature in which the fans of original literature develop stories about characters, the settings, or plots of the original books.

Check out these fanfiction sites connected to children's and young adult series books:

- AO3: http://archiveofourown.org;

- Fanfiction.net: https://www.fanfiction.net/;

- Wattpad: https://www.wattpad.com;

- FicWad: http://ficwad.com;

- Harry Potter Fanfiction: http://www.harrypotterfanfiction.com.

Fanart is often included with some fanfics, but there are other sites that focus specifically on the art (Figure 7.13):

- Deviantart: http://www.deviantart.com/;

- Tumblr: https://www.tumblr.com;

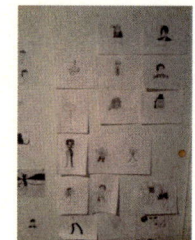

Figure 7.13
My daughter creates fanart for anime, manga, and cartoons. She posts it on her bedroom wall, closet doors, and in notepads. Not all fanfic and fanart is made public. Photo copyright 2015 by Jenifer Schneider.

Fanfiction is popular among teenage youth and it is frequently studied by literary scholars. Fanfiction is also popular among adults. In fact, some very famous adult writers create fanfiction.

- Meg Cabot: Author of the *Princess Diaries* wrote *Star Wars* fanfic as a teen.

- Cassandra Clare: Author of *Mortal Instruments*, wrote very popular fanfic based on *Lord of the Rings*.

- S.E. Hinton: Author of *The Outsiders*, writes *Supernatural* fanfiction.

- Neil Gaiman: Author of *Coraline* writes a number of strands of fanfiction.

In contrast to the authors who write or encourage fanfiction, some fight the practice with their poison pens and, on occasion, with legal action. The Copyright Act of 1976 gives a copyright owner the exclusive right to reproduce, adapt, distribute, perform, and display his or her work. The Copyright Act prevents others from doing the same. However, when someone wants to recreate or extend their experience with characters, plots, and images, there are some exceptions made when the reproduction or adaptation meets the criteria for fair use:

> If a writer of fan fiction (sic) is sued for infringement the writer can make an argument of fair use. Under fair use, there is a four factor test that the courts apply: 1) the purpose and character of the use (commercial in nature or nonprofit educational purposes), 2) the nature of the copyrighted work, 3) the amount and substantiality of the portion used in relation to the copyrighted work, and 4) the effect of the use on the potential market of the copyrighted work. (Fan Fiction and Copyright Law by Sam T. http://lawblog.usfca.edu/internetjustice/2013/fan-fiction-and-copyright-law/)

For example, throughout this textbook, I worked with a copyright librarian to determine if I met the conditions of fair use when I wanted to include cover art of children's books. I also worked with her to seek permission to perform (i.e., read aloud) certain works. According to Michael Thomas, founding partner of Creative Vision Legal,(http://www.creativevisionlegal.com), "there is no bright-line rule; fair use analysis is really tricky and complex" (personal communication).

At one point, before Web 2.0 and the prevalence of platforms conducive to participatory culture, literary/musical/artistic "remixing" and "borrowing" were clearly viewed as plagiarism. Rap music borrows rhythms, lyrics, and beats. But now it's hard to control and difficult to decide. For now, most fanfiction seems to go unchallenged and it continues to thrive.

Revisiting a Number of Things

In the beginning of this chapter I discussed the popularity of series books in connection to the number of sales, promotions, critiques, uses, and readers. Clearly, a book's success is much more complicated than one good promotion or one noteworthy critique. Although there are mechanistic processes surrounding the production of many series, there is no single recipe for a series success, unless, of course, you give credit to the creators.

I ended the chapter with a look at serial writing and illustrating. Whether prolific and profound, ghostly, celebrity, or fan, children's literature creators are in high demand. All sources indicate that children's and young adult series are holding up markets in both print and ebook sales as well as Internet traffic and fandoms (Bluestone, 2015). Of course, increased production might impact quality; but increased production and alternative publishing also create space for new ideas and challenging conventions. In the next chapter, I further explore children's book publishing and marketing trends.

CHAPTER 08

BEYOND THE PAGE AND BEHIND THE SCENES

(WRITING, PUBLISHING, AND MARKETING CHILDREN'S LITERATURE: BOOKS, CINEMA, CARTOONS, TOYS AND APPS)

Since 1998, I have served as the Director of an annual literature conference for children. *The Children's Literature Collection of Know-how* (CLICK) provides an opportunity for professional authors and illustrators to speak to youth and provide tips for writing and drawing (Figure 8.1). In addition to learning from professionals, the children and youth share their own writing with each other and receive feedback from the audience (Figure 8.2). The attendees work with a journalist to create the CLICK blog (Figure 8.3).

Figure 8.1

The Children's Literature Collection of Know-how (CLICK) is an annual conference featuring authors and illustrators. Joyce Carol Thomas presented to the crowd of children and adults in 2006. In the photo, she shares images from *The Gospel Cinderella* as she talks about her writing process. *The Gospel Cinderella* by Joyce Carol Thomas and illustrated by David Diaz, 2004, New York, NY: Amistad. Photo copyright 2006 by Jenifer Schneider.

Children's Literature Collection of Know-how:

Website: www.coedu.usf.edu/syac

Facebook:
- https://www.facebook.com/ClickChildrensLiteratureCollectionOfKnowHow
- https://www.facebook.com/Suncoast-Young-Authors-Celebration-Alumni-550145618363135/timeline/

Twitter: https://twitter.com/usfclick

Figure 8.2

Attendees share their writing during a break out session at the CLICK Conference. Photo copyright 2014 by Jenifer Schneider.

Figure 8.3

Youth work with journalist-in-residence, Anne Worthwine Anderson, to create the CLICK Chronicle, a conference blog. Photo copyright 2015 by Jenifer Schneider.

They also participate in several breakout sessions that showcase their artistic responses to the books featured during the conference.

Drawing (Figure 8.4 and Figure 8.5);

Figure 8.4
Children create guerilla art in response to reading books and listening to the author and illustrator talks. Photo copyright 2015 by Jenifer Schneider.

Figure 8.5
CLICK artist-in-residence, Csaba Osvath, poses with the guerilla art that he helped the participants create (http://www.csabaosvath.com/). Photo copyright 2015 by Jenifer Schneider.

Bookmaking (Figure 8.6);

Figure 8.6
Students create blank books to take home from the CLICK Conference. Photo copyright 2015 by Jenifer Schneider.

Filmmaking (Figure 8.7);

Figure 8.7
Students use Play-doh and iPads to create stop-motion versions of the books they read during the CLICK Conference. Photo copyright 2015 by Jenifer Schneider.

Performance activities (Figure 8.8).

Figure 8.8
Dramatist, Margaret Branscombe, works with children during the CLICK Conference. Students use tableau and other theater games to revisit the books discussed by the CLICK authors and illustrators. For more information about Margaret and her techniques, visit http://www.learnthroughdrama.com/. Photo copyright 2015 by Jenifer Schneider.

Over the years, approximately 10,000 youth from over 75 public, private, and home schools have attended the conference. In addition, hundreds of parents, teachers, librarians and volunteers have chaperoned. With all those children and adults, you might be surprised to learn that every year, without fail, they ask the guest authors and illustrators the same exact questions:

- How did you learn to write or draw?
- Where do you get your ideas?
- How do I get published?

In this chapter, I further explore children's literature beyond the page and behind the scenes. I take a look at children's book authors and illustrators to understand the nature of their processes. I link to resources for aspiring writers and illustrators and provide insider perspectives on the publication process. I also connect the origins of ideas with the marketing of movies, toys, games, and apps in order to provide an expansive view of children's literature markets beyond the books. As you will discover, no aspect of children's literature is as simple, as glamorous, or as textual as it may seem.

The Work of Authors and Illustrators: Learning to Write or Draw

"A work of art is essentially the internal made external, resulting from a creative process operating under the impulse of feeling, and embodying the combined product of the poet's perceptions, thoughts, and feelings" (Abrams, 1953, p. 22). Much of the attention on children's literature focuses on the work of art—the written text or the illustrated image. Readers read the resulting products. Critics dwell on text and images. In this section, I explore the creation of these works of art—the internal made external.

Professional writers and illustrators of children's and young adult literature often articulate their "tools of the trade" and share insightful reflections about their creative processes. In turn, their tips provide their readers and fans with specific methods and suggestions that can be imitated.

Here is a collection of resources for aspiring writers. Warning! These articles contain conflicting ideas:

- 8 Habits of Highly Successful Young Adult Fiction Authors:
  http://www.theatlantic.com/entertainment/archive/2013/10/the-8-habits-of-highly-successful-young-adult-fiction-authors/280722/

- How to Write a Picture Book:
  http://www.buzzfeed.com/macbarnett/how-to-write-a-picture-book-i066#.ck4mkDrg8

- C.S. Lewis on the Three Ways of Writing for Children and the Key to Authenticity in All Writing by Maria Popova: http://www.brainpickings.org/2014/06/18/c-s-lewis-writing-for-children/

- The Hundred Best Websites for Writers in 2015:
  http://thewritelife.com/100-best-websites-for-writers-2015/#.2f65qk:kGK2

- Writing Young Adult Fiction for Dummies:
  http://www.dummies.com/how-to/content/writing-young-adult-fiction-for-dummies-cheat-shee.html

- Writing Children's Books for Dummies:
  http://www.dummies.com/how-to/content/writing-childrens-books-for-dummies-cheat-sheet.html

- How To Create A Fantastic Picture Book:
  https://www.writersandartists.co.uk/writers/advice/327/dedicated-genre-advice/writing-for-children/

Some writers engage in familiar routines that can be approximated by the general public, but others have developed habits that may be impractical for most of us (e.g., Roald Dahl wrote in a backyard hut). Professional methods are not recipes for guaranteed success, but they are practices that may take the mystery, and often the misery, out of writing words or making art.

The Writers

Several years ago I surveyed children's book authors and illustrators to get a sense of their backgrounds, educational training, and approaches to children's book creation (Schneider, 2010). Eighty-five people responded to the anonymous survey and I synthesized their reflections on several components of the process of writing children's books. Below, I share their responses and highlight major points with examples from other writers who have publically revealed elements of their process.

 Funding for the survey research was provided by the International Reading Association, Elva Knight Research Grant.

Forms and Feedback. Although we may have romantic visions of authors as spending their days writing in cafes and sipping coffee (see Mo Willems writing in a Paris cafe http://www.cbsnews.com/news/for-kids-book-author-mo-willems-childhood-is-an-awful-time/), the authors I surveyed consistently indicated that their most predominant form of writing was email followed by letters or formal correspondence. Remember, most authors (and illustrators) are independent contractors who must manage the business end of children's book creation along with the creative components.

When I book authors or illustrators for the CLICK Conference, I send an email to determine the person's availability. Once we agree to the terms of the presentation, then I email a contract, which the creator must read, sign, and return along with tax forms and other documentation. The authors/illustrators typically book their own air fare and hotel room and then they must obtain reimbursement from the CLICK Conference (more documentation and email correspondence). We exchange emails or schedule phone calls to discuss the nature of the presentation, their needs for materials (microphones, easels, markers, chair and room arrangement, etc.)

I work with the university bookstore to manage the sale of books; however, when authors and illustrators make school visits, they have more of a role in the book sale process. They select the books they want to sell, but often these books are not ready for sale or there is some snag in distribution. Therefore, they must contact the publisher to intervene and push the process along.

On the day of the CLICK Conference, the authors and illustrators present to groups of children, interact with attendees, and sign autographs. I have observed illustrators using "down time" to sketch illustrations or write notes. A school visit can take 2 or more days out of the week (plus the prep and follow up). The authors' and illustrators' days are filled with school visits and talks to promote their books and increase sales which leaves very little time for creating new ones.

None of what I have just described includes the many ways in which the authors and illustrators communicate with editors, graphic designers, book production staff, etc. To create a book, the author and illustrator is involved in much more than "creation."

As for their creative writing efforts, the authors most frequently write in narrative and poetic genres. The authors write in home offices and they rarely "collaborate" in the co-writing sense of the word. Of course some of the authors participate in writing groups, or they consult with editors, but they do not consider their writing process to be collaborative. Authors receive feedback and then make further writing decisions on their own.

Some authors use writing groups and various organizations provide networking opportunities for people who want to write books for children.

- Society of Children's Book Writers and Illustrators http://www.scbwi.org/frequently-asked-questions/

- Children's Book Author Meetups http://childrens-book-authors.meetup.com/

Processes and Procedures. If you were to observe a writer during the active creation of a text, you would not witness much action beyond typing on a keyboard or letter formation on a notepad. The behaviors of writers are not grandiose and magnificent; they are often subtle. For example, you might see a writer create several revisions of the same text. The writer might play with alternative words or sayings, or create alternative beginnings, middles, and ends.

Often, a writer's work is invisible and unrelated to the act of writing. Writers may revise their work inside their heads, which leaves their bodies free to behave in other ways. Writers can work while they are painting, listening to music, driving a car or taking a shower. Some authors have to write while lying down on a sofa or in bed. Others need special objects around them (e.g., Roald Dahl sat in big chair, covered his feet with a sleeping bag, and surrounded himself with travel souvenirs and photos—Figure 8.9). The "quirks" of writers are often humorous and unusual but they remind us that writing is a compilation of the writer's entire being. Writing is a mental, emotional and physical act.

Figure 8.9
Roald Dahl's hut at the Road Dahl Museum and Story Centre. Photo copyright 2013 by Jenifer Schneider.

 Read Maria Popova's article, "The Odd Habits and Curious Customs of Famous Writers" (http://www.brainpickings.org/2013/09/23/odd-type-writers/)

The authors I surveyed revealed that they mentally plan for writing, rarely using webs or organizers, but occasionally creating lists or outlines of their texts. The authors do not focus on fonts or layout, nor do they focus on "correctness." Font, color, graphics, and other visual aspects of children's literature are not considerations in the writing process because book design and artwork are separate procedures. Instead, the authors stated that they attend to language and ideas. They value other writing skills that develop their personal writing styles such as reading good examples and understanding audience. The authors revealed that they rely on editors to catch and correct grammar and mechanics errors. They also acknowledge the contributions of copy-editors in "cleaning up" their writing.

Authors hardly rely on the writing strategies most people learn in school (Video 8.1). Watch Kate DiCamillo and Katherine Paterson dismiss common instructional strategies as they discuss their writing processes. https://www.youtube.com/watch?v=GprltUiL-YQ

Also, the following writers share tips and tricks:

- Mem Fox: http://memfox.com/for-writers-hints/for-writer-hints/
- Pat Mora: http://www.patmora.com/tips/
- Emma Walton Hamilton: http://emmawaltonhamilton.com/the-6-common-

Video 8.1 The Evolution of an Author's Manuscript: Luna by Julie Anne Peters http://www.kaltura.com/tiny/zul3z

Writing Instruction and Training. Most of the authors stated that they learned writing skills in high school or college and they learned how to refine their texts by reading and analyzing their teachers' written comments. The authors frequently stated that writers must learn to "accept feedback and criticism." They suggested that those who aspire to become writers should "read extensively in order to know the field" and, given the amount of rejection in children's book publishing, new writers should "choose the career path only if writing is a passion."

Interpreting written feedback might seem like a no-brainer but it is actually good advice. For some reason many people do not learn this strategy. In addition, it's hard to do. Writers must understand the reviewer's advice and then figure out how to act on it.

The authors I surveyed unanimously valued reading and writing as tools for improving writing skills. They suggested that aspiring authors read quality examples and study the writing styles of other published authors. One author stated, "Read, read, read." Another one wrote, "Write, write, write."

Here is a short list of authors and illustrators who share tips and tricks. I think these resources are particularly helpful:

- Doreen Marts: http://www.creativebloq.com/illustration/5-tips-illustrating-childrens-book-5132983
- David MacIntosh: http://www.theguardian.com/childrens-books-site/2014/mar/11/david-mackintosh-top-10-illustration-and-design-tips
- Jim Harris: http://www.jimharrisillustrator.com/ChildrensBooks/TipsforIllustrators.html

Although many of the authors earned college degrees in diverse fields such as psychology, business, and education, most of the authors had backgrounds in writing or took college courses in creative writing. There are several colleges and universities that offer specific programs in "Writing for Children."

- Columbia University School of the Arts offers courses in Writing Children's Books.
  http://arts.columbia.edu/summer/writing/course/childrens-books

- Hamline University offers an MFA in Writing for Children and Young Adults.
  http://www.hamline.edu/cla/mfac/

- Hollins University offers an MFA in Children's Book Writing & Illustrating.
  https://www.hollins.edu/academics/graduate-degrees/childrens-book-writing-illustrating/

- Lesley College offers an MFA degree in Writing for Young People.
  http://www.lesley.edu/master-of-fine-arts/creative-writing/low-residency/writing-for-young-people/

- Simmons College offers an MFA in Writing for Children.
  http://www.simmons.edu/academics/graduate-programs/writing-for-children-mfa

- Vermont College of Fine Arts offers an MFA in Writing for Children & Young Adults.
  http://vcfa.edu/wcya

Through my survey, I attempted to capture and synthesize successful writers' processes in relation to their education, training, and writing strategies. Outside of the advice to "read" and "write," the authors communicated many other unique suggestions. Rather than revealing a blueprint of effective writing strategies, the survey responses reiterated the fact that writing is an idiosyncratic process. In other words, there isn't one way to write a children's book.

The Illustrators

Illustrators share many similarities with the writers of children's literature. Illustrators work in their studios and they function as independent contractors. Many illustrators also work as contract employees for publishers. Just like children's book authors, the illustrators manage the business components of their careers and they must engage in correspondence, contract negotiation, billing, public relations, and marketing. Hiring an agent and management personnel can relieve some of the publication responsibilities; however, hiring people costs money.

Forms and Feedback. Most illustrators have worked in formal art settings, gaining experiences in corporate art production before working as freelance children's book illustrators. For example, many illustrators have experience creating greeting cards, film animation, or producing artwork for magazines (Figure 8.10).

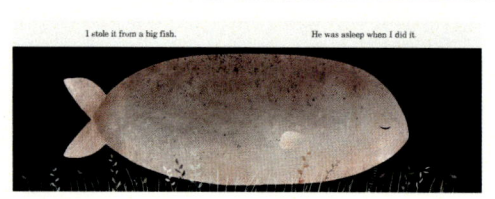

Figure 8.10

Jon Klassen worked as a film animator. His book, *This Is Not My Hat*, won the Caldecott Medal. Image from *This Is Not My Hat* by Jon Klassen, 2012, Somerville, MA: Candlewick Press. Copyright 2012 by Jon Klassen.

The reading public is generally unaware that children's book writers and illustrators do not work together when developing children's books. In addition, publishers do not want writers to find their own illustrators. Of course, there are some illustrators who are also talented writers, but, generally, the writer writes and the illustrator illustrates, leaving each person to create spaces for interpretation in the final product.

Generally, the author and illustrator come together through the publisher's production staff. Editors work with the writers and different editors/art directors work with the illustrators. The publishers match the artist to a particular text. The art director (or similar type of personnel) is the person who selects the appropriate illustrator for a book project. The art director communicates with the illustrator and "directs" his/her visual work, providing feedback on the evolution of the product.

Processes and Procedures. For illustrators, art making is a mental, emotional, and physical act. Although many people would think about illustration as a primarily physical process, the artistic process is an embodied reaction to thinking and visualization. Illustrators explore ideas on canvases using various media and mock-ups, but their processes capture mental imagery. As with the writers, an observer can't see visualizing, but an observer can see composing and revision.

Some illustrators use sketchpads; some compile photographic images; others draw on the computer. Most artists work in a studio or on a large desk on which they can assemble materials and maintain works in progress because an illustrator's work is not always movable, neat, or small. Again, an illustrator's process is idiosyncratic.

For an excellent discussion on the importance of an artist's sketchpad, read "Chris Raschka: The Habits of an Artist" http://www.hbook.com/2012/06/creating-books/chris-raschka-the-habits-of-an-artist/#

For a glimpse at the variety of artists' desks and workspaces, read, "The Creative and Colorful Desks of Children's Book Illustrators" by Jordan G. Teicher. http://www.slate.com/blogs/behold/2015/08/10/jake_green_photographs_emerging_children_s_illustrators_in_his_book_the.html

Once an illustrator is selected for a children's book, he or she creates a rough sketch of the book illustration. These rough sketches or dummies provide the editor with enough detail regarding the artist's point of view, color scheme, page layout, and illustrative focus to understand the overall look and feel of the book. Based on the editor's feedback and the publisher's specific production process, the artist makes changes and continues the process until the final images are approved.

Jane Massy describes the book development process: http://www.artistsandillustrators.co.uk/how-to/family-art/281/how-to-illustrate-a-childrens-book

The Children's Literature Research Collection at the University of Minnesota presented an online exhibit about the engineering of a picture book, featuring Melissa Sweet's "Balloons Over Broadway." http://gallery.lib.umn.edu/exhibits/show/balloons-over-broadway

Allison Jay describes the book illustration process in this blog post: https://kathytemean.wordpress.com/2014/05/17/illustrator-saturday-alison-jay/

Art Instruction and Training. Although many people might assume children's book art is predominantly cartoon art or digitized illustration, children's book artists work in all forms of media: collage, gouache, pencil, watercolor, oil, paper, construction, and pastels. An artist may use one type of media and consistently work in one particular style. Other successful artists use multiple media and create illustrations in many different styles.

Children's book illustrators attend top design schools. Top design schools teach children's book illustration.

- Pratt Institute
  (https://www.pratt.edu/the-institute/);
- Rhode Island School of Design
  (http://www.risd.edu/);
- School of the Art Institute of Chicago
  (http://www.saic.edu/index.html)
- Hollins University
  (https://www.hollins.edu/);
- Ringling College of Art and Design
  (http://www.ringling.edu/);
- Columbia University School of the Arts
  (http://arts.columbia.edu/);
- Simmons College of Arts and Sciences
  (http://www.simmons.edu/academics/schools/college-of-arts-and-sciences).

The quality of children's book illustrations are so high, illustrations are shown in galleries and museums across the world.

- The Eric Carle Museum of Picture Book Art (http://www.carlemuseum.org/) collects, preserves, presents, and celebrates picture books and picture book illustrations from around the world (Figure 8.11).

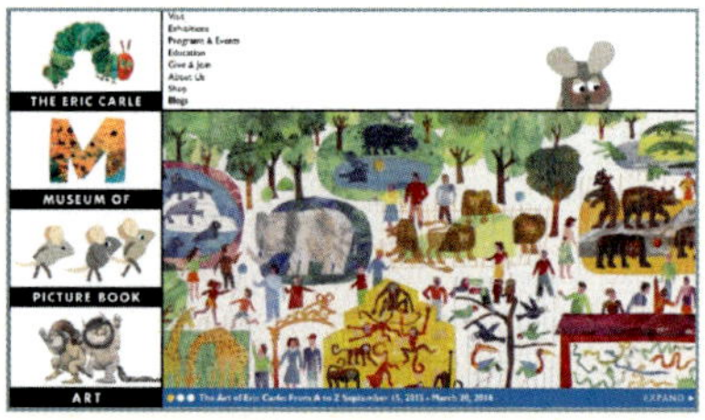

Figure 8.11
The Eric Carle Museum of Picture Book Art (http://www.carlemuseum.org/).

- The Mazza Museum (http://www.mazzamuseum.org/) promotes literacy and enriches the lives of all people through the art of children's literature. Located on the campus of the University of Findlay, the museum features thousands of pieces of art from hundreds of artists.

- The de Grummond Children's Literature Collection (http://digilib.usm.edu/cdm/landingpage/collection/degrum) at the University of Southern Mississippi Collection features American and British children's literature, historical and contemporary.

- The Kerlan Collection at the University of Minnesota (https://www.lib.umn.edu/clrc/kerlan-collection) includes original illustrations from various artists and historical illustrations as well.

- The Victoria and Albert Museum (http://www.vam.ac.uk/content/articles/n/national-art-library-childrens-literature-collections/) in the UK holds over 100,000 books from the 16th entry to the present day.

- The Norman Rockwell Museum (http://www.nrm.org/) hosts a Distinguished Illustrator Series.

- Maurice Sendak's illustrations are exhibited in the Rosenbach Museum in Philadelphia, PA (https://www.rosenbach.org/learn/collections/maurice-sendak-collection) (Figure 8.12). Sendak was also featured on the American Masters series on PBS (http://www.pbs.org/wnet/americanmasters/maurice-sendak-about-maurice-sendak/701/).

Figure 8.12

The Maurice Sendak Collection at the Rosenbach Museum (https://www.rosenbach.org/learn/collections/maurice-sendak-collection).

- Seven Stories is the National Centre for Children's Books in the UK (http://www.sevenstories.org.uk/). The collection features authors and illustrators, thousands of books, and rotating exhibits.

- Trinity College Dublin Library holds over 150,000 children's books. The collection is accessible through the National Collection of Children's Books (https://nccb.tcd.ie/about) and features periodic exhibits such as *Upon the Wild Waves: A Journey through Myth in Children's Books* (https://www.tcd.ie/Library/about/exhibitions/wild-waves/).

In contrast to the laborious methods of illustration that were in place during the early years of children's literature publication (Video 8.2), modern digitalization and printing processes have created countless possibilities for children's book illustration.

> The following online resources provide viewers with access to the illustration process of many children's book artists. Illustrators use these websites to network and showcase their work. Some of the sites provide opportunities for continuing education as well:
>
> - Artists & Illustrators- how to guide http://www.artistsandillustrators.co.uk/how-to
> - Children's Illustrators http://www.childrensillustrators.com/
> - Children's Books Guide http://childrensbooksguide.com/illustrators
> - Illustration http://www.illustrationweb.us/artists
> - Artists Network http://www.artistsnetwork.com/

Video 8.2 Chromolithography and Early Methods for Color Illustrations http://www.kaltura.com/tiny/lnlwj

CHROMOLITHOGRAPHY & EARLY METHODS FOR COLOR ILLUSTRATIONS

WITH MELANIE GRIFFIN

THE INSIDE, OUTSIDE, AND UPSIDE DOWNS OF CHILDREN'S LITERATURE | From Poets and Pop-ups to Princesses and Porridge

There is no particular style or media that is more successful than others. Children still prefer color rather than black and white. And they tend to gravitate toward realistic, detailed illustration rather than sparse, surreal interpretive scenes. But there are many exceptions to these general preferences (Figure 8.13). Yes, grocery store books (common, lower-quality books) may have similar looks, but the children's books that have literary value, artistic value, maintain a reader's interest, and stand the test of time are illustrated from a broad spectrum of styles and media. Any medium can be found in children's literature.

Figure 8.13
Beth Krommes' scenic, folk-art illustrations are predominantly black and white, but they capture readers' attention and draw them into the story. Image from *The House in the Night* by Susan Marie Swanson and illustrated by Beth Krommes, 2009, New York, NY: HMH Books for Young Readers. Illustration copyright 2009 by Beth Krommes.

Acrylics (Figure 8.14)

Figure 8.14
Acrylic paints are water-soluble, synthetic paints. They can have a gloss or matte finish and a thin or thick opacity. Jim Harris describes the pros and cons of painting with acrylics (http://www.jimharrisillustrator.com/ChildrensBooks/Books/threelittledinos.html#oilpainting). He used acrylic and oil paint to create his book, *The Three Little Dinosaurs*. Image from *The Three Little Dinosaurs* by Jim Harris, 1999, Gretna, LA: Pelican Publishing. Copyright 1999 by Jim Harris.

Crayon (Figure 8.15)

Figure 8.15
Oliver Jeffers uses all types of media, but *The Day the Crayons Quit* is an example of crayon illustration. You will enjoy his website (http://oliverjeffersworld.com/) and his short film about his artistic process (https://vimeo.com/57472271). *The Day the Crayons Quit* by Drew Daywalt and illustrated by Oliver Jeffers, 2013, New York, NY: Philomel. Illustration copyright 2013 by Oliver Jeffers.

Collage (Figure 8.16)

Figure 8.16
Collage is a process of assembling images from different materials. Chris Haughton used collage and digital illustration to create *Shh! We Have A Plan*. He describes the making of his book and the details of his writing and illustration process on his blog (http://blog.chrishaughton.com/the-making-of-shh-we-have-a-plan/). *Shh! We Have A Plan* by Chris Haughton, 2014, Somerville, MA: Candlewick. Copyright 2014 by Chris Haughton.

Digital (Figure 8.17)

Figure 8.17
Digital illustration is quite pervasive as many new artists are trained using digital tools. Illustrators often combine digital techniques with handmade illustration, but some work completely electronically. Bob Staake is a prolific, digital illustrator who creates children's books and much more. Read about his art and books on his website (http://www.bobstaake.com/). Image from *The First Pup: The Real Story of How Bo Got to the White House* by Bob Staake, 2010, New York, NY: Feiwel & Friends. Copyright 2010 by Bob Staake.

Gouache (Figure 8.18)

Figure 8.18

Gouache is a water-based paint that is more color-dense than watercolors. Wendell Minor creates beautiful paintings using gouache (http://www.minorart.com/childrensbooks.html). A recent example is *Trapped! A Whale's Rescue* by Robert Burleigh with paintings by Wendell Minor, 2015, Boston, MA: Charlesbridge. Illustration copyright 2015 by Wendell Minor.

Oil (Figure 8.19)

Figure 8.19

Oil paint is a slow-drying paint in which the pigment is suspended in oil. Jim Kay is an illustrator who uses oil along with other media. He was selected by J.K. Rowling to create the illustrated version of *Harry Potter and the Philosopher's Stone*. His illustrations allow Harry fans to revisit the story in a whole new way. Amazing! Watch a video of Jim's process (https://www.youtube.com/watch?v=GmhDRHIix48&feature=youtu.be). Image from *Harry Potter and the Philosopher's Stone Deluxe Illustrated Edition* by J.K. Rowling and illustrated by Jim Kay, 2015, London, UK: Bloomsbury Children's. Illustration copyright 2015 by Jim Kay.

Pastels (Figure 8.20)

Figure 8.20

Pastels are a powdered pigment that is formed into a stick. Pastels have a powdery property similar to chalk. Lynne Chapman creates illustrations using pastels. She shares her techniques through a series of videos (http://www.lynnechapman.co.uk/talking-about-work.php). Image from *Rumble, Roar, Dinosaur!* By Tony Mitton and illustrated by Lynne Chapman, 2010, New York, NY: Macmillan. Illustration copyright 2010 by Lynn Chapman. Retrieved from https://s-media-cache-ak0.pinimg.com/originals/1d/1b/a1/1d1ba155de585d46fd7adbf64e858494.jpg.

Pen and Ink (Figure 8.21)

Figure 8.21

Pen, ink, and graphite are familiar media for most people; they are the writing tools we commonly use. However, in the hands of an artist, new worlds are created. Arnold Lobel illustrated some of the most memorable characters using graphite, ink, and watercolor. You might know Frog and Toad, but this is Arnold's self-portrait from *The Book of Pigericks* by Arnold Lobel, 1983, New York, NY: HarperCollins. Copyright 1983 by Arnold Lobel.

Scratchboard (Figure 8.22)

Figure 8.22

Scratchboard is an illustrative technique in which the artist uses tools to scratch into clay covered by ink. Beth Krommes shares further details and examples on her website (http://www.bethkrommes.com/illustration/what-is-scratchboard). Image from *The Lamp, the Ice, and the Boat Called Fish* by Jacqueline Briggs Martin and illustrated by Beth Krommes, 2001, New York, NY: HMH Books for Young Readers. Illustration copyright 2001 by Beth Krommes.

Watercolor (Figure 8.23)

Figure 8.23

Watercolors are pigments suspended in a water-based solution. Jerry Pinkney is a master storyteller using watercolor. Most of his books include words, but *The Lion and the Mouse* is a wordless book. Jerry shares his process in several videos available on his website (http://www.jerrypinkneystudio.com/frameset.html). Image from *The Lion and the Mouse* by Jerry Pinkney, 2009, New York, NY: Little, Brown Books for Young Readers. Copyright 2009 by Jerry Pinkney.

Getting Published

There isn't one way to write a children's book. There isn't one way to illustrate text. Hone your craft. Seek feedback. Expect rejection. Work to accept criticism with an open mind. If children's book publishing is your passion and goal, I wish you the best of luck! It is a complicated industry. I have not published children's literature, and I can't claim insider experience. However, I have published academic texts and I have talked to many authors and illustrators. I can share their advice.

Learn from Mentors

Many years ago, scholars tried to capture the individual experiences of writers and artists in order to share their advice with novices (Cott, 1981; Murray, 1992; Wachtel, 1994). Similarly, children's book writers and illustrators published their own reflections on their composing activities to inform others about the book creation process (Paterson, 1981; Rylant, 1989). One of the most consistent resources for "letting the authors talk about their work themselves" has been *The Paris Review* (http://www.theparisreview.org/). Since 1953, founding editor, George Plimpton, and other contributors, interviewed prominent children's authors such as E.B. White (Plimpton & Crowther, 1969, No. 48), P.L. Travers (Burness & Griswold, 1982, No. 86), and Paula Fox (Broudy, 2004, No. 170). Through these exchanges, the interviewers explored the authors' childhoods and motivations for writing as well as their processes.

Mentoring and publication advice is available online. Watch out for self-promotion and those seeking financial gain. You can usually spot the artists from the con-artists, but be cautious. Here are a few examples of good advice and mentoring.

Jane Massy describes the book development process:
http://www.artistsandillustrators.co.uk/how-to/family-art/281/how-to-illustrate-a-childrens-book

The Children's Literature Research Collection at the University of Minnesota presented an online exhibit about the engineering of a picture book, featuring Melissa Sweet's "Balloons Over Broadway."
http://gallery.lib.umn.edu/exhibits/show/balloons-over-broadway

Allison Jay describes the book illustration process in this blog post:
https://kathytemean.wordpress.com/2014/05/17/illustrator-saturday-alison-jay/

More recently, *The Paris Review* launched *The Paris Review for Young Readers* (http://www.theparisreview.org/blog/2015/04/01/the-paris-review-for-young-readers/) and featured Eric Carle as their first interviewee. This blog "offers the same caliber of fiction, poetry, art, and interviews you expect from *The Paris Review*, for readers age eight to twelve." Although *The Paris Review* blog is written for children, the creators insist that it will not condescend to children and, therefore, the blog is positioned to provide insider views about the creation of children's literature for all audiences.

Similarly, *The Horn Book* posts monthly *Talks with Roger* that feature interviews by Roger Sutton (editor-in-chief) with some of the most well-known and successful writers and illustrators in children's literature (http://www.hbook.com/talks-with-roger/).

Getting published is hard work. Read interviews. Watch videos. Peruse literary magazines and websites. Learn about the art and business of children's literature.

Engage in Professional Networks

Today, aspiring authors and illustrators have unprecedented access to writers and illustrators through digital resources that provide up-close and personal accounts of children's literature creation. In addition, many authors and illustrators use social networks to interact with fans and share their illustrations outside the pages of books.

Here are some suggestions for following illustrators of children's books.

18 Illustrators to Follow on Instagram
http://www.buzzfeed.com/mallorymcinnis/follow-these-illustrators-on-instagram#.gj2ajWgbY

Picture Book Authors & Illustrators on Twitter
http://taralazar.com/2009/04/08/childrens-picture-book-authors-on-twitter/

Check Out the Children's Illustrators Showcase
https://twitter.com/cillustrators

Find Information Through Author & Illustrator Websites
Search the professional Society of Children's Books Writers and Illustrators:
http://www.scbwi.org/

Don't Follow the Pigeon
Follow Mo Willems on Twitter https://twitter.com/The_Pigeon

Following, liking, and friend-ing authors and illustrators is a great way for aspiring writers and illustrators to enter children's literature networks and learn who's who and what's what.

Listen to Good Advice

Publishing success is a combination of individual talent, unique ideas, dogged persistence, and luck. It's hard to capture exact measurements of an organic, flexible, and nuanced process; and, unfortunately, it's easy to be misled or fall victim to predatory agents and publishers. For very clear specifics about publishing children's books, the following resources provide helpful information:

- *The Society of Children's Book Writers and Illustrators* (SCBWI) is an organization for new and established authors and illustrators. SCBWI offers workshops, blogs, and services to support children's book creators. SCBWI also has regional chapters which offer critique groups, newsletters, boot camps, and networking opportunities at the local level (http://www.scbwi.org/).

- *The Children's Writer's & Illustrator's Market* (CWIM) by Chuck Sambuchino, is a reference book that is published annually. The CWIM provides market and submission/contact information for book publishers, art representatives, international publishers, literary agents, contests, magazines, and conferences. The book also includes interviews with experienced writers and illustrators, interviews with debut authors and illustrators, and instructional articles and webinar links. You can buy the newest version from the publisher (Writers Digest) or from booksellers. You can also access older versions from Google Books and most university libraries (http://www.writersdigestshop.com/2016-childrens-writers-and-illustrators-market).

- *The Artist's & Graphic Designer's Market* by Mary Burzlaff Bostic is a reference book for those who want a career in fine art, illustration, or graphic design. Similar to the CWIM, the Artist's & Graphic Designer's Market publishes interviews and insider information. It also provides contact information for art resources including galleries, book publishers, greeting card companies, and other outlets (http://www.amazon.com/2016-Artists-Graphic-Designers-Market/dp/144034261X).

- Neil Gaiman offers very specific advice about getting published (http://www.neilgaiman.com/FAQs/Advice_to_Authors).

- Neil Gaiman also offers very good advice about getting an agent (http://journal.neilgaiman.com/2005/01/everything-you-wanted-to-know-about.asp).

- Find out the difference between traditional publishing, vanity publishing, and self-publishing (http://theworldsgreatestbook.com/self-publishing-vanity-publishing/).

Get informed. Stay informed. Follow up and follow through. Although many resources provide good advice, each situation is different and you must exercise due diligence to protect yourself and make decisions in your best interest.

Where Do Authors and Illustrators Get Their Ideas?

Ideas are peculiar. They are ephemeral and permanent, fluid and specific. They come from nowhere and from everywhere. As Neil Gaiman wrote, "Where do I get my ideas from? I make them up. Out of my head" (http://www.neilgaiman.com/Cool_Stuff/Essays/Essays_By_Neil/Where_do_you_get_your_ideas%3F).

If you have a good idea for a children's book, it's important to know if it's been done before. To find out, do your homework! Read, look, write, and draw.

Read, Read, Read

Authors and illustrators overwhelmingly suggest that aspiring book creators need to read (http://writeforkids.org/2014/05/start-here-writing-for-children-step-one/). Reading literature is the writer's or illustrator's greatest tool. Reading other books gives creators ideas in the forms of images, memories and words. Reading also allows authors and illustrators to study language, phrasing, story structure, and design. Many authors and illustrators have been inspired by the work, style, or voice of another creator.

Look, Look, Look

Writers and illustrators also get ideas by paying attention to the world around them. Through personal interactions and conversations, many children's book creators find ideas in their daily encounters. Ideas can also arrive from faraway places and from different periods in time. Events or stories that are reported on the news or in newspapers can trigger a writer or illustrator into action. In case you missed this earlier, Oliver Jeffers perfectly explains idea sources (https://vimeo.com/57472271).

Write, Write, Write or Draw, Draw, Draw

Many writers keep personal journals, blogs, or diaries. Others may use Twitter, Instagram, and other sites to record words, images, and phrases. Some illustrators keep digital or paper sketch pads. Others use nothing at all. Through multiple text forms or mental remembering, writers and illustrators collect and curate their thoughts, feelings, observations and reactions to daily events. They may also store dreams and recollections in some tangible way. Many children's book creators state that specific words and passages will enter their minds and never leave. Some writers rely on their memories to hold these words, others put them in safe paper and digital places.

Whether writing or illustrating, it is hard to trace a creator's ideas. We rely on their personal recollections to know what they were thinking, who they've read or watched, or what they know. We can also try some idea sleuthing ourselves!

Whose idea is it anyway? Big ideas in *Jurassic Park, Jumanji,* and *The Cat in the Hat*

By Anne W. Anderson

The June 2015 release of *Jurassic World*, the fourth movie in the *Jurassic Park* series, takes the dinosaur-cloning-breeds-disaster premises of the previous movies (*Jurassic Park*, 1993; *The Lost World: Jurassic Park*, 1997; and *Jurassic Park, III*, 2001) a step further. Instead of just cloning dinosaurs from prehistoric DNA, *Jurassic World* explores the idea of genetically engineering dinosaurs. Unlike the previous three movies, which were based on Michael Crichton's novels *Jurassic Park* (1990) and *The Lost World* (1995), *Jurassic World* was not based on a novel. Crichton, who died in 2008 and who wrote about genetic engineering in his 2006 book *Next* (Figure 8.24), didn't link genetic engineering to dinosaurs. Instead, after some legal wrangling, the screen credits read: "Screenplay by Rick Jaffa & Amanda Silver and Colin Trevorrow & Derek Connolly; Story by Rick Jaffa & Amanda Silver; Based on characters created by Michael Crichton" (Robb, 2015, para. 1). Here is how the Internet Movie Database lists the writers on each of the four movies (Table 1).

Figure 8.24

Michael Crichton wrote about genetic engineering in his book, *Next* by Michael Crichton, 2006, New York, NY: HarperCollins. Cover copyright 2006 by HarperCollins.

Table 1. This table shows how the idea for the *Jurassic Park* films began with Michael Crichton's novels but then took on a life of its own as other people built other stories around the characters Crichton created.

Film	Writing Credits
Jurassic Park (1993)	Novel by Michael Crichton; Screenplay by Michael Crichton and David Koepp http://www.imdb.com/title/tt0107290/
The Lost World: Jurassic Park (1997)	Novel by Michael Crichton; Screenplay by David Koepp http://www.imdb.com/title/tt0119567/
Jurassic Park III, 2001	Based on characters created by Michael Crichton; Written by Peter Buchman and Alexander Payne & Jim Taylor* http://www.imdb.com/title/tt0163025/fullcredits?ref_=tt_ov_wr#writers
Jurassic World (2015)	Screenplay by Rick Jaffa & Amanda Silver and Colin Trevorrow & Derek Connolly; Story by Rick Jaffa & Amanda Silver; Based on characters created by Michael Crichton http://www.imdb.com/title/tt0369610/fullcredits/

*According to the Writers Guild of America (2015), the ampersand (&) between names indicates a team of writers. When more than one team works together or when individual writers work together, the word "and" is used. (*Theatrical Credits Procedures* A,1D)

So whose idea was *Jurassic World*? Not listed in the writing credits are the directors, Steven Spielberg (*Jurassic Park* and *The Lost World: Jurassic Park*), Joe Johnston (*Jurassic Park III*), and Colin Trevorrow (*Jurassic World*) who "wrote" the words of the screenplay onto film. Money—maybe millions of dollars—and reputations are at stake in who is credited with what in Hollywood films. But is an idea ever just the product of one person's brain? And what about other types of adaptations such as theme parks, video games, and toys based on books and films? Whose ideas are they?

Another book that became a 1995 film—also directed by Joe Johnston, who later directed *Jurassic Park III*—that became a board game, video game, television series, and more—is Chris Van Allsburg's *Jumanji*, which won the Caldecott Medal (1981) for its illustrations. Van Allsburg's black-and-white illustrations show the reader the story of Judy and Peter and a troublesome board game, *Jumanji*, from various perspectives. At one point, the reader seems to be on the floor looking up at Peter who is kneeling on a chair as he watches his train travel underneath the chair and around the room (p. 2) (Figure 8.25). After the children, whose parents have gone out, have become bored playing with their toys, the reader is positioned at an upstairs window watching the children leave the yard for the park across the street (p. 4). Next, the reader watches from above as the children begin to play the board game they have found in the park (p. 6) (Figure 8.26).

Figure 8.25
Peter, a main character in *Jumanji*, kneels on a chair as he watches his train travel underneath the chair and around the room. Image from *Jumanji* by Chris Van Allsburg, 1981, New York, NY: Houghton Mifflin. Copyright 1981 by Chris Van Allsburg.

Figure 8.26
The reader watches from above as Judy and Peter begin to play the board game they have found in the park. Image from *Jumanji* by Chris Van Allsburg, 1981, New York, NY: Houghton Mifflin. Copyright 1981 by Chris Van Allsburg.

In the book, the story is only about Judy and Peter whose parents have left them at home with instructions to keep the house tidy. There is no Alan Parish who had argued with his parents and was running away from home when he was sucked into the game a quarter of a decade earlier. Only when the film version of Judy and Peter, orphans living with their aunt, find the game and resume play is Alan freed from the Jumanji jungle. But he is no longer a child and the house he once knew as home is no longer his. The game in the book says it is "especially designed for the bored and restless" (p. 5), not, as the game in the movie says, "for those who seek to find a way to leave their world behind." Unlike in the movie, where the giant mosquitoes, stampeding rhinos, and other creatures leave the house and wreak havoc on the town, all the adventures occur inside the house in the book version. Whereas in the movie Van Pelt is a murderous hunter, the unnamed jungle guide in the book is merely confused and lost.

How and why did the movie change so much? Chris Van Allsburg is listed in the screen credits as helping to write the screen story that was based on his book (IMDB). But the movie exaggerates what happens, heightening the suspense and suggesting that, no matter what people do to try to get rid of the game, the game is alive and waiting for a new set of victims. The movie also adds another element not in the book: a romance between the adult Alan, played by Robin Williams, and Sarah Whittle, played by Bonnie Hunt.

> Although books and movies are viewed as the same story, they are not. Books aren't movies. Movies aren't books. We are seeing and experiencing narratives through two different media.

Joel Chaston (1997), writing about children's books adapted to films, noted that "classical Hollywood narration" (p. 14), meaning the plot lines in films that Hollywood has found to be successful, often combine "[a]dult heroes... whose narrative progress ranges from a restoration of the status quo ante to the development of a completely new order of things, frequently coupled with a second plot trajectory that works toward the fulfillment of heterosexual romance" (p. 14). Romantic love, to many people, seems an "inappropriate" storyline involving children, and Chaston said, "certain aspects of psychological realism appear to dictate a desire [for child protagonists] to return to a more familiar and manageable environment such as home" (p. 14). Hollywood reflects a more typical adult understanding of what is considered appropriate for children, whereas children's books "frequently delight in subverting precisely these conventions" (p. 13). In other words, when Hollywood writers make a movie of a children's book, they either tweak the plot so the child realizes he/she has misjudged his/her parents and wants nothing more than to get *safely* home—with all the word implies—or they add an adult romance, or they do both.

> Anne brings up an interesting point here. Think about it, do the professionals who make movies—the writers, directors, actors, casting agents, camera crew—have expertise in "childhood" or degrees in child-focused fields of study? Do they understand children's social, emotional, cognitive and physical developmental trajectories? Of course not. They may have children in their own homes, but they haven't studied filmmaking from a child's perspective. Film schools aren't focused on children so the individuals who create films bring adult sensibilities to the product. They add adult backstories.

In the case of *Jumanji*, they did both. Instead of a bored Judy and Peter looking for a little excitement, Hollywood adds Alan who was beaten up by bullies who took his bike, has fought with his parents, and is in the process of running away. Just as he gets ready to leave, however, he is sidetracked by the game . . . and by Sarah, a schoolmate, who has found and returned his bike. When Alan returns after years of being rumored as either missing or murdered, he wants nothing more than to find his parents, i.e., to return safely "home." He also reconnects with a now grown-up Sarah, with predictable results. Cinematically, the film *Jumanji* has much in common with the *Jurassic Park* films. In addition to being directed by Joe Johnston, who also directed *Jurassic Park III*, the film version of *Jumanji* features hordes of flying, crawling, and stampeding animals who, like those in *Jurassic Park*, have been taken out of their original "natural" setting—prehistoric times for the Jurassic-era dinosaurs and Africa for the modern-era beasts—by the plot devices of science fiction or fantasy. Additionally, *Jurassic Park* was the first film to use computer-generated imagery in some shots; *Jumanji* was the second film to use CGI.

The *Jumanji* film plot also echoes elements of the plot of *Where the Wild Things Are* by Maurice Sendak.

The ideas in the book version of *Jumanji*, however, have more in common with an earlier story, one that also features a brother and sister left alone at home (Figure 8.27), this time on a cold, rainy day that leaves them sitting and looking out the window. When the boy says, "How I wish we had something to do" (Seuss, 1957, p. 4), they hear a "BUMP!" (p. 5). In walks the Cat in the Hat (Figure 8.28) who proceeds to cause all sorts of mayhem with his games and tricks—and with his own mini-horde of creatures, i.e., Thing One and Thing Two, who fly kites in the house and get into the mother's bedroom. In the book version of *Jumanji*, it is a lion that chases Peter into the parents' bedroom and is trapped there by Peter's quick thinking.

Figure 8.27

The Cat in the Hat features a brother and sister left alone at home, on a cold, rainy day. *The Cat in the Hat* by Dr. Seuss, 1957, New York, NY: Random House. Copyright 1957 by Dr. Seuss.

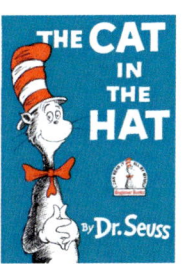

Figure 8.28

The Cat from *The Cat in the Hat* by Dr. Seuss, 1957, New York, NY: Random House. Copyright 1957 by Dr. Seuss.

Both *Jumanji* and *The Cat in the Hat* feature "bored and restless" (Van Allsburg, 1981, p. 5) children whose parents have left them at home with either explicit instructions to tidy up (*Jumanji*) or with the expectation that they will (*The Cat in the Hat*) behave, i.e., that they will keep the house tidy. Far from yearning to be safely at home, the children *are* home. As most children begin to do, they long for the excitement they think is to be found in the outside, grownup world. Van Allsburg and Seuss grant their wishes, providing mayhem of a magnitude to satisfy even the most skeptical child. Both books even invade the parents' sacred domains—their bedrooms—all without the parents' knowledge. Both books end with all the creatures gone from the house and everything tidy by the time the adults return home. Both mothers ask what the children did while the adults were gone. Peter (*Jumanji*) begins to tell his parents about the adventures, but the adults laugh and think he has just been dreaming. Sally and her brother (*The Cat in the Hat*) just look at each other, trying to decide what to say. Seuss ends his story by asking the reader, "Should we tell her about it? Now, what SHOULD we do? Well . . . What would YOU do if your mother asked you?" (p. 61).

Van Allsburg and Seuss depict children who have been lured by a board game or by a Cat with a game into a kind of wild rampage. Both authors subvert the adult expectations that children want to be safely at home and that children obey instructions when they are left alone by showing what happens when the adults are absent. Seuss, in particular, draws attention to what the children "SHOULD" do by repeating the word and by writing it once in all capital letters. But then he turns the question back to the reader, suggesting, perhaps, that the reader wouldn't tell, either.

Did Van Allsburg get the idea for his story from Dr. Seuss? Where did Dr. Seuss get the idea for his story?

If we go way back, we might think about the myth of Pandora, who disobeyed Zeus, opened a jar he had told her not to open, and released all the evils into the world. Or we might think about Eve in the Garden of Eden disobeying the instruction not to eat of the fruit of the Tree of the Knowledge of Good and Evil—or, to flip the story, about Eve and Pandora longing to know what would happen if they went against or subverted what the person in charge said to do. Psychologist Carl Jung's theory about the "collective unconsciousness" suggests all people and all cultures share common story patterns, like the similarities between the stories of Pandora and Eve. Does that mean there is no truth in them? Or does it mean there is a truth that is too big to be confined to a single story? Is that why so many stories seem to be retelling the same few big ideas?

Jumanji and *The Cat in the Hat* seem to tell similar stories about the conflict between parents and children and between what we should do and what we want to do, but what about *Jurassic Park*? In some sense, Michael Crichton and the writers who have followed him seem to be depicting some scientists as bored with the conventional ways of doing things and who are curious about what would happen if they tried something different. Unlike in *Jumanji* and *The Cat in the Hat*, however, the resulting death and destruction are very real and they don't go away because the game never really ends.

In the end, it may not matter whose idea it is or who had it first. Instead, what matters is that we stop to listen and to think deeply about the stories we hear and see and to think about the big ideas contained in them.

As you read stories and watch films, think about the big ideas the authors are presenting. Also think about the ways in which the illustrators or visual artists visualize their ideas. Whose perspective is told? How are you positioned as the reader?

Take Offs, Spin Offs, and Paraphernalia

As Anne delineated, ideas are hard to trace. Origins are not always clear. For these reasons, copyright law exists. Permissions are expensive, but business entities are willing to pay the price for intact fan bases and guaranteed sales.

Children's literature often functions as the source text for movies, toys, clothing, games, and apps. Walt Disney famously mined children's literature for his most successful animated films. Other movie studios followed suit and have created films to follow a book's success. A successful film will yield a toy line, a clothing line, and a series of games, puzzles, apps and licensed products. Even unsuccessful films will yield product lines.

Here is a short selection of children's books that have accompanying adaptations. Peruse the list and choose your favorite to read, watch, or play.

Shrek

Book: *Shrek!* by William Steig (Figure 8.29)
- Steig, W. (1990). *Shrek!*. New York: Farrar, Straus, Giroux.

Movie: *Shrek* by Dreamworks
- Adamson, A., Jenson, V., Warner, A., Williams, J. H., Katzenberg, J., Elliott, T., Rossio, T., ... DreamWorks Home Entertainment (Firm). (2006). *Shrek*. Glendale, CA: DreamWorks Animation.

Apps: *Pocket Shrek* (2015) by No Yetis Allowed.
- https://itunes.apple.com/us/app/pocket-shrek/id886216658?mt=8

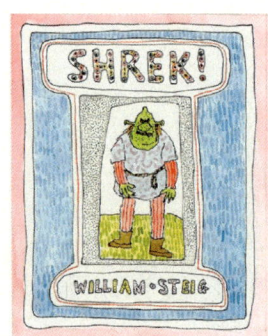

Figure 8.29

Shrek was popularized by Mike Myers film version. But Mike Myers got his idea from *Shrek!* By William Steig. *Shrek!* By William Steig, 1990, New York, NY: Farrar, Straus, & Giroux. Copyright 1990 by William Steig.

Peter Pan

Play: *Peter Pan in Kensington Gardens* by J.M. Barrie
- Barrie, J. M., & Rackham, A. (1910). *Peter Pan in Kensington gardens*. New York: C. Scribner's Sons.

Book: *Peter and Wendy* by J.M. Barrie (Figure 8.30)
- Barrie, J. M., & Oliver Wendell Holmes Collection (Library of Congress). (1911). *Peter and Wendy*. New York: Charles Scribner's Sons.

Movie: *Hook* by Amblin Entertainment, TriStar
- Spielberg, S., Hart, J. V., Marmo, M. S., Castle, N., Kennedy, K., Marshall, F., Molen, G. R., ... Columbia TriStar Home Video (Firm). (2000). *Hook*. Burbank, CA: Columbia TriStar Home Video.

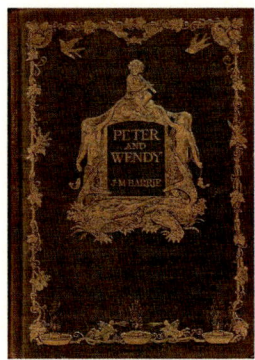

Figure 8.30

Peter Pan: The Boy Who Wouldn't Grow Up by J.M. Barrie, 1904, London, England: Hodder & Stoughton. Copyright 1988 by Great Ormond Street Hospital.

Movie: *Peter Pan* by Walt Disney Co.
- Disney, W., Luske, H. S., Geronimi, C., Jackson, W., Driscoll, B., Beaumont, K., Conried, H., ... Buena Vista Home Entertainment (Firm). (2007). *Peter Pan*. Burbank, CA: Walt Disney Home Entertainment.

Movie: *Pan* by Dune Entertainment
- Wright, J., Fuchs, J., Jackman, H., Hedlund, G., Mara, R., & Warner Home Video (Firm),. (2015). *Pan*.

eBook: Peter Pan Adventures (2015) by TabTale LTD.
- https://itunes.apple.com/us/app/peter-pan-adventures-classic/id588311104?mt=8

Winnie the Pooh

Book: *Winnie the Pooh* by A.A. Milne (Figure 8.31)
- Milne, A. A., Milne, A. A., Milne, A. A., & Shepard, E. H. (1957). *The World of Pooh: The complete Winnie-the-Pooh and the House at Pooh Corner*.

Movie: *Winnie the Pooh* by Walt Disney Co.
- Milne, A. A., Milne, A. A., Anderson, S., Hall, D., Del, V. P., Spencer, C., Lasseter, J., ... Walt Disney Studios Home Entertainment (Firm). (2011). *Winnie the Pooh*. Burbank, CA: Walt Disney Studios Home Entertainment.

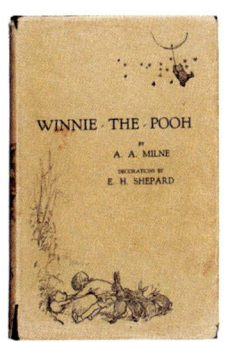

Figure 8.31
Winnie the Pooh by A.A. Milne and decorations by E.H. Shepard, 1926, London, UK: Methuen & Co. Ltd. Copyright 1988 Dutton.

Television: The New Adventures of Winnie the Pooh by American Broadcasting Co.
- Clemmons, L., Lounsbery, J., Reitherman, W., Walmsley, J., Cabot, S., Winchell, P., Milne, A. A., ... Buena Vista Home Entertainment (Firm). (2013). *The many adventures of Winnie the Pooh*. United States: Buena Vista Home Entertainment.

Apps: Letters with Pooh (2015) by Disney
- https://itunes.apple.com/us/app/letters-with-pooh/id535661652?mt=8

Mary Poppins

Book: *Mary Poppins* by P.L. Travers (Figure 8.32)
- Travers, P. L., & Shepard, M. (1962). *Mary Poppins*. New York: Harcourt, Brace & World.

Movie: *Mary Poppins* by Walt Disney Co.
- Stevenson, R., Walsh, B., DaGradi, D., Andrews, J., Van, D. D., Tomlinson, D., Johns, G., ... Buena Vista Home Entertainment (Firm). (2004). *Mary Poppins*. Burbank, Calif: Walt Disney Home Entertainment.

Movie: *Saving Mr. Banks* by Walt Disney Co.
- Hancock, J. L., Marcel, K., Smith, S., Owen, A., Collie, I., Steuer, P., Newman, T., ... Buena Vista Home Entertainment (Firm),. (2014). *Saving Mr. Banks*. Burbank, Calif: Walt Disney Home Entertainment.

Toy: Mary Poppins Pop Vinyl
- http://www.amazon.com/Funko-POP-Disney-Poppins-Figure/dp/B00BV1P5H0/ref=sr_1_1?s=toys-and-games&ie=UTF8&qid=1451846742&sr=1-1&refinements=p_lbr_characters_browse-bin%3AMary+Poppins

Figure 8.32

Mary Poppins by P.L. Travers and illustrated by Mary Shepard, 1934, London, UK: HarperCollins. Copyright 1962 by P.L. Travers.

Are children's books an adequate basis for films and other adaptations? Do you expect the film to stay true to the book or vary from the original? Two researchers, Amit Joshi and Huifang Mao decided to study the relationship between best-selling books and motion picture adaptations. Joshi and Mao analyzed over 700 movies and found that book-based movies performed better at the box office on the opening weekend than non-book movies. They also discovered that "the opening weekend performance of book-based movies is positively driven by book equity, book-movie similarity, and recency between the book's peak equity and movie release" (Joshi & Mao, 2012, p. 558). In other words, if audiences loved the book, they want the movie to bring the book to life.

This may be why Steven Spielberg declined to direct *Harry Potter*. He wanted to make Harry an animated film and he ended up backing out. He stated:

> I purposely didn't do the *Harry Potter* movie because for me, that was shooting ducks in a barrel. It's just a slam dunk. It's just like withdrawing a billion dollars and putting it into your personal bank accounts. There's no challenge
> http://www.hollywood.com/general/quote-of-the-day-spielberg-on-not-making-harry-potter-57179290/

Just like the artists and writers who create children's literature, movie directors and actors bring a level of interpretation to their adaptations. When the book is just like the movie, some of the creative, interpretive work is reduced in favor of consistency with the original. As mentioned in a previous chapter, young children like to hear the same stories over and over again. I guess the same is true for older children and adults as well. The dolls, games, toys, costumes, and other paraphernalia function as reminders of the original and allow each of us to enter the story through new modes. Once there, we like things to be as we expect—close to the "original" idea.

1. **Choose** your favorite piece of children's literature published within the last three years. I selected the three-year time frame in the hopes you find a book without other adaptations or sequels.
2. **Create** an artistic response to the book. Choose one of the following. Click on the links to see samples and tutorials:

- **Make a pop-up book**
  - Watch this to see a sample:
    - You definitely want to click here: http://wp.robertsabuda.com/make-your-own-pop-ups/
    - https://www.youtube.com/watch?v=0XNV9oVf_pU
- **Create a movie trailer or short film**
  - https://www.youtube.com/watch?v=yT9V2aN8OYQ
  - https://www.youtube.com/watch?v=t1emxcttgKE
- **Develop a line of toys**
  - http://www.babble.com/home/keep-it-handmade-23-diy-toy-projects/
  - Make the toys and take pictures.
- **Cast the movie**
  - How to: http://www.howcast.com/videos/60027-How-to-Make-Your-First-Movie-Phase-3-Casting
  - Complete a casting sheet.
- **Create a movie poster**
  - http://bighugelabs.com/poster.php
  - https://www.lucidpress.com/pages/examples/free-online-poster-maker

Why did you choose this medium? How did your product connect to or diverge from your reading of the book? Did this product give you any insight into the characters, the plot, the writing style, the illustrations, etc.? Any negative impressions?

Please, Sir. I Want Some More.

In the words of Oliver Twist, audiences, and therefore, publishers, "want more" of a good thing. Audiences read a book and they want the author to write a sequel. Audiences read a book and they wait for the movie to premiere—even though most readers will find the book is better. When readers find a book they love, the publishers do not have to wait for a movie production; they search for similar plots, characters, and themes to push to publication. When a book is successful, trends follow suit.

> Although Twilight was not the first vampire series, it sparked a trend in the publication of monster fantasy. The Hunger Games was not the first dystopian novel but it initiated a resurgent interest in dystopian fiction. Success attracts copycats, adaptations, and paraphernalia.

The repetitive occurrence of books, adaptations, and marketing paraphernalia give off the impression that writing and illustrating books can be bottled and sold. Many people believe if they can come up with "one great idea" the book and its successive adaptations will lead to fortunes.

As Neil Gaiman wrote:

> The Ideas aren't the hard bit. They're a small component of the whole. Creating believable people who do more or less what you tell them to is much harder. And hardest by far is the process of simply sitting down and putting one word after another to construct whatever it is you're trying to build: making it interesting, making it new (http://www.neilgaiman.com/Cool_Stuff/Essays/Essays_By_Neil/Where_do_you_get_your_ideas%3F).

Children's book writing and illustrating are creative enterprises that are focused on creating new literary, aesthetic objects—new characters, novel ideas, different plots, persuasive arguments, or unique presentations of content. Children's book publishing and product marketing are businesses—businesses focused on providing goods and services for a profit and occasionally not-for-profit. A peek behind the scenes of the children's book industry often reveals a cookie-cutter sameness that business processes have brought to bear on what begins as compositional art and turns it into product sales. Don't get me wrong, the writers and artists want to make money too. However, the children's book publishing engine is trendy, regimented, and focused on tested models and proven results, until something new comes along (self-publishing, fanfiction, Netflix, literary talent, artistic skill) and recalibrates the system. Keep these competing agendas in mind as you read children's literature. Understand the impact on the process and product when business, literature, and art combine.

TEXTUAL TENDENCIES AND OPEN AND CLOSE READINGS

SECTION 3

CHAPTER 09 | GORE & GRIMM, PRINCESSES & PORRIDGE

(THE ROOTS OF STORY AND NARRATION)

In this chapter, I'm going to put you to work. You are going to create a story, play with a story, and fracture a story. Along the way, pay attention to your process but also keep track of your products. When you are done, I will use your creations to discuss the roots of story and the traditions of narrative.

Passing Down Stories

Your first assignment is to "tell" a story that creates a communal explanation of an observed phenomenon. Much like ancient people who did not have modern science to explain the physical world around them, you are going to use your bodily senses, along with your sense of story, to develop a tale, legend, or myth to describe one of four events.

I would like for you to select one of the four visual images from *The Mysteries of Harris Burdick* by Chris Van Allsburg (Figure 9.1). Each one of the mysteries includes a title and a small clue.

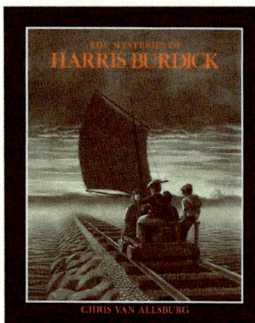

Figure 9.1

The Mysteries of Harris Burdick is a collection of stories, but the reader must determine the beginning, middle, and end of each one. *The Mysteries of Harris Burdick* by Chris Van Allsburg, 1984, New York, NY: Houghton Mifflin. Copyright 1984 by Chris Van Allsburg.

Figure 9.2 The Seven Chairs: The fifth one ended up in France.

Figure 9.2

The Seven Chairs: The fifth one ended up in France. Image from *The Mysteries of Harris Burdick* by Chris Van Allsburg, 1984, New York, NY: Houghton Mifflin. Copyright 1984 by Chris Van Allsburg.

Figure 9.3 Mr. Linden's Library: He had warned her about the book. Now it was too late.

Figure 9.3

Mr. Linden's Library: He had warned her about the book. Now it was too late. Image from *The Mysteries of Harris Burdick* by Chris Van Allsburg, 1984, New York, NY: Houghton Mifflin. Copyright 1984 by Chris Van Allsburg.

[Figure 9.4](#) Archie Smith, Boy Wonder: A tiny voice asked, "Is he the one?"

[Figure 9.5](#) Under the Rug: Two weeks passed and it happened again.

Figure 9.4
Archie Smith, Boy Wonder: A tiny voice asked, "Is he the one?"
Image from *The Mysteries of Harris Burdick* by Chris Van Allsburg, 1984, New York, NY: Houghton Mifflin. Copyright 1984 by Chris Van Allsburg.

Figure 9.5
Under the Rug: Two weeks passed and it happened again.
Image from *The Mysteries of Harris Burdick* by Chris Van Allsburg, 1984, New York, NY: Houghton Mifflin. Copyright 1984 by Chris Van Allsburg.

Each visual image represents an event that you can observe, but which you may not readily understand. You can see who is involved (characters) and what has occurred (plot event), but the story is incomplete. It's up to you to narrate this event to help others make sense of what they are seeing and feeling.

To begin the process, select one image/event and read the corresponding caption. To build on this initial statement, use one or two sentences of your own to narrate the unbelievable event before your eyes.

Verbally share your story amongst your family or a group of friends. Invite one person to create the next sequence of events in the story. Then invite another. The sentence building should continue until everyone has had a chance to contribute and the story is told.

Your short story may twist and turn or end abruptly. But that's what happens in myths, legends, tales, and fables that are spun from oral traditions. Each teller takes the tale in a slightly different direction than the previous teller. Each teller remembers something new or embellishes different details to create intrigue, to foreshadow outcomes, to provide moral guidance, or to entertain.

Now that you have a story, how will you remember it?

 Without the aid of writing tools or recording devices, how did ancient people hold on to oral stories? There are many groups of people in the world today who rely on storytelling to maintain their cultural history. Do you come from a family of storytellers? How are stories passed from generation to generation in your circles of family and friends?

GORE & GRIMM, PRINCESSES & PORRIDGE
(THE ROOTS OF STORY AND NARRATION)

Writing Down Stories

What happens to oral stories when they get written down? Well, sometimes the author gets is right, and sometimes the author gets it wrong.

 Is this possible? Is there a right and wrong way to story? Is there a right and wrong story to tell?

If you want to find out how famous authors interpreted the visual images you selected, read *The Chronicles of Harris Burdick* (Figure 9.6). In this book, professional writers such as Stephen King, Lois Lowry, and Walter Dean Myers, recorded their interpretations of the events. Did the professional authors capture a similar story to yours? Where did your stories converge or diverge? What did you notice? You "witnessed" the same exact event, so what are the sources of any discrepancies?

Figure 9.6

The Chronicles of Harris Burdick is the attempt of 14 famous authors to solve the mysteries of Harris Burdick. You can also find out how other readers have responded to the Burdick mysteries (http://www.houghtonmifflinbooks.com/features/harrisburdick/).

The Chronicles of Harris Burdick by Chris Van Allsburg, 2011, New York, NY: Houghton Mifflin. Cover art copyright 2011 by Chris Van Allsburg.

> Now what happens as an oral tradition arises about an historical event or an historical person is that, strangely enough, the first oral tradition is not an attempt to remember exactly what happened, but is rather a return into the symbols of the tradition that could explain an event. Therefore, one has to imagine that legend and myth and hymn and prayer are the vehicles in which oral traditions develop. The move into a formulated tradition that looks as if it was a description of the actual historical events is actually the end result of such a development….So oral tradition develops as the community looks for a recreation of memory in community life. (Helmut Koester, 1998)

Folk tales, fairy tales, legends, myths, tall tales, and fables are just a few of the recognizable forms of story that "originated in oral traditions throughout the world and still exist" (Zipes, 2012, p. 114).

 For an extensive collection of folklore and mythology texts, visit the digital archive created by Emeritus Professor D.L. Ashliman at the University of Pittsburgh, Department of German: http://www.pitt.edu/~dash/folktexts.html

"Traditional literature" is the collective name for the text types that began through oral storytelling and are now preserved in iterations of writing. With oral origins, there were no "original" versions to track down and no identifiable authors to credit. However, as time passed, many individuals decided to collect, organize, and write these stories for collection and distribution.

Jacob and Wilhelm Grimm (Figure 9.7), two German brothers who were aspiring lawyers with a hobby of collecting folktales, took positions as librarians in 1808 and became linguists, folklorists, and scholars of medieval studies (Ashliman, 2015). They traveled through Germany and spoke with families to acquire stories and document the language with which the stories were told. They published a collection of *Children's and Household Tales* for wider distribution and their names became synonymous with these stories (Figure 9.8). The Brothers Grimm did not create the stories; they collected and interpreted them. Now the stories are preserved in time. The Grimms' collections are often considered the originals, but the Grimms altered the stories across versions (Video 9.1).

Figure 9.7

Image of the Brothers Grimm. Retrieved from http://monumente-online.de/wAssets/img/ausgaben/2012/1/466/fotogrimm_Br__der_Grimm_Museum_Kassel_1_765x715.jpg

Figure 9.8

The Brothers Grimm published this version of *Children's and Household Tales* in 1882. This version was illustrated by Walter Crane and translated by Lucy Crane. The text is available from The Project Gutenberg http://www.gutenberg.org/files/19068/19068-h/19068-h.htm and http://www.archive.org/stream/grimmsfairytal00grim#page/n5/mode/2up.

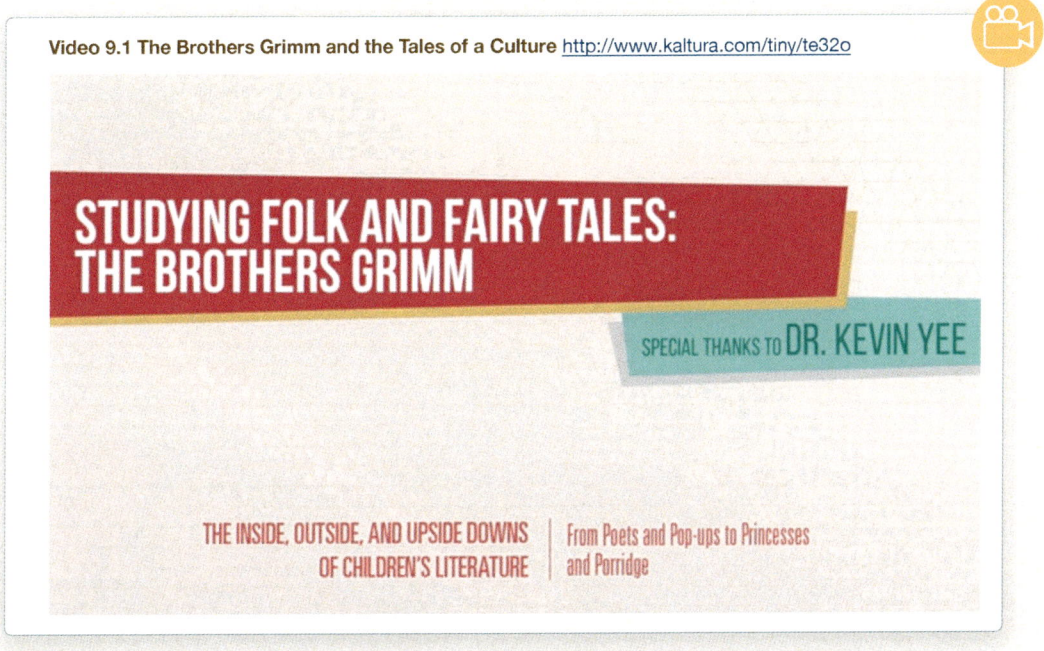

Video 9.1 The Brothers Grimm and the Tales of a Culture http://www.kaltura.com/tiny/te32o

In a different country, Charles Perrault (Figure 9.9), a respected academic who lived almost 100 years before the Brothers Grimm, engaged in the preservation of stories told in France. In 1697, he published a volume of *Stories or Tales from Times Past: Tales of Mother Goose* (Figure 9.10) and included the stories of *Cinderella*, *Sleeping Beauty*, and *Little Red Riding Hood*.

In another time and place, Joseph Jacobs (Figure 9.11), an Australian, Jewish scholar, folklorist, and literary critic compiled collections of English tales and legends (Bergman, 1983). Capturing stories such as *Jack and the Beanstalk* and *The Three Bears*, Joseph Jacobs preserved English legends as well as Jewish, Celtic, and Indian folklore (Figure 9.12).

http://www.archive.org/stream/morecelticfairyt00jaco#page/n7/mode/2up

Figure 9.9

Charles Perrault by Lallemand, 1693, de 'Académie Française, Source=New York Public Library Digital Gallery, Retrieved from http://digitalgallery.nypl.org/nypldigital/dgkeysearchdetail.cfm?trg=1&strucID=1018746&imageID=1555918&word=Perrault&s=1&notword=&d=&c=&f

Figure 9.10

Puss in Boots, from a handwritten and illustrated version of Charles Perrault's Contes de ma mère l'Oye (Mother Goose Tales). Retrieved from https://commons.wikimedia.org/wiki/File:Puss-in-Boots-1695.jpg

Figure 9.11

Joseph Jacobs was a distinguished Jewish historian and linguist who published folktales of English, Celtic, Indian, and European cultures. Retrieved from http://www.folklore-network.folkaustralia.com/images/image0012.gif.

Figure 9.12

More Celtic Fairy Tales, Jacobs, J., 1895 New York : Grosset & Dunlap (2nd edition) Copy scan by nicole-Deyo, a trusted source, from copy held by New York Public Lib., obtained from http://www.archive.org/stream/morecelticfairyt00jaco#page/n7/mode/2up

Comment: Professor D.L. Ashliman created a website for Charles Perrault. http://www.pitt.edu/~dash/perrault.html

Project Gutenberg has published a 1922 version of *The Tales of Charles Perrault* http://www.gutenberg.org/files/29021/29021-h/29021-h.htm

Collections of Joseph Jacobs work can be found at http://www.sacred-texts.com/neu/eng/eft/

Joseph Jacobs wrote explicitly about the people who passed down these tales from generation to generation. He noted, "in dealing with Folk-lore, much was said of the Lore, almost nothing was said of the Folk" [Jacobs, 1893: 233]: http://england.prm.ox.ac.uk/englishness-Joseph-Jacobs.html

Oral traditions occur across all cultures, countries and time periods. The European origins of the Brothers Grimm, Charles Perrault, and Joseph Jacobs reflect Anglo-Saxon preferences in publishing and its corresponding impact on U.S. literary history.

Scholars have collected African, Russian, South American, Asian, and Native people's stories as well. http://www.worldoftales.com/index.html http://www.unc.edu/~rwilkers/title.htm

I am focusing on the traditions of Grimm, Perrault, and Jacobs because I want to make a point about the evolution of oral stories into print and across time.

Exploring Story

Variants of oral tales provide interesting comparisons and opportunities for exploring the parallel development of stories across cultures and the divergence of stories across time, people, and languages. For your next assignment, you will read a selection of folktales to compare and contrast. (Click on the form to help you explore the story.)

Step 1. Choose one of the following folktales, which began in the oral tradition.
Select one story and use it for steps 2-6.

- Cinderella/ The Little Glass Slipper
- Sleeping Beauty
- Jack and the Bean Stalk
- The Three Bears
- The Three Little Pigs
- Little Red Riding Hood/ Little Red Cap
- Hansel and Gretel

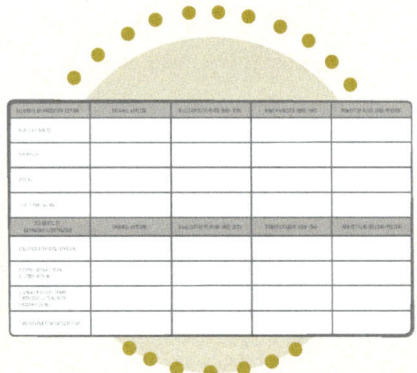

Step 2: Find a version of the selected folktale as it was first published by the Brothers Grimm, Charles Perrault, or Joseph Jacobs.

- Brothers Grimm: http://www.pitt.edu/~dash/grimmtales.html
- Charles Perrault: http://www.pitt.edu/~dash/perrault.html
- Joseph Jacobs: http://www.sacred-texts.com/neu/eng/eft/
- Project Gutenberg (https://www.gutenberg.org/). Project Gutenberg offers over 50,000 free ebooks that were originally published by legitimate publishers. You can search by Perrault, Grimm, or Joseph Jacobs.

Examine the elements of story:

Plot: The events and action within a story. The plot has a beginning, middle, and end connected through rising action, a climax, and falling action. Conflict drives the plot. Conflict typically occurs as character vs. character, character vs. nature, character vs. society, or character vs. self.

Characters: The actors in the plot. Characters are round, dynamic, flat or static. In other words, they grow, change, and evolve or they are limited, stereotypical, and unlearning. Characters are also identified as protagonists and antagonists. The author or illustrator characterizes the actors directly through description and direct statements or indirectly through thoughts, words, and actions.

Setting: The location of the events in the plot. The setting positions the action in time and space. The setting can also project the mood and develop the atmosphere.

Theme: The main point or essence of the story. The theme reflects the author and illustrator's central message.

Style and Perspective: The way in which a story is presented and the perspective from which the story is told or illustrated. The point of view can be omniscient (all knowing), limited omniscient (through one character), or first person. The author and illustrator's voice and techniques come into play as well.

> To evaluate narrative books (i.e., chapter books) based primarily on the text, such as contemporary realistic fiction, historical fiction, fantasy, or novels in verse, I use a combination of criteria from the *Newbery Medal (ALA)* and the *Printz Award (ALA)*. Depending on the book, one or more of these criteria apply:
>
> - Development of a plot
> - Delineation of characters
> - Delineation of a setting
> - Distinctive interpretation of the theme or concept
> - Excellent presentation of information including accuracy, clarity, and organizational flow
> - Appropriateness of style for the audience
> - Design
>
> If the narrative is presented in the form of a picturebook or graphic novel, I use the following criteria from the *Caldecott Medal (ALA)* as well.
>
> - Excellence of execution in the artistic technique employed;
> - Excellence of pictorial interpretation of story or theme;
> - Appropriateness of style of illustration to the story or theme;
> - Delineation of plot, theme, characters, setting, mood through the pictures;
> - Excellence of presentation in recognition of the intended audience.

What do you notice about the Grimm/Perrault/Jacobs version in comparison to your personal experience and recollection of the selected folktale?

If you are surprised by the content of the folktale you read, you aren't alone. Walt Disney versions of these stories pervade your experience. For an excellent discussion of the sex, violence, witches, and beasts of folktales, read *The Hard Facts of the Grimms' Fairy Tales* by Maria Tatar (2003).

What do you notice about the recurring themes?

For example, I notice fear. Fear is part of our lives. Throughout our collective history, we have used fear (and story) to teach, convince, coerce, and control what happens in society. Fear rhetoric and scary stories are pervasive in adult literature (Check out this collection of classic horror: http://www.underworldtales.com/classic.htm). And if it happens in society, and if it happens in adult literature, it happens in children's literature. Ever read the Goosebumps series by R.L. Stine? (http://rlstine.com). What techniques do you notice?

Step 3: Find Something Old

Find another old version, and I mean really old! Yes, you already found an old written version of a fairytale, but now I want you to find another old illustrated version intended for children. Using the following database, find a children's book version of your selected folktale published between 1800 and 1899.

- The Baldwin Library of Historical Children's Literature (http://ufdc.ufl.edu/juv) at the University of Florida houses a searchable database filled with old examples of children's literature. In fact, the Baldwin includes individual stories and anthologies of the Grimm's fairy tales.

Read the old version.

What do you notice about a children's book version of your selected folktale published before 1900? What do you notice about the illustrations? Can you see evidence of different cultural expectations? What do you notice about the language?

Step 4: Find Something New

The story you selected is famous and it has been retold and interpreted by many authors and illustrators over the years. Find two "newer" versions of your story written for children.

Authors and illustrators who publish folktales:

Jan Brett	Paul Galdone	Jerry Pinkney
Anthony Brown	Virginia Hamilton	Cynthia Rylant
Marc Brown	Trina Shart Hyman	Jon Scieszka
Marcia Brown	Steven Kellogg	Paul O. Zelinsky

- Find a version published between 1900 and 1999.
- Find a version published between 2000 and today.

Hint: Search your public library's database. Check Amazon for popular versions and then search for those titles in your library as well. Or head to the public library and search the stacks. That's always a fun option.

Please note the folktale may appear in a collection of tales. The story may be illustrated by any individual and categorized by the illustrator's last name. The story might be retold by someone other than the Brothers Grimm, Charles Perrault, or Joseph Jacobs, but the new author should credit the old author in some way.

What do you notice about the children's book versions of your selected folktale published between 1900-1999 and 2000 to present? What do you notice about the illustrations? What happened to the plot? What happened to the characters? What happened to the language?

Can you infer anything about the folk, by examining the lore?

Step 5: Find Something Borrowed

Find at least one "borrowed" variation of your folktale. In other words, many authors and illustrators have borrowed the basic plot structure or characters from your selected folktale and reinterpreted them from a different perspective. These variants, also known as "fractured fairy tales," share similarities with the well-known story you have read, but the author or illustrator has made changes along the way. Below, I have listed a few examples. There are many more.

Cinderella:

- *Cinder Edna* by Ellen Jackson and illustrated by Kevin O'Malley, 1998, New York, NY: HarperCollins (Figure 9.13)
- *Cinderella Skeleton* by Robert D. San Souci and illustrated by David Catrow, 2000, New York, NY: Silver Whistle.
- *Cindy Ellen: A Wild Western* by Susan Lowell and illustrated by Jane Manning, 2001, New York, NY: HarperCollins.
- *Ella Enchanted* by Gail Carson Levine, 2011, New York, NY: HarperCollins.

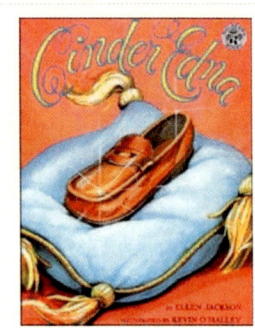

Figure 9.13
Cinder Edna is the story of Cinderella's neighbor. *Cinder Edna* by Ellen Jackson and illustrated by Kevin O'Malley, 1998, New York, NY: HarperCollins. Cover art copyright 1998 by Kevin O'Malley.

Read Aloud: Fractured Fairy Tales
Watch this wonderful selection of fractured fairy tales. The name, "Fractured Fairy Tales," originated during these shorts shown during the *Rocky and Bullwinkle Show*.

Cinderella
https://www.youtube.com/watch?v=-xnYcKHl8E4

Sleeping Beauty
https://www.youtube.com/watch?v=edS6i-2z4H0

Jack and the Bean Stalk
https://www.youtube.com/watch?v=YB1EE-FDgMk

The Three Bears
https://www.youtube.com/watch?v=Kby4oA1nQZM

The Three Little Pigs
https://www.youtube.com/watch?v=pYiCM35V7_w

Little Red Riding Hood
https://www.youtube.com/watch?v=RksxFR-uMaI

Hansel and Gretel
https://www.youtube.com/watch?v=csdZQZmgKfQ

Sleeping Beauty:

- *Sleeping Ugly* by Jane Yolen and illustrated by Diane Stanley, 1997, New York, NY: Puffin.

- *Awake: The Story of Sleeping Beauty with Espresso* by Karleen Tauszik, 2014, Seattle, WA: Amazon (Figure 9.14).

- *Ugly Sleeping Beauty* by Jamie Campbell, 2014, Seattle, WA: Amazon Digital Services.

Jack and the Bean Stalk:

- *Waynetta and the Cornstalk* by Helen Ketteman and illustrated by Diane Greenseid, 2007, Morton Grove, IL: Albert Whitman & Co.

- *Jack and the Beanstalk* by Nina Crews, 2011, New York, NY: Henry Holt & Co.

- *Juan y Los Frijoles Magicos* by Carol Ottolenghi, 2005, Greensboro, NC: Brighter Child.

- *Jack and the Baked Beanstalk* by Colin Stimpson, 2012, New York, NY: Templar (Figure 9.15).

The Three Bears:

- *Deep in the Forest* by Brinton Turkle, 1992, New York, NY: Puffin.

- *I Thought This Was a Bear Book* by Tara Lazar and illustrated by Benji Davies, 2015, New York, NY: Aladdin (Figure 9.16).

- *Goldilocks and Just One Bear* by Leigh Hodgkinson, 2012, Nosy Crow.

Figure 9.14
Awake has the modern sensibilities of high-priced coffee. *Awake: The Story of Sleeping Beauty with Espresso* by Karleen Tauszik, 2014, Seattle, WA: Amazon. Copyright 2014 by Karleen Tauszik.

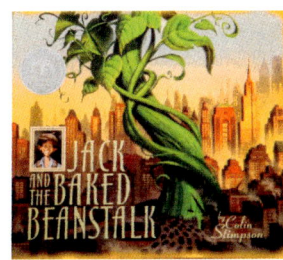

Figure 9.15
This is the story of Jack in the big city during an economic downturn. *Jack and the Baked Beanstalk* by Colin Stimpson, 2012, New York, NY: Templar. Copyright 2012 by Colin Stimpson.

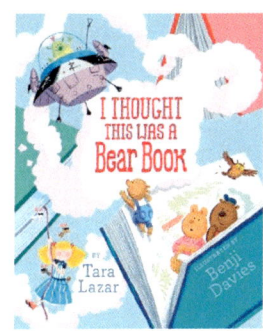

Figure 9.16
An alien has landed in the story of the three bears. No problem, right? *I Thought This Was a Bear Book* by Tara Lazar and illustrated by Benji Davies, 2015, New York, NY: Aladdin. Cover art copyright 2015 by Benji Davies.

The Three Little Pigs:

- *The Three Pigs* by David Wiesner, 2001, New York, NY: Clarion (Figure 9.17)

- *The Three Little Wolves and the Big Bad Pig* by Eugene Trivizas and illustrated by Helen Oxenbury, 1997, New York, NY: Margaret K. McElderry.

- *The True Story of the Three Little Pigs* by Jon Scieszka and illustrated by Lane Smith, 1989, New York, NY: Viking.

- *Pig, Pigger, Piggest* by Rick Walton and illustrated by Jimmy Holder, 2003, Layton, UT: Gibbs Smith.

Little Red Riding Hood:

- *Honestly Red Riding Hood was Rotten* by Trisha Speed Shaskan and illustrated by Gerald Guerlais, 2011, Mankato, MN: Picture Window Books.

- *Lon Po Po* by Ed Young, 1989, New York, NY: Philomel.

- *Good Little Wolf* by Nadia Shireen, 2011, New York, NY: Knopf Books (Figure 9.18).

Hansel and Gretel:

- *Hansel and Gretel* by Cynthia Rylant and illustrated by Jen Corace, 2008, New York, NY: Hyperion.

- *Hansel and Gretel* by Neil Gaiman and illustrated by Lorenzo Mattotti, 2014, London, UK: Bloomsbury.

- *Hansel and Gretel* by Rachel Isadora, 2009, New York, NY: G.P. Putnam's Sons (Figure 9.19).

Figure 9.17

David Wiesner turns the story of the three pigs inside out. *The Three Pigs* by David Wiesner, 2001, New York, NY: Clarion. Copyright 2001 by David Wiesner.

Figure 9.18

Nadia Shireen explores what happens when the bad guy is good. *Good Little Wolf* by Nadia Shireen, 2011, New York, NY: Knopf Books. Copyright 2011 by Nadia Shireen.

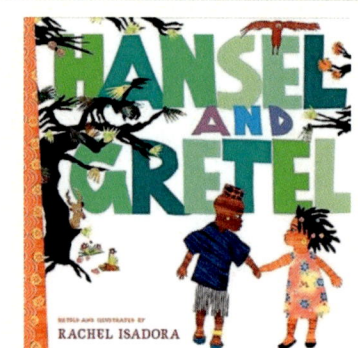

Figure 9.19

Rachel Isadora's illustrative style gives Hansel and Gretel a completely different feel. *Hansel and Gretel* by Rachel Isadora, 2009, New York, NY: G.P. Putnam's Sons. Copyright 2009 by Rachel Isadora.

Step 6: Comparing Characteristics

The versions, variants, and examples of old and new books exemplify the ways in which narrative elements (plot, setting, character, point of view, theme) impact the story arc and the reader's experience. Using different examples of your selected folktale, compare and contrast the stories. You can compare

- whole-to-whole
- similarities to differences
- Female antagonists vs. Male antagonists

What do you notice about the scare? What do you notice about the characters and plot events? Short or elaborated, realistic or imaginative, the same standards of quality apply.

To evaluate narrative books (i.e., chapter books) based primarily on the text, such as contemporary realistic fiction, historical fiction, fantasy, or novels in verse, I use a combination of criteria from the *Newbery Medal (ALA)* and the *Printz Award (ALA)*. Depending on the book, one or more of these criteria apply:

- Development of a plot
- Delineation of characters
- Delineation of a setting
- Distinctive interpretation of the theme or concept
- Excellent presentation of information including accuracy, clarity, and organizational flow
- Appropriateness of style for the audience
- Design

If the narrative is presented in the form of a picturebook or graphic novel, I use the following criteria from the *Caldecott Medal (ALA)* as well.

- Excellence of execution in the artistic technique employed;
- Excellence of pictorial interpretation of story or theme;
- Appropriateness of style of illustration to the story or theme;
- Delineation of plot, theme, characters, setting, mood through the pictures;
- Excellence of presentation in recognition of the intended audience.

From Tradition to Modern Fiction

We make sense of the world through story. Children's language usage indicates their development of the concept of story (Applebee, 1978). The oral, abbreviated folktales from centuries ago serve as short story archetypes for today's fully developed novels. Many people view fantasy as the natural progression of traditional literature, but other forms of fiction follow suit as well. For an excellent overview of fictional genres, visit Pauline Dewan's website http://childliterature.net/childlit/index.html. She describes the differences between genres of fiction: adventure fiction, realistic fiction, animal fiction, historical fiction, toy fiction, and fantasy fiction.

The traditional and modern stories written for children and young adults are structured around characters who live in particular places and times, who experience a series of events that are revealed through narration, character action, and dialogue. Although stories can have elaborate plots that defy chronologies or narrative practices, they all have a basic beginning, middle, and an end. Otherwise, we wouldn't be able to follow along as readers. Some people feel we are born with an understanding of story structure; others believe we are socialized into the practice. Either way, story has a grammar and it's a tool for thinking and understanding. The Brothers Grimm, Charles Perrault, and Joseph Jacobs represent the many people who have attended to story and recognized its value in culture and human development.

CHAPTER 10

WAXING POETIC WITH DELIBERATE DESCRIPTION AND AESTHETIC ARGUMENTATION

(POETS AND POETIC TEXTS, READING ALOUD, CHORAL READING, PERFORMANCE)

Poetry

What is poetry? Who knows?

Not the rose, but the scent of the rose;

Not the sky, but the light in the sky;

Not the fly; but the gleam of the fly;

Not the sea; but the sound of the sea;

Not myself, but what makes me

See, hear, and feel something that prose

Cannot; and what it is who knows?

(Eleanor Farjeon, 1938)

In her poem, Poetry, Eleanor Farjeon used imagery, sensory details, repetition, and a series of metaphors to communicate her message. Her purpose was to define poetry, and in doing so, she engaged in a succinct form of writing to describe an elusive genre. Farjeon was not the first person to attempt such a definition.

Aristotle also tried to capture the essence of poetry. In *Poetics* (c. 335 BCE) Aristotle formed categories and organized various kinds of poetry into systems, identifying the "essential quality" of each (Telford, 1961, p. 1). His list of poetic forms included "Epic poetry and Tragedy, Comedy also and Dithyrambic poetry."

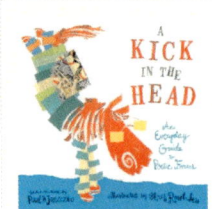

Figure 10.1

Kids are still required to identify poetic forms. But the process can be more entertaining in the hands of a poet such as Paul Janeczko. *A Kick in the Head: An Everyday Guide to Poetic Forms* by Paul B. Janeczko and illustrated by Chris Raschka, 2005, Somerville, MA: Candlewick. Copyright 2005 by Chris Raschka.

As children, teenagers, and college students, many of us have experienced poetry as an approximation of Aristotle's method: we categorized the types of poetry, conducted close analyses of the language in poetry, and discovered the aesthetic representations within the words (Figure 10.1). We memorized poems and we also read the great poets: Wordsworth, Yeats, Frost (Figure 10.2), Whitman, Poe, Keats, Shakespeare, Eliot, Thoreau.

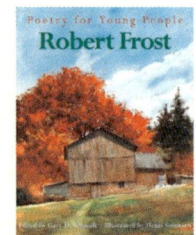

Figure 10.2

Classic poetry is often republished with modern illustrations. Poetry for Young People is a popular series. *Poetry for Young People: Robert Frost* by Gary D. Schmidt and Illustrated by Henri Sorensen, 2008, New York, NY: Sterling. Copyright 2008 by Henri Sorensen.

In 5th grade, Sr. Margaret required my class to memorize and recite "The Charge of the Light Brigade" by Alfred Lloyd Tennyson. The poem is about the Battle of Balaclava during the Crimean War. Here is the first stanza.

Half a league half a league,
Half a league onward,
All in the valley of Death Rode the six hundred:
'Forward, the Light Brigade!
Charge for the guns' he said:
Into the valley of Death Rode the six hundred. - See more at:
http://www.nationalcenter.org/ChargeoftheLightBrigade.html#sthash.YvI72enH.dpuf

I still remember the experience and I can recite some of the poem. Do you think that's a good thing?

Here is one example.

To A Young Girl

My dear, my dear, I know

More than another

What makes your heart beat so;

Not even your own mother

Can know it as I know,

Who broke my heart for her

When the wild thought,

That she denies

And has forgot,

Set all her blood astir

And glittered in her eyes.

(William Butler Yeats, 1919)

If we were extra lucky, our teachers also introduced us to poetry by great women: Dickenson (Figure 10.3), Barrett Browning, Plath, Brontë.

These great poets were excellent wordsmiths. They crafted lyrical phrases about people, places, events, and feelings in ways that were uncommon. Their abilities to use precise, descriptive language gave readers new insight and an opportunity to re-see the world (Figure 10.4).

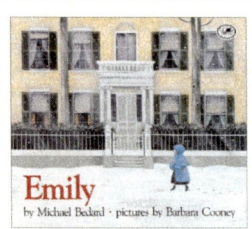

Figure 10.3
Emily Dickenson is one of the most important poets, male or female. Details about her work and life are told by storytellers and illustrators. *Emily* by Michael Bedard and illustrated by Barbara Cooney, 2002, New York, NY: Dragonfly. Cover art copyright 2002 by Barbara Cooney.

Figure 10.4
Although this isn't a book of poetry, the *Henry Hikes* series is inspired by the writing of Henry David Thoreau. *Henry Hikes to Fitchburg* by D.B. Johnson, 2006, New York, NY: HMH Books for Young Readers. Copyright 2006 by D.B. Johnson.

To evaluate descriptive books based primarily on the text, I use a combination of criteria from the *NCTE Award for Excellence in Poetry for Children (ALA)*, the *John Burroughs Riverby Award* (American Museum of Natural History), and the *Newbery Medal and Printz Award (ALA)*. Depending on the book, one or more of these criteria will apply:

- Perceptive and artistic accounts of direct experiences in the world
- Demonstrate authenticity of voice
- Use language and form in fresh ways
- Excellent, engaging, and distinctive use of clear and concise language.
- Excellent, engaging and distinctive use of vivid language.
- Excellent, engaging and distinctive use of sensory language.
- Appropriate structure to highlight the topic
- Appropriate organization with clear sequencing and logical development

If the description is presented in the form of a picturebook, I use the following criteria from the *Caldecott Medal* (ALA) as well.

- Excellence of execution in the artistic technique employed;
- Excellence of pictorial interpretation of theme or topic;
- Appropriateness of style of illustration to the theme or topic;
- Delineation of information through the pictures;
- Excellence of presentation in recognition of the intended audience.

How Do I Love Thee?

How do I love thee? Let me count the ways.

I love thee to the depth and breadth and height

My soul can reach, when feeling out of sight

For the ends of Being and ideal Grace.

I love thee to the level of every day's

Most quiet need, by sun and candlelight.

I love thee freely, as men strive for Right;

I love thee purely, as they turn from Praise.

I love with a passion put to use

In my old griefs, and with my childhood's faith.

I love thee with a love I seemed to lose

With my lost saints, I love thee with the breath,

Smiles, tears, of all my life! and, if God choose,

I shall but love thee better after death.

(Elizabeth Barrett Browning, 1850)

The women's perspectives certainly added new twists to the content of poetry. In addition to writing about love and sexuality, female poets also wrote about injustice, death, and darker motifs (Figure 10.5). They tackled history and social issues alongside explorations of human existence. But their language and ways with words were not necessarily relatable to us—the youth who were required to read them.

Figure 10.5

Dark, dreary, and dead. These are the poets of my youth. *Complete Works of Elizabeth Barrett Browning* (Delphi Poets Series), 2013, Delphi Classics, Amazon Digital Services.

Therefore, those of us who were super lucky may have been introduced to more accessible, but simultaneously more challenging, poets from different cultural, racial, and ethnic backgrounds: Hughes (Figure 10.6), Angelou, Wheatley, Brooks, McKay, Clifton, Cisneros, Soto, Neruda, Marti, Mora, Harjo.

By reading poetry from diverse poets, we could see how difficult topics were tackled differently. Poetic language changed. The sensibilities and diction of Victorian England or 19th Century New England gave way to urban, immigrant, disenfranchised, powerful, and hopeful voices who intended to describe and persuade.

Figure 10.6

Langston Hughes was one of many influential poets of the Harlem Renaissance. *The Collected Poems of Langston Hughes*, edited by Arnold Rampersad, 1995, New York, NY: Vintage. Copyright 1995 by Arnold Rampersad and Langston Hughes.

For example, in *Harriet*, Lucille Clifton challenges poetic and descriptive traditions with her content (celebrating strong Black women at the height of the Civil Rights movement), her language (using Black English vernacular to create the sounds of speech), and conventions (using lower case letters throughout to create the informal feeling of a private note or journal entry).

Modern poets may be more relatable to modern audiences (Figure 10.7), but not necessarily to young audiences. I'm certainly not one to prohibit youth from reading adult poetry; however, there is something missing from adult poetry that children need—the experiences and perspectives of youth.

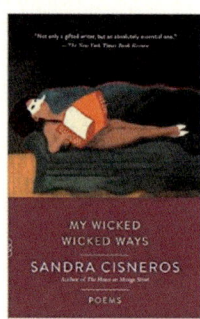

Figure 10.7

Sandra Cisneros' poetry reflected her human experience. *My Wicked Wicked Ways* by Sandra Cisneros, 1987, Berkeley, CA: Third Women Press. Cover for 3rd edition copyright by Vintage.

Those of you who are lottery lucky know what I mean. You have read poetry written specifically for children and adolescents: Silverstein, Prelutsky, Greenfield, Ciardi, Grimes, Adoff, Fisher, McCord, Merriam, Kuskin, Worth, Kennedy, Florian (Figure 10.8).

Figure 10.8

Poets, such as Douglas Florian, create topical and thematic books of poetry for children. *Shiver Me Timbers! Pirate Poems and Paintings* by Douglas Florian and illustrated by Robert Neubecker, 2012, New York, NY: Beach Lane Books. Cover art copyright 2012 by Robert Neubecker.

To evaluate argumentation based primarily on the text, I use a combination of criteria from awards designed to address a point of view or perspective [e.g., Jane Addams Peace Award (http://www.janeaddamspeace.org/jacba/subguide.shtml), Scott O'Dell Award for Historical Fiction (http://www.scottodell.com/pages/scotto'dellawardforhistoricalfiction.aspx), Sibert Medal (http://www.ala.org/alsc/awardsgrants/bookmedia/sibertmedal/sibertterms/sibertmedaltrms) and the Orbis Pictus Award (http://www.ncte.org/awards/orbispictus)].

- Depending on the book, one or more of these criteria apply:
- Establishes a central claim;
- Provides clear and accurate evidence to support the claim;
- Appropriate organization with clear sequencing and logical development;
- Appropriate style of presentation for subject and for intended audience;
- Honest and intimate accounts of experience that are relevant.

If the argumentation is presented in the form of a picture book, or if it includes sufficient illustration, I use the following criteria from the Caldecott Medal as well (http://www.ala.org/alsc/awardsgrants/bookmedia/caldecottmedal/caldecottterms/caldecottterms).

- Excellence of execution in the artistic technique employed;
- Excellence of pictorial interpretation of theme or argument;
- Appropriateness of style of illustration to the theme or argument;
- Delineation of argument through the pictures;
- Excellence of presentation in recognition of the intended audience.

How To Eat A Poem

Don't be polite.

Bite in.

Pick it up with your fingers and lick the juice that

may run down your chin.

It is ready and ripe now, whenever you are.

You do not need a knife or fork or spoon

or plate or napkin or tablecloth.

For there is no core

or stem

or rind

or pit

or seed

or skin

to throw away.

(Eve Merriam, 1964)

WAXING POETIC WITH DELIBERATE DESCRIPTION AND AESTHETIC ARGUMENTATION
(POETS AND POETIC TEXTS, READING ALOUD, CHORAL READING, PERFORMANCE)

Just because poetry is written for children does not mean it will be fluffy and light. In Eve Merriam's poem, *How To Eat a Poem*, she doesn't condescend to readers with simplistic language or forced rhyme. She describes poetry through a metaphor that is easily relatable (eating) but also quite deep—a poem leaves nothing to throw away. She also portrays poetry as delicious, sloppy, and ill-mannered, sending readers the message that youthful interactions are encouraged.

The content of children's poetry spans the gamut of human experience—just like adult poetry. Also, the language of children's poetry varies depending on the intended audience. Poetry for young children (Figure 10.9) is different than poetry for older children (Figure 10.10); and poetry for older children is different than poetry for adolescents (Figure 10.11).

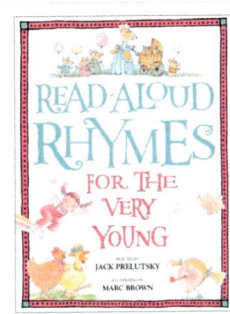

Figure 10.9

Poetry for very young children is playful and features rhyme, repetition, and memorable illustrations. *Read Aloud Rhymes for the Very Young*, written and selected by Jack Prelutsky and illustrated by Marc Brown, 1986, New York, NY: Knopf Books for Young Readers. Cover art copyright 1986 by Marc Brown.

In US schools and universities, there is always the temptation to continue a structural approach to poetry. Analysis is familiar. Close reading is scholarly. Familiarity is the reason why the general public calls for a return "back to basics." Identifying the mechanics of a poem is one way people make sense of poetry. However, the elaboration, sensory detail, and descriptive language of poetry creates spaces for different ways to find meaning. I like to go into those spaces.

Figure 10.10

Poetry for older children reflects their growing sense of themselves and their world. *Giant Children* by Brod Bagert and illustrated by Ted Arnold, 2005, New York, NY: Puffin Books. Cover art copyright 2005 by Ted Arnold.

In this chapter, I explore who's writing poetic texts looking specifically at the content of poetry and examining texts that describe, persuade, and elicit embodied ways of reading.

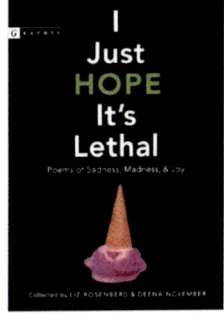

Figure 10.11

Poetry for young adults covers content that reflects their emotional range and the angst of adolescence. *I Just Hope It's Lethal* selected by Liz Rosenberg and Deena November, 2005, New York, NY: HMH Books for Young Readers. Copyright 2005 by Liz Rosenberg and Deena November.

Who's Who?

When searching for lists of "best" poetry or the "top ten poets" of all time, why do the search results look like a collection from the *Dead Poet's Society* (Schulman, 1988)? Try to find a good list of recommended poets or poems and the lists are more classic than contemporary.

Here is a list of 30 Great Poems Everyone Should Know:
http://www.thetimes.co.uk/tto/public/poetrycompetition/article3229711.ece

These poems come from poets who qualify for membership in the "Dead Poets Society." However, if you watch the film, the teacher, Mr. Keating (played by the late Robin Williams), challenges the orthodox, academic view on poetry:

> "We don't read and write poetry because it's cute. We read and write poetry because we are members of the human race. And the human race is filled with passion. Medicine, law, business, engineering, these are all noble pursuits, and necessary to sustain life. But poetry, beauty, romance, love, these are what we stay alive for."

Then Mr. Keating lowers his voice and paraphrases Walt Whitman's poem, reciting:

> "O me, o life of the questions of these recurring, of the endless trains of the faithless, of cities filled with the foolish. What good amid these, o me, o life? Answer: that you are here. That life exists, and identity. That the powerful play goes on, and you may contribute a verse..." Then the Mr. Keating stops for a brief moment, looks at his students and asks, "What will your verse be?"

(Haft, et. al., 2006, Touchstone Home Entertainment).

If you want to find a strong selection of poetry, you have to visit a public library or independent bookstore. Or you have to know specific titles and poets. Most adults' unfamiliarity with modern poetry creates a perpetual void in what is offered to youth. If parents, librarians, and teachers do not read or value poetry, then children are not exposed to poetry. In addition, I am frequently dismayed by the utter lack of poetry in major bookstores and retailers. In major retailers you will only find the most popular books based on sales history or holiday themes. It's true. Look for yourself.

The Popular Ones: Shel Silverstein, Jack Prelutsky

Award for Most Popular

Without question, Shel Silverstein is the most well-known and beloved poet for children (Figure 10.12). Here's why:

Shel Silverstein wrote poetry that entertains. Watch him: (https://www.youtube.com/watch?v=Bv2LUva-fo0)

Shel Silverstein wrote poetry that is relatable. Read *Sick* (https://www.poets.org/poetsorg/poem/sick).

Shel Silverstein wrote poetry that is meaningful. Read *The Little Boy and the Old Man* (http://poems.writers-network.com/shel-silverstein/the-little-boy-and-the-old-man.html).

Shel Silverstein wrote poetry that sounds good (Figure 10.13).

Shel Silverstein did not condescend to children. Although some librarians and teachers critique his poetry as simplistic (e.g., Kutiper & Wilson, 1993), he actually wrote from a playful, ironic, truthful place. Shel Silverstein understood what children wanted and needed in a poem.

Plus, listen to him read (https://www.youtube.com/watch?v=CNiaYHZme_U). He knows how language works.

Figure 10.12

Where the Sidewalk Ends is a standard book in any library collection. *Where the Sidewalk Ends* by Shel Silverstein, 1974, New York, NY: Harper & Row. Copyright 1974 by Shel Silverstein.

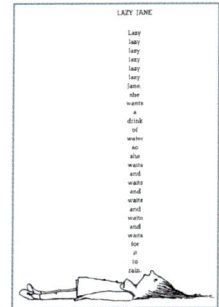

Figure 10.13

Shel Silverstein drew his own illustrations so he used words and images to create the sound, feel, and mood with which he wanted his poems read. "Lazy Jane" from *Where the Sidewalk Ends* by Shel Silverstein, 1974, New York, NY: Harper & Row. Copyright 1974 by Shel Silverstein.

Award for Funniest

Jack Prelutsky shares similar qualities with Shel Silverstein.

Jack Prelutsky writes poetry that entertains. Watch this (https://www.youtube.com/watch?v=nVJX845OLuA).

Jack Prelutsky writes poetry that is relatable. Read *The Bogeyman* (http://www.poetryfoundation.org/poem/177559).

Jack Prelutsky writes poetry that is meaningful (Figure 10.14).

Jack Prelutsky writes poetry that sounds good. Read here: (http://jackprelutsky.com/jacks-poems/).

Watch here: Jack reads at 08:50 (http://www.loc.gov/today/cyberlc/feature_wdesc.php?rec=4187).

I love the poetry of Jack Prelutsky. Poetry doesn't need iambic pentameter or linguistic metaphors to impress me (although Jack has both). Prelutsky's poetry is mostly humorous; and who doesn't like humor? Plus, children and young adults love it (Figure 10.15).

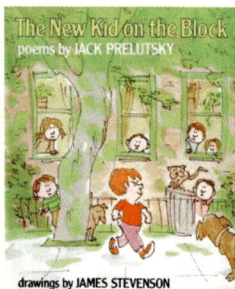

Figure 10.14

Have you ever been the victim of a bully? Jack Prelutsky knows how it feels. *The New Kid on the Block* by Jack Prelutsky and illustrated by James Stevenson, 1984, New York, NY: Greenwillow. Cover art copyright 1984 by James Stevenson.

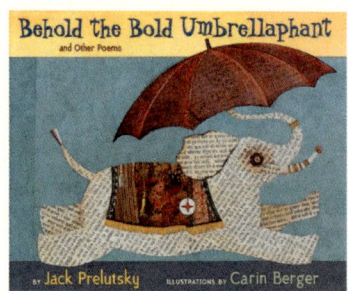

Figure 10.15

As demonstrated by the title of this book, Jack Prelutsky likes to play with the meaning and sound of words. Plus, he makes up words too. *Behold the Bold Umbrellaphant* by Jack Prelutsky and illustrated by Carin Berger, 2006, New York, NY: Greenwillow. Cover art copyright 2006 by Carin Berger.

When selecting poetry for children, the popular poets, such as Jack Prelutsky and Shel Silverstein, are a great place to start. Why? Youth are drawn to their humor.

Way back in 1974, Ann Terry surveyed 422 students in 4th, 5th, and 6th grade to determine their poetry preferences. She found that the students liked contemporary poems with humorous content, familiar experiences, and animals (Sounds about right!). The students also preferred narrative poems and poems with rhythm and rhyme (Yes, they sound better). Students disliked the poems they couldn't understand (Who doesn't?) and they disliked poems with visual imagery and figurative language (I get it).

Follow-up studies in the early 1990s supported Ann Terry's research. Kutiper and Wilson (1993) examined surveys of students in different grade levels and they also examined research using circulation records to determine what books students checked out of the library. The students consistently preferred rhythm, rhyme, excitement, and humor.

Recently, Jonda McNair (2012) found some expansion in children's interest in poetic forms (e.g., children enjoyed free verse), but the content of poetry preferences still holds true: youth like humorous, familiar, and rhythmic poetry. For these reasons, and many more, Uncle Shelby and Jackie P. are two of children's most loved poets.

 Hmm, contemporary topics, familiar experiences, humor. Sounds like a perfect description of "Charge of the Light Brigade." (Are you detecting my sarcasm?)

The Award Winners

In previous chapters, I debated the value of using awards to determine the quality of a book. Awards have their issues, but they also have some benefits. In the case of poetry, given its limited availability in bookstores, award winners are helpful guides that can direct your attention to the good stuff.

The *National Council of Teachers of English* offers the *Award for Excellence in Poetry for Children*. This award was created in 1977 to honor a living American poet for his or her aggregate work for children ages 3-13. The award is given to a poet or anthologist (someone who creates poetry collections) for his or her literary merit, contributions, and appeal to children.

NCTE defines literary merit and appeal to children in the following way:

Literary Merit (art and craft of aggregate work--as poet or anthologist)

Creating books of poetry that demonstrate imagination, authenticity of voice, evidence of a strong persona, and universality / timelessness are essential. In short, we're looking for a poet who creates poetry books that contain clean, spare lines; use language and form in fresh ways; surprise the reader by using syntax artistically; excite the reader's imagination with keen perceptions and sharp images; touch the reader's emotions. A maker of word events is what we're looking for.

Appeal to Children

Although the appeal to children of a poet's or anthologist's work is an important consideration, the art and craft must be the primary criterion for evaluation. Evidence of students' excitement for the poetry and evidence of childlike quality, yet poem's potential for stirring fresh insights and feelings should be apparent.
http://www.ncte.org/awards/poetry

The poets who won this award are among the who's who in children's poetry. Below, I listed the year they won the award and links to their collections via Goodreads.com (if available). Goodreads is a quick way to scan through most of their books.

- David McCord, 1977 (Figure 10.16) (http://www.goodreads.com/author/show/6883654.David_T_W_McCord)

- Aileen Fisher, 1978 (http://www.goodreads.com/search?utf8=%E2%9C%93&query=aileen+fisher)

- Karla Kuskin, 1979 (http://www.goodreads.com/search?utf8=%E2%9C%93&q=karla+kuskin&search_type=books)

Figure 10.16

David McCord won the first NCTE Award for Excellence in Poetry for Children. *Every Time I Climb a Tree* includes 25 memorable poems and engaging illustrations. *Every Time I Climb a Tree* by David McCord and illustrated by Marc Simont, 1967, New York, NY: Little, Brown and Company. Cover art copyright 1967 by Marc Simont.

- Myra Cohn Livingston, 1980 (http://www.goodreads.com/search?utf8=%E2%9C%93&query=myra+cohn+livingston)

- Eve Merriam, 1981 (http://www.goodreads.com/search?utf8=%E2%9C%93&query=eve+merriam)

- John Ciardi, 1982 (http://www.goodreads.com/search?utf8=%E2%9C%93&query=john+ciardi)

- Lillian Moore, 1985 (http://www.goodreads.com/search?utf8=%E2%9C%93&q=lilian+moore&search_type=books)

- Arnold Adoff, 1988 (http://www.goodreads.com/search?utf8=%E2%9C%93&q=arnold+adoff&search_type=books)

- Valerie Worth, 1991 (http://www.goodreads.com/search?utf8=%E2%9C%93&q=valerie+worth&search_type=books)

- Barbara Juster Esbensen, 1994 (http://www.goodreads.com/search?utf8=%E2%9C%93&q=barbara+juster+esbensen&search_type=books)

- Eloise Greenfield, 1997 (Figure 10.17) (http://www.goodreads.com/search?utf8=%E2%9C%93&q=eloise+greenfield&search_type=books)

As a child, I always wondered about love. What is love? How do you know when you are in love? (Figure 10.17). In these poems, Eloise Greenfield uses very small moments from normal, everyday life, to show children what love means, how it feels, and how someone-who-loves acts.

Love Don't Mean
Love don't mean all that kissing
Like on television
Love means Daddy
Saying keep your mama company
till I get back
And me doing it.

Keepsake
Before Mrs. Williams died
She told Mr. Williams
When he gets home
To get a nickel out of her
Navy blue pocket book
And give it to her
Sweet little gingerbread girl
That's me
I ain't never going to spend it

Figure 10.17

Eloise Greenfield wrote my two favorite love poems in *Honey, I Love and Other Poems* by Eloise Greenfield, illustrations by Diane and Leo Dillon, from Harper Collins Publishers, NY, 1978. Cover art copyright 1978 by Diane and Leo Dillon.

- X.J. Kennedy, 2000 (http://www.goodreads.com/search?utf8=%E2%9C%93&q=x.j.+kennedy&search_type=books)

- Mary Ann Hoberman, 2003 (http://www.goodreads.com/search?utf8=%E2%9C%93&q=mary+ann+hoberman&search_type=books)

- Nikki Grimes, 2006 (http://www.goodreads.com/search?utf8=%E2%9C%93&q=nikki+grimes&search_type=books)

- Lee Bennett Hopkins, 2009 (http://www.goodreads.com/search?utf8=%E2%9C%93&q=lee+bennett+hopkins&search_type=books)

- J. Patrick Lewis, 2011 (Figure 10.18) (http://www.goodreads.com/search?utf8=%E2%9C%93&q=j.+patrick+lewis&search_type=books)

- Joyce Sidman, 2013 (http://www.goodreads.com/search?utf8=%E2%9C%93&q=joyce+sidman&search_type=books)

- Marilyn Singer, 2015 (http://www.goodreads.com/search?utf8=%E2%9C%93&q=marilyn+singer&search_type=books)

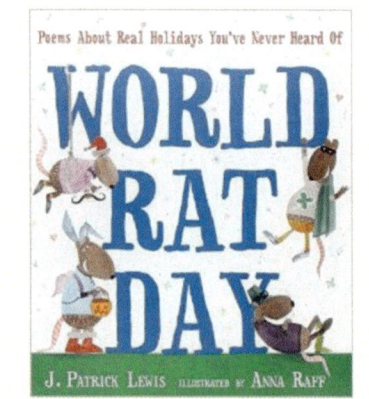

Figure 10.18

J. Patrick Lewis is a prolific poet with collections about chocolate moustaches, animal epitaphs, and little known holidays such as Cow Appreciation Day in *World Rat Day* by J. Patrick Lewis and illustrated by Anna Raff, 2013, Somerville, MA: Candlewick. Cover art copyright 2013 by Anna Raff.

The NCTE Award winners are not an exhaustive list of poets; but the list provides a good resource for exploration.

Another place to find award-winning poets is the list of Poet Laureates (http://www.loc.gov/poetry/laureate-2011-present.html). The Poet Laureate is a consultant in poetry to the Library of Congress. The poet is appointed for a year term and the person is responsible for raising "the national consciousness to a greater appreciation of the reading and writing of poetry" (http://www.loc.gov/poetry/about_laureate.html). The selected poets initiate special projects (e.g., Poetry 180 http://www.loc.gov/poetry/180/) and engage in talks, readings, and dramatic performances. Of course, the Poet Laureates write poetry for adults, but many of them also write poetry for youth. In addition, the line between youth and adults is a blurry one. If the poetry inspires and interests you, it might do the same for children and young adults.

There is no official Children's Poet Laureate for the Library of Congress. However, The Poetry Foundation awards the Young People's Poet Laureate title every two years (http://www.poetryfoundation.org/resources/poet-laureate/). The award recognizes poets who write for children and youth, and it attempts to raise awareness and promote poetry for young people.

The Weirdos, Novelties, and Outliers

Between Shel, Jack, and the award winners, I've mentioned some of the big names in poetry for children. But there are many more. There are poets for every single taste and interest—every sense and sensibility.

Just for the fun of it, I categorized my favorite poets by their content. They are the weirdos, novelties, and outliers. I assign these labels with great affection. These poets have carved out poetry niches and they have moved the sound and look of poetry in new directions.

   The Weirdos. The Weirdos are the poets who often write about scary, dark, and mysterious events. They may refer to a monster or two, including those that are imagined and real.

Roald Dahl (Figure 10.19)
Jack Prelutsky
Marilyn Singer
Christine Heppermann
Edgar Allan Poe
Liz Rosenberg

Figure 10.19
Roald Dahl is known for his fantasy novels, but he also liked to write wicked poetry. One example is *Revolting Rhymes* by Roald Dahl and illustrated by Quentin Blake, 1982, New York, NY: Alfred A. Knopf. Cover art copyright 1982 by Quentin Blake.

If you love scary, there is a website for scary poetry for children (http://www.scaryforkids.com/scary-poems/). If you can get past the ads and design, the poetry is good.

Poetry Soup also sorts poetry by scary type (http://www.poetrysoup.com/poems/horror).

The Novelties. The Novelty poets are interesting and charming. They pursue their own topic strands and establish lines of poetry about school, lunchrooms, siblings, body functions, etc. They are the serial poets.

Bruce Lansky
Alison Lester
Dennis Lee
Natalie Finnigan
C.J. Heck
Kenn Nesbitt (Figure 10.20)
Brod Bagert

Figure 10.20
Kenn Nesbitt is a popular poet who typically publishes humorous poetry. One example is *Revenge of the Lunch Ladies: The Hilarious Book of School Poetry* by Kenn Nesbitt and illustrated by Mike Gordon and Carl Gordon, 2007, New York, NY: Meadowbrook. Cover art 2007 by Mike and Carl Gordon.

Kenn Nesbitt created a website where users can search for poems by category and reading level. The website also includes games, apps, word lists, and videos (http://www.poetry4kids.com).

The Outliers. The Outliers are the poets who are unconventional. They are the poets who think with poetry and challenge the status quo. They write about social justice, food justice, and the environment. They explore our ways of being.

Paul Fleischman
Douglas Florian
Jacqueline Woodson
X.J. Kennedy
Paul Janeczko
Judith Viorst
Joyce Sidman
Naomi Shihab Nye (Figure 10.21)

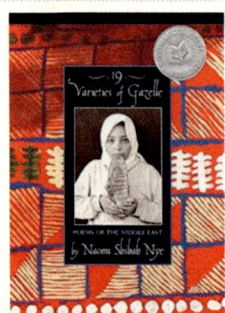

Figure 10.21
Naomi Shihab Nye received a lot of attention for her poetry for girls but she writes a broad range of poetry. *19 Varieties of Gazelle: Poems of the Middle East* by Naomi Shihab Nye, 2002, New York, NY: HarperCollins. Copyright 2002 by Naomi Shihab Nye.

Jacqueline Woodson is the Young People's Poet Laureate from 2015-2017. Her website includes samples of poetry as memoir, poetry as fiction, poetry as picture book, poetry as history, and poetry as empathy (http://www.jacquelinewoodson.com/books-ive-written/poetry/).

Whether popular, award-winning, or weird, poetry can be used to describe, inform, persuade, and tell stories. Poets describe human emotions and experiences, pushing readers toward new ways of thinking.

Finding Poetry

Quite honestly, poets are difficult to categorize and they rarely focus all of their writing efforts on one theme or a single form of poetry. For this reason poetry is often assembled into anthologies, featuring the work of many people.

- Anthologies are collections of poetry.
    - Single-authored anthologies are collections of poetry by one poet (Figure 10.22).
    - Edited anthologies are collections of poetry by many different poets and an editor makes the selection of which poets and what poems to include in the collection (Figure 10.23).
    - Picture books are also used to showcase poetry collections (Figure 10.24).
- Single poems can be segmented to span the length of a picture book.
- Picture books are often used to showcase an illustrator's interpretation of poetry.
- Entire novels can be written in verse, with or without illustration (Figure 10.25).

Children's poetry comes in all shapes, sizes, and formats to cover any topic (Video 10.1). There are many poetry websites that make it easy to find poets and their poetry.

Figure 10.22

All of the poems in this book were written by Nikki Giovanni. Then Ashley Bryan created illustrations that integrate the text. *The Sun Is So Quiet* by Nikki Giovanni and illustrated by Ashley Bryan, 1996, New York, NY: Henry Holt and Co. Cover art copyright 1996 by Ashley Brya

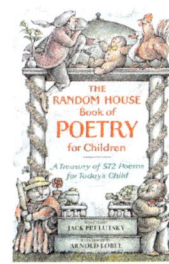

Figure 10.23

Jack Prelutsky edited my favorite poetry anthology of all time—*The Random House Book of Poetry*. Search for poetry by topic, title, author, and first line. There are poems about everything—from Abraham Lincoln to rainy days. It is a beautiful collection illustrated by Arnold Lobel. *The Random House Book of Poetry for Young Children* selected by Jack Prelutsky and illustrated by Arnold Lobel, 1983, New York, NY: Random House. Cover art copyright 1984 by Arnold Lobel.

Figure 10.24

Collections, such as *Pass It On*, gather selections from poets who use their voices to point out injustice and to inspire people. *Pass It On: African American Poetry for Children* selected by Wade Hudson and illustrated by Floyd Cooper, 1993, New York, NY: Scholastic. Cover art copyright 1993 by Floyd Cooper.

Figure 10.25

The Crossover is a verse novel, telling the story of Josh and JB, basketball and life. *The Crossover* by Kwame Alexander, 2014, New York, NY: Houghton Mifflin. Copyright 2014 by Kwame Alexander.

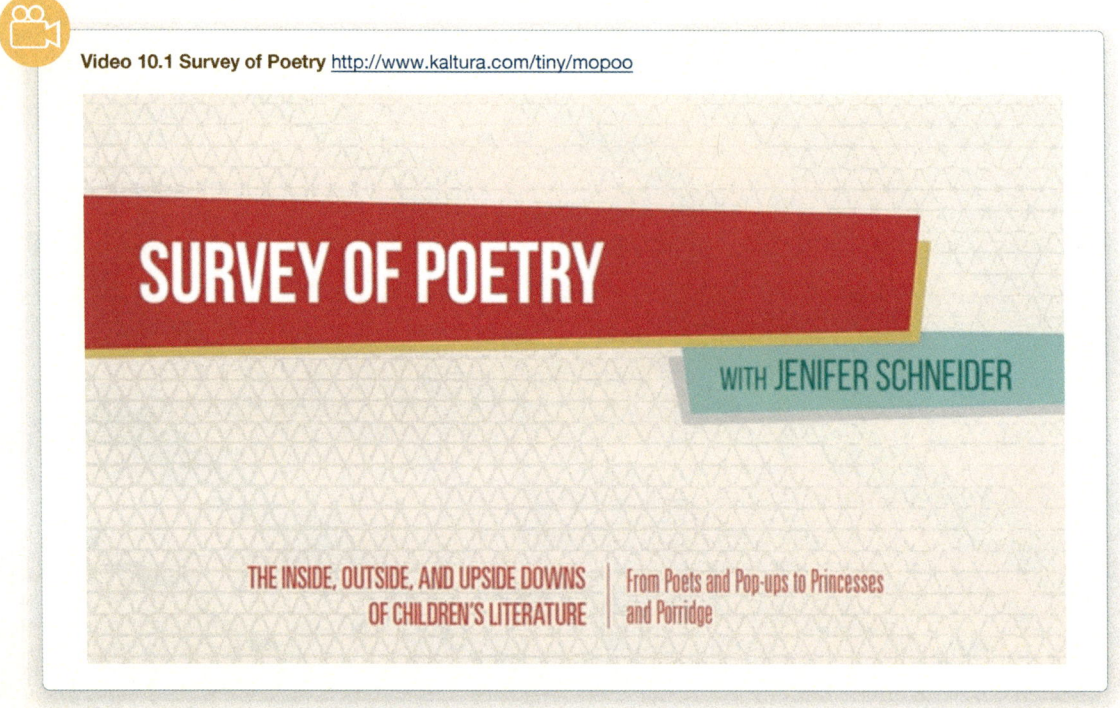

Video 10.1 Survey of Poetry http://www.kaltura.com/tiny/mopoo

For Extensive Biographies and Information About Poets:

- The Poetry Foundation (http://www.poetryfoundation.org/children/) features children's poets, videos, articles, newsletters, and social media links about children's poetry.

To Search For Complete Poems:

- The Academy of American Poets provides a search tool to find poetry by occasion, theme, or form (https://www.poets.org/poetsorg/browse-poems-poets).

- Poem Hunter allows searchers to find poems and poets by title and theme (http://www.poemhunter.com).

- The Poetry Archive is a comprehensive, searchable website where you can find famous poets (http://childrenspoetryarchive.org/).

To Search "Best Of" Lists

- This Goodreads collection features excellent examples of poetry for children and youth (http://www.goodreads.com/list/show/1340.Best_children_s_poetry_books).

- The Public Broadcasting Service (PBS) compiled a list of top ten children's poets (http://www.pbs.org/parents/education/bookfinder/popular-poets-for-kids/).

- Here is another list that is more contemporary and diverse (http://www.buzzfeed.com/krystieyandoli/life-changing-poems-everyone-should-read#.IaYZ2DnVw).

Sharing Poetry

With an understanding of who writes poetry, let's take a look at how to read and share poetry for children and youth.

Poetry Is Not A Math Problem

Poetry should NOT be

Structurally dissected

Linguistically torn apart

Or quantifiably syllabified

Without a focus on enjoyment, engagement, and reading.

Poetry should not be

Forcibly

Memorized

Or contrived to fit some outdated conception of literariness.

Children's poetry should be READ ALOUD!

Experienced.

Savored.

Acted upon.

Reading Aloud and Recitations

Poetry readings are not a new concept. Poetry is best experienced when it is read aloud.

Poetic language is intended for savoring, enunciating, stretching, and emphasizing.

Reading aloud entertains children, youth, and adults.

Reading a shared text gives the group a central focus and a cohesive focal point.

Reading aloud elicits conversations and further insight about the poem.

Reading aloud helps children learn how to read (this is really true). They develop an ear for poetry, language, and words.

> I couldn't understand Shakespeare until my high school English teacher read it out loud. Listen to Shel Silverstein, Maya Angelou, and Langston Hughes read their poems. Their reading techniques add to my comprehension of their messages.

The web exhibit, *Poetry Through The Ages*, provides excellent suggestions for reading aloud (http://www.webexhibits.org/poetry/home_reading.html). The exhibit also explains the basic measurements of poetic forms (e.g., hexameter, pentameter, etc.) and the most common types of meter used. In addition, the exhibit outlines tools for reading poetry.

Reading poetry is so important the Library of Congress developed Poetry 180 (http://www.loc.gov/poetry/180/), a resource intended to help high school students read a poem a day during the school year. Hosted by Billy Collins, U.S. Poet Laureate from 2001-2003, Poetry 180 includes a list of 180 poems (one for each school day), ideas for ways to share the poems, and helpful hints for how to read a poem effectively.

> Read the poem slowly.
> Read in a normal, relaxed tone.
> Pause only where there is punctuation, not at the end of every line.
> Know what the poem means so the message is communicated
> (From http://www.loc.gov/poetry/180/p180-howtoread.html).

For those who like competition, Poetry Out Loud is a national competition sponsored by the National Endowment for the Arts and the Poetry Foundation (http://www.poetryoutloud.org). The official contest is for high school students in participating states, but the poetry and materials are free for anyone to use. Poetry Out Loud also offers tips for reading and video examples of voice, physical presence, and dramatic appropriateness (http://www.poetryoutloud.org/poems-and-performance/tips-on-reciting).

Choral Reading

Choral reading or speaking is a term that describes an oral performance in which two or more people read or speak as one voice. Choral reading or speaking requires the performers to read for fluency and listen to the nuances of written language. In other words, through performance, the reader attends to the descriptive and structural elements of the text. Paul Fleischman created books of poetry for two voices (Figure 10.26) and four voices (Figure 10.27).

Figure 10.26

This book is quite remarkable. *Joyful Noise* tells the stories and secret lives of insects. The words are perfectly placed on the page, telling readers when to read alone or as two voices. *Joyful Noise: Poems for Two Voices* by Paul Fleischman and illustrated by Eric Beddows, 1988, New York, NY: Harper Trophy. Cover art copyright 1988 by Eric Beddows.

There are no specific criteria for selecting a text to read chorally. Instead, let the text determine the choral speaking method. Although poetry is perfect for choral speaking, not all poems are suitable for it. Choose your text carefully. Use the following general descriptions as a basis for your decisions.

Before you begin, read the poem once or twice to hear the flow of the language and understand the poem's meaning. Then use Poetry 180 for tips for reading effectively (From http://www.loc.gov/poetry/180/p180-howtoread.html).

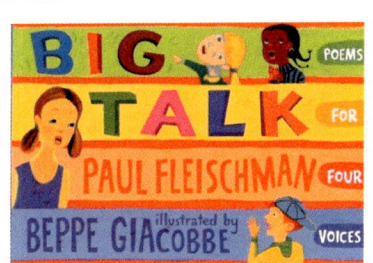

Figure 10.27

Paul Fleischman kicks it up a notch with poetry for four voices. The text and illustrations in *Big Talk* orchestrate choral reading. *Big Talk: Poems for Four Voices* by Paul Fleischman and illustrated by Beppe Giacobbe, 2008, Somerville, MA: Candlewick. Cover art copyright 2008 by Beppe Giacobbe.

Refrain. Choose a text in which the refrain repeats and is important. Typically, a selected person reads most of the lines while other participants read lines or stanzas that repeat. Here is an example (Video 10.2).

Video 10.2   Choral Reading   peak F R   Chapter
https://www.youtube.com/watch?v=Cp-VTHGIKWA

Line a person/group. Choose a text in which different voices need to be heard. Divide the text into segments (e.g., lines, stanzas, refrains). Individuals or small groups are assigned to read one segment. Each person reads only his or her segment. You may also assign small groups to read one segment. Here is an example (Video 10.3).

ViVideo 10.3 Choral Reading   xample https://www.youtube.com/watch?v=LFRzl2Oe_Bs

Here is another one (Video 10.4).

Video 10.4 Changing the World One Word at a Time https://www.youtube.com/watch?v=YshUDa10JYY

Cumulative. Choose a text in which the message builds or circles around concepts or phrases. Divide the poem into segments and assign to a person/group. The first reader begins and then others join in when it is their turn. Everyone reads his or her segment and continues reading until the end of the poem. Here is an example (Video 10.5).

Video 10.5 Old Lady Who Swallowed A Fly https://www.youtube.com/watch?v=qC_xO2aN_IA

Here is another one (Video 10.6).

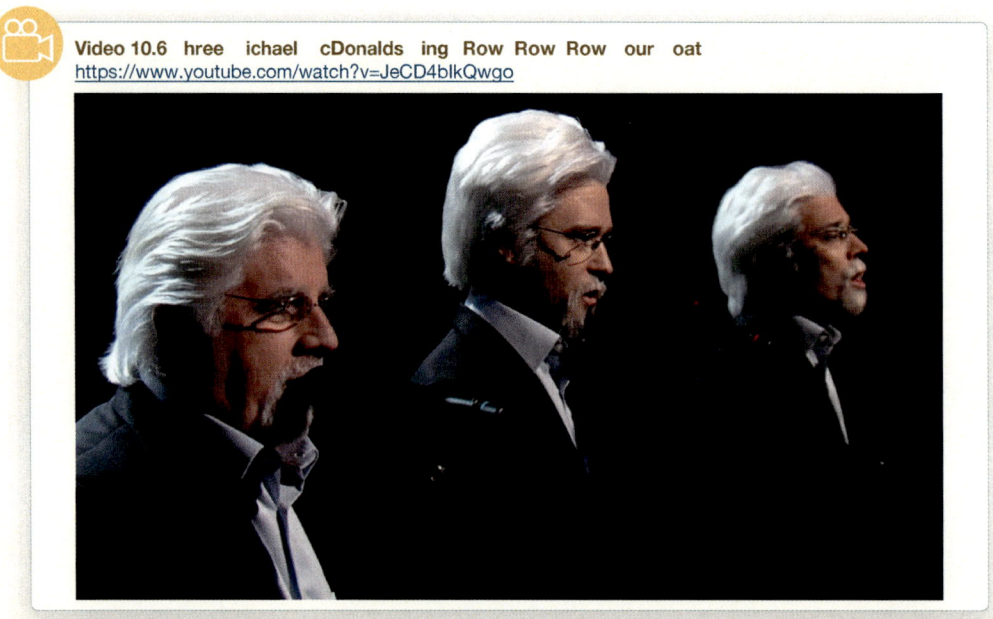

Video 10.6 Three Michael McDonalds Sing Row Row Row Your Boat
https://www.youtube.com/watch?v=JeCD4blkQwgo

Antiphonal. Select a text in which the message is emphasized by different voices, tones, and sounds. Divide the text into segments and determine the "voice" for each segment (Ex. high-low, soft-loud, squeaky-strong, male-female, etc.). Then divide the group to read their corresponding parts. Here is an example (Video 10.7).

Video 10.7   Choral Reading 4th Chapter https://www.youtube.com/watch?v=gbtMDrxi9JY

Unison. Choose a text that feels communal and more powerful when read by many voices. To me, unison reading is the most difficult type of choral speaking because the entire group reads the poem at one time. It takes practice to get many voices reading at the same time. Here is an example (Video 10.8).

Video 10.8 Valentine's Day Poem Moon Whole Class
https://www.youtube.com/watch?v=HJK2Lg5NfmM

Poetry Slams and Spoken Word

Poetry Slams are performance opportunities for individuals or teams of poets to present their work on stage. Audience members and/or a panel of judges rate the performance and select winners. Poetry Slams are live events, but slams can also occur via social networks (https://www.youtube.com/watch?v=lpPASWlnZIA) and curated collections such as TED talks (https://www.youtube.com/watch?v=cxGWGohIXiw).

 Watch this Ted Talk about writing slam poetry.
http://ed.ted.com/lessons/become-a-slam-poet-in-five-steps-gayle-danley

Youth Speaks (http://youthspeaks.org/) is an organization that produces local and national youth poetry slams, festivals, and reading events, as well as arts-education programming.

Spoken Word poetry is similar to a Poetry Slam in that the poetry is performed in front of an audience. However, there is no winner or contest. The Power Poetry website provides advice for writing and performing Spoken Word poetry (http://www.powerpoetry.org/actions/5-tips-spoken-word).

Performing and Embodying Poetry

In addition to sharing poetry through recitation and poetry slams, poetry is also a source for embodied performance. Poetic texts elicit different responses and emotions. To act on those responses, readers often use arts-based modalities as a way of understanding. In particular, performing arts allow readers to use their voices and body movements to convey their interpretations.

 Recitation of poetry can be a good thing—with the right poem for the right reader at the right time. Here is someone who obviously loves the poems she memorized (https://www.youtube.com/watch?v=0pg6BFDpJ4g).

Dramatic interpretation. Dramatic engagement can take many forms, from a scripted play to an improvised scene. Poetic texts can serve as the foundation for dramatic performances or as the basis for informal theater games. For example, tableaux are frozen scenes created by participants' bodies, gestures, and facial expressions. Tableau can be used as a form of illustration as readers enact scenes with their bodies. Tableau also provides a structure in which the participants can explore characters, emotions, and roles from within the text (See Figures 10.28 and 10.29).

Figure 10.28

Marilyn Singer creates poetry that has one meaning when read down one side of the page and a different meaning when read on the other. Through this structure, she shares new perspectives on familiar fairy tales. *Mirror Mirror: A Book of Reverso Poems* by Marilyn Singer and illustrated by Josee Masse, 2010, New York, NY: Dutton. Cover art copyright 2010 by Josee Masse.

Figure 10.29

Tableau gives readers an opportunity to experience poetry from the characters' perspectives. In this frozen scene, the participants explore the perspectives of a girl and a wolf using the positions of their bodies, gestures, and facial expressions. Photo copyright 2014 by Randi Meyer.

Musical interpretation. Musical performance is another medium for reading and sharing poetry because the poetry can be rhythmically, linguistically, and vocally interpreted. Many people equate song lyrics with poetry, but there may be more intricate connections with regard to content and sound (Figure 10.30). Musical instruments, including the voice, can be explored in relation to the rhythm, tone, and cadence of a poem. Watch this video for an excellent example of musical interpretation of poetry (Video 10.9).

Figure 10.30

When a poet is also an illustrator, really cool things can happen between image and text. For example, Douglas Florian uses art to understand celestial objects and find just-right words to describe them. Image of Saturn from *Comets, Stars, the Moon, and Mars* by Douglas Florian, 2007, New York, NY: HMH Books for Young Readers. Copyright 2007 by Douglas Florian.

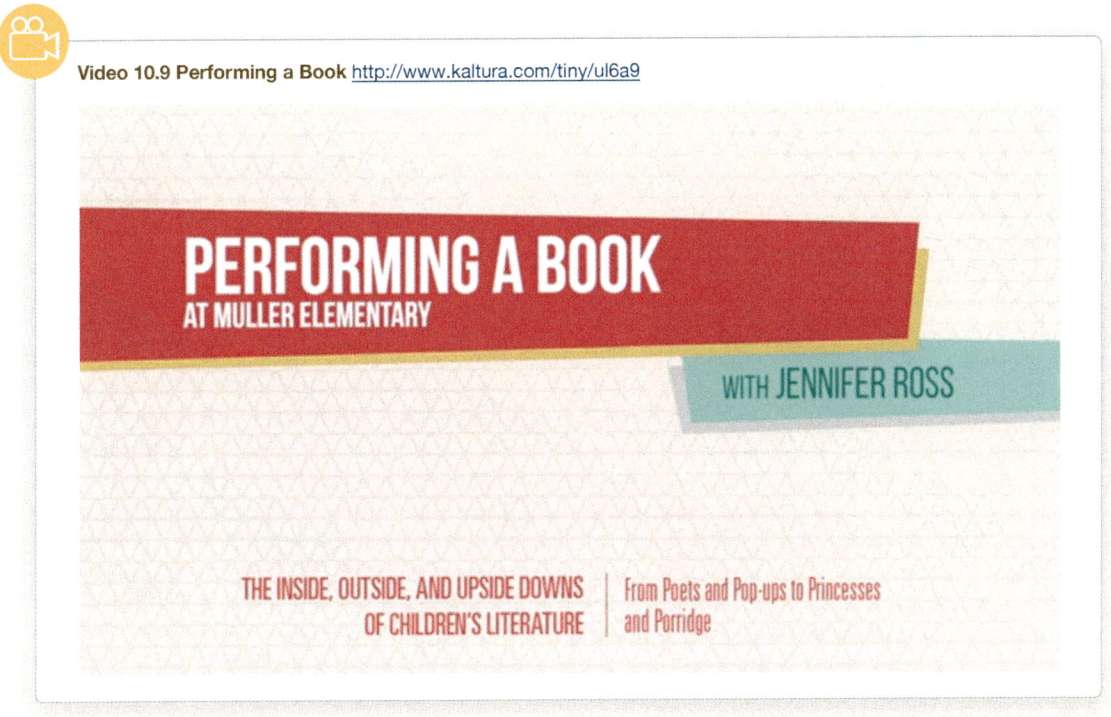

Video 10.9 Performing a Book http://www.kaltura.com/tiny/ul6a9

Visual interpretation. If you explore children's poetry, you will discover that most publications contain visual elements, pictures, or nontraditional uses of typeface and layout. Consequently, many poems published for children are visual poems or presented in a form of a picture book in which images and text are equally important and interrelated (Figure 10.31).

Although visual responses such as drawing, painting, or photography, are not typically considered to be performing arts, the act of creating images is an embodied experience. In creating an image the reader can reveal his or her understanding of the text. Altering different media (crayons, markers, paint, chalk, photographs) have an impact on comprehension and interpretation as well (Video 10.10).

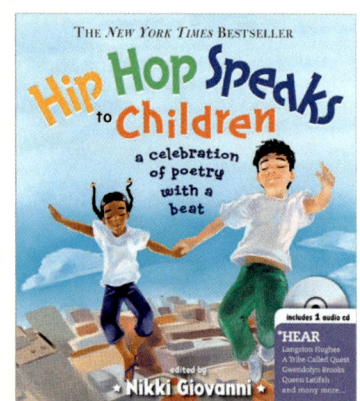

Figure 10.31

As Nikki Giovanni states in her introduction, Hip Hop is modern opera, with truthful tales surrounded by public commentary. This collection of poetry includes celebrated children's poets, musicians, and rappers telling stories. *Hip Hop Speaks to Children: A Celebration of Poetry* with a Beat selected by Nikki Giovanni and illustrated by Michele Noiset and Jeremy Tugeau, 2008, Naperville, IL: Sourcebooks. Cover art copyright 2008 by Michele Noiset and Jeremy Tugeau.

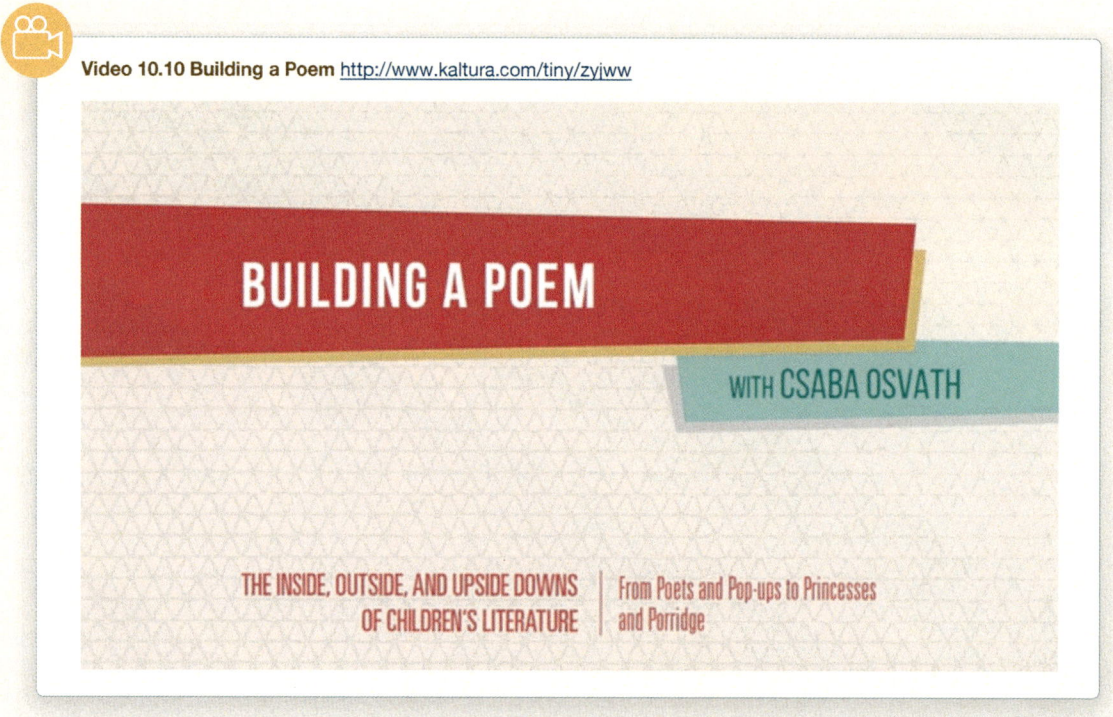

Video 10.10 Building a Poem http://www.kaltura.com/tiny/zyjww

Creating Poetry
by Csaba Osvath

In children's poetry, there are poets who construct visual or concrete poetry by creating visual compositions where the text and visual elements (e.g., pictures, typeface, colors, layout, balance) are inseparable. A famous example is Lewis Carroll's 'Mouse's Tale' in *Alice's Adventures in Wonderland*, where the text is shaped as a long, curving tail (Figure 10.32).

Another type of visual poetry is graphic poetry, where images are intentionally matched with a text to aid comprehension and interpretation. In the production of filmed, spoken-word poetry, many poets will augment their recitation with images and words to enhance the experience of engaging with their poems on the screen. As such, visual and concrete poems offer layers of interaction with the reader (Figure 10.33). By creating visual, graphic, or concrete poems the poet offers new approaches to communicate or to connect with the audience.

Poetry: A Slippery Slide. Of course, as a mature person, you might think that your beliefs about poetry are irrelevant in the context of poetry in an academic course in children's literature. Additionally, you might think that learning about poetry related to children's literature has little connection to your "adult" life and the problems related to adulthood. However, consider Lemony Snicket's introduction to a children's poetry portfolio, 'All Good Slides Are Slippery', in *Poetry* magazine where he wrote:

Figure 10.32
Lewis Carroll showed readers how text has illustrative function through page arrangement. The Mouse's Tail from *Alice's Adventures in Wonderland* by Lewis Carroll, 1865, New York, NY: Macmillan. Copyright expired.

Figure 10.33
Concrete poets use shape, page layout, font, and other aspects of design to communicate meaning. One example is *Meow Ruff: A Story in Concrete Poetry* by Joyce Sidman and illustrated by Michelle Berg, 2006, New York, NY: HMH Books for Young Readers. Cover art copyright 2006 by Michelle Berg.

The poems contained in this children's poetry portfolio are not made for children. Poetry is like a curvy slide in a playground – an odd object, available to the public – and, as I keep explaining to my local police force, everyone should be able to use it, not just those of a certain age (See more at http://www.poetryfoundation.org/poetrymagazine/article/246328).

I personally agree with Snicket. Poetry is a kind of functional architecture or a transportation device that is asking us to inhabit it and to use it with the added possibility of joy, thrill, or even fear. Snicket does not mention the intellectual abilities of children when it comes to poetry. He never writes that these poems are too complex, or too difficult, or too challenging for a young audience. He suggests that *understanding* might not even be a necessary prerequisite for engaging with poetry. In fact, even if you don't understand what the author meant to say, the poem still communicates to you. The poem can still reach you and impact your life, incite and ignite feelings, reveal ideas, etc. Consider, the short poem from the portfolio by Eileen Myles, titled "Uppity" (http://www.poetryfoundation.org/poetrymagazine/poem/246366).

Uppity

Roads around mountains

cause we can't drive

through

That's Poetry

to Me.

(Eileen Myles, 2013)

What does the poet mean in this poem? Are the roads a metaphor for words? Or are the roads a metaphor for contemplation? Is there a point to explain this poem, or is the experience of reading the poem, simply, meaningful? Again, Snicket hits the mark when he writes about the essence of poetry in the context of a children's literature:

If you are a child, you might like these poems. Of course, you might not. Poems, like children, are individuals, and will not be liked by every single person who happens to come across them. So you may consider this portfolio a gathering of people in a room. It does not matter how old they are, or how old you are yourself. What matters is that there are a bunch of people standing around in a room, and you might want to look at them.

Ars Poetica. All this leads to some important conclusions. Poetry is communal, regardless of the age or the "maturity" of its audience. Poetry does not function in isolation. Poetry thrives on interpersonal connections and on the use of voice and speech. Poetry thrives when it is "said out loud" and heard by "a bunch of peoples standing around." So the questions loop back around and pose questions that answer, "What do you believe about poetry?" "Do you need poetry in your life?" And most importantly, "What can poetry offer you?"

When I now ponder these questions, I recall the story of a young boy, Gregory Orr, who is now a college professor of English. Through a project organized by National Public Radio (NPR) he tells a poignant, but inspiring story about a tragic childhood accident in his life and the role of poetry. Orr goes as far as to elevate poetry and the writing of poems as tools for survival. Orr reveals that for him, poetry and the making of poems are a "way of surviving the emotional chaos, spiritual confusion, and traumatic events that come with being alive" (http://www.npr.org/templates/story/story.php?storyId=5221496). The author shares how traumatic violence isolates us and makes us numb. For him, the act of writing and actively sharing poetry with others became the essential tool to process his painful experiences and translate them into words. And when we are able to translate experiences into words, we realize that we are no longer powerless. Instead, we can actively shape our memories and our pain into poems. And through the act of sharing, we realize that we are no longer alone. We are, indeed, part of humanity.

- by Csaba Osvath

Exploring Poetry

The work of the great poets often serve as our introduction to poetry, but irrelevant teaching practices may have taken many of us away. Take a look at poetry for children and young adults. Revisit the classics and modern adult poetry as well. But do so by creating embodied experiences, reading aloud, and playing with the words, shapes, and meaning of poetry. Bottom line: you will find new meaning.

Sharing great poetry with children is not only a catalyst of change, but it is a valuable and diverse tool that poets (even emergent or amateur ones) can master and utilize in order to express their feelings, ideas, thoughts, dreams. Poetry allows us to connect with others, which eliminates fear from the "other." The key or the foundation for this responsibility begins with our willingness to engage with and to learn about poetry that is written, created, spoken, and intended for children or youth.

CHAPTER 11

PAST PRESIDENTS AND EVADING INVENTORS: NOT YOUR GRANDMOTHER'S INFORMATION BOOKS

(PORTRAYING PEOPLE, ARGUING POSITIONS, AND PRESENTING DISCIPLINARY CONTENT)

Unlike the poet or the storyteller, the nonfiction writer is often viewed as less of an artist and more of a technician. The poet is a "responsible commentator" (Smith, 2010), sending persuasive and descriptive messages that are personal, political, or playful. The fiction writer is a storyteller, using description and narration to build imagined worlds that are realistic and fantastic. In contrast, the nonfiction writer is instructive, logical, and factual; using text structures to build concepts, present information, and clarify concepts. Where's the art in that? Well, there's plenty.

Poorly written information books are boring and overly simplified or filled with lifeless chronologies of events and factual statements. They are often written by experts with little knowledge of youth or written by no-name technical writers with stock knowledge of content. Expertise is essential in the creation of nonfiction texts, and so is strong writing—after all, we are talking about the creation of books. Contemporary information books are cleverly written, they feature amazing photographs and illustrations, and they focus on important material that interests and challenges readers.

The purpose of this chapter is to explore modern approaches to informational writing for children, which may include argumentative, descriptive, and narrative elements as well. In doing so, I dispel some myths about nonfiction texts as boring, bland, and basic. I identify how nonfiction literature can be used to enhance learning across disciplinary areas. I also share examples of the literature that reflect current trends.

The iNK Think Tank (http://inkthinktank.com) is focused on creating interesting nonfiction for kids. The authors and illustrators who are members of this community write blogs, visit schools, and create content to share in the Nonfiction Minute (http://www.nonfictionminute.com).

The Quest for Information

Nonfiction books clarify content and reveal the subject through accuracy, documentation, organization, visual material and book design. Such books display respect for children's understanding, abilities, and aesthetic appreciation. They also appeal to adults.

Relevant Topics and Professional Interests

Think about your college major, your current professional position, or your future aspirations. Are you in health sciences, social work, business, art, engineering, hospitality? What are your professional interests?

Find two children's information books that relate to your profession. Yes, that's right—a children's book. The content of nonfiction children's literature spans all disciplines.

Find award-winning nonfiction books categorized by discipline:
History: http://www.ncte.org/library/NCTEFiles/About/Awards/OPBooks-Historical.pdf
Science: http://www.ncte.org/library/NCTEFiles/About/Awards/OPBooks-Science.pdf
Biography: http://www.ncte.org/library/NCTEFiles/About/Awards/OPBooks-Biographical.pdf

For example, if your career is in English, language, or linguistics maybe these books are right for you?

- *The Right Word: Roget and His Thesaurus* written by Jen Bryant and illustrated by Melissa Sweet, 2014, New York, NY: Eerdmans.

- *Sequoyah: The Cherokee Man Who Gave his People Writing* by James Rumford and translated by Anna Sixkiller Huckaby, 2004, New York, NY: HMH Books for Young Readers (Figure 11.1).

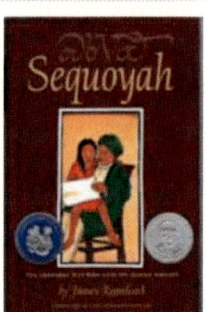

Figure 11.1

If you are interested in languages, Sequoyah provides a glimpse into Cherokee history. *Sequoyah: The Cherokee Man Who Gave his People Writing* by James Rumford and translated by Anna Sixkiller Huckaby, 2004, New York, NY: HMH Books for Young Readers. Cover image copyright 2004 by Anna Sixkiller Huckaby.

- If your career is in fashion, marketing, art direction, or performance, check out the following:

  - *Balloons Over Broadway* written and illustrated by Melissa Sweet, 2011, New York, NY: HMH Books for Young Readers.

  - *My Story, My Dance: Robert Battle's Journey to Alvin Ailey* by Lesa Cline-Ransome, illustrated by James E. Ransome, 2015, New York, NY: Simon & Schuster (Figure 11.2).

Figure 11.2

Read about Robert Battle in *My Story, My Dance: Robert Battle's Journey to Alvin Ailey* by Lesa Cline-Ransome, illustrated by James E. Ransome, 2015, New York, NY: Simon & Schuster. Illustration copyright 2015 by James E. Ransome.

- If your career aspirations are in business, politics, or economics, look for books on related topics.

  - *Growing Money: A Complete Investing Guide for Kids* written by Gail Karlitz and Debbie Honig, 2010, New York, NY: Price Stern Sloan.

  - *So You Want to be President* written by Judith St. George and illustrated by David Small, 2004/2012, New York, NY: Philomel (Figure 11.3).

Figure 11.3

If you like quirky facts about the Presidency and the Presidents of the US, this book is for you. *So You Want to be President* written by Judith St. George and illustrated by David Small, 2004/2012, New York, NY: Philomel. Illustration copyright 2004/2012 by David Small.

- Or, do you just love numbers and math? Read about number people and math problems.

  - *Money Madness* by David A. Adler and illustrated by Edward Miller, 2010, New York, NY: Holiday House.

  - *Mystery Math: A First Book of Algebra* written by David A. Adler and illustrated by Edward Miller, 2011, New York, NY: Holiday House. (Figure 11.4).

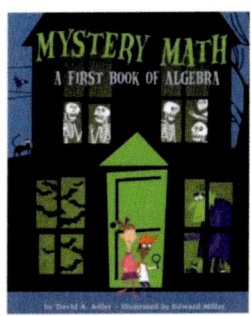

Figure 11.4

Part story, part mystery, part math. This book integrates mathematical thinking with narrative. *Mystery Math: A First Book of Algebra* written by David A. Adler and illustrated by Edward Miller, 2011, New York, NY: Holiday House. Cover art copyright 2011 by Edward Miller.

- Focused on law, civil rights, and cultures? Read about others like you.

  - *Funny Bones: Posada and His Day of the Dead Calaveras* by Duncan Tonatiuh, 2015, New York, NY: Harry N. Abrams (Figure 11.5).

  - *Drowned City: Hurricane Katrina & New Orleans* written by Don Brown, 2015, New York, NY: HMH Books for Young Readers.

- Perhaps you are an historian or your career is in the military.

  - *Bomb: The Race to Build—and Steal—the World's Most Dangerous Weapon* written by Steve Sheinkin, 2012, New York, NY: Flash Point (Figure 11.6).

  - *Hitler Youth: Growing Up in Hitler's Shadow* written by Susan Campbell Bartoletti, 2005, New York, NY: Scholastic.

- Are you an environmentalist or scientist? Look for books that address your issues and concerns.

  - *The Elephant Scientist* by Caitlin O'Connell and Donna M. Jackson/photographs by Caitlin O'Connell and Timothy Rodwell, 2011, New York, NY: HMH Books for Young Readers.

  - *Kakapo Rescue: Saving the World's Strangest Parrot*, written by Sy Montgomery, photographs by Nic Bishop, 2010, New York, NY: Houghton Mifflin Books for Children (Figure 11.7).

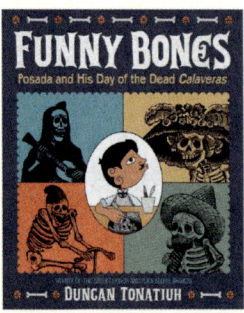

Figure 11.5
Learn about the Day of the Dead. *Funny Bones: Posada and His Day of the Dead Calaveras* by Duncan Tonatiuh, 2015, New York, NY: Harry N. Abrams. Copyright 2015 by Duncan Tonatiuh.

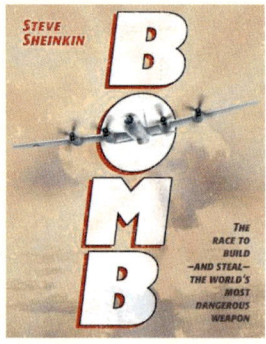

Figure 11.6
Bomb is a combination of history and military science. *Bomb: The Race to Build—and Steal—the World's Most Dangerous Weapon* written by Steve Sheinkin, 2012, New York, NY: Flash Point. Copyright 2012 by Steve Sheinkin.

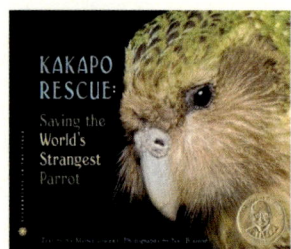

Figure 11.7
You won't forget the images in this book. *Kakapo Rescue: Saving the World's Strangest Parrot*, written by Sy Montgomery, photographs by Nic Bishop, 2010, New York, NY: Houghton Mifflin Books for Children. Cover art copyright 2010 by Nic Bishop.

Your Personal Interests and Passions

I'm sure you expected children's books to cover "school" topics, but what about your personal interests and hobbies? Children's literature spans a range of topics of interest to many different audiences. Are you into sports, drama, religion, charity work? Find children's information books that relate to your personal interests and passions.

- If you like to fish, check out animals of the sea.

    - *Neighborhood Sharks: Hunting with the Great Whites of California's Farallon Islands* by Katherine Roy, 2014, New York, NY: David Macaulay Books (Figure 11.8).

Figure 11.8
Roy writes about sharks with great expertise and in simple terms. *Neighborhood Sharks: Hunting with the Great Whites of California's Farallon Islands* by Katherine Roy, 2014, New York, NY: David Macaulay Books. Copyright 2014 by Katherine Roy.

- If you enjoy traveling and learning about different people, places, and times, there are plenty of books for you.

    - *The Grand Mosque of Paris: A Story of How Muslims Rescued Jews during the Holocaust* by Karen Gray Ruelle and Deborah Durland Desaix, 2009, New York, NY: Holiday House (Figure 11.9).

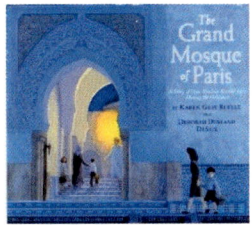

Figure 11.9
If you enjoy learning about different religions and historical sites, read *The Grand Mosque of Paris: A Story of How Muslims Rescued Jews during the Holocaust* by Karen Gray Ruelle and Deborah Durland Desaix, 2009, New York, NY: Holiday House. Cover art copyright 2009 by Deborah Durland Desaix.

- If you love birdwatching, there are many amazing options.

    - *Look Up! Bird-Watching in Your Own Backyard* by Annette LeBlanc Cate, 2013, Somerville, MA: Candlewick (Figure 11.10).

Figure 11.10
Look Up! Is a helpful guide for identifying birds and their features. *Look Up! Bird-Watching in Your Own Backyard* by Annette LeBlanc Cate, 2013, Somerville, MA: Candlewick. Copyright 2013 by Annette LeBlanc Cate.

- Are you an artist? Read about museums, different media, art installations, or the artists themselves.

    - *Drawing from Memory* by Allen Say, 2011, New York, NY: Scholastic (Figure 11.11).

Figure 11.11
Allan Say takes readers on his journey as an illustrator. *Drawing from Memory* by Allen Say, 2011, New York, NY: Scholastic. Copyright 2011 by Allen Say.

- Love the cosmos? Look for books about our constantly evolving universe.

  - *A Black Hole is NOT a Hole* by Carolyn Cinami DeCristofano, illustrated by Michael Carroll, 2012, Boston, MA: Charlesbridge (Figure 11.12).

- Do you scrapbook? Yes, there are kids books about scrapbooking.

  - *The Scraps Book* by Lois Ehlert, 2014, New York, NY: Beach Lane Books (Figure 11.13).

- Love amusement parks? Look for books that share your interest in rollercoasters, cotton candy, and entertainment.

  - *Mr. Ferris and His Wheel* by Kathryn Gibbs Davis and illustrated by Gilbert Ford, 2014, New York, NY: HMH Books for Young Readers (Figure 11.14).

Figure 11.12
Black holes are difficult to understand but this book explains their features with words and images. *A Black Hole is NOT a Hole* by Carolyn Cinami DeCristofano, illustrated by Michael Carroll, 2012, Boston, MA: Charlesbridge. Cover art copyright 2012 by Michael Carroll.

Figure 11.13
Lois Ehlert shares colorful scraps. *The Scraps Book* by Lois Ehlert, 2014, New York, NY: Beach Lane Books. Copyright 2014 by Lois Ehlert.

Figure 11.14
Not only does this book provide the history of Mr. Ferris, but the illustrations provide readers with a unique viewing experience of the wheel. *Mr. Ferris and His Wheel* by Kathryn Gibbs Davis and illustrated by Gilbert Ford, 2014, New York, NY: HMH Books for Young Readers. Illustration copyright 2014 by Gilbert Ford.

If you think children's books are too simple to add to your knowledge base, think again. Experts across all major fields of study recognize the depth and quality of the content in children's books. Authors and illustrators consult with experts and conduct extensive research to present accurate information. If a book includes detailed information and advanced knowledge, look at the credits for recognition of the consultants, museums, libraries, and organizations who contributed to the book's content.

Now that you've located books that represent your areas of interest and expertise, what do you notice? Did you learn something new?

Video 11.1 Survey of Information Books http://www.kaltura.com/tiny/xhgpm

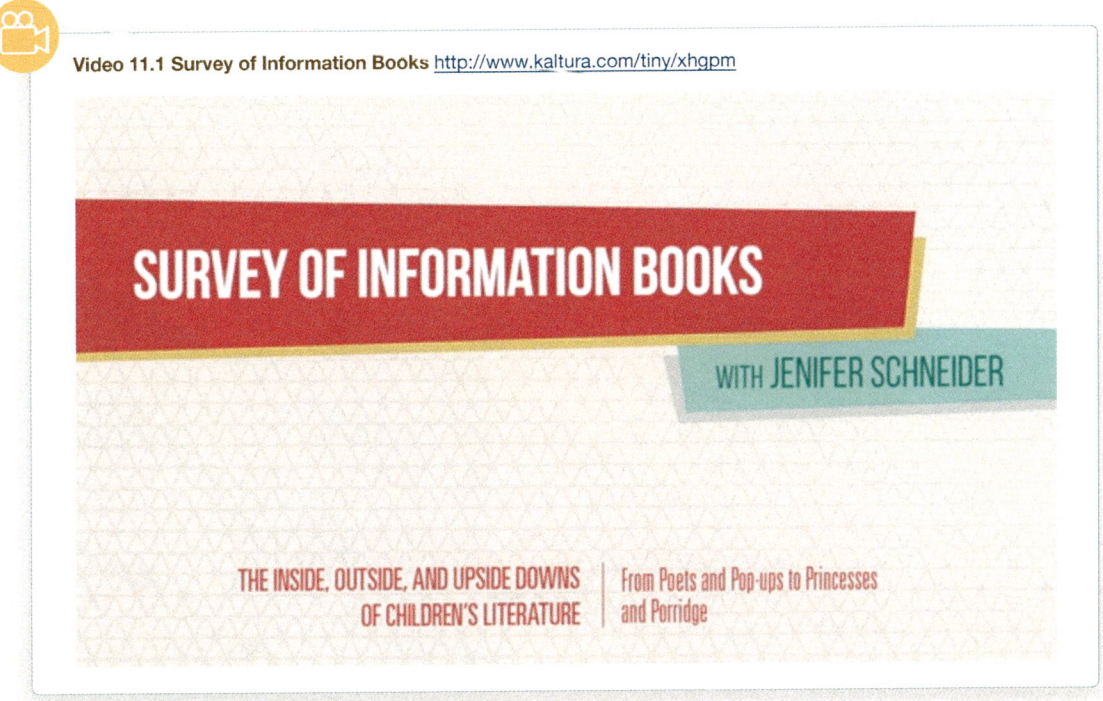

Limited Topics and Perspectives

The publishing world has produced fabulous examples of nonfiction books for children. Almost every topic is covered, but not every perspective is explored. For example, I love biographies.

I read celebrity biographies (Figure 11.15),

Figure 11.15
Bossypants by Tina Fey, 2014, Boston, MA: Back Bay Books. Copyright 2014 by Tina Fey.

musicians' biographies (Figure 11.16),

Figure 11.16
Heroin Diaries by Nikki Sixx and Ian Gittins, 2007, New York, NY: Pocket Books. Copyright 2007 by Nikki Sixx and Ian Gittins.

PAST PRESIDENTS AND EVADING INVENTORS: NOT YOUR GRANDMOTHER'S INFORMATION BOOKS (PORTRAYING PEOPLE, ARGUING POSITIONS, AND PRESENTING DISCIPLINARY CONTENT)

athletes' biographies (Figure 11.17),

Figure 11.17
Open by Andre Agassi, 2009, New York, NY: Knopf. Copyright 2009 by Andre Agassi.

political biographies (Figure 11.18),

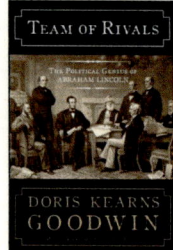

Figure 11.18
Team of Rivals: The Political Genius of Abraham Lincoln by Doris Kearns Goodwin, 2006, New York, NY: Simon & Schuster. Copyright 2006 by Doris Kearns Goodwin

historical biographies (Figure 11.19),

Figure 11.19
All But My Life: A Memoir by Gerda Weissman Klein, 1995, New York, NY: Hill and Wang. Copyright 1995 by Gerda Weissman Klein

and spiritual biographies (Figure 11.20).

Figure 11.20
The Story of My Experiments with Truth: An Autobiography by Mohandas Karamchand (Mahatma) Gandhi, 2014, Seattle WA: CreateSpace. Copyright 2014 by Mohandas Karamchand (Mahatma) Gandhi.

Of course, these examples are not written for children. Yet, when I examine children's biographies, I see dead people. In fact, I see a lot of dead, white, male people. Where is the children's equivalent of my Tina Fey or Nikki Sixx?

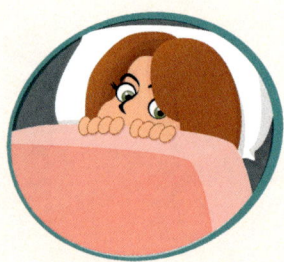

I am not asking for explicit content, but I am calling for information about interesting people beyond the corporate propaganda for the latest movie release or music album. Certainly a series, such as *Who Was?/What Was?*, attempts to bridge the gap by featuring a wide array of individuals from the present and the past. But how can an individual's unique characteristics come through in a book series with formulaic structures and illustrations that look the same? I want to read a biography on Rev. Lennox Yearwood Jr. and the creation of the Hip Hop Caucus (http://www.hiphopcaucus.org/) written by Jacqueline Woodson and illustrated by Chris Raschka (it doesn't exist, but that's what I want to read). Or how about a book on the environment that traces the work of Adrianna Quintero, executive director of Voces Verdes (http://www.vocesverdes.org/) and senior attorney at the Natural Resources Defense Council. This book doesn't exist either. But I want to read it.

I am not alone in seeing dead people, or archaic ideas, reiterated across texts. In a study about gender roles in children's science biographies, Trevor Owens (2009) determined that Marie Curie and Albert Einstein are the two most frequent subjects of science biographies for children yet they are constructed in gendered ways. He points out that neither of these individuals was from the United States and they are continually portrayed as hating school. He wrote:

> Children's books on Curie have changed in emphasis. Now, instead of simply describing Curie's accomplishments without context, children's books have adapted to explain the genderbiased world of science and thus demonstrate the further greatness of those accomplishments. Alongside this transition, books on Einstein have begun to offer a much more sympathetic portrayal of Mileva, both as a wife and in most cases as a physicist. Interestingly, the changes in tone in the Curie books began in the late seventies while the change in portrayal of Mileva did not occur until the mid nineties. Despite the increasingly conscious and explicit treatment of gender relations in such children's books, subtle attitudes towards gender emerge in other contexts, sometimes with much less reformatory potential; in particular, in persistently stereotypical—and gendered—treatments of both Curie's and Einstein's relations to authority in school. (Owens, 2009, p. 937)

In the world of children's literature, portrayals are still gendered and so are the editor's choices in whose story gets told. For example, by the end of 2015, readers of the *Who Was?* series could choose from 26 biographies about women (Figure 11.21) and 71 biographies about men (Figure 11.22). In the *What Was?* series, there were 14 books about topics such as *What Was Pompeii?* and *What Was the Alamo?* Of these 14 books, only four books featured a person of color on the cover (*The March on Washington, The Underground Railroad* (Figure 11.23), *The Panama Canal, The First Thanksgiving*), and four books featured an image of a woman on the cover (*The Underground Railroad, Pompeii, Ellis Island, The Statue of Liberty*). If this very popular series is any indication of the status of the field, the field is racist and sexist (and other things that I can't easily see or count). In fact, Thomas Crisp (2015) reviewed the winners of the Orbis Pictus Award for Nonfiction. Using categories of "populations identified frequently as being under-represented and/or marginalized within children's literature" (p. 244), he found deficits in portrayals of sexual identities, religions, ages, and regions of the world. For those who think race, gender, sexual, economic, and social inequality is solved. Think again.

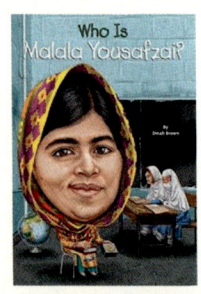

Figure 11.21
The Who Is series publishes biographies of interesting women much less frequently than biographies of men. *Who is Malala Yousafzai?* By Dinah Brown and illustrated by Andrew Thomson, 2015, New York, NY: Grosset & Dunlap. Cover art copyright 2015 by Andrew Thomson.

Figure 11.22
Michael Jackson and Jesus were two of the many male biographies published in the same year. *Who was Michael Jackson?* By Megan Stine and illustrated by Joseph J.M. Qiu, 2015, New York, NY: Grosset & Dunlap. Cover art copyright 2015 by Joseph J.M. Qiu.

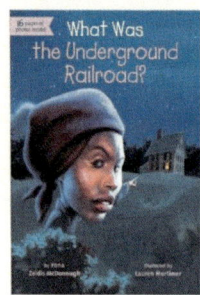

Figure 11.23
What was the Underground Railroad? By Yona Zeldis McDonough and illustrated by Lauren Mortimer and James Bennett, 2013, New York, NY: Grosset & Dunlap. Cover art copyright 2013 by Lauren Mortimer and James Bennett.

Children are not vacuous. Children need nonfiction books that address their issues and the concerns of their generation—the environment, Internet safety, bullying. All youth, boys and girls, need to read about the women who shaped history and science. We all need to know about important contributions from people of color.

PAST PRESIDENTS AND EVADING INVENTORS: NOT YOUR GRANDMOTHER'S INFORMATION BOOKS (PORTRAYING PEOPLE, ARGUING POSITIONS, AND PRESENTING DISCIPLINARY CONTENT)

To explore some of the better examples of contemporary biographies (even though most of the people are still dead), I have selected a range of books highlighting different approaches.

Choose ONE from the following:

- *Amelia and Eleanor Go For a Ride* by Pam Munoz Ryan and illustrated by Brian Selznick, 1999, New York, NY: Scholastic (Figure 11.24).

Figure 11.24
On their own, Amelia and Eleanor are immensely important. Together, they are unstoppable trailblazers. *Amelia and Eleanor Go For a Ride* by Pam Munoz Ryan and illustrated by Brian Selznick, 1999, New York, NY: Scholastic. Cover art copyright 1999 by Brian Selznick.

- *The Watcher: Jane Goodall's Life with the Chimps* by Jeanette Winter, 2011, New York, NY: Schwartz and Wade (Figure 11.25).

Figure 11.25
Jane Goodall is an amazing scientist and conservationist. *The Watcher: Jane Goodall's Life with the Chimps* by Jeanette Winter, 2011, New York, NY: Schwartz and Wade. Copyright 2011 by Jeanette Winter.

- *Harlem's Little Blackbird* by Renee Watson, 2012, New York, NY: Random House (Figure 11.26).

Figure 11.26
I like biographies of lesser known people such as *Harlem's Little Blackbird* by Renee Watson, 2012, New York, NY: Random House. Copyright 2012 by Renee Watson.

- *Wilma Unlimited: How Wilma Rudolph Became the Fastest Woman* by Kathleen Krull and illustrated by David Diaz, 2000, New York, NY: HMH Books for Young Readers (Figure 11.27).

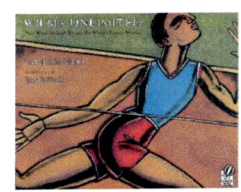

Figure 11.27
From braces to winning races. Women are sports heroes too. *Wilma Unlimited: How Wilma Rudolph Became the Fastest Woman* by Kathleen Krull and illustrated by David Diaz, 2000, New York, NY: HMH Books for Young Readers. Cover art copyright 2000 by David Diaz.

- *Here Come the Girl Scouts!: The Amazing All True Story of Juliette 'Daisy' Gordon Low and Her Great Adventure* by Shana Corey and illustrated by Hadley Hooper, 2012, New York, NY: Scholastic (Figure 11.28).

Figure 11.28
How many people know about the origins of the girl scouts? *Here Come the Girl Scouts!: The Amazing All True Story of Juliette 'Daisy' Gordon Low and Her Great Adventure* by Shana Corey and illustrated by Hadley Hooper, 2012, New York, NY: Scholastic. Cover art copyright 2012 by Hadley Hooper.

- *Almost Astronauts: 13 Women Who Dared to Dream* written by Tanya Lee Stone, 2009, Somerville, MA: Candlewick (Figure 11.29).

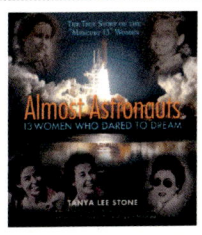

Figure 11.29
This collection of stories features brave women who changed the space industry. *Almost Astronauts: 13 Women Who Dared to Dream* written by Tanya Lee Stone, 2009, Somerville, MA: Candlewick. Cover art copyright 2009 by Tanya Lee Stone.

Choose ONE from the following:

- *Nelson Mandela* by Kadir Nelson, 2013, New York, NY: Katherine Tegen Books (Figure 11.30).

- *Hanging Off Jefferson's Nose: Growing Up on Mount Rushmore* by Tina Coury and illustrated by Sally Wern Comport, 2012, New York, NY: Dial (Figure 11.31).

- *Jim Henson: The Guy Who Played with Puppets* by Kathleen Krull and illustrated by Steve Johnson and Lou Fancher, 2011, New York, NY: Random House (Figure 11.32).

- *Lou Gehrig* by David A. Adler and illustrated by Terry Widener, 2001, New York, NY: HMH Books for Young Readers (Figure 11.33).

- *It Jes' Happened: When Bill Traylor Started to Draw* by Don Tate and illustrated by R. Gregory Christie, 2012, New York, NY: Lee & Low (Figure 11.34).

- *Freedom Riders: John Lewis and Jim Zwerg on the Front Lines of the Civil Rights Movement* by Ann Bausum, 2005, Washington, D.C.: National Geographic Books (Figure 11.35).

Figure 11.30

He never lost hope. *Nelson Mandela* by Kadir Nelson, 2013, New York, NY: Katherine Tegen Books. Copyright 2013 by Kadir Nelson.

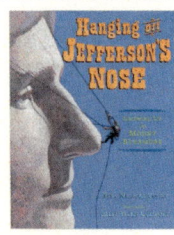

Figure 11.31

I've never thought about the creation of Mount Rushmore; just the final result. Here is the inside story. *Hanging Off Jefferson's Nose: Growing Up on Mount Rushmore* by Tina Coury and illustrated by Sally Wern Comport, 2012, New York, NY: Dial. Cover art copyright 2012 by Sally Wern Comport.

Figure 11.32

He created characters that millions of people have loved for decades. *Jim Henson: The Guy Who Played with Puppets* by Kathleen Krull and illustrated by Steve Johnson and Lou Fancher, 2011, New York, NY: Random House. Cover art copyright 2011 by Steve Johnson.

Figure 11.33

David Adler tells Lou Gehrig's story from his childhood to his becoming the luckiest man on the face of the Earth. *Lou Gehrig* by David A. Adler and illustrated by Terry Widener, 2001, New York, NY: HMH Books for Young Readers. Cover art copyright 2001 by Terry Widener.

Figure 11.34

Here is a story of untapped talent. *It Jes' Happened: When Bill Traylor Started to Draw* by Don Tate and illustrated by R. Gregory Christie, 2012, New York, NY: Lee & Low. Cover art copyright 2012 by R. Gregory Christie.

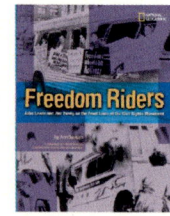

Figure 11.35

The Freedom Riders exhibited extraordinary bravery and changed the world. *Freedom Riders: John Lewis and Jim Zwerg on the Front Lines of the Civil Rights Movement* by Ann Bausum, 2005, Washington, D.C.: National Geographic Books. Copyright 2005 by Ann Bausum.

Here are some questions to guide your thinking and analysis:

- How are the individuals portrayed?

- Pay attention to the language in the two books you selected. Do you notice differences and similarities in how the main character is described?

- Compare the content of both books. Do you notice any differences or similarities in the topics covered? What events are highlighted?

- What personal strengths or challenges are featured?

- How did the illustrations affect your reading?

- How did the illustrator's choices impact your view and understanding of each person?

It's also interesting to compare different approaches to the same person/topic. Here are a few to examine:

I Am Malala: How One Girl Stood Up for Education and Changed the World by Malala Yousafzai and Patricia Mccormick

Who is Malala Yousafzai by Dinah Brown and Andrew Thomson

Marcel Marceau: Master of Mime by Gloria Spielman and Manon Gauthier

Monsieur Marceau: Actor Without Words by Leda Schubert and Gerard DuBois

Do biographies for children/youth have to be about a famous person's childhood? No. My daughter watched an episode of *Cosmos* in which Clair Patterson was featured (http://natgeotv.com/uk/cosmos-a-spacetime-odyssey/videos). Clair Patterson was the man who fought big oil and big research to expose the high concentrations of lead in gasoline and its impact on the environment. *Cosmos* did not highlight Clair's childhood; they told the story of his work, his science, and the politics of truth. Based on their portrayal, my daughter selected Clair Patterson as the person for her National History Day project.

Do biographies for children/youth have to censor the information and focus on positive experiences? No. Contemporary biographies are showing signs of wrestling with difficult issues and tragic experiences. Many books have been written about the Holocaust. Fewer books have been written about history since World War II. Shouldn't children and youth know more about Vietnam, Watergate, or 9/11? Perhaps these topics are too big and complicated? Maybe they are too new? Well, take a look at *Hitler Youth: Growing Up in Hitler's Shadow* by Susan Campbell Bartoletti (2005) and you will see an example of how to focus on parts of a complex situation.

Do biographies and nonfiction texts have to focus on serious issues? No. Youth like to read about topics that are relevant to their lives. Sometimes kids want to know who invented Cheetos. Heck, I want to know who invented Cheetos. We know who invented the lightbulb, but who were the people (women and men) who invented the smartphone the iPad, *Space Invaders, Super Mario,* or *Call of Duty*?

Biographies and other forms of narrative nonfiction shed light on the past and present. They help us understand events and put them in context of the time. If we all ask for, buy, and check out more interesting biographies and nonfiction books, then more interesting choices will come (Video 11.2).

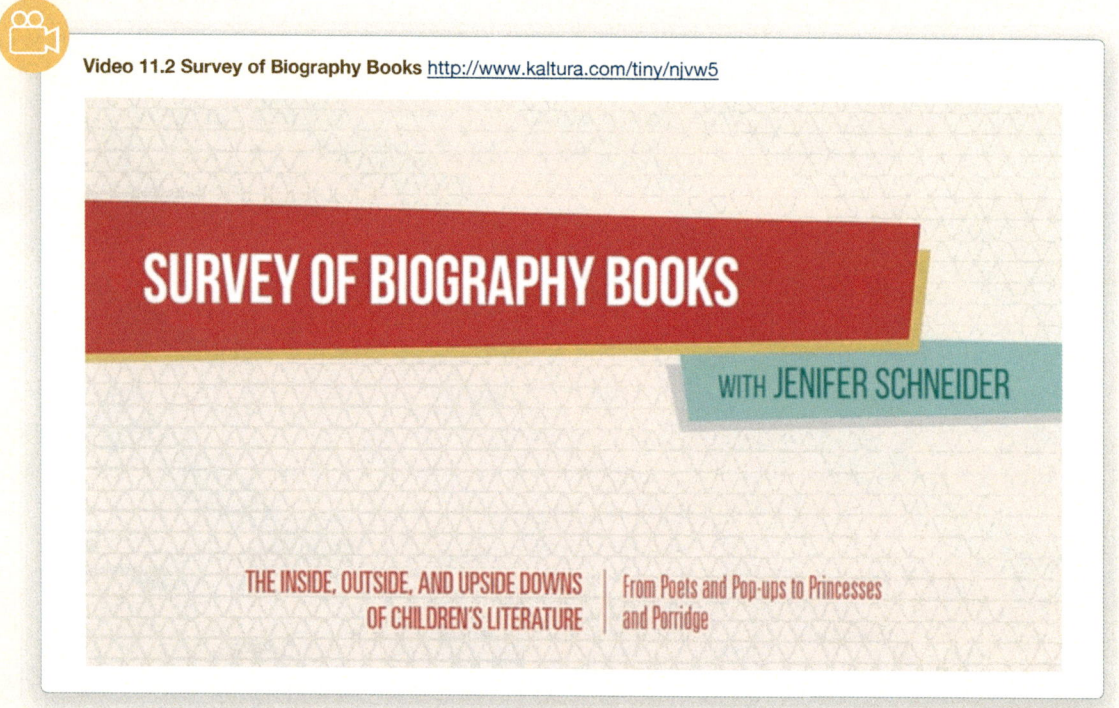

Video 11.2 Survey of Biography Books http://www.kaltura.com/tiny/njvw5

Expertise and Interesting Writing

Nonfiction writers conduct extensive research and consult with experts, bridging the gap between a field of study and the intended audience of children. In other words, the nonfiction writer is an information translator, recasting details in a different way. Of course, there are always bad examples of nonfiction. But, you might also be surprised by the depth and breadth of what is available.

Author Expertise
Many writers of nonfiction for children have professional backgrounds and training in the area in which they write. Many of them also have careers in teaching and working with children. Below, I've highlighted a few individuals.

- Seymour Simon studied Science at the City College of New York. He has a Masters in Comparative Psychology, which is the study of Animal Behavior. He taught middle school science for over 20 years, developing his knowledge of what interests youth and the ways in which children learn about the world (http://www.seymoursimon.com/index.php/about_seymour_simon/faq/).

- David A. Adler graduated from Queens College with a BA in economics and education with licenses to teach mathematics and history. He was a New York City mathematics teacher for nine years. While teaching he earned his MBA in marketing and began a PhD in marketing when he was inspired to write books (http://www.davidaadler.com/bio.htm).

- Susan Campbell Bertoletti has a Bachelors in English and Secondary Education from Marywood University in Scranton, PA. She taught Eighth Grade English (composition, grammar, and literature) for 18 years. She has a Masters in English from the University of Scranton where she also taught courses in composition. She earned a Ph.D. in English from Binghamton University, State University of New York with a creative nonfiction dissertation (*Black Potatoes: The Story of the Great Irish Famine, 1845 to 1850*. (Published by Houghton Mifflin). She taught courses in creative writing at the college level (http://www.scbartoletti.com/downloads/CV_2010.pdf).

- Vicki Cobb graduated from Barnard College with a major in zoology and a Master's degree in Secondary Science Education. After an early career as a laboratory researcher, she eventually worked as a science teacher, and then she became a full-time writer of science books for children (http://www.vickicobb.com/aboutvicki.html).

I selected these four award-winning, nonfiction writers because I personally value their work. I am especially impressed with their **depth of research**, their **perspectives** on the topics on which they write, their abilities to ***write for the targeted age level***, and their ***literary styles***. As these selected individuals demonstrate, nonfiction writers have personal expertise in the subjects about which they write, and if they don't have formal training, they have the education and advanced skills necessary to conduct research. As Seymour Simon wrote,

> Whenever I want to write about a subject, I need to study. I start by looking at research that other people have done. What experiments have they run? What animals have they observed? By studying all the work that others have already done, I learn about the subjects that I write about in my books. As the great scientist Sir Isaac Newton once wrote, 'If I have seen further than others, it is because I have stood on the shoulders of giants' (http://www.seymoursimon.com/index.php/about_seymour_simon/faq/).

It is not a coincidence that each of these successful writers was also a teacher. I didn't select these individuals because they were teachers, but I believe their extraordinary success in writing for children is a direct result of years of talking with, listening to, and learning from children and youth. As teachers, they learned how to help students access complex disciplinary information by breaking down concepts, modeling ways of thinking, and using writing across the disciplines as a method of communication. They also honor children as intelligent, thoughtful individuals who appreciate accurate information that is written in respectful and interesting ways.

Language Features and Readability

There is an art to writing interesting nonfiction. When presenting information, an author needs to engage the reader while also explaining the content with detail and accuracy. Some authors err on the side of entertainment. For example, when describing how blood flows through the body, an author might animate the blood cells and portray them as talking to one another (Figure 11.36).

Figure 11.36
Fictional storytelling techniques are frequently used in Basher books. *Human Body: A Book with Guts!* By Dan Green and Simon Basher and illustrated by Simon Basher, 2011, New York, NY: Kingfisher. Text copyright 2011 by Dan Green and Simon Basher.

Although anthropomorphism and personification appear to add character and interest to nonfiction topics, they are authorial techniques for fictional storytelling. If the purpose of the text is to present information, then the author should use effective nonfiction techniques while maintaining accuracy and authentic information.

In Chapter 5, I combined criteria from national nonfiction awards to guide you in the selection of quality nonfiction.

Criteria to evaluate information books:
- Interesting and timely subject matter
- Excellent, engaging, and distinctive use of language.
- Excellent, engaging, and distinctive use of visuals in illustrated texts (for picturebooks see below).
- Appropriate organization with clear sequencing and logical development
- Thorough documentation and author's qualifications
- Clear, accurate, and stimulating presentation of facts, concepts, and ideas.
- Appropriate style of presentation for subject and for intended audience.
- Supportive features (index, table of contents, maps, timelines, etc).
- Respectful and of interest to intended audience.

Anthropomorphism is the attribution of human form or other characteristics to beings other than humans, particularly deities and animals. People attribute human-like mental states, for example, to God and non-human animals.

Personification is the related attribution of human form and characteristics to abstract concepts such as nations and natural forces such as the seasons and the weather.

Both anthropomorphism and personification have ancient roots as storytelling and artistic devices. Most cultures have traditional fables with anthropomorphized animals as characters.

Here is a short list of nonfiction technques:
http://www.fionabayrock.com/ARTICLEeleventips.htm

Some information should be narrated. In these instances, there is a dual purpose: to present information and narrate a series of events. Seymour Simon wrote, "I write stories for children that happen to be non-fiction. I don't write textbooks, or encyclopedias, I'm telling stories" (http://www.seymoursimon.com/index.php/about_seymour_simon/faq/). In the technical sense, Seymour Simon does not tell stories (plot, setting, characters), but he does use narration and argumentation to present information.

The content of nonfiction texts is expansive. With so much to cover, authors may use different formats and text structures to highlight information, isolate important ideas, and make connections across the text. The author's use of text features can help the reader locate information and make sense of the content. Text features include headings and subheadings, captions, diagrams, labels, text boxes, images, indexes, glossaries, and key words (Figure 11.37). Although these features are used in children's books, many readers skip over text boxes, diagrams and other features that assist comprehension. Children, youth, and many adults need guidance to understand how the text features work to help them understand the information in a book.

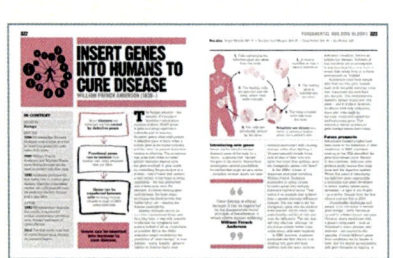

Figure 11.37

Headings and subheadings, captions, diagrams, labels, text boxes, images, indexes, glossaries, and key words help readers understand *The Science Book: Big Ideas Simply Explained* by Dan Green, 2014, Washington, D.C.: DK Books. Excerpt copyright 2014 by Dan Green.

> Reading aloud nonfiction text is extremely important. Children need to develop an ear for nonfiction as well as for story and poetry.
>
> Jennifer Wharton, a blogger for the Children's and Young Adult Bloggers' Literary Awards has compiled a list of nonfiction read aloud books: http://www.cybils.com/2015/02/list-fun-read-aloud-non-fiction.html.
>
> Many public librarians have developed helpful lists and suggestions for nonfiction reading: http://www.aadl.org/user/lists/61527
>
> Pinterest also includes several lists for nonfiction read alouds: https://www.goodreads.com/shelf/show/non-fiction-read-aloud

Children and youth enjoy reading nonfiction books, but they are often dissuaded by teachers who tend to prefer fictional texts. Children typically receive very little time to read nonfiction in school. In fact, in 2000, Nell Duke made the literacy world stand up and take notice of the paucity of attention given to nonfiction texts. In a study of 20 first-grade classrooms, Duke found that children spent an average of 3.6 minutes per day with informational texts during classroom written language activities. This study initiated a series of follow-up studies and additional attention to the role of nonfiction texts in schools. More recently, the *Common Core State Standards* (National Association of Governors, 2014) have emphasized the reading of nonfiction text, given that most college and career paths require extensive nonfiction reading.

In addition to more reading time, teachers, librarians, and parents should read aloud nonfiction texts. Reading aloud gives the reader an "ear" for nonfiction and explicit instruction provides direct information about the strategies to use (Video 11.3).

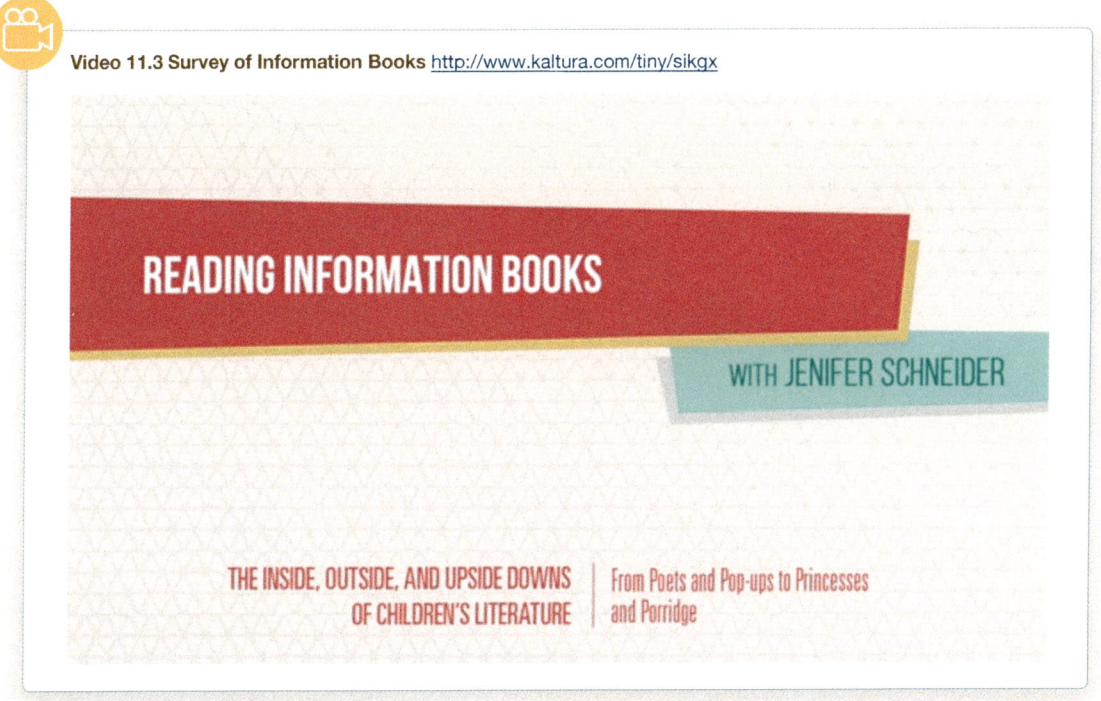

Video 11.3 Survey of Information Books http://www.kaltura.com/tiny/sikgx

If you select the right book, the reading is easy. If not, the reading is snoozy. Pay attention to the language choices in the following excerpts from different books about wind.

I Face The Wind by Vicki Cobb, illustrated by Julia Gorton (2003)

Ever face a strong wind?

Your hair blows away from your face.

You could lose your hat.

And if the wind is blowing hard enough, you may even have to walk at a slant.

You can't see this force that's pushing you. But you can feel it. And you can see what wind does to other things.

It makes dust swirl in a circle.

It makes flags stick out straight and flutter.

Can you name some things you see wind do?

Go outside and watch.

Leaves on trees shake.

A kite stays in the sky...

Vicki Cobb received a Sibert Honor Award for this book. I feel it is an outstanding example of nonfiction writing. The reader is engaged. He or she must make references to windy experiences in his or her own life. This is a classic example of showing the reader, not telling the reader. Instead of saying, "wind has energy—here's the evidence," Vicki Cobb showed us through examples.

Wind by Marion Dane Bauer, illustrated by John Wallace (2003)

The earth we live on is a spinning ball.

When the earth spins, the air around it moves too.

When air moves we call it "wind."

As the sun heats the air, the air grows lighter. Light air rises.

Cool air is heavy. It falls...

Marion Dane Bauer's book is more simplistic than Cobb's, but not as engaging. The concepts are presented as statements without any explanation of the science. Why does hot air get lighter? Why does hot air rise?

Wind Energy Engineering by Pramod Jain (2010, p. 9-10)

The energy of wind has been exploited for thousands of years. The oldest applications of wind energy include extracting water from wells, making flour out of grain, and other agricultural applications. In recent times, the use of wind energy has evolved to, primarily, generation of electricity (p. 1) ... The kinetic energy contained in wind is:

$E = \frac{1}{2} mv^2$ where m is mass and v is speed; units of energy are kg m2/s2 = Joule.

The mass (m) from which energy is extracted is the mass contained in the volume of air that will flow through the rotor.

Pramod Jain wrote this book for audiences interested in higher levels of science content. The information is straightforward and easy to understand. Jain also uses real life examples and practical applications for the science. However, he is not engaging with the audience as much as he is presenting the information.

The Importance of Illustration

As you might imagine, illustrations play a central role in nonfiction texts for youth. Even the most dense nonfiction narratives will include some photographs and illustrations. For example, look at the examples of the books about wind. In each book, the illustrations play a different role.

In Vicki Cobb's book, the images help the reader think about the words she wrote. They guide the reader to pay attention to the examples in their own world (Figure 11.38).

In Marion Dane Bauer's book, the images add interest to the text, but they do not necessarily add informational content (Figure 11.39).

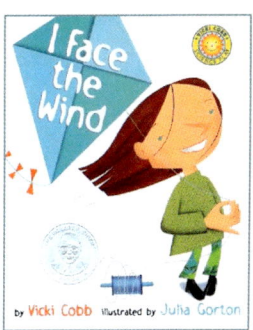

Figure 11.38

In Vicki Cobb's book, the images help the reader think about the words. *I Face the Wind* by Vicki Cobb and illustrated by Julia Gorton, 2003, New York, NY: HarperCollins. Cover art copyright 2003 by Julia Gorton.

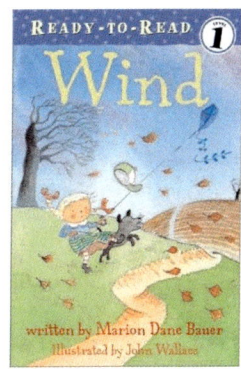

Figure 11.39

In Marion Dane Bauer's book, the images add interest to the text. *Wind* by Marion Dane Bauer and illustrated by John Wallace, 2003, New York, NY: Simon Spotlight. Cover art copyright 2003 by John Wallace.

In Pramod Jain's book, the images are selected to illustrate concepts that require visualization. For example, how is a turbine constructed? In this case, it's easier to show the visual than describe or inform through text. The illustrations take the place of needless technical writing (Figure 11.40).

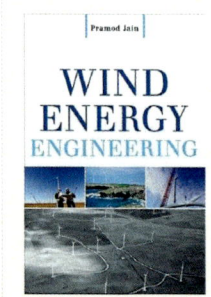

Figure 11.40

In Pramod Jain's book, the images illustrate concepts that require visualization. *Wind Energy Engineering* by Pramod Jain, 2010, New York, NY: McGraw Hill. Copyright 2010 by Pramod Jain.

Unlike a young adult novel, the purpose of a nonfiction text is to share information. Therefore, photographs, drawings, illustrations and other forms of media are useful in presenting the information across various modes.

With informational texts, the same standards for artistic quality apply as for any picture book. Illustrated nonfictional texts are similar to, but different from, illustrated fiction.

If the information is presented in the form of a picture book, I use the following criteria from the Caldecott Medal (ALA) to determine the book's quality.

- Excellence of execution in the artistic technique employed;
- Excellence of pictorial interpretation of theme or concept;
- Appropriateness of style of illustration to the theme or concept;
- Delineation of information through the pictures;
- Excellence of presentation in recognition of the intended audience.

Video 11.4 Survey of Books Illustrated http://www.kaltura.com/tiny/noij4

DETERMINING THE COMMUNICATIVE PURPOSE OF TEXT AND ILLUSTRATION

WITH JENIFER SCHNEIDER

THE INSIDE, OUTSIDE, AND UPSIDE DOWNS OF CHILDREN'S LITERATURE | From Poets and Pop-ups to Princesses and Porridge

Looking Past Dead Presidents and the Same Ol' Inventors

Good examples of nonfiction are written about all aspects of disciplinary content—from the microscopic (atom) to the enormous (universe). Good examples of nonfiction are also written about all kinds of people who have contributed to society across time periods and across the globe. Modern, effective writers and illustrators accurately inform readers through beautiful language and detailed illustrations. But there is work to do. Nonfiction books continue to feature a lot of dead white people involved in lifeless events that have little relevance to youth. We need to choose nonfiction books carefully and demand excellence and diversity in the coverage of topics for children.

For more on this topic, here is an opinion on the topic: http://www.buzzfeed.com/hannahjewell/inventions-by-women-that-changed-the-world#.lmBWaw2Nx. Caution, this article contains offensive language.

CHAPTER 12

BANNED AND BURNED: WHY WORRY? IT'S JUST KIDDIE LIT

(CHILDREN, BANNED BOOKS, AND THE RIGHT TO READ)

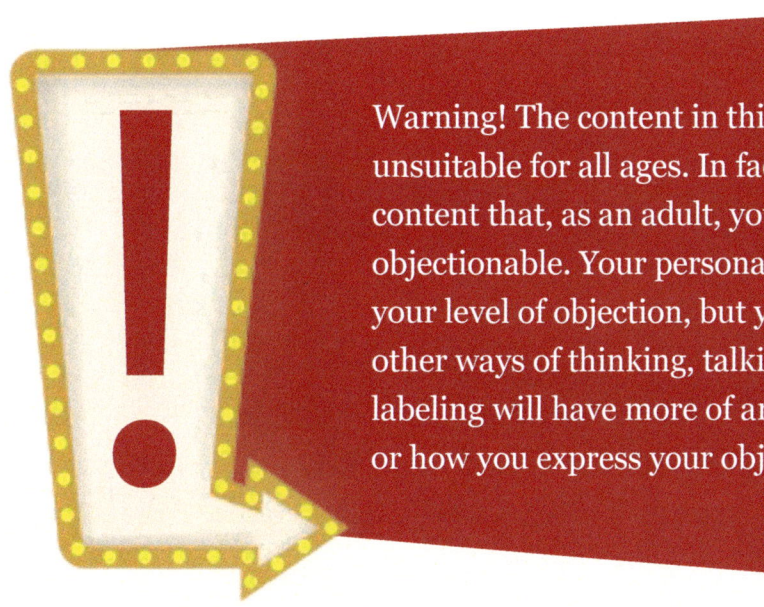

Warning! The content in this chapter may be unsuitable for all ages. In fact, you may read content that, as an adult, you find highly objectionable. Your personal beliefs will determine your level of objection, but your tolerance for other ways of thinking, talking, behaving, and labeling will have more of an impact on if, when, or how you express your objections.

If you don't want to read a list of curse words or offensive terms used in children's literature, skip the next page.

BANNED AND BURNED: WHY WORRY? IT'S JUST KIDDIE LIT
(CHILDREN, BANNED BOOKS, AND THE RIGHT TO READ)

Are you offended by words such as fuck, bitch, fag, lez, or whore?

Let's take it down a notch and try the following: snot, butt, booger, fart, or burp?

If penis or vagina make you feel uncomfortable, how about caca, pee pee, tinkle, and poo poo?

Wait, I'm not done. What do you think about names for groups of people from various ethnicities or regions? People who might be described as "off the boat": Dago, Polak, Spic, or Yank? Are these too old-fashioned?

OK, let's try some other old-fashioned words that are currently used: nigger, redskin, wetback, cracker.

Too harsh? Would you use the following: illegals, aliens, berry pickers, border jumpers?

Here are a just a few more labels: feminist, hetero, trans, Nazi, Confederate, terrorist, Christian, atheist, Muslim, Jew, wizard, witch?

BANNED AND BURNED: WHY WORRY? IT'S JUST KIDDIE LIT
(CHILDREN, BANNED BOOKS, AND THE RIGHT TO READ)

As I mentioned, your personal beliefs dictate your level of offense or comfort with the previous terms. You might hear some of these words daily or read them across text sources. Your reactions to these terms are personal and may be connected to your spiritual, moral, ethical, or individual beliefs; yet the terms carry pervasive meanings that sort and label people or objects. The terms, and the people they categorize, exist in real life. They also exist in children's and young adult literature (Click here for examples—Figure 12.1).

Figure 12.1

Click thumbnail for examples.

 Bad words are everywhere. Here is just one example in daily life: http://www.esquire.com/news-politics/news/a29318/redskin-name-update/

The big question is this: how do you feel about children reading objectionable words?

Are these words okay for teenagers to read?

If words are used in our homes and in society, why should children's books exclude the same concepts and words?

Where do your feelings end and the rights of others begin?

Can you accept difference even when you profoundly disagree?

Welcome to Banned Books! The place in which opinions, beliefs, morals, values, and judgments bump up against freedom, difference, rights, responsibilities, and positions. Although you will read some of the actual "banned" books that correspond to this chapter, the issues reach far beyond the books themselves. Critiquing, selecting, purchasing, displaying, censoring, and banning books are behaviors that reflect views about childhood and children, a child's right to read, a parent's right to parent, an author's freedom of speech, the role of libraries and librarians in providing equitable access to information, and the necessity of intellectual freedom as a basic right in a democratic society.

Most Wanted

Across children's and young adult literature there are some high-profile offenders who consistently push the boundaries of what is acceptable for children to read. For example, Judy Blume is notorious for writing about real life situations, including sex, using explicit terms and language (Figure 12.2). Similarly, David Levithan writes fictional stories about the lives of teenagers with a particular focus on characters that are gay (Figure 12.3). Other authors, such as Alvin Schwartz, write scary books that feature supernatural events, mythical monsters, and evil beings that engage in violent and disturbing acts (Figure 12.4). And award-winning authors, such as Phillip Pullman, push boundaries with cultural and religious critiques underlying their texts (Figure 12.5). Provocative books garner quick and intense attention for controversial content. However, there is one author and one book series that draws surprising and consistent protest.

What serial offender is more "unsuitable for the age group" than a book that features a man and woman who engage in bondage and sadomasochistic sex?

What cartoon character is more destructive than a male protagonist with mommy issues and his mentally disturbed stalker?

Who is more damaging to youth than a weak female protagonist in love with a "Prince Charming" who dominates her?

Figure 12.2
Sexually explicit content makes *Forever* one of the most challenged books. *Forever* by Judy Blume, 1975, Scarsdale, N.Y.: Bradbury Press. Cover art copyright 2007 by Simon & Schuster.

Figure 12.3
Homosexual themes often trigger parental challenges. One example is *Boy Meets Boy* by David Levithan, 2003, New York: Alfred A. Knopf. Copyright 2003 by David Levithan.

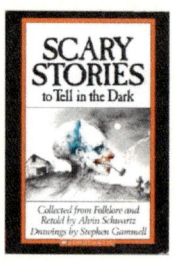

Figure 12.4
Violence and the occult are a cause for concern for those who challenge *Scary Stories To Tell in the Dark* by Alvin Schwartz, and illustrated by Stephen Gammell, 1981, New York: Lippincott. Cover art copyright 1981 by Stephen Gammell.

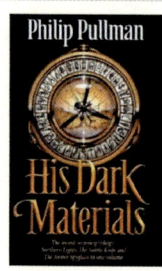

Figure 12.5
Religious groups often challenge *His Dark Materials* by Philip Pullman, 2007, New York: Alfred A. Knopf. Copyright 2007 by Philip Pullman.

That's right, it's *Captain Underpants*!

Drawing loathe and contempt from people across the US, *Captain Underpants* beat out *Fifty Shades of Gray* as the most challenged book in 2012 and 2013 and it continues to appear on frequently challenged lists (http://www.ala.org/bbooks/).

Let's take a look at *Captain Underpants* (Figure 12.6)—a villainous superhero featured in a book filled with "disrespectful" dialogue, bodily functions, and men's underwear. *Captain Underpants* is a book that is challenged for teaching children to question authority, to recognize that bullies come in all sizes (including adult), and to value the imagination over societal rules. Most people love it; some people hate it. You decide.

Figure 12.6 & 12.7
George and Harold disobey school rules and undermine authority in *The Adventures of Captain Underpants: An Epic Novel* by Dav Pilkey, 1997, New York: Blue Sky Press.

Dav Pilkey once said: I guess I really shouldn't be surprised that my *Captain Underpants* series continues to top banned books lists around the world. After all, my very first *Captain Underpants* stories were "banned" by my second grade teacher.
http://www.theguardian.com/childrens-books-site/2015/aug/31/banned-books-captain-underpants-dav-pilkey

Read *The Adventures of Captain Underpants*.

Why is *Captain Underpants* so frequently challenged? In a nutshell, the main characters dislike school and they disrupt and disturb the people who run the school (Figure 12.7). In addition, the main characters disrupt and disturb the students (nerds) who do well in school. The boys, George and Harold, act badly. Parents and library patrons reject the content because they do not want children to emulate George and Harold. However, character emulation is complex. The mediating factors that create the conditions for emulation exist within the person, not the book character. According to Cohen (2001):

> Identification is an imaginative process through which an audience member assumes the identity, goals, and perspective of a character… It is fairly clear that different types of media and media texts promote different responses from audiences (e.g., film vs. television, print vs. visual, first-person vs. third-person narration, and narrative texts vs. nonnarrative texts), but it is equally probable that there is variance in the responses of different groups to a given text (differentiated by social groups and psychological variables). Thus, a comprehensive theory of identification will necessarily incorporate propositions about texts and audiences (p. 261).

> Parents have every right to raise their children in ways that match their personal beliefs (as long as those beliefs are in keeping with the law). There is some research and anecdotal evidence that youth may emulate characters from books, television, and video games (e.g., Strouse & Troseth, 2008). However, the research and anecdotal evidence must be considered in the context of the whole child (Dubow, Huesmann, & Boxer, 2009; Ferguson, 2013). Exposure to domestic violence has effects on a person, but those effects are different when the violence is experienced in real life or experienced through video games. Additionally, exposure to detrimental events (violence, trauma, poverty) can be mediated by other intervening circumstances. Take, for example, copycat crimes. Most people do not engage in copycat crimes. It is not the mere exposure to violence that begets violence; there are other factors at play.
>
>> The assumption of traditional character educators that children build moral literacy from reading or hearing moral stories is challenged based on research findings. First, research in text comprehension indicates that readers do not understand texts the same way due to differences in reading skill and background knowledge. Second, moral comprehension research indicates that moral arguments are understood differently based on differences in moral schema development. Third, moral texts (e.g., that contain embedded moral reasoning) are understood and distorted differently by readers with different moral schemas. Fourth, children do not extract moral story themes as intended by the writer (Narvaez, 2002, p. 155).

For further elaboration on the reasons Captain Underpants is challenged, read http://www.businessinsider.com/why-captain-underpants-is-the-most-banned-book-in-america-2013-9

In addition to the proposal that *Captain Underpants* characters function as bad influences, some people challenge the books for their lack of literary qualities. Certainly, the *Captain Underpants* series is written for elementary aged children. The plots are funny and entertaining. Many individuals believe the books are perfect for boys, but girls enjoy the series as well. However, not all boys like the stories. Neither do all girls.

Here is one response to the question-- Why are parents opposed to a book that gets young kids (especially boys) excited about reading? Read: One Nation, Underpants http://www.slate.com/articles/arts/family/2012/09/dav_pilkey_s_captain_underpants_books_why_kids_love_them_and_parents_should_make_peace_with_them_.html

There aren't "boy" books or "girl" books. There are books. There aren't "boy" colors/toys/sports or "girl" colors/toys/sports. Let's go for equal opportunity and access.

Captain Underpants is no magical potion for struggling readers either. As discussed in a previous chapter, the right book needs to get into the right hands at the right time. The genre of "silly" fiction and comic-book illustration is not a perfect match for everyone. But the book series is humorous and it is different than most school reading that is selected by teachers who are one, two, or even three generations older than the targeted Second to Fourth-Grade reader. In other words, Dav Pilkey writes books for his Second Grade self—a child who struggled with learning to read (http://www.publishersweekly.com/pw/by-topic/childrens/childrens-book-news/article/67784-dav-pilkey-wants-to-give-you-superpowers.html).

For the most part, people are incredulous when they discover that *Captain Underpants* is one of the most challenged books. They feel the books are harmless. I agree. But what if I did not agree? Who gets to decide?

The Right to Read

There are layers in the decision-making process when it comes to a child's right to read. At the macro level, youth who live in the United States have First Amendment rights.

Amendment I
Congress shall make no law respecting an establishment of religion, or prohibiting the free exercise thereof; or abridging the freedom of speech, or of the press; or the right of the people peaceably to assemble, and to petition the Government for a redress of grievances. (Retrieved from http://www.archives.gov/exhibits/charters/bill_of_rights_transcript.html)

First Amendment protections apply to all youth in the context of their homes, their schools, and in public spaces. First Amendment rights also apply to literature and other media. The Supreme Court continues to operate by the following mantra: "It can hardly be argued that either students or teachers shed their constitutional rights to freedom of speech or expression at the schoolhouse gate" (Tinker v Des Moines Independent School District, 393 U.S. 503 (1969), p. 506.) However, the First Amendment seems to require Supreme Court interpretation when it comes to minors.

Supreme Court Rulings
In several cases, the Supreme Court of the United States has ruled on youth's rights to read or view material that might be considered objectionable. In the case of Erznoznik vs. Jacksonville, Richard Erznoznik, a drive-in movie theater manager, was charged with violating a city ordinance that prohibited the showing of movies containing nudity if the films were visible from public streets. The Supreme Court struck down the Jacksonville law stating that the state could not be the arbiters of what is "offensive" and the state could not single out one form of media or one type of content.

> Minors are entitled to a significant measure of First Amendment protection, and only in relatively narrow and well-defined circumstances may government bar public dissemination of protected materials to them... Speech that is neither obscene as to youths nor subject to some other legitimate proscription cannot be suppressed solely to protect the young from ideas or images that a legislative body thinks unsuitable for them.
>
>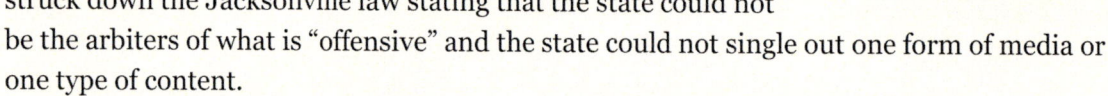
> *Erznoznik v. City of Jacksonville*, 422 U.S. 205, 212-14 (1975).

In Board of Education v. Pico, 457 U.S. 853 (1982), The Island Trees Union School District in New York removed several books from school libraries because the school board members determined the books were inappropriate. The court ruled that school officials could not remove books based on the ideas contained within.

> The Court has long recognized that local school boards have broad discretion in the management of school affairs.... At the same time, however, we have necessarily recognized that the discretion of the States and local school boards in matters of education must be exercised in a manner that comports with the transcendent imperatives of the First Amendment.
>
> *Board of Education v. Pico*, 457 U.S. 853 (1982, pp. 864-5).

However, the Court has also ruled to limit access to materials if they are viewed as obscene. In other words, controversial ideas fall under the protection of the First Amendment, but youth need to be "protected" when the content is "obscene."

> Currently, obscenity is evaluated by federal and state courts alike using a tripartite standard established by Miller v. California 413 U.S. 15 (1973). The Miller test for obscenity includes the following criteria: (1) whether 'the average person, applying contemporary community standards' would find that the work, 'taken as a whole,' appeals to 'prurient interest' (2) whether the work depicts or describes, in a patently offensive way, sexual conduct specifically defined by the applicable state law, and (3) whether the work, 'taken as a whole,' lacks serious literary, artistic, political, or scientific value.
>
> (Retrieved from https://www.law.cornell.edu/wex/obscenity)

For previous generations, "obscene" materials were curated by librarians, teachers, or store owners who often served as gatekeepers. Sometimes editors and publishers altered texts to conform to societal expectations. Sometimes the authors fought back (Video 12.1).

Video 12.1 Authors Fight Back: Censorship and Editorial Control in My Brother Sam is Dead
http://www.kaltura.com/tiny/swt56

With the advent of digital media and the networked capabilities of the Internet, access to information, books, videos, and images is more easily obtained by youth. In order to protect children from obscene materials, some attempts have been made to restrict transmissions. For example, in 1996 Congress passed the Telecommunications Act and with it some legislators tried to include the Communications Decency Act (CDA) which attempted to restrict pornography. The Supreme Court rejected the CDA as overly broad. In response, Congress passed the Child Online Protection Act (COPA).

> The ACLU again filed suit, which became Ashcroft v. Civil Liberties Union (00-1293) 535 U.S. 564 (2002) 217 F.3d 162 ("ACLU II"). Aschcroft upheld the Constitutionality of COPA and deemed its use of "'community standards' to identify 'material that is harmful to minors'" acceptable practice under the first amendment. However, the Court also demanded that COPA be enjoined and the case be remanded to the Third Circuit, where the Court found COPA created a content-ban on adult transmissions, was overly broad, intrusive, and restrictive in its efforts to protect children from adult speech. (Retrieved from https://www.law.cornell.edu/wex/obscenity)

In the end, the proposed child protections interfered with adult freedom and information exchange. Therefore, Internet restrictions violated First Amendment rights and the COPA never took effect.

Throughout this book, I have clearly stated my anti-censorship position. However, when I wrote this chapter and searched for children's literature that contained the controversial terms listed in Figure 12.1, I was shocked by the results of some of my searches. I did not search for "pornography" but I found pornographic images and video when I searched for "lesbian; YA novels" or words such as "penis" and "vagina." I expected the results for certain words, but something as simple as "butt" triggered graphic images.

I do not support Internet restrictions nor do I want to limit access to information, but I am concerned about children and young adult exposure to images, videos, and texts that are intended for adults. I would love to think that all parents parent, and all children listen, but this is not the case. Some adults simply do not know what is available online. Some adults are too trusting. And some adults bury their own faces in their own smartphones without noticing their children are visiting obscene spaces.

To create a safe space for youth, there are obscenity laws in place in which the "state" acts in the best interest of the child. In addition, many agencies and entities are working to protect children.

> Please read the FBI Parents' Guide to Internet Safety: https://www.fbi.gov/stats-services/publications/parent-guide. Some of you might be thinking- yeah, yeah, whatever, but you should read this document if you have children or work with children in any capacity.

> The Digital Future Project has been tracking Internet usage and digital evolution since 1993. If you are interested in data regarding online trends and technology and media usage, visit their site: http://www.digitalcenter.org/

> The Pew Research Center provides extensive publications, interactives, presentations, and data sets on media usage and technology as well as expert reports on privacy, regulation, and responsibility. http://www.pewinternet.org/

In a more recent case, the Supreme Court ruled on the content of video games and laws meant to regulate their sales.

> Like the protected books, plays, and movies that preceded them, video games communicate ideas—and even social messages—through many familiar literary devices (such as characters, dialogue, plot, and music) and through features distinctive to the medium (such as the player's interaction with the virtual world). That suffices to confer First Amendment protection.
> *Brown v. Entertainment Merchants Association,* 564 U.S. (2011)

This series of cases demonstrates the intricacies of the First Amendment in relation to the intentions of individuals who want to protect children. Whereas the First Amendment appears straightforward, the evolution of children's literature, digital texts, and developing technologies push against "community standards." But whose community decides?

Public Library Rulings

As an elaboration on our Constitutionally protected First Amendment rights, the American Library Association developed the Library Bill of Rights to support local libraries and patrons exert their freedom of choice.

The American Library Association affirms that all libraries are forums for information and ideas, and that the following basic policies should guide their services.

I. Books and other library resources should be provided for the interest, information, and enlightenment of all people of the community the library serves. Materials should not be excluded because of the origin, background, or views of those contributing to their creation.

II. Libraries should provide materials and information presenting all points of view on current and historical issues. Materials should not be proscribed or removed because of partisan or doctrinal disapproval.

III. Libraries should challenge censorship in the fulfillment of their responsibility to provide information and enlightenment.

IV. Libraries should cooperate with all persons and groups concerned with resisting abridgment of free expression and free access to ideas.

V. A person's right to use a library should not be denied or abridged because of origin, age, background, or views.

VI. Libraries which make exhibit spaces and meeting rooms available to the public they serve should make such facilities available on an equitable basis, regardless of the beliefs or affiliations of individuals or groups requesting their use.

Adopted June 19, 1939, by the ALA Council; amended October 14, 1944; June 18, 1948; February 2, 1961; June 27, 1967; January 23, 1980; inclusion of "age" reaffirmed January 23, 1996. (Retrieved from http://www.ala.org/advocacy/intfreedom/librarybill)

Children have a right to read and the authors/illustrators have a right to create, but there is a circuitous route to the point where the two meet.

Although students have rights, so do teachers, administrators, and schools. School librarians are not required to purchase all of the books ever written; therefore, a librarian makes choices within the constraints of the budget and the curriculum. Teachers also make choices about the books they choose to bring into their classrooms. Similarly, administrators use blockers and controls to regulate Internet access and the types of materials students can view on school computers.

Outside of school, children can access books and other media through public libraries and bookstores. Similar to school libraries, the catalog of books depends on the library, bookstore, or youth's budget. Libraries also use Internet controls to block certain content.

Parents exert their influence in out-of-school contexts as well. For example, juveniles cannot obtain library cards without their parents or guardians' permission. Youth may also have difficulty visiting a library or bookstore (online or brick and mortar) due to transportation constraints, limited Internet access, or financial reasons.

The publishing industry also exerts control over what children read. Editors choose which books to develop. Production logistics restrict forms and materials. Marketing and publicity campaigns highlight particular authors, illustrators, or texts. Then reviewers and critics share their opinions. These factors, and others, impact librarians or teachers' choices.

By the time books or other media get into children's hands, the books have made it through layers of review, critique, and selection. Therefore, youth make choices within parameters.

In spite of protective roadblocks, books and media can be subjected to additional challenges. In these cases, the challenge begins at the library.

For a rundown of the most frequently challenged books, check these out:
Read the American Library Association's (ALA) list of the Top Ten Challenged Books by Decade.
http://www.ala.org/bbooks/frequentlychallengedbooks/top10
Read the ALA's list of most challenged authors.
http://www.ala.org/bbooks/frequentlychallengedbooks/challengedauthors
Read the ALA's list of the most challenged authors of color.
http://www.ala.org/bbooks/frequentlychallengedbooks/challengedauthors/authorsofcolor

The Challenging Process

The Office for Intellectual Freedom of the American Library Association provides extensive information about challenges and how libraries should handle them. To be very clear, the library does not ban books. In fact, the library's central tenets are freedom and access to information. Yet, intellectual freedom and the right to express opinions work both ways. Therefore, the library created a process to allow patrons to express their concerns and file complaints.

I repeat— the library does not ban books. In fact, the American Library Association and many other coalitions, associations, and centers have joined together to fight censorship and celebrate the freedom to read (See http://www.bannedbooksweek.org/about).

Since 1982, September marks the month for Banned Books Week. Libraries, bookstores, and other venues sponsor film festivals, workshops, lectures, and virtual read outs to promote the freedom to read and the right to choose (See http://www.ala.org/bbooks/bannedbooksweek/events/virtualreadout).

If a patron finds a book to be of concern, he or she may express his or her objection in a number of ways:

- **Expression of Concern.** An inquiry that has judgmental overtones.

- **Oral Complaint.** An oral challenge to the presence and/or appropriateness of the material in question.

- **Written Complaint.** A formal, written complaint filed with the institution (library, school, etc.), challenging the presence and/or appropriateness of specific material.

- **Public Attack.** A publicly disseminated statement challenging the value of the material, presented to the media and/or others outside the institutional organization in order to gain public support for further action.

- **Censorship.** A change in the access status of material based on the content of the work and made by a governing authority or its representatives. Such changes include exclusion, restriction, removal, or age/grade level changes.
  (Retrieved from the Intellectual Freedom Committee http://www.ala.org/bbooks/challengedmaterials)

A challenge does not necessarily result in a formal complaint, a hearing, or outright censorship. Occasionally, a complaint ends with the mere expression of concern. On other occasions the challenge is pursued. The American Library Association provides suggested policies and procedures for dealing with book challenges and it offers advice for librarians who must oversee collections and respond to complaints (see http://www.ala.org/bbooks/challengedmaterials/support).

For those who are particularly interested in the library's rationale for defending the freedom of choice or for others interested in media relations, read "Strategies and Tips for Dealing with Challenges to Library Materials."
http://www.ala.org/bbooks/challengedmaterials/support/strategies

What are they complaining about now?

Across the thousands of complaints and challenges the ALA registers each year, the following list captures the most common reasons for concern about the content of children's literature:

- Sexually explicit;
- Offensive language;
- Unsuitable to age;
- Violence;
- Homosexuality;
- Religious viewpoints.

These reasons are somewhat generic and function to categorize the complaints rather than describe the specific content. Alternatively, the television, movie, and video game industry have taken different approaches in their content descriptors.

For example, the music industry created the Parental Advisory Label (PAL) system. In this self-policing program, "individual record companies and artists decide which of their releases should receive a "PAL Notice" indicating that the release contains explicit content....The recording industry's PAL Program lets parents undertake [selection] responsibility for their families and respects the core American value of freedom of expression that tolerates unpopular speech and frowns upon censorship."
(Retrieved from https://www.riaa.com/toolsforparents.php?content_selector=parental_advisory)

I was in high school when a group of moms attempted to ban certain records from music stores. The parents, who were wives of Washington politicians, formed a committee (Parents Music Resource Center) and they pushed the music industry to censor lyrics or ban songs. Eventually, the PMRC exploited their Washington connections (i.e., husbands) and found a way to have their concerns heard by a Senate committee. Famous musicians testified before the Senate, but before any legislative action occurred, the Recording Industry Association of America (RIAA) agreed to a labeling program.

For further details about the "filthy fifteen" records and the PMRC's attempt to ban music, click here: https://en.wikipedia.org/wiki/Parents_Music_Resource_Center

Occasionally, record companies may ask an artist to re-record certain songs or to revise lyrics. Sometimes artists remove songs or re-record edited versions. The artist and recording company determine if the product requires the Recording Industry Association of America/Parental Advisory Label. Other industries have taken different approaches to label or describe their content.

Is labeling and warning a form of censorship?

Music (https://www.riaa.com/toolsforparents.php?content_selector=parental_advisory)

- PAL: Parental Advisory Logo

Television (http://www.tvguidelines.org/ratings.htm)

- D: suggestive dialogue (usually means talks about sex);
- L: course or crude language;
- S: sexual situations;
- V: violence;
- FV: fantasy violence (children's programming only).

Movies (http://filmratings.com/downloads/rating_rules.pdf)

- Mature themes;
- Language;
- Depictions of violence;
- Nudity;
- Sensuality;
- Depictions of sexual activity;
- Adults activities (i.e., activities that adults, but not minors, may engage in legally);
- Drug use.

Video Games (http://www.esrb.org/ratings/ratings_guide.jsp)

- Alcohol Reference—Reference to and/or images of alcoholic beverages;
- Animated Blood—Discolored and/or unrealistic depictions of blood;
- Blood—Depictions of blood;

- Blood and Gore—Depictions of blood or the mutilation of body parts;

- Cartoon Violence—Violent actions involving cartoon-like situations and characters. May include violence where a character is unharmed after the action has been inflicted;

- Comic Mischief—Depictions or dialogue involving slapstick or suggestive humor;

- Crude Humor—Depictions or dialogue involving vulgar antics, including "bathroom" humor;

- Drug Reference—Reference to and/or images of illegal drugs;

- Fantasy Violence—Violent actions of a fantasy nature, involving human or non-human characters in situations easily distinguishable from real life;

- Intense Violence—Graphic and realistic-looking depictions of physical conflict. May involve extreme and/or realistic blood, gore, weapons and depictions of human injury and death;

- Language—Mild to moderate use of profanity;

- Lyrics—Mild references to profanity, sexuality, violence, alcohol or drug use in music;

- Mature Humor—Depictions or dialogue involving "adult" humor, including sexual references;

- Nudity—Graphic or prolonged depictions of nudity;

- Partial Nudity—Brief and/or mild depictions of nudity;

- Real Gambling—Player can gamble, including betting or wagering real cash or currency;

- Sexual Content—Non-explicit depictions of sexual behavior, possibly including partial nudity;

- Sexual Themes—References to sex or sexuality;

- Sexual Violence—Depictions of rape or other violent sexual acts;

- Simulated Gambling—Player can gamble without betting or wagering real cash or currency;

- Strong Language—Explicit and/or frequent use of profanity;

- Strong Lyrics—Explicit and/or frequent references to profanity, sex, violence, alcohol or drug use in music;

- Strong Sexual Content—Explicit and/or frequent depictions of sexual behavior, possibly including nudity;

- Suggestive Themes—Mild provocative references or materials;

- Tobacco Reference—Reference to and/or images of tobacco products;

- Use of Alcohol—The consumption of alcoholic beverages;

- Use of Drugs—The consumption or use of illegal drugs;

- Use of Tobacco—The consumption of tobacco products;

- Violence—Scenes involving aggressive conflict. May contain bloodless dismemberment;

- Violent References—References to violent acts.

Is the entirety of this chapter written in defense of violence and sex? Am I in favor of the obscene?

To the contrary, public school students can read the Bible, Torah, Koran or other religious texts as "literature." Given our First Amendment rights, these texts may be interpreted for their literary qualities.

Public schools can restrict the texts available in school libraries based on budget constraints and curricular goals— all in keeping with the First Amendment as well.

In addition to the extensive list of content descriptors, the video game industry (through the Entertainment Software Rating Board) elected to list the game's interactive elements on its warning labels as well:

- Shares Info—Indicates that personal information provided by the user (e.g., e-mail address, phone number, credit card info, etc.) is shared with third parties;

- Shares Location—Includes the ability to display the user's location to other users of the app;

- Users Interact—Indicates possible exposure to unfiltered/uncensored user-generated content, including user-to-user communications and media sharing via social media and networks. (Retrieved from http://www.esrb.org/ratings/ratings_guide.jsp)

To date, books do not come with warning labels or content descriptors. Nor are they subject to a ratings system such as those used with television, movies, video games or fan fiction (see Figure 12.8 for other ratings systems).

Figure 12.8
Ratings systems for fanfiction, movies, television, music, and video games.

However, children's book covers or endpapers may contain information about the age level of the intended reader and a synopsis of the content. Board books, picturebooks, nonfiction, and young adult literature are frequently housed in different sections of a library or bookstore to encourage age-appropriate corralling.

Also, children's literature is heavily reviewed in formal and informal ways, providing librarians, teachers, parents, and other adults with extensive information about a book's content.

 School Library Journal (SLJ): http://www.slj.com/#

SLJ produces resources, services, and reviews for library and education professionals. However, the materials are also relevant for any adult with an interest in children's and young adult literature. SLJ originated as a print magazine and still exists as such. However, they also produce extensive content, including an amazing network of blogs, that is freely available online.

 Molly Wetta.(@mollywetta) curates SLJ's banned books Pinterest board. Check it out! https://www.pinterest.com/sljournal/banned-books-week/

Click here for SLJ's blog network: http://www.slj.com/slj-blog-network/

Common Sense Media: https://www.commonsensemedia.org/

Unlike *SLJ*, which supports librarians, Common Sense Media originated to rate, educate, and advocate, not for youth's First Amendment rights, but for parents, teachers, and policymakers. According to their mission statement, "Common Sense Media helps families make smart media choices. We offer the largest, most trusted library of independent age-based and educational ratings and reviews for movies, games, apps, TV shows, websites, books, and music" (Retrieved from https://www.commonsensemedia.org/about-us/our-mission).

Common Sense Media provides detailed information for those individuals who want to know more about the content of children's literature and other forms of media. They also engage in education, policy, and lobbying efforts.

 Goodreads: http://www.goodreads.com/

Goodreads is a website in which 40 million users post lists of the books they are reading and survey the lists of their friends and family. In other words, Goodreads is a book recommendation site. Unlike *SLJ* or Common Sense Media, Goodreads is curated by the users. Yes, there are places to access expert opinions (blogs) and author pages, but Goodreads predominantly functions on locating book recommendations based on the users' preferences.

There are thousands of blogs and websites dedicated to children's literature. I featured these three resources because they are popular and consistent sources of information. Yet, I clearly understand there is no way to capture all opinions and satisfy the sensibilities of every child, youth, or concerned adult.

The Final Word

In the United States, we don't ban books, but when some people are offended by what they read they often make efforts to limit or restrict what others, especially children, can read, view, watch, and play. The following statement is an excerpt from Supreme Court Justice Antonin Scalia's Opinion of the Court on the matter of video games and vulgarity. He specifically draws connections to children's literature and the Brothers Grimm to make his points.

> Certainly the books we give children to read—or read to them when they are younger—contain no shortage of gore. Grimm's Fairy Tales, for example, are grim indeed. As her just deserts for trying to poison Snow White, the wicked queen is made to dance in red hot slippers "till she fell dead on the floor, a sad example of envy and jealousy." The Complete Brothers Grimm Fairy Tales 198 (2006 ed.). Cinderella's evil stepsisters have their eyes pecked out by doves. Id. , at 95. And Hansel and Gretel (children!) kill their captor by baking her in an oven. Id. , at 54.
>
> High-school reading lists are full of similar fare. Homer's Odysseus blinds Polyphemus the Cyclops by grinding out his eye with a heated stake. The Odyssey of Homer, Book IX, p. 125 (S. Butcher & A. Lang transls. 1909) ("Even so did we seize the fiery-pointed brand and whirled it round in his eye, and the blood flowed about the heated bar. And the breath of the flame singed his eyelids and brows all about, as the ball of the eye burnt away, and the roots thereof crackled in the flame"). In the Inferno, Dante and Virgil watch corrupt politicians struggle to stay submerged beneath a lake of boiling pitch, lest they be skewered by devils above the surface. Canto XXI, pp. 187–189 (A. Mandelbaum transl. Bantam Classic ed. 1982). And Golding's Lord of the Flies recounts how a schoolboy called Piggy is savagely murdered by other children while marooned on an island. W. Golding, Lord of the Flies 208–209 (1997 ed.)...
>
> Excerpt from Note 4:
> Reading Dante is unquestionably more cultured and intellectually edifying than playing Mortal Kombat. But these cultural and intellectual differences are not constitutional ones. Crudely violent video games, tawdry TV shows, and cheap novels and magazines are no less forms of speech than The Divine Comedy, and restrictions upon them must survive strict scrutiny—a question to which we devote our attention in Part III, infra. Even if we can see in them "nothing of any possible value to society . . . , they are as much entitled to the protection of free speech as the best of literature." *Winters v. New York, 333 U. S. 507, 510 (1948).*

From Justice Scalia's Opinion of the Court, *Brown v. Entertainment Merchants Association*, 564 U.S., 8-9 (2011).

Did you think I would give Justice Antonin Scalia the final word? Of course not! Although, in this instance, I completely agree with him.

But I do offer Justice Scalia's statement as the second-to-last word because we don't often read about Supreme Court Justices' literary diets nor do we glimpse the breadth of their children's literature knowledge.

For the rest of the court's opinion, click here: https://www.law.cornell.edu/supct/html/08-1448.ZO.html#ref-- it's a very interesting read.

Children's literature. If Supreme Court Justices read it, you can too.

In a less litigious and more practical application of readers' rights, I will end this chapter, and this book, with a visual representation of Daniel Pennac's manifesto regarding the *Rights of the Reader* (Figure 12.9).

Daniel Pennac created this list of reader-considerate practices that disregards well-intentioned adults and focuses on the interaction between a reader and the text—a privileged place where children and youth have choices and select literature for personal, private reasons.

After reading this book, I hope you understand the depth and complexity of children's and young adult literature—the texts, the writers and illustrators, the markets, the awards, the wars, and everything in between. I also hope you will advocate for children and youth so they are afforded the opportunity to read what they like, when they like, and how they like. Finally, I hope you read children's literature too—it's a big deal!

Figure 12.9

I think Daniel Pennac sums up my views perfectly; children are young, but they have rights as readers. *The Rights of the Reader* by Daniel Pennac, translated by Sarah Hamp Adams, and illustrated by Quentin Blake, 2006, London, UK: Walker Books. Images copyright 2006 by Quentin Blake.

CHAPTER 05 | APPENDIX

Exploring Literary Analysis: Techniques for Understanding Complex Literature

by: Lindsay Persohn

Understanding how texts fit into the world can help readers make connections with familiar and new ideas. An analysis is a critique, or a response to literature, helping readers position texts in individual, cultural, and sociological spheres. Readers see a text through an overlapping set of lenses, relating the text to their personal experiences, other texts they have read, and sociocultural systems in their worlds. Critical literary analyses can come in many forms. Analysis of a text occurs through iterative processes of identifying a comment on a text, relating the comment to a larger theory, then providing evidence from the text to substantiate the comment. But, performing an analysis or critique of literature can be a challenge. How does a reader begin? What does a reader say? Why does it matter?

In this section, I offer some framing explanation for why literature is studied critically, an introduction to some ways in which literature could be studied, and four example analyses I wrote based on one short story, 'The Spring Tune' by the award-winning Finnish author and illustrator Tove Jansson. This illustrated short story is published in Jansson's *Tales from Moominvalley*, originally in Swedish in 1962, translated to English in 1964, and more recently republished by Square Fish in 2010. This book is readily available in many libraries or for purchase online through retailers like indiebound.org and amazon.com. 'The Spring Tune' complexity, brief length, and engaging content make it an appealing text for sample analyses.

An Introduction to Strategies for Studying Literature

Shining light on a piece of literature through a selected theoretical lens can produce questions, responses, and ideas that help readers situate literature within its field. A literary analysis could discuss how components of a literary work relate to personal experience, to other literary components (within a single work), how two literary works relate to each other, and how a literary work relates to larger sociocultural contexts. The reader's interpretation is supported by connecting the text with a critical theory. It is important for readers to understand there are many ways to interpret literature. Meyer (1999) reminds critics of all experience levels, "New voices do not drown out the past; they build on it and eventually become part of the past as newer writers take their place beside them" (p. 2025). Budding critics can find their way to meaning and significance in literature by bearing in mind there are many possible frameworks for analysis to explore, their ideas will often spring from the ideas of others, and ideas about literature can change over time as various contexts influence the lenses brought to literature.

As a starting point for thinking about literary analysis, readers might think about different perspectives through which a work could be viewed. Any of the following perspectives might be used to critically respond to a text:

- **biographical strategies** - Knowledge of an author's life can be used to serve as a gauge on an interpretation of a work. Biographical analyses can open the possibilities of interpretation and raise questions without resolving them. For example, knowledge of Lewis Carroll's (aka Charles Dodgson's) life helps a reader understand *Alice's Adventures in Wonderland* (1865) as a search for personal identity.

- **gender strategies** - Ideas about masculinity and femininity are the main focus of gender strategies. Readers can work to understand how gender is socially constructed in cultures, including how men and women write and read about each other. These strategies are based on feminist theory. This approach could also include topics related to sexuality (i.e., queer theory, LGBTQ perspectives). As one example, a reader could examine how gender is constructed in variant editions of Cinderella tales.

- **historical strategies** - Readers can use history to better understand the original context of a work of literature, use literature to understand the nuances of history, or read with an eye for the stories untold by traditional history (as a new historicist). For example, a reader could investigate the ties between Harper Lee's *To Kill a Mockingbird* (1960) and the racial climate of Alabama in the 1930s.

- **ideological strategies** - Ideological strategies examine an ideograph (e.g., liberty, equality, family values, freedom of speech, etc.) in a work through an understanding of the social, political, and intellectual systems (e.g., realism, Marxism, religious faith, etc.) in which the author wrote it. For example, a reader might study family structure in J.M. Barrie's *Peter Pan* (1911) in order to contrast Victorian and modern ideas about families.

- **mythological strategies** - Myths focus on hopes, fears, and expectations of entire cultures, providing "a strategy for understanding how human beings try to account for their lives symbolically" (Meyer, 1999, p. 2037). This kind of analysis could focus on ideas about the potentially unexplainable (i.e., origins, destiny, purpose, etc.) or utilize archetypes to connect with folk tales, heroes, tricksters, spirits, etc. As an example, a reader could compare the main characters in Suzanne Collins' *Hunger Games* (2008) to the gladiators of ancient Rome.

- **psychological strategies** - Psychology has been greatly influenced by Sigmund Freud's theories including levels of consciousness (id, ego, superego), dreams (often said to reveal the unconscious), defense mechanisms, etc. Psychological strategies are influenced by many other psychologists throughout history, including Carl Jung's theory of the collective consciousness. In this kind of work, a reader could analyze Charlotte Brontë's *Jane Eyre* (1847) through her use of defense mechanisms.

- **reader-response strategies** - Reader-response strategies view reading as a creative act and emphasize what happens in the reader's mind (Iser, 1974; Rosenblatt, 1994/1978). A reader-response interpretation is based in the original text, so it should come after several close readings of a text. For example, a reader might examine how J.K. Rowling's Harry Potter experienced school, quoting passages and citing incidents from the book to contrast to his or her views of school.

- **structuralist strategies** - A structuralist might attend to the relationships between form and meaning in the work—its language, structure and tone through elements such as diction, irony, paradox, metaphor, and symbol as well as plot, characterization, and narrative technique. The focus of a structuralist analysis is on literary devices over content (i.e., the *way* a text is written, over *what* is written). A reader could use structuralist strategies to examine Ernest Hemingway's writing style in *The Old Man and the Sea* (1952).

This list of strategies is not exhaustive; there are many ways scholars study literature. Each approach to making meaning in a text has limitations and advantages. Readers should select a text and an approach to meet their interests and skill levels. With the knowledge that many approaches overlap and supplement each other, readers can record observations, questions, and ideas about connections to a text during reading to begin analysis.

Approaching the Text: Logic and Process

Developing an analysis, critique, or comment is not writing a summary— analysis begins with a comment on the text, the reader relates the comment to a larger theory, then provides evidence from the text to substantiate the comment. It is important to choose a compelling text.

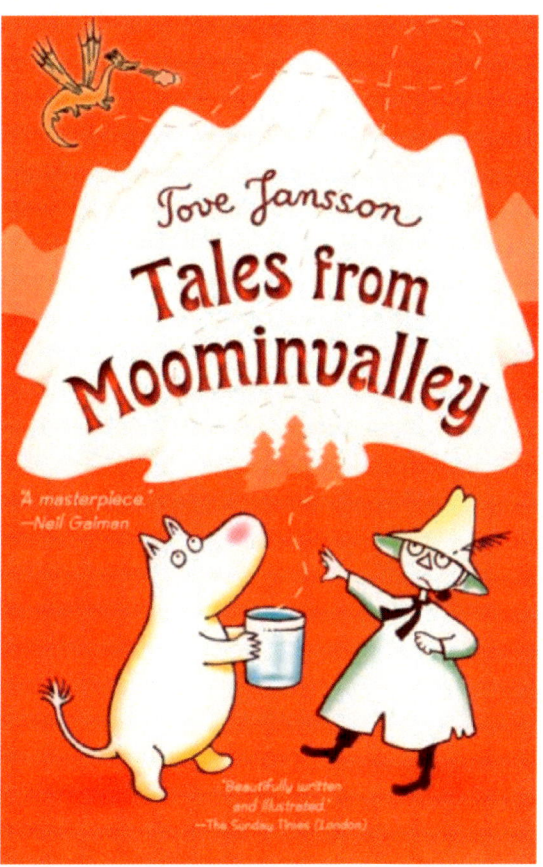

Figure 1 The Spring Tune is one story in a collection called Tales from Moominvalley by Tove Jansson and translated by Thomas Warburton, 1962, New York, NY: Farrar, Straus & Giroux.

As I read Tove Jansson's 'The Spring Tune' for the first time, I saw evidence of layered meanings through meticulous word choices, unusual phrase construction, and the story's complex structure. I also chose to study this story because I enjoy it. Jansson's expressive, sensory writing carries her distinct and Nordic viewpoint. Her Moomin characters each have distinguishable personalities, revealed over time through their stories to give readers an understanding of the many facets of each character. Tove Jansson is a key player in Finnish children's literature and won the Hans Christian Andersen Award in 1966 for her writing. The Moomin series has been translated into over 30 languages (Jansson, 1964/2010). Translated literature provides a unique opportunity for an international exchange of ideas. Complex, entertaining stories like these are a good place for novice literary critics to begin.

Step 1: Read, Note, Repeat

Rereading the text and making notes are important first steps in the analysis process. Rereading helps a reader develop an understanding of the text through an open-ended process of studying words and illustrations for their literal and figurative meanings, which may differ from understandings developed during a first reading (Eagleton, 2008). Making notes in the text encourages a reader to spend more time with each page, engage in recording in-the-moment thoughts, and document details and overarching ideas. Notes allow a reader to revisit germane ideas and questions as he or she develops a comment for formalized analysis.

- To begin my analysis, I copied 'The Spring Tune' in an enlarged format (11"x17") to allow extra space for writing my notes during repeated readings.
- During the rereading process, I marked each iteration of my notes with a different color or method to distinguish my thoughts after each iteration. (See Figure 1 for a photographed example of my notes.)
- During my first rereading, I made no marks in the text; rather I read for nuanced comprehension of the story and enjoyment.
- During my second re-reading, I used a yellow highlighter, highlighting words and phrases that seemed to carry more than surface-level meanings.
- On my next re-readings, I developed a subtext in the margins, including my observations, questions, and connections as I read, attending to my own reading processes as well as the author's writing.
- I marked my notes in purple pen during my third rereading, blue pen for the fourth, purple highlighter for the fifth, and black ink for the sixth rereading.

APPENDIX

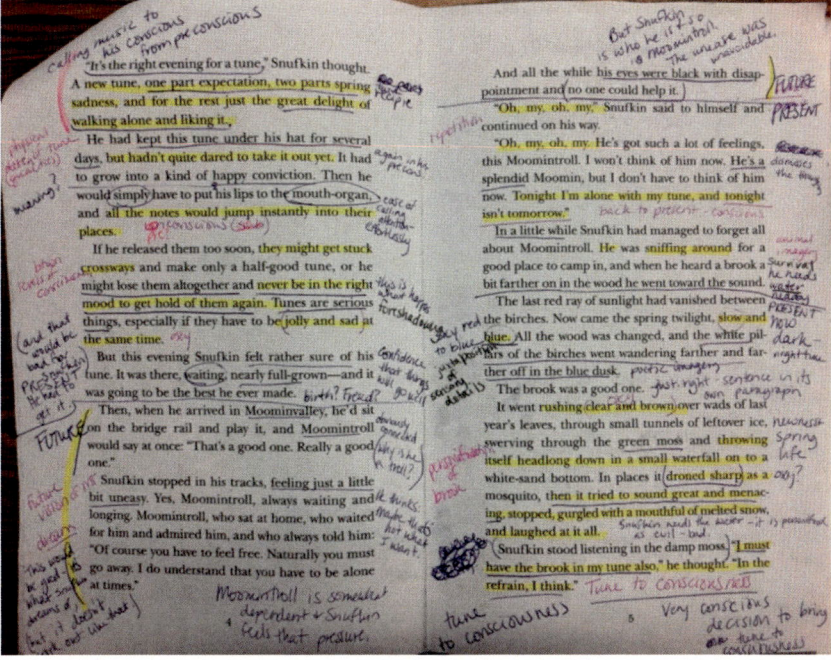

Figure 2 The analysis involves several readings using different color pens, highlighters, and note locations.

During these readings over time, my notes helped me build an understanding of particular words, phrases, and passages in the story, as well as how those words, phrases, and passages work together throughout the story in details of the plot, character development, sociocultural structures, humor, and enchantment in 'The Spring Tune'.

Step 2: Investigate, Write, Read, Repeat

I researched my selected perspectives, revisited the text, and recorded my thoughts. I reread the short story as published (i.e., not from my notes, but from my copy of the book) to myself, then aloud I as focused on ideas at the forefront of my mind after reading and noting my ideas— form, myth, dreams, and illustrations. I made notes on a separate notepad as I read the short story again. I solidified my ideas about Snufkin's encounter with the Creep and I wrote complete and incomplete sentences to "account for phenomena — the text— without distorting or misrepresenting what it describes" (Meyer, 1999, p. 2023). As I wrote about my ideas, I continued to go back to my annotations and notes when questions arose and clarification was needed. I consulted primary and secondary sources about the ideas I discerned from the text (literary form, myth, dreams, and descriptive illustrations in this story) to help develop my strands of thinking. The process resulted in the four analyses following the synopsis of 'The Spring Tune' by Tove Jansson.

Jansson's 'The Spring Tune'

Familiarity with Tove Jansson's short story 'The Spring Tune' in *Tales from Moominvalley* (1964/2010) is useful for readers of the following examples. Though I highly recommend reading the short story in its entirety, here I provide a synopsis:

> In 'The Spring Tune', characters Snufkin and a small, initially unnamed wood creature (known as a Creep), engage in a complex exchange of power and subjectivity. Snufkin, the vagabond and musician, is on his way back to Moominvalley after Winter Sleep. He is irritated by the small Creep, dismissive of his attempts at conversation and his requests to hear some of Snufkin's famous mouth-organ music. Feeling his evening of solitude is ruined and the tune he had "under his hat" (Jansson, 1964/2010, p. 4) is gone, Snufkin engages in dialogue with the Creep and gives Teety-Woo his name before it/he scurries off. The next day, Snufkin can think of nothing but Teety-Woo and returns to the wood, wishing to find him again. When Snufkin encounters Teety-Woo for a second time, Teety-Woo is dismissive of Snufkin.

While I strive to address structural, cultural, and psychological ideas in a straightforward way, I hope my discussion evokes further investigation into the intricacies of these perspectives for readers. Following each example, I say more about how I developed the commentary from my notes into these literary comments.

Example Analysis 1: Jansson's Notable Use of Language

> *"The Little Creep stared at him with yellow eyes in the firelight. It thought its name over, tasted it, listened to it, crawled inside it, and finally turned its nose to the sky and softly howled its new name, so sadly and ecstatically that Snufkin felt a shiver along his back."*
> *(Jansson, 1964/2010, p. 12)*

Tove Jansson's stories bring readers' awareness to matters of psychology and sociology through diction and syntax. Her descriptions are highly sensory and her word choices often juxtapose ideas, drawing attention to not only *what* she writes, but the *way* she writes. Linguistic devices in Jansson's works emphasize feelings and thoughts.

In the opening paragraphs of 'The Spring Tune', Jansson brings readers' awareness to the present, using language resembling that of meditation:

> Walking had been easy, because his knapsack was nearly empty and he had no worries on his mind. He felt happy about the wood and the weather, and himself. Tomorrow and yesterday were both at a distance, and just at present the sun was shining brightly red between the birches, and the air was cool and soft. (Jansson, 1964/2010, p. 3)

Sensory language describing the sun as "shining brightly red" and the air as "cool and soft" connect the reader to Snufkin's surroundings and his contented state of mind. Commas draw attention to the description of Snufkin's personal satisfaction, found through his travels and his presence in the moment's details.

When Snufkin begins to settle into the woods for the evening, readers catch a glimpse of his pensive ways through his view on mealtimes (Jansson, 1964/2010, p. 6):

> Snufkin was used to cooking his own dinner. He never cooked a dinner for other people if he could avoid it, nor did he care much for other people's dinners. So many people insisted on talking when they had a meal.
>
> Also they had a great liking for chairs and tables, and some of them used napkins. He even had heard of a Hemulen who changed his clothes everytime he was about to eat, but that was probably slander.

The fact that he cooks for himself and avoids other people's cooking isolates Snufkin from social dinners, evidencing his persona as a loner and wanderer. Snufkin's thoughts counter the ideals of a civilized meal, but when narrated through his viewpoint, these conventions of mealtime become defamiliarized and subject to scrutiny. The use of *slander* points to the relative absurdity in the old tradition of dressing for dinner. Snufkin's point of view, brought to light by a distinctive syntactic rhythm and crisp word choice, gives readers a glimpse Snufkin's innermost thoughts about himself and his relationship with society.

Jansson's diction and syntax bring readers' awareness to matters of psychology and sociology. As she wrote the Moomin stories in her native language, Swedish, one could argue many of these noteworthy word choices are selected by a translator. But books in the Moomin series have been translated by several writers, and all works maintain poetic rhythm, illustrative vocabulary, and detailed yet concise phrasing. The ideas and diction are Jansson's creations, and the translated versions would, of course, not exist without her original works. Her descriptions are highly sensory, often juxtapose ideas, and Jansson's distinctive construction of sentences draws attention to not only the content of her stories, but the way she tells them.

Reflections on Developing Example Analysis 1

My initial highlights and notes in 'The Spring Tune' became the basis for the structural analysis presented here in Example 1. Many of the phrases I highlighted provided sensory details, carried a rhythmic nature, and conveyed human emotions. Rereading the story aloud helped me identify particularly poetic, sensory, and descriptive phrases, good candidates for development in my analysis. Example 1 came to fruition as I studied the phrases I highlighted in my early readings of 'The Spring Tune', by identifying, naming, and describing the richness in Jansson's writing.

Example Analysis 2: Snufkin and Teety-Woo; or Prometheus and Io, Reimagined

> *"He puffed a few clouds of smoke toward the night sky and waited for the spring tune.*
> *It didn't come. Instead he felt the Creep's eyes upon him."*
>
> *(Jansson, 1964/2010, p. 7)*

Myths are ancient ways of answering questions about the universe from people who had a much stronger connection to nature than today's "civilized man" (Hamilton, 1942/2011, p. 1). In 'The Spring Tune', I identify several of Snufkin's characteristics that relate to the mythological figure Prometheus. The wood Creep of 'The Spring Tune' shares some symbolism with the mythological figure Io. I suggest links between the two stories by first summarizing the pertinent points of each story, then drawing parallels between them.

Prometheus and Io. Prometheus is considered a "champion of humankind" and one of the wisest Titans (Daly, 1992/2009, p. 121). He stole the gift of fire from heaven to give to man. Prometheus was bound to a rock by Zeus as punishment for bringing fire to man, where a bird picked off his liver throughout the day. Each night, he healed so his punishment would go on forever. Prometheus had a "strange visitor" described by Hamilton (1942/2011) as a "distracted fleeing creature . . . clambering awkwardly over the cliffs and crags…" (p. 95). Prometheus recognized this visitor as Io, the beautiful woman turned into a heifer. Prometheus told Io to look to the future to cope with her plight of the gad-fly's ceaseless buzzing which forced her to wander aimlessly near the Ionian sea.

Snufkin and Teety-Woo. Snufkin is a vagabond and musician, wood-famous for his travel stories and his mouth-organ music. 'The Spring Tune' begins as Snufkin searches for dry firewood. As he sits by his fire, smoking his pipe, he feels the eyes of a small wood Creep "[watching] everything he did, admiringly" (Jansson, 1964/2010, p. 7). Snufkin feels uneasy. The wood Creep recognizes Snufkin and reaches him by wading across a brook, stumbling and freezing all the way. After some conversation, Snufkin names the Creep Teety-Woo, a name based on the song of a passing bird. Once Teety-Woo is named, he sees a future for himself.

Prometheus : Io : : Snufkin : Teety-Woo. The following two-column comparison of Prometheus and Io, and Snufkin and Teety-Woo evidences similarities between the two stories.

- Prometheus speaks Io's name
- a bird provides Prometheus's punishment
- Io is caught between human and animal

- Snufkin gives Teety-Woo his name
- a bird provides Snufkin's inspiration
- Teety-Woo is caught between animal and human

When Io first comes upon Prometheus, bound to the rock at Caucasus, she says:

> This that I see—
> A form storm-beaten,
> Bound to a rock.
> Do you do wrong?
> Is this your punishment?
> Where am I?
> Speak to the wretched wanderer.
> Enough— I have been tried enough—
> My wandering— my long wandering.
> Yet I have found nowhere
> To leave my misery.
> I am a girl who speak to you,
> But horns are on my head.
> (Hamilton, 1942/2011, p. 96)

In the same style, I respond through the voice of The Creep:

> This that I see—
> A form weather-worn,
> Unbound from Establishment.
> Do you do song?
> Is this your freedom?
> Who am I?
> Name the curious wanderer.
> Enough— I have been ignored enough—
> My reality— my small reality.
> Yet I have found no name
> To leave my anonymity.
> I am a person who speak to you,
> But fur is on my body.
> (Persohn, 2015)

Though Jansson's story is decidedly less morbid than the myth, similarities between the stories exist on several levels. Prometheus is considered to mean "forethought', and Snufkin mentions the new moon, wishes, and new beginnings. According to Daly (1992/2009), Gothe saw Prometheus as a symbol of "rebellion against the restraints of society" (p. 121), a strong characteristic of Snufkin's persona, who rejects personal property and authority figures. Io is a woman changed to a heifer, and the wood Creep, Teety-Woo in 'The Spring Tune' similarly wavers between animal and human. References to fire, strange visitors, real and perceived constraints, ceaseless wandering, and nods to the future run through the myth of Prometheus and Io and the tale of Snufkin and Teety-Woo.

Reflections on Developing Example Analysis 2

My comparison of 'The Spring Tune' to the myth of Prometheus and Io only developed after I read the story six or seven times. Example 2 came together when I realized I was familiar with a myth involving a strange visitor and references to fire. I toured Edith Hamilton's *Mythology* (1942/2011) and found the familiar tale of Prometheus and Io. After reading the myth three times, I identified and described essential elements in the Prometheus and Io myth, then returned to 'The Spring Tune' to write about analogous concepts. I began to see the conversation Prometheus and Io had at Caucasus could mirror the conversation Snufkin and Teety-Woo had by the campfire. I recognized words and phrasing in passages from the myth I could substitute with ideas and actions from 'The Spring Tune' to create a parody.

Example Analysis 3: Tove Jansson's 'The Spring Tune' as 'The Spring Dream'

> *The tune was quite near at hand, easy to catch by the tail. But there was time enough to wait: it was hedged in and couldn't get away. No, better to wash the dishes first, then light a pipe -- and afterwards, when the campfire was burning down and the night creatures started calling for each other, then he'd have it.*
>
> *Snufkin was washing his saucepan in the brook when he caught sight of the Creep. It was sitting on the far side below a tree root, looking at him.*
>
> -- *(Jansson, 1964/2010, p. 6-7)*

Tove Jansson's 'The Spring Tune' is wrought with dream imagery, ambivalent details, and non-sequitur conversations. Jansson's illustration on the opening page of the story supports the conception of the story as a dream with the main character, Snufkin, lying in the grass, arms folded behind his head, eyes closed (Jansson, 1964/2010, p. 3). Jansson uses phrasing like "rested his eyes" (p. 6), characters talk about dreaming (p. 9), and the story closes with Snufkin again lying in the grass, looking at the "clear, dark blue straight above him..." (Jansson, 1964/2010, p. 16). I selected a Freudian dream analysis (Freud, 1900) to deconstruct Snufkin's encounter with a wood Creep in this story. Freud's psychoanalytic dream-work enables me to explore the text as condensed, displaced, and visualized to understand the story through manifest meaning of latent content (Dimitriadis & Kamberelis, 2006; Freud, 1900; Eagleton, 2008).

Dream-work. According to Sigmund Freud, the first job of dream-work is *condensation*, whereby some elements of thought are omitted from representation altogether, fragments of complex thoughts manifest, and elements of thought combine into a single unit (Freud, 1916 as cited in Rice & Waugh, 2001). The second action in dream-work is *displacement*. Displacement might replace a thought with an allusion or shift an idea so it appears differently centered and strange (Freud, 1916/2001). Thirdly, a *transformation* occurs, whereby dream-work must shape condensed and displaced thoughts as sensory images, mostly visual.

Freud offers some caution in interpreting dreams: "In general one must avoid seeking to explain one part of the manifest dream by another, as though the dream had been coherently conceived and was a logically arranged narrative" (Freud, 1916 as cited in Rice & Waugh, 2001, p. 31). Sometimes the meaning of thoughts and images in dreams is distorted to the point of reversal (e.g., Climbing up a staircase can mean the same thing as coming down) (Freud, 1916/2001). Freud warns against overestimating the dream-work by attributing too much to it. I proceeded in my analysis with this in mind.

Freudian Interpretations. Snufkin, the vagabond and musician of Moominvalley, walks through the woods just before twilight, with a new song just "under his hat" (Jansson, 1964/2010, p. 4). The task of catching this tune can not be forced or rushed. Instead of his tune, Snufkin encounters a small admirer in the woods. He is dismissive and irritated at the interruption to his thoughts. The admirer (a shy, scared Creep) walks across the icy creek, falling several times to reach Snufkin, while Snufkin watches with an uneasy feeling, unable to move, as in a dream. Snufkin, his evening of solitude ruined, gives in to conversation with the Creep after he shares his intense interest in Snufkin's wood-famous musical talents. The Creep has never heard music before.

In his questions that follow, the Creep requests Snufkin give him a name, as he is too small to have one yet. After "someone flew across the brook on long pointed wings and gave a long, sad cry among the trees: *Yo-yooo, yo-ooo, tee-woo…*", Snufkin dubs him 'Teety-Woo' because it has a "light beginning, sort of, and a little sadness to round it off" (Jansson, 1964/2010, p. 11), focusing energy on the way sounds relate to emotion and mimicking the song of the passing creature. The Creep's interest in Snufkin quickly wanes and the newly-named Teety-Woo almost immediately exits the scene.

The naming of Teety-Woo is possibly the moment when a Tune would emerge for Snufkin; instead he names the Creep. Snufkin misses the opportunity to capture his song and the Tune is forever lost to his unconscious. Though it is a lesser known topic of Freud's work, songs, like dreams, are associated with repressed thoughts (Diaz de Chumacerio, 1990).

Freudian Conclusions. At the end of the story, Teety-Woo moves to the foreground, assuming power and individual identity, while Snufkin recedes. Snufkin's eventual interest in Teety-Woo could approximate how Snufkin might react if his softhearted friend, Moomintroll, assumed the power in their relationship and forego his "waiting and longing" (Jansson, 1964/2010, p. 4) for Snufkin's return to Moominhouse. When they first meet, Snufkin and the Creep talk of Snufkin's best friend, Moomintroll:

> 'Isn't it a nice thing to know that someone's longing for you and waiting and waiting to see you again?'
> 'I'm coming when it suits me!' Snufkin cried violently. 'Perhaps I shan't come at all. Perhaps I will go somewhere else.'
> 'Oh. Then he'll be sad,' said the Creep. (Jansson, 1964/2010, p. 11)

As Teety-Woo points out, the privilege of friendship comes with an obligation to satisfy someone else's needs. As Snufkin says, "'You can't ever really be free if you admire somebody too much… I know.'" (Jansson, 1964/2010, p. 8). Snufkin and Teety-Woo's conversation about Moomintroll could point to the strain Snufkin feels about his best friend, manifest in the dream. Snufkin rebuffs Teety-Woo's admiration, just as he thinks he might with Moomintroll. In the case of Teety-Woo, however, Snufkin finds as soon as the admiration fades, he desperately seeks it. Through Snufkin's dream-like state I see the forest as a place of dreams, and Snufkin's experience through Freud's dream-work.

Reflections on Developing Example Analysis 3

After my second rereading of this story, I wondered, "Is this Snufkin's dream?" So on my third rereading, I began to attend more heavily to what I saw as dream references, the foundation for Example 3. I worked first on formalizing the dream analysis, the most-referenced idea in my notes. I refreshed my memory about Sigmund Freud's dreamwork by reading his original works (1900) and Rice and Waugh's (2001) presentation of Freud (1916). Rand and Torok (1993) discuss Freud's interpretation of dreams as "personal free association" and, on the other hand, "a world of fixed and universal meanings" (p. 575). Eagleton, citing Freud, refers to dreams as the 'royal road' to the unconscious (Eagleton, 2008, p. 137). I worked to develop rational parallels between Freud's psychoanalytic dream interpretation and 'The Spring Tune', locate sufficient support in those texts, and record my connections in sentences.

Example Analysis 4: Jansson's Pencil Alongside Her Pen in 'The Spring Tune'

"The last red ray of sunlight had vanished between the birches. Now came the spring twilight, slow and blue. All the wood was changed, and the white pillars of the birches went wandering farther and farther off in the blue dusk."
-- (Jansson, 1964/2010, p. 5)

Tove Jansson, illustrator and author, includes many interior illustrations with her stories. Her detailed black line sketches are charged with emotion and indicative of her rich narrative writing style. The fact that her pictures illustrate her words creates a unique relationship between text and image. Jansson illustrates the short story 'The Spring Tune' with seven separate but variously linked images of Snufkin, Teety-Woo, the moon, and the landscape that helps shape the emotional influences in this story.

The image before the first page of 'The Spring Tune' shows Snufkin alone, facing a large but light and rising full moon along his wide, open path. The illustration evokes feelings of solitude, peace, and renewed wonder at the surrounding world. The illustration on the next page, just before the start of the story shows Snufkin reclined on a leafy bed, a peaceful face, arms folded behind his head, resting on his knapsack. Snufkin (a recurring character in Jansson's stories) is often pictured in other illustrations with a large, triangular nose, making him appear old, firm, and wise, but in this reclined position, viewers see his face in small, soft outline, giving Snufkin an air of child-like ease.

Several pages into the story, Jansson visually introduces "a rather thin and miserable Creep" (Jansson, 1964/2010, p. 8) as he crawls through the cold, deep brook to meet Snufkin on the other side. Jansson's third illustration in this short story shows a close shot of the Creep from the waist up, with wide, intense eyes and paws held out of the water that surrounds him. Jansson tells readers "the Creep stepped straight into the water and started to wade across. The brook was rather too broad for it, and the water was ice-cold. A couple of times the Creep lost its foothold and tumbled over. . ." (Jansson, 1964/2010, p. 8). Finally, with chattering teeth, the Creep reaches Snufkin at the other shore. On the next page, a full-page illustration reveals a dense wood with trees so tall their tops do not enter the picture. In the bottom third of the illustration, the Creep, highlighted in the center of the image by an absence of surrounding forms, talks to a contemplative Snufkin who sits on a dark log nearby, holding his hands in his lap and his pipe in his mouth. Through his wondering expression and his outstretched arms, the Creep seems to be revealing his deepest thoughts to Snufkin. Jansson's text confirms this idea, revealing the Creep's admiration for Snufkin's worldly experiences and wisdom: "'I know you know everything,' the Little Creep prattled on, edging closer still. 'I know you've seen everything. You're right in everything you say, and I'll always try to become as free as you are . . . So now you're on your way to Moominvalley to have a rest and meet your friends . . . .'" (Jansson, 1964/2010, p. 9-11).

As soon as the conversation turns to expectations of Snufkin's return to Moominvalley, Snufkin snaps, "I'm coming when it suits me!" (Jansson, 1964/2010, p. 11).

Silence follows until a night bird flies over head and inspires Snufkin to give the Little Creep a name, as he requested when they first met. Snufkin names the Creep 'Teety-Woo' and "the Little Creep stared at him with yellow eyes in the firelight. It thought its name over, tasted it, listened to it, crawled inside it, and finally turned its nose to the sky and softly howled its new name, so sadly and ecstatically that Snufkin felt a shiver along his back" (Jansson, 1964/2010, p. 12). The illustration above this description shows the newly-named Teety-Woo, void of surroundings, stretched upright, eyes cast skyward, mouth open as if howling. After this moment in the story, Teety-Woo disappears to Snufkin's surprise and chagrin. The next page shows Snufkin alone and void of surroundings except the rock he sits on. Under his distinctive wide-brimmed and crumpled hat, Snufkin's expression is forlorn and bewildered. Though Jansson presents Snufkin or Teety-Woo alone in five of the seven images in this story, only this sixth image conveys a loneliness in being alone. Snufkin's form indicates a completive posture, with his hands folded in his lap and his shapeless clothing covering all but his feet and face. His gaze is cast on the reader, as if he may be hoping for direction and reassurance from an outside source.

The closing image in this short story shows a crescent-shaped moon above pointed treetops. Perhaps this illustration is indicative of a lunar eclipse, significant in astrology and culture as a good or bad omen, depending on which traditions one follows. A lunar eclipse can only occur during a full moon, which links this closing illustration to Jansson's very first picture, before the opening of this story. The full moon depicted initially is expectant of hope and renewed energies, just as Snufkin is expectant of a new Spring Tune at the close of the story as he lays on his back, looks up at the sky, and delights in being by himself once again.

Developing Example Analysis 4

This analysis was the last I developed from Jansson's short story. Throughout my readings and re-readings, I made notes about Jansson's illustrations, but the details and connections I propose here came after careful and systematic consideration of the drawings. When looking closely at art, I begin by asking myself three questions: What do I see? What do I think? What do I feel? Principles of visual literacy (i.e., how we read images; see Bang, 2000; Kress & van Leeuwen, 2006) influence how I understand the parts and wholes of images in illustration. Not surprisingly, as I make observations, I develop questions and thoughts about the images I see. These questions and thoughts cause me to look more closely at what I see and respond to and interpret my questions and ideas. With illustration (opposed to some other forms of visual art), the accompanying text provides great insights and directions for interpretation. As I make sense of my observations and questions about illustrations I see, I revisit textual accompaniments to better understand an author/illustrator's verbal/visual messages.

From Commentary to Comment

I followed similar nonlinear processes through all three analyses: developing a comment, locating support in the texts, checking my logic, then further developing the comment, adding support, and again checking my logic. I selected quotes from Jansson's (1964/2010) text to frame each of my analyses. Identifying parts of the original text related to the ideas I present in my analyses helped me solidly anchor my analyses in the original text. I drafted introductory and concluding paragraphs with the goal of tracing my thinking and following my connections. I considered potential objections to my interpretations and added comments to address some counter-interpretations. I reread my analyses for logical development, cohesion, and flow. Then, I asked other readers to read and comment on my work. I revised my writing to address their questions and concerns, then checked for coherence and corrected typographical errors.

Concluding Thoughts

Literary analysis is complex and nonlinear. These understandings of 'The Spring Tune' developed over time, with my attention vacillating between details and broader strokes of this story and supporting texts (i.e., the myth of Prometheus and Io, Freud's dream interpretation framework, texts about literary analysis, visual messages in illustration, etc. in these examples). Formalizing a literary comment, with sufficient support from both the original text and supporting sources, is a challenging undertaking that caused me to think deeply about the story, the theories, my reading processes, and the author's writing processes.

To be sure, there are may be other possible interpretations of 'The Spring Tune'. But the purpose of this book segment is to demonstrate why it is important to move beyond sentence level comprehension of a text and provide examples of how readers might accomplish this goal. Understanding how a text fits into the landscape of literature can help readers make real-world connections with texts in their broadest conceptions. Additionally, critical readings of literature can spark new investigations into various writing structures, histories, and theories.

References

Bang, M. (2000). *Picture this: How pictures work.* San Francisco, CA: Chronicle Books.

Daly, K.N. (1992/2009). *Greek and Roman mythology A to Z.* (3rd ed. Revised by Marian Rengel). New York, NY: Chelsea House Publishers.

Diaz de Chumacerio, C.L. (1990). Songs of the countertransference in psychotherapy dyads. *The American Journal of Psychoanalysis*, 50 (1), 75-89.

Dimitriadis, G. & Kamberelis, G. (2006). 'Sigmund Freud'. *Theory for education.* New York, NY: Routledge.

Eagleton, T. (2008). *Literary Theory: An Introduction.* Minneapolis, MN: University of Minnesota Press.

Freud, S. (1900). *The interpretation of dreams.* Available online at http://psychclassics.yorku.ca/Freud/Dreams/dreams.pdf.

Freud, S. (1916/2001). 'Sigmund Freud'. In Rice, P., & Waugh, P. (Eds.). *Modern literary theory.* New York, NY: Bloomsbury.

Hamilton, E. (1942/2011). *Mythology: Timeless tales of gods and heroes.* New York, NY: Grand Central Publishing.

Iser, W. (1974). *The Implied Reader.* Baltimore, MD: John Hopkins University Press.

Jansson, T. (1964/2010). The Spring Tune. In *Tales of Moominvalley* (pp. 3-16). (T. Warburton, Trans.) New York, NY: Square Fish. (Original work published 1962)

Kress, G. & van Leeuwen, T. (2006). *Reading images: The grammar of visual design* (2nd ed.). New York, NY: Routledge.

Meyer, M. (1999). *The Bedford introduction to literature: Reading, thinking, and writing.* New York, NY: St. Martin Press.

Rand, N., & Torok, M. (1993). Questions to Freudian psychoanalysis: Dream interpretation, reality, fantasy. *Critical Inquiry*, 19 (3), 567-94.

Rice, P., & Waugh, P. (Eds.). (2001). *Modern literary theory.* New York, NY: Bloomsbury.

Rosenblatt, L. (1994/1978). *The reader, the text, the poem: The transactional theory of the literary work (*2nd ed.). Carbondale, IL: Southern Illinois University Press.

CHAPTER 09 | APPENDIX

Exploring Story. For this assignment, you will compare and contrast a selection of folktales using this form.

ELEMENTS OF NARRATIVE FICTION	ORIGINAL VERSION	ILLUSTRATED VERSION 1800-1899	NEWER VERSION 1900-1999	NEWEST VERSION 2000-PRESENT
PLOT DEVELOPMENT				
CHARACTERS				
SETTING				
STYLE & PERSPECTIVE				

APPENDIX

ELEMENTS OF NARRATIVE ILLUSTRATION	ORIGINAL VERSION	ILLUSTRATED VERSION 1800-1899	NEWER VERSION 1900-1999	NEWEST VERSION 2000-PRESENT
EXECUTION OF ARTISTIC TECHNIQUE				
PICTORAL INTERPRETATION OF STORY OR THEME				
DELINEATION OF PLOT, THEME, CHARACTERS, SETTING, MOOD THROUGH PICTURES				
CONSIDERATION OF INTENDED AUDIENCE				

Click here to return back to Chapter 9.

CHAPTER 12 | APPENDIX (12.1)

List of objectionable words or labels and the children's and YA books in which they are found.

WORD/LABEL	BOOK 1	BOOK 2
ALIENS	Alvarez, Julia. 2009. *Return to sender*. New York, NY: Alfred A. Knopf.	Nazario, Sonia. 2006. *Enrique's journey*. New York, NY: Random House. (Figure 12.1.1) **Figure 12.1. 1** *Enrique's journey* by Sonia Nazario, 2006, New York, NY: Random House.
ATHEIST	Seidman, David. 2015. *What if i'm an atheist?: a teen's guide to exploring a life without religion*. New York, NY: Simon Pulse.	Paterson, Katherine. 1977. *Bridge to Terabithia*. New York, NY: T.Y. Crowell.
BERRY PICKERS	Fried, Marc B. 1995. *The huckleberry pickers: a raucous history of the Shawangunk Mountains*. Hensonville, NY: Black Dome Press Corp.	Williams, Sherley Anne, Carole M. Byard. 1992. *Working cotton*. San Diego, CA: Harcourt.
BITCH	O'Hara, Mary. 2007. *My friend Flicka*. London: Egmont.	Blume, Judy. 1974. *Blubber*. Scarsdale, N.Y.: Bradbury Press.

APPENDIX

WORD/LABEL	BOOK 1	BOOK 2
BOOGER	Bolger, Kevin. 2008. *Sir Fartsalot hunts the booger*. New York, NY: Razorbill.	Joyce, William. 2015. *Billy's booger: a memoir (which is a true story, which this book is)*. New York, NY: Monbot Books. (Figure 12.1.2) **Figure 12.1.2** *Billy's booger: a memoir (which is a true story, which this book is)* by William Joyce, 2015, New York, NY: Monbot Books.
BORDER JUMPERS	Cruz, Maria Colleen. 2003. *Border crossing: a novel*. Houston, TX: Piñata Books.	Tonatiuh, Duncan. 2014. *Separate is never equal: Sylvia Mendez & her family's fight for desegregation*. New York, NY: Abrams.
BURP	Goodman, Susan E., and Michael H. Slack (illustrator). 2013. *How do you burp in space?: and other tips every space tourist needs to know*. New York, NY: Bloomsbury Pub. (Figure 12.1.3)	Stangl, Jean. 2000. *What makes you cough, sneeze, burp, hiccup, blink, yawn, sweat, and shiver?* New York, NY: Franklin Watts. **Figure 12.1.3** *How do you burp in space?: and other tips every space tourist needs to know* by Susan E. Goodman and illustrated by Michael H. Slack, 2013, New York, NY: Bloomsbury Pub.
BUTT	Griffiths, Andy. 2003. *The day my butt went psycho*. New York, NY: Scholastic.	Mackler, Carolyn. 2003. *The earth, my butt, and other big, round things*. Cambridge, MA: Candlewick Press.
CACA	Behar, Joy, and Gene Barretta (illustrator). 2006. *Sheetzucacapoopoo: my kind of dog*. New York, N.Y.: Dutton Children's Books.	Toscani, Oliviero. 1998. *Cacas: the encyclopedia of poo*. Koln: Colors.

APPENDIX

WORD/LABEL	BOOK 1	BOOK 2
CAMEL JOCKEY	Jahanbin, Payman and Clifford Lyon (editor), 2010, *Camel Jockey Go Home*. Seattle, Washington: Amazon Digital Services.	Pál, Erika. 2010. *Azad's camel*. London: Frances Lincoln Children's Books.
CHRISTIAN	Philip Pullman. 2012. *His dark materials*. London: Scholastic.	Alexie, Sherman, and Ellen Forney (illustrator). 2009. *The absolutely true diary of a part-time Indian*. New York, NY: Little, Brown.
CRACKER	Smith, Patrick D. 1984. *A land remembered*. New York, NY: Penguin Group.	Rawlings, Marjorie Kinnan. n.d. *The yearling*. London: Heinemann.
CUNT	Haddon, Mark. 2003. *The curious incident of the dog in the night-time*. New York, NY: Doubleday. (Figure 12.1.4)	Kelly, Brendan. 2013. *The Runt Who Said C#nt*. Seattle, WA: Amazon Digital Services.  **Figure 12.1. 4** *The curious incident of the dog in the night-time* by Mark Haddon, 2003, New York, NY: Doubleday.
DAGO	Bondanella, Peter E. 2004. *Hollywood Italians: dagos, palookas, romeos, wise guys, and Sopranos*. New York, NY: Continuum.	Fante, John, and Valenti Angelo. 1940. *Dago red*. New York, NY: Viking Press.

APPENDIX

WORD/LABEL	BOOK 1	BOOK 2
DICK	Doherty, Meghan. 2013. *How not to be a dick: an everyday etiquette guide.* San Francisco, California: Zest Books. (Figure 12.1.5)	Levithan, David. 2003. *Boy meets boy.* New York, NY: Alfred A. Knopf. **Figure 12.1.5** *How not to be a dick: an everyday etiquette guide* by Meghan Doherty, 2013, San Francisco, California: Zest Books.
FAG	Sanchez, Alex. 2001. *Rainbow boys.* New York, NY: Simon & Schuster.	Woodson, Jacqueline. 1995. *From the notebooks of Melanin Sun.* New York, NY: Blue Sky Press.
FART	O'Neil, J. B. 2013. *Ninja farts: silent but deadly.* Vestal, NY: J.J. Fast Publishing.	Dawson, Jim. 1999. *Who cut the cheese?: a cultural history of the fart.* Berkeley, Calif: Ten Speed
FEMINIST	Schatz, Kate, and Miriam Klein Stahl. 2015. *Rad American women A-Z.* San Francisco, Calif: City Lights Books.	Cole, Babette. 1987/2005. *Princess Smartypants.* New York, NY: Putnam.
FUCK	Dawe, Ted. 2012. *Into the river.* [Auckland, N.Z.]: M.U.P.	Conaghan, Brian. 2014. *When Mr. Dog bites.* New York, NY: Bloomsbury. (Figure 12.1.6) **Figure 12.1.6** *When Mr. Dog bites* by Brian Conaghan, 2014, New York, NY: Bloomsbury.
HOMO	Bauer, Marion Dane. 1994. *Am I blue?: coming out from the silence.* New York, NY: HarperCollins.	Chbosky, Stephen. 1999. *The perks of being a wallflower.* New York, NY: Pocket.

APPENDIX

WORD/LABEL	BOOK 1	BOOK 2
ILLEGALS	Nazario, Sonia. 2006. *Enrique's journey*. New York, NY: Random House.	Mateo, José Manuel, and Javier Martínez Pedro. 2014. *Migrant: the journey of a Mexican worker*. New York, NY: Abrams.
INDIAN	Lenski, Lois. 1941. *Indian captive: the story of Mary Jemison*. New York, NY: Frederick A. Stokes Co.	Wilder, Laura Ingalls, and Garth Williams (illustrator). 1953. *Little house on the prairie*. New York, NY: Harper & Bros.
JEW	Lowry, Lois. 1989. *Number the stars*. Boston: Houghton Mifflin Harcourt.	Zusak, Markus. 2006. *The book thief*. New York, NY: Alfred A. Knopf.
LEZ	Garden, Nancy. 1982. *Annie on my mind*. New York, NY: Farrar, Straus, Giroux.	George, Madeleine. 2012. *The difference between you and me*. New York, NY: Viking.
MUSLIM	Saeed, Aisha. 2015. *Written in the stars*. New York, NY: Penguin. (Figure 12.1.7)	Latham, Jennifer. 2015. *Scarlett undercover*. New York, NY: Little, Brown, and Company. Figure 12.1. 7 *Written in the stars* by Aisha Saeed, 2015, New York, NY: Penguin.
NAZI	Bartoletti, Susan Campbell. 2005. *Hitler Youth: growing up in Hitler's shadow*. New York, NY: Scholastic Nonfiction.	Naylor, Phyllis Reynolds. 1999. *Walker's Crossing*. New York, N.Y.: Atheneum Books for Young Readers.

APPENDIX

WORD/LABEL	BOOK 1	BOOK 2
NIGGER	Shakur, Sanyika. 1993. *Monster: the autobiography of an L.A. gang member*. New York, NY: Atlantic Monthly Press.	Myers, Walter Dean, and Christopher Myers (illustrator). 1999. *Monster*. New York, N.Y.: HarperCollins Publishers.
PEE PEE	Willems, Mo. 2003. *Time to pee!* New York, NY: Hyperion Books for Children.	Marciuliano, Francesco. 2012. *I could pee on this: and other poems by cats*. San Francisco: Chronicle Books.
PENIS/PRICK	Honowitz, Stacey. 2010. *Genius with a penis, don't touch!* Indianapolis, IN: Dog Ear Publishing.	Green, John, and David Levithan. 2010. *Will Grayson, Will Grayson*. New York, NY: Dutton. (Figure 12.1.8) **Figure 12.1.8** *Will Grayson, Will Grayson* by John Green and David Levithan, 2010, New York, NY: Dutton.
POLAK/POLACK	Wilde, Larry. 1983. *The absolutely last official Polish joke book*. Toronto, CA: Bantam.	Krech, Bob. 2006. *Rebound*. New York, NY: Marshall Cavendish.
POO POO	Blake, Stephanie. 2011. Poo bum. Wellington, N.Z.: Gecko Press.	Gomi, Tarō. 1993. *Everyone poops*. Brooklyn, N.Y.: Kane/Miller Book Publishers.
REDSKIN	Alexie, Sherman, and Ellen Forney (illustrator). 2007. *The absolutely true diary of a part-time Indian*. New York, NY: Little, Brown.	Red Hawk, Richard. 1988. *A, B, C's: the American Indian way*. Sacramento, Calif: Sierra Oaks Pub. Co.

WORD/LABEL	BOOK 1	BOOK 2
SAND NIGGER	Barua, Bula. 2011. *Sand Nigga A Collection of Stories*. Authorhouse.	Joseph, Lawrence. 2005. *Codes, precepts, biases and taboos: poems, 1973-1993*. New York, NY: Farrar, Straus and Giroux.
SKINHEAD	Picciolini, Christian. 2015. *Romantic violence: memoirs of an American skinhead*. Chicago, IL: Goldmill Group.	Jacobs, Evan. 2015. *Skinhead Birdy*. Costa Mesa, CA: Saddleback.
SNOT	Cronin, Doreen, and Renata Liwska (illustrator). 2014. *Boom, Snot, Twitty*. New York, NY: Penguin. (Figure 12.1.9)	Krulik, Nancy, and Aaron Blecha. 2015. *'Snot funny!* New York, NY: Grossett & Dunlap. Figure 12.1.9 *Boom, Snot, Twitty* by Doreen Cronin and illustrated by Renata Liwska, 2014, New York, NY: Penguin.
SPIC	Cisneros, Sandra. 1991. *The house on Mango Street*. New York, NY: Vintage Books. (Figure 12.1.10)	Medina, Meg. 2013. *Yaqui Delgado wants to kick your ass*. Somerville, Mass: Candlewick Press. Figure 12.1.10 *The house on Mango Street* by Sandra Cisneros, 1991, New York, NY: Vintage Books.
TERRORIST	Satrapi, Marjane. 2003. *Persepolis*. New York, NY: Pantheon Books.	Vaughan, Brian K., Niko Henrichon, and Todd Klein. 2006. *Pride of Baghdad*. New York, NY: DC Comics.

WORD/LABEL	BOOK 1	BOOK 2
TINKLE	Lansky, Bruce, Robert Pottle, and Anne Catharine Blake (illustrator). 2005. *Tinkle, tinkle, little tot: songs and rhymes for toilet training.* Minnetonka, Minn: Meadowbrook Press.	Richman, Josh, and Anish Sheth. 2009. *What's my pee telling me?* San Francisco, CA: Chronicle Books.
TITS	Mark Monmonier. 2006. *From Squaw Tit to Whorehouse Meadow: How Maps Name, Claim, and Inflame.* University of Chicago Press.	Murdock, Catherine Gilbert. 2006. *Dairy queen: a novel.* Boston: Houghton Mifflin. (Figure 12.1.11) 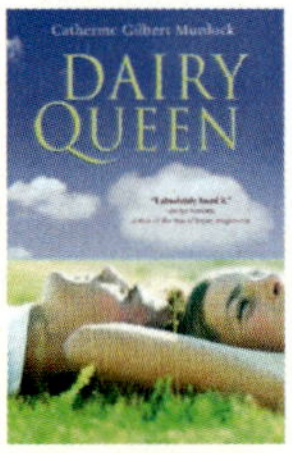 **Figure 12.1. 11** *Dairy queen: a novel* by Catherine Gilbert Murdock, 2006, Boston, MA: Houghton Mifflin.
TRANS	Peters, Julie Anne. 2004. *Luna: a novel.* New York, NY: Little, Brown.	Wittlinger, Ellen. 2007. *Parrotfish.* New York, NY: Simon & Schuster Books for Young Readers.
TWAT	Conaghan, Brian. 2014. *When Mr. Dog bites.* New York, NY: Bloomsbury.	Wilson, Jacqueline, and Nick Sharratt (illustrator) 2008. *My sister Jodie.* London: Doubleday.
VAGINA	Blume, Judy. 1975. *Forever ...: a novel.* Scarsdale, N.Y.: Bradbury Press.	Saltz, Gail, and Lynne Woodcock Cravath. 2005. *Amazing you: getting smart about your private parts.* New York, NY: Dutton Children's Books.

APPENDIX

WORD/LABEL	BOOK 1	BOOK 2
WETBACK	Birdseye, Tom. 1993. *Just call me stupid*. New York, NY: Holiday House. (Figure 12.1.12)	Beatty, Patricia. 1981. *Lupita Mañana*. New York, NY: Morrow. 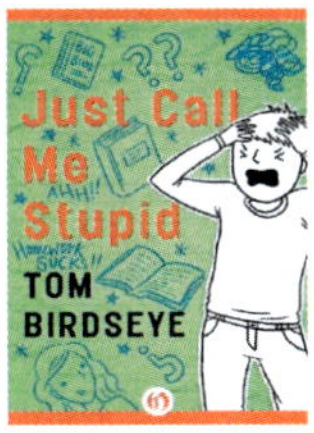 **Figure 12.1. 12** *Just call me stupid* by Tom Birdseye, 1993, New York, NY: Holiday House.
WHORE	Dahl, Roald, and Quentin Blake (illustrator). 1982. *Roald Dahl's Revolting rhymes*. New York, NY: Knopf.	Lee, Harper. 1960. *To kill a mockingbird*. Philadelphia, PA: Lippincott.
WITCH	Speare, Elizabeth George. 1958. *The witch of Blackbird Pond*. Boston, MA: Houghton Mifflin.	Schanzer, Rosalyn. 2011. *Witches!: the absolutely true tale of disaster in Salem*. Washington, D.C.: National Geographic Society.
WIZARD	Rowling, J. K., and Mary GrandPré. 1998. *Harry Potter and the sorcerer's stone*. New York, NY: A.A. Levine Books.	Baum, L. Frank, and W. W. Denslow (illustrator). 1956. *The Wizard of Oz*. Chicago, IL: Reilly & Lee.
YANK	Nathan, Amy. 2001. *Yankee doodle gals: women pilots of World War II*. Washington, D.C.: National Geographic Society.	Rodman, Mary Ann. 2004. *Yankee girl*. New York, NY: Farrar, Straus and Giroux. (Figure 12.1.13)  **Figure 12.1. 13** *Yankee girl* by Mary Ann Rodman, 2004, New York, NY: Farrar, Straus and Giroux.

CHAPTER 12 | APPENDIX (12.8)

Ratings systems for fanfiction, movies, television, music, and video games.

To date, books do not come with warning labels or content descriptors. Nor are they subject to a ratings system such as those used with television, movies, video games or fan fiction (see the following pages for other ratings systems).

APPENDIX

ENTERTAINMENT SOFTWARE RATINGS

The Entertainment Software Rating Board (ESRB) developed ratings for the content in video games and apps. (Retrieved from http://www.esrb.org/ratings/ratings_guide.jsp)

EARLY CHILDHOOD
Content is intended for young children.

EVERYONE
Content is generally suitable for all ages. May contain minimal cartoon, fantasy or mild violence and/or infrequent use of mild language.

EVERYONE 10+
Content is generally suitable for ages 10 and up. May contain more cartoon, fantasy or mild violence, mild language and/or minimal suggestive themes.

TEEN
Content is generally suitable for ages 13 and up. May contain violence, suggestive themes, crude humor, minimal blood, simulated gambling and/or infrequent use of strong language.)

MATURE
Content is generally suitable for ages 17 and up. May contain intense violence, blood and gore, sexual content and/or strong language.

ADULTS ONLY
Content suitable only for adults ages 18 and up. May include prolonged scenes of intense violence, graphic sexual content and/or gambling with real currency.

The Recording Industry Association of America has provided record companies and artists with labeling tools that alert parents to explicit content (https://www.riaa.com/toolsforparents.php?content_selector=parental_advisory)

- PAL: Parental Advisory Logo

TELEVISION RATINGS

The television industry designed a ratings system regarding the content and age-appropriateness of TV programs. (Retrieved from http://www.tvguidelines.org/ratings.htm)

TVY — ALL CHILDREN

This program is designed to be appropriate for all children. Whether animated or live-action, the themes and elements in this program are specifically designed for a very young audience, including children from ages 2-6. This program is not expected to frighten younger children.

TVY7 — DIRECTED TO OLDER CHILDREN

This program is designed for children age 7 and above. It may be more appropriate for children who have acquired the developmental skills needed to distinguish between make-believe and reality. Themes and elements in this program may include mild fantasy violence or comedic violence, or may frighten children under the age of 7. Therefore, parents may wish to consider the suitability of this program for their very young children.

TVG — GENERAL AUDIENCE

Most parents would find this program suitable for all ages. Although this rating does not signify a program designed specifically for children, most parents may let younger children watch this program unattended. It contains little or no violence, no strong language and little or no sexual dialogue or situations.

TVPG — PARENTAL GUIDANCE SUGGESTED

This program contains material that parents may find unsuitable for younger children. Many parents may want to watch it with their younger children. The theme itself may call for parental guidance and/or the program may contain one or more of the following: some suggestive dialogue (D), infrequent coarse language (L), some sexual situations (S), or moderate violence (V).

TV14 — PARENTS STRONGLY CAUTIONED

This program contains some material that many parents would find unsuitable for children under 14 years of age. Parents are strongly urged to exercise greater care in monitoring this program and are cautioned against letting children under the age of 14 watch unattended. This program may contain one or more of the following: intensely suggestive dialogue (D), strong coarse language (L), intense sexual situations (S), or intense violence (V).

TVMA — MATURE AUDIENCE ONLY

This program is specifically designed to be viewed by adults and therefore may be unsuitable for children under 17. This program may contain one or more of the following: crude indecent language (L), explicit sexual activity (S), or graphic violence (V).

MOTION PICTURE RATINGS

The Motion Picture Association of America rates films as follows (Retrieved from http://www.mpaa.org/film-ratings/):

G — GENERAL AUDIENCES

Nothing that would offend parents for viewing by children.

PG — PARENTAL GUIDANCE

Parents urged to give "parental guidance." May contain some materials parents might not like for their young children.

PG13 — PARENTS STRONGLY CAUTIONED

Parents are urged to be cautious. Some materials maybe inappropriate for pre-teenagers.

R — RESTRICTED

Contains some adult material. Parents are urged to learn more about the film before taking their young children with them.

NC17 — NO ONE 17 AND UNDER ADMITTED

Clearly adult.
Children are not admitted.

FICTION RATINGS

On fanfiction.net uses the ratings system from fictionratings.com. The criteria are as follows (Retrieved from https://www.fictionratings.com/):

K — FOR KIDS
Suitable for all ages
(Equivalent to a G-Rating or a U in Britain)

K+ — FOR OLDER KIDS
Suitable for children 9 and older
(Equivalent to a PG-Rating)

T — FOR TEEN
Suitable for teens 13 and older
(Equivalent to a PG-13Rating or a 12A in Britain or a M Rating in Australia)

M — FOR MATURE
Suitable for teens 16 and older
(Equivalent to anR-Rating or a 15 in Britain or a MA15+ Rating in Australia)

MA — FOR MATURE ADULTS
Limited only to adults 18 and older
(Equivalent to an NC-17 Rating or a 18 in Britain or a R Rating in Australia)

List of Figures

Figure i. Bethany's reading about dirty dogs before naptime. Copyright 2002 by Jenifer Schneider.

Figure ii. Mary's reading before bedtime. Copyright 2011 by Jenifer Schneider.

Figure iii. Troy is my "fox" in socks. Copyright 2003 by Jenifer Schneider.

Figure iv. The girls love to "hop on their pop!" They also love to read with their pop. Copyright 2003 by Jenifer Schneider.

Figure v. My mom and dad with me. Copyright 1968 by Al Scanio.

Figure vi. *Inside, Outside, Upside Down* by Stan and Jan Berenstain, 1968, New York, NY: Random House. Copyright 1968 Stan and Jan Berenstain.

Figure vii. Hanging out in my bookpen. Copyright 1969 by Zygmunt Jasinski.

Figure viii. My dad in role as "Iggy." Copyright 1976 by Jenifer Jasinski.

Figure ix. Ohio State doctoral students meet with Jeanne Chall in 1994. Copyright unknown.

Figure x. Got butterbeer? Escaping into The Wizarding World of Harry Potter™. Copyright 2010 by Troy Schneider.

Figure xi. The members of the Media Innovation Team at the University of South Florida. Copyright 2015 by William Tillis.

Figure xii. Just like Olivia, the Literacy Studies doctoral students wear me out. But I love them anyway! Illustration from *Olivia,* by Ian Falconer, 2000, New York, NY: Simon & Schuster. Copyright 2000 by Ian Falconer. Reprinted with permission.

Chapter 1

Figure 1.1. A classic image from *The Polar Express,* by Chris Van Allsburg, 1983, New York, NY: Scholastic. Copyright 1983 by Chris Van Allsburg.

Figure 1.2. If you haven't read G. Neri's books, give them a try. Cover art from *Ghetto Cowboy* by G. Neri and illustrated by Jesse Joshua Watson, 2013, New York, NY: Candlewick Press. Copyright 2013 by Jesse Joshua Watson.

Figure 1.3. Explore newer books. *Hana Hashimoto, Sixth Violin* by Chieri Uegaki and illustrated by Qin Leng, 2014, Toronto, CA: Kids Can Press. Copyright 2014 by Qin Leng.

Figure 1.4. A wonderful book, perfect for reading aloud. *Ida B... and Her Plans to Maximize Fun, Avoid Disaster, and Save the World* by Katherine Hannigan and cover illustration by Dana Tezarr, 2004, New York, NY: Greenwillow/HarperCollins. Copyright 2004 by Greenwillow/HarperCollins.

Figure 1.5. Peter H. Reynolds' *The Dot* demonstrates how small moments can make significant changes to a child's life. *The Dot* by Peter H. Reynolds, 2003, New York, NY: Candlewick Press. Copyright 2003 by Peter H. Reynolds.

Figure 1.6. The waiting room at the office of Gerald Copeland, D.D.S., Tampa, FL. Copyright 2015 by Jenifer Jasinski Schneider.

Figure 1.7. One example of the big business impact on children's books is found in The Walt Disney Company. For an overview of the Disney industry, Jim Fanning's *The Disney Book* provides visual highlights and an historical synopsis. *The Disney Book*, by Jim Fanning, 2015, New York, NY: DK. Copyright 2015 by Disney.

Figure 1.8. Explore what can happen when boys love dolls. *William's Doll* by Charlotte Zolotow and illustrated by William Pene du Bois, 1972, New York, NY: Harper & Row. Copyright 1972 by William Pene du Bois.

Figure 1.9. If you think children's books are "easy," think again. One example of young adult fiction with complex plots and characters is *A Wrinkle In Time* by Madeleine L'Engle, 1962, New York, NY: Farrar, Straus, and Giroux. Cover illustration copyright 1979 by Leo and Diane Dillon.

Figure 1.10. With thousands of children's and young adult books published each year, it's important to know how to select books. Copyright 2015 by Jenifer Jasinski Schneider.

Figure 1.11. Avatars of the Media Innovation Team who created the visual media and graphic designs in this book. Copyright 2015 by William Tillis.

Figure 1.12. What would you rather read? *Dick and Jane* by William S. Gray and illustrated by Zerna Sharp, 2004, New York, NY: Grosset & Dunlap. Copyright 2004 by Zerna Sharp. *Leonardo the Terrible Monster* by Mo Willems, 2005, New York, NY: Hyperion. Copyright 2005 by Mo Willems.

Chapter 2

Figure 2.1. Dorothy Kunhardt's *Pat the Bunny* is a classic example of a predictable baby book in which the content, layout, illustration, and language are designed to match young children's developmental levels. *Pat the Bunny* by Dorothy Kunhardt, 1940/2001, New York, NY: Golden Books. Copyright 1940 by Dorothy Kunhardt.

Figure 2.2. The McGuffey Readers were a popular series beginning in the early 1800's and used until the 1950's. *McGuffey's Second Eclectic Reader (revised edition)* by William H. McGuffey, 1879, Van Antwerp, Bragg & Co. (https://archive.org/stream/mcguff2ndeclreader02mcguf#page/n3/mode/2up).

Figure 2.3. Current basal readers include "real" children's literature in their collections. The publishers rewrite the stories, controlling for content and embedding vocabulary words. *Treasures* by Macmillan/McGraw-Hill, 2011, New York, NY: Macmillan/McGraw-Hill. Copyright 2011 by Macmillan/McGraw-Hill.

Figure 2.4. *A Game of Thrones* by George R. R. Martin, 1996, New York, NY: Random House. Cover art copyright 2011 by Bantam Books.

Figure 2.5. *The Kite Runner* by Khaled Hosseini, 2003, New York, NY: The Berkeley Publishing Group. Cover art copyright 2003 by Honi Werner.

Figure 2.6. *Unspoken: A Story from the Underground Railroad* by Henry Cole, 2012, New York, NY: Scholastic. Copyright 2012 by Henry Cole.

Figure 2.7. A full-page spread from *Unspoken: A Story from the Underground Railroad* by Henry Cole, 2012, New York, NY: Scholastic. Copyright 2012 by Henry Cole.

Figure 2.8. Panel illustrations from *Unspoken: A Story from the Underground Railroad* by Henry Cole, 2012, New York, NY: Scholastic. Copyright 2012 by Henry Cole.

Figure 2.9. *The Littlest Bitch* by David Quinn and Michael Davis, illustrated by Devon Devereaux, 2010, Portland, ME: Sellers Publishing. Cover art copyright 2010 by Devon Devereaux.

Figure 2.10. Gutenberg invented movable type printing around 1439 and children's books evolved alongside changes in the printing process. Although not the very first children's book, *A Little Pretty Pocket Book* was an influential publication. *A Little Pretty Pocket Book* by John Newbery, 1744, Worcester, MA: Isaiah Thomas. Copyright expired.

Figure 2.11. *Don't Let the Pigeon Run This App* by Mo Willems and you, 2011, Glendale, CA: Disney Enterprises Inc. Cover art copyright 2011 by Disney Enterprises Inc.

Figure 2.12. *Grump, Groan, Growl* by bell hooks and illustrated by Chris Raschka, 2008, New York, NY: Disney-Hyperion. Cover art copyright 2008 by Chris Raschka.

Figure 2.13. *Hitler Youth: Growing Up in Hitler's Shadow* by Susan Campbell Bartoletti, 2005, New York, NY: Scholastic. Copyright 2005 by Susan Campbell Bartoletti.

Figure 2.14. *Marcel the Shell: The Most Surprised I've Ever Been* by Dean Fleischer-Camp and Jenny Slate, 2014, New York, NY: Razorbill. Copyright 2014 by Dean Fleischer-Camp.

Figure 2.15. *The Death of the Hat: A Brief History of Poetry in 50 Objects* by Paul B. Janeczko and Illustrated by Chris Raschka, 2015, New York, NY: Candlewick. Cover art copyright 2015 by Chris Raschka.

Figure 2.16. *Maps* by Aleksandra Mizielinski and Daniel Mizielinski, 2013, New York, NY: Big Picture Press. Copyright 2013 by Aleksandra Mizielinski and Daniel Mizielinski.

Figure 2. 17. *The Borrowers* by Mary Norton and illustrated by Beth Krush and Joe Krush, 1953, New York, NY: Harcourt Brace. Cover art copyright 1953 by Beth Krush and Joe Krush.

Figure 2.18. *Where the Sidewalk Ends* by Shel Silverstein, 1974, New York, NY: Harper & Row Publishers. Copyright 1974 by Shel Silverstein.

Figure 2.19. *Matilda* by Roald Dahl and illustrated by Quentin Blake, 1988, New York, NY: Penguin. Cover art copyright 1988 by Quentin Blake.

Figure 2.20. *From Seed to Plant* by Gail Gibbons, 1993, New York, NY: Holiday House. Copyright 1993 by Gail Gibbons.

Figure 2.21. *No, David!* by David Shannon, 1998, New York, NY: Blue Sky Press. Copyright 1998 by David Shannon.

Figure 2.22. *I am Malala: The Girl Who Stood Up for Education and Was Shot by the Taliban* by Malala Yousafzai and Christina Lamb, 2013, New York, NY: Little, Brown and Company. Copyright 2013 by Malala Yousafzai and Christina Lamb.

Figure 2.23. *Jumanji* by Chris Van Allsburg, 1981, New York, NY: Houghton Mifflin Harcourt. Copyright 1981 by Chris Van Allsburg.

Figure 2.24. *Encyclopedia Prehistorica Dinosaurs: The Definitive Pop-Up* by Robert Sabuda and Matthew Reinhart, 2005, New York, NY: Candlewich. Copyright 2005 by Robert Sabuda and Matthew Reinhart.

Figure 2.25. *It's a Book* by Lane Smith, 2010, New York, NY: Roaring Brook Press. Copyright 2010 by Lane Smith.

Figure 2.26. *Peter Pan: The Boy Who Wouldn't Grow Up* by J.M. Barrie, 1904, London, England: Hodder & Stoughton. Copyright 1988 by Great Ormond Street Hospital.

Figure 2.27. The Fault in Our Stars by John Green, 2012, New York, NY: Penguin. Copyright 2012 by John Green.

Figure 2.28. *Guys Write for Guys Read* edited by Jon Scieszka, 2005, New York, NY: Viking Press. Copyright 2005 by Jon Scieszka.

Figure 2.29. Delores Huerta: A Hero to Migrant Workers by Sarah Warren and illustrated by Robert Casilla, 2012, Seattle, WA: Two Lions. Cover art copyright 2012 by Robert Casilla.

Figure 2.30. *Mr. Happy* by Roger Hargreaves, 1971, London, England: Price Stern Sloan. Copyright 1971 by Roger Hargreaves.

Figure 2.31. *Sad Underwear and Other Complications* by Judith Viorst and illustrated by Richard Hull, 2000, New York, NY: Antheneum. Cover art copyright 2000 by Richard Hull.

Figure 2.32. *Scary Stories to Tell in the Dark* by Alvin Schwartz and illustrated by Stephen Gammell, 1981, New York, NY: Scholastic. Cover art copyright 1981 by Stephen Gammell.

Figure 2.33. *Babymouse #14: Mad Scientist* by Jennifer Holm and illustrated by Matthew Holm, 2011, New York, NY: Random House Books for Young Readers. Cover art copyright 2011 by Matthew Holm.

Figure 2.34. *Locomotive* by Brian Floca, 2013, New York, NY: Atheneum Books for Young Readers. Copyright 2013 by Brian Floca.

Figure 2.35 An Italian translation of Aesop's Fables was published as *Aesopus Moralisatus* by Bernardino di Benalli, 1485, Venezia, Italy. Copyright 1485 by Bernardino di Benalli. The book is available for viewing at https://en.wikipedia.org/wiki/Aesop%27s_Fables#/media/File:Aesopus_-_Aesopus_moralisatus,_circa_1485_-_2950804_Scan00010.tif.

Figure 2.36. *Abckiria* is the first children's book in Finnish, written by Bishop Michael Agricola (c. 1510-1557), 1559, Helsinki, Finnland: Finnish Literature Society. Copyright 1559 by Michael Agricola. The complete book is available for viewing at http://www.childrenslibrary.org/icdl/BookPreview?bookid=agrabck_00070001&route=advanced_327_326_0_English_0_all&lang=English&msg=&ilang=English.

Figure 2.37. Johannes Amos Comenius' *Orbis Pictus*, 1657, is widely considered to be the first picturebook school book (Comenius, 1896). *Orbis Pictus* by Johannes Amos Comenius, 1685, London, England: Charles Mearne. Copyright 1685 by Johannes Amos Comenius. The 1728 edition is available for viewing at http://www.gutenberg.org/files/28299/28299-h/28299-h.htm.

Figure 2.38. *The Catechism of Nature for the Use of Children* by Dr. Martinet was published in 1793. Figure 2.38 is an English version translated from Dutch. *The Catechism of Nature for the Use of Children* by Dr. Martinet, 1793, Boston, MA: Young and Etheridge. Copyright 1793 by Doctor Martinet.

Figure 2.39. *A Description of Three Hundred Animals* by Thomas Boreman, 1730, London, England: Thomas Boreman. Copyright 1730 by Thomas Boreman.

Figure 2.40. Image from *Tommy Thumb's Pretty Song Book* by Mary Cooper, 1788, Worcester, MA: Isaiah Thomas. Copyright 1744 by Mary Cooper.

Figure 2.41. John Newbery published A Little Pretty Pocket-Book Intended for the Instruction and Amusement of Little Master Tommy and Pretty Miss Polly in 1744. Image from A Little Pretty Pocket-Book Intended for the Instruction and Amusement of Little Master Tommy and Pretty Miss Polly by John Newbery, 1770, London, England: Newbery and Carnan.

Figure 2.42. *The Adventures of Robinson Crusoe* written by Daniel Defoe and illustrated by Paul Adolphe Kauffman, 1884, London, England: T. Fisher Unwin. Cover art copyright 1884 by Paul Adolphe Kauffman. The book is available for viewing at http://www.childrenslibrary.org/icdl/BookPage?bookid=defthea_00360697&pnum1=1&twoPage=false&route=advanced_329_326_0_English_0_all&size=0&fullscreen=false&lang=English&ilang=English.

Figure 2.43. *El Capitán* by Liliana Santirso and illustrated by Patricio Gómez, 1998, Mexico: Celta Amaquemecan. Cover art copyright 1998 by Patrico Gómez. The book is available for viewing at http://www.childrenslibrary.org/icdl/BookPreview?bookid=sntcptn_00160004&route=advanced_335_326_0_English_0_all&lang=English&msg=&ilang=English.

Figure 2.44. *All We Need Are Dragons* by Ljubivoje Ršumović and illustrated by Dušan Petričić, 1990, Serbia: Rad. Cover art copyright 1990 by Rad. The book is available for viewing at http://www.childrenslibrary.org/icdl/BookPreview?bookid=rsujosn_00380094&route=advanced_335_326_0_English_0_all&lang=English&msg=&ilang=English.

Figure 2.45. *Intik'a: How the Taquileo island was not an island but a very tall mountain that was called Intik'a* by Cronwell Jara Jiménez, 1995, Lima, Peru: Ironyodla. Copyright 1995 by Cronwell Jara Jiménez. The book is available for viewing at http://www.childrenslibrary.org/icdl/BookPreview?bookid=jarinti_00510025&route=advanced_335,389_326,359_0_English_0_all&lang=English&msg=&ilang=English.

Figure 2.46. *Mbegu Ya Ajabu* (The Amazing Seed) by Deus. M. Richard, 1997, Kenya: Sasa Sema. Copyright 1997 by Readit Books. The book is available for viewing at http://www.childrenslibrary.org/icdl/BookPreview?bookid=ricmbeg_00590008&route=advanced_335,380_326,359_0_English_0_all&lang=English&msg=&ilang=English.

Chapter 3

Figure 3.1. Reading lesson in segregated African American elementary school in Washington, D.C., by Marjory Collins, 1942. Library of Congress Prints and Photographs Division Washington, D.C. 20540 USA. No known restrictions.

Figure 3.2 The oldest known library in the world is in Ebla, Syria, 2008. Photograph by Effi Schweizer. Reprinted with permission.

Figure 3.3 Excerpt of catalog from the Old North Church, 1752. Photograph by Percival Merritt. The parochial library of the eighteenth century in Christ Church, Boston. Boston: Merrymount Press, 1917. Public domain.

Figure 3.4. American Indian cultures included literate and artistic practices; yet they were ignored in favor of European trends. "The Red Child of the Forest" by Eleanor Stackhouse Atkinson in *The How and Why Library*, 1909. Public domain.

Figure 3.5. The Library Company of Philadelphia was founded in 1731 by Benjamin Franklin. Image scan of "A Short Account of the Library," in *A Catalogue of Books Belonging to the Library Company of Philadelphia* (Philadelphia: B. Franklin, 1741). No known restrictions.

Figure 3.6. An exhibit featuring Thomas Jefferson's library in the Thomas Jefferson Building at the Library of Congress in Washington, DC, 2015. Photograph by Smash the Iron Cage. Reprinted with permission.

Figure 3.7. The West Tampa Free Public Library is a Carnegie Library built in 1913. The library continues to serve the West Tampa community. Photograph by Ebyabe, 2007. Reprinted with permission.

Figure 3.8. Carnegie libraries featured large reading rooms to encourage extended visits. Carnegie Library, Coshocton, Ohio / E.W. Hart, architects, 1903. Library of Congress Prints and Photographs Division Washington, D.C. 20540 USA. No known restrictions.

Figure 3.9. Librarians frequently debated library design. Competitive design for the New York Public Library / Brite & Bacon, architects, 1897. Library of Congress Prints and Photographs Division Washington, D.C. 20540 USA. No known restrictions.

Figure 3.10. View of library with stacks and skylight by George Gardner Rockwood, 1832-1911. Image scan of Robert N. Dennis collection of stereoscopic views. Stephen A. Schwarzman Building / Photography Collection, Miriam and Ira D. Wallach Division of Art, Prints and Photographs. Public domain.

Figure 3.11. Library patrons agreed to follow the rules and often signed certificates of character, which were intended to guarantee the return of books. Rules for Public Library, Hertfordshire, 1930. No known restrictions.

Figure 3.12 African-American children line up outside of Albemarle Region bookmobile. Colored Children's Library [sic], North Carolina Digital Collections, 1950s. No known restrictions.

Figure 3.13 Branch libraries segregated immigrant populations. Art and Picture Collection, The New York Public Library. *[Interior of the Aguilar Library, Lower East side, ca. 1898.]* Public domain.

Figure 3.14 When we think about libraries, we think about open stacks. In the late 1800s and early 1900s, librarians pulled reading materials for patrons. Children were not the priority. Inside the Buffalo Public Library, New York, 1900s. Public domain.

Figure 3.15 Mechanics institute and free libraries were intended to educate the working class, nd. Public domain.

Figure 3.16 Caroline Hewins is credited with creating the first children's story hour. Image of Caroline Hewins – Hartford History Center, Hartford Public Library - See more at: http://connecticuthistory.org/the-public-library-movement-caroline-hewins-makes-room-for-young-readers/#sthash.w7rJY3hV.dpuf

Figure 3.17. Library rules for the Cooper Union Reading Room, nd. Cooper Union for the Advancement of Science and Art. No known restrictions.

Figure 3.18. Anne Carroll Moore, nd, was hired by the Pratt Institute and she altered the library program to secure services for children. No known restrictions.

Figure 3.19 Anne Carroll Moore was a pioneering librarian. Her story is told in a children's book: *Miss Moore Thought Otherwise: How Anne Carroll Moore Created Libraries for Children* by Jan Pinborough and illustrated by Debby Atwell, 2013, New York, NY: HMH Books for Young Readers. Copyright 2013 by Debby Atwell.

Figure 3.20. The reading room for the Peter Pan Collection at the Great Ormond Street Hospital. Copyright 2015 by Jenifer Schneider.

Figure 3.21 Original program artwork for the performance of *Peter Pan* by J.M. Barrie, 1904, London, England: Hodder & Stoughton. Copyright 1988 by Great Ormond Street Hospital. Copyright 2015 by Jenifer Schneider.

Figure 3.22 *Peter Pan* memorabilia in the Peter Pan Collection at the Great Ormond Street Hospital. Copyright 2015 by Jenifer Schneider.

Figure 3.23 Programs from various *Peter Pan* pantomimes are available in the Peter Pan Collection at the Great Ormond Street Hospital. Copyright 2015 by Jenifer Schneider.

Figure 3.24 Inkwood Books in Tampa, Florida. Copyright 2015 Stefani Beddingfield. Reprinted with permission.

Figure 3.25 The Roald Dahl Museum and Story Centre in Great Missendon, England is a short train ride away from London. Copyright 2015 by Jenifer Schneider.

Figure 3.26 I'm as tall as a Twit if I measure myself using the heights of characters from Roald Dahl's books. Copyright 2015 by Jenifer Schneider.

Figure 3.27 Visitors to the Roald Dahl Museum and Story Centre can walk through his writing hut! Copyright 2015 by Jenifer Schneider.

Figure 3.28 My visit to Louisa May Alcott's Orchard House. Copyright 2015 by Jenifer Schneider.

Figure 3.29 My visit to the Eric Carle Museum of Picture Book Art. Copyright 2015 by Jenifer Schneider.

Figure 3.30 The bathrooms tiles are a space for art at the Eric Carle Museum of Picture Book Art. Copyright 2015 by Jenifer Schneider.

Figure 3.31 The Mazza Museum gallery, an amazing collection of children's book illustration. Copyright 2015 by Jenifer Schneider.

Figure 3.32 Different illustrative styles and techniques are on display at the Mazza Museum. Copyright 2015 by Jenifer Schneider.

Chapter 4

Figure 4.1. *A Little Pretty Pocket Book* by John Newbery, 1744, Worcester, MA: Isaiah Thomas. Copyright 1744 by John Newbery.

Figure 4.2. The first Newbery Medal was awarded to *The Story of Mankind* by Hendrik Willem van Loon, 1922, New York, NY: Boni and Liveright. Copyright 1922 by Hendrik Willem van Loon.

Figure 4.3. Kwame Alexander won the Newbery for *The Crossover* by Kwame Alexander, 2014, New York, NY: Houghton Mifflin. Copyright 2014 by Kwame Alexander.

Figure 4.4 Randolph Caldecott was a prominent illustrator of his time. For example, one of his early books was *The Diverting History of John Gilpin* by William Cowper and illustrated by Randolph Caldecott, 1878, London, England: George Routledge & Sons. Reprinted with permission from http://www.randolphcaldecott.org.uk/gilpin.htm.

Figure 4.5 Did you know that back covers were used by the publisher to advertise other books? Visit the Randolph Caldecott Society website for other details about various editions (http://www.randolphcaldecott.org.uk/editions.htm).

Figure 4.6 The Caldecott Medal was created several years after the Newbery. The first Caldecott was awarded to *Animals of the Bible, A Picture Book*, illustrated by Dorothy P. Lathrop with text selected by Helen Dean Fish, 1938, New York, NY: Lippincott. Cover art copyright by Dorothy P. Lathrop.

Figure 4.7 Artwork and illustrative styles have changed over the years. A more recent Caldecott winner is *The Adventures of Beekle: The Unimaginary Friend* by Dan Santat, 2014, New York, NY: Little, Brown Books for Young Readers. Copyright 2014 by Dan Santat.

Figure 4.8 The 2015 Pura Belpre Award was given to *I Lived on Butterfly Hill* by Marjorie Agosín and illustrated by Lee White, 2014, New York, NY: Atheneum Books for Young Readers. Cover art copyright 2014 by Lee White.

Figure 4.9 The 2015 Sibert Medal was awarded to *The Right Word: Roget and His Thesaurus* by Jen Bryant and illustrated by Melissa Sweet, 2014, New York, NY: Eerdmans Books for Young Readers. Cover art copyright 2014 by Melissa Sweet.

Figure 4.10 The Printz Award is given to young adult literature. A recent winner was *I'll Give You the Sun* by Jandy Nelson, 2014, New York, NY: Dial Books. Copyright 2014 by Jandy Nelson.

Figure 4.11 The first Coretta Scott King Author Award was given to *Martin Luther King, Jr.: Man of Peace* by Lillie Patterson, 1969, New York, NY: Dell. Copyright 1969 by Lillie Patterson.

Figure 4.12 The first Coretta Scott King Illustrator Award was given to George Ford for illustrating *Ray Charles* by Sharon Draper. *Ray Charles* by Sharon Draper and illustrated by George Ford, 1973, New York, NY: Crowell. Cover art copyright 1973 by George Ford.

Figure 4.13 *Goose* by Molly Bang won the Phoenix Award from ChLA. *Goose* by Molly Bang, 1996, New York, NY: Blue Sky Press. Copyright 1996 by Molly Bang.

Figure 4.14 *Rain Reign* won the inaugural Charlotte Huck Award. *Rain Reign* by Ann M. Martin, 2014, New York, NY: Feiwel & Friends. Copyright 2014 by Ann M. Martin.

Figure 4.15 The winner of the first Orbis Pictus Award was *The Great Little Madison* by Jean Fritz, 1988, New York, NY: Puffin. Copyright 1988 by Jean Fritz.

Figure 4.16 A recent Orbis Pictus winner is *The Family Romanov: Murder, Rebellion & the Fall of Imperial Russia* by Candace Fleming, 2014, New York, NY: Schwartz & Wade. Copyright 2014 by Candace Fleming.

Figure 4.17 Eloise Greenfield is one of my favorite poets of all time. And my favorite Eloise Greenfield book is *Honey I Love and Other Love Poems* by Eloise Greenfield and illustrated by Diane and Leo Dillon, 1978, New York, NY: HarperCollins. Cover art copyright 1978 by Diane and Leo Dillon.

Figure 4.18 NBGS books are selected because they accurately portray diverse cultures and groups of people. *No Crystal Stair: A Documentary Novel of the Life and Work of Lewis Michaux, a Harlem Bookseller* by Vaunda Michaux Nelson and illustrated by R. Gregory Christie, 2012, Minneapolis, MN: Carolrhoda Lab/Lerner. Cover art copyright 2012 by R. Gregory Christie.

Figure 4.19 A nonfiction NBGS book is *Denied, Detained, Deported: Stories from the Dark Side of Immigration* by Ann Bausum, 2009, Washington, D.C.: National Geographic. Copyright 2009 by Ann Bausum.

Figure 4.20 Poetry books are also included in the NBGS selection process. An example is *Dare to Dream.. Change the World* edited by Jill Corcoran and illustrated by J. Beth Jepson, 2012, Tulsa, OK: Kane/Miller. Cover art copyright 2012 by J. Beth Jepson.

Figure 4.21 Science books are recognized by the National Science Teachers Association. *Egg: Nature's Perfect Package* by Robin Page and Steve Jenkins, 2015, New York, NY: Houghton Mifflin Harcourt. Copyright 2015 by Robin Page and Steve Jenkins.

Figure 4.22 Advanced science trade books are published for high school students as well. *Food Engineering: From Concept to Consumer* by Michael Burgan, 2015, Framingham, MA: C. Press/F. Watts Trade. Copyright 2015 by Michael Burgan.

Figure 4.23 Math books have come a long way. Check out a Mathica winner, *Really Big Numbers* by Richard Schwartz, 2014, Providence, RI: American Mathematical Society. Copyright 2014 by Richard Schwartz.

Figure 4.24 A Golden Kite Award for Fiction was awarded to *Revolution* by Deborah Wiles, 2014, New York, NY: Scholastic Press. Copyright 2014 by Deborah Wiles.

Figure 4.25 A Golden Kite Award for Picture Book Text was awarded to *A Dance Like Starlight*: *One Ballerina's Dream* written by Kristy Dempsey and illustrated by Floyd Cooper, 2014, New York, NY: Philomel. Cover art copyright 2014 by Floyd Cooper.

Figure 4.26 Humor wasn't often recognized as a literary quality until the Sid Fleischman Humor Award came along. One of Sid Fleischman's books was *Sir Charlie: Chaplin, the Funniest Man in the World* by Sid Fleischman, 2010, New York, NY: Greenwillow. Copyright 2010 by Sid Fleischman.

Figure 4.27 The *Evil Librarian* is one example of a humorous book recognized by the Sid Fleischman Humor Award. *Evil Librarian* by Michelle Knudsen, 2014, New York, NY: Candlewick. Copyright 2014 by Michelle Knudsen.

Figure 4.28 The Aesop Prize was awarded to *Chinese Fables: The Dragon Slayer and Other Timeless Tales of Wisdom,* by Shiho S. Nunes and illustrated by Lak-Khee Tay-Audouard, 2013, Tokyo/Rutland, Vermont: Tuttle Publishing. Cover art copyright 2013 by Lak-Khee Tay-Audouard.

Figure 4.29 The inaugural Boston Globe-Horn Book Award for Fiction was given to *The Little Fishes* by Erik Christian Haugaard in 1967. *The Little Fishes* by Erik Christian Haugaard and illustrated by Milton Johnson, 1967, Boston, MA; Houghton Mifflin. Cover art copyright 1967 by Milton Johnson.

Figure 4.30 The inaugural Boston Globe-Horn Book Award for Picture Books was given to *London Bridge is Falling Down* by Peter Spier in 1967. *London Bridge is Falling Down* by Peter Spier, 1967, London, England: Doubleday and Company. Copyright 1967 by Peter Spier.

Figure 4.31 The inaugural Boston Globe-Horn Book Award for Nonfiction was given to *Voyaging to Cathay: Americans in the China Trade* by Alfred Tamarin and Shirley Glubok, 1976, New York, NY: Viking Press. Copyright 1976 by Alfred Tamarin and Shirley Glubok.

Figure 4.32 A contemporary winner of the Boston Globe-Horn Book Award for Fiction is *Cartwheeling in Thunderstorms* by Katherine Rundell, 2014, New York, NY: Simon & Schuster. Copyright 2014 by Katherine Rundell.

Figure 4.33 A contemporary winner of the Boston Globe-Horn Book Award for Picture Books is a wordless book, *The Farmer and the Clown* by Marla Frazee, 2014, New York, NY: Beach Lane Books. Copyright 2014 by Marla Frazee.

Figure 4.34 A contemporary winner of the Boston Globe-Horn Book Award for Nonfiction is *The Family Romanov: Murder, Rebellion & the Fall of Imperial Russia* by Candace Fleming, 2014, New York, NY: Schwartz & Wade. Copyright 2014 by Candace Fleming.

Figure 4.35 The inaugural Kirkus Prize for Young Readers was awarded to *Aviary Wonders Inc. Spring Catalog and Instructional Manual* by Kate Samworth, 2014, New York, NY: Clarion. Copyright 2014 by Kate Samworth.

Figure 4.36 E.B. White wrote our most beloved contributions to children's literature, and the ABA named their read aloud award in honor of his collection of books. Here's one example, *Charlotte's Web* by E.B. White and illustrated by Garth Williams, 1952, New York, NY: HarperCollins. Copyright 1952 by Garth Williams.

Figure 4.37 *brown girl dreaming* has won many awards, including the E.B. White Read-Aloud Award. *brown girl dreaming* by Jacqueline Woodson, 2014, New York, NY: Penguin. Copyright 2014 by Jacqueline Woodson.

Figure 4.38 Book fans meet Henry Cole at the USF CLICK Conference (Children's Literature Collection of Know How). Photo copyright 2015 by Jenifer Schneider.

Figure 4.39 Yes, I flew through platform 9 ¾ in London's Kings Cross Station. Photo copyright 2015 by Troy Schneider.

Figure 4.40 The Cybils selected *Kalley's Machine Plus Cats* as the best book app of 2014 (https://itunes.apple.com/us/app/kalleys-machine-plus-cats/id905722643?mt=8&ign-mpt=uo%3D). *Kalley's Maching Plus Cats* by Jon, Carrie, Corbett, & Kalley Alexander, 2014, RocketWagon: Retrieved from http://rocketwagon.com/app/kalleys-machine/.

Figure 4.41 You don't see many awards for easy readers or early chapter books. The Cybils categorizes their awards based on ages and stages in reading development. A Cybils Early Chapter Book winner was *Lulu's Mysterious Mission* by Judith Viorst and illustrated by Kevin Cornell, 2014, New York, NY: Atheneum. Cover art copyright 2014 by Kevin Cornell.

Figure 4.42 The Cybils also gives awards to graphic novels for children and young adults. A recent winner was *In Real Life* by Cory Doctorow and Jen Wang, 2014, New York, NY: First Second. Copyright by Cory Doctorow and Jen Wang.

Figure 4.43 The 2015 Lammy was awarded to *Five, Six, Seven, Nate!* By Tim Federle, 2015, New York, NY: Simon & Schuster Books for Young Readers. Copyright 2015 by Tim Federle.

Figure 4.44 The novel, *Two Boys Kissing*, won a Lammy for fiction in 2014. *Two Boys Kissing* by David Levithan, 2013, New York, NY: Alfred A. Knopf Books for Young Readers. Copyright 2013 by David Levithan.

Figure 4.45 The novel, *If You Could Be Mine*, also won a Lammy in 2014. *If You Could Be Mine* by Sara Farizan, 2013, New York, NY: Algonquin Books. Copyright 2013 by Sara Farizan.

Figure 4.46 An award that focuses on the portrayal of disability is the Schneider Family Book Award. *Girls Like Us* by Gail Giles, 2014, New York, NY: Candlewick Press. Copyright 2014 by Gail Giles.

Figure 4.47 A recent Jane Addams Children's Book Award was given to *The Girl From the Tar Paper School: Barbara Rose Johns and the advent of the Civil Rights Movement* by Teri Kanefield, 2014, New York, NY: Abrams Books for Young Readers.Copyright 2014 by Teri Kanefield.

Figure 4.48 The Batchelder Award goes to a publisher. Eerdmans Books won the 2015 award for *Mikis and the Donkey*, written by Bibi Dumon Tak, illustrated by Philip Hopman, translated by Laura Watkinson, 2014, Grand Rapids, MI: Eerdmans Books. Copyright 2014 by Philip Hopman.

Figure 4.49 Thomas Crisp wrote about the impact of reading *Rainbow Boys*. *Rainbow Boys* by Alex Sanchez, 2003, New York, NY: Simon & Schuster Books for Young Readers. Copyright 2003 by Alex Sanchez.

Figure 4.50 Gary Paulsen, a White man, wrote Nightjohn, a story about a Black slave. *Nightjohn* by Gary Paulsen and illustrated by Jerry Pinkney, 1993, New York, NY: Delacorte Press. Cover art copyright 1993 by Jerry Pinkney.

Figure 4.51 bell hooks, a Black woman, wrote *Happy to be Nappy*, a book about girls' hair. *Happy to be Nappy* by bell hooks and illustrated by Chris Raschka, 1999, New York, NY: Jump at the Sun. Cover art copyright by Chris Raschka.

Chapter 5

Figure 5.1 Fictional stories *could* happen, but they haven't actually happened. An example of a fictional story with an authentically flawed protagonist and realistic plot twists is *Pointe* by Brandy Colbert, 2014, New York, NY: G.P. Putnam's Sons Books for Young Readers. Copyright 2014 by Brandy Colbert.

Figure 5.2 *Tuck Everlasting* is a story about living forever. *Tuck Everlasting* by Natalie Babbitt, 1975, New York, NY: Farrar, Straus and Giroux. Copyright 1975 by Natalie Babbitt.

Figure 5.3 Fictionalized biographies are stories based on the true lives of real people. The story of Neftalí Reyes (also known as Pablo Neruda, the Nobel Prize-winning poet) is recreated by Pam Muñoz Ryan and illustrated by Peter Sís. *The Dreamer* by Pam Muñoz Ryan and illustrated by Peter Sís, 2010, New York, NY: Scholastic Press. Cover art copyright 2010 by Peter Sís.

Figure 5.4 Nonfiction authors use expository text structures to present information. For example, Melissa Stewart used labels and short explanations to explore different types of feathers in *Feathers Not Just for Flying* by Melissa Stewart and illustrated by Sarah S. Brannen, 2014, Watertown, MA: Charlesbridge Publishing. Cover art copyright 2014 by Sarah S. Brannen.

Figure 5.5 Rosalyn Schanzer uses honest prose and straightforward examples to describe numerous people, places, and events surrounding the Salem Witch Trials. Excerpt from *Witches!: The Absolutely True Tale of Disaster in Salem,* by Rosalyn Schanzer, 2011, Washington, DC: National Geographic Books. Copyright 2011 by Rosalyn Schanzer.

Figure 5.6 Jane Yolen's text for *Owl Moon* captures the main character's feelings as she embarks on her first owling with her father. Yolen's writing also reflects the quiet of the snow and the still of the late night. Excerpt from *Owl Moon* by Jane Yolen and illustrated by John Schoenherr, 1987, New York, NY: Philomel Books. Cover art copyright 1987 by Jane Yolen.

Figure 5.7 Peter Sís uses his father's diary as inspiration for *Tibet Through the Red Box* by Peter Sís, 1998, New York, NY: Farrar, Straus and Giroux. Copyright 1998 by Peter Sís.

Figure 5.8 Poetic language is often descriptive. For example, Langston Hughes uses sensory detail in his poem, Mother to Son, in *The Dream Keeper and Other Poems* by Langston Hughes and illustrated by Brian Pinkney, 1994, New York, NY: Alfred A. Knopf. Text copyright 1932/1960 by Langston Hughes and 1994 by the Estate of Langston Hughes, illustrations copyright 1994 by Brian Pinkney.

Figure 5.9 Duncan Tonatiuh tells the story of Sylvia Mendez using narrative techniques and argumentation. *Separate is Never Equal: Sylvia Mendez and her Family's Fight for Desegregation* by Duncan Tonatiuh, 2014, New York, NY: Abrams. Copyright 2014 by Duncan Tonatiuh.

Figure 5.10 A scene from *Make Way for Ducklings* shows elaborate detail of the setting and tells the story from the perspective of the ducks. *Make Way for Ducklings* by Robert McCloskey, 1941, New York, NY: Viking Press. Copyright 1969 by Robert McCloskey.

Figure 5.11 Another scene from *Make Way for Ducklings* by Robert McCloskey shows the progression of the plot. *Make Way for Ducklings* by Robert McCloskey, 1941, New York, NY: Viking Press. Copyright 1969 by Robert McCloskey.

Figure 5.12 *Pink and Say* tells a big story using illustrations of small details and events. *Pink and Say* by Patricia Polacco, 1994, New York, NY: Philomel. Copyright 1994 by Patricia Polacco.

Figure 5.13 Sarah S. Brannen used panels and labels to highlight the features of different types of feathers in *Feathers Not Just for Flying* by Melissa Stewart and illustrated by Sarah S. Brannen, 2014, Watertown, MA: Charlesbridge Publishing. Copyright 2014 by Sarah S. Brannen.

Figure 5.14 Katherine Roy's illustrations provide visual details that help the reader understand the text in *Neighborhood Sharks: Hunting with the Great Whites of California's Farallon Islands* by Katherine Roy, 2014, New York, NY: David Macaulay Studio.

Figure 5.15 The cover image features the use of photographs and primary sources in *The Family Romanov: Murder, Rebellion & the Fall of Imperial Russia* by Candace Fleming, 2014, New York, NY: Schwartz & Wade. Copyright 2014 by Candace Fleming.

Figure 5.16 Roget's lists are viewable at the Karpeles Manuscript Library. The online site includes an interactive tool that allows users to view the document's transcription (http://www.rain.org/~karpeles/index.html). Roget's entry for Existence, 1805, Retrieved from http://www.rain.org/~karpeles/rogfrm.html.

Figure 5.17 Melissa Sweet uses collage to represent Roget's process of collecting words in *The Right Word: Roget and his Thesaurus* by Jen Bryant and illustrated by Melissa Sweet 2014, New York, NY: Eerdmans Books for Young Readers. Cover art copyright 2014 by Melissa Sweet.

Figure 5.18 Sweet's illustrations are highly detailed and accessible to readers. *The Right Word: Roget and his Thesaurus* by Jen Bryant and illustrated by Melissa Sweet 2014, New York, NY: Eerdmans Books for Young Readers. Excerpt art copyright 2014 by Melissa Sweet.

Figure 5.19 Seymour Simon has written approximately 300 books for children. Most of his books focus on a particular concept such as snakes, planets, and coral reefs. *Coral Reefs* by Seymour Simon, 2013, New York, NY: HarperCollins. Copyright 2013 by Seymour Simon.

Figure 5.20 In *Drowned City*, Don Brown illustrates the tragedy of Hurricane Katrina with a perspective that is more disturbing than the media coverage of the storm and its aftermath. *Drowned City: Hurricane Kartrina & New Orleans* by Don Brown, 2015, New York, NY: HMH Books for Young Readers. Copyright 2015 by Don Brown.

Figure 5.21 Captions, labels, titles, and charts are a few of the text features used in informative illustrations. Excerpt from *First Flight Around the World: The Adventures of the American Fliers Who Won the Race* by Tim Grove and the National Air and Space Museum, 2015, New York, NY: Henry N. Abrams. Copyright 2015 by Tim Grove and the National Air and Space Museum.

Figure 5.22 John Schoenherr's illustrations for *Owl Moon* capture more than a story. They explore human interaction in nature. Excerpt from *Owl Moon* by Jane Yolen and illustrated by John Schoenherr, 1987, New York, NY: Philomel Books. Illustration copyright 1987 by John Schoenherr.

Figure 5.23 Rosalyn Schanzer uses color, line, and a scratching technique to illustrate the events surrounding the Salem Witch Trials. Excerpt from *Witches!: The Absolutely True Tale of Disaster in Salem*, by Rosalyn Schanzer, 2011, Washington, DC: National Geographic Books. Copyright 2011 by Rosalyn Schanzer.

Figure 5.24 Illustrator, LeUyen Pham, creates the details of math obsession in *The Boy Who Loved Math* by Deborah Heiligman, 2013, New York, NY: Roaring Book Press. Illustration copyright 2013 by LeUyen Pham.

Figure 5.25 If you know someone who loves math, you will recognize the math-centric behaviors of the main character, Paul Erdős in *The Boy Who Loved Math* by Deborah Heiligman, 2013, New York, NY: Roaring Book Press. Illustration copyright 2013 by LeUyen Pham.

Figure 5.26 Seriously. My husband loves math and he sees the world in numbers and formulas. This is real. *The Boy Who Loved Math* by Deborah Heiligman, 2013, New York, NY: Roaring Book Press. Illustration copyright 2013 by LeUyen Pham.

Figure 5.27 Debbie Tilley uses comparison in her illustrations of the characters in *Hey, Little Ant* by Phillip M. Hoose and Hannah Hoose and illustrated by Debbie Tilley, 1998, New York, NY: Tricycle Press. Illustration copyright 1998 by Debbie Tilley.

Figure 5.28 Duncan Tonatiuh manipulates the reader's point of view to alter our relationship to the character and our interpretation of the courtroom scene in *Separate is Never Equal: Sylvia Mendez and her Family's Fight for Desegregation* by Duncan Tonatiuh, 2014, New York, NY: Abrams. Copyright 2014 by Duncan Tonatiuh.

Figure 5.29 Was it an accidental sneeze or an intentional blow? Illustrators, such as Lane Smith, appeal to the reader's ethics, reason, and emotions. Excerpt from *The True Story of the Three Little Pigs* by Jon Scieszka and illustrated by Lane Smith, 1989, New York, NY: Penguin. Illustration copyright 1989 by Lane Smith.

Figure 5.30 Douglas Florian has a series of poetry books (*Poem Depot, Poem Runs, Poetrees*) in which the illustrations alter the ways in which the titles are read. Cover from *Poem Runs* by Douglas Florian, 2012, New York, NY: HMH Books for Young Readers. Copyright 2012 by Douglas Florian.

Figure 5.31 Magical, beautiful, interesting, and just overall lovely! I'm sure you have read *The Very Hungry Caterpillar* by Eric Carle, 1969, New York, NY: World Publishing Company. Image from a later publication, 1982, New York, NY: Penguin. Copyright 1969/1982 by Eric Carle.

Figure 5.32 I don't know of any artist who paints faces like Floyd Cooper. I am drawn to his artwork. He is able to capture an internal spirit that is indescribable. This example is a book of poetry *The Blacker the Berry* by Joyce Carol Thomas and illustrated by Floyd Cooper, 2008, New York, NY: Amistad. Cover art copyright 2008 by Floyd Cooper.

Figure 5.33 In wordless books, the illustrations do all of the work. Most illustrators don't have a whole career in wordless books, but David Wiesner's has had several and his are famous. Here is a page from *Flotsam* by David Wiesner, 2006, New York, NY: Clarion. Copyright 2006 by David Wiesner.

Figure 5.34 Eloise Greenfield's poetic texts are written from different perspectives and focus on unique characters, but they all relate powerful emotions and stories. *Nathaniel Talking* is one example of Eloise Greenfield's many contributions. *Nathaniel Talking* by Eloise Greenfield and illustrated by Jan Spivey Gilchrist, 1998, London, England: Writers & Readers. Cover art copyright 1998 by Jan Spivey Gilchrist.

Figure 5.35 J. Patrick Lewis and Kenn Nesbitt are award-winning, prolific poets. In *Bigfoot is Missing*, they take on the creatures of childhood nightmares. MinaLima's illustrations play with all of the hype. *Bigfoot is Missing* by J. Patrick Lewis and Ken Nesbitt and illustrated by MinaLima, 2015, New York, NY: Chronicle Books. Illustration copyright 2015 by MinaLima.

Figure 5.36 Steven Kellogg wrote and illustrated several tall tales and legends as separate books. One example is *Jack and the Beanstalk* by Steven Kellogg, 1997, New York, NY: HarperCollins. Copyright 1997 by Steven Kellogg.

Figure 5.37 Virginia Hamilton wrote a collection of Black folktales in *The People Could Fly: American Black Folktales* by Virginia Hamilton and illustrated by Leo and Diane Dillon, 1993, New York, NY: Knopf Books for Young Readers. Cover art copyright 1993 by Leo and Diane Dillon.

Figure 5.38 James Marshall put his own spin on well-known fairy tales such as The Three Pigs, Goldilocks, and Hansel & Gretel. Check out *Little Red Riding Hood* by James Marshall, 1993, New York, NY: Puffin. Copyright 1993 by James Marshall.

Figure 5.39 Roald Dahl was simply fantastic and his book are still loved and read all over the world. One of my favorites is *James and the Giant Peach* by Roald Dahl and illustrated by Nancy Ekholm Burkert, 1961, New York, NY: Penguin. Cover image copyright 1961 by Nancy Ekholm Burkert.

Figure 5.40 One of the most important and impactful writers of contemporary fiction is Walter Dean Myers. Although his books span 40 years, his stories are relevant today. One award winning example is *Monster* by Walter Dean Myers and illustrated by Christopher Myers, 1999, New York, NY: HarperCollins. Cover art copyright 1999 by Christopher Myers.

Figure 5.41 Katherine Patterson is probably best known for writing *Bridge to Terebithia* or *The Great Gilly Hopkins*, but my favorite book of all time is *Jacob Have I Loved*. I have read it over and over again. This is an older cover, but it's the one I love. *Jacob Have I Loved* by Katherine Paterson, 1980, New York, NY: HarperCollins. Cover art copyright 2007 by Chris Sheban.

Figure 5.42 *Roll of Thunder, Hear My Cry* is one of a series of novels set during the time of segregation in the US. *Roll of Thunder, Hear My Cry* by Mildred Taylor, 1976, New York, NY: Dial Books. Frontispiece copyright 1976 by Dial Books.

Figure 5.43 G. Neri writes all types of fiction, but *Yummy* was one of the first graphic novels I read. *Yummy* by G. Neri and illustrated by Randy DuBurke, 2010, New York, NY: Lee & Low Books. Cover art copyright 2010 by Randy DuBurke.

Figure 5.44 Graphic novels are insanely popular for young adults. The illustrations are elaborate and intense with developed characters and quick dialogue. Jullian Tamaki created *This One Summer* with her cousin, Mario Tamaki. *This One Summer* by Jullian Tamaki and Mario Tamaki, 2014, New York, NY: First Second Books. Copyright 2014 by Jullian Tamaki and Mario Tamaki.

Figure 5.45 David Adler is a prolific writer of biographies. Check out *A Picture Book of Cesar Chavez* by David A. Adler and Michael S. Adler and illustrated by Marie Olofsdotter, 2011, New York, NY: Holiday House. Cover art copyright 2011 by Marie Olofsdotter.

Figure 5.46 Kadir Nelson creates amazing illustrations and he also writes incredible tributes for important individuals. One example is *We Are The Ship: The Story of Negro League Baseball* by Kadir Nelson, 2008, New York, NY: Jump at the Sun. Copyright 2008 by Kadir Nelson.

Figure 5.47 Gail Gibbons writes information books for youth of all ages, but she is particularly strong at creating concept books for young children. She writes about a range of topics as well. *Tornadoes* by Gail Gibbons, 2010, New York, NY: Holiday House. Copyright 2010 by Gail Gibbons.

Figure 5.48 Allen Say often creates paintings and tells stories that reflect his Japanese heritage. He won the Caldecott for *Grandfather's Journey*, which is a must-read about his grandfather's emigration to the US, but he has many other books as well. *Kamishibai Man* is about a man who performs the dying art of paper theater. *Kamishibai Man* by Allen Say, 2005, New York, NY: HMH Books for Young Readers. Copyright 2005 by Allen Say.

Figure 5.49 Alma Flor Ada writes books in English that focus on Latina/o culture. *My Name is Maria Isabel* is about a girl whose teacher calls her Mary, not Maria, and the struggle the child feels about her name and her identity. *My Name is Maria Isabel* by Alma Flor Ada and illustrated by K. Dyble Thompson, 1995, New York, NY: Atheneum Books for Young Readers. Cover art copyright by K. Dyble Thompson.

Figure 5.50 Alma Flor Ada translates children's books from English to Spanish. She translated *My Name is Maria Isabel* into *Me Llamo María Isabel* by Alma Flor Ada and illustrated by K. Dyble Thompson, 1996, New York, NY: Atheneum Books for Young Readers. Copyright by K. Dyble Thompson.

Figure 5.51 Cover of the first, privately printed edition of *The Tale of Peter Rabbit* by Beatrix Potter Retrieved from http://www.abebooks.com/servlet/BookDetailsPL?bi=1374463542&searchurl=an%3DBeatrix%2BPotter%26sortby%3D1%.

Figure 5.52 Images of Max's "wild rumpus" are immediately recognizable by people across generations. Image from *Where the Wild Things Are* by Maurice Sendak, 1963, New York, NY: Harper & Row. Copyright 1963 by Maurice Sendak.

Figure 5.53 Babies read differently than older children. Copyright 2015 by Aimee Frier.

Figure 5.54 Babies read with their eyes. Copyright 2000 by Jenifer Schneider.

Figure 5.55 Babies exhibit emergent reading behaviors when they have access to books. They learn how to hold books, turn the pages, and follow along. Copyright 2015 by Aimee Frier.

Figure 5.56 Family members, including older siblings and cousins, who recognize and encourage reading behaviors can significantly affect a child's attitude toward reading. Copyright 2015 by Aimee Frier.

Figure 5.57 Soft books work well for many reasons. Babies can read, chew, or throw them. *Find the Ball* by Manhattan Toy, nd, Minneapolis, MN. Copyright 2015 by Manhattan Toy Company.

Figure 5.58 Sandra Boynton has collections of board books that feature simple illustrations and funny, rhythmic, and repetitive text. *Moo, Baa, La La La* by Sandra Boynton, 1982, New York, NY: Little Simon. Copyright 1982 by Sandra Boynton.

Figure 5.59 Dr. Seuss' Beginner Books have repetitive, rhyming language that is easy for toddlers to memorize. Excerpt from *Hop on Pop* by Dr. Seuss, 1963, New York, NY: Random House. Copyright renewed 1991 by Dr. Seuss Enterprises L.P.

Figure 5.60 Elmo is a favorite, recognizable character. This lift the flap book features letters, characters, and labels. *Sesame Street: Elmo's ABC Lift-the-Flap* by Sesame Street, 2014, New York, NY: Reader's Digest. Copyright 2014 by Sesame Street.

Figure 5.61 I loved Richard Scarry as a child. His illustrations were intricate with hidden sub-plots. Excerpt from *What Do People Do All Day?* by Richard Scarry, 1968, New York, NY: Random House. Copyright 1968 by Richard Scarry.

Figure 5.62 Most of you might remember *The Wreck of the Zephyr* or *The Z was Zapped*, but Chris Van Allsburg has new books too. *The Misadventures of Sweetie Pie* by Chris Van Allsburg, 2014, New York, NY: HMH Books for Young Readers. Copyright 2014 by Chris Van Allsburg.

Figure 5.63 Jacqueline Woodson writes about Lonnie, a boy in foster care who finds hope through poetry. *Locomotion* by Jacqueline Woodson, 2003, New York, NY: G.P. Putnam & Sons. Copyright 2003 by Jacqueline Woodson.

Figure 5.64 My daughters' dentist, Dr. Gerald Copeland, is an exception—his office has a large selection of books for children of all ages. He also has an extensive array of interesting magazines of all types. He invests in his patients' literacy and he is thoughtful about parent, child, and teen wait time. Copyright 2015 by Jenifer Schneider.

Figure 5.65 Edgy and authentic are two words that describe Philip Pullman's books. For example, His Dark Materials are best selling books that continue to be read by new generations. The 20th anniversary edition of *Northern Lights* was published in 2015. *Northern Lights (His Dark Materials)* by Philip Pullman, 1995, London, England: Scholastic UK. Copyright 1995 by Philip Pullman.

Chapter 6

Figure 6.1 If you were in school in the 60s or 70s, you may have met Mister M with the munching mouth. The Letter People represent a systematic approach to teaching the alphabet letter names and corresponding sounds. A brief history of The Letter People is available at http://www.retrojunk.com/article/show/1448/the-letter-people.

Figure 6.2 Teachers used basal readers, workbook pages, and assessments to teach reading. My elementary school used the Holt Reading Series, and I specifically remember feeling happy when I moved through different levels. *People Need People* by Eldonna L. Evertts, 1973, Holt Basic Reading System Level 9, New York, NY: Holt, Rinehart and Winston. Copyright 1973 by Holt, Rinehart and Winston.

Figure 6.3 Flash cards were a prevalent instructional material for teachers who used basal readers. Image retrieved from https://cdn.shopify.com/s/files/1/0817/7493/files/blog_vintage-flashcards.jpg?2371429416518442553.

Figure 6.4 *Reading with Phonics* by Julie Hay and Charles Wingo was a reading series using phonics lessons. The teacher's edition included directions for teaching single sounds, blending, recognizing digraphs, dipthongs, and silent letters, and word lists for practice. Excerpt from *Reading with Phonics* by Julie Hay and Charles Wingo, 1954, Philadelphia, PA: Lippincott. Copyright 1954 by Julie Hay and Charles Wingo.

Figure 6.5 The Language Experience Approach was based on the development of student-created texts with the intention of helping students learn to read the words they knew and used. The method is described in *The Language Experience Approach to Reading* by Denise D. Nessel and Margaret B. Jones, 1981, New York, NY: Teachers College Press. Copyright 1981 by Teachers College Press. Click here to see a more recent example of the method (http://edp1f2012.blogspot.com/2012_03_01_archive.html).

Figure 6.6 Linguistic methods included a focus on grammar and the structure of language. Excerpt from *Patterns and Spelling in Writing* by Morton Botel, Cora Holsclaw, and Aileen Brothers, 1964, Chicago, IL: Follett Publishing Company. Copyright 1964 by Morton Botel, Cora Holsclaw, and Aileen Brothers.

Figure 6.7 A basic chart of the Pitman Initial Teaching Alphabet (i.t.a.). The i.t.a. included Roman and Latin characters and it was a semi-phonetic orthography of English mainly intended to make learning to read easier by connecting.

Figure 6.8 Mrs. Miles (in green) taught me to read in the first grade using reading groups, workbook pages, and SRA kits. She also sang to us, recited poetry every morning and afternoon, taught us how to make Rice Krispy treats, and she took us out to play.

Figure 6.9 The SRA Reading Laboratory kits were used extensively in schools. The materials included tests and color-coded levels. I remember working through the books and levels on my own. Image from https://s-media-cache-ak0.pinimg.com/736x/87/a7/aa/87a7aadf278dba630ddc441a1e226442.jpg.

Figure 6.10 Literature collections and reading materials were limited in their representation of writers from different races, ethnicities, and genders. *Norton Anthology of English Literature* (3rd Ed.), 1975, New York, NY: Norton & Co.

Figure 6.11 Racist literature still exists. *An African Fable* by Reading Horizons Staff, 2012, North Salt Lake, Utah: Reading Horizons. Copyright 2012 by Reading Horizons.

Figure 6.12 Miscue analysis was an important tool in helping teachers identify a reader's use of cueing systems (syntactic/semantic/graphophonemic or meaning/structure/visual). Teachers used the symbols to take notes on reading passages as the student reads them aloud. *Running Record Symbols and Marking Conventions,* 2015, Reading A-Z, Retrieved from https://www.readinga-z.com/guided/runrecord.html#markingsample.

Figure 6.13 A completed running record gives a teacher qualitative data about reading errors (meaning/structure/visual) and quantitative information about a student's errors, self-corrections, and strategies. *Running Record Symbols and Marking Conventions,* 2015, Reading A-Z, Retrieved from https://www.readinga-z.com/guided/runrecord.html#scoring.

Figure 6.14 Literacy experts, such as Bernice Cullinan, helped teachers understand how to use real books to teach reading. Her book, which has successive editions, includes chapter contributions from leading literacy researchers. *Children's literature in the reading program*, by Bernice Cullinan, 1987, Newark, DE: International Reading Association.

Figure 6.15 Charlotte Huck and Doris Young Kuhn, first published their comprehensive overview of children's literature in 1961. They helped teachers find a place for children's literature across the curriculum, providing book suggestions and genre overviews. Although Charlotte Huck passed away, iterations of her book continue by her co-author, Barbara Kiefer. *Children's Literature in the Elementary School* by Charlotte S. Huck and Doris Young Kuhn, 1968, New York, NY: Holt, Rinehart and Winston.

Figure 6.16 Whole language instruction prioritizes book reading and writing activities that have relevance to children's lives. Teachers use big books and charts for whole class instruction. Teachers reread texts frequently, helping children remember the words they read. Image retrieved from http://www.tunstallsteachingtidbits.com/wp-content/uploads/2014/08/IMG_4295.jpg.

Figure 6.17 Remember Sylvia Mendez? *Separate is Never Equal: Sylvia Mendez and her Family's Fight for Desegregation* by Duncan Tonatiuh, 2014, New York, NY: Abrams. Copyright 2014 by Duncan Tonatiuh.

Figure 6.18 April 12th is Beverly Cleary's birthday and national DEAR day. She is the author of *Ramona Quimby, Henry Huggins, Dear Mr. Henshaw, Ralph S. Mouse* and so many more (http://www.beverlycleary.com/characters.aspx#Ramona). Ramona Quimby, Age 8 by Beverly Cleary, 1981/1982, New York, NY: Dell. Cover art copyright by Joanne Scribner.

Figure 6.19 Jennifer Frances, founder of Bess the Book Bus, stocks her bus shelves with hundreds of books, which she gives away to underprivileged children. Photo copyright 2015 by Jenifer Schneider.
Figure 6.20 Bess the Book Bus travels all over the US, distributing books to children who don't own many, if any, of their own. Photo copyright 2015 by Jenifer Schneider.

Chapter 7

Figure 7.1 Shannon Hale writes an excellent essay on boys and series books. *The Princess in Black Series* by Shannon and Dean Hale and illustrated by LeUyen Pham, 2015, New York, NY: Random House. Cover art copyright 2015 by LeUyen Pham.

Figure 7.2 Come on! Who isn't laughing at this cover and concept? Artie Bennett also wrote *Poopendous* and *Belches, Burps, and Farts, Oh My!* Cover from *The Butt Book* by Artie Bennett and illustrated by Mike Lester, 2009, London, UK: Bloomsbury. Copyright 2009 by Mike Lester.

Figure 7.3 You may not know that Harry's British title is *Harry Potter and the Philosopher's Stone*. Either way, critics on both sides of the pond wrote mixed reviews. *Harry Potter and the Philosopher's Stone* by J.K. Rowling and illustrated by Thomas Taylor, 1997, London, UK: Bloomsbury. Cover art copyright 1997 by Thomas Taylor.

Figure 7.4 *Harry Potter* was re-titled, repackaged, and re-illustrated for the US market. *Harry Potter and the Sorcerer's Stone* by J.K. Rowling and illustrated by Mary GrandPré, 1998, New York, NY: Scholastic. Cover art copyright 1998 by Mary GrandPré.

Figure 7.5 Dyamonde Daniel is a memorable character, and Nikki Grimes' series focuses on her normal, everyday life experiences. *Almost Zero: A Dyamonde Daniel Book* by Nikki Grimes and illustrated by R. Gregory Christie, 2010, New York, NY: G.P. Putnam's Sons Books for Young Readers. Cover art copyright 2010 by R. Gregory Christie.

Figure 7.6 Elephant & Piggie books are one of several series written and illustrated by Mo Williams. *I Broke My Trunk (An Elephant & Piggie Book)* by Mo Willems, 2011, New York, NY: Disney-Hyperion.

Figure 7.7 Anthony Browne, a prolific and award-winning artist, created an illustrated series based on Willy a wimpy chimp. *Willy the Wimp* by Anthony Browne, 2008, London, UK: Walker Books. Cover from 2014 edition, copyright 2014 by Anthony Browne.

Figure 7.8 Nina Crews takes familiar folk tales and sets them in modern, urban settings. One example is *Jack and the Beanstalk* by Nina Crews, 2011, New York, NY: Henry Holt and Co. Copyright 2011 by Nina Crews.

Figure 7.9 R.L. Stine created one of the most famous series of children's books—the Goosebump Series. *The Curse of the Mummy's Tomb*, by R.L. Stine, 1993, New York, NY: Scholastic. Cover art copyright 2003 by Scholastic.

Figure 7.10 *Freckleface Strawberry* started as a successful book by a celebrity author and now there is a book series and musical. *Freckle Face Strawberry* by Julianne Moore and illustrated by LeUyen Pham, 2007, London, UK: Bloomsbury. Cover art copyright 2007 by LeUyen Pham.

Figure 7.11 LeUyen Pham illustrates several series. One series is by Jabari Asim. *Whose Toes Are Those?* By Jabari Asim and illustrated by LeUyen Pham, 2006, New York, NY: LB Kids. Cover art copyright 2006 by LeUyen Pham.

Figure 7.12 Jimmy Fallon is an example of a celebrity author who has a writing background as a comedian. He also writes children's books from his personal experience as a father. But notice that this picture book does not list the illustrator, Miguel Ordóñez, on the front cover. *Your Baby's First Word Will Be Dada* by Jimmy Fallon and illustrated by Miguel Ordóñez, 2015, New York, NY: Feiwel & Friends. Cover art copyright 2015 by Miguel Ordóñez.

Figure 7.13 My daughter creates fanart for anime, manga, and cartoons. She posts it on her bedroom wall, closet doors, and in notepads. Not all fanfic and fanart is made public. Copyright 2015 by Jenifer Schneider.

Chapter 8

Figure 8.1 The Children's Literature Collection of Know-how (CLICK) is an annual conference featuring authors and illustrators. Joyce Carol Thomas presented to the crowd of children and adults in 2006. In the photo, she shares images from *The Gospel Cinderella* as she talks about her writing process. *The Gospel Cinderella* by Joyce Carol Thomas and illustrated by David Diaz, 2004, New York, NY: Amistad. Photo copyright 2006 by Jenifer Schneider.

Figure 8.2 Attendees share their writing during a break out session at the CLICK Conference.

Figure 8.3 Youth work with journalist-in-residence, Anne W. Anderson, to create the CLICK Chronicle, a conference blog.

Figure 8.4 Children create guerilla art in response to reading books and listening to the author and illustrator talks.

Figure 8.5 CLICK artist-in-residence, Csaba Osvath, poses with the guerilla art that he helped the participants create (http://www.csabaosvath.com/).

Figure 8.6 Students create blank books to take home from the CLICK Conference.

Figure 8.7 Students use Play-doh and iPads to create stop-motion versions of the books they read during the CLICK Conference.

Figure 8.8 Dramatist, Margaret Branscombe, works with children during the CLICK Conference. Students use tableau and other theater games to revisit the books discussed by the CLICK authors and illustrators. For more information about Margaret and her techniques, visit http://www.learnthroughdrama.com/.

Figure 8.9 Roald Dahl's hut at the Road Dahl Museum and Story Centre. Photo copyright 2013 by Jenifer Schneider.

Figure 8.10 Jon Klassen worked as a film animator. His book, *This Is Not My Hat*, won the Caldecott Medal. Image from *This Is Not My Hat* by Jon Klassen, 2012, New York, NY: Candlewick Press. Copyright 2012 by Jon Klassen.

Figure 8.11 The Eric Carle Museum of Picture Book Art (http://www.carlemuseum.org/).

Figure 8.12 The Maurice Sendak Collection at the Rosenbach Museum (https://www.rosenbach.org/learn/collections/maurice-sendak-collection).

Figure 8.13 Beth Krommes' scenic, folk-art illustrations are predominantly black and white, but they capture readers' attention and draw them into the story. Image from *The House in the Night* by Susan Marie Swanson and illustrated by Beth Krommes, 2009, New York, NY: HMH Books for Young Readers. Copyright 2009 by Beth Krommes.

Figure 8.14 Acrylic paints are water-soluble, synthetic paints. They can have a gloss or matte finish and a thin or thick opacity. Jim Harris describes the pros and cons of painting with acrylics (http://www.jimharrisillustrator.com/ChildrensBooks/Books/threelittledinos.html#oilpainting). He used acrylic and oil paint to create his book, *The Three Little Dinosaurs*. Image from *The Three Little Dinosaurs* by Jim Harris, 1999, Gretna, LA: Pelican Publishing. Copyright 1999 by Jim Harris.

Figure 8.15 Crayon is the medium of childhood, but it's infrequently used in children's books. Oliver Jeffers uses all types of media, but *The Day the Crayons Quit* is an example of crayon illustration. You will enjoy his website (http://oliverjeffersworld.com/) and his short film about his artistic process (https://vimeo.com/57472271). *The Day the Crayons Quit* by Drew Daywalt and illustrated by Oliver Jeffers, 2013, New York, NY: Philomel.

Figure 8.16 Collage is a process of assembling images from different materials. Chris Haughton used collage and digital illustration to create *Shh! We Have A Plan*. He describes the making of his book and the details of his writing and illustration process on his blog (http://blog.chrishaughton.com/the-making-of-shh-we-have-a-plan/). *Shh! We Have A Plan* by Chris Haughton, 2014, New York, NY: Candlewick. Copyright 2014 by Chris Haughton.

Figure 8.17 Digital illustration is quite pervasive as many new artists are trained using digital tools. Illustrators often combine digital techniques with handmade illustration, but some work completely electronically. Bob Staake is a prolific, digital illustrator who creates children's books and much more. Read about his art and books on his website (http://www.bobstaake.com/). Image from *The First Pup: The Real Story of How Bo Got to the White House* by Bob Staake, 2010, New York, NY: Feiwel & Friends. Copyright 2010 by Bob Staake.

Figure 8.18 Gouache is a water-based paint that is more color-dense than watercolors. Wendell Minor creates beautiful paintings using gouache (http://www.minorart.com/childrensbooks.html). A recent example is *Trapped! A Whale's Rescue* by Robert Burleigh with paintings by Wendell Minor, 2015, Boston, MA: Charlesbridge. Copyright 2015 by Wendell Minor.

Figure 8.19 Oil paint is a slow-drying paint in which the pigment is suspended in oil. Oil paints add depth of color. Jim Kay is an illustrator who uses oil along with other media. He was selected by J.K. Rowling to create the illustrated version of *Harry Potter and the Philosopher's Stone*. His illustrations allow Harry fans to revisit the story in a whole new way. Amazing! Watch a video of Jim's process (https://www.youtube.com/watch?v=GmhDRHIix48&feature=youtu.be). Image from *Harry Potter and the Philosopher's Stone Deluxe Illustrated Edition* by J.K. Rowling and illustrated by Jim Kay, 2015, London, UK: Bloomsbury Children's.

Figure 8.20 Pastels are a powdered pigment that is formed into a stick. Pastels have a powdery property similar to chalk. Lynne Chapman creates illustrations using pastels. She shares her techniques through a series of excellent videos posted on her website (http://www.lynnechapman.co.uk/talking-about-work.php). Image from *Rumble, Roar, Dinosaur!* By Tony Mitton and illustrated by Lynne Chapman, 2010, New York, NY: Macmillan. Copyright 2010 by Lynn Chapman. Retrieved from https://s-media-cache-ak0.pinimg.com/originals/1d/1b/a1/1d1ba155de585d46fd7adbf64e858494.jpg.

Figure 8.21 Pen, ink, and graphite are familiar media for most people; they are the writing tools we commonly use. However, in the hands of an artist, new worlds are created. Arnold Lobel illustrated some of the most memorable characters using graphite, ink, and watercolor. You might know Frog and Toad, but this is Arnold's self-portrait from *The Book of Pigericks* by Arnold Lobel, 1983, New York, NY: HarperCollins. Copyright 1983 by Arnold Lobel.

Figure 8.22 Scratchboard is an illustrative technique in which the artist uses tools to scratch into clay covered by ink. Beth Krommes shares further details and examples on her website (http://www.bethkrommes.com/illustration/what-is-scratchboard). Image from *The Lamp, the Ice, and the Boat Called Fish* by Jacqueline Briggs Martin and illustrated by Beth Krommes, 2001, New York, NY: HMH Books for Young Readers. Copyright 2001 by Beth Krommes.

Figure 8.23 Watercolors are pigments suspended in a water-based solution. Jerry Pinkney is a master storyteller using watercolor. Most of his books include words, but *The Lion and the Mouse* is a wordless book. Jerry shares his process in several videos available on his website (http://www.jerrypinkneystudio.com/frameset.html). Image from *The Lion and the Mouse* by Jerry Pinkney, 2009, New York, NY: Little, Brown Books for Young Readers. Copyright 2009 by Jerry Pinkney.

Figure 8.24 Michael Crichton wrote about genetic engineering in his book, *Next* by Michael Crichton, 2006, New York, NY: HarperCollins. Cover copyright 2006 by HarperCollins.

Figure 8.25 Peter, a main character in *Jumanji*, kneels on a chair as he watches his train travel underneath the chair and around the room. Image from *Jumanji* by Chris Van Allsburg, 1981, New York, NY: Houghton Mifflin. Copyright 1981 by Chris Van Allsburg.

Figure 8.26 The reader watches from above as Judy and Peter begin to play the board game they have found in the park. Image from *Jumanji* by Chris Van Allsburg, 1981, New York, NY: Houghton Mifflin. Copyright 1981 by Chris Van Allsburg.

Figure 8.27 *The Cat in the Hat* features a brother and sister left alone at home, on a cold, rainy day. *The Cat in the Hat* by Dr. Seuss, 1957, New York, NY: Random House. Copyright 1957 by Dr. Seuss.

Figure 8.28 The Cat from *The Cat in the Hat* by Dr. Seuss, 1957, New York, NY: Random House. Copyright 1957 by Dr. Seuss.

Figure 8.29 Shrek was popularized by Mike Myers film version. But Mike Myers got his idea from *Shrek!* By William Steig. *Shrek!* By William Steig, 1990, New York, NY: Farrar, Straus, & Giroux. Copyright 1990 by William Steig.

Figure 8.30 *Peter Pan: The Boy Who Wouldn't Grow Up* by J.M. Barrie, 1904, London, England: Hodder & Stoughton. Copyright 1988 by Great Ormond Street Hospital.

Figure 8.31 *Winnie the Pooh* by A.A. Milne and decorations by E.H. Shepard, 1926, London, UK: Methuen & Co. Ltd. Copyright 1988 Dutton.

Figure 8.32 Mary Poppins by P.L. Travers and illustrated by Mary Shepard, 1934, London, UK: HarperCollins. Copyright 1962 by P.L. Travers.

Chapter 9

Figure 9.1 *The Mysteries of Harris Burdick* is a collection of stories, but the reader must determine the beginning, middle, and end of each one. *The Mysteries of Harris Burdick* by Chris Van Allsburg, 1984, New York, NY: Houghton Mifflin. Copyright 1984 by Chris Van Allsburg.

Figure 9.2 The Seven Chairs: The fifth one ended up in France.
Image from *The Mysteries of Harris Burdick* by Chris Van Allsburg, 1984, New York, NY: Houghton Mifflin. Copyright 1984 by Chris Van Allsburg.

Figure 9.3 Mr. Linden's Library: He had warned her about the book. Now it was too late.
Image from *The Mysteries of Harris Burdick* by Chris Van Allsburg, 1984, New York, NY: Houghton Mifflin. Copyright 1984 by Chris Van Allsburg.

Figure 9.4 Archie Smith, Boy Wonder: A tiny voice asked, "Is he the one?"
Image from *The Mysteries of Harris Burdick* by Chris Van Allsburg, 1984, New York, NY: Houghton Mifflin. Copyright 1984 by Chris Van Allsburg.

Figure 9.5 Under the Rug: Two weeks passed and it happened again.
Image from *The Mysteries of Harris Burdick* by Chris Van Allsburg, 1984, New York, NY: Houghton Mifflin. Copyright 1984 by Chris Van Allsburg.

Figure 9.6 *The Chronicles of Harris Burdick* is the attempt of 14 famous authors to solve the mysteries of Harris Burdick. You can also find out how other readers have responded to the Burdick mysteries (http://www.houghtonmifflinbooks.com/features/harrisburdick/). *The Chronicles of Harris Burdick* by Chris Van Allsburg, 2011, New York, NY: Houghton Mifflin. Cover art copyright 2011 by Chris Van Allsburg.

Figure 9.7 Image of the Brothers Grimm. Retrieved from http://monumente-online.de/wAssets/img/ausgaben/2012/1/466/fotogrimm_Br___der_Grimm_Museum__Kassel_1_765x715.jpg

Figure 9.8 The Brothers Grimm published this version of *Children's and Household Tales* in 1882. This version was illustrated by Walter Crane and translated by Lucy Crane. The text is available from The Project Gutenberg http://www.gutenberg.org/files/19068/19068-h/19068-h.htm and http://www.archive.org/stream/grimmsfairytal00grim#page/n5/mode/2up.

Figure 9.9 Charles Perrault by Lallemand, 1693, de 'Académie Française, Source=New York Public Library Digital Gallery, Retrieved from http://digitalgallery.nypl.org/nypldigital/dgkeysearchdetail.cfm?trg=1&strucID=1018746&imageID=1555918&word=Perrault&s=1&notword=&d=&c=&f

Figure 9.10 Puss in Boots, from a handwritten and illustrated version of Charles Perrault's Contes de ma mère l'Oye (Mother Goose Tales). Retrieved from https://commons.wikimedia.org/wiki/File:Puss-in-Boots-1695.jpg

Figure 9.11 Joseph Jacobs was a distinguished Jewish historian and linguist who published folktales of English, Celtic, Indian, and European cultures. Retrieved from http://www.folklore-network.folkaustralia.com/images/image0012.gif.

Figure 9.12 *More Celtic Fairy Tales*, Jacobs, J., 1895 New York : Grosset & Dunlap (2nd edition?) Copy scan by nicole-Deyo, a trusted source, from copy held by New York Public Lib., obtained from morecelticfairyt00jaco

Figure 9.13 Cinder Edna is the story of Cinderella's neighbor. *Cinder Edna* by Ellen Jackson and illustrated by Kevin O'Malley, 1998, New York, NY: HarperCollins.

Figure 9.14 Awake has the modern sensibilities of high-priced coffee. *Awake: The Story of Sleeping Beauty with Espresso* by Karleen Tauszik, 2014, Seattle, WA: Amazon.

Figure 9.15 This is the story of Jack in the big city during an economic downturn. *Jack and the Baked Beanstalk* by Colin Stimpson, 2012, New York, NY: Templar.

Figure 9.16 An alien has landed in the story of the three bears. No problem, right? *I Thought This Was a Bear Book* by Tara Lazar and illustrated by Benji Davies, 2015, New York, NY: Aladdin.

Figure 9.17 David Wiesner turns the story of the three pigs inside out. *The Three Pigs* by David Wiesner, 2001, New York, NY: Clarion.

Figure 9.18 Nadia Shireen explores what happens when the bad guy is good. *Good Little Wolf* by Nadia Shireen, 2011, New York, NY: Knopf Books. (Figure

Figure 9.19 Rachel Isadora's illustrative style gives Hansel and Gretel a completely different feel. *Hansel and Gretel* by Rachel Isadora, 2009, New York, NY: G.P. Putnam's Sons

Chapter 10

Figure 10.1 Kids are still required to identify poetic forms. But the process can be more entertaining in the hands of a poet such as Paul Janeczko. *A Kick in the Head: An Everyday Guide to Poetic Forms* by Paul B. Janeczko and illustrated by Chris Raschka, 2005, New York, NY: Candlewick. Copyright 2005 by Chris Raschka.

Figure 10.2 Classic poetry is often republished with modern illustrations. Poetry for Young People is a popular series. *Poetry for Young People: Robert Frost* by Gary D. Schmidt and Illustrated by Henri Sorensen, 2008, New York, NY: Sterling. Copyright 2008 by Henri Sorensen.

Figure 10.3 Although this isn't a book of poetry, the *Henry Hikes* series is inspired by the writing of Henry David Thoreau. *Henry Hikes to Fitchburg* by D.B. Johnson, 2006, New York, NY: HMH Books for Young Readers. Copyright 2006 by D.B. Johnson.

Figure 10.4 Emily Dickenson is one of the most important poets, male or female. Details about her work and life are told by storytellers and illustrators. *Emily* by Michael Bedard and illustrated by Barbara Cooney, 2002, New York, NY: Dragonfly. Cover art copyright 2002 by Barbara Cooney.

Figure 10.5 Dark, dreary, and dead. These are the poets of my youth. *Complete Works of Elizabeth Barrett Browning* (Delphi Poets Series), 2013, Delphi Classics, Amazon Digital Services.

Figure 10.6 Langston Hughes was one of many influential poets of the Harlem Renaissance. *The Collected Poems of Langston Hughes*, edited by Arnold Rampersad, 1995, New York, NY: Vintage.

Figure 10.7 Sandra Cisneros' poetry reflected *her* human experience. *My Wicked Wicked Ways* by Sandra Cisneros, 1987, Berkeley, CA: Third Women Press. Cover for 3rd edition by Vintage.

Figure 10.8 Poets, such as Douglas Florian, create topical and thematic books of poetry for children. *Shiver Me Timbers! Pirate Poems and Paintings* by Douglas Florian and illustrated by Robert Neubecker, 2012, New York, NY: Beach Lane Books. Cover art copyright 2012 by Robert Neubecker.

Figure 10.9 Poetry for very young children is playful and features rhyme, repetition, and memorable illustrations. *Read Aloud Rhymes for the Very Young*, written and selected by Jack Prelutsky and illustrated by Marc Brown, 1986, New York, NY: Knopf Books for Young Readers. Cover art copyright 1986 by Marc Brown.

Figure 10.10 Poetry for older children reflects their growing sense of themselves and their world. *Giant Children* by Brod Bagert and illustrated by Ted Arnold, 2005, New York, NY: Puffin Books. Cover art copyright 2005 by Ted Arnold.

Figure 10.11 Poetry for young adults covers content that reflects their emotional range and the angst of adolescence. *I Just Hope It's Lethal* selected by Liz Rosenberg and Deena November, 2005, New York, NY: HMH Books for Young Readers. Copyright 2005 by Liz Rosenberg and Deena November.

Figure 10.12 *Where the Sidewalk Ends* is a standard book in any library collection. *Where the Sidewalk Ends* by Shel Silverstein, 1974, New York, NY: Harper & Row. Copyright 1974 by Shel Silverstein.

Figure 10.13 Shel Silverstein drew his own illustrations so he used words and images to create the sound, feel, and mood with which he wanted his poems read. "Lazy Jane" from *Where the Sidewalk Ends* by Shel Silverstein, 1974, New York, NY: Harper & Row. Copyright 1974 by Shel Silverstein.

Figure 10.14 Have you ever been the victim of a bully? Jack Prelutsky knows how it feels. *The New Kid on the Block* by Jack Prelutsky and illustrated by James Stevenson, 1984, New York, NY: Greenwillow.

Figure 10.15 As demonstrated by the title of this book, Jack Prelutsky likes to play with the meaning and sound of words. Plus, he makes up words too. *Behold the Bold Umbrellaphant* by Jack Prelutsky and illustrated by Carin Berger, 2006, New York, NY: Greenwillow. Cover art copyright 2006 by Carin Berger.

Figure 10.16 David McCord won the first NCTE Award for Excellence in Poetry for Children. *Every Time I Climb a Tree* includes 25 memorable poems and engaging illustrations. *Every Time I Climb a Tree* by David McCord and illustrated by Marc Simont, 1967, New York, NY: Little, Brown and Company. Cover art copyright 1967 by Marc Simont.

Figure 10.17 Eloise Greenfield wrote my two favorite love poems in *Honey, I Love and Other Poems* by Eloise Greenfield, illustrations by Diane and Leo Dillon, from Harper Collins Publishers, NY, 1978. Cover art copyright 1978 by Diane and Leo Dillon.

Figure 10.18 J. Patrick Lewis is a prolific poet with collections about chocolate moustaches, animal epitaphs, and little known holidays such as Cow Appreciation Day in *World Rat Day* by J. Patrick Lewis and illustrated by Anna Raff, 2013, New York, NY: Candlewick. Cover art copyright 2013 by Anna Raff.

Figure 10.19 Roald Dahl is known for his fantasy novels, but he also liked to write wicked poetry. One example is *Revolting Rhymes* by Roald Dahl and illustrated by Quentin Blake, 1982, New York, NY: Alfred A. Knopf. Cover art copyright 1982 by Quentin Blake.

Figure 10.20 Kenn Nesbitt is a popular poet who typically publishes humorous poetry. One example is *Revenge of the Lunch Ladies: The Hilarious Book of School Poetry* by Kenn Nesbitt and illustrated by Mike Gordon and Carl Gordon, 2007, New York, NY: Meadowbrook. Cover art 2007 by Mike and Carl Gordon.

Figure 10.21 Naomi Shihab Nye received a lot of attention for her poetry for girls but she writes a broad range of poetry. *19 Varieties of Gazelle: Poems of the Middle East* by Naomi Shihab Nye, 2002, New York, NY: HarperCollins.

Figure 10.22 All of the poems in this book were written by Nikki Giovanni. Then Ashley Bryan created illustrations that integrate the text. *The Sun Is So Quiet* by Nikki Giovanni and illustrated by Ashley Bryan, 1996, New York, NY: Henry Holt and Co. Cover art copyright 1996 by Ashley Bryan.

Figure 10.23 Jack Prelutsky edited my favorite poetry anthology of all time—*The Random House Book of Poetry*. Search for poetry by topic, title, author, and first line. There are poems about everything—from Abraham Lincoln to rainy days. It is a beautiful collection illustrated by Arnold Lobel. *The Random House Book of Poetry for Young Children* selected by Jack Prelutsky and illustrated by Arnold Lobel, 1983, New York, NY: Random House. Cover art copyright 1984 by Arnold Lobel.

Figure 10.24 Collections, such as *Pass It On*, gather selections from poets who use their voices to point out injustice and to inspire people. *Pass It On: African American Poetry for Children* selected by Wade Hudson and illustrated by Floyd Cooper, 1993, New York, NY: Scholastic.

Figure 10.25 *The Crossover* is a verse novel, telling the story of Josh and JB, basketball and life. *The Crossover* by Kwame Alexander, 2014, New York, NY: Houghton Mifflin. Copyright 2014 by Kwame Alexander.

Figure 10.26 This book is quite remarkable. *Joyful Noise* tells the stories and secret lives of insects. The words are perfectly placed on the page, telling readers when to read alone or as two voices. *Joyful Noise: Poems for Two Voices* by Paul Fleischman and illustrated by Eric Beddows, 1988, New York, NY: Harper Trophy.

Figure 10.27 Paul Fleischman kicks it up a notch with poetry for four voices. The text and illustrations in *Big Talk* orchestrate choral reading. *Big Talk: Poems for Four Voices* by Paul Fleischman and illustrated by Beppe Giacobbe, 2008, New York, NY: Candlewick. Cover art copyright 2008 by Beppe Giacobbe.

Figure 10.28 Marilyn Singer creates poetry that has one meaning when read down one side of the page and a different meaning when read on the other. Through this structure, she shares new perspectives on familiar fairy tales. *Mirror Mirror: A Book of Reverso Poems* by Marilyn Singer and illustrated by Josee Masse, 2010, New York, NY: Dutton. Cover art copyright 2010 by Josee Masse.

Figure 10.29 Tableau gives readers an opportunity to experience poetry from the characters' perspectives. In this frozen scene, the participants explore the perspectives of a girl and a wolf using the positions of their bodies, gestures, and facial expressions. Photo copyright 2014 by Randi Meyer.

Figure 10.30 As Nikki Giovanni states in her introduction, Hip Hop is modern opera, with truthful tales surrounded by public commentary. This collection of poetry includes celebrated children's poets, musicians, and rappers telling stories. *Hip Hop Speaks to Children: A Celebration of Poetry with a Beat* selected by Nikki Giovanni and illustrated by Michele Noiset and Jeremy Tugeau, 2008, Naperville, IL: Sourcebooks. Cover art copyright 2008 by Michele Noiset and Jeremy Tugeau.

Figure 10.31 When a poet is also an illustrator, really cool things can happen between image and text. For example, Douglas Florian uses art to understand celestial objects and find just-right words to describe them. Image of Saturn from *Comets, Stars, the Moon, and Mars* by Douglas Florian, 2007, New York, NY: HMH Books for Young Readers. Copyright 2007 by Douglas Florian.

Figure 10.32 Lewis Carroll showed readers how text has illustrative function through page arrangement. The Mouse's Tail from *Alice's Adventures in Wonderland* by Lewis Carroll, 1965, New York, NY: Macmillan.

Figure 10.33 Concrete poets use shape, page layout, font, and other aspects of design to communicate meaning. One example is *Meow Ruff: A Story in Concrete Poetry* by Joyce Sidman and illustrated by Michelle Berg, 2006, New York, NY: HMH Books for Young Readers. Cover art copyright 2006 by Michelle Berg.

Chapter 11

Figure 11.1 If you are interested in languages, *Sequoyah* provides a glimpse into Cherokee history. *Sequoyah: The Cherokee Man Who Gave his People Writing* by James Rumford and translated by Anna Sixkiller Huckaby, 2004, New York, NY: HMH Books for Young Readers.

Figure 11.2 Read about Robert Battle in *My Story, My Dance: Robert Battle's Journey to Alvin Ailey* by Lesa Cline-Ransome, illustrated by James E. Ransome, 2015, New York, NY: Simon & Schuster

Figure 11.3 If you like quirky facts about the Presidency and the Presidents of the US, this book is for you. *So You Want to be President* written by Judith St. George and illustrated by David Small, 2004/2012, New York, NY: Philomel

Figure 11.4 Part story, part mystery, part math. This book integrates mathematical thinking with narrative. *Mystery Math: A First Book of Algebra* written by David A. Adler and illustrated by Edward Miller.

Figure 11.5 Learn about the Day of the Dead. *Funny Bones: Posada and His Day of the Dead Calaveras* by Duncan Tonatiuh, 2015, New York, NY: Harry N. Abrams

Figure 11.6 Bomb is a combination of history and military science. Bomb: The Race to Build—and Steal—the World's Most Dangerous Weapon written by Steve Sheinkin, 2012, New York, NY: Flash Point.

Figure 11.7 You won't forget the images in this book. *Kakapo Rescue: Saving the World's Strangest Parrot*, written by Sy Montgomery, photographs by Nic Bishop, 2010, New York, NY: Houghton Mifflin Books for Children

Figure 11.8 Roy writes about sharks with great expertise and in simple terms. Neighborhood Sharks: Hunting with the Great Whites of California's Farallon Islands by Katherine Roy, 2014, New York, NY: David Macaulay Books.

Figure 11.9 If you enjoy learning about different religions and historical sites, read *The Grand Mosque of Paris: A Story of How Muslims Rescued Jews during the Holocaust* by Karen Gray Ruelle and Deborah Durland Desaix, 2009, New York, NY: Holiday House.

Figure 11.10 *Look Up!* Is a helpful guide for identifying birds and their features. *Look Up! Bird-Watching in Your Own Backyard* by Annette LeBlanc Cate, 2013, New York, NY: Candlewick.

Figure 11.11 Allan Say takes readers on his journey as an illustrator. *Drawing from Memory* by Allen Say, 2011, New York, NY: Scholastic.

Figure 11.12 Black holes are difficult to understand but this book explains their features with words and images. *A Black Hole is NOT a Hole* by Carolyn Cinami DeCristofano, illustrated by Michael Carroll, 2012, Boston, MA: Charlesbridge.

Figure 11.13 Lois Ehlert shares colorful scraps. *The Scraps Book* by Lois Ehlert, 2014, New York, NY: Beach Lane Books.

Figure 11.14 Not only does this book provide the history of Mr. Ferris, but the illustrations provide readers with a unique viewing experience of the wheel. *Mr. Ferris and His Wheel* by Kathryn Gibbs Davis and illustrated by Gilbert Ford, 2014, New York, NY: HMH Books for Young Readers.

Figure 11.15 *Bossypants* by Tina Fey, 2014, Boston, MA: Back Bay books.

Figure 11.16 *Heroin Diaries* by Nikki Sixx and Ian Gittins, 2007, New York, NY: Pocket Books.

Figure 11.17 *Open* by Andre Agassi, 2009, New York, NY: Knopf.

Figure 11.18 *Team of Rivals: The Political Genius of Abraham Lincoln* by Doris Kearns Goodwin, 2006, New York, NY: Simon & Schuster.

Figure 11.19 *All But My Life: A Memoir* by Gerda Weissman Klein, 1995, New York, NY: Hill and Wang.

Figure 11.20 *The Story of My Experiments with Truth: An Autobiography* by Mohandas Karamchand (Mahatma) Gandhi, 2014, Seattle WA: CreateSpace.

Figure 11.21 The Who Is series publishes biographies of interesting women much less frequently than biographies of men. *Who is Malala Yousafzai?* By Dinah Brown and illustrated by Andrew Thomson, 2015, New York, NY: Grosset & Dunlap.

Figure 11.22 Michael Jackson and Jesus were two of the many male biographies published in the same year. *Who was Michael Jackson?* By Megan Stine and illustrated by Joseph J.M. Qiu, 2015, New York, NY: Grosset & Dunlap.

Figure 11.23 *What was the Underground Railroad?* By Yona Zeldis McDonough and illustrated by Lauren Mortimer and James Bennett, 2013, New York, NY: Grosset & Dunlap.

Figure 11.24 On their own, Amelia and Eleanor are immensely important. Together, they are unstoppable trailblazers. *Amelia and Eleanor Go For a Ride* by Pam Munoz Ryan and illustrated by Brian Selznick, 1999, New York, NY: Scholastic

Figure 11.25 Jane Goodall is an amazing scientist and conservationist. *The Watcher: Jane Goodall's Life with the Chimps* by Jeanette Winter, 2011, New York, NY: Schwartz and Wade

Figure 11.26 I like biographies of lesser known people such as *Harlem's Little Blackbird* by Renee Watson, 2012, New York, NY: Random House

Figure 11.27 From braces to winning races. Women are sports heroes too. *Wilma Unlimited: How Wilma Rudolph Became the Fastest Woman* by Kathleen Krull and illustrated by David Diaz, 2000, New York, NY: HMH Books for Young Readers

Figure 11.28 How many people know about the origins of the girl scouts? Here Come the Girl Scouts!: The Amazing All True Story of Juliette 'Daisy' Gordon Low and Her Great Adventure by Shana Corey and illustrated by Hadley Hooper, 2012, New York, NY: Scholastic.

Figure 11.29 This collection of stories features brave women who changed the space industry. *Almost Astronauts: 13 Women Who Dared to Dream* written by Tanya Lee Stone, 2009, New York, NY: Candlewick

Figure 11.30 He never lost hope. *Nelson Mandela* by Kadir Nelson, 2013, New York, NY: Katherine Tegen Books

Figure 11.31 I've never thought about the creation of Mount Rushmore; just the final result. Here is the inside story. *Hanging Off Jefferson's Nose: Growing Up on Mount Rushmore* by Tina Coury and illustrated by Sally Wern Comport, 2012, New York, NY: Dial

Figure 11.32 He created characters that millions of people have loved for decades. *Jim Henson: The Guy Who Played with Puppets* by Kathleen Krull and illustrated by Steve Johnson and Lou Fancher, 2011, New York, NY: Random House

Figure 11.33 David Adler tells Lou Gehrig's story from his childhood to his becoming the luckiest man on the face of the Earth. *Lou Gehrig* by David A. Adler and illustrated by Terry Widener, 2001, New York, NY: HMH Books for Young Readers

Figure 11.34 Here is a story of untapped talent. *It Jes' Happened: When Bill Traylor Started to Draw* by Don Tate and illustrated by R. Gregory Christie, 2012, New York, NY: Lee & Low

Figure 11.35 The Freedom Riders exhibited extraordinary bravery and changed the world. Freedom Riders: John Lewis and Jim Zwerg on the Front Lines of the Civil Rights Movement by Ann Bausum, 2005, Washington, D.C.: National Geographic Books

Figure 11.36 Fictional storytelling techniques are frequently used in Basher books. *Human Body: A Book with Guts!* By Dan Green and Simon Basher and illustrated by Simon Basher, 2011, New York, NY: Kingfisher.

Figure 11.37 Headings and subheadings, captions, diagrams, labels, text boxes, images, indexes, glossaries, and key words help readers understand *The Science Book: Big Ideas Simply Explained* by Dan Green, 2014, Washington, D.C.: DK Books.

Figure 11.38 In Vicki Cobb's book, the images help the reader think about the words. *I Face the Wind* by Vicki Cobb and illustrated by Julia Gorton, 2003, New York, NY: HarperCollins.

Figure 11.39 In Marion Dane Bauer's book, the images add interest to the text. *Wind* by Marion Dane Bauer and illustrated by John Wallace, 2003, New York, NY: Simon Spotlight.

Figure 11.40 In Pramod Jain's book, the images illustrate concepts that require visualization. *Wind Energy Engineering* by Pramod Jain, 2010, New York, NY: McGraw Hill.

Chapter 12

Figure 12.1 Table of "objectionable" words found in children's literature.

Figure 12.2 Sexually explicit content makes *Forever* one of the most challenged books. *Forever* by Judy Blume, 1975, Scarsdale, N.Y.: Bradbury Press. Cover art copyright 2007 by Simon & Schuster.

Figure 12.3 Homosexual themes often trigger parental challenges. One example is *Boy Meets Boy* by David Levithan, 2003, New York: Alfred A. Knopf.

Figure 12.4 Violence and the occult are a cause for concern for those who challenge *Scary Stories To Tell in the Dark* by Alvin Schwartz, and illustrated by Stephen Gammell, 1981, New York: Lippincott.
Figure 12.5 Religious groups often challenge *His Dark Materials* by Philip Pullman, 2007, New York: Alfred A. Knopf.

Figure 12.6 The Adventures of Captain Underpants: An Epic Novel by Dav Pilkey, 1997, New York: Blue Sky Press.

Figures 12.6 and 12.7 George and Harold disobey school rules and undermine authority in *The Adventures of Captain Underpants: An Epic Novel* by Dav Pilkey, 1997, New York: Blue Sky Press.

Figure 12.8 Ratings systems for fanfiction, movies, television, music, and video games.

Figure 12.9 I think Daniel Pennac sums up my views perfectly; children are young, but they have rights as readers. *The Rights of the Reader* by Daniel Pennac, translated by Sarah Hamp Adams, and illustrated by Quentin Blake, 2006, London, UK: Walker Books. Images copyright 2006 by Quentin Blake.

List of Videos

Chapter 1

Video 1.1
Schneider, J.J. & USF Media Innovation Team. (2016, March 15). *Overview of The Inside, Outside, and Upside Downs of Children's Literature: From Poets and Pop-ups to Princesses and Porridge.* [Video file]. Retrieved from http://www.kaltura.com/tiny/yn1jr

Chapter 2

Video 2.1.
MacmillanChildrens. (2010, August 16). *It's a Book by Lane Smith.* [Video file]. Retrieved from https://www.youtube.com/watch?v=x4BK_2VULCU

Video 2.2
Schneider, J.J. & USF Media Innovation Team. (2016, March 15). *Look, touch, shake, and swipe: Pop up books and interactive ebooks.* [Video file]. Retrieved from http://www.kaltura.com/tiny/wlrn1

Video 2.3
Griffin, M., Schneider, J.J. & USF Media Innovation Team. *The didactic origins of children's literature.* [Video file]. Retrieved from http://www.kaltura.com/tiny/vnmbg

Chapter 3

Video 3.1
Schneider, J.J. & USF Media Innovation Team. (2016, March 15). *Jenny's tour through the wackety stacks.* [Video file]. Retrieved from http://www.kaltura.com/tiny/rr3ev

Video 3.2
The New York Public Library. (2010, December 3). *Toddler story time. Webster Library.* [Video file]. Retrieved from http://www.nypl.org/audiovideo/toddler-story-time-webster-library

Video 3.3
Griffin, M., Schneider, J.J. & USF Media Innovation Team. (2016, March 15). *Using special collections.* [Video file]. Retrieved from http://www.kaltura.com/tiny/pcd3b

Video 3.4
Griffin, M., Schneider, J.J. & USF Media Innovation Team. (2016, March 15). *Nancy Drew: Then and now.* [Video file]. Retrieved from http://www.kaltura.com/tiny/u8z8v

Video 3.5
Griffin, M., Schneider, J.J. & USF Media Innovation Team. (2016, March 15). *The evolution of an author's manuscript: Luna by Julie Anne Peters.* [Video file]. Retrieved from http://www.kaltura.com/tiny/zul3z

Video 3.6
Griffin, M., Schneider, J.J. & USF Media Innovation Team. (2016, March 15). *The Alice in Wonderland Collection at the University of South Florida.* [Video file]. Retrieved from http://www.kaltura.com/tiny/vbkud

Video 3.7
Beddingfield, S., Schneider, J.J. & USF Media Innovation Team. (2016, March 15). *Inkwood Books*. [Video file]. Retrieved from http://www.kaltura.com/tiny/zk58b

Video 3.8
Hurley, A., Brown, J. & USF Media Innovation Team. (2016, March 15). *Inkwood Books Reading Groups*. [Video file]. Retrieved from http://www.kaltura.com/tiny/vnwmn

Chapter 4

Video 4.1
Schneider, J.J. & USF Media Innovation Team. (2016, March 15). *Frog and Toad Are Friends by Arnold Lobel*. [Video file]. Retrieved from http://www.kaltura.com/tiny/x7ypm

Video 4.2
TEDGlobal. (2009, July). *Chimamanda Ngozi Adichie: The danger of a single story*. [Video file]. Retrieved from http://www.ted.com/talks/chimamanda_adichie_the_danger_of_a_single_story?language=en.

Chapter 5

Video 5.1
Schneider, J.J. & USF Media Innovation Team. (2016, March 15). *Determining the communicative purpose of text and illustration*. [Video file]. Retrieved from http://www.kaltura.com/tiny/x1tmd

Video 5.2
Schneider, J.J. & USF Media Innovation Team. (2016, March 15). *How to read a picture book: Olivia by Ian Falconer*. [Video file]. Retrieved from http://www.kaltura.com/tiny/m79l0

Video 5.3
Schneider, J.J. & USF Media Innovation Team. (2016, March 15). *Visual purpose and illustrative style*. [Video file]. Retrieved from http://www.kaltura.com/tiny/lfhu3

Video 5.4
Schneider, J.J. & USF Media Innovation Team. (2016, March 15). *Reading development and selecting texts for children: birth to adolescence*. [Video file]. Retrieved from http://www.kaltura.com/tiny/v2fwj

Video 5.5
Margarella, E., Margarella, B., Schneider, J.J. & USF Media Innovation Team. (2016, March 15). *Reading to a newborn*. [Video file]. Retrieved from http://www.kaltura.com/tiny/m3fdp

Video 5.6
Cross, M., Cross, M., Cross, H., Schneider, J.J. & USF Media Innovation Team. (2016, March 15). *Reading to a baby*. [Video file]. Retrieved from http://www.kaltura.com/tiny/ol2hj

Video 5.7
Frier, A., Blanton, A., Frier-Blanton, H., Schneider, J.J. & USF Media Innovation Team. (2016, March 15). *Reading with a toddler*. http://www.kaltura.com/tiny/mg2he

Video 5.8
Margarella, E., Margarella, E., Margarella, B., Margarella, B., Schneider, J.J. & USF Media Innovation Team. (2016, March 15). *Reading with young children*. [Video file]. Retrieved from http://www.kaltura.com/tiny/k4ktd

Video 5.9
Han, H.J., Oh, C., Oh, A., Schneider, J.J. & USF Media Innovation Team. (2016, March 15). *Reading with older children*. [Video file]. Retrieved from http://www.kaltura.com/tiny/ng9aq

Chapter 6

Video 6.1.1
Edwards, K., Schneider, J.J., & USF Media Innovation Team. (2016, March 15). *Interactive school library video series: The Rudolph Library introduction*. [Video file]. Retrieved from http://www.kaltura.com/iny/j1b7w

Video 6.1.2
Edwards, K., Schneider, J.J., & USF Media Innovation Team. (2016, March 15). *Interactive school library video series: The Rudolph Library Teaching area*. [Video file]. Retrieved from http://www.kaltura.com/tiny/ogxtt

Video 6.1.3
Edwards, K., Schneider, J.J., & USF Media Innovation Team. (2016, March 15). *Interactive school library video series: The Rudolph Library Computer Stations*. [Video file]. Retrieved from http://www.kaltura.com/tiny/qbm2m

Video 6.1.4
Edwards, K., Schneider, J.J., & USF Media Innovation Team. (2016, March 15). *Interactive school library video series: The Rudolph Library read around the world*. [Video file]. Retrieved from http://www.kaltura.com/tiny/s7hyu

Video 6.1.5
Edwards, K., Schneider, J.J., & USF Media Innovation Team. (2016, March 15). *Interactive school library video series: The Rudolph Library Storytime area*. [Video file]. Retrieved from http://www.kaltura.com/tiny/jgue8

Video 6.1.6
Edwards, K., Schneider, J.J., & USF Media Innovation Team. (2016, March 15). Interactive school library video series: The Rudolph Library collections development. [Video file]. Retrieved from http://www.kaltura.com/tiny/o63fo

Video 6.2
Schneider, J.J., & USF Media Innovation Team. (2016, March 15). *Jean Ann Cone Library at Berkeley Preparatory School*. [Video file]. Retrieved from http://www.kaltura.com/tiny/sfnp6

Video 6.3
Frances, J.H., Schneider, J.J., & USF Media Innovation Team. (2016, March 15). *Bess the Book Bus*. [Video file]. Retrieved from http://www.kaltura.com/tiny/yiq4t

Chapter 7

Video 7.1
Schneider, J.J. & USF Media Innovation Team. (2016, March 15). *Olivia by Ian Falconer*. [Video file]. Retrieved from http://www.kaltura.com/tiny/rtws0

Video 7.2
Schneider, J.J. & USF Media Innovation Team. (2016, March 15). *Olivia Saves the Circus by Ian Falconer*. [Video file]. Retrieved from http://www.kaltura.com/tiny/xpz02

Video 7.3
Schneider, J.J. & USF Media Innovation Team. (2016, March 15). *Math Curse by Jon Scieszka and illustrated by Lane Smith*. [Video file]. Retrieved from http://www.kaltura.com/tiny/jfcxf

Video 7.4
Schneider, J.J. & USF Media Innovation Team. (2016, March 15). *Science Verse by Jon Scieszka and illustrated by Lane Smith*. [Video file]. Retrieved from http://www.kaltura.com/tiny/s4rlm

Video 7.5
Schneider, J.J. & USF Media Innovation Team. (2016, March 15). *Click, Clack, Moo: Cows that Type by Doreen Cronin and illustrated by Betsy Lewin*. [Video file]. Retrieved from http://www.kaltura.com/tiny/t57dm

Video 7.6
Schneider, J.J. & USF Media Innovation Team. (2016, March 15). *Dooby Dooby Moo by Doreen Cronin and illustrated by Betsy Lewin*. [Video file]. Retrieved from http://www.kaltura.com/tiny/v3gb1

Video 7.7
Griffin, M., Schneider, J.J. & USF Media Innovation Team. (2016, March 15). *Series books for girls and boys*. [Video file]. Retrieved from http://www.kaltura.com/tiny/ypxbq

Video 7.8
Schneider, J.J. & USF Media Innovation Team. (2016, March 15). *Meeting authors and illustrators: Autographs, materials, and tweets*. [Video file]. Retrieved from http://www.kaltura.com/tiny/z8k2b

Chapter 8

Video 8.1
Griffin, M., Schneider, J.J. & USF Media Innovation Team. (2016, March 15). *The evolution of an author's manuscript: Luna by Julie Anne Peters*. [Video file]. Retrieved from http://www.kaltura.com/tiny/zul3z

Video 8.2
Griffin, M., Schneider, J.J. & USF Media Innovation Team. (2016, March 15). *Chromolithography and early methods for color illustrations*. [Video file]. Retrieved from http://www.kaltura.com/tiny/lnlwj

Chapter 9

Video 9.1
Yee, K., Schneider, J.J., & USF Media Innovation Team. (2016, March 15). *Studying folk and fairy tales: The Brothers Grimm*. [Video file]. Retrieved from http://www.kaltura.com/tiny/te32o

Chapter 10

Video 10.1
Schneider, J.J. & USF Media Innovation Team. (2016, March 15). *Survey of poetry*. [Video file]. Retrieved from http://www.kaltura.com/tiny/m0p00

Video 10.2
Glenn, D. (2013, January 31). *IGNITE choral speaking: Speak first chapter* [Video file]. Retrieved from https://www.youtube.com/watch?v=Cp-VTHGIKWA

Video 10.3
Schubert, J. (2008, April 8). *Choral reading example* [Video file]. Retrieved from https://www.youtube.com/watch?v=LFRzl2Oe_Bs

Video 10.4
Queen Latifah (2014, November 4). *Changing the world, one word at a time! The Queen Latifah Show* [Video file]. Retrieved from https://www.youtube.com/watch?v=YshUDa10JYY

Video 10.5
Beta Hi-Fi Archive (2009, June 5). *Judy Collins "Old Lady Who Swallowed a Fly" Muppet Show- 1977* [Video file]. Retrieved from https://www.youtube.com/watch?v=qC_xO2aN_IA&list=RDqC_xO2aN_IA#t=4

Video 10.6
The Tonight Show Starring Jimmy Fallon (2013, March 13). *Three Michael McDonalds sing "Row, Row, Row Your Boat" (with Jimmy Fallon & Justin Timberlake)* [Video file]. Retrieved from https://www.youtube.com/watch?v=JeCD4bIkQwg

Video 10.7
Glenn, D. (2013, January 31). *IGNITE choral speaking: Speak 4th chapter* [Video file]. Retrieved from https://www.youtube.com/watch?v=gbtMDrxi9JY

Video 10.8
Moon, W. (2013, February 24). *Valentine's Day poem/Moon whole class* [Video file]. Retrieved from https://www.youtube.com/watch?v=HJK2Lg5NfmM

Video 10. 9
Ross, J., Brown, C., Schneider, J.J., & USF Media Innovation Team. (2016, March 15). *Performing a Book.* [Video file]. Retrieved from http://www.kaltura.com/tiny/ul6a9

Video 10.10
Osvath, C., Schneider, J.J., & USF Media Innovation Team. (2016, March 15). *Building a poem.* [Video file]. Retrieved from http://www.kaltura.com/tiny/zyjww

Chapter 11

Video 11.1
Schneider, J.J. & USF Media Innovation Team. (2016, March 15). *Survey of information books.* [Video file]. Retrieved from http://www.kaltura.com/tiny/xhgpm

Video 11.2
Schneider, J.J. & USF Media Innovation Team. (2016, March 15). *Survey of biography books.* [Video file]. Retrieved from http://www.kaltura.com/tiny/njvw5

Video 11.3
Schneider, J.J. & USF Media Innovation Team. (2016, March 15). *Information book read aloud.* Retrieved from http://www.kaltura.com/tiny/sikgx

Video 11.4
Schneider, J.J. & USF Media Innovation Team. (2016, March 15). *Survey of information book illustration.* [Video file]. Retrieved from http://www.kaltura.com/tiny/noij4

Chapter 12

Video 12.1
Griffin, M., Schneider, J.J. & USF Media Innovation Team. (2016, March 15). *Authors fight back: Censorship and editorial control in My Brother Sam is Dead.* [Video file]. Retrieved from http://www.kaltura.com/tiny/swt56

Contributors

The following individuals contributed to this book by sharing their ideas, experiences, and perspectives on children's literature through writing, art, demonstration, and discussion.

Anne W. Anderson, a doctoral candidate at the University of South Florida, Tampa, is also the Director of Blended and Online Learning for Eckerd College's Program for Experienced Learners. She studies the Big Ideas of Life found in children's literature and other texts and admits to bouts of binge reading mysteries set in other times and places.
awanderson@mail.usf.edu

Stefani Beddingfield has been an avid reader ever since she promised her mother she would stay outside and read in her treehouse all summer if she didn't have to go to Lazy W Summer Camp and ride horses. The rest is history. She knows some Spanish, was a Peace Corps volunteer in Ecuador, built an accessible playground, got married, got unmarried and has two adorable daughters who are really good at math but like to read too. She's been the owner of Inkwood Books since April 1, 2013 and doesn't feel like it was a foolish decision at all.
inkwoodbooks@gmail.com

Kathleen Edwards is the Lower Division Librarian at Berkeley Preparatory School in Tampa, Florida. She has been a teaching librarian for 13 years. Kathleen has a Bachelor of Arts degree in Sociology with a minor in Anthropology from the University of New Orleans. She earned a Master of Library and Information Science degree from the University of South Florida.
edwarkat@berkeleyprep.org

Jennifer E. Frances founded Bess the Book Bus, a mobile literacy outreach, in 2002. She named the bus in honor of her Nana, Bess O'Keefe, the person who taught Jennifer the joy of reading. Bess the Book Bus was founded on one simple premise - bring that same joy of reading to children everywhere. From humble beginnings with a Volkswagen van, Bess the Book Bus has traveled across 48 states, serving 30,000 children and giving away over 50,000 books a year.
bessthebookbus@gmail.com

Melanie Griffin is Special Collections Librarian at the University of South Florida, where she serves as curator of the science fiction and children's literature collections. Melanie holds an MLIS with a concentration in Rare Books Librarianship and an MA in British Literature, both from the University of South Carolina, and she is currently pursuing a PhD in Children's Literature at the University of South Florida.
griffin@usf.edu

Csaba Osvath is a doctoral student in the College of Education at University of South Florida, pursuing a specialization in literacy studies with a focus on qualitative methods and arts-based research. His research explores the epistemological and pedagogical roles/functions of art making in the context of literacy education. Csaba also maintains a Children's Literature Facebook page:
https://www.facebook.com/Csaba-Osvath-On-Childrens-Literature-126746794107934/.
csabaosvath@mail.usf.edu

Lindsay Persohn likes to read books, articles, magazines, websites, and even her student's papers. She is former elementary school teacher, a former school librarian, a teacher of people who will be teachers, and an aspiring bookseller. When she is not reading or teaching, Lindsay likes to spend time with her kindhearted,

hilarious family and friends.
lindsayfromhp@gmail.com

Jennifer Ross is an alumna of Stetson University, earning a Bachelor of Arts degree. In her current position at Muller Elementary Magnet School, she established a large children's chorus, Muller Chorale, transformed a traditional children's theater program into a children's musical theater ensemble aptly named, Broadway Bound, and led multiple instrumental ensembles all while teaching general music classes that integrate all subject areas. She also accompanies the Muller Chorale and the Muller String Orchestra in concert. Jennifer Ross has experience teaching voice privately and working with adult learners. She is also an accomplished soprano who performs professionally whenever possible.
jennyross_tampa@gmail.com

Bethany Schneider is a student, artist, athlete, musician, scientist, bug watcher, reader, and all around Renaissance woman. Her favorite book of all time is Animals, but she is also partial to *Dune, The Hobbit, Harry Potter* (of course), anime, manga, and all things Whovian, Supernatural, mysterious, and interesting.

Mary Schneider is a word girl (spelling bee champ), math whiz, book battler, and storywriter. She is also a player of bagpipes and piano, softball and volleyball. Mary is also an expert in creating persuasive texts and oral arguments. Her favorite book is *Harry Potter* and she's partial to the 11th Doctor. But who isn't?

Kevin Yee is the Director of the Academy of Teaching and Learning Excellence at the University of South Florida and has worked in faculty development since 2004. He earned his PhD in German from UC Irvine. Dr. Yee has taught courses on German Romanticism, fairy tales, and Walt Disney World.
kyee@usf.edu

References

Abrams, J.C. (1970). Learning disabilities: A complex phenomenon. *The Reading Teacher, 23*(4), 299–367. Retrieved from http://www.jstor.org/stable/20196309.

Abrams, M. (1953). *The mirror and the lamp.* New York: Oxford University Press.

Abrams, M.H. (Ed.). (1975). *Norton anthology of English literature.* New York, NY: Norton & Co.

Allington, R.L. (2002). *Big brother and the national reading curriculum: How ideology trumped evidence.* Portsmouth, NH: Heinemann.

Allington, R.L. & Gabriel, R. (2012). Every child, every day. *Educational Leadership, 69*(6), 10-15.

Allington, R., & Pearson, P.D. (2011). The casualties of policy on early literacy development. *Language Arts, 89*(1), 70.

Alvarez, M.C., & Risko, V.J. (1988). Using a thematic organizer to facilitate transfer learning with college developmental studies students. *Literacy Research and Instruction, 28*(2), 1-15. http://dx.doi.org/10.1080/19388078909557964

Alvermann, D.E. (1987). *Using discussion to promote reading comprehension.* International Reading Association, Newark, DE.

American Federation of Teachers (2014). Testing, testing. *Educational Leadership, 71*(6), 8.

American Library Association (n.d.). Sibert Informational Book Award: Terms and criteria. Retrieved from http://www.ala.org/alsc/awardsgrants/bookmedia/sibertmedal/sibertterms/sibertmedaltrms.

American Library Association Council. (1996). *Library Bill of Rights.* Chicago, IL: ALA.

Anderson, R.C., & Pearson, P.D. (1984). A schema-theoretic view of basic processes in reading comprehension. *Handbook of reading research, 1,* 255-291.

Applebee, A.N. (1978). *A child's concept of story.* Chicago: University of Chicago Press.

Applebee, A.N. (1993). *Literature in the secondary school: Studies of curriculum and instruction in the United States.* Urbana, IL: National Council of Teachers of English.

Aristotle, Buckley, T.W.A., & Hobbes, T. (1900). *Aristotle's treatise on rhetoric.* London: George Bell & Sons.

Ashcroft v. Civil Liberties Union (00-1293) 535 U.S. 564 (2002) 217 F.3d 162 ("ACLU II").

Ashliman, D. (2013). *Brothers Grimm home page.* Retrieved from http://www.pitt.edu/~dash/grimm.html

Ashliman, D. (2015). *Grimm Brothers' home page: Chronology of their life.* Retrieved from http://www.pitt.edu/~dash/grimm.html.

Atwell, N. (1987). *In the middle: Writing, reading, and learning with adolescents.* Portsmouth, NY: Heinemann Educational Books.

Bain, A. (1866). *English composition and rhetoric* (enlarged ed.). New York, NY: D. Appleton.

Bang, M. (2000). *Picture this: How pictures work.* San Francisco, CA: Chronicle Books.

Barr, R., Pearson, P.D., Kamil, M.L., & Mosenthal, P.B. (1996). *Handbook of reading research* (Vol. 2). London, England: Psychology Press.

Beach, J.D. (2015). Do children read the children's literature adults recommend? A comparison of adults' and children's annual "best" lists in the United States 1975–2005. *New Review of Children's Literature & Librarianship, 21*(1), 17. http://dx.doi.org/10.1080/13614541.2015.976075

Beach, R. (1993). *A teacher's introduction to reader-response theories. NCTE teacher's introduction series*. Urbana, IL: National Council of Teachers of English.

Bell, B.W. (1917). The Colored branches of the Louisville Free Public Library. *Bulletin of the American Library Association*, 169-173.

Bergman, G.F.J. (1983). 'Jacobs, Joseph (1854–1916)', *Australian dictionary of biography,* National Centre of Biography, Australian National University. Retrieved from http://adb.anu.edu.au/biography/jacobs-joseph-6817/text11797.

Berman, R.A., & Katzenberger, I. (2004). Form and function in introducing narrative and expository texts: A developmental perspective. *Discourse Processes: A Multidisciplinary Journal, 38*(1), 57-94. http://dx.doi.org/10.1207/s15326950dp3801_3

Biancarosa, G. & Snow, C. (2004). *Reading next: A vision for action and research in middle and high school literacy: A report from the Carnegie Corporation of New York*. New York, NY: Alliance for Excellent Education.

Bishop, R.S. (1990). Mirrors, windows, and sliding glass doors. *Perspectives, 6*(3), ix–xi.

Bissett, D.J. (1969). *The usefulness of children's books in the reading program*. Paper presented at the International Reading Association Conference, Kansas City, MO.

Bluestone, M. (2015). *U.S. publishing industry's annual survey reveals $28 billion in revenue in 2014.* Association of American Publishers. Retrieved from http://publishers.org/news/us-publishing-industry%E2%80%99s-annual-survey-reveals-28-billion-revenue-2014.

Board of Education v. Pico, 457 U.S. 853 (1982, pp. 864-5).

Bogart, D. (Ed.). (2015). *The Bowker Annual 2015: Library and Book Trade Almanac.* Information Today.

Bond, G.L. & Dykstra, R. (1967). The cooperative research study in first-grade reading instruction, *Reading Research Quarterly, 2*(4), 9-142. http://dx.doi.org/10.2307/746948

Bostic, M.B. (2016). *Artist's & graphic designer's market*. Blue Ash, OH: F+W Media.

Bostwick, A.E. (1910). *The American public library*. New York, NY: D. Appleton and Company.

Botel, M., Holsclaw, C. & Brothers, A. (1964). *Patterns and spelling in writing*. Chicago, IL: Follett Publishing Company.

Bowditch, L.P. (1976). Why the whats are when: Mutually contextualizing realms of narrative. *Berkeley Linguistic Society, 2,* 59-77.

Brenner, R. (2011). Comics and graphic novels. In S. Wolf, K. Coats, P. Enciso, & C. Jenkins (Eds.), *Handbook of Research on Children's and Young Adult Literature,* (pp. 256-266), New York, NY: Routledge.

Broudy, O. (2004). Paula Fox: The art of fiction No. 181. *The Paris Review, 170*. Retrieved from http://www.theparisreview.org/interviews/1/the-art-of-fiction-no-181-paula-fox.

Brown v. Entertainment Merchants Association, 564 U.S. (2011).

Brownell, K.D. & Warner, K.E. (2009). The perils of ignoring history: Big Tobacco played dirty and millions died. How similar is Big Food? *Milbank Quarterly, 87*(1), 259-294. http://dx.doi.org/10.1111/j.1468-0009.2009.00555.x

Buchwald, E., (1988). *Emilie Buchwald talk at the Hennepin County Library*. Minnetonka, MN: Hennepin County Library.

Bullock, E.D. (1901). Practical cataloging. *Public Libraries, 6,* 135-6.

Burnes, S. (2014). Why this grown-up reads YA. *The Paris Review.* Retrieved from http://www.theparisreview.org/blog/2014/10/24/why-this-grown-up-reads-ya/

Burness, E. & Griswold, J. (1982). P.L. Travers: The art of fiction No. 63. *The Paris Review, 86.* Retrieved from http://www.theparisreview.org/interviews/3099/the-art-of-fiction-no-63-p-l-travers.

Bus, A.G., Van Ijzendoorn, M.H., & Pellegrini, A.D. (1995). Joint book reading makes for success in learning to read: A meta-analysis on intergenerational transmission of literacy. *Review of educational research, 65*(1), 1-21. http://dx.doi.org/10.3102/00346543065001001

Bush, G.W. (2001, February 27). *Address to the Joint Session of Congress.* Retrieved from http://georgewbush-whitehouse.archives.gov/infocus/bushrecord/documents/Selected_Speeches_George_W_Bush.pdf

Butler, F. (1973). The editor's high chair: Children's literature and the humanities. *Children's Literature* 2(1), 8-10. *Project MUSE.* Retrieved from https://muse.jhu.edu/. http://dx.doi.org/10.1353/chl.0.0461.

Campione, J. (1981, April). *Learning, academic achievement, and instruction.* Paper delivered at the Second Annual Conference on Reading Research of the Center for the Study of Reading, New Orleans, LA.

Carden, M. (1949). *The Carden method.* Place of publication not identified: Mae Carden, Incorporated.

Carson, J. (1912). The children's share in a public library. *Library Journal, 37,* 254.

Casson, L. (2001). Libraries in the ancient world. *New Haven-London,* 16.

Caswell, L.J., & Duke, N.K. (1998). Non-narrative as a catalyst for literacy development. *Language Arts, 75,* 108–117.

Chall, J. (1967). *Learning to read: The great debate.* New York: McGraw Hill.

Chaston, J.D. (1997). The "Ozification" of American children's fantasy films: The blue bird, Alice in Wonderland, and Jumanji. *Children's Literature Association Quarterly, 22*(1), 13-20. http://dx.doi.org/10.1353/chq.0.1124

Cho, K.S., & Krashen, S.D. (1994). Acquisition of vocabulary from the Sweet Valley Kids series: Adult ESL acquisition. *Journal of Reading,* 662-667.

Clark, S.K., Jones, C.D., & Reutzel, D.R. (2013). Using the text structures of information books to teach writing in the primary grades. *Early Childhood Education Journal, 41,* 265-271. http://dx.doi.org/10.1007/s10643-012-0547-4

Clay, M.M. (1972). *Reading: The patterning of complex behaviour.* Portsmouth, NH: Heinemann.

Clay, M.M. (1985). *The early detection of reading difficulties.* Portsmouth, NH: Heinemann.

Clay, M.M. (1989). Concepts about print in English and other languages. *The Reading Teacher 42*: 268-276.

Cohen, D. (2000). Andrew Carnegie and academic library philanthropy: The case of Rollins College, Winter Park, Florida. *Libraries & Culture, 35*(3), 389-413.

Cohen, J. (2001). Defining identification: A theoretical look at the identification of audiences with media characters. *Mass Communication & Society, 4*(3), 245-264.

Comenius, J.A. (1887). *The Orbis Pictus*. (11th ed.). (trans. Charles Hoole, 1658). Syracuse, NY: C.W. Bardeen.

Comenius, J.A. (1896). *The great didactic of John Amos Comenius*. (trans. M.W. Keatinge). London, UK: Adam and Charles Black.

Cott, J. (1981). *Pipers at the gates of dawn*. New York, NY: Random House.

Cox, D. (2012). Is Accelerated Reader best practice for all?. *California Reader, 46*(2).

Crichton, M. (1993). *Jurassic Park*. London, UK: Arrow.

Crichton, M. (1995). *The Lost World: A Novel*. New York, NY: Knopf.

Crisp, T. (2011). It's not the book, it's not the author, it's the award: The Lambda Literary Award and the case for strategic essentialism. *Children's Literature in Education, 42*(2), 91-104. http://dx.doi.org/10.1007/s10583-010-9126-8

Crisp, T. (2015). A content analysis of Orbis Pictus award-winning nonfiction, 1990-2014. *Language Arts, 92*(4), (241-155).

Crowley, P., & Marshall, F. (Producers), & Trevorrow, C. (Director). (2015). *Jurassic World* [Motion Picture]. United States of America: Universal.

Crusius, T.W. & Channell, C.E. (2009). *The aims of argument: A brief guide* (6th ed.). Boston, MA: McGraw.

Cullinan, B.E. (1987). *Children's literature in the reading program*. International Reading Association, Newark, DE.

Cutler, M.S. (1892). What a woman librarian earns. *Library Journal, 18*, 89-9.

Daly, K.N. (1992/2009). *Greek and Roman mythology A to Z*. (3rd ed. Revised by Marian Rengel). New York, NY: Chelsea House Publishers.

Darling-Hammond, L. (2011). Excessive testing is a dangerous obsession. *The New York Times*. Retrieved from http://www.nytimes.com/roomfordebate/2011/05/30/testing-students-to-grade-teachers/execessive-testing-is-a-dangerous-obsession.

Dennis, D.V. (2013). Heterogeneity or homogeneity What assessment data reveal about struggling adolescent readers. *Journal of Literacy Research, 45*(1), 3-21. http://dx.doi.org/10.1177/1086296X12468431

Dewey, M. (1891). *Decimal classification and relative index for libraries, clippings, notes, etc*. New York, NY: Library Bureau.

Diaz de Chumacerio, C.L. (1990). Songs of the countertransference in psychotherapy dyads. *The American Journal of Psychoanalysis, 50* (1), 75-89.

Dimitriadis, G. & Kamberelis, G. (2006). Sigmund Freud. *Theory for education*. New York, NY: Routledge.

DiPardo, A. (1990). Narrative knowers, expository knowledge: Discourse as a dialectic. *Written Communication, 7*(1), 59-95. http://dx.doi.org/10.1177/0741088390007001003

Donovan, C.A. & Smolkin, L.B. (2011). Supporting informational writing in the elementary grades, *The Reading Teacher, 64*(6), 406-416. http://dx.doi.org/10.1598/RT.64.6.2

Dubow, E.F., Huesmann, L.R., & Boxer, P. (2009). A social-cognitive-ecological framework for understanding the impact of exposure to persistent ethnic-political violence on children's psychosocial adjustment. *Clinical Child And Family Psychology Review, 12*(2), 113-126. http://dx.doi.org/10.1007/s10567-009-0050-7

Dubrovin, V. (1979). The new hi/lo books: Stepping stones to reading success. *Curriculum Review, 18*(5), 384-85.

Dudak, C. (2013). 10 works you didn't know were ghostwritten. *Mandatory*. Retrieved from http://www.mandatory.com/2013/06/17/10-works-you-didnt-know-were-ghostwritten/4

Duke, N.K. (2000). 3.6 minutes per day: The scarcity of informational texts in first grade. *Reading Research Quarterly*, 202-224. http://dx.doi.org/10.1598/RRQ.35.2.1

Dupuis, M.M., Askov, E.N., & Lee, J.W. (1979). Changing attitudes toward content area reading: The content area reading project. *The Journal of Educational Research, 73*(2), 66-74. http://dx.doi.org/10.1080/00220671.1979.10885210

Dutro, E. & McIver, M.C. (2011). Imagining a writer's life: Extending the connection between readers and books. *Handbook of Research on Children's and Young Adult Literature,* (pp. 92-107), New York, NY: Routledge.

Dykstra, R. (1968). *Classroom implications of the first-grade reading studies.* Paper presented at the College Reading Association Conference, Knoxville, TN.

Eagleton, T. (2008). *Literary theory: An introduction*. Minneapolis, MN: University of Minnesota Press.

Eddy, J. (2006). *Bookwomen: Creating an empire in children's book publishing, 1919–1939*. Madison, WI: University of Wisconsin Press. *Project MUSE*. Retrieved from https://muse.jhu.edu/.

Edelstein, R.R. (1970). Use of group processes in teaching retarded readers. *The Reading Teacher, 23*(4), 318–393. Retrieved from http://www.jstor.org/stable/20196312

Eeds, M., & Wells, D. (1989). Grand conversations: An exploration of meaning construction in literature study groups. *Research in the Teaching of English, 23*(1), 4-29.

Ellis, A. (1963). *A history of children's reading and literature: The commonwealth and international library: Library and technical information division*. London, UK: Elsevier.

Emma, C. (2015). Education department: Too much testing, Partly our fault. *Politico*, 10-24-15, Retrieved from http://www.politico.com/story/2015/10/education-department-too-much-testing-215131.

Erznoznik v. City of Jacksonville, 422 U.S. 205, 212-14 (1975).

Everhart, N. (2013). Defining a vision of outstanding school libraries. *Teacher Librarian, 41*(1), 14.

Ferguson, C.J. (2013). Violent video games and the Supreme Court: Lessons for the scientific community in the wake of Brown v. Entertainment Merchants Association. *American Psychologist, 68*(2), 57-74. http://dx.doi.org/10.1037/a0030597

Fisher, C.J., & Natarella, M.A. (1982). Young children's preferences in poetry: A national survey of first, second and third graders. *Research in the Teaching of English, 16*(4), 339-354.

Flanzraich, G.L. (1990). *The role of the Library Bureau and Gaylord Brothers in the development of library technology, 1876-1930*. New York, NY: Columbia University.

Fletcher, W.I. (1894). *Public libraries in America*. Boston, MA: Roberts Brothers.

Francis, B.H., & Lance, K.C. (2011). The impact of library media specialists on students and how it is valued by administrators and teachers: Findings from the latest studies in Colorado and Idaho. *TechTrends, 55*(4), 63-70. http://dx.doi.org/10.1007/s11528-011-0513-9

Franco, L., & Kennedy, K. (Producers), & Johnston, J. (Director). (2001). *Jurassic Park III* [Motion Picture]. United States of America: Universal.

Freud, S. (1900). *The interpretation of dreams*. Retrieved from http://psychclassics.yorku.ca/Freud/Dreams/dreams.pdf.

Freud, S. (1916/2001). Sigmund Freud. In Rice, P., & Waugh, P. (Eds.). *Modern literary theory*. New York, NY: Bloomsbury.

Gallagher, K. (2009). *Readicide: How schools are killing reading and what you can do about it*. Portland, ME: Stenhouse.

Gambrell, L.B., & Heathington, B.S. (1981). Adult disabled readers' metacognitive awareness about reading tasks and strategies. *Journal of literacy research, 13*(3), 215-222. http://dx.doi.org/10.1080/10862968109547409

Gates, A.I. (1961). Results of teaching a system of phonics. *The Reading Teacher, 14*(4), 248–252. Retrieved from http://www.jstor.org/stable/20197386

Gay, C. (n.d.). *ChLA: 1973-1983*. Retrieved from http://www.childlitassn.org/assets/docs/resources-carol_gay_history_5pages.pdf.

Genette, G. (1980/1988). *Narrative discourse*. New York, NY: Cornell University Press.

Godfrey, C.B. (1892). *U.S. Patent No. 478,509*. Washington, DC: U.S. Patent and Trademark Office.

Goodman, K. (1969). Analysis of oral reading miscues: Applied psycholinguistics. *Reading Research Quarterly, 5,* 9-30. http://dx.doi.org/10.2307/747158

Goodman, K.S. (1986). *What's whole in whole language? A parent/teacher guide to children's learning*. Portsmouth, NH: Heinemann Educational Books.

Goodman, K.S. & Goodman, Y.M. (1977). Learning about psycholinguistic processes by analyzing oral reading. *Harvard Educational Review, 47,* 317-333. http://dx.doi.org/10.17763/haer.47.3.528434xv67l534x8

Goodman, Y.M. (1978). Kid watching: An alternative to testing. *National Elementary Principal, 57*(4), 41-5.

Goodman, Y.M. & Burke, C.L. (1972). *Reading miscue inventory*. New York, NY: MacMillan.

Graham, R. (2014a). Against YA. *The Slate Book Review*. Retrieved from http://www.slate.com/articles/arts/books/2014/06/against_ya_adults_should_be_embarrassed_to_read_children_s_books.html

Graham, R. (2014b). Should adults be embarrassed to read young-adult books? *National Public Radio*. [Audio transcript] Retrieved from http://www.npr.org/2014/06/08/320024790/should-adults-be-embarrassed-to-read-young-adult-books.

Graham, S., McKeown, D., Kiuhara, S.A., Harris, K.R. (2012). A meta-analysis of writing instruction for students in the elementary grades. *Journal of Educational Psychology, 104,* 879-896.

Greene, S. (2008). *Literacy as a civil right: Reclaiming social justice in literacy teaching and learning* (Vol. 316). London, UK: Peter Lang.

Gregory, L.P., & Morrison, T.G. (1998). Lap reading for young at-risk children: Introducing families to books. *Early Childhood Education Journal, (26)*2, pp. 67-77. http://dx.doi.org/10.1023/A:1022995027819

Grenby, M.O. (2015). *The origins of children's literature* [Online museum exhibit]. The British Library. Retrieved from http://www.bl.uk/romantics-and-victorians/articles/the-origins-of-childrens-literature

Gross, D.A. (2015). The mystery of the hardy boys and the invisible authors. *The Atlantic*. Retrieved from http://www.theatlantic.com/entertainment/archive/2015/05/hardy-boys-nancy-drew-ghostwriters/394022/

Guthrie, J.T. (1980). Research views: The 1970s' comprehension research. *The Reading Teacher, 33*(7), 880–882. Retrieved from http://www.jstor.org/stable/20195137.

Haft, S., Weir, P., Witt, P.J., Thomas, T., Schulman, T., Williams, R., Leonard, R.S., ... Buena Vista Home Entertainment (Firm). (2006). *Dead Poets Society*. Burbank, CA: Touchstone Home Entertainment.

Hamilton, E. (1942/2011). *Mythology: Timeless tales of gods and heroes*. New York, NY: Grand Central Publishing.

Hammill, E. (2011). Listening for the scratch of a pen: Museums devoted to children's and young adult literature. In S. Wolf, K. Coats, P. Enciso, & C. Jenkins (Eds.), *Handbook of Research on Children's and Young Adult Literature,* (pp. 508-524), New York, NY: Routledge.

Hammond, M. (2002). "The great fiction bore": Free libraries and the construction of a reading public in England, 1880-1914. *Libraries & Culture, 37*(2), 83-108. http://dx.doi.org/10.1353/lac.2002.0026

Hanaway, E.S. (1887). The children's library in New York. *Library Journal,* p. 185.

Harris, R.D. (1915). The advantages of colored branch libraries. *Southern Workman, 44*(7), 385.

Harris, V.J. (1992). *Teaching multicultural literature in grades K-8*. Christopher-Gordon Pub.

Hay, J. & Wingo, C. (1954). *Reading with phonics*. Philadelphia, PA: Lippincott.

Hayes, K.J. (2008). Benjamin Franklin's library. *Mulford, Cambridge Companion to Benjamin Franklin*, 11-23.

Hazeltine, A.I. (Ed.). (1917). *Library work with children*. New York, NY: HW Wilson Company.

Hazeltine, A.I. (1921). What is a children's librarian?. *Public Libraries, 26*, 513.

Hewins, C.M. (1882). Boys' and girls' reading. *Library Journal,* p. 182.

Hewins, C.M. (1888). The history of children's books. *The Atlantic Monthly, 61*(363), 112-126.

Hewins, C.M. (1896). *Reading of the young*. U.S. Bureau of Education Papers prepared for the World's Library Congress held at the Columbian Exposition; ed. by M. Dewey, p. 944.

Hewins, C.M. (1915). *Books for boys and girls: A selected list*. Boston, MA: American Library Association Publishing Board.

High, P.C., Klass, P., Donoghue, E., Glassy, D., DelConte, B., Earls, M., ... & Schulte, E.E. (2014). Literacy promotion: An essential component of primary care pediatric practice. *Pediatrics, 134*(2), 404-409.

Horning, K.T. (2014). Children's books: Still an all-white world? *School Library Journal.* Retrieved from http://www.slj.com/2014/05/diversity/childrens-books-still-an-all-white-world/

Hoyle, K.N. (2011) Archives and special collections devoted to children's and young adult literature. In S. Wolf, K. Coats, P. Enciso, & C. Jenkins (Eds.), *Handbook of Research on Children's and Young Adult Literature,* (pp. 386-392), New York, NY: Routledge.

Huang, S. (2012). A mixed method study of the effectiveness of the Accelerated Reader program on middle school students' reading achievement and motivation. *Reading Horizons, 51*(3), 5.

Huck, C.S. (1992). Literacy and literature. *Language Arts,* 520-526.

Hynds, S.D. (1985). Interpersonal cognitive complexity and the literary response processes of adolescent readers. *Research in the Teaching of English, 19*(4), 386-402.

Ibis World. (2015). *Children's Book Publishing in the US: Market Research Report.* Retrieved from http://www.ibisworld.com/industry/childrens-book-publishing.html

International Reading Association. (2005). *Literacy development in the preschool years* [Position statement]. Newark, DE: Author.

International Reading Association. (2014). *Leisure reading* [Position statement]. Newark, DE: Author.

Iser, W. (1974). *The implied reader.* Baltimore, MD: John Hopkins University Press.

Ishikawa, M. (2012). Young people's encounters with museum collections: Expanding the range of contexts for art appreciation. *International Journal of Education through Art, 8*(1), 73-89.

Jacobs, J. (1893). The folk. *Folklore,* 4(2), 233-238. http://dx.doi.org/10.1080/0015587X.1893.9720155

Jansson, T. (1964/2010). The spring tune. In *Tales of Moominvalley* (pp. 3-16). (T. Warburton, Trans.) New York, NY: Square Fish. (Original work published 1962)

Jarrod, S. (2015). *Ci3: A Bright Future for Children's Book Market.* Retrieved from American Booksellers Association; Bookselling This Week, http://www.bookweb.org/news/ci3-bright-future-children%E2%80%99s-book-market

Jefferson, T., & Wilson, D.L. (2010). *Thomas Jefferson's Library.* The Lawbook Exchange, Ltd.

Jevons, W.S. (1881). The rationale of free public libraries. *Contemporary Review, 39,* 385-402.

Jones, T.J. (1917). *Negro education: A study of the private and higher schools for colored people in the United States* (Vol. 1). US Government Printing Office.

Jordan, A.M. (1913). A chapter in children's libraries. *Library Journal,* 20.

Joshi, A. & Mao, H. (2012). Adapting to succeed? Leveraging the brand equity of best-sellers to succeed at the box office. *Journal of the Academy of Marketing Science, 40,* 558-571. http://dx.doi.org/10.1007/s11747-010-0241-2

Kamil, M.L., Mosenthal, P.B., Pearson, P.D. & Barr, R. (2000). *Handbook of reading research* (Vol. 3). London, England: Psychology Press.

Kamil, M.L., Pearson, P.D., Moje, E.B., & Afflerbach, P. (Eds.). (2011). *Handbook of reading research* (Vol. 4). London, England: Routledge.

Karabell, Z. (2014). Why indie bookstores are on the rise again. *Slate.* Retrieved from http://www.slate.com/articles/business/the_edgy_optimist/2014/09/independent_bookstores_rising_they_can_t_compete_with_amazon_and_don_t_have.html.

Kennedy, K., & Molen, G.R. (Producers), & Speilberg, S. (Director). (1993). *Jurassic Park* [Motion Picture]. United States of America: Universal.

Kidd, K. (2009). Not censorship but selection: Censorship and/as prizing. *Children's Literature in Education, 40*(3), 197-216. http://dx.doi.org/10.1007/s10583-008-9078-4

Kiefer, B.Z., Hepler, S.I., Hickman, J., Huck, C.S. (2007). *Charlotte Huck's children's literature*. Boston, MA: McGraw-Hill.

Kiefer, B.Z. (2010). *Charlotte Huck's children's literature* (10th ed.). New York, NY: McGraw Hill.

Kinlock, L.M. (1935). The menace of the series books. *Elementary English Review, 12,* 9-11.

Knoblauch, A. (2011). A textbook argument: Definitions of argument in leading composition textbooks. *College Composition & Communication, 63*(2), 244-268.

Koester, H. (1998). Importance of the oral tradition: Oral tradition. *PBS Frontline, From Jesus to Christ*. Retrieved from http://www.pbs.org/wgbh/pages/frontline/shows/religion/story/oral.html.

Korat, O. (2010). Reading electronic books as a support for vocabulary, story comprehension and word reading in kindergarten and first grade. *Computers & Education, 55*(1), 24-31. http://dx.doi.org/10.1016/j.compedu.2009.11.014

Koutsoubou, M. (2010). The use of narrative analysis as a research and evaluation method of atypical language: The case of deaf writing. *International Journal of Bilingual Education and Bilingualism, 13*(2), 225–241.

Krashen, S.D. (1993). *The power of reading*. Santa Barbara, CA: Libraries Unlimited.

Krashen, S.D. (2011). *Free voluntary reading*. Santa Barbara, CA: Libraries Unlimited.

Kress, G. & van Leeuwen, T. (2006). *Reading images: The grammar of visual design* (2nd ed.). New York, NY: Routledge.

Kutiper, K., & Wilson, P. (1993). Updating poetry preferences: A look at the poetry children really like. *The Reading Teacher, 47*(1), 28-35.

Labov, W. (1972). *Language in the inner city*. Philadelphia, PA: University of Pennsylvania Press.

Lance, K.C., & Kachel, D. (2013). Achieving academic standards through the school library program. *Teacher Librarian, 40*(5), 8-13.

Larrick, N. (1965). The all-white world of children's books. *The Saturday Review,* 63-65.

Lauer, J.M., Lundsford, A., Atwill, J., … Uber-Kellogg, N. (2000). *Four worlds of writing: inquiry and action in context*. Boston, MA: Pearson Custom Publishing.

Lee, D.R. (1991). Faith cabin libraries: A study of an alternative library service in the segregated south, 1932-1960. *Libraries & Culture,* 169-182.

Lee, D.R. (1998). From segregation to integration: library services for blacks in South Carolina, 1923–1962. *Tucker, Untold Stories, 99*.

Liang, T. (2015). The effects of keyword cues and 3r strategy on children's e-book reading. *Journal of Computer Assisted Learning, 31*(2), 176-187. http://dx.doi.org/10.1111/jcal.12072

Lipson, M.Y., Valencia, S. W., Wixson, K. K., & Peters, C. W. (1993). Integration and thematic teaching: Integration to improve teaching and learning. *Language Arts,* 252-263.

Lonsdale, M. (2003). *Impact of school libraries on student achievement: a review of the research.* Australian Council for Educational Research, Victoria. Retrieved from http://www.asla.org.au/research/.

Lord, I.E., & Willcox, E.S. (1908). Open shelves and book losses. *Bulletin of the American Library Association*, 231-254.

Louie, B., & Sierschynski, J. (2015). Enhancing English learners' language development using wordless picture books. *The Reading Teacher, 69*(1), 103-111. http://dx.doi.org/10.1002/trtr.1376

Mabillard, A. (2000). *Why Study Shakespeare? Shakespeare Online.* Retrieved from http://www.shakespeare-online.com/biography/whystudyshakespeare.html.

Magary, D. (2012). If you give a mouse a cookie, you're fucked: 10 tips for avoiding terrible children's books. *Deadspin,* Retrieved from http://deadspin.com/5889376/if-you-give-a-mouse-a-cookie-youre-fucked-10-tips-for-avoiding-terrible-childrens-books

Malone, C.K. (1995). Louisville Free Public Library's racially segregated branches, 1905-35. *The Register of the Kentucky Historical Society*, 159-179.

Marcus, L.S. (2011). Point of departure. In S. Wolf, K. Coats, P. Enciso, & C. Jenkins (Eds.), *Handbook of Research on Children's and Young Adult Literature,* (pp. 393-394), New York, NY: Routledge.

Martinez, M., & Roser, N. (1985). Read it again: The value of repeated readings during storytime. *The Reading Teacher, 38*(8), 782-786.

Martinez, M.G., & Teale, W.H. (1993). Teacher storybook reading style: A comparison of six teachers. *Research in the Teaching of English*, 175-199.

Matthews, C. (1908). The growing tendency to over-emphasize the children's side. *Library Journal, 33,* 135-138.

Matthews, C. (1917). The growing tendency to over-emphasize the children's side. In A. Hazeltine (Ed.). *Library work with children,* (pp. 91-98). New York, NY: HW Wilson Company.

Mathiews, F.K. (1914). Blowing out the boy's brains. *Outlook.* 653.

May, V. (1917). Public libraries in the South. *Library Journal, 42*(1-6), 163.

McKenzie, J. (2005). Bums, poos and wees: carnivalesque spaces in the picture books of early childhood. or, has literature gone to the dogs?. *English Teaching: Practice And Critique, 4*(1), 81-94.

McNair, J.C. (2012). Poems about sandwich cookies, jelly, and chocolate: poetry in k-3 classrooms. *Young Children, 67*(4), 94-100.

Medley, M. (2014). Ruth Graham doesn't go far enough: Adults and kids should only read books aimed directly at their demographic. *National Post.* Retrieved from http://news.nationalpost.com/2014/06/11/stick-with-your-kind-getting-adults-off-ya-books-doesnt-go-nearly-far-enough/.

Meyer, M. (1999). *The Bedford introduction to literature: Reading, thinking, and writing.* New York, NY: St. Martin Press.

Miller v. California 413 U.S. 15 (1973).

Miller, G.E. (2015). Fan fiction writers speak out against 'Fifty Shades of Grey.' *New York Post.* Retrieved from http://nypost.com/2015/02/07/fan-fiction-writers-speak-out-against-50-shades-of-grey/.

Moebius, W. (1986). Introduction to picturebook codes. *Word & Image, 2*(2), 141-158. http://dx.doi.org/10.1080/02666286.1986.10435598

Moeller, R.A. and Becnel, K.E. (2015). You are what you read: young adult literacy and identity in rural America. *Journal of Research on Libraries & Young Adults, 6*, n. page.

Molen, G.R., & Wilson, C. (Producers), & Speilberg, S. (Director). (1997). *The Lost World: Jurassic Park* [Motion Picture]. United States of America: Universal.

Moore, D.W., Readence, J. E., & Rickelman, R. J. (1983). An historical exploration of content area reading instruction. *Reading Research Quarterly*, 18(4), 419-438. http://dx.doi.org/10.2307/747377

Morris, V.I. (2012). *The readers' advisory guide to street literature*. Chicago, IL: ALA Editions.

Moses, M.J. (1907). *Children's books and reading*. New York, NY: Mitchell Kennerley.

Moulton, L.W. (1935). Library card printing machine. *U.S. Patent No. 1,986,352*. Washington, DC: U.S. Patent and Trademark Office.

Murray, D. (1992). *Writing for your readers* (2nd ed.). Old Saybrook, CT: The Globe Pequot Press.

Myers, C. (2014). The apartheid of children's literature. *New York Times, 15*. Retrieved from http://www.nytimes.com/2014/03/16/opinion/sunday/the-apartheid-of-childrens-literature.html.

Myers, W.D. (2014). Where are the people of color in children's books? *The New York Times*. Retrieved from http://www.nytimes.com/2014/03/16/opinion/sunday/where-are-the-people-of-color-in-childrens-books.html.

Narvaez, D. (2002). Does reading moral stories build character?. *Educational Psychology Review, 14*(2), 155-171.

National Center for Education Statistics (2013). *The Nation's Report Card: Trends in Academic Progress 2012* (NCES 2013–456). National Center for Education Statistics, Institute of Education Sciences, U.S. Department of Education, Washington, D.C.

National Council of Teachers of English (1970). *Criteria for teaching materials in Reading and Literature*. Urbana, IL: NCTE.

National Council of Teachers of English. (2004). *A call to action: What we know about adolescent literacy and ways to support teachers in meeting students' needs* [Position statement]. Urbana, IL: NCTE. Retrieved from http://www.ncte.org/positions/statements/adolescentliteracy.

National Governors Association Center for Best Practices & Council of Chief State School Officers. (2010). *Common Core State Standards for English language arts and literacy in history/social studies, science, and technical subjects*. Washington, DC: Authors.

National Institute of Child Health and Human Development. (2000). Report of the National Reading Panel. Teaching children to read: an evidence-based assessment of the scientific research literature on reading and its implications for reading instruction. Retrieved from https://www.nichd.nih.gov/publications/pubs/nrp/pages/smallbook.aspx.

National Reading Panel. (2000). *Teaching children to read: An evidence-based assessment of the scientific research literature on reading and its implications for reading instruction, reports of the subgroups*. Rockville, MD: National Institute of Child Health and Human Development. Retrieved from http://www.nichd.nih.gov/publications/nrp/report.cfm

Nessel, D.D. & Jones, M.B. (1981). *The Language Experience Approach to reading*. New York, NY: Teachers College Press.

Neuman, S.B., & Celano, D. (2001). Access to print in low-income and middle-income communities: An ecological study of four neighborhoods. *Reading Research Quarterly, 36*(1), 8-26.

Neumeyer, P. (1987). Children's literature in the English department. *Children's Literature Association Quarterly, 12*(3), 146-150. http://dx.doi.org/10.1353/chq.0.0422

No Child Left Behind Act of 2001, Title I: *Improving the Academic Achievement of the Disadvantaged.* (2001). Washington, DC: National Clearinghouse for Bilingual Education, George Washington University.

Nodelman, P. (1988). *Words about pictures: The narrative art of children's picture books.* University of Georgia Press.

Norton, D.E. (1992). *The impact of literature-based reading.* Prentice Hall.

Nowell, J. (2015). Children's print books sales buck the trend. *Publisher's Weekly,* http://www.publishersweekly.com/pw/by-topic/childrens/childrens-industry-news/article/66291-children-s-print-book-sales-buck-the-trend.html

Olshavsky, J.E. (1976). Reading as problem solving: An investigation of strategies. *Reading Research Quarterly, 12,* 654-674. http://dx.doi.org/10.2307/747446

Owens, T. (2009). Going to school with Madame Curie and Mr. Einstein: gender roles in children's science biographies. *Cultural Studies Of Science Education, 4*(4), 929-943. http://dx.doi.org/10.1007/s11422-009-9177-6

Pappas, C.C. (1990). *An integrated language perspective in the elementary school: Theory into action.* Reading, MA: Addison-Wesley-Longman.

Paris, S.G. (2005). Reinterpreting the development of reading skills. *Reading Research Quarterly, 40*(2), 184-202. http://dx.doi.org/10.1598/RRQ.40.2.3

Paris, S.G., Cross, D.R., & Lipson, M.Y. (1984). Informed strategies for learning: A program to improve children's reading awareness and comprehension. *Journal of Educational Psychology, 76*(6), 1239. http://dx.doi.org/10.1037/0022-0663.76.6.1239

Parr, J.M., & Maguiness, C. (2005). Removing the *silent* from SSR: Voluntary reading as social practice. *Journal of Adolescent & Adult Literacy, 49*(2), 98–107. http://dx.doi.org/10.1598/JAAL.49.2.2

Paterson, K. (1981). *The gates of excellence.* New York: Elsevier/Nelson Books.

Pearson, P.D., Barr, R., & Kamil, M.L. (1984). *Handbook of reading research* (Vol. 1). London, England: Psychology Press.

Pearson, P.D., & Gallagher, M.C. (1983). The instruction of reading comprehension. *Contemporary educational psychology, 8*(3), 317-344. http://dx.doi.org/10.1016/0361-476X(83)90019-X

Pennac, D. (2008). *The rights of the reader.* London, UK: Candlewick Press.

Pilgreen, J.L. (2000). *The SSR handbook: How to organize and manage a sustained silent reading program.* Portsmouth, NH: Boynton/Cook.

Pinnell, G.S., Lyons, C.A., Deford, D.E., Bryk, A.S., & Seltzer, M. (1994). Comparing instructional models for the literacy education of high-risk first graders. *Reading Research Quarterly,* 9-39.

Plimpton, G. & Crowther, F.H. (1969). E.B. White, The art of the essay. *The Paris Review, 48.* Retrieved from http://www.theparisreview.org/interviews/4155/the-art-of-the-essay-no-1-e-b-white.

Plummer, M.W. (1897). The work for children in free libraries. *Library Journal, 22*(11), 684.

Powell, S.H.H. (1917). *The children's library, a dynamic factor in education.* New York, NY: HW Wilson.

Putnam, H. The woman in the library. *Library Journal, 41*(880), 401-31.

Quincy, J.P. (1876). Free libraries. *William I. Fletcher. Public Libraries in the United States of America.* Washington, DC, GP. O, 402.

Rand, N., & Torok, M. (1993). Questions to Freudian psychoanalysis: Dream interpretation, reality, fantasy. *Critical Inquiry*, *19*(3), 567-94. http://dx.doi.org/10.1086/448686

Raphael, T.E., & McMahon, S.I. (1994). Book club: An alternative framework for reading instruction. *The Reading Teacher*, 102-116.

Rasinski, T.V. (1989). Adult readers' sensitivity to phrase boundaries in texts. *The Journal of Experimental Education*, *58*(1), 29-40. http://dx.doi.org/10.1080/00220973.1989.10806520

Ratekin, N., Simpson, M.L., Alvermann, D.E., & Dishner, E.K. (1985). Why teachers resist content reading instruction. *Journal of Reading*, 432-437.

Reading Horizons. (2012). *An African Fable*. Salt Lake, Utah: Reading Horizons.

Reed, J.C. (1970). The deficits of retarded readers: Fact or artifact?. *The Reading Teacher*, *23*(4), 347-393.

Reutzel, D.R., Fawson, P.C., & Smith, J.A. (2008). Reconsidering silent sustained reading: An exploratory study of scaffolded silent reading. *The Journal of Educational Research*, *102*(1), 37–50. http://dx.doi.org/10.3200/JOER.102.1.37-50

Reutzel, D.R., Jones, C.D., Fawson, P.C., & Smith, J.A. (2008). Scaffolded silent reading: A complement to guided repeated oral reading that works! *The Reading Teacher*, *62*(3), 194–207. http://dx.doi.org/10.1598/RT.62.3.2

Reutzel, D.R., Jones, C.D., & Newman, T.H. (2010). Scaffolded silent reading: Improving the conditions of silent reading practice in classrooms. In E.H. Hiebert & D.R. Reutzel (Eds.), *Revisiting silent reading: New directions for teachers and researchers* (pp. 129–150). Newark, DE: International Reading Association.

Roback, D. (2013). Facts & Figures 2012: 'Hunger Games' still rules in children's. *Publisher's Weekly*. Retrieved from http://www.publishersweekly.com/pw/by-topic/childrens/childrens-industry-news/article/56411-hunger-games-still-rules-in-children-s-facts-figures-2012.html.

Robb, D. (2015, April 7). 'Jurassic World' script credits resolved; Helmer Colin Trevorrow speaks on arbitration process. *Deadline Hollywood*. Retrieved from http://deadline.com/2015/04/jurassic-world-script-credits-resolved-colin-trevorrow-speaks-on-arbitration-process-1201406086/

Romano, A. (2014) 10 famous authors who write fanfiction. *Daily Dot*. Retrieved from http://www.dailydot.com/culture/10-famous-authors-fanfiction/.

Rose, E. (1922). Work with negroes round table. *Bulletin of the American Library Association*, 361-366.

Rosenblatt, L. (1994/1978). *The reader, the text, the poem: The transactional theory of the literary work* (2nd ed.). Carbondale, IL: Southern Illinois University Press.

Ross, C.S. (1995). "If they read Nancy Drew, so what?": Series book readers talk back. *Library & Information Science Research*, *17*(3), 201-236. http://dx.doi.org/10.1016/0740-8188(95)90046-2

Rylant, C. (1989). *But I'll be back again*. New York, NY: Orchard.

Sambuchino, C. (2016). *Children's writer's & illustrator's market*. Blue Ash, OH: F+W Media/Writers Digest.

Sanden, S. (2014). Out of the shadow of SSR: Real teachers' classroom independent reading practices. *Language Arts*, *91*(3), 161–175.

Sanders, J. & Moudy, J. (2008). Literature apprentices: Understanding nonfiction text structures with mentor texts. *Journal of Children's Literature, 34*(2), 31-42.

Sayers, F. C. (1963). The American origins of public library work with children. *Library Trends, 12*(8).

Schaffner, E., Schiefele, U., & Ulferts, H. (2013). Reading amount as a mediator of the effects of intrinsic and extrinsic reading motivation on reading comprehension. *Reading Research Quarterly, 48*(4), 369-385.

Schneider, J.J. (2010, December). *Read Strunk & White: Results from a survey of successful adults and their writing practices in the workplace.* Paper presented at the meeting of the Literacy Research Association, Fort Worth, TX.

Schulman, T.H. 1988. *The dead poets society.* Hollywood, CA: Script City.

Schurman, L.C., & Johnson, D. (2002). *Scorned literature: Essays on the history and criticism of popular mass-produced fiction in America.* Santa Barbara, CA: ABC-CLIO, Praeger.

Senn, N. (2012). Effective approaches to motivate and engage reluctant boys in literacy. *The Reading Teacher, 66*(3), 211-220. http://dx.doi.org/10.1002/TRTR.01107

Serafini, F. (2010). Reading multimodal texts: Perceptual, structural and ideological perspectives. *Children's Literature in Education, 41*(2), 85-104. http://dx.doi.org/10.1007/s10583-010-9100-5

Serafini, F. (2011). Expanding perspectives for comprehending visual images in multimodal texts. *Journal of Adolescent & Adult Literacy, 54*(5), 342-350. http://dx.doi.org/10.1598/JAAL.54.5.4

Short, K.G. (1995). *Research & professional resources in children's literature: piecing a patchwork quilt.* Newark, DE: International Reading Association.

Short, K. (2011). Reading literature in elementary classrooms. In S. Wolf, K. Coats, P. Enciso, & C. Jenkins (Eds.), *Handbook of Research on Children's and Young Adult Literature,* (pp. 48-62), New York, NY: Routledge.

Silverstein, S. (2015). Shel Silverstein. *Biography.com.* Retrieved from http://www.biography.com/people/shel-silverstein-9483912.

Singer, H. (1970). *Theories, models, and strategies for learning to read.* ERIC, EBSCO*host*, Retrieved from http://files.eric.ed.gov/fulltext/ED049006.pdf.

Sipe, L. (1998). How picture books work: A semiotically framed theory of text-picture relationships. *Children's Literature in Education, 29*(2), 97-108. http://dx.doi.org/10.1023/A:1022459009182

Sipe, L. (2008). *Storytime: Young children's literary understanding in the classroom.* New York, NY: Teachers College Press.

Sipe, L. (2011). The art of the picturebook. In S. Wolf, K. Coats, P. Enciso, & C. Jenkins (Eds.), *Handbook of Research on Children's and Young Adult Literature,* (pp. 48-62), New York, NY: Routledge.

Slavin, R.E., Cheung, A., Groff, C., & Lake, C. (2008). Effective reading programs for middle and high schools: A best-evidence synthesis. *Reading Research Quarterly, 43*(3), 290-322.

Smith, F.R., & Feathers, K.M. (1983). Teacher and student perceptions of content area reading. *Journal of Reading,* 348-354.

Smith, P. (2010). *Just kids.* Feltrinelli Editore.

Sonnenschein, S., Baker, L., Serpell, R., & Schmidt, D. (2000). Reading is a source of entertainment: The importance of the home perspective for children's literacy development. In K.A. Roskos & J.F. Christie (Eds.), *Play and literacy in early childhood: Research from multiple perspectives* (pp. 107–124). Mahwah, NJ: Erlbaum.

Stanovich, K.E. (1990). A call for an end to the paradigm wars in reading research. *Journal of Literacy Research, 22*(3), 221-231. http://dx.doi.org/10.1080/10862969009547708

Starr, C. (2015). *Brief history of the young adult services division*. Retrieved from http://www.ala.org/yalsa/aboutyalsa/history/briefhistory.
Stearns, L.E. (1894). Report on reading for the young. *Library Journal, 19*(12), 81-87.

Steiner, B.C. (1896). Rev. Thomas Bray and his American libraries. *The American Historical Review, 2*(1), 59-75. http://dx.doi.org/10.2307/1833614

Sternberg, M. (2010). Narrativity: From objectivist to functional paradigm. *Poetics Today, 31*(3), 507-659. http://dx.doi.org/10.1215/03335372-2010-004

Stevenson, D. (2011) History of children's and young adult literature. In S. Wolf, K. Coats, P. Enciso, & C.A. Jenkins (Eds.), *Handbook of Research on Children's and Young Adult Literature* (pp. 179-192). New York, NY: Routledge.

Strouse, G.A., & Troseth, G.L. (2008). "Don't try this at home": Toddlers' imitation of new skills from people on video. *Journal of Experimental Child Psychology, 101*(4), 262-280.

Sulzby, E., & Teale, W.H. (1991). The development of the young child and the emergence of literacy. *Handbook of Research on Teaching the English Language Arts* (pp. 273-285). New York, NY: Macmillan.

Swann, B., & Krupat, A. (1987). *Recovering the word: Essays on Native American literature*. University of California Press.

Tatar, M. (2003). *The hard facts of the Grimms' fairy tales*. Princeton, NJ: Princeton University Press.

Taylor, D. (1983). *Family literacy: Young children learning to read and write*. Portsmouth, NH: Heinemann.

Taylor, M.A. (1978). Children's literature and the English department. *ADE Bulletin, 56*, 17-19. http://dx.doi.org/10.1632/ade.56.17

Taylor, B.M., & Frye, B.J. (1992). Comprehension strategy instruction in the intermediate grades. *Literacy Research and Instruction, 32*(1), 39-48. http://dx.doi.org/10.1080/19388079209558104

Teale, W.H., & Sulzby, E. (1986). *Emergent literacy: Writing and Reading*. Norwood, NJ: Ablex Publishing Corporation.

Telford, K.A. (1961). *Aristotle's poetics : Translation and analysis* (Gateway ed.). Chicago, IL: Henry Regnery.

Terry, A. (1974). *Children's poetry preferences: A national survey of upper elementary grades*. Urbana, IL: NCTE Research Report No. 16.

Tierney, R.J. (1985). *Reading strategies and practices. A compendium*. Old Tappan, NJ: Allyn and Bacon.

Tierney, R.J., & Pearson, P.D. (1983). Toward a composing model of reading. *Language Arts*, 568-580.

Tinker v Des Moines Independent School District, 393 U.S. 503 (1969), p. 506.

Tyson, N.D. (2004). A conversation with Neil Tyson. *NOVA Online*. Retrieved from http://www.pbs.org/wgbh/nova/space/conversation-with-neil-tyson.html

United Nations Human Rights. (1989). *Convention on the rights of the child.* Retrieved from http://www.ohchr.org/en/professionalinterest/pages/crc.aspx.

United States Citizenship and Immigration Services. (2015). *Definition of child for citizenship and naturalization.* Retrieved from http://www.uscis.gov/policymanual/HTML/PolicyManual-Volume12-PartH-Chapter2.html.

United States Criminal Code (18 U.S. Code § 2256) (2015). *Sexual exploitation and other abuse of children: Definitions for chapter.* Retrieved from Legal Information Institute, Cornell University Law School https://www.law.cornell.edu/uscode/text/18/2256.

U.S. Department of Education, Institute of Education Sciences, National Center for Education Statistics, *National Assessment of Educational Progress (NAEP),* 2015 Reading Assessment.

Valance, E.J. (2007). Main Street as art museum: Metaphor and teaching strategies. *Journal of Aesthetic Education, 41*(2), 25-38. http://dx.doi.org/10.1353/jae.2007.0021

Van Slyck, A.A. (1995). *Free to all: Carnegie libraries & American culture, 1890-1920.* Chicago, IL: University of Chicago Press.

Wachtel, E. (1994). *Writers & company.* New York: Harcourt, Brace & Co.

Walker, K.P. (2013). Scaffolded silent reading (ScSR): Advocating a policy for adolescents' independent reading. *Journal of Adolescent & Adult Literacy, 57*(3), 185–188. http://dx.doi.org/10.1002/JAAL.235

Wallace, K. (2015). Parents all over U.S. 'opting out' of Standardized Student Testing. *CNN.* Retrieved from http://www.cnn.com/2015/04/17/living/parents-movement-opt-out-of-testing-feat/

Warner, K.E. (2005). The role of research in international tobacco control. *American Journal of Public Health, 95*(6), 976. http://dx.doi.org/10.2105/AJPH.2004.046904

Weaver, C. (1990). *Understanding Whole Language: From Principles to Practice.* Portsmouth, NH: Heinemann.

Wellisch, H.H. (1981). Ebla: The world's oldest library. *Journal of Library History (1974-1987), 16*(3), 488-500.

West, M.I. (1985). Not to be circulated: The response of children's librarians to dime novels and series books. *Children's Literature Association Quarterly, 10*(3), 137-139. http://dx.doi.org/10.1353/chq.0.0120

Williamson, C.C. (1919). Some present-day aspects of library training. *Bulletin of the American Library Association,* 120-126.

Wilson, P.J., & Kutiper, K. (1994). Beyond Silverstein and Prelutsky: Enhancing and promoting the elementary and middle school poetry collection. *Journal of Youth Services in Libraries, 7*(3), 273-81.

Wineman, J.D., & Peponis, J. (2010). Constructing spatial meaning spatial affordances in museum design. *Environment and Behavior, 42*(1), 86-109. http://dx.doi.org/10.1177/0013916509335534

Winerip, M. (1999). Children's books: Harry Potter and the Sorcerer's Stone. *New York Times Book Review.* Retrieved from https://www.nytimes.com/books/99/02/14/reviews/990214.14childrt.html

Wolitzer, M. (2014). Look homeward, reader: A not so young audience for young adult books. *New York Times.* Retrieved from http://www.nytimes.com/2014/10/19/fashion/a-not-so-young-audience-for-young-adult-books.html?_r=0

Wright, W.E. (2010). *Foundations for Teaching English Language Learners: Research, Theory, Policy, and Practice.* Philadelphia, PA: Caslon Publishing.

Writers Guild of America. (2015). *Theatrical Credits Procedures Guide*. Retrieved from http://www.wga.org/content/default.aspx?id=4370#e

Yatvin, L. (2000). Minority view. In National Reading Panel, *Teaching children to read: An evidence-based assessment of the scientific research literature on reading and its implications for reading instruction, reports of the subgroups*. Rockville, MD: National Institute of Child Health and Human Development. Retrieved from http://www.nichd.nih.gov/publications/nrp/report.cfm

Youngs, S., & Serafini, F. (2011). Comprehension strategies for reading historical fiction picturebooks. *The Reading Teacher*, 65(2), 115-124. http://dx.doi.org/10.1002/TRTR.01014

Yust, W.F. (1913). What of the black and yellow races?. *Bulletin of the American Library Association*, 158-170.

Zipes, J. (2002). *Sticks and stones: The troublesome success of children's literature from Slovenly Peter to Harry Potter*. Routledge.

Zipes, J. (2012). A fairy tale is more than just a fairy tale. *Book 2.0*, 2(1-2), 113-120. http://dx.doi.org/10.1386/btwo.2.1-2.113_1

Children's, Young Adult, and Adult Literature Cited

Ada, A. F. (1993). *My name is María Isabel* (K.D. Thompson, Illustrator). New York, NY: Atheneum.

Ada, A. F. (1996). *Me Llamo María Isabel* (K.D. Thompson, Illustrator). New York, NY: Atheneum.

Adamson, A., Jenson, V., Warner, A., Williams, J. H., Katzenberg, J., Elliott, T., Rossio, T., ... DreamWorks Home Entertainment (Firm). (2006). *Shrek*. Glendale, CA: DreamWorks Animation.

Adler, D. A. (2001). *Lou Gehrig: The luckiest man* (T. Widener, Illustrator). New York, NY: HMH Books for Young Readers.

Adler, D. A., (2010). *Money madness* (E. Miller, Illustrator). New York, NY: Holiday House.

Adler, D. A. (2011). *Mystery math: A first book of algebra* (E. Miller, Illustrator). New York, NY: Holiday House.

Adler, D. A., & Adler, M. S. (2010). *A picture book of Cesar Chavez* (M. Olofsdotter, Illustrator). New York, NY: Holiday House.

Agassi, A. (2009). *Open: An autobiography*. New York, NY: A. Knopf.

Agosín, M. (2014). *I lived on Butterfly Hill* (L. White, Illustrator). New York, NY: Atheneum Books for Young Readers.

Agricola, M. (1559). *Abckiria*. Helsinki, Finnland: Finnish Literature Society.

Alexander, J., Alexander, C., Alexander, C., & Alexander, K. (2014). Kalley's machine plus cats [App, Illustrator]. Retrieved from http:// rocketwagon.com/app/ kalleys-machine/

Alexander, K. (2014). *The crossover*. Boston, MA: Houghton Mifflin.

Asim, J. (2006). *Whose toes are those?* (L.U. Pham, Illustrator). New York, NY: Little, Brown.

Auxier, J. (2014). *The Night Gardener*. New York, NY: Amulet Books.

Babbitt, N. (1975). *Tuck everlasting*. New York, NY: Farrar, Straus, Giroux.

Bagert, B. (2002). *Giant children* (T. Arnold, Illustrator). New York, NY: Dial Books for Young Readers.

Bang, M. (1996). *Goose*. New York, NY: Blue Sky Press.

Barnett, M. (2014). *Sam & Dave dig a hole* (J. Klassen, Illustrator). Somerville, MA: Candlewick Press.

Barrie, J.M. (1904). Peter Pan: The boy who wouldn't grow up. London, England: Hodder & Stoughton.

Barrie, J. M. (1911). *Peter and Wendy*. New York, NY: Charles Scribner's Sons.

Barrie, J. M., & Rackham, A. (1910). *Peter Pan in Kensington gardens*. New York, NY: C. Scribner's Sons.

Bartoletti, S. C. (2005). Hitler Youth: Growing up in Hitler's shadow. New York, NY: Scholastic Nonfiction.

Basher, S., & Green, D. (2011). Basher Human Body: A Book With Guts. New York, NY: Kingfisher.

Bauer, M. D. (2003). *Wind* (J. Wallace, Illustrator). New York, NY: Aladdin.

Bausum, A. (2006). Freedom Riders: John Lewis and Jim Zwerg on the front lines of the civil rights movement. Washington, D.C: National Geographic.

Bausum, A. (2009). Denied, detained, deported: Stories from the dark side of American immigration. Washington, DC: National Geographic.

Bedard, M. (1992). *Emily* (B. Cooney, Illustrator). New York, NY: Dragonfly.

Bennett, A. (2009). *The butt book* (M. Lester, Illustrator). New York, NY: Bloomsbury.

Bennett, A. (2012). Poopendous!: The inside scoop on every type and use of poop. (M. Moran, Illustrator). Maplewood, NJ: Blue Apple.

Bennett, A. (2014). *Belches, burps and farts, oh my!* (P.T. Naujokaitis, Illustrator). Maplewood, NJ: Blue Apple.

Berenstain, S. & Berenstain, J. (1968). *Inside outside upside down*. New York, NY: Bright & Early Books, a division of Random House.

Blume, J. (1975). *Forever: A novel*. Scarsdale, N.Y: Bradbury Press.

Boreman, T. (1968). A description of three hundred animals. Wakefield: S.R. Publishers.

Boynton, S. (1995). *Moo, baa, la la la!*. New York, NY: Little Simon.

Brandt, L. (2014). *Maddi's fridge* (V. Vodel, Illustrator). Brooklyn, NY: Flashlight Press.

Brannon, T. (2000). *Elmo Likes*. New York, NY: Random House Books for Young Readers.

Brown, D. (2015). Drowned city: Hurricane Katrina & New Orleans. New York, NY: HMH Books for Young Readers.

Brown, D. (2015). *Who is Malala Yousafzai?* (A. Thomson, Illustrator). New York, NY: Grosset & Dunlap.

Browne, A. (1984). *Willy the wimp*. New York, NY: Knopf.

Browning, E.B. (2013). How do I love thee? In *Complete Works of Elizabeth Barrett Browning* (Delphi Classics). Seattle, WA: Amazon Digital Services.

Bryant, J. (2014). *The right word: Roget and his thesaurus* (M. Sweet, Illustrator). New York, NY: Eerdmans Books for Young Readers.

Burgan, M. (2016). *Food engineering: From concept to consumer*. Framingham, MA: C. Press/F. Watts Trade.

Burleigh, R. (2015). *Trapped!: A whale's rescue*. (W. Minor, Illustrator). Boston, MA: Charlesbridge.

Cabot, M. (2000). *The princess diaries*. New York, NY: Harper Avon.

Campbell, J. (2014). *Ugly Sleeping Beauty*. Seattle, WA: Amazon Digital Services.

Carle, E. (1972). *The Very Hungry Caterpillar*. New York, NY: World/Penguin.

Carroll, L. (1965). Alice's adventures in Wonderland (J. Tenniel, Illustrator). New York, NY: Macmillan. (Originally published 1865).

Cate, A. (2013). Look up!: Bird-watching in your own backyard. Somerville, MA: Candlewick.

Chocolate, D. (1999). The piano man (E. Velasquez, Illustrator). New York, NY: Walker and Co.

Cisneros, S. (1987). *My wicked, wicked ways* (3rd ed.). Berkeley, CA: Third Women Press.

Clare, C.(2010). *Mortal instruments*. New York, NY: Margaret K. McElderry Books.

Clements, A., (1996). *Frindle* (B. Selznick, Illustrator). New York, NY: Simon & Schuster.

Clemmons, L., Lounsbery, J., Reitherman, W., Walmsley, J., Cabot, S., Winchell, P., Milne, A. A., ... Buena Vista Home Entertainment (Firm). (2013). *The many adventures of Winnie the Pooh*. United States: Buena Vista Home Entertainment.

Cline-Ransome, L. (2015). *My story, my dance: Robert Battle's journey to Alvin Ailey* (J.E. Ransome, Illustrator). New York, NY: Simon & Schuster.

Cobb, V. (2003). *I face the wind* (J. Gorton, Illustrator). New York, NY: HarperCollins.

Colbert, B. (2014). *Pointe*. New York, NY: G.P. Putnam's Sons.

Cole, H. (2012). Unspoken: A story from the Underground Railroad. New York, NY: Scholastic Press.

Collins, S. (2008). *The Hunger Games*. New York, NY: Scholastic.

Comenius, J.A. (1887). *The Orbis Pictus*. (11th ed.). (trans. Charles Hoole, 1658). Syracuse, NY: C.W. Bardeen.

Cooper, M. (1744). Tommy Thumb's pretty song book. Worcester, MA: Isaiah Thomas.

Copeland, M. (2014). Firebird (C. Myers, Illustrator). New York, NY: G.P. Putnam's Sons.

Corcoran, J. (2012). *Dare to dream-- change the world* (J.B. Jepson, Illustrator). Tulsa, OK: Kane Miller.

Corey, S. (2012). Here come the Girl Scouts!: The amazing all-true story of Juliette "Daisy" Gordon Low and her great adventure (H. Hooper, Illustrator). New York, NY: Scholastic Press.

Cormier, R. (1974). *The chocolate war: A novel*. New York, NY: Pantheon Books.

Coury, T. N. (2012). *Hanging off Jefferson's nose: Growing up on Mount Rushmore* (S.W. Comport). New York, NY: Dial Books for Young Readers.

Cowper, W. (1878). *The diverting history of John Gilpin* (R. Caldecott, Illustrator). London, England: George Routledge & Sons.

Crews, N. (2011). *Jack and the beanstalk*. New York, NY: Henry Holt.

Crichton, M. (2006). *Next: A novel*. New York, NY: HarperCollins Publishers.

Dahl, R. (1961). *James and the giant peach* (N.E. Burkert, Illustrator). New York, NY: Penguin.

Dahl, R. (1982). *Roald Dahl's Revolting rhymes* (Q. Blake, Illustrator). New York, NY: Knopf.

Dahl, R., (1988). *Matilda* (Q. Blake, Illustrator). New York, N.Y: Viking Kestrel.

Daywalt, D. (2013). *The day the crayons quit* (O. Jeffers, Illustrator). New York, NY: Philomel.

Defoe, D., (1884). *The adventures of Robinson Crusoe*. (Illus. P.A. Kauffmann). London, England: T. Fisher Unwin.

Dempsey, K. (2014). *A dance like starlight: One ballerina's dream* (F. Cooper, Illustrator). New York, NY: Philomel.

Di Benalli, B. (1485). *Aesopus Moralisatus*. Venezia, Italy.

Dickens, C. (1838). Oliver Twist. London, England: Bentley.

DeCristofano, C. C. (2012). *A black hole is not a hole* (M. Carroll, Illustrator). Boston, MA; Charlesbridge.

Disney. (2015). *Letters with Pooh* [App, Illustrator]. Retrieved from https://itunes.apple.com/us/app/letters-with-pooh/id535661652?mt=8

Disney, W., Luske, H. S., Geronimi, C., Jackson, W., Driscoll, B., Beaumont, K., Conried, H., ... Buena Vista Home Entertainment (Firm). (2007). *Peter Pan*. Burbank, CA: Walt Disney Home Entertainment.

Davis, K. (2014). *Mr. Ferris and his wheel* (G. Ford, Illustrator). New York, NY: HMH Books for Young Readers.

Dixon, F. W. (1969). The twisted claw (Hardy Boys Series). New York, NY: Grosset & Dunlap.

Doctorow, C., & Wang, J. (2014). *In real life*. New York, NY: First Second.

Draper, S. (1973). *Ray Charles* (G. Ford, Illustrator). New York, NY: Crowell.

Draper, S. M. (1994). *Tears of a tiger*. New York, NY: Atheneum Books for Young Readers.

Dumon, T. B. (2014). *Mikis and the donkey* (P. Hopman, Illustrator). Grand Rapids, MI: Eerdmans Books for Young Readers.

Ehlert, L. (2013). The scraps book: Notes from a colorful life. New York, NY: Beach Lane Books.

Evertts, E. L. (1973). *People need people*. New York, NY: Holt, Rinehart and Winston.

Falconer, I. (2000). *Olivia*. New York, NY: Simon & Schuster.

Fallon, J. (2015). *Your baby's first word will be Dada* (M. Ordóñez, Illustrator). New York, NY: Feiwel & Friends.

Fanning, J. (2015). *The Disney Book*. New York, NY: DK.

Farjeon, E. (1983). Poetry. In J. Prelutsky (Ed.), *The Random House book of poetry for children* (A. Lobel, Illustrator). New York, NY: Random House.

Farizan, S. (2013). If you could be mine: A novel. Chapel Hill, NC: Algonquin.

Federle, T. (2014). *Five, six, seven, Nate!*. New York, NY: Simon & Schuster.

Fey, T. (2011). *Bossypants*. Boston, MA: Back Bay Books.

Fish, H. D. (1938). *Animals of the Bible: A picture book* (D.P. Lathrop, Illustrator). Philadelphia, PA: Lippincott.

Fleischer-Camp, D., & Slate, J. (2014). Marcel the shell: The most surprised I've ever been. New York, NY: Razorbill.

Fleischman, P. (1988). *Joyful noise: Poems for two voices* (E. Beddows, Illustrator). New York, NY: Harper & Row.

Fleischman, P. (2000). *Big talk: Poems for four voices* (B. Giacobbe, Illustator). Cambridge, MA: Candlewick Press.

Fleischman, S. (2010). Sir Charlie Chaplin: The funniest man in the world. New York, NY: Greenwillow Books.

Fleming, C., (2014). The family Romanov: Murder, rebellion & the fall of Imperial Russia. New York, NY: Schwartz & Wade.

Floca, B., (2013). *Locomotive*. New York, NY: Atheneum Books for Young Readers.

Florian, D. (2007). Comets, stars, the Moon, and Mars: Space poems and paintings. New York, NY: HMH Books for Young Readers.

Florian, D. (2012). Poem runs: Baseball poems and paintings. Boston: Harcourt Children's Books.

Florian, D. (2012). *Shiver me timbers: Pirate poems & paintings* (R. Neubecker, Illustrator). New York, NY: Beach Lane Books.

Frazee, M. (2014). *The farmer and the clown*. New York, NY: Beach Lane Books.

Fritz, J. (1989). The great little Madison. New York, NY: Putnam.

Frost, R., Schmidt, G. D. (1994). *Poetry for young people: Robert Frost* (H. Sorenson, Illustrator). New York, NY: Sterling Publishers.

Gaiman, N. (2002). *Coraline* (D McKean, Illustrator). New York, NY: HarperCollins.

Gaiman, N., (2014). *Hansel & Gretel* (L. Mattiotti, Illustrator). London, UK: Bloomsbury.

Gandhi, M. (2014). The story of my experiments with truth: An autobiography. Seattle, WA: Create Space.

Gibbons, G. (1991). *From seed to plant*. New York, NY: Holiday House.

Gibbons, G. (2009). *Tornadoes!*. New York, NY: Holiday House.

Giles, G. (2014). *Girls like us*. Somerville, MA: Clarion.

Giovanni, N. (1996). *The sun is so quiet* (A. Bryan, Illustrator). New York, NY: Henry Holt.

Giovanni, N. (Ed.). (2008). *Hip hop speaks to children: A celebration of poetry with a beat* (M. Noiset & J. Tugeau, Illustrators). Naperville, Ill: Sourcebooks.

Goodwin, D. K. (2005). Team of rivals: The political genius of Abraham Lincoln. New York, NY: Simon & Schuster.

Gray, W.S. (2003). *Dick and Jane*. (Z. Sharp, Illustrator). New York, NY: Grosset & Dunlap

Green, D. (2014). The Science book: Big ideas simply explained. (2014). Washington, DC: DK.

Green, D. & Basher, S. (2011). Basher Human Body: A Book With Guts. New York, NY: Kingfisher.

Green, J. (2012). *The fault in our stars*. New York, NY: Dutton.

Greenfield, E. (1978). *Honey, I love: And other love poems* (D. Dillon & L. Dillon, Illustrator). New York, NY: HarperCollins.

Greenfield, E. (1988). *Nathaniel talking* (J.S. Gilchrist, Illustrator). New York, NY: Black Butterfly Children's Books.

Grimes, N. (2010). *Almost zero: A Dyamonde Daniel book* (R.G. Christie, Illustrator). New York, NY: G.P. Putnam's Sons.

Grimm, J., & Grimm, W. (1882). Children's and household tales. [Trans. L. Crane, Illustrator). New York, NY: Dover.

Grimm, J., Grimm, W., & Ashliman, D. (2013). Cinderella. In J. Grimm & W. Grimm *Children and Household Tales*. Retrieved from http://www.pitt.edu/~dash/type0510a.html.

Grove, T., & National Air and Space Museum. (2015). First flight around the world: The adventures of the American fliers who won the race. New York, NY: Henry N. Abrams.

Hale, S., Hale, D. (2014). *The Princess in Black* (L.U. Pham, Illustrator). New York, NY: Random House.

Hall, K. (2014). Polar bears and penguins: A compare and contrast book. Mount Pleasan, SC: Sylvan Dell Publishing.

Hamilton, V. (1985). *The people could fly: American Black folktales* (L. Dillon & D. Dillon, Illustrator). New York, NY: Knopf.

Hancock, J. L., Marcel, K., Smith, S., Owen, A., Collie, I., Steuer, P., Newman, T., ... Buena Vista Home Entertainment (Firm),. (2014). *Saving Mr. Banks*. Burbank, Calif: Walt Disney Home Entertainment.

Hannigan. K. (2004). Ida B... and her plans to maximize fun, avoid disaster, and save the world. New York, NY: HarperCollins.

Haugaard, E. C. (1967). *The little fishes* [M. Johnson, Illustrator]. Boston: Houghton Mifflin.

Haughton, C. (2014). *Shh! We have a plan*. New York, NY: Candlewick.

Hargreaves, R. (1980). *Mr. Happy*. Baltimore, MD: Ottenheimer.

Harris, J. (1999). The three little dinosaurs. Gretna, LA: Pelican Pub.

Hay, J., & Wingo, C. E. (1968). *Reading with phonics*. Philadelphia, PA: Lippincott.

Heiligman, D., (2013). *The boy who loved math: The improbable life of Paul Erdős* (L.U. Pham, Illustrator). New York, NY: Roaring Brook Press.

Herron, C. (1997). *Nappy hair* (J. Cepeda, Illustrator). New York, NY: Knopf.

Hill, L. C. (2013). When the beat was born: DJ Kool Herc and the creation of hip hop (T. Taylor, Illustrator). New York, NY: Roaring Brook Press.

Hinton, S. E. (1967). *The outsiders*. New York, NY: Viking Press.

Hodgkinson, L. (2012). Goldilocks and just one bear. Somerville, MA: Nosy Crow.

Holm, J. L., & Holm, M. (2011). *Babymouse: 14*. New York, NY: Random House.

hooks, b. (1999). *Happy to be nappy* [C. Raschka, Illustrator]. New York, NY: Hyperion Books for Children.

hooks, b., (2008). *Grump groan growl* [C. Raschka, Illustrator]. New York, NY: Hyperion Books for Children.

Hoose, P. M. & Hoose, H. (1998). *Hey little ant* (D. Tilley, Illustrator). Berkeley, Calif: Tricycle Press.

Hope, L. L. (1927). *The Bobbsey Twins Series*. New York, NY: Grosset & Dunlap.

Hosseini, K. (2003). *The kite runner*. New York, NY: Riverhead Books.

Hudson, W. (1993). *Pass it on: African-American poetry for children* (F. Cooper, Illustrator). New York, NY: Scholastic Inc.

Hughes, L. (1932/1994). *The Dream Keeper and other poems* (Brian Pinkney, Illustrator). New York, NY: Alfred A. Knopf.

Hughes, L. (1994). The collected poems of Langston Hughes. In A. Rampersad (Ed.). The Collected Poems of Langston Hughes. New York, NY: Vintage.

Isadora, R. (2009). *Hansel and Gretel*. New York, NY: G.P. Putnam's Sons.

Jackson, E. (1994). *Cinder Edna* (K. O'Malley, Illustrator). New York, NY: HarperCollins.

Jacobs, J. (1895). *More Celtic fairy tales* (2nd ed.). New York, NY: Grosset & Dunlap.

Jain, P. (2011). *Wind energy engineering*. New York, NY: McGraw-Hill.

James, E.L. (2011). *Fifty shades of Grey*. New York, NY: Vintage Books.

Janeczko, P. B. (2005). *A kick in the head: An everyday guide to poetic forms* (C. Raschka, Illustrator). Cambridge, MA: Candlewick Press.

Janeczko, P. B. (2015). The death of the hat: A brief history of poetry in 50 objects (C. Raschka, Illustrator). New York, NY: Candlewick.

Jenkins, S., & Page, R. (2015). *Egg: Nature's perfect package*. New York, NY: Houghton Mifflin Harcourt.

Jiménez, C.J. (1995). *Intik'a: How the Taquileo island was not an island but a very tall mountain that was called Intik'a*. Lima, Peru: Ironyodla.

Johnson, D. B. (2000). *Henry hikes to Fitchburg*. Boston, MA: Houghton Mifflin.

Kanefield, T., & Abrams Books for Young Readers,. (2014). The girl from the tar paper school: Barbara Rose Johns and the advent of the civil rights movement. New York, NY: Abrams Books.

Karlitz, G. (1999). *Growing money: A complete investing guide for kids* (D. Honig, Illustrator). New York, NY: Price Stern Sloan.

Keene, C. (2004). *Nancy Drew collection*. New York, NY: Aladdin Paperbacks.

Kellogg, S. (1991). *Jack and the beanstalk*. New York, NY: Morrow Junior Books.

Ketteman, H. (2007). *Waynetta and the cornstalk: A Texas fairy tale* (D. Greenseid, Illustrator). Morton Grove, IL: Albert Whitman.

Kinney, J. (2007). *Diary of a wimpy kid*. New York, NY: Amulet Books.

Klassen, J. (2012). *This is not my hat*. New York, NY: Candlewick Press.

Klein, G. W. (1995). *All but my life*. New York, NY: Hill and Wang.

Knudsen, M. (2014). *Evil librarian*. Somerville, MA: Candlewick Press.

Krull, K. (1996). Wilma unlimited: How Wilma Rudolph became the world's fastest woman (D. Diaz, Illustrator). New York, NY: HMH Books for Young Readers.

Krull, K. (2011). *Jim Henson: The guy who played with puppets* (S. Johnson & L. Fancher, Illustrators). New York, NY: Random House.

Kunhardt, D. (1940/2001). *Pat the Bunny*. New York, NY: Golden Books.

Lazar, T. (2015). *I thought this was a bear book* (B. Davies, Illustrator). New York, NY: Aladdin.

L'Engle, M. (1963/2012). *A wrinkle in time*. New York, NY: Random House.

Lee, H. (1960). *To kill a mockingbird*. Philadelphia, NY: Lippincott.

Lee, H. (2015). *Go set a watchman*. New York, NY: Harper.

Levine, G. C. (1997). *Ella enchanted*. New York, NY: HarperCollinsPublishers.

Levithan, D. (2003). *Boy meets boy*. New York, NY: Alfred A. Knopf.

Levithan, D. (2013). *Two boys kissing*. New York, NY: Alfred A. Knopf.

Lewis, J. P. (2013). World rat day: Poems about real holidays you've never heard of (A. Raff, Illustrator). Somerville, MA: Candlewick Press.

Lewis, J. P. & Nesbitt, K. (2015). *Bigfoot is missing!* (MinaLima, Illustrator). New York, NY: Chronicle.

Lobel, A. (1970). *Frog and toad are friends*. New York, NY: Harper & Row.

Lobel, A. (1983). The book of pigericks: Pig limericks. New York, N.Y: Harper & Row.

Look, L. (2008). *Alvin Ho: Allergic to girls, school, and other scary things* (L.U. Pham, Illustrator). New York, NY: Schwartz & Wade Books.

Lowell, S. (2000). *Cindy Ellen: A wild western Cinderella* (J. Manning, Illustrator). New York, NY: HarperCollins Publishers.

Macmillan/McGraw-Hill (2011). *Treasures*. New York, NY: Author.

Manhattan Toy Company. (nd). *Find the Ball*. Minneapolis, MN: Author.

Marshall, J. (1987). *Red Riding Hood*. New York, NY: Puffin.

Martin, A. M. (1994). The babysitters club collection 1. London, England: Hippo.

Martin, A. M. (2014). *Rain reign*. New York, NY: Feiwel & Friends.

Martin, G.R.R. (2011). *A game of thrones*. New York, NY: Bantam.

Martin, G.R.R., Garcia, E. & Antonsson, L. (2014). The world of ice and fire: The untold history of Westoros and the game of thrones. New York, NY: Bantam.

Martin, J. B. (2001). *The lamp, the ice, and the boat called Fish* (B. Krommes, Illustrator). Boston, Mass: Houghton Mifflin.

Martinet, Dr. (1783). The catechism of nature for the use of children. Boston, MA: Young and Etheridge.

McBratney, S. (1995). *Guess how much I love you* (A. Jeram, Illustrator). Cambridge, MA: Candlewick Press.

McCloskey, R. (1941). *Make way for ducklings*. New York, NY: Viking Press.

McCloskey, R. (1948). *Blueberries for Sal*. New York, NY: Viking Press.

McCord, D. T. W. (1967). *Every time I climb a tree* (M. Simont, Illustrator). New York, NY: Little, Brown and Co.

McDonough, Y. Z. (2013). *What was the Underground Railroad?* (L. Mortimer, Illustrator). New York, NY: Grosset & Dunlap.

McGuffey, W.H. (1879). McGuffey's second eclectic reader (revised edition). New York, NY: Van Antwerp, Bragg & Co.

Merriam, E. (1966). How to eat a poem. *It doesn't always have to rhyme*. New York, NY: Atheneum.

Meyer, S. (2005). *Twilight*. Boston, MA: Little, Brown & Co.

Milne, A. A., & Shepard, E. H. (1957). The World of Pooh: The complete Winnie-the-Pooh and the House at Pooh Corner.

Mitton, T. (2010). Rumble, roar, dinosaur!: More prehistoric poems with lift-the-flap surprises! (L Chapman, Illustrator). New York, NY: Macmillan.

Mizielińska, A., Mizieliński, D., & Lloyd-Jones, A. (2013). *Maps*. Somerville, MA: Big Picture Press.

Montgomery, S. (2010). *Kakapo rescue: Saving the world's strangest parrot* (N. Bishop, Photographer). New York, NY: Houghton Mifflin Books for Children.

Moore, J. (2007). *Freckleface Strawberry* (L.U. Pham, Illustrator). London, UK: Bloomsbury Children's Books.

Mullenbach, C. (2014). The industrial revolution for kids: The people and technology that changed the world : with 21 activities. Chicago IL: Chicago Review Press.

Munsch, R. N. (1986). *Love you forever*. (S. McGraw, Illustrator). Scarborough, ON: Firefly.

Myles, E. (2001). Uppity. *Skies: Poems*. Santa Rosa, CA: Black Sparrow Press.

Myers, W. D. (1999). *Monster* (C. Myers, Illustrator). New York, N.Y: HarperCollins Publishers.

Nelson, J. (2014). *I'll give you the sun*. New York, NY: Dial Books.

Nelson, K. (2008). *We are the ship: The story of Negro League baseball*. New York, NY: Jump at the Sun/Hyperion Books for Children.

Nelson, K. (2013). *Nelson Mandela*. New York, NY: Katherine Tegen Books.

Nelson, V. M. (2012). No crystal stair: A documentary novel of the life and work of Lewis Michaux, Harlem bookseller (R.G. Christie, Illustrator). Minneapolis: Carolrhoda Lab.

Neri, G. (2013). *Ghetto Cowboy*. (illus. by J.J. Watson). New York, NY: Candlewick Press.

Neri, G., & DuBurke, R. (2010). Yummy: The last days of a Southside shorty. New York, NY: Lee & Low Books.

Nesbitt, K. (2007). *Revenge of the lunch ladies: The hilarious book of school poetry* (M. Gordon & C. Gordon, Illustrators). Minnetonka, MN: Meadowbrook Press.

Newbery, J. (1770). A little pretty pocket- book intended for the instruction and amusement of little Master Tommy and pretty Miss Polly. London, England: Newbery and Carnan.

No Yetis Allowed (2015). *Pocket Shrek*. [App, Illustrator). Retrieved from https://itunes.apple.com/us/app/pocket-shrek/id886216658?mt=8

Norton, M. (1953). *The Borrowers* (J. Krush, & B. Krush, Illustrator). New York, NY: Harcourt, Brace & World.

Numeroff, L. J., (1985). *If you give a mouse a cookie* (F. Bond, Illustrator). New York, NY: Harper & Row.

Nunes, S. S. (2013). Chinese fables: "the Dragon Slayer" and other timeless tales of wisdom (L.K. Tay-Audouard, Illustrator). Tokyo: Rutland, Vt.

Nye, N. S. (2002). 19 varieties of gazelle: Poems of the Middle East. New York, NY: Greenwillow Books.

O'Connell, C. & Jackson, D. M (2011). *The elephant scientist* (D.M. Jackson & C. O'Connell, Photographers). New York, NY: HMH Books for Young Readers.

Osborne, M. P. (1996). Magic tree house collection #1: The mystery of the tree house. (S. Murdocca, Illustrator). New York, NY: Random House.

Ottolenghi, C., (2005). *Jack and the beanstalk =: Juan y frijoles magicos* (G. Porfirio, Illustrator). Greensboro, NC: Brighter Child.

Paterson, K. (1977). *Bridge to Terabithia*. New York, NY: Harper.

Paterson, K. (1978). *The great Gilly Hopkins*. New York, NY: T.Y. Crowell.

Paterson, K. (1980). *Jacob have I loved*. New York, NY: T.Y. HarperCollins.

Patterson, L. (1969). *Martin Luther King, Jr: Man of peace* (V. Mays, Illustrator). New York, NY: Dell.

Paulsen, G. (1985). *Dogsong*. New York, N.Y: Bradbury Press.

Paulsen, G. (1987). *Hatchet*. New York, NY: Bradbury Press.

Paulsen, G. (1989). *The winter room*. New York, NY: Orchard Books.

Paulsen, G. (1993). *Nightjohn*. New York, NY: Delacorte Press.

Perrault, C. (1922). *The tales of Mother Goose as first collected by Charles Perrault*. Retrieved from http://www.gutenberg.org/files/29021/29021-h/29021-h.htm (Original work published 1697).

Pilkey, D. (1997). The adventures of Captain Underpants: An epic novel. New York, NY: Blue Sky Press.

Pinborough, J., (2013). Miss Moore thought otherwise: How Anne Carroll Moore created libraries for children (D. Atwell, Illustrator). Boston, MA: HMH Books for Children.

Pinkney, J., & Aesop. (2009). *The lion & the mouse*. New York, NY: Little, Brown Books for Young Readers.

Polacco, P. (1994). *Pink and Say*. New York, NY: Philomel Books.

Potter, B. (1902). *The Tale of Peter Rabbit*. London, England: Frederick Warne & Co. Retrieved from https://www.gutenberg.org/files/14838/14838-h/14838-h.htm

Prelutsky, J. (1983). *The Random House book of poetry for children* (A. Lobel, Illustrator). New York, NY: Random House.

Prelutsky, J. (1984). *The new kid on the block: Poems* (J. Stevenson, Illustrator). New York, NY: Greenwillow Books.

Prelutsky, J. (1986). *Read-aloud rhymes for the very young* (M. Brown, Illustrator). New York, NY: Knopf Books for Young Readers.

Prelutsky, J. (2006). *Behold the bold umbrellaphant: And other poems* (C. Berger, Illustrator). New York, NY: Greenwillow Books.

Pullman, P. (1995). *Northern lights*. London, England: Scholastic.

Pullman, P. (2007). *His dark materials*. New York, NY: Alfred A. Knopf.

Quinn, D. B., & Devereaux, D. (2010). *The littlest bitch*. Portland, Me: Sellers.

Raschka, C. (1999). *Like likes like*. New York, NY: DK Pub.

Reading Horizons. (2012). *An African Fable*. Salt Lake, Utah: Reading Horizons.

Reynolds, J. (2014). *When I was the greatest*. New York, NY: Atheneum Books for Young Readers.

Reynolds, P.H. (2003). *The Dot*. New York, NY: Candlewick Press.

Richard, D.M. (1997). Mbegu Ya Ajabu (The Amazing Seed). Kenya: Sasa Sema.

Rosenberg, L., & November, D. (2005). I just hope it's lethal: Poems of sadness, madness, and joy. New York, NY: HMH Books for Young Readers.

Rowling, J.K. (1997). *Harry Potter and the philosopher's stone* (T. Taylor, Illustrator). London, England: Bloomsbury Books.

Rowling, J.K. (1998). *Harry Potter and the sorcerer's stone* (M. GrandPré, Illustrator). New York, NY: A.A. Levine Books.

Rowling, J. K. (2016). Harry Potter and the Philosopher's Stone Deluxe Illustrated Edition (J. Kay, Illustrator). London, UK: Bloomsbury Children's.

Roy, K. (2014). Neighborhood sharks: Hunting with the great whites of California's Farallon Islands. New York, NY: David Macaulay Studio.

Ršumović, L. (1990). *All We Need Are Dragons* (D. Petričić, Illustrator). Serbia: Rad.

Ruelle, K. G., & DeSaix, D. D. (2009). The grand mosque of Paris: A story of how Muslims rescued Jews during the Holocaust. New York, NY: Holiday House.

Rumford, J. (2004). Sequoyah: The Cherokee man who gave his people writing. New York, NY: HMH Books for Young Readers.

Rundell, K. (2014). *Cartwheeling in thunderstorms*. New York, NY: Simon & Schuster.

Ryan, P. M. (1999). *Amelia and Eleanor go for a ride: Based on a true story* (B. Selznick, Illustrator). New York, NY: Scholastic Press.

Ryan, P.M. (2010). *The Dreamer* (Peter Sís, Illustrator). New York, NY: Scholastic Press.

Rylant, C. (2008). *Hansel and Gretel* (J. Corace, Illustrator). New York, NY: Hyperion Books for Children.

Sabuda, R., & Reinhart, M. (2005). Encyclopedia prehistorica: Dinosaurs. London: Walker.

St. George, J. (2000). *So you want to be president?* (D. Small, Illustrator). New York, NY: Philomel Books.

Samworth, K. (2014). Aviary Wonders Inc. Spring Catalog and Instruction Manual. New York, NY: Clarion.

Sanchez, A. (2001). *Rainbow boys*. New York, NY: Simon & Schuster.

San Souci, R. D. (2000). *Cinderella Skeleton* (D. Catrow, Illustrator). San Diego, CA: Silver Whistle/Harcourt.

Santat, D. (2014). *The adventures of Beekle: The unimaginary friend*. New York, NY: Little Brown Books for Young Readers.

Santirso, L. (1998). *El Capitán* (P. Gomez, Illustrator). Mexico: Celta Amaquemecan.

Say, A. (1993). *Grandfather's journey*. Boston: Houghton Mifflin Company.

Say, A. (2005). *Kamishibai man*. New York, NY: HMH Books for Young Readers.

Say, A. (2011). *Drawing from memory*. New York, NY: Scholastic Press.

Scarry, R. (1968). *What do people do all day?*. New York, NY: Random House.

Schanzer, R. (2011). Witches!: The absolutely true tale of disaster in Salem. Washington, D.C: National Geographic Society.

Schubert, L. (2012). *Monsieur Marceau* (G. Dubois, Illustrator). New York, NY: Roaring Brook Press.

Schwartz, A., (1981). *Scary stories to tell in the dark* [S. Gammell, Illustrator]. New York, NY: Lippincott.

Schwartz, R. E. (2014). *Really big numbers*. Providence, RI: American Mathematical Society.

Scieszka, J. (1989). *The true story of the 3 little pigs*. (L. Smith, Illustrator). New York, NY: Penguin.

Scieszka, J. (2005). Guys write for guys read. New York, NY: Viking.

Sendak, M. (1963). *Where the wild things are*. New York, NY: Harper & Row.

Sesame Street. (2014). *Elmo's ABC: Lift-the-flap*. New York, NY: Reader's Digest.

Seuss, Dr. (1957). *The cat in the hat*. New York, NY: Random House.

Seuss, Dr. (1963). *Hop on Pop*. New York, NY: Beginner Books, a division of Random House.

Seuss, Dr. (1965). *Fox in socks*. New York, NY: Beginner Books, a division of Random House.

Seuss, Dr. (2015). *What pet should I get?*. New York, NY: Random House.

Shannon, D. (1998). *No, David!*. New York, NY: Blue Sky Press.

Shaskan, T. S. (2012). Honestly, Red Riding Hood was rotten!: The story of Little Red Riding Hood as told by the wolf (G. Guerlais, Illustrator). Mankato, MN: Picture Window Books.

Sheinkin, S. (2012). Bomb: the race to build—and steal—the world's most dangerous weapon. New York, NY: Flash Point.

Shireen, N. (2011). *Good little wolf*. New York, NY: Alfred A. Knopf.

Sidman, J. (2006). *Meow ruff: A story in concrete poetry*. (M. Berg, Illustrator). New York, NY: HMH Books for Young Readers.

Silverstein, S. (1974). Where the sidewalk ends: The poems & drawings of Shel Silverstein. New York, NY: Harper and Row.

Simon, S. (2013). *Coral reefs*. New York, NY: Harper.

Singer, M. (2010). *Mirror mirror: A book of reverso poems* (J. Masse, Illustrator). New York, N.Y: Dutton Children's Books.

Sís, P. (1998). *Tibet: Through the red box*. New York, NY: Farrar Straus Giroux.

Sixx, N., & Gittins, I. (2008). The heroin diaries: A year in the life of a shattered rock star. New York, NY: Pocket Books.

Smith, L. (2010). *It's a book*. New York, NY: Roaring Brook Press.

Spielberg, S., Hart, J. V., Marmo, M. S., Castle, N., Kennedy, K., Marshall, F., Molen, G. R., … Columbia TriStar Home Video (Firm). (2000). *Hook*. Burbank, CA: Columbia TriStar Home Video.

Spielman, G. (2011). *Marcel Marceau: Master of mime* (M. Gauthier, Illustrator). Minneapolis: Kar-Ben Pub.

Spier, P. (1967). *London Bridge is falling down!*. Garden City, N.Y: Doubleday.

Staake, B. (2010). The First Pup: The Real Story of How Bo Got to the White House. New York, NY: Feiwel & Friends.

Steig, W. (1990). *Shrek!*. New York, NY: Farrar, Straus, Giroux.

Steptoe, J. (1969). *Stevie*. New York, NY: Harper & Row, Publishers.

Steptoe, J. (1984). *The story of Jumping Mouse: A native American legend* (L. Braswell, Illustrator). New York, NY: Lothrop, Lee & Shepard Books.

Steptoe, J. (1987). *Mufaro's beautiful daughters: An African tale* (J. Stevens, Illustrator). New York, NY: Lothrop, Lee & Shepard Books.

Stevenson, R. L. (1911).*Treasure Island*. New York, NY: C. Scribner's Sons.

Stevenson, R., Walsh, B., DaGradi, D., Andrews, J., Van, D. D., Tomlinson, D., Johns, G., … Buena Vista Home Entertainment (Firm). (2004). *Mary Poppins*. Burbank, Calif: Walt Disney Home Entertainment.

Stewart, M. (2014). *Feathers: Not just for flying*. (S.S. Brannen, Illustrator). Boston, MA: Charlesbridge.

Stimpson, C. (2012). *Jack and the baked beanstalk*. New York, NY: Templar Books.

Stine, M. (2015). *Who was Michael Jackson?* (J. J. M. Qiu, Illustrator). New York, NY: Grosset & Dunlap.

Stine, R. L. (1992). Welcome to dead house (Goosebumps Series). New York, NY: Scholastic Inc.

Stine, R. L. (1993). The curse of the mummy's tomb. New York, NY: Scholastic.

Stone, T. L. (2009). Almost astronauts: 13 women who dared to dream. Somerville, MA: Candlewick Press.

Swanson, S. M. (2008). *The house in the night*. (B. Krommes, Illustrator). Boston: Houghton Mifflin Company.

Sweet, M. (2011). Balloons over Broadway: The true story of the puppeteer of Macy's Parade. New York, NY: HMH Books for Young Readers.

TabTale LTD (2015). *Peter Pan Adventures*. [App, Illustrator]. Retrieved from https://itunes.apple.com/us/app/peter-pan-adventures-classic/id588311104?mt=8

Tamaki, M., Tamaki, J. (2014). *This one summer*. New York, NY: FirstSecond.

Tamarin, A. H., & Glubok, S. (1976). Voyaging to Cathay: Americans in the China trade. New York, NY: Viking Press.

Tate, D. (2012). *It jes' happened: When Bill Traylor started to draw* (R.G. Christie, Illustrator). New York, NY: Lee & Low Books.

Tauszik, K. (2014). Awake: The story of sleeping beauty with espresso. Seattle, WA: Amazon.

Taylor, M. D. (1976). Roll of thunder, hear my cry. New York, NY: Dial Press.

Tennyson, A.L. (1854). *The Charge of the Light Brigade*. Retrieved from http://www.poetryfoundation.org/poem/174586

Thomas, J. C. (2008). *The blacker the berry: Poems* (F. Cooper, Illustrator). New York, NY: HarperCollins.

Tolkien, J. R. R. (1937/1966). The hobbit, or, There and back again. Boston: Houghton Mifflin.

Tonatiuh, D. (2014). Separate is never equal: Sylvia Mendez and her family's fight for desegregation. New York, NY: Abrams.

Tonatiuh, D. (2015). Funny bones: Posada and his Day of the Dead calaveras. New York, NY: Abrams.

Travers, P. L. (1962). *Mary Poppins* (M. Shepard, Illustrator). New York, NY: Harcourt, Brace & World.

Trivizas, E., (1993). *The three little wolves and the big bad pig* (H. Oxenbury, Illustrator). New York, NY: Margaret K. McElderry.

Turkle, B. (1992). *Deep in the forest*. New York, NY: Puffin.

Uegaki, C. (2014). *Hana Hashimoto, Sixth Violin* (illus. by Qin Leng). Toronto, Canada: Kids Can Press.

Van Allsburg, C. (1981). *Jumanji*. Boston, MA: Houghton Mifflin Co.

Van Allsburg, C. (1983). *The Polar Express*. New York, NY: Scholastic.

Van Allsburg, C. (1983). *The wreck of the Zephyr*. Boston, MA: Houghton Mifflin.

Van Allsburg C. (1984). The mysteries of Harris Burdick. Boston, MA: Houghton Mifflin.

Van Allsburg, C. (1987). The Z was zapped: A play in twenty-six acts. Boston, MA: Houghton Mifflin.

Van Allsburg, C. (2014). *The misadventures of Sweetie Pie*. Boston, MA: Houghton Mifflin Harcourt.

Van Allsburg, C. (Ed.) (2011). The chronicles of Harris Burdick: Fourteen amazing authors tell the tales. Boston, MA: Houghton Mifflin Books for Children.

Van Loon, H.W. (1922). The story of mankind. New York, NY: Boni and Liveright.

Van Wagenen, M. (2014). Popular: A memoir : vintage wisdom for a modern geek. New York, NY: Dutton.

Viorst, J., (1995). Sad underwear: And other complications more poems for children and their parents (R. Hull, Illustrator). New York, NY: Atheneum Books for Young Readers.

Viorst, J. (2014). *Lulu's mysterious mission* (K. Cornell, Illustrator). New York, NY: Atheneum.

Walton, R. (1997). *Pig, pigger, piggest* (J. Holder, Illustrator). Salt Lake City: Gibbs-Smith.

Warren, S. (2012). *Delores Huerta: A hero to migrant workers* (R. Casilla, Illustrator). Seattle, WA: Two Lions.

Waters, T. (2014). *Beauty of the broken*. New York, NY: Simon Pulse.

Watson, R., (2012). *Harlem's little blackbird* (C. Robinson, Illustrator). New York, NY: Random House.

Wells, R. (1979). Max: Series of Board Books. New York, NY: Dial.

White, E. B. (1952). *Charlotte's web* (G Williams, Illustrator). New York, NY: Harper & Brothers.

White, E. B. (1970). *The trumpet of the swan* (E. Frascino, Illustrator). New York, NY: Harper & Row.

White, E. B. (1973). *Stuart Little* (G Williams, Illustrator). New York, NY: Harper & Row.

Wiesner, D. (2001). *The three pigs*. New York, NY: Clarion Books.

Wiesner, D. (2006). *Flotsam*. New York, NY: Clarion Books.

Wiles, D. (2014). *Revolution*. New York, NY: Scholastic.

Willems, M. (2003). Don't let the pigeon drive the bus. New York, NY: Hyperion.

Willems, M. (2004). Knuffle Bunny: A cautionary tale. New York, NY: Hyperion.

Willems, M. (2005). Leonardo the terrible monster. New York, NY: Hyperion.

Willems, M. (2011). *Don't let the pigeon run this app*. Gledale, CA: Disney Enterprises Inc.

Willems, M. (2011). *I broke my trunk!*. New York, NY: Hyperion Books for Children.

Winter, J. (2011). The watcher: Jane Goodall's life with the chimps. New York, NY: Schwartz & Wade Books.

Woodson, J. (2003). *Locomotion*. New York, NY: G.P. Putnam's Sons.
Woodson, J. (2014). *brown girl dreaming*. New York, NY: Nancy Paulsen Books.

Wright, J., Fuchs, J., Jackman, H., Hedlund, G., Mara, R., & Warner Home Video (Firm). (2015). *Pan*.

Yeats, W.B. (1919). To a young girl. In W.B. Yeats, *The wild swans at Coole*. London, England: Macmillan.

Yolen, J. (1987). *Owl moon* (J. Schoenherr, Illustrator). New York, NY: Philomel.

Yolen, J. (1997). *Sleeping ugly* (D. Stanley, Illustrator). New York, N.Y: Puffin.

Young, E. (1989). Lon Po Po: A Red-Riding Hood story from China. New York, NY: Philomel Books.

Yousafzai, M., & Lamb, C., (2013). I am Malala: The girl who stood up for education and was shot by the Taliban. New York, NY: Little, Brown and Company.

Zion, G. (1956/2002). *Harry the dirty dog*. (illus. M.B. Graham). New York, NY: Harper & Bros.

Zolotow, C. (1972) *William's doll* (illus. by William Pene du Bois). New York, NY: Harper & Row.

Key Words Index

The following terms and topics are found throughout the book. Use these key words to search for more information about people, places, and things associated with children's and young adult literature.

Academy of American Poets

Achievement

Acrylics

Adichie, Chimamanda

Adolescents

Adults who read YA

Aesop Prize

Aesthetics

African American literature

Age levels

ALA: American Library Association

Alphabet

ALSC: Association for Library Service to Children

Amazon Best Sellers

American Booksellers Association

American Education Research Association

American Folklore Society

American Indian

American Indian culture

American Library Association: ALA

Ancient libraries

Animal books

Antagonist

Anthologies

AO3 Archive of our Own

Appreciation

Apps

Argument

Argumentation

Art instruction

Artistic styles

Artists

Asian

Asian American

Association for Library Service to Children: ALSC

Audience
Authors
Author's purpose
Author/illustrator visits
Authorship
Award for Excellence in Poetry for Children
Awards
Babies
Balanced literacy
Baldwin Collection
Banned Books Week
Basal readers
Battle of the Books
Beatrix Potter's Hill Top Farm
Belpre Medal
Bess the Book Bus
Best-of lists
Biography
Black/White
Book clubs
Book fairs
Book Launch Award
Book mobiles
Book orders
Book talks
Bookmaking
Booksellers
Bookstores
Boston Globe-Horn Book Award
Boston Public Library
Boys
Bray, Thomas
Brothers Grimm
Bullying
Caldecott Medal
Caldecott, Randolph
Carnegie libraries
Carnegie, Andrew
Carter G. Woodson Book Awards
Caucasian

CCSS: Common Core State Standards
Celebrity authors
Censorship
Character
Charles Perrault
Charlotte Huck Award for Outstanding Fiction for Children
Child Online Protection Act (COPA)
Children
Children's Award Winning Books
Children's Book Council (CBC)
Children's Choice Book Award
Children's Library Association
Children's Literature Collection of Know-how
Children's Literature Research Collection
Children's reading rooms
Children's Story Hour
ChLA Children's Literature Association
ChLA Notables Award
Choral Reading
Chromolithography
Circulation reports
Civil rights
CLA Children's Literature Assembly of the National Council of Teachers of English
Class
Classics
CLICK Conference
Close reading
Cognitive factors
Collage
Collections
Common Core State Standards: CCSS
Common Sense Media
Comprehension
Concrete poetry
Contemporary Realistic Fiction
Content
Copyright
Coretta Scott King Awards
Crayon
Criteria

Critiques
Cultural factors
Curriculum
Curse words
Cussing
Cybils
Cycles of illiteracy
Database
De Grummond Collection
DeBary Children's Science Book Award
Definition of children's literature
Degree programs
Description
Design
Dialogue
Digital
Digital Future Project
Disney
Diverse books
Doctors
Dolly Parton Imagination Library
Dr. Seuss
Drama
Dramatic interpretation
Dromkeen
E.B. White Read Aloud Awards
Ebooks
Embodiment
EMIERT: Ethnic Materials Information Exchange Round Table Task Force
Emotional factors
Emotions
Employment level
Entertainment
Entertainment Software Rating Board
Eric Carle Museum of Picture Book Art
Ethnic Materials Information Exchange Round Table Task Force: EMIERT
Evaluation
Fairy tales
Family
Fanfiction

Fantasy
FBI Parent's Guide to Internet Safety
Fiction
Film
Filmmaking
First-grade studies
Five pillars of reading
Fluency
Folktales
Format
Formulaic texts
Fractured fairy tales
Franklin, Benjamin
Free speech
Gay literature
Geisel Award
Genres
Ghostwriting
Girls
Golden Kite Awards
Goodreads
Gouache
Grade levels
Graphic design
Graphic novels
Grimm
Habits of writers
Harris Burdick
Hazeltine, Alice
Hewins, Caroline
High school libraries
Historical fiction
Hollywood
Homosexuality
Horn Book Magazine
i.t.a. Initial Teaching Alphabet
Ideas
ILA Children's and Young Adults' Book Award
ILA: International Literacy Association
Illustration

Illustrations
Illustrators
Imagination
Indies Choice
Information
Informational texts
Inkwood Books
Instruction
Intergenerational literacy
International Children's Digital Library
International Literacy Association: ILA
International Youth Library
Internet
Jane Addams Children's Book Award
Jefferson, Thomas
John Steptoe New Talent Award
Jordan, Alice
Joseph Jacobs
Junior Library Guild
Kerlan Collection
Kiddie/Kiddy lit
Kids Like Us
Kirkus
Kirkus Prize
Knight, Valerie
Lambda Literary Award
Language
Language Experience Approach
Learning disabilities
Leisure Reading
Lesbian
Letter People
Leveled books
LGBT
Libraries
Library budget
Library collection development
Library collections
Library of Congress
Library programming

Library space
Linguistics
Literacy
Literary elements
Literary theory
Look Say Method
Many languages literature
Market research
Matching books to readers
Math
Mathical Prize
Matthews, Caroline
Mazza Museum
McGuffey Readers
Media
MFA Masters in Fine Arts
Michael L. Printz Award
Mildred L. Batchelder Award
Moore, Anne Carroll
Motivation
Movie adaptation
Museums
Music
Musical interpretation
NAEP National Assessment of Educational Progress
Narration
National Collection of Children's Books Dublin
National Council of Teachers of English: NCTE
NCTE Award for Excellence in Poetry for Children
NCTE Charlotte Huck Award for Outstanding Fiction for Children
NCTE National Council of Teachers of English
NCTE Orbis Pictus Award for Outstanding Nonfiction for Children
Negro libraries
New York Public Library
New York Times
Newbery Medal
Newbery, John
No Child Left Behind (NCLB)
Nonfiction
Nonfiction Award

Norton Award
Notable authors and illustrators
Notable Books for a Global Society (NBGS)
Notable Social Studies Trade Books for Young People
Novels
NRP National Reading Panel
Objectionable content
Obscene
Oil
Online access
Online retailers
Oral language
Oral tradition
Orbis Pictus Award for Outstanding Nonfiction for Children
Organization
Page arrangement
Parental Advisory Label
Parents Music Resource Center PMRC
Paris Review
Pastels
Pediatricians
Pen and ink
Performance
Peter Pan Collection
Pew Research Center
Phoenix Award
Phoenix Picture Book Award
Phonemic awareness
Phonics
Photographs
Physical factors
Plagiarism
Plot
Plummer, Mary Wright
Poem Hunter
Poetry
Poetry 180
Poetry Archive
Poetry Foundation
Poetry slams

Politics
Pop up books
Popular
Poverty
Powell, Sophy
Pratt Institute
Promotions
Protagonist
Public Broadcasting Service PBS
Publishing industry
Race
Read aloud
Readability
Reader response
Reader's Choice
Reading
Reading development
Reading incentives
Reading Rainbow
Reading strategies
Reading teachers
Reading to a baby
Reading to a toddler
Reading to older children
Reading to young children
Reading wars
Recording Industry Association of America
Relatable action
Religion
Religious libraries
Representations
RIF Reading is Fundamental
Right book
Right book for the right reader
Rights of the Reader
Roald Dahl Museum and Story Centre
Rosetta Project
Sales
SCBWI Society of Children's Book Writers and Illustrators
Schneider Family Book Award

School boards
School Library Journal
Science
Science fiction
Science Fiction and Fantasy Writers of America (SFWA)
Scientists
Scratchboard
Scripted instruction
Second language learners
Segregation
Selection
Self-publishing
Series
Series books
Setting
Seven Stories Centre
Sex
Sibert Medal
Sid Fleischman Humor Award
Sketchpads
Social
Social factors
Social status
Society of Illustrators
Spark Award
Speaking
Special collections
Spoken word
Sports
Status
Stories
Story
Story time
Strategies for reading
Stratemeyer series
Street literature
Style
Supreme Court
Sustained silent reading
Talks with Roger

TED talks
Teen Choice Book Award
Teenagers
Television
Testing
Text analysis
Text structures
Theme
Time
Toddlers
Traditional literature
Trinity College Dublin
University libraries
University of South Florida Special Collections
US Presidents
Victoria and Albert Museum
Video
Video games
Virginia Hamilton Award for Lifetime Achievement
Visual
Visual interpretation
Vocabulary
Watercolor
We Need Diverse Books
White/Black
Whole Language
Wilder Medal
Word Choice
Wordless books
Writing
Writing tips
YALSA Young Adult Library Services Association
Young Adults
Youth

Made in the USA
Monee, IL
24 December 2019